HIMACHAL PRADESH
DEVELOPMENT REPORT

सत्यमेव जयते

PLANNING COMMISSION
GOVERNMENT OF INDIA

Himachal Pradesh Development Report

सत्यमेव जयते

PLANNING COMMISSION
GOVERNMENT OF INDIA
NEW DELHI

Published by

ACADEMIC FOUNDATION
NEW DELHI

First Published in 2005 by
Academic Foundation
4772-73 / 23 Bharat Ram Road, (23 Ansari Road), Darya Ganj, New Delhi - 110 002 (India).
Phones : 23245001 / 02 / 03 / 04. Fax : +91-11-23245005. E-mail : academic@vsnl.com
www : academicfoundation.com

Published under arrangement with :
Planning Commission,
Government of India,
New Delhi.

Himachal Pradesh Development Report
ISBN 81-7188-445-8

Designed and typeset by Italics India, New Delhi
Printed and bound in India.

Contents

...CONTD. ...

...CONTD. ...

...CONTD. ...

एम. एस. आहलुवालिया
MONTEK SINGH AHLUWALIA

सत्यमेव जयते

उपाध्यक्ष
योजना आयोग
भारत
DEPUTY CHAIRMAN
PLANNING COMMISSION
INDIA

MESSAGE

One of the important Tenth Plan initiatives of the Planning Commission was to sponsor the preparation of the State Development Reports with much of the work being done by reputed national level institutes. This exercise was undertaken in recognition of the fact that economic circumstances and performance in individual States varied considerably and it was necessary to examine development challenges for individual States in the light of State specific constraints and circumstances. The basic idea is to produce quality reference documents on development profiles of individual States and the possible strategies for accelerating growth, and reducing poverty and inequality.

The Himachal Pradesh Development Report reviews Himachal Pradesh's experience and highlights issues critical for the State's development in the years ahead. I hope its publication wil stimulate debate on growth strategies appropriate for Himachal Pradesh. I am sure the road map indicated in the Report will stimulate a broader awareness of the critical policy issues facing the State and will assist the State to move to a higher growth path and to achieve all round human and economic development.

(M.S. AHLUWALIA)

योजना भवन, संसद मार्ग, नई दिल्ली – 110001 दूरभाष : 23096677, 23096688 फैक्स : 23096699
Yojna Bhawan, Parliament Street, New Delhi : 110001 Phones: 23096677, 23096688 Fax : 23096699, E-mail : dch@yojana.nic.in

डॉ. सईदा हमीद
Dr. Syeda Hameed

सत्यमेव जयते

सदस्य
योजना आयोग
योजना भवन
नई दिल्ली–110 001
MEMBER
PLANNING COMMISSION
YOJNA BHAWAN
NEW DELHI-110 001

PREAMBLE

In keeping with the Central Plan Scheme of the "50th Year Initiative for the Planning", the Planning Commission has been preparing Development Reports (SDRs) for each State. These SDR's are an attempt to compile quality reference documents on the profile and strategy for accelerating the pace of development in the respective States.

The Himachal Pradesh State Development Report (HPSDR) has been prepared by the Planning Commission with the assistance of the Centre for Research in Rural & Industrial Development (CRRID), Chandigarh, in partnership with the Government of Himachal Pradesh. A Core Committee reviewed the dimensions of the various developmental issues and helped to chart out the scope and coverage of the SDR for Himachal Pradesh in association with the State Government and the CRRID, Chandigarh.

I am sure this Report will serve as a resource material not only for the State and Central Government but also for all the Non-Governmental Organisations working for Himachal Pradesh.

I would like to place on record my appreciation for the work of Prof. Rashpal Malhotra, Founder Director, Centre for Research in Rural & Industrial Development, Chandigarh. I would like to thank Principal Adviser Smt. Kasturi Gupta Menon and Shri J.P. Vijay, Deputy Adviser, Planning Commission, as well as the officers of the Himachal Pradesh Government for their help in the preparation of this document.

Syeda Hameed

(SYEDA HAMEED)

दूरभाष : 23096570 फैक्स : 23096571
Telephone: 23096570 Fax : 23096571, email: s.hameed@yojana.nic.in

CHIEF MINISTER

ELLERSLIE
SHIMLA-171002

MESSAGE

It gives me immense pleasure to learn that the Centre for Research in Rural and Industrial Development, Chandigarh, has prepared the State Development Report of Himachal Pradesh at the behest of the Planning Commission, Government of India, New Delhi, in close coordination with the various departments of the Government of Himachal Pradesh. The Planning Commission is to be congratulated for its innovative initiative in sponsoring such studies for various states of India. These exercises not only unfold the development scene and needs of different states but also underline the imperative of interdependence in realising their development goals in the interest of nation-building.

Himachal Pradesh has made highly commendable progress since its formation in 1948. The State is widely acclaimed for its outstanding achievements in social development, leading to a visible social transformation. It is a notable success story born out of the progressive policies and programmes of the successive governments. This is no less a tribute to its relative political stability and efficacy of administrative delivery.

The discourse of the Report is a testimony to all this. I am happy to observe the critical issues which the State has to resolve and possible strategies towards that end are also indicated by the Report. It is a document of immense value for changing the course of development of the State. The State Planning Department performed the function of nodal department in coordinating the study at the State level and facilitating data inputs and interaction with various departments. I hope the report will prove helpful for policy planning, both at the Centre and State level, and also lead to better appreciation of the constraints of development at the level of the Central Government.

(Virbhadra Singh)

List of Tables and Figures

Tables

Appendix Tables

Figures

Preparing the State Development Report on Himachal Pradesh

The State Development Report (SDR) on Himachal Pradesh is different from the earlier report on Punjab, though both were prepared by the Centre for Research in Rural and Industrial Development (CRRID), Chandigarh. The report on Punjab has taken into account the history of 2000 years of the region and focuses on the past, the present and the future. The one on Himachal Pradesh has its focus primarily on the future.

The present of what constitutes Himachal Pradesh today can be best understood in the context of the socio-cultural and economic progress made by it in the process of its overall development during the last half-a-century. Members of the faculty of CRRID and a team of experts critically examined different sectors and sub-sectors of the socio-economic development of the state. What has emerged clearly is the success achieved in the social sector. The state of economic development, however, is a matter of concern. The weak financial health of the economy is reflected in the rising fiscal deficit. This condition has been analysed in depth to make a case for the Government of Himachal Pradesh to look for ways and means for fully exploiting its existing sources of revenue and tapping fresh resources, so as to improve the financial health of the state and minimise its fiscal deficit.

The Chief Minister of Himachal Pradesh, Hon'ble Shri Virbhadra Singh, shared his perspective, knowledge and understanding of the problems and prospects of the state in an open interactive session with members of the faculty and eminent advisers engaged in the preparation of the SDR. He expressed his confidence that notwithstanding the natural, constitutional and traditional constraints, the financial health of the state could be considerably improved and the pace of development accelerated. This would, however, require constitutional and institutional support to the state from the central agencies. Placed as it is, the state cannot be economically self-sufficient when compared with the neighbouring states of Punjab, Haryana, Rajasthan, and even Delhi. The distinctive environmental and geographical characteristics of the state need to be harnessed intensively and extensively to ensure a sustainable pace of social development by uplifting and upgrading the human and technical resources which are available in abundance.

Highly commendable success has been achieved in some social sector parameters such as primary education, female literacy and health. But this is not adequately reflected in the state's economic progress. Obviously, much more needs to be done to enrich the social sectors, which require effective professionalism and a technological base. The World Human Development Reports have emphatically stressed that economic progress has strong linkages with social sector development. The agenda for it should be well conceived and implemented, taking into consideration local needs and aspirations of the people. A turn-around in the economy will then follow.

The social development of Himachal Pradesh is both a precondition and a component of economic progress and will have to be the primary focus of the next five-year plan for constructing a strong economic base. The state can neither emulate nor sustain the same pattern of industrial and urban development, as adopted by Punjab and Haryana or any other state, except those in the hilly regions of the country.

Another critical measure, which could help accelerate the pace of economic development, would be to develop long-term co-operation with other states in the region for a common programme of development so as to realise fully the potential of Himachal Pradesh. This report has, in this context, drawn particular attention to the possibilities that exist in such areas as forestry, hydel power and tourism sectors. Other areas calling for special attention include management of water resources, roads and markets. Himachal Pradesh could also take advantage of the advanced educational, technological and medical facilities of the neighbouring states, to upgrade further the quality of its technological and human resource base.

This, as would be evident from a perusal of this report, does not require much investment beyond the resources normally made available by the Central ministries and institutions.

Himachal Pradesh, as stated above and as spelt out through their analyses by the contributors to this report, cannot compromise on its environmental and ecological status. These have not only to be protected but also their development has to be so conceptualised and planned that it extends the benefits to the neighbouring states of the region as well. In this context, one might draw attention to the impact of the forests of Venezuela on the ecology of the USA. What needs to be emphasised is co-operation within the region for mutual benefit. Himachal Pradesh should not try to compete with the agriculturally and industrially developed states of the region. Nor should it allow itself to become the victim of competition from them. On the contrary, entrepreneurs and other stakeholders should look upon Himachal Pradesh as a source of energy. A long-term perspective of interdependence, institutionalised through a Memorandum of Understanding among the neighbouring states, would strengthen the concept of mutual environmental and ecological planning for holistic development. Should they choose to initiate such a process of co-operative development, based on the sound and just principles of interdependence and interconnectivity, it would change the course of development not only in Himachal Pradesh but also in the neighboring states. In this context, the decisive role of the central agencies, particularly the Planning Commission, in initiating, encouraging, nurturing and regulating this process cannot be over-emphasised. This would help realise the full potential of every state in the region. This would also go a long way towards achieving the goal of improving not only the financial and administrative health of Himachal Pradesh but also the quality of life of the people of the entire region.

The newly constituted Planning Commission with Dr. Montek Singh Ahluwalia as its Chairman and his colleague Dr. (Smt.) Syeda Hameed, Chairperson, Core Committee of the State Development Report and their colleagues have spent considerable time in going through the Report and making some valuable suggestions which have been incorporated, as desired. In fact the idea of involving independent institutions, universities and research organisations in preparing such State Development Reports was initiated by none other than Dr. Montek Singh Ahluwalia as Member of the Planning Commission. These reports including the one prepared by Centre for Research in Rural and Industrial Development (CRRID) have been commissioned to focus objectively as well as constructively on the problems, prospects and development of state concerned and also to highlight the human, technological and scientific potentials, as well as those which have not been tapped, particularly pertaining to the social sector.

Finally, Himachal Pradesh has another distinctive feature worthy of special note. It is the political culture of the people of the state. The state has consistently supported national political parties. This pattern of behaviour is an evidence of their sagacity. It also indicates the existence of a social structure which can be protected and developed through its integration with, but not subservience to, economic development. Such a paradigm should surely invite the interest and concern of social scientists, planners, administrators, and politicians, in particular. Himachal Pradesh, as the Chief Minister emphasised during his valuable interactive session with members of the faculty on 26 June 2003, is committed to involving the community in the management of the state and society through the devolution of powers to the Panchayati Raj Institutions. These very institutions are going to reform the shape of events to come. They will mobilise the people for improving their own quality of life through a purposeful and effective relationship with the educational, technological, administrative and other institutions. These institutions, in turn, will have to be upgraded and made more efficient and effective so as to fulfil their obligations to the people and also meet the competitive environment thrown up by the market economy.

The process of preparing the State Development Report began with the then Member, Planning Commission, Shri Kamaluddin Ahmed, who shared his deep insight and wide range of experience, while chairing the first meeting of the officials and member of the team. Thereafter, it was Dr. D N Tewari, Member, Planning Commission who replaced Shri Kamaluddin Ahmed as Chairperson of the Core Committee under whose advice the Report was finalised. A number of highly educative and meaningful interactive sessions followed with the senior officials of the Planning Commission headed by the then Principal Adviser, Shri S P Arya; Shri T P Biswas, Director and also by Shri M Ranjan, Principal Adviser and Shri J P Vijay, currently Deputy Adviser. The senior officials of the Government of Himachal Pradesh had actively participated in a number of interactive sessions taken place at Chandigarh as well as at Shimla. These were not only stimulating but also rewarding, particularly because of the meaningful response and unhesitating co-operation of the senior officials of the Himachal Pradesh Government extended to the members of the team of CRRID engaged in preparing of the State Development Report.

Subsequently, Dr. (Smt.) Syeda Hameed, Member, Planning Commission and Chairperson of the Core Committee took keen interest in pursuing the Report and sent some suggestions to the Planning Commission which have been incorporated.

Finally, a concluding interactive session with the then Chairman of the Governing Body of CRRID, Dr. Manmohan Singh, currently the Prime Minister of India and also member of the Governing Body some of whom had served as member of the Planning Commission and in senior positions in the Government of India was organised. They enriched our efforts with valuable inputs given in the form of their advice during these meetings.

May I avail of this opportunity to express my sincere thanks to the following members of the CRRID team, officials of the Planning Commission and the State Government of the Himachal Pradesh besides several well-known experts for their valuable contributions in preparing the State Development Report. Himachal Pradesh: A Profile, *Pawan Kumar Sharma;* Natural Resources, *Surya Kant, Sameer Lakhwara, Gurcharan Singh and Anil Sinha;* Natural Disaster Management, *Surya Kant, Sameer Lakhwara, Gurcharan Singh and Anil Sinha;* Forestry, *Sunil Bansal;* Population, *Aswini Kumar Nanda;* Fiscal and Financial Management, *J.P. Gupta;* Education, *Bindu Duggal;* Health, *Rajesh Kumar Aggarwal;* Nutrition, *Komila Parthi;* Gender Empowerment, *B.K. Pattanaik and Kulwinder Singh;* Agriculture, *R.K. Grover;* Livestock, *Krishna Mohan;* Rural Development, *Kesar Singh and Sukhwinder Singh;* People's Participation, *Kesar Singh and Sukhwinder Singh;* Public Distribution System, *B.K. Pattanaik;* Industry, *S.S. Agarwal;*

Infrastructure, *D.P.S. Sandhu;* Information Technology, *S.K. Mangal and Sanjay Gupta;* Tourism, *D.P.S. Sandhu;* Urban Development, *M.K. Teotia;* Employment and Unemployment, *Himal Chand;* Wages and Prices, *Neetu Gaur;* Science and Technology, *S.K. Bijlani and* Sectoral Perspectives and Development Strategy, *Gopal Krishan.* The contributions made by Shri Harsh Gupta, Advisor CRRID, and Former Chief Secretary, Government of Himachal Pradesh, Shri Subarata Banerjee and Shri Anand Sarup, Advisors at CRRID and Shri Jaswant Singh, Editorial Advisor were commendable.

– RASHPAL MALHOTRA

Founder Director

CRRID

Core Committee

1. **Dr. Syeda Hameed** — **Chairperson**
   Member, Planning Commission
   New Delhi

2. **Smt. Kasturi Gupta Menon** — **Member**
   Principal Adviser (SP-N)
   Planning Commission, New Delhi

3. **Shri D.K. Sharma** — **Member**
   Principal Adviser-cum-Secretary (Plg.)
   Government of Himachal Pradesh, Shimla

4. **Shri Rashpal Malhotra** — **Member**
   Founder Director
   Centre for Research in Rural and
   Industrial Development (CRRID), Chandigarh

5. **Shri J.P. Vijay** — **Member-Secretary**
   Dy. Advisor (SP-N), Planning Commission
   New Delhi

Executive Summary

Introduction

The State Development Report (SDR) on Himachal Pradesh focuses primarily on the future.

Himachal Pradesh of today can best be understood in the context of the socio-cultural and economic progress it has made in the past four decades. Analytical studies of different sectors and sub-sectors of the socio-economic development of the state by members of the faculty of Centre for Research in Rural and Industrial Development, (CRRID), Chandigarh and its team of experts clearly show the success achieved in the social sector. As for economic development, the weak financial health of the economy, reflected in the rising fiscal deficit, is disturbing. This has been analysed in depth to make a case for the government of Himachal Pradesh to look for ways and means to exploit fully its existing sources of revenue and to tap fresh sources.

The Chief Minister of Himachal Pradesh, Shri Virbhadra Singh, shared his knowledge and understanding of the problems and prospects of the state in an open interactive session with members of the faculty and experts engaged in the preparation of the SDR. He was confident that notwithstanding the natural, constitutional and traditional constraints, the financial health of the state could be considerably improved and the pace of development accelerated. This would, however, require constitutional and institutional support to the state from central agencies. Placed as it is, the state cannot be economically self-sufficient like its neighbouring states of Punjab, Haryana, Delhi and Rajasthan. The distinctive environmental and geographical characteristics of the state call for an intensive and extensive study to ensure sustainable social development by uplifting and upgrading its human and technical resources which are in abundance.

Social development of Himachal Pradesh is both a precondition and a component of economic progress. It will have to be the primary focus of the next five-year plan for constructing a strong economic base. No other state in the country, except possibly the hilly regions, can provide a suitable model of development for Himachal. A long-term understanding with other states in the region for a common programme of development, can accelerate the pace of its economic development. This report has drawn particular attention to the possibilities that exist in such areas as forests, hydel power and tourism sectors. Other areas could be the management of water, roads and markets. Himachal Pradesh can also take advantage of the advanced educational, technological and medical facilities of the neighbouring states, to uplift and upgrade its own technological human resources. This, as this report shows, does not require investment of resources normally made available by Central ministries and institutions.

Himachal Pradesh cannot compromise on its environmental and ecological status which must be protected. Development in this regard has to be designed in co-operation with other states of the region for mutual benefit. Himachal Pradesh should not try to compete with the agriculturally and industrially developed states of the region, nor allow itself to be the victim of competition from them. On the contrary, entrepreneurs and other stakeholders should look upon Himachal Pradesh as a source of energy. A long-term perspective of interdependence, institutionalised through a Memorandum of Understanding with the neighbouring states, would strengthen mutual planning for holistic development. The overall role of the central agencies, particularly the Planning Commission, would, however, be decisive in realising the full potential of each neighbouring state. This would go a long way towards improving the financial and administrative health of Himachal Pradesh, and, as a consequence, the quality of life of the people of the region as a whole.

Finally, a distinctive feature of Himachal is the political culture of its people. Their continuing support to national political parties testifies to their sagacity and is also indicative of a social structure which can be protected and developed through its integration with, but not subservience to, economic development. Such a paradigm should surely invite the interest and concern of social scientists, planners, economists, and administrators. Himachal Pradesh, as the Chief Minister emphasised in his interaction with members of the faculty of CRRID, is committed to people's participation in governance through devolution to Panchayati Raj Institutions, which would have to be upgraded and made more efficient.

Himachal Pradesh: A Profile

Himachal is one of the most dynamic hill states of India with significantly high indicators of human development. Its natural resources and physiography, separate administrative identity, and notable accomplishments in literacy hold the promise of great progress. One of the smaller states of India inhabited by Hindi-speaking people, it was granted full statehood on 25 January, 1971. In the 2001 census, the state recorded a population of 60.8 lakh, distributed over an area of 55,673 sq.km. Almost half of this population lives in three districts (among a total of 12) — Kangra, Mandi and Shimla — and 7.54 per cent in the three bottom districts of Lahaul and Spiti, Kinnaur and Bilaspur. The socio-economic base of the state at the time of its formation and even earlier has a bearing on the level of its development. Like other hill areas, it has been neglected in the past because of its peripheral location. Himachal Pradesh started with a weak economic and institutional base and a low level of human skills essential for modern development. The state has tried to overcome this inadequacy by turning to horticulture, power generation and tourism.

Himachal Pradesh now is one of the eleven special category states, eligible for special central assistance. Starting with a growth rate lower than that of the national economy and Punjab and Haryana, the state reversed this trend during the nineties. The per capita income too has been consistently rising in the nineties. A structural change was experienced with a significant decline in the share of the primary sector and a rise in that of the secondary and tertiary sectors. The percentage of population below the poverty line declined to well below the national average. The thrust of planning has gradually shifted from agriculture and transport to social services, with power generation receiving prime attention. A drastic decline in development expenditure in the state in recent years is highly disturbing. At the same time, spatial equity is being generated by a reduction in the income level and literacy. Regional disparity in industrial development, however, calls for correction. The major challenge before the state is to deploy its human resources effectively for economic development, employment generation and the well-being of its people.

Natural Resources

Land

Given the large expanse of snow-covered, uninhabitable mountains, considerable forest cover and permanent pastures and grasslands, along with the remaining small area under settlements, roads, water reservoirs and so on, the state is left only with a tiny share of land per person, if distributed equally. Hardly 10 per cent of the total area is cultivated; 26 per cent is under forests; and pastures and grasslands account for 24 per cent. Himachal Pradesh can be divided into three broad regions on the basis of land use: i) the intensively cultivated and moderately forested southern region with marginal pastures and other grazing lands; ii) the moderately cultivated and highly forested central region, with enough pastures and other grazing lands; and iii) the poorly cultivated and sparsely forested, northern region with a high proportion of pastures and other grazing lands. Institutional changes for optimum utilisation of land resources are obviously urgent. The transfer of management of common lands from the community to the state has to be reversed, as it has reduced the scope of people's participation in resource management. The State Land Use Board has to be rejuvenated and strengthened to ensure proper land-use by the departments concerned. The unsurveyed parts of the state need to be studied and mapped through remote sensing.

Water

Himachal Pradesh is rich in water resources, with perennial rivers receiving water from snowcapped mountains. The major rivers flow into the Indus basin, except the Yamuna, which flows into the Ganga system. The seasonal concentration of rainfall makes irrigation in Himachal Pradesh essential, but hardly one-fifth of the cultivated land is irrigated largely because of physiographic constraints. The major rivers and their tributaries form a virtually unlimited hydel power potential. Seasonal fluctuations in the discharge of water, however, necessitate construction of big reservoirs. Only one-fifth of the state's hydel-power potential has so far been harnessed. Efforts are on to make bigger use of this resource in the near future. Fish culture is widespread because of the numerous rivers and streams. The perennial snow-fed streams are suitable for the culture of trout (the most famous sporting species). Properly-managed ponds can yield 2000 kg to 2500 kg of fish per hectare annually. The farmers can be encouraged to adopt the latest techniques of fish culture. An integrated watershed and river basin development programme will ensure regular water supply to the rural areas, augment water supply to the overburdened urban systems and help integrate water, soil and vegetation cover. The following measures are recommended in particular:

- *In situ*-water harvesting on a war footing is essential to maximise the utilisation of rainwater by the habitations, for augmenting drinking water supply and for irrigation on mountain slopes.
- Identification of all micro watersheds/watersheds in each river basin/sub-basin and preparation of their development plans for execution on priority basis.
- Creation of a Traditional Water Sources Cell in the IPH Department for the development of traditional sources of water.
- Large-scale installation of hydraulic rams or hydrams in the rural areas, with government subsidy for needy habitations in hilly areas.
- An extensive programme of installation of deep tubewells for effective utilisation of untapped groundwater to create the necessary irrigation potential.
- Conducting river basin/sub-basinwise estimate of water resources and setting up an Institute of Mountain Hydrology to collect and generate hydrological data base.
- Involving government officials and the public in the planning process to educate them on the importance of developing ground-water resources for sustainable development.
- Involving the NGOs in the collection of data and information on all sources of water and the pattern of their utilisation.

Minerals

According to preliminary investigations of the Geological Survey of India, salt, gypsum, limestone, barytes, clays, mica, iron pyrites, slate and lead are the major minerals of Himachal Pradesh. The geological wing in the state's Directorate of Industries is actively engaged in mineral prospecting. For effective utilisation of all mineral resources of the state, the geological wing must be strengthened for a complete survey of actual availability; fuel and transport links to connect mineral-rich sites have to be established; mining and quarrying need attention to minimise irreparable damage to the environment; and greater care must be taken when mining and dumping waste so that the problems of soil erosion and induced landslides are not aggravated.

Natural Disaster Management

Himachal Pradesh needs to develop a holistic approach to manage the entire gamut of natural and man-made disasters, which include quakes, landslides, avalanches, cloudbursts, flash floods and forest fires. All development projects in the vulnerable areas should be so formulated as to minimise the adverse effects of natural disasters and should be linked with disaster mitigation. A cost-benefit analysis is essential to meet the economic impact of a natural disaster. Linkages between environment, natural disasters and development must be clearly established to mitigate disasters and to improve the environment.

Forestry

The emphasis on conservation and regeneration of forests with the involvement of the communities and others living in and around these areas has led to an increase in the percentage of forest cover from 21.16 in 1991 to 25.79 in 2001. Now a holistic approach is required to reduce the dependence of communities on forests directly, by encouraging the use of alternatives to fuel-wood and timber and indirectly, by raising their economic status. Monoculture should give way to multiple species culture so as to encourage biodiversity at different levels of forest regeneration.

The traditional migration of the *Gujjar* communities with their cattle to the high alpine pastures during the summer and return to the lower hills during the winter, degrades and destroys pasture lands and forests, with consequent impact on soil erosion. Rehabilitation in permanent *Gujjar* settlements has not succeeded because of their mindset. Training and vocational skill-upgradation, social welfare services for their women and children, coupled with a mechanism to collect their produce are necessary to motivate the *Gujjars* to settle down permanently, so as to prevent degradation of pasture lands and forests. Conservation of medicinal and aromatic plants, very few of which are available elsewhere and perfection of their multiplication techniques should be a major task of the Forest Department, backed by a strong, modern, research-based organisational support. In the changing conditions of global trade, India can successfully face the challenge of better quality and lower priced timber from Malaysia and Thailand through efficient forest management and interdependence and interconnectivity of the forest-producer states and the user states in the country. *Panchayats* should be made responsible for monitoring forest development and conservation.

Medicinal plants of value, which can be propagated in the state, include *Chirata* and *Katki* (for liver disorder), *Jatamani* (for nervous ailments) and Indian Barberry (for digestive disorders), in addition to sea buck thorn and lavender.

Population

Because of the interdependence of population dynamics in the state and events outside, such as spread of private health-care services and in-migration, population planning in Himachal Pradesh must go beyond the elementary goals set in the draft State Population Policy or outlined in Health Vision 2020 and should cover larger issues of human development. In ecologically-sensitive Himachal Pradesh, population and development linkages which envelop environmental concerns have to be addressed satisfactorily. The public health services have to be improved considerably and their optimum utilisation ensured, particularly because the success of the family planning programme also depends on their performance. A major task is to ensure greater private sector participation in the health sector. Greater public participation in both policy formulation and implementation through the Panchayati Raj Institutions, can aid efforts to stabilise the population if the functions, functionaries and funds are used in tune with the expectations of the public at all levels. Creating adequate opportunities for the marginalised groups would help achieve demographic goals. Programme interventions must also adequately address gender disparities. Indigenous data generation is particularly essential in Himachal for reliable, long-term and cross-sectional demographic assessment, policy formulation and a well-focused programme of intervention. Such efforts demand strong institutional and financial support. Himachal can succeed in maintaining a healthy balance between social development and the pace of demographic development by fully utilising the assets created by achieving a high rank in human development.

Fiscal and Financial Resources

The total revenue receipt of the state has increased about four times between 1991-92 and 2002-03, but the corresponding revenue expenditure has increased nearly five times. This is unsustainable and requires strategic fiscal restructuring of the tax and non-tax base. The debt of the state, including guarantees, has also reached a worrisome high. The increase in the total debt stock and the trend of higher interest payments have resulted in high committed liability, adversely affecting the financial position of the state. The total tax revenue of the state as percentage of the GSDP is persistently low. The committed expenditure on salaries, pensions, grants-in-aid and interest payment has reached more than 116 per cent of its revenue receipts. The balance of the current revenue in each year of the Ninth Plan and 2002-2003 has been consistently showing a deficit and has been financed by borrowings and increased plan assistance. The Plan performance of the state in financial terms has exceeded the approved outlay and transfers by the Government of India have been increasing steadily with current transfers being higher than those of the neighbouring states of Punjab and Haryana.

Hydro Power Potential as a Resource

The income generated from free power as royalty from all non-HPSEB-power generated in the state and its share of the total power generated from Nathpa-Jhakri will constitute an increasing financial resource. This could be further augmented by helping the HPSEB become a well-performing board by breaking even through VRS or redeployment of one-third of its staff.

Public Sector Reforms

Speedy disinvestment or closure of loss-making PSUs is urgently needed for improving the poor financial health of Himachal. Swapping high-interest loans with low-cost loans will reduce the interest liability of the state. The national policy of one-time settlement (OTS) of non-performing assets of loans advanced by the state-sector financing agencies should be implemented and the first charge on such receipts should be the disbursement of retrenchment compensation under the voluntary retirement scheme (VRS).

Measures for Stabilising the Financial Position of Himachal Pradesh

Measures have to be taken to control factors which have adversely affected the state's fiscal position over the past ten years. The tax collection mechanism should be restructured to plug leakages in revenue collection and increase the revenue from the existing base of taxation by at least five per cent per year over the next four-five years. The swapping of expensive debts with cheaper ones, a targeted reduction in the current expenditure level, minimum reliance on borrowings are measures that can reduce the fiscal stress of the state. A major percentage of the borrowings of the state government has been used to fill the revenue gap. Capital expenditure as percentage of the GDP has declined and revenue expenditure constitutes about 60 per cent of the plan expenditure. The state government should gradually withdraw from several unproductive sectors including unmerited subsidies, but continue budgetary support to social-sector activities that enrich human capital. The Himachal Pradesh government is faced with an unsustainable macro fiscal situation. It has been deprived of the Central revenue deficit grant, recommended by the Eleventh Finance Commission, because of the state's inability to sign the MoU to implement the 'fiscal policy objectives' set forth by the Commission.

Measures for Correcting Revenue and Fiscal Deficits

Measures for correcting the revenue and fiscal deficits to be taken by the state should include: Fixing reasonable caps on public debt and outstanding guarantees; creating a sinking fund and guarantee redemption fund for timely repayment of debts; implementing 'fiscal objectives and reforms', power sector reforms, public sector restructuring programme and budgetary reforms. A Fiscal Responsibility and Financial Management Act aimed at giving the state long–term financial stability by controlling, in particular, revenue and fiscal deficits should be enacted. Greater attention must also be paid to additional resource mobilisation for the Tenth Plan (2002-07). The revenue of this high per capita income state has the potential to go up much higher than that projected in the Tenth Plan. The state's representation to the Central Government for a tax on hydro power generated in the state is justified, to help augment its income from the sale of the state's share of free power as already envisaged. User charges for higher education, medical education, technical education and secondary health service, drinking water, sewerage, etc., are an untapped but justifiable source of resource mobilisation.

Education

From the lowest literacy level at the time of independence, Himachal today ranks 11th among the states and UTs in India. Its literacy rate was recorded at 77.1 per cent as against the national average of 65.4 per cent in the 2001 census. Education receives priority in the state and allocation of resources is much higher in Himachal Pradesh than in Punjab, Haryana, Kerala and at the all-India level. The age-specific enrolment rate is also much higher. The state has also reduced its dropout rates considerably up to the elementary level. Despite fairly adequate teacher-pupil ratio at all levels, absenteeism of teachers and untrained teachers (at the primary level) has affected the quality of education. The present mode of teaching/learning is a matter of concern when one considers more than 50 per cent failure rate at the matriculation level and 60 per cent at the 10+2 level. Very few children go in for higher education and a large number of those who do, select general courses instead of technical/professional education. Efforts must be made to motivate students to opt for such courses to bridge the existing gap between the skill-type being produced and the actual demand in the market. Himachal Pradesh should formulate its own 'Education Policy' with priority to its specific requirements to create suitable manpower to harness the available natural resources and the vast hydel potential in the state. The state should focus on pre-service/in-service teacher training and provide a suitable guidance and counselling mechanism to assist the students to seek admission to courses suited to their aptitude and interests. It is important to introduce new courses and upgrade some of the existing institutions and promote interaction between industry and the institutions.

Health

From virtually primitive medical and health facilities at the time of its formation, Himachal Pradesh has made considerable progress with focus on the development of the Indian system of medicine and homoeopathy (ISM&H), particularly *ayurveda*, and by ensuring greater community participation through the Panchayati Raj Institutions (PRIs). The health infrastructure of the state today includes, among other things, two medical colleges, 50 general hospitals, 66 community health centres, 441 primary health centres, 2067 sub-centres, two regional *ayurvedic* hospitals, 20 *ayurvedic* hospitals, and 1,109 *ayurvedic* health centres. A great deal remains to be done for providing tertiary health care services and a wider and varied health management system, including both public and private effort. Outlay and expenditure on health has been uneven over the years and has been receiving priority since the Eighth Plan. Morbidity records in Himachal are inadequate. Available data indicate that the health problems that the state faces are high morbidity, particularly among the aged and acute respiratory and intestinal infections. A large percentage of women and a majority of children continue to be anaemic, with many chronically undernourished. Most of the deliveries take place at home, mostly attended by a traditional birth attendant. The number of HIV-positive cases and AIDS patients is rising. The public sector plays a crucial role in all spheres of health and allopathy is the most preferred system.

Himachal Pradesh has to reach parity in provision and quality of health services at all levels, with the neighbouring states of Punjab and Haryana. The health care system of the future should be more scientific and technologically advanced, with better services through selected health-sector reforms. Immediate state interventions are necessary for the vulnerable sections, and for bringing about an attitudinal and behavioural change regarding the reproductive health of women. Greater inter-sectoral and inter-departmental co-ordination would ensure effective and optimal utilisation of the existing and future health-care programmes and increased public awareness towards healthy practices.

Nutrition

The nutritional status of the population of Himachal Pradesh reveals that the percentage of underweight children at birth has gone up from 28.2 in 1992-93 to 35.1 in 1998-99. Malnutrition persists among 43.6 per cent of the children under three years. No less than 30 per cent of the women in the 15-49 years age group are chronically energy-deficient. This is the highest figure among the neighbouring states of Punjab, Haryana and Jammu & Kashmir. Thus, nutrition planning for Himachal Pradesh has to take into account the diverse structure and composition of its population and differences in food needs. The state should adopt a SMART (S- Sustainable, M- Manageable, A- Actionable, R-Reliable and T-Time bound) action plan for nutrition, covering a nutritional surveillance and monitoring system. New nutritive care institutions need to be established at various levels and the existing ones strengthened. Nutrition-rich local foods need to be identified and their production increased. *Anganwari* Leaving Certificate should be made mandatory for admission to a primary school and there should be networking with school authorities to enhance the nutrition level of the children and a cost-effective public distribution system providing a wider range of nutritious products.

Gender Empowerment

Himachal should use its high position in the Women Empowerment Index among 16 major states to reduce some of the weaknesses that continue to exist. Special efforts should be made to provide education to women and girl children belonging to the Scheduled Castes and Scheduled Tribes. As women are highly concentrated in lower cadre jobs, the participation of women needs to be promoted in decision-making positions. Special measures are necessary for the speedy disposal of cases of crime against women and for the proper rehabilitation of war widows. For effective participation in grassroots democracy, women members of the Panchayati Raj Institutions must be trained and encouraged to participate in all their activities, including contesting elections to various positions. Women need to be involved actively in social forestry and farm forestry activities through formation of self-help groups, provided with economic support and the necessary training. Himachal should formulate a Women Empowerment Policy (WEP) to integrate women effectively into the process of development. A Women's Resource Centre (WRC) should be set up to act as a documentation and information dissemination unit and conduct capacity-building programmes and other activities, aimed at raising the status of women.

Agriculture

A concerted effort has to be made to overcome the limitation that agriculture suffers because of the physiographic characteristics of Himachal. Agrarian reforms are needed to boost agricultural and horticultural production in the state. The existing potential for improving the land-use pattern and minor irrigation schemes has to be fully realised and emphasis given to dissemination of suitable and practical technologies which are available. Urgent measures are necessary to make available quality and certified HYV seeds of different crops to a larger number of farmers than at present. The pattern of land use has to be changed to ensure availability of land for commercial cultivation, mechanisation and wider use of agrochemicals. Land reforms, with the possibility of large holdings would encourage contract and commercial farming with corporate investment, thereby increasing productivity. Himachal must encourage minor irrigation and watershed development wherever possible. The micro hydel projects for power generation should be integrated with irrigation projects, for rapid increase of the state's irrigation potential and for bringing drought-prone areas under improved cultivation. Rainwater harvesting and water conservation must be encouraged. Given the advantage of topography and climate, where all kinds of crops can be grown, there is scope for changing the excessive cultivation of foodgrain crops to greater emphasis on vegetables and other crops with potential for good productivity and higher returns. This demands investment in modern technology and management inputs, as also growing exotic vegetables, with support from extension agencies and agricultural universities.

Since the agro-climatic conditions of the state are ideally suited for horticulture, all efforts should be made to extend the area under quality fruits and vegetables. Some caution has to be exercised with regard to diversion to new crops that demand higher technical inputs to achieve economic productivity. Extra attention should be paid to improving the quality and productivity of the existing fruits through professional management, new technologies and infrastructure back-up, particularly for cost-management and securing best quality rootstocks, seeds and tubers from the international market and their multiplication through tissue culture. For effective implementation of such policies, the management of horticulture produce should be transferred to the Horticulture Department from the Marketing Board. Economic gains from flower cultivation require strong infrastructural support for marketing, including an international airport, and extensive cold storage and roads network, all of which are lacking. Nevertheless, taking advantage of climatic factors, professional flower cultivation, leading to production of seeds and bulbs/rhizomes, can be profitable, especially with the production of cut flowers for the nearby markets. Concerted efforts are needed to organise tea plantations on a commercial basis, with support to extensive cultivation and processing on modern lines. Medicinal and aromatic plants need special attention, as these are valuable for health or cosmetic use and also are foreign exchange earners. A full package of practices for the cultivation of commonly used medicinal and aromatic plants, without over exploitation, should be developed and popularised among the farmers, with assured marketing by government or private agencies.

Organic Farming

Small farmers, who do not use chemical fertilisers, can be helped to increase production and incomes through organic farming, particularly vegetable and fruit cultivation, besides tea. Technological and management inputs must be provided by the agricultural universities and the Department of Agriculture. Urgent measures are necessary for the extension network of the universities and the Department of Agriculture and Horticulture to reach the farmers with modern technology, appropriate seeds and other inputs. Infrastructural facilities have to be developed to provide for cold storage and quick marketing of perishable foods and their processing.

Livestock

Nineteen out of every twenty households in Himachal Pradesh keep at least one of the livestock species, especially cattle, goats and sheep. Their productivity is, however, inordinately low. A two-pronged effort, involving both conservation and improvement of the indigenous breeds and crossbreeding on a large scale, is required to improve the situation. The government's proposal to arrange veterinary services through the private sector might not be economically viable, because of the topographic conditions, scattered habitations and the practice of transhumance. The experience of the Dagshai Army Dairy Farm of mixing apple peel with the feed, to increase the daily milk yield of cows, could be adopted in apple-rich Himachal Pradesh as part of the feed management for improving the quality of the livestock. Scientific research should be conducted for upgrading the alpine pastures and the quality of grass in village common lands. Training courses for proper management of livestock at the household level, particularly for women, need to be organised through the local Panchayati Raj Institutions. These measures call for co-ordination between different government departments concerned, in particular the Department of Biotechnology and veterinary science education institutions.

Rural Development

Successful implementation of various strategies and projects have made a dent in rural poverty in Himachal. Availability of basic amenities and rural infrastructure has improved considerably. The state government has been generally following the planning strategies evolved by the central government.

Rural Development and Panchayati Raj

The state government has devolved powers, functions and responsibilities for 15 departments to the PRIs, mainly for the planning, execution and monitoring of schemes. The *panchayats* are empowered to hear and decide cases relating to minor offences under the Indian Penal Code (IPC). They have been given powers to report on the physical attendance of grassroots level functionaries. The social factors that dominate the style of living and working of the state are in some respects better than the standard prevailing in the country as a whole, but they need restructuring, particularly in the areas of rural education and industrialisation. Attention also needs to be paid to specific problems of rural Himachal and to the introduction of modern-technology-based industries and micro-planning at the *Panchayat* level to provide for gainful employment and utilisation of local resources and indigenous skills. Information technology will have to be made an integral part of the future development process of Himachal, particularly for generating and maintaining a database for use in decision-making down to the village level. In this context, information technology must be part of the training of the rural youth.

Himachal has already taken measures to promote people's participation in development works, under various schemes. Further efforts, however, have to be made to activise the *Gram Sabha*/Ward Committee to ensure participation of the people from all sections of rural society. Wider access to a variety of information, necessary for rural development, has to be ensured, as also exchange of experiences among different local bodies at different levels. For continuing and making further advances in people's participation in development, the subject should form part of the curriculum of institutions training elected representatives of local bodies and government departments.

Public Distribution System

A number of public distribution schemes have been functioning in Himachal. A study of the utilisation of PDS and consumer satisfaction, conducted by CRRID in some parts of rural and urban Himachal, has revealed some inherent weaknesses of the system and its utilisation, mainly by APL families. The PDS in Himachal Pradesh is catering to the foodgrain needs of BPL families. However, the needs of the poorest of the poor cannot be better served unless E mistakes "Exclusion of deserving" and I mistakes "Inclusion of non-deserving" are avoided. There is scope for more effective utilisation of the PDS, through careful categorisation of the beneficiaries through effective participation of local institutions including the PRIs. Efficient self-help groups could also be utilised for implementing the PDS, including the running of fair price shops.

Industry

Himachal has only two industrially developed districts — Solan and Sirmaur. As the remaining ten are industrially backward, the state faces the challenges of decentralising industry by providing necessary financial support, technical inputs, and marketing facilities. This refers particularly to small, tiny and cottage industries, which hold the key to large-scale employment generation and expansion of the economy. The possibility of the New Industrial Policy, 2003, notified by the Government of India, attracting a large number of entrepreneurs to the periphery of the adjoining states of Punjab and Haryana can make the state complacent. It should keep in mind that the new units might not be sustainable, being incentive-linked. Necessary pre-emptive steps should be taken to ensure the sustainability of such units.

As an effective facilitator, enabler and co-ordinator, the state government must promote public-private partnership. It must also harness financial institutions and industrial development agencies for modernising the existing infrastructure and creating new technical facilities. 'Rural industrial clusters' in the backward areas, with centralised facilities and Agri-Export Zones (AEZs) and Export Promotion Parks in the developed areas would open opportunities for new units with prospects of long-term sustainability. A suitable monitoring system is necessary for timely detection of sickness in the SSI sector and taking early preventive and remedial measures. Skill upgradation and training linkages between the industry and the technical institutions and setting up of new research and development centres should be encouraged. In particular, in-house R&D and training centres should be set up in large and medium industries. Graded incentives, in favour of the industrially backward districts and small and tiny industries are the need in Himachal.

Infrastructure

Infrastructure development is particularly important and also a challenge in a hill state. The tremendous hydel power potential of the state has yet to be fully harnessed to meet growing development needs. It is not a power-surplus state. Being a seasonal power producer, it sells power in summer and buys in winter. For the overall economic development of the state, the State Electricity Board must reduce its cost of production by improving generation-efficiency, and cutting transmission and generation losses. Efficient generation, particularly through renovation and modernisation, could reduce the per unit generation cost and as a consequence bring down the 'manpower cost' by cost-effective deployment. While unbundling generation, transmission and distribution through immediate implementation of the Electricity Act 2003, the state must take immediate measures to equip the SERC to fulfil its expanded statutory role. It may seek central government notifications on a national policy for permitting stand-alone systems on decentralised purchase and distribution in rural electrification. There is need also for steps to ensure that mini/micro hydel schemes are kept out of CEA purview, to facilitate quicker decision-making. Such reforms can be successful only through the people's and employees' participation, particularly because the efficiencies take time to establish, and the benefits to reach the consumer. Himachal should also come to a long-term understanding with Jammu & Kashmir, Punjab, Haryana and Delhi to integrate the varying seasonal demands and supply requirements for mutual financial benefit. Major initiatives to initiate the reform process should be started without delay.

Transport

The transport sector in Himachal Pradesh has assumed key importance to meet the construction demands of the hydel power projects and widespread, balanced industrial development, particularly to meet the need for quick movement of material and short-life agricultural and horticultural products. An efficient transport network is also essential for the success of the tourism industry.

Though Himachal is the leader in road development among the hill states, it has yet to implement its own targets and meet its requirements. Only half the roads are all-weather roads, large stretches are unmetalled and of inferior quality with poor compacting and drainage. The road system is totally inadequate to meet the needs of the greatly expanded tourist industry which has to become a dynamic component of the economic development of Himachal. In this context, it is necessary to emphasise the importance of taking adequate care to preserve the environment of this beautiful hill state when constructing roads.

The operations of the HRTC, which has a wide reach in the state and in the neighbouring states of Punjab, Haryana, Rajasthan, Uttar Pradesh, Jammu & Kashmir, and the Union Territories of Chandigarh and Delhi, are of tremendous importance for linking distant areas within and outside the state for its all-round development. It can fulfil its potential role in the coming days only if it is run as a profitable commercial unit. This calls for aggressive technical training programmes. Equally important is to improve safety and bring down maintenance and operational costs, rationalise the staffing pattern, including redeployment in other government departments, increase kilometres per bus per day, and render punctuality to lift occupancy ratios. Vigorous pursuit of the initiatives already taken to improve the service and reduce the cost should be the motto.

Attention also needs to be paid to the expansion of the railway system as part of the new strategy for the development of Himachal Pradesh. The ongoing line-works should be completed without delay. The state needs to encourage containerisation for direct shipping of agro-products to international markets. With Himachal's vision of a high growth curve, alternative means of transport must be developed to take the pressure off the roads; otherwise tourists will simply not be able to reach, and goods delivery schedules will go haywire. The possibility of using ropeways, onward air linkages to the existing airports by helicopters and introduction of cable cars for tourists must be evaluated. Himachal must be ready for the future and set up a multi-modal transport plan, woven into a logistics plan to provide efficient transport. Cargo containerisation must form an important element of this logistics plan. Special Purpose Vehicles (SPVs) for investment in project-specific transport systems should also be evaluated to enhance the transport capacity for bulk moves and prevent serious traffic bottlenecks in the existing system.

Information Technology

Recognising its role in socio-economic development, Himachal Pradesh engaged NASSCOM (National Association of Software and Service companies), a premier national body, to suggest a plan for developing the IT industry in the state. The state government has accepted the recommendations of NASSCOM. Himachal has made some progress in the implementation of its IT policy during the last three years, but there is a huge gap between the recommendations made by NASSCOM and the achievements. This is probably because of the widening resource gap in terms of financial allocations made by the state government and the availability of human resources. The projections for the IT industry in Himachal Pradesh by 2009-10 need to be reduced to one-third of NASSCOM recommendation. Even to achieve this target, the government must aggressively market the infrastructure and create an atmosphere conducive to setting up an IT industry in the state and develop quality human resources for it by upgrading the professional level of the existing training facility to meet international standards. An Indian Institute of Information Technology should be set up for this purpose. The state must also monitor the quality and standardisation in both government and private institutions. It must take every measure for the use of IT in rural development through Community Information Dissemination Centres (CIDCs). IT should also be used for setting up an education network in the rural areas and implementing e-governance in a holistic and integrated manner.

Tourism

The tourism policy of Himachal recognises the endless possibilities of its development as an important labour-intensive sector, capable of making a larger contribution to the state's domestic product. It has identified important areas of action for expanding the scope of tourism, breaking seasonal and destination barriers. It favours the entry of the private sector, alongside the HPTDC. Unfortunately, the follow-up of the policy is inadequate and demands development of new tourist attractions, change in the land policy to encourage tourism entrepreneurship and aggressive marketing and advertising policies in this regard. It also calls for early action to market the wider scope of tourism, location-wise and for all seasons, and to improve the quality of the services at every level of contact with the tourist. The tourism sector has to be seen as an industry, re-orienting its entire philosophy to a marketing concept, focusing singularly on the customer, that is the tourist. It is important to realise that the development of Himachal will take place as a by-product of viewing the tourist as a customer. In a larger context, Himachal Pradesh should take the lead in looking at Jammu & Kashmir, Punjab, Uttar Pradesh, Haryana, and Delhi as an area with large possibilities of regional co-operation. These states have some of the best economic indicators in India and they can participate in a regional plan for power and transport infrastructure to their mutual benefit.

Urban Development

Although only one-tenth of the state's population is urban, yet all is not well with the quality of life in the urban areas. There are serious deficiencies in the urban infrastructure, mainly because of the poor fiscal health of the ULBs. Disparities in the level and quality of the infrastructure between the small and large towns are expected to increase in the future because of the planning bias in favour of the latter. Plan outlays for urban development have been inadequate. The coverage of water supply and sewerage systems should be enhanced. Common waste treatment facilities would help small and medium ULBs overcome financial constraints for creating such facilities. Specific funds should be provided for the maintenance of municipal roads and streets and the Central Finance Commission and the Tourism Department should fund augmentation of parking facilities, especially in towns with a heavy tourist influx. Other municipal services should also be upgraded. The Himachal Pradesh Infrastructure Development Board (HPIDB) should invest the specific-purpose funds raised by it in identified critical sectors of urban infrastructure.

The traditional sources of municipal income have been grossly inadequate, because of the lack of fiscal discipline among the ULBs, poor autonomy to raise resources, stagnation in most of the sources of tax and non-tax revenues and higher municipal expenditure on establishment. Budgetary allocations, fiscal transfers and grants, have also been inadequate to meet the growing needs of the urban infrastructure and need to be enhanced, backed by monitoring and regular evaluation/assessment of the CSSs for their effective implementation, better utilisation of grants and greater quantitative and qualitative impact on the quality of life in the urban areas. The dependence of the state on the central government is increasing due to poor revenue generation at the local level and the increasing non-development expenditure. The changing urban scene and the financing mechanism demand diversification of revenue sources of the ULBs and mobilisation of non-budgetary resources including external aid for urban infrastructure. With the implementation of the reforms, the state could take advantage of the Urban Reform Incentive Fund (URIF) and the City Challenge Fund (CCF) for financing urban infrastructure.

There is need for a state level *urbanisation strategy* and *urban development/urban infrastructure policy* for overall planning, monitoring and securing alternative financial resources in the urban areas of this ecologically sensitive state, for sustainable development of urban infrastructure and municipal services. The strategy/policy should comprise long-term city/environment-friendly goals such as empowerment of the ULBs by transferring funds, functions and functionaries and adequate urban infrastructure/services. Proper land use/development is necessary to promote eco-friendly sustainable development of urban areas. Environment conservation should be a major thrust area for the urban policymakers and stakeholders in infrastructure development. The development of commercial areas, industrial focal points and new towns should be allowed to grow in harmony with the surrounding environment, and ecologically sensitive areas should not be affected by their activities. Suitable institutional, legal, legislative and managerial environment should be created to promote rationalisation of user charges, accessing the capital market in the form of municipal bonds and maintaining the services with a greater role for the private sector. Municipal financial reporting, budgeting and accounting practices should be upgraded to promote better urban management in the state. The functioning of local self-government institutions at various levels should be strengthened. The major functions listed in the Twelfth Schedule should be transferred to the ULBs, along with funds and functionaries. People's participation must be promoted for development and maintenance of community infrastructure. The urban development policy must emphasise capacity building of the elected and appointed functionaries of local self-governments and other officers responsible for urban governance/infrastructure development.

Employment

Though the NSS unemployment rate of three per cent in Himachal is lower than the seven per cent in India, it has been increasing. It is higher in the urban areas, especially for women. Higher productive employment has to be generated in the rural areas through conscious policy intervention. The lowest growth of employment in the state, despite significantly high economic growth, indicates lack of strong linkage between growth and employment. Appropriate intervention in the industrially advanced districts is necessary for enhancing employment opportunities. In the backward districts, employment should be generated through productive use of the local resource base. The major challenge is the replacement of the existing low-quality jobs with high-quality jobs. Appropriate employment opportunities have to be created to face the serious problem of educated unemployment. This demands a fresh look at the present education policy for manpower planning.

Though the rate of female work-participation has been high in the state, much of the work is in a subsidiary capacity in low productivity activities, mostly self-employment in the agricultural sector, which suffers from severe underemployment. Efforts need to be made to provide employment to women in non-farm activities. The private sector has to be encouraged for the generation of employment in the state removing various bottlenecks that exist. Simultaneously, adequate policy steps have to be taken to promote self-employment. Excessive dependence on the agricultural sector has to be reduced for better quality of employment and incomes in the non-agricultural sector. Improvements in the fast-expanding service sector can create quality employment. Extensive economic and social infrastructure development is the need of the hour. Private investment needs to be encouraged in extensive economic and social infrastructure development. Expansion of village industries will ensure an increase in income levels and the quality of life of rural workers and craftsmen. For this, the KVIC programme needs restructuring to enhance the design and quality of its products. The unorganised sector assumes greater significance for future expansion of employment, as the growth of employment in the organised sector has substantially declined. However, to promote wage- and self-employment in this sector, its different needs, especially finance and marketing, must be met. ITIs and other technical institutions need upgradation and modernisation to absorb the large unmet need for vocational training to new entrants to the labour force. Specialised higher technical education has to be strengthened to enable the technical manpower to take advantage of the opportunities in the international labour market. Institutions like IITs and IIMs, which are known for the quality of their talent, need to be promoted. Appropriate manpower planning and judicious use of human resources need to be ensured. A higher investment rate, along with increase in efficiency of capital use, is essential to ensure growth-led employment generation.

Wages and Prices

Assuming that the actual minimum wage of Rs. 26 per day in Himachal Pradesh in 1995-96 was as desired, its continuance till 1999-00 was below the desired level of Rs. 39.23 per day (calculated using CPIAL). The actual minimum wage was raised to Rs. 51 per day in

2000-01 against the notional desired wage of Rs. 40.24 per day. It was a commendable social welfare measure by the government. The revision of the minimum wage, however, has not been regular. The increase in the real wages of workers, other than agricultural labourers, has also been far less than the warranted wage. Although labourers in Himachal Pradesh are better placed than at the all-India level and in the neighbouring states, unskilled labourers are most vulnerable to rising prices. This applies more to unskilled women labourers.

With fundamental changes in the labour market in the name of globalisation, wage determination cannot be left entirely to the interplay of market forces. Government intervention is necessary to provide social security at least to the least privileged sections of society, particularly when a majority of the population is engaged in the highly unorganised agricultural sector.

Science and Technology

While the state has undergone transformation from subsistence agriculture to commercial-horticulture based development, in the last 30 years this has also created problems of depleting forests, increasing pressure on common property resources and deterioration in the quality of water and air.

There is need for a major input of science and technology, not only for correcting such distortions but also for invigorating every sector of the economy and society. Science and technology in Himachal Pradesh has special relevance for organic cultivation of appropriate species of medicinal plants, remote sensing of crop acreage and production, use of solar passive construction technology for buildings and industry, status assessment of roads and bridges, communicational connectivity between dispersed settlements, and identification of optimal locations for industry.

Sectoral Perspectives and Development Strategy

The territorial evolution of Himachal Pradesh from a patchwork of feudatory states to full statehood in 1971 has had a profound influence on the structure and style of its politics and administration. This also defined the priorities and pace of development in different phases. Himachal has the potential to emerge as a 'model' hill state in terms of just socio-economic development, effective decentralised polity and efficient e-governance. This would demand a 'modern' hill state culture represented by the best quality of physical and social infrastructure; a combination of a highly diversified farm economy, industrial clusters, tourism circuits and hydel-power complexes; an investment climate which is conducive to the entry of multinationals, in particular; and a society responsive to the emerging global scene. Himachal has to enhance its natural endowment to build a 'beautiful' state through professional management of land use and its landscape. It has also to emerge as a 'local governance' state, with development based on local resources, requirements, aspirations, adaptive technology and above all salience of the people. The state also has to cohere to tradition and modernity meaningfully, to invigorate the native culture.

For enunciating an effective development strategy for Himachal, the specificities of the state have to be understood. These include its disposition as a macro-watershed for the entire northwest region, the history of frequent and extensive changes in its territorial contours, and dependence on liberal financial assistance from the Centre. Political stability, which gave continuity to the development process and ensured minimal caste and class conflicts, led to relative efficiency of governance, with easy access of the people to those in political power or the administration. A large number of in-service army personnel, as also ex-servicemen, generates an inflow of sizeable financial resources through remittances and pensions. This is further augmented by a tradition of male out-migration in search of employment in the organised sector, public or private. Himachal Pradesh has come to be assessed as a 'trailblazing success story in human development and social infrastructure scripted by a remarkable synergy between government initiative and community participation'.

This success story is not without its problems and constraints. The per unit cost of development is high in Himachal Pradesh due to the peculiarities of physiography, population distribution and long distances. This adversely affects public access to health, educational, administrative and other services. Its climate, though highly conducive to the promotion of tourism, horticulture and forestry, has negative features affecting the daily life of the people, particularly causing seasonal isolation in some parts. Natural disasters in the form of landslides, flash floods, and even earthquakes are not infrequent. Forests, a natural wealth of Himachal Pradesh, are no longer a source of non-tax revenue because of the legal restrictions on their harvesting. These are to be preserved for the sake of the ecological health, not only its own but also of the neighbouring states. The minerals in the state, particularly limestone, cannot be fully exploited because of the constraints of transport and concern for ecology. Its water resource, as a source of hydel-power, is not easy to exploit because of the need for massive investment, large rehabilitation costs and extensive damage to the forest cover. The scattered pattern of its population increases the cost of public utilities and basic services. Finally, its distance from the large and lucrative markets of the country and a highly dispersed and small internal market are disincentives to investment from outside.

Taking into consideration the strengths and weaknesses of the specificities of Himachal Pradesh and the level of socio-economic and political development achieved, it is now possible to identify the core concerns of the state. These include a progressive rise in the standard of living and the quality of life of the people; correction of fiscal imbalance; acceleration in the implementation of hydel-power generation projects; diversification of subsistence agriculture towards horticulture, with enhanced productivity; dispersal of horticulture to new areas; and promotion of tourism. Additional imperatives include generation of employment opportunities, especially for the educated youth and ex-servicemen; upgradation of the quality of service provision; sustaining ecology; and strengthening grass roots institutions.

Governance

It is ultimately the quality of governance that determines the functional quality and dynamics of every system. Although, Himachal Pradesh has a relatively committed and efficient administration, adoption of the new economic policy and structural reforms have made reinvention of governance critical. The opening of the economy to a competitive culture in the sprit of globalisation is posing an additional challenge. The effort of the state at present is, however, piecemeal. It needs a holistic perspective and integrated approach through the establishment of an 'Economic, Fiscal and Administrative Reforms Division' for co-ordinating and monitoring the reforms. Some specific tasks for governance in Himachal Pradesh include: optimal utilisation of development funds; investment of surplus capital generated in the apple belt; wider induction of the private sector in the economy; and training of the youth towards self-employment by providing them with necessary facilities. A reform of the administrative map of the state needs consideration. This calls for rationalisation of the boundaries of the administrative areas, such as districts and development blocks, and resiting of highly scattered habitations in remote areas to some planned central locations. The latter strategy will economise on the provision of services and reduce the cost of development.

The prominent rivers, either originating in or traversing through Himachal Pradesh and being the source of water and power to its neighbouring states as well, is a reality that needs to be at the centre of any effort at harnessing and enhancing interconnectivity between and among the states involved. This is a situation of both competition and complementarity. Himachal must weigh its relative strengths and weaknesses in each specific case of relationship with its neighbours and devise appropriate strategies. The interconnectivity already established among some of the emerging dynamic centres of industries in Himachal Pradesh, Haryana, Punjab and Chandigarh need to be carried forward through organised collaborative efforts. Every care should be taken to see that this process of collaboration does not lead to the domination of the stronger economy over a relatively weaker one, but is of mutual benefit.

A Northwest Council, on the pattern of the Northeast Council, would help in designing development projects for member states in a co-ordinated manner. This will facilitate preparation of an integrated and sustainable regional plan for the constituent states.

Salient Messages

These, as distilled from the foregoing discussion and can be succinctly put as follows:

- Politico-administrative peculiarities of Himachal Pradesh demand a continuing big role for the state, but future investment in development depends largely upon the private sector. The state has to acquire professional competence in managing the private sector and privatisation.
- Factors of topography, scattered pattern of habitations, and distances make the involvement of Panchayati Raj Institutions indispensable for effective and sustained development. Simultaneously, the elected members need to be trained regularly for their capacity building.
- Bio-business, based on medicinal and aromatic plants, particularly lavender *kutki*, *jatamansi*, and *sugandhwalla*, calls for promotion on a priority basis. In addition, extension of area under bamboo can prove a gold mine for the state.

- Entrepreneurship, as against the urge for government jobs, should be generated and nurtured among the educated youth.
- The existing land policy has to be changed for attracting external investment, especially in industries, tourism and hydel projects.
- The watershed principle is most appropriate for organisation of space for administration and development. The boundaries of the districts and blocks should preferably coincide with those of the watersheds.
- A sub-regional perspective internally and an extra-regional perspective *vis-à-vis* the neighbouring states, are imperative for the state's integrated development.
- The role of science and technology is emerging as paramount for the preparation of watershed plans, identification of appropriate tourism sites, and assessment of glacial retreat; use of bio-fertilisers in horticulture; and promotion of interconnectivity between various localities and government departments.
- A review should be made of the existing legal provisions relevant to different sectors, and all cases that restrain the development process should be revised.

Chapter 1

Himachal Pradesh: A Profile

A brief overview of the evolution of Himachal Pradesh as a state, its geographical location and economy, can provide the background to issues discussed in the *State Development Report of Himachal Pradesh*. This chapter places the state in the national context and also deals with the problems of its intra-regional disparities, resources and the physical, social and economic infrastructures necessary for its all round development.

The history of human settlement in Himachal Pradesh goes back to the palaeolithic period of which stone tools and flakes have been discovered in the valleys of the Sutlej and Beas rivers and also in the foothill zone of the Shivalik hills. Numerous tribes settled in different parts of the region. The recorded history begins with effect from the Maurya period, that is 4th Century B.C., when this part of India was an outlier of Chandragupta's kingdom. Throughout its history, the present territory of Himachal Pradesh remained segmented into a number of principalities, usually under the hegemony of an empire centered at Delhi. The area has also been a refuge for several freedom-loving population groups/castes, particularly *Rajputs* and *Brahmins* who refused to live under the imperial authority centered at Delhi. They settled in specific parts of this region, which took the form of small/tiny states under the chiefdom of *Rajput* princes. The colonial empire brought them under the hegemony of the British Crown in 1859. They continued enjoying a degree of autonomy but were essentially in the nature of feudatory states. On the eve of Independence of India, half of the present territory of Himachal Pradesh was divided into 30 princely states and the other half was a part of the Punjab province of the British Empire. Himachal Pradesh acquired its present disposition in phases over time after independence.

Himachal now is one of the most dynamic hill states of India. It scores significantly high on indicators of human development. Its resources of forests, fruits, minerals, health resorts, and hydel power hold the promise of great progress. Natural assets for tourism in the state are ideal. It has its own rich culture, physiography suited to almost all types of crops and fruits, and an independent administrative identity. Its notable accomplishments have been in literacy, agriculture, horticulture, roads, forests, hydel power generation and tourism. The state is called 'the apple belt' of India. Its vast potential for hydel power generation, because of its locational advantage, has attracted the attention of the entire nation, as a major resource awaiting full exploitation. Its physical diversity, its climate and its peaceful environment can derive high economic value from the development of the tourist industry.

Himachal Pradesh in the National Context

Himachal Pradesh with an area of 55,673 sq. km. is one of the smaller states of India (Table 1.1). It ranks 17th among the States and Union Territories in terms of area, which is one-sixth of the largest state - Rajasthan. With a population of 60.8 lakh, Himachal Pradesh ranks 21st among the States and Union Territories. That its population is 27 times below that of the most populous state, Uttar Pradesh, is an indicator of its smallness.

The state accounted for 1.7 per cent of the total area of the country and 0.59 per cent of the total population in 2001. With a density of 109 persons per sq. km., it ranks 28th among the states and Union Territories which is much below the all-India average of 324 persons per sq. km.

The urban population constitutes 9.79 per cent of the total population of the state, the lowest among all States and Union Territories. Almost eight out of every

TABLE 1.1

Status of Himachal Pradesh on Selected Parameters in India, 1999-2001

States/Union Territories	*Area*(in sq. km.)*	*Population#*	*Density# (persons per sq. km.)*	*Urban Population# (in per cent)*	*Literate# (in per cent)*	*Per Capita Income## (Rs.) 2000-01 (P) at 1993-94 Base*
India	**32,87,263**	**102,70,15,247**	**324**	**27.78**	**65.38**	**10306**
States						
Andhra Pradesh	2,75,069	7,57,27,541	275	28.08	61.11	9697
Arunachal Pradesh	83,743	10,91,117	13	20.41	54.74	—
Assam	78,438	2,66,38,407	340	12.72	64.28	6157
Bihar	94,163	8,28,78,798	880	10.47	47.53	4345
Chhattisgarh	1,35,133	2,07,95,956	154	20.08	65.18	*
Goa	3,702	13,43,998	363	47.77	82.32	26106
Gujarat	1,96,024	5,05,96,992	258	37.35	69.97	12975
Haryana	44,212	2,1,082,989	477	29	68.59	14331
Himachal Pradesh	**55,673**	**60,77,248**	**109**	**9.79**	**77.13**	**10942**
Jammu and Kashmir	2,22,236	1,00,69,917	99	24.88	54.46	7383
Jharkhand	79,714	2,69,09,428	338	22.25	54.13	*
Karnataka	1,91,791	5,27,33,958	275	33.98	67.04	11910
Kerala	38,863	3,18,38,619	819	25.97	90.92	10712
Madhya Pradesh	3,08,000	6,03,85,118	196	26.67	64.11	7003
Maharashtra	3,07,713	9,67,52,247	314	42.4	77.27	15,172
Manipur	22,429	23,88,634	107	23.88	68.87	—
Meghalaya	22,429	23,06,069	103	19.63	63.31	8460
Mizoram	21,087	8,91,058	42	49.5	88.49	—
Nagaland	16,579	19,88,636	120	17.74	67.11	—
Orissa	1,55,707	3,67,06,920	236	14.97	63.61	5187
Punjab	50,362	2,42,89,296	482	33.95	69.95	14916
Rajasthan	3,42,239	5,64,73,122	165	23.38	61.03	7932
Sikkim	7,096	5,40,493	76	11.1	69.98	—
Tamil Nadu	1,30,058	6,21,10,839	478	43.86	73.47	—
Tripura	10,491	31,91,168	304	17.02	73.66	9372
Uttar Pradesh	2,38,566	16,60,52,859	689	20.78	57.36	5770
Uttaranchal	53,484	84,79,562	159	25.59	72.28	*
West Bengal	88,752	8,02,21,171	904	28.03	69.22	9778
Union Territories						
Andaman and Nicobar Islands	8,249	3,56,265	43	32.67	81.18	*
Chandigarh	114	9,00,914	7903	89.78	81.76	29208
Dadra and Nagar Haveli	491	2,20,451	449	22.89	60.03	*
Daman and Diu	112	1,58,059	1411	36.26	81.09	*
Delhi	1,483	1,37,82,976	9294	93.01	81.82	*
Lakshadweep	32	60,595	1894	44.47	87.52	*
Pondicherry	492	9,73,829	2029	66.57	81.49	*

Source: # - *Census of India, 2001, Provisional Population Totals, Paper-1 of 2001*, DCO, Punjab.
- *Statistical Abstract of Punjab, 2002*, Economic Advisor to Government of Punjab, Chandigarh.
* - Ministry of Information and Broadcasting (2003): *India 2002, A Reference Annual*, Publication Division, Government of India, New Delhi.

ten persons in the state are literate, and it ranks 11th in terms of literacy.

Evolution of the State

Historically, Himachal Pradesh has not only experienced different stages of social transformation, but has also seen many changes in its size and administrative structure. Comprising 30 princely states, it came into existence as a Chief Commissioners Province in 1948, and graduated through a number of stages of administrative transformation to a full-fledged state of the Indian Union in 1971. To start with, it consisted of four districts — Chamba, Mahasu, Mandi and Sirmaur. Under the rule of the princes, this region suffered from the worst kind of feudal exploitation. The rulers did not consider it necessary to develop their territories, by utilising the available wealth of natural resources (M.G. Singh, 1985). Since its formation

MAP 1.1

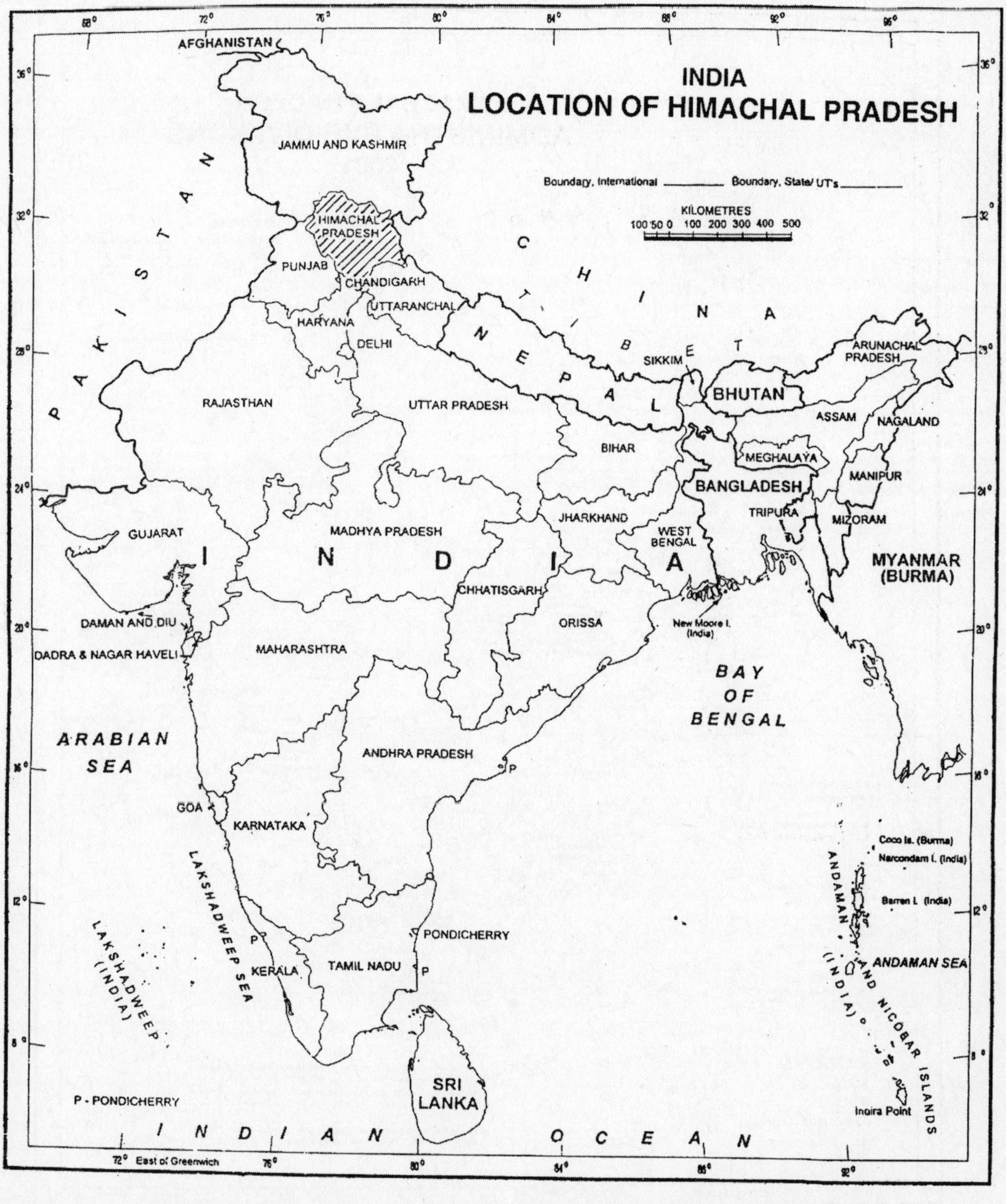

Source: Census of India, 2001, Provisional Population Totals, Paper 1 of 2001, Himachal Pradesh, *Directorate of Census Operations,* Himachal Pradesh.

MAP 1.2

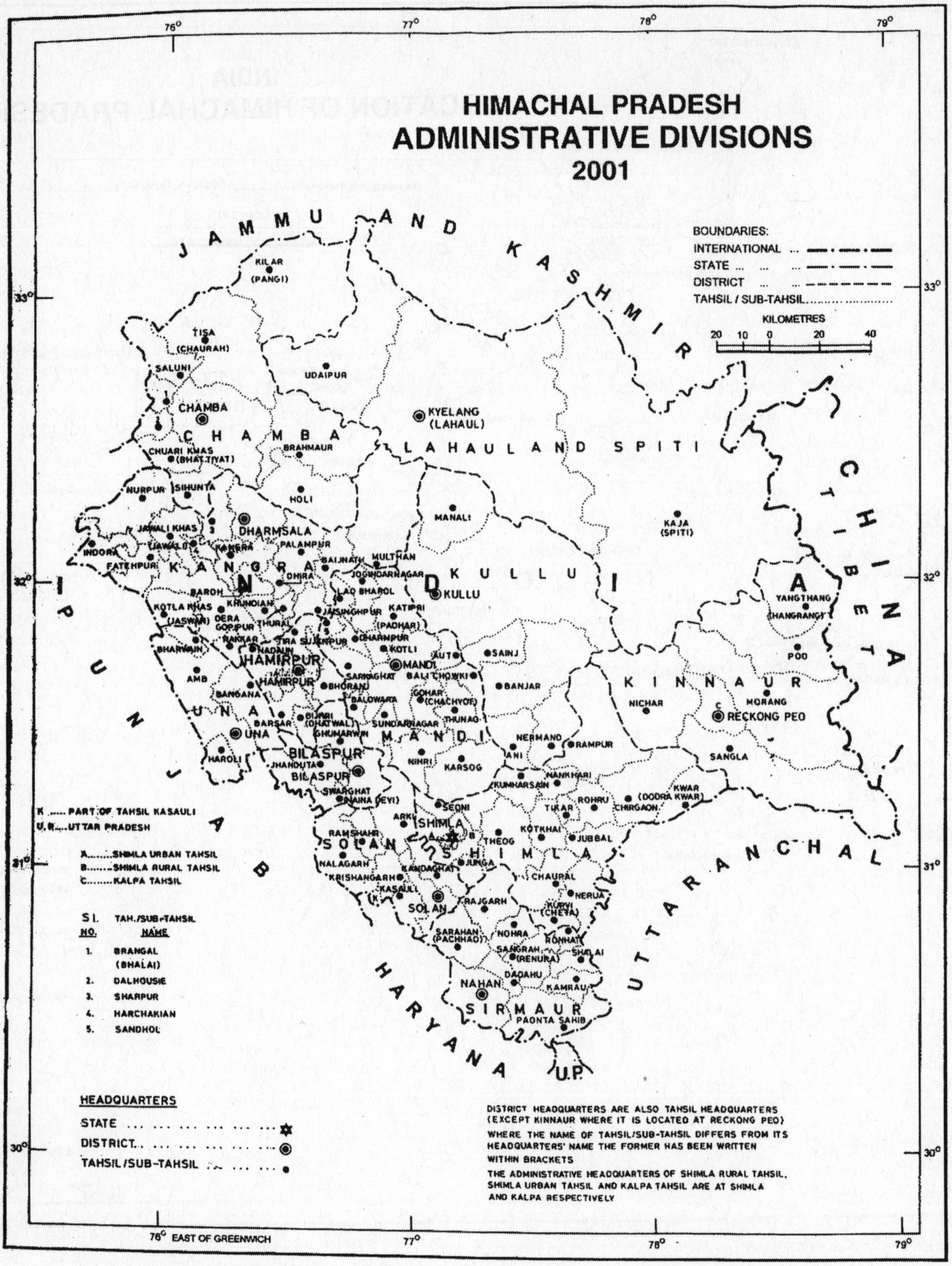

Source: *Census of India, 2001, Provisional Population Totals, Paper 1 of 2001*, Himachal Pradesh, *Directorate of Census Operations*, Himachal Pradesh.

Himachal has, however, attained a high level of overall development.

The changes in size and the administrative structure that the state has gone through between 1948 and 1971 have influenced the level and pace of its development. Himachal inherited a primitive economic system from its feudal structure, and an inadequate institutional framework, which constituted a weak base for socio-economic development. Thus, at the initial stages the state was at a disadvantage in relation to the rest of the country in pursuing the process of development. In this context, the institutional task of setting up an integrated administration, transforming a feudal system into a modern democratic one, necessitating the abolition of all feudal practices and laws, was certainly fairly difficult (L.R. Sharma, 1985).

The merger of the princely state of Bilaspur in 1954 enlarged the geographical area of Himachal Pradesh and increased the number of its districts to five. In 1960, a new district of Kinnaur was carved out of Mahasu district.

The states reorganisation of 1966 transferred parts of Punjab (Ambala, Hoshiarpur and Gurdaspur) to Himachal Pradesh, adding three more districts, namely, Kangra, Kullu, and Lahaul and Spiti. These areas were under the direct administration of the British Government before independence and were far behind the other progressive regions of Punjab and failed to achieve substantial economic development, until their integration with Himachal Pradesh (M.G. Singh, 1985).

On 25 January 1971, the state was granted full-fledged statehood. Una and Hamirpur districts were carved out of Kangra district and Mahasu district was divided into Shimla and Solan districts on September 1, 1972. The people of the state classify themselves into two sub-regional identities: the old Himachal Pradesh and the new Himachal Pradesh. The erstwhile princely states constitute the old Himachal and territories that were earlier part of Punjab, form the new areas. The former is less developed than the latter.

There has been no change in the number of districts since 1972, even though there are substantial variations in area and population of the districts. Lahaul and Spiti, with an area of 13,835 sq. km. is the largest district. It contains 24.85 per cent of the state's area followed by Chamba with 11.72 per cent (Table 1.2). Hamirpur with 2.01 per cent of the area of the state is at the bottom with Bilaspur (2.1 per cent) coming next. However, these rankings become totally different, once the population is taken into account. Lahaul and Spiti, which occupies the first place in terms of area, is relegated to the last position with a population of 33,224, Kinnaur with 83,950 coming next. Chamba, the second largest in area, occupies the fifth position in terms of population. Almost half the population lives in three districts — Kangra, Mandi and Shimla and the bottom three districts of Lahaul and Spiti, Kinnaur and Bilaspur, share 7.54 per cent of the state's population. These variations in the land-man ratio are reflected in the density of population. The low density of population in the larger districts is due to the limited arable land, unfavorable physio-geographical conditions, poor means of transport and communication, hostile climate and the low level of economic development.

TABLE 1.2

District-wise Status of Selected Parameters in Himachal Pradesh, 2001

District	*Area (in 000 sq. km.)*	*Population*	*Density (persons per sq. km.)*	*Urban Population (in per cent)*	*Literates (in per cent)*
Kangra	5,739	13,38,536	233	5.39	80.68
Mandi	3,950	9,00,987	228	6.77	75.86
Shimla	5,131	7,21,745	141	23.12	79.68
Solan	1,936	4,99,380	258	18.26	77.16
Chamba	6,528	4,60,499	71	7.50	63.73
Sirmaur	2,825	4,58,351	162	10.38	70.85
Una	1,540	4,47,967	291	8.80	81.09
Hamirpur	1,118	4,12,009	369	7.32	83.16
Kullu	5503	3,79,865	69	7.92	73.36
Bilaspur	1,167	3,40,735	292	6.44	78.80
Kinnaur**	6,401	8,3,950	13	—	NA
Lahaul and Spiti	13,835	33,224	2	—	73.17

Source: Census of India, 2001, Provisional Population Totals, Paper 1 of 2001, Himachal Pradesh, *Directorate of Census Operations,* Himachal Pradesh.

Note: ** - Based on projected population, N.A. – Not available

Shimla with a population of 1,44,578 is the only class 1 town (with a population of more than 1,00,000) in the state. Lahaul and Spiti and Kinnaur districts have no urban centres. The pattern of urbanisation in Himachal Pradesh is different from that of the neighbouring states of Punjab and Haryana. Its undulating topography prevents the development of big towns and is more conducive to smaller towns. One-fourth of the state's urban population lives in Shimla and 31 per cent in Class V and Class VI towns. Shimla, Solan and Kangra districts together share half the urban population of the state.

Hamirpur district with 83 per cent of literates is at the top of the literacy chart, closely followed by Una

(81.1 per cent) and Kangra (80.1 per cent) while Chamba with 64 per cent literates is at the bottom.

The state is a linguistic unit inhabited by Hindi speaking people. It had a population of 60.7 lakh in 2001 distributed in 20,729 villages and 57 towns. Administratively, it is divided into 12 districts, 75 *tehsils* and 75 blocks. The city of Shimla is the capital of the state.

Physical Setting

The state took its name Himachal from the Himalayas. Himachal Pradesh is a hilly and mountainous state situated between 30° 22′ and 33° 12′ north latitude and 75° 47′ and 79° 4′ east longitude. Its neighbours are Jammu and Kashmir in the north, Punjab in the west and southwest, Haryana and Uttar Pradesh in the south and Tibet in the east. The territory of the state is mountainous, except for a few pockets bordering Punjab and Haryana, which have a sub-mountainous topography. Altitude in different areas ranges from 350 to 7000 metres above the mean sea level. Wide differences in geo-physical features account for considerable variation in the climate and rainfall of different sub-regions of the state. Physiographically, the state is part of the Himalayan system. From south to north it can be topographically divided into three zones:

1) The Shivaliks or outer Himalayas,

2) Inner Himalayas or mid-mountains, and

3) Alpine zone or the greater Himalayas.

The lower hills of Kangra, Hamirpur, Una, Bilaspur and the lower parts of Mandi, Solan and Sirmaur districts are part of the Shivalik range. The altitude of this zone varies from 350 metres to 1500 metres above the mean sea level. The annual rainfall varies from 1500 mm. to 1800 mm. Since it is made up of consolidated deposits, which can erode easily, the zone experiences deforestation and a high rate of soil erosion. It is suitable for the cultivation of maize, wheat, ginger, sugarcane, paddy, table potatoes and citrus fruits.

The altitude of the inner Himalayas or the mid-mountains ranges between 1500 metres and 4500 metres above mean sea level. This zone includes areas such as the upper parts of Pachhad and Renuka in Sirmaur district, Chachiot and Karsog *tehsil* of Mandi district, and upper parts of Churah *tehsil* of Chamba district. The quality of soil in these areas ranges from silty loam to clay loam to dark brown colour and is useful for seed potatoes and temperate fruits. From the horticultural point of view, this area is suitable for stone and soft fruits.

The greater Himalayas or the Alpine zone has an altitude of 4500 metres above mean sea level. This area comprises Kinnaur district, Pangi *tehsil* of Chamba district and some areas of Lahaul and Spiti. Rainfall is scanty in this zone. The soil has high texture with variable fertility. The climate is temperate and semi-arctic in winter. The climate and the soil are best suited to the cultivation of dry fruits. From October to March-April, this zone remains cut off from the rest of the world.

The climate of Himachal Pradesh varies from semi-tropical to the semi-arctic depending on the altitude. It has three seasons, which have an impact on its economic development. The rainy season lasts from July to September, winter from October to March and summer from April to June. During summer, there is an influx of tourists to the state both from within the country and abroad.

Five perennial rivers — Sutlej, Beas, Ravi, Chenab and Yamuna — flow through the state. The river system in the Himalayas cannot be exploited for irrigation as fully as in the plains, but it is the source of water for the Indus river basin. The undulating terrain limits the utility of these rivers for irrigation. During the rains, the flow in the rivers is heavy and in winter, with snowfall and the water frozen at higher altitudes, they shrink into narrow streams. These rivers, however, provide ample scope for the generation of hydel power.

The diversity of altitude and climate has given Himachal Pradesh a rich variety of flora. Covering nearly two-thirds of the total area of the state, forests form an important source of income, providing raw material for industries, fodder and nutritious grasses for livestock and resources to meet the needs of agriculturists and other people. They are also a source of herbs and drugs. The physiography of the state also determines its economic potential. Agriculture in general is handicapped by the steep and hilly terrain, hazards of climate, small and scattered holdings, thin stony soil, limited irrigation and a limited cultivated area, only about 10 per cent. There is little scope for expanding the cultivated area. However, the state has overcome absence of adequate land, by resort to horticulture and optimal use of the cultivated area.

Despite sufficient resources in particular areas, Himachal's industrial potential is one of the least in India. Only a small proportion of the population is engaged in industry. Its remote location, geographic conditions, such as difficult terrain and severe winter, lack of transport facilities and other infrastructure, have thwarted industrial development. However, industry is gradually picking up, even in these difficult conditions.

There are some additional constraints, associated with the geographical features and climate of a hilly region. These are for instance, shorter productive man-years and lower physical productivity at high altitudes, and the difficulty in developing alternative means of transport and communication with the existing technology.

Economic Development

In this section we have tried to explain the long-term economic development trends through such indicators as income-growth, structural composition of the income, per capita income and poverty.

It is important to have an understanding of the socio-economic base of the state at the time of its formation and even before that. Himachal Pradesh requires a different kind of approach for its economic development. The hill areas, because of their peripheral location have been neglected in the past. Himachal Pradesh was no exception and the state started with the disadvantage of a weak economic and institutional base, and a low level of catalytic skills of the people to provide services such as roads and transport, banking, medical and health, which can create conditions for modern development. In fact, Himachal's surfaced road-length per one lakh population (8.5 km.) in 1950-51 was the lowest in India. Per capita consumption of electricity in 1948 was 0.99 kwh as against the national average of 17.8 kwh (L. R. Sharma, 1987). It was only after the formation of Himachal Pradesh that the people and government of this hilly region began to make concerted efforts to improve their own economic condition and that of the state (M.G. Singh, 1985).

The planning process at the national and the state level aimed at achieving a more balanced growth. The attempt through the five year plans has been to give a boost to economies of states by investing in relatively backward areas. Himachal Pradesh is one of the eleven special category states in the country, eligible for such special assistance.

During the First Five Year Plan, Himachal grew at an annual rate of 1.6 per cent as against the national average of 3.6 per cent (Table 1.3). In the Third Plan, the growth rate was slightly higher at the national level.

TABLE 1.3

Growth Rate of Himachal Pradesh and National Economy During Five Year Plans

Plan Period	*Himachal Pradesh*	*All India*	*H.P./India Ratio*
First Plan (1951-56)	1.6	3.6	0.44
Second Plan (1956-61)	4.4	4.1	1.07
Third Plan (1961-66)	3.0	2.4	1.25
Annual Plans	–	4.1	
Fourth Plan (1969-74)	3.0	3.4	0.88
Fifth Plan (1974-78)	4.6	5.2	0.88
Annual Plans (1978-79 to 1979-80)	3.6	0.2	18.00
Sixth Plan (1980-85)	3.0	5.3	0.57
Seventh Plan (1985-90)	8.8	6.0	1.47
Annual Plan (1990-91)	3.9	5.4	0.72
Annual Plan (1991-92)	0.4	0.8	0.50
Eighth Plan (1992-97)	6.3	6.2	1.02
Ninth Plan (1997-2002)	6.2	5.4	1.15
1997-98	6.4	5.0	1.28
1998-99	7.2	6.6	1.09
1999-00	6.6	6.6	1.00
2000-01 (revised)	6.2	4.4	1.41
2001-02 (quick)	5.1	5.6	0.91

Source: *Economic Survey, 2002-03*, Department of Economics and Statistics, Himachal Pradesh.

Its recognition as a full-fledged state of the Indian Union in 1971 gave a new direction to the pace of development in Himachal Pradesh. So far the Union Government had treated it as any other Union Territory, from each one of which Himachal differed greatly in many respects. (Planning Commission, H.P., Fourth Plan). The rate of economic growth was slower than that of the national economy, because the development of Himachal Pradesh in its initial stages, required heavy investments in certain fields without considerations of immediate results. It was visualised that if those fields were fully developed, the rest would follow. In the post-1971 period up to the Sixth Plan (1980-85), the state economy grew at a slower pace than the national. Then, as visualised, it picked up and grew at a rate faster than the national average. In the Sixth Plan, the rate of growth of the state's economy was almost half the national average. By the Seventh Plan, the scenario had reversed. Economic growth of the state was almost 1.5 times that of the national average. In the Ninth Plan, the state's economy grew at an annual rate of 6.4 per cent as against 5.4 per cent at the national level (Figure 1.1).

A comparison of the economic growth with neighbouring Haryana and Punjab indicated that the

FIGURE 1.1

Growth Rate of Himachal Pradesh and Indian Economy During Five Year Plans

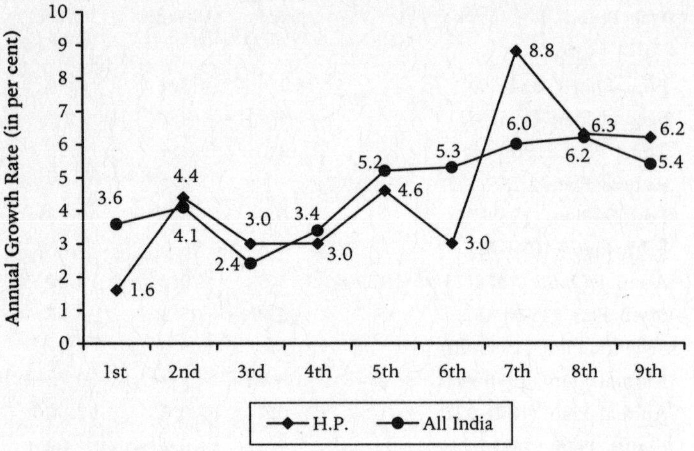

Source: *Economic Survey, 2002-03*, Department of Economics and Statistics, Himachal Pradesh.

economy of Himachal grew at a relatively faster rate during the decade of the nineties (Table 1.4) than in the eighties. In the eighties, the state's economy grew at an annual rate of five per cent per annum, which increased to 6.7 per cent by the nineties. The corresponding figures at the national level were 5.6 per cent and 6.8 per cent. During the same decade, the growth rate in the neighbouring hilly state of Jammu and Kashmir was lower than that of Himachal Pradesh.

TABLE 1.4

Trends in the Rate of Growth in Gross Domestic Product in Himachal Pradesh, Neighbouring States and India During the Eighties and Nineties

States	*1980-81 to 1990-91*	*1993-94 to 1998-99*
Himachal Pradesh	**5.0**	**6.7**
Haryana	6.2	5.8
Punjab	5.4	5.0
Jammu and Kashmir	2.2	4.7
India	**5.6**	**6.8**

Source: *Tenth Five Year Plan*, Planning Commission, Government of India, New Delhi.

State Domestic Product

The growth of a state's domestic product (SDP) is considered the single most important indicator of economic development. For want of comparable data on a single base since 1950-51, a detailed analysis has been done only for the period after the formation of the state. However, on the 1950-51 base, the average annual growth rate of the Himachal Pradesh income during 1950-51 to 1965-66 was 3.4 per cent as against 3.9 per cent at the all-India level.

The new series data on the 1993-94 base indicate that during the last three decades, since the formation of the state (1970-71 to 2000-01), the SDP has grown at an annual rate of 4.27 per cent (Table 1.5). A breakdown of the SDP growth reveals that the annual rate has been the highest (6.39%) between 1985-86 and 1990-91 as against lowest of 2.44 per cent between 1975-76 and 1980-81.

The primary sector has grown at an annual rate of 1.56 per cent, the secondary at 6.11 per cent and the tertiary at 6.17 per cent during the last three-decades. The growth of the state's economy has depended mostly on the performance of the agricultural sector. The state's economic growth was the highest (6.4%) between 1985-86 and 1990-91. This was the time when the growth of the agricultural sector was also the highest (4.72%). Similarly, between 1975-76 and 1980-81, the annual rate of growth was the lowest (2.44%). This was the period when the agricultural sector experienced a negative growth (-0.34%).

The rate of growth of real estate, ownership of dwellings and business services (2.83%) and agricultural and animal husbandry (1.89%) has been below the state average during the last three decades. Forestry and logging experienced a negative growth (-0.15%), because of the state policy of conservation. The mid-eighties marked a significant turning point in the management of forests in the state. Conservation assumed importance and green felling for commercial purposes was banned. From 1980-81 to 1985-86, this sector experienced a negative growth of –8.23 per cent.

Sectors that recorded a rate of growth higher than the state average were electricity, gas and water supply (21%), mining and quarrying (13.46%), banking and insurance (11.69%), fishing (8.72%), trade, hotels and restaurants (7.93%), manufacturing (6.91%), public administration (6.52%), transport, storage and communication (4.89%) and construction (4.74%) (Figure 1.2).

The production structure of the state in 1950-51 was highly unbalanced, even more than what it was at the national level. Agriculture, industry and services contributed 69.4 per cent, 17.3 per cent and 13.2 per cent respectively to the state domestic product. The corresponding figures at the national level were 51.3 per cent, 33.1 per cent and 15.8 per cent respectively.

TABLE 1.5

Sectoral Rates of Growth in Himachal Pradesh, 1970-71 to 2000-01

(At 1993-94 Constant Prices)

	1970-71 to 1975-76	*1975-76 to 1980-81*	*1980-81 to 1985-86*	*1985-86 to 1990-91*	*1990-91 to 1995-96*	*1995-96 to 2000-01*	*1970-71 to 2000-01*
A. Primary							
Agriculture and animal husbandry	4.63	-1.10	2.70	4.37	-0.75	1.67	1.89
Forestry and logging	-1.87	0.56	-8.23	5.52	4.40	-0.63	-0.15
Fishing	7.78	33.02	4.87	10.30	0.67	-1.10	8.72
Mining and quarrying	15.56	41.04	15.65	8.12	-4.64	9.77	13.46
Total (A)	**2.85**	**-0.34**	**0.68**	**4.72**	**0.06**	**1.47**	**1.56**
B. Secondary							
Manufacturing	-1.59	-9.36	15.07	15.59	15.82	8.69	6.91
Registered	-5.91	-4.28	22.48	19.46	16.39	9.17	8.97
Unregistered	1.39	-12.72	6.54	7.20	14.02	7.03	3.56
Construction	4.11	7.75	-0.85	2.83	8.63	6.28	4.74
Electricity, gas and water supply	26.01	15.79	48.22	13.54	16.89	3.47	20.97
Total (B)	**2.75**	**4.16**	**4.35**	**6.99**	**12.10**	**6.58**	**6.11**
C. Tertiary							
Transport, storage and communication	3.57	-0.17	5.31	-3.62	9.48	15.93	4.89
Railways	5.51	1.71	2.21	0.00	-4.36	17.04	3.48
Transport by other means and storage	2.24	-11.14	3.82	4.93	14.82	15.88	4.70
Communication	6.78	14.95	6.51	-10.77	2.56	15.91	5.60
Trade, hotel and restaurants	8.05	17.24	4.33	7.74	5.03	5.73	7.93
Banking and insurance	11.46	12.27	13.94	17.29	5.10	10.44	11.69
Real estate and ownership of dwellings and business services	2.73	3.55	2.20	3.11	2.98	2.42	2.83
Public administration	6.17	3.45	5.87	9.28	0.76	14.10	6.52
Other services	2.93	4.59	3.22	9.55	4.99	11.60	6.10
Total (C)	**4.52**	**6.40**	**4.49**	**7.99**	**4.05**	**9.68**	**6.17**
Total net state domestic product at factor cost	3.25	2.44	2.70	6.39	4.66	6.28	4.27

Source: Computed from different volumes of *State Domestic Product*, Department of Economics and Statistics, Himachal Pradesh.

FIGURE 1.2

Sectoral Rate of Growth in Himachal Pradesh, 1970-71 to 2001
(At 1993-94 Constant Prices)

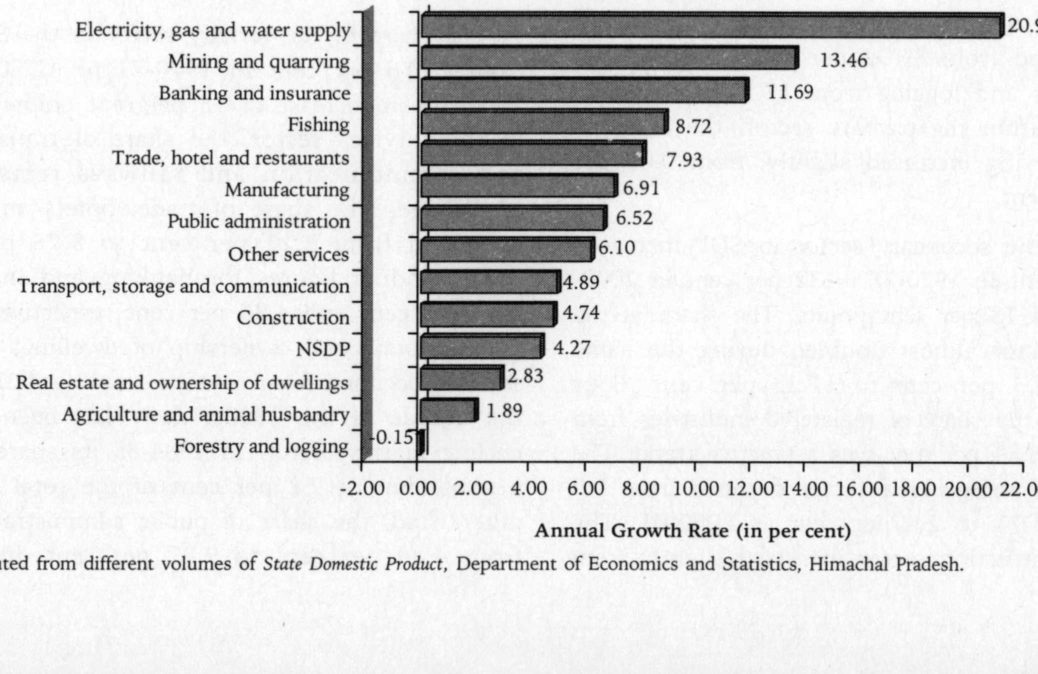

Source: Computed from different volumes of *State Domestic Product*, Department of Economics and Statistics, Himachal Pradesh.

TABLE 1.6

Sectoral Distribution of SDP of Himachal Pradesh, 1970-71 to 2000-01

(At 1993-94 Constant Prices)

	1970-71	1975-76	1980-81	1985-86	1990-91	1995-96	2000-01
A. Primary							
Agriculture and animal husbandry	39.02	41.68	34.95	34.97	31.77	24.37	19.52
Forestry and logging	17.13	13.28	12.11	6.90	6.62	6.54	4.67
Fishing	0.06	0.07	0.27	0.30	0.36	0.30	0.21
Mining and quarrying	0.09	0.15	0.76	1.38	1.49	0.94	1.10
Total (A)	**56.29**	**55.19**	**48.09**	**43.54**	**40.24**	**32.14**	**25.50**
B. Secondary							
Manufacturing	5.30	4.17	2.26	3.99	6.05	10.04	11.23
Registered	2.36	1.48	1.05	2.54	4.54	7.73	8.84
Unregistered	2.95	2.69	1.21	1.45	1.51	2.31	2.40
Construction	13.58	14.16	18.23	15.29	12.90	15.54	15.54
Electricity, gas and water supply	0.06	0.16	-0.40	2.48	3.44	5.97	5.22
Total (B)	**18.95**	**18.49**	**20.09**	**21.76**	**22.38**	**31.55**	**32.00**
C. Tertiary							
Transport, storage and communication	2.01	2.04	1.79	2.03	1.24	1.55	2.40
Railways	0.09	0.10	0.10	0.10	0.07	0.05	0.07
Transport by other means and storage	1.43	1.36	0.67	0.71	0.66	1.05	1.61
Communication	0.49	0.58	1.02	1.23	0.51	0.46	0.71
Trade, hotel and restaurants	3.11	3.90	7.66	8.29	8.83	8.99	8.76
Banking and insurance	0.62	0.91	1.43	2.41	3.93	4.01	4.86
Real estate and ownership of dwellings and business services	6.41	6.25	6.60	6.44	5.51	5.08	4.22
Public administration	4.89	5.62	5.90	6.87	7.86	6.50	9.27
Other services	7.72	7.60	8.43	8.65	10.01	10.17	12.99
Total (C)	**24.76**	**26.32**	**31.82**	**34.69**	**37.38**	**36.30**	**42.50**

Source: Computed from different volumes of *State Domestic Product*, Department of Economics and Statistics, Himachal Pradesh.

The production structure of the state has since changed. The share of the primary sector in SDP declined sharply from 56.29 per cent in 1970-71 to 25.50 per cent in 2000-01, a decrease of 31 per cent points (Tables 1.6 & 1.7). Agriculture and animal husbandry declined from 39.02 per cent to 19.52 per cent, and forestry and logging from 17.13 per cent to 4.67 per cent. Within the primary sector, the share of mining and quarrying increased slightly, from 0.09 per cent to 1.1 per cent.

The share of the secondary sector in SDP increased from 18.95 per cent in 1970-71 to 32 per cent in 2000-01, an increase of 13 per cent points. The share of the manufacturing sector almost doubled during the same duration, from 5.3 per cent to 11.23 per cent. Four times increase in the share of registered industries from 2.36 per cent to 8.84 per cent was a positive trend. The proportion in the unregistered sector declined from 2.9 per cent in 1970-71 to 2.4 per cent in 2000-01. The share of the construction sector increased slightly from 13.58 per cent in 1970-71 to 15.54 per cent in 2000-2001. The corresponding figures for electricity, gas and water supply were 0.06 per cent and 5.22 per cent respectively.

The share of the tertiary sector in the SDP increased from 24.76 per cent in 1970-71 to 42.50 per cent in 2000-01, an increase of 18 per cent points (Figure 1.3). In the services sector, the share of transport, storage and communication and railways remained almost unchanged. The share of trade, hotels and restaurants increased from 3.11 per cent to 8.76 per cent. The corresponding figures for banking and insurance were 0.62 per cent and 4.86 per cent respectively. The share of real estate and ownership of dwellings and business services declined from 6.41 per cent to 4.22 per cent. In the decade of the 1990s, there has been a consistent decline in this sector. In 1984-85 its share increased to a maximum of 7.2 per cent of the total SDP. On the other hand, the share of public administration increased from 4.89 per cent to 9.27 per cent during the last

TABLE 1.7

Share of Primary, Secondary and Tertiary Sectors in the SDP of Himachal Pradesh, 1970-71 to 2000-01

(At 1993-94 Constant Prices)

Years	Primary	Secondary	Tertiary
1970-71	56.29	18.95	24.76
1971-72	54.88	19.55	25.56
1972-73	52.84	21.37	25.79
1973-74	53.69	20.25	26.05
1974-75	53.09	19.83	27.09
1975-76	55.19	18.49	26.32
1976-77	50.68	21.38	27.94
1977-78	52.04	21.82	26.14
1978-79	52.83	19.43	27.74
1979-80	46.65	20.50	32.85
1980-81	48.09	20.09	31.82
1981-82	49.24	19.46	31.30
1982-83	44.37	21.44	34.19
1983-84	47.59	18.68	33.74
1984-85	43.81	19.04	37.14
1985-86	43.54	21.76	34.69
1986-87	43.88	20.00	36.12
1987-88	37.98	22.86	39.16
1988-89	37.88	24.36	37.76
1989-90	41.99	18.85	39.17
1990-91	40.24	22.38	37.38
1991-92	38.53	22.70	38.76
1992-93	36.99	24.14	38.87
1993-94	35.99	25.29	38.72
1994-95	33.27	30.41	36.32
1995-96	32.14	31.55	36.30
1996-97	30.84	32.49	36.67
1997-98	29.23	32.21	38.56
1998-99	27.57	32.03	40.40
1999-00	24.61	32.49	42.90
2000-01	25.50	32.00	42.50

Source: Computed from different volumes of *State Domestic Product*, Department of Economics and Statistics, Himachal Pradesh.

three decades. The share of other services increased from 7.72 per cent to 12.99 per cent during the same period.

From a highly unbalanced structure of economy, the state is moving towards a more balanced one, which would help it to achieve a higher level of development.

Per Capita Income

The level and growth of per capita income is used to measure the economic development of a state. Himachal, in 2000-01, had a per capita income of Rs. 10,942, slightly higher than the national average of Rs. 10,306.

FIGURE 1.3

Net State Domestic Product at Factor Cost by Sectors in Himachal Pradesh: 1970-71 to 2000-01 (At 1993-94 Constant Prices)

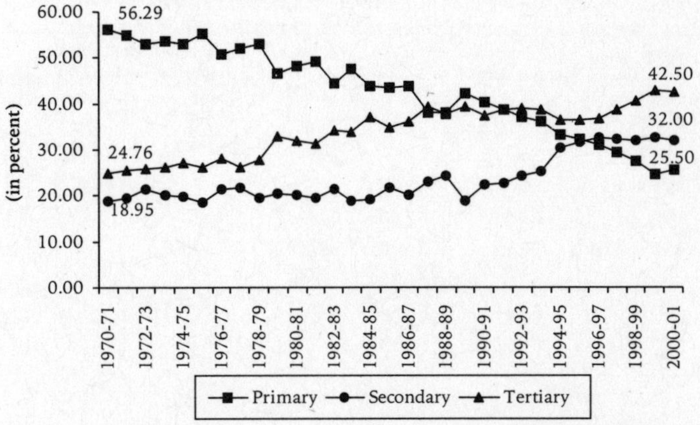

Source: Computed from different volumes of *State Domestic Product*, Department of Economics and Statistics, Himachal Pradesh.

Taking a longer-term view, during the last three decades, the per capita income of the state has nearly doubled and has continued to be higher than at the all-India level (Table 1.8 and Figure 1.4). However, there have been variations in the level of per capita income. Between 1970-71 and 1982-83, the per capita income of the state was higher than the all-India average, and lower in the period, 1983-84 to 1991-92. Since then, it has always been higher than the all-India average. In comparison, the per capita incomes of the neighbouring states of Punjab and Haryana, have always been higher than that of Himachal Pradesh. Jammu and Kashmir has always had a lower per capita income.

FIGURE 1.4

Per Capita Income of Selected States, 1970-71 to 2000-01 (At 1993-94 Prices)

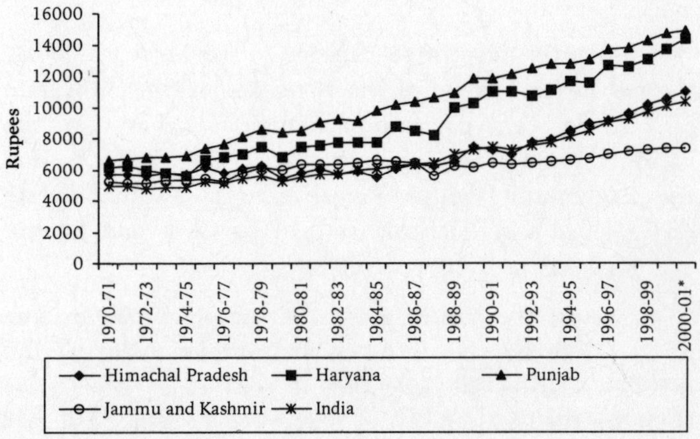

Source: Computed from different volumes of *Statistical Abstracts of Punjab and Haryana.*

TABLE 1.8

Per Capita Income of Selected States, 1970-71 to 2000-2001

(At 1993-94 Constant Prices)

Year	*Himachal Pradesh*	*Haryana*	*Punjab*	*Jammu and Kashmir*	*India*
1970-71	5659	6141	6591	5165	4967
1971-72	5676	6267	6677	5155	4920
1972-73	5584	5923	6764	5071	4739
1973-74	5784	5734	6819	5269	4873
1974-75	5659	5608	6899	5335	4849
1975-76	6160	6575	7343	5401	5186
1976-77	5726	6834	7644	5212	5100
1977-78	6085	6939	8131	5759	5438
1978-79	6193	7450	8550	6107	5618
1979-80	5392	6757	8408	5966	5202
1980-81	5792	7429	8501	6343	5469
1981-82	6035	7510	9032	6329	5650
1982-83	5707	7758	9183	6364	5643
1983-84	5864	7702	9145	6407	5972
1984-85	5516	7720	9749	6561	6083
1985-86	6042	8708	10172	6543	6214
1986-87	6362	8507	10283	6461	6311
1987-88	6202	8144	10571	5611	6408
1988-89	6553	9915	10880	6200	6972
1989-90	7420	10200	11787	6179	7237
1990-91	7280	10999	11794	6379	7455
1991-92	6986	10968	12087	6339	7297
1992-93	7734	10723	12422	6443	7512
1993-94	7870	11090	12710	6543	7690
1994-95	8489	11617	12784	6619	8070
1995-96	8966	11570	12989	6732	8498
1996-97	9140	12664	13705	6978	9007
1997-98	9625	12544	13812	7128	9242
1998-99	10131	13003	14279	7296	9647
1999-00	10514	13709	14698	7384	10067
2000-01*	10942	14331	14916	7383	10306

Source: Computed from different volumes of *Statistical Abstracts of Punjab and Haryana*.

Note: Provisional

During the last three decades, 1970-71 to 2000-01, the per capita income of the state has grown at the rate of 2.22 per cent per annum, which is lower than the national average of 2.46 per cent (Table 1.9). Among the neighbouring states, Punjab grew at an annual rate of 2.87 per cent, Haryana at 2.76 per cent and Jammu and Kashmir at 1.20 per cent.

However, the rate of growth of the per capita income of the state has been the most impressive during the nineties. During the seventies, it grew at a slower pace than in the neighbouring states (0.23 per cent per annum) and by the nineties its rise was the highest, growing at an annual rate of 4.16 per cent as compared to 3.29 per cent at the all-India level. The growth rate in the neighbouring states, Punjab (2.38%), Haryana (2.68%) and Jammu and Kashmir (1.47%) was lower than Himachal and the all-India average. The state's performance was even better during the period 1990-91 to 1995-96 (4.25%).

TABLE 1.9

Annual Rate of Growth of Per Capita Income in Himachal Pradesh, Neighbouring States and India

States	*1970-71 to 1980-81*	*1980-81 to 1990-91*	*1990-91 to 2000-2001*	*1970-71 to 2000-01*
Himachal Pradesh	**0.23**	**2.31**	**4.16**	**2.22**
Haryana	1.92	4.00	2.68	2.87
Punjab	2.58	3.33	2.38	2.76
Jammu and Kashmir	2.08	0.06	1.47	1.20
India	**0.97**	**3.15**	**3.29**	**2.46**

Source: Computed from different volumes of *Statistical Abstracts of Punjab and Haryana*.

Further, from 1995-96 to 2000-01, the rate of growth in the per capita income of Punjab, Haryana and Jammu and Kashmir increased over the previous years, while in Himachal Pradesh it decreased slightly.

Poverty

Economic growth has crucial implications for poverty reduction. It is expected that the faster growing states would experience a rapid reduction in the proportion of their population below the poverty line. This section attempts to analyse the existing level of poverty and the performance of programmes for its alleviation in Himachal as compared to other states and Union Territories. Poverty has been a matter of national concern. Various agencies, both private and government, have been estimating poverty levels from time to time following different methodologies and drawing different conclusions. This has led to controversies over the reliability of the data. The Planning Commission, has been providing estimates on poverty from time to time. These too are not free from controversy, yet these have been accepted as official and hence are analysed in this section.

The proportion of Himachal's population below the poverty line declined from 26.39 per cent in 1973-74 to 7.63 per cent in 1999-2000, when the corresponding figures at the national level were 54.88 per cent and 26.1 per cent, 3.5 times higher than that of the state. Himachal was ranked sixth among the states and Union Territories during 1999-2000, after Jammu and Kashmir (3.48%), Goa (4.4%), Daman and Diu (4.44%), Chandigarh (5.75%) and Punjab (6.16%). The neighbouring state of Haryana had a higher poverty ratio than Himachal Pradesh. Himachal Pradesh with 7.94 per cent of its rural population below the poverty line ranks seventh among the states and Union Territories, only below Delhi (0.4%), Goa (1.35%), Lakshadweep (1.35%), Jammu and Kashmir (3.93%), Chandigarh (5.75%) and Punjab (6.35%) and with 4.63 per cent of such population in the urban areas, it ranks second only below Jammu and Kashmir (1.98%).

TABLE 1.10

Poverty Alleviation Performance Index of States and Union Territories, 1973-74 to 1999-2000

States/Union Territories	*Values of Poverty Alleviation Performance Index** *Total*	*Rural*	*Urban*
States			
Andhra Pradesh	0.67	0.77	0.47
Arunachal Pradesh	0.36	0.24	0.80
Assam	0.30	0.24	0.80
Bihar	0.31	0.30	0.38
Goa	0.90	0.97	0.80
Gujarat	0.71	0.72	0.70
Haryana	0.75	0.76	0.75
Himachal Pradesh	**0.71**	**0.71**	**0.65**
Jammu and Kashmir	0.91	0.91	0.91
Karnataka	0.63	0.68	0.52
Kerala	0.79	0.84	0.68
Madhya Pradesh	0.39	0.41	0.33
Maharashtra	0.53	0.59	0.39
Manipur	0.43	0.36	0.80
Meghalaya	0.33	0.36	0.80
Mizoram	0.61	0.24	0.80
Nagaland	0.36	0.24	0.80
Orissa	0.29	0.29	0.23
Punjab	0.78	0.77	0.79
Rajasthan	0.67	0.69	0.62
Sikkim	0.28	0.24	0.80
Tamil Nadu	0.62	0.64	0.55
Tripura	0.32	0.24	0.80
Uttar Pradesh	0.45	0.45	0.49
West Bengal	0.57	0.56	0.57
All India	**0.52**	**0.52**	**0.52**
Union Territories			
Delhi	0.83	0.98	0.82
A & N Islands	0.62	0.64	0.55
Chandigarh	0.79	0.79	0.79
Dadra and Nagar Haveli	0.63	0.62	0.64
Lakshadweep	0.74	0.98	0.68
Pondicherry	0.60	0.84	0.85
Daman and Diu			
All India	**0.52**	**0.52**	**0.52**

Source: Computed from the data provided by Government of India, Planning Commission, New Delhi.

Note: * Poverty Alleviation Performance Index = $\frac{\{1973-74 - 1999-00\}}{1973-74}$

Levels of poverty in the different states have declined at varying rates. Noteworthy are the cases of Jammu and Kashmir and Kerala, which beginning as high poverty-ratio states, have joined states with a low percentage of population below the poverty line. Himachal Pradesh has not lagged behind in alleviating poverty.

A poverty alleviation performance index has been formulated for measuring the rate of its decline (Krishan, G., 1999). It indicates that Jammu and Kashmir (0.91), Goa (0.90), Delhi (0.83), Kerala (0.79), Punjab (0.78) and Haryana (0.75) had achieved tremendous success in alleviating poverty in almost three decades (Table 1.10). Himachal Pradesh ranked 9th among the states and union territories in reducing poverty ratios, 12th in the rural areas and 19th in the urban areas.

The performance of poverty alleviation in the state has varied during different points of time. During the period 1973-74 and 1977-78 and 1987-88 to 1993-94, poverty in Himachal had increased (Table 1.11). From 1993-94 to 1999-2000, its pace of poverty reduction was the highest among the neighbouring states of Haryana and Punjab also as compared to the national level.

TABLE 1.11

Poverty Alleviation Performance Index of Himachal Pradesh, Neighbouring States and India at Different Points of Time, 1973-74 to 1999-2000

States/India	*1973-74 to 1977-78*	*1977-78 to 1983-84*	*1983-84 to 1987-88*	*1987-88 to 1993-94*	*1993-94 to 1999-2000*
Himachal Pradesh	**-0.23**	**0.49**	**0.06**	**-0.84**	**0.73**
Haryana	0.16	0.28	0.22	-0.51	0.65
Punjab	0.32	0.16	0.18	0.11	0.48
Jammu and Kashmir	0.05	0.38	0.02	-0.06	0.86
All India	**0.43**	**-0.42**	**0.13**	**0.07**	**0.27**

Source: Computed from data provided by Planning Commission, New Delhi.

The growth-poverty reduction linkage holds true in Himachal Pradesh unlike the neighbouring states of Punjab and Haryana.

Expenditure Pattern

The state has implemented a series of development plans to create an infrastructure based on its requirements and potential. It initially focused on creating transportation and communication facilities, which were considered basic for the development of the hilly areas. Emphasis was also laid on creating facilities for water, irrigation, power and agricultural growth. Over a period, the emphasis has shifted to creating and providing social services.

Plans-wise Expenditure: Spending on different sectors has had a direct bearing on the growth of the state's economy. In the First Plan, expenditure on transportation and communication was more than half the total. The power sector got a meagre share of 4.6 per cent in the First Plan. By Third Plan it had increased to seven per cent. Expenditure on agriculture and allied activities was 14.4 per cent in the First Plan and increased to 32 per cent in the Third Plan. Expenditure on social services was one-fifth of the total expenditure in the First and Third Plans.

Since the formation of the state, expenditure on agriculture and allied activities has decreased considerably from 24 per cent in the Fourth Plan to 11 per cent in Ninth Plan. Allocations made for this sector in the Tenth Plan are on a still lower side (9.6%). Expenditure on energy has decreased from 27 per cent in the Sixth Plan to 18.4 per cent in the Ninth Plan. The increased allocation in the Tenth Plan (24.2%) indicates the importance given to this sector. Expenditure on transportation and communication has decreased from 29 per cent in the Fourth Plan to 14 per cent in the Ninth Plan. The Tenth Plan has allocated 16 per cent to this sector.

The social sector has received top priority. Expenditure on this sector has more than doubled during the Fourth and Ninth Plans. During the Fourth Plan, expenditure on social services was 18 per cent, which by the Ninth Plan increased to 41.3 per cent. However, allocation to this sector has been slightly less (39%) in the Tenth Plan, but continues to be the most important sector.

Pattern of Expenditure: Budgetary expenditure by the government during the period 1970-71 to 2001-02 increased 73 times from Rs. 62 crore to 4,510 crore. At the time of the formation of the state, development expenditure was more than four-fifths of the total expenditure, which over the last three decades has decreased by almost 30 per cent points. During the period 1970-71 to 1975-76, the proportion of development expenditure consistently decreased and reached 65 per cent in 1975-76. Thereafter, it increased till 1980-81, reaching almost 80 per cent. During 2000-01 and 2001-02, the proportion of development expenditure decreased by nine per cent points. This is a worrisome phenomenon.

TABLE 1.12

Budgetary Expenditure in Himachal Pradesh, 1970-71 to 2001-02

(Rs. in Crore)

Year	*Budgetary Expenditure*	*Development Expenditure*	*Non-development Expenditure*
1970-71	62	51 (82.26)	11 (17.74)
1971-72	65	53 (81.54)	12 (18.46)
1972-73	68	53 (77.94)	15 (22.06)
1973-74	75	57 (76.00)	18 (24.00)
1974-75	80	55 (68.75)	25 (31.25)
1975-76	87	57 (65.52)	30 (34.48)
1976-77	96	65 (67.71)	31 (32.29)
1977-78	99	71 (71.72)	28 (28.28)
1978-79	126	94 (74.60)	32 (25.40)
1979-80	150	115 (76.67)	35 (23.33)
1980-81	188	149 (79.26)	39 (20.74)
1981-82	213	168 (78.87)	45 (21.13)
1982-83	264	191 (72.35)	72 (27.27)
1983-84	284	211 (74.30)	74 (26.06)
1984-85	344	251 (72.97)	93 (27.03)
1985-86	412	291 (70.63)	120 (29.13)
1986-87	464	321 (69.18)	143 (30.82)
1987-88	608	435 (71.55)	174 (28.62)
1988-89	768	560 (72.92)	208 (27.08)
1989-90	783	543 (69.35)	240 (30.65)
1990-91	902	617 (68.40)	284 (31.49)
1991-92	983	643 (65.41)	340 (34.59)
1992-93	1146	753 (67.71)	393 (34.29)
1993-94	1351	887 (65.66)	464 (34.34)
1994-95	1615	1105 (68.42)	509 (31.52)
1995-96	1904	1270 (66.70)	634 (33.30)
1996-97	2147	1456 (67.82)	691 (32.18)
1997-98	2699	1758 (65.14)	941 (34.86)
1998-99	3334	2157 (64.70)	1177 (35.30)
1999-00	3822	2240 (58.61)	1582 (41.39)
2000-01	4376	2704 (61.79)	1672 (38.21)
2001-02	4510	2372 (52.59)	2138 (47.41)

Source: Department of Finance (Budget), Government of Himachal Pradesh.

Note: The figures in parenthesis are in per cent.

Regional Disparities

The above sections have analysed variations in the development process of Himachal Pradesh in relation to other states and Union Territories. However, development within the state has not been homogeneous. Disparities exist between different districts. In this section, an effort has been made to understand these disparities in the context of the level and growth of infrastructural facilities in relation to population and area. This is important because efforts have been made to create physical facilities by investing

FIGURE 1.5

Budgetary Expenditure in Himachal Pradesh, 1970-71 to 2000-01

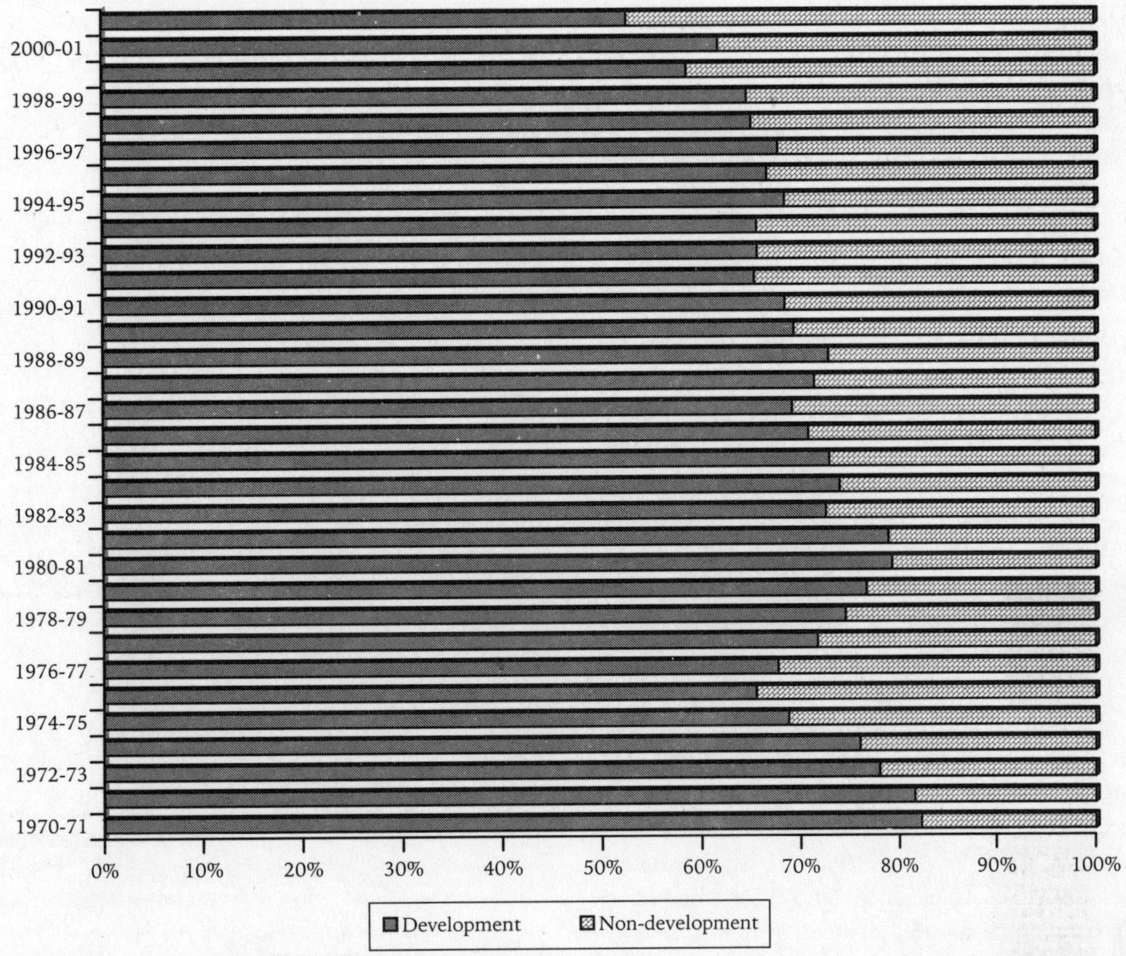

Source: Department of Finance (Budget), Government of Himachal Pradesh.

heavily in these sectors. The indicators discussed to measure the level of socio-economic development at the district level are:

1) per capita income
2) female literacy rate
3) credit-deposit ratio
4) number of industrial workers per thousand of population
5) medical and public health facilities
6) means of communication, and
7) banking sector

These indicators have been used to measure various dimensions of development. Economic development at the district level has been gauged through per capita income, and the state of social development through variations in female literacy rates. Credit-deposit ratio signifies the enterprising nature of the local people. A relatively higher number of industrial workers in the population signifies a higher level of industrial development. Such indicators as percentage of villages with primary health centres, sub-centres, post-offices and banks within a distance of one kilometre, have been used to measure the level of infrastructure essential for social development.

The selection of the indicators was greatly hampered by lack of access, non-comparability and reliability of data at the district level. The data available on infant mortality rate at the district level were not reliable and hence were excluded from the analysis. However, the indicators discussed here represent a fairly balanced level of development. An exercise was undertaken to get a combined development index. It was assumed that these indictors would be positively correlated but the results were not in line with our hypothesis. This shows state-specific peculiarities in the pattern of development. Per capita income, infrastructure and CD ratio were negatively correlated with the female literacy rate, whereas we had assumed that these would be positively correlated. Only the number of industrial workers per thousand of population and the CD ratio were significantly (.744) correlated. Per capita income and the number of industrial workers per thousand of population were also positively correlated, but not significantly. This prompted us to analyse these indicators separately.

Per Capita Income

Himachal had an average per capita income of Rs. 6,507 in 1999-2000 at 1990-91 constant prices (Table 1.13). The district of Lahaul and Spiti with Rs. 12,559 was at the top and Hamirpur with Rs. 4,243 at the bottom. Low density of population and high value- added cash crops in Lahaul and Spiti were the reasons for the high per capita income. The state average in 1990-91 was Rs. 4,618. Lahaul and Spiti was again at the top and Una was at the bottom. Shimla, the state capital, ranked third at both points of time. Solan, being the centre of industrial activity, ranked second in 1999-2000. During the nineties, the per capita income in the state as a whole increased by Rs. 1,889. The highest increase in quantitative terms was in Solan district (Rs. 5,179). In Kinnaur, it decreased by Rs. 816 during 1990-91 and 1999-00. In Kinnaur, because of the failure of rains and natural disasters the production of horticultural and agricultural crops was low, and that had an impact on its per capita income (HPHDR, 2002).

During the nineties, the per capita income in Himachal grew at an annual rate of 3.88 per cent. Every district, with the exception of Kinnaur (-1.08%) had a positive growth of per capita income. It was the highest in Una district (7.21%) closely followed by Solan (7.11%). The per capita income in Una district, which was almost at the bottom at both points of time was small, but even this small increase of Rs. 2,086 amounted to a faster growth. The per capita income of Solan district was 2.5 times that of Una in 1999-00. This was significant. The secondary sector has dominated the economy of Solan district and the tertiary sector in Una. The growth of per capita income in Lahaul and Spiti and Shimla, which otherwise ranked first and third respectively, was among the slowest among all districts (1.06% and 1.10% respectively).

Regional disparities in terms of per capita income in all districts decreased during the decade of the nineties (Table 1.14). In 1990-91, the per capita income of the highest ranked district was almost five times that of the lowest ranked district, which came down to three times in 1999-2000. The values of coefficient of variability calculated separately for 1990-91 and 1999-2000, further confirm this.

TABLE 1.13

District-wise Per Capita Income, 1990-91 to 1999-2000 at 1990-91 Prices

Districts/State	*1999-2000 (in Rupees)*	*Rank 2000*	*1990-1991 (in Rupees)*	*Rank 1991*	*Annual Growth Rate (1990-1991 to 1999-2000)*
Una	4480	11	2394	12	7.21
Solan	11231	2	6052	4	7.11
Bilaspur	7547	5	4515	7	5.87
Mandi	5313	10	3394	10	5.11
Hamirpur	4243	12	2753	11	4.92
Sirmaur	5650	9	3934	9	4.10
Kangra	5736	8	4128	8	3.72
Chamba	6058	7	4822	6	2.57
Shimla	8304	3	7525	3	1.10
Lahaul and Spiti	12559	1	11417	1	1.06
Kullu	6098	6	6039	5	0.11
Kinnaur	7930	4	8746	2	-1.08
Himachal Pradesh	**6507**		**4618**		**3.88**

Source: Computed from *Human Development Report of Himachal Pradesh, 2002*.

Note: The districts are arranged in descending order of annual growth rate.

TABLE 1.14

Coefficient of Variability of Per Capita Income, 1990-91 and 1999-2000 At 1990-91 Prices

Year	*Coefficient of Variability*	*Regional Disparity*
1990-1991	48.51	↓
1999-2000	36.42	

Female Literacy

At the state level, almost seven out of every ten females were literate in 2001 as against five in every ten in 1991 (Table 1.15). The district of Hamirpur with three-fourths of its females being literate, was at the top and Chamba with only half was at the bottom at both points of time. The corresponding figures in 1991 were 66 per cent and 29 per cent. Female literacy rate in Lahaul and Spiti, Kullu, Sirmaur and Chamba districts have increased by more than 20 per cent points during the last decade. This has been attributed to the fact that these four were the lowest ranked districts in

TABLE 1.15

District-wise Female Literacy Rates in Himachal Pradesh, 1991 and 2001

Districts/State	*Literacy Rate 2001 (in per cent)*	*Rank 2001*	*Literacy Rate 1991 (in per cent)*	*Rank 1991*	*Change in per cent Points During 1991-2001*
Lahaul and Spiti	60.94	9	38.05	11	22.85
Kullu	61.24	8	38.53	9	22.71
Sirmaur	60.93	10	38.45	10	22.48
Chamba	49.7	11	28.57	12	21.13
Shimla	70.68	4	51.75	5	18.93
Solan	67.48	6	50.69	6	16.79
Mandi	65.36	7	49.12	7	16.24
Bilaspur	70.53	5	56.55	4	13.98
Una	73.85	2	61.01	3	12.84
Kangra	73.57	3	61.39	2	12.18
Hamirpur	76.41	1	65.9	1	10.51
Kinnaur	NA		42.04	8	-
Himachal Pradesh	**68.08**		**52.13**		**15.95**

Source: *Census of India (2001) Provisional Population Totals, Paper-1 of 2001, Series-3*, Directorate of Census Operations, Himachal Pradesh.

1991 and had greater scope for improving their female literacy rates.

A comparison of the values of the coefficient of variability at both points of time indicates a decrease in regional disparities (Table 1.16). The districts are moving towards homogeneity in terms of social development, as reflected in female literacy rates.

TABLE 1.16

Coefficient of Variability of Female Literacy Rates, 1991 and 2001

Year	*Coefficient of Variability*	*Regional Disparity*
1991	24.18	
2001	11.76	↓

Credit-Deposit Ratio

Credit-Deposit ratio in 2000 was 21.7 per cent as against 33.4 per cent in 1990 (Table 1.17). Solan district, with a CD ratio of 49.7 per cent, stood at the top and Lahaul and Spiti, with 11.6 per cent, was at the bottom. The district of Solan with a very high CD ratio of 87.1 per cent in 1990 was ranked at the top, and Hamirpur with 15.3 per cent at the bottom. There has been a sharp decline of almost 37 per cent points in the CD ratio between 1990 and 2000.

A comparison of the values of the coefficient of variability at both points of time indicates a decrease in regional disparities (Table 1.18). The districts are moving towards homogeneity but at a very slow pace. It is important to mention that this homogeneity is because of a fall in the CD ratio of the top-ranking districts, which is not a good sign. The situation would have been better had the lower-ranking districts moved upwards.

TABLE 1.17

District-wise Credit-Deposit Ratio in Himachal Pradesh, 1990 2000

		2000			*1990*			*Rank 1990*
Rank 2000	*Districts/State*	*Credit*	*Deposit*	*CD Ratio*	*Credit*	*Deposit*	*CD Ratio*	
1.	Solan	28332	57052	49.7	11203	12869	87.1	1
2.	Sirmaur	10373	23893	43.4	3296	5209	63.3	2
3.	Kullu	11416	32797	34.8	2838	7851	36.1	4
4.	Mandi	14904	66954	22.3	4644	13622	34.1	5
5.	Shimla	29287	162286	18.0	12486	36803	33.9	6
6.	Bilaspur	4951	27599	17.9	1410	5373	26.2	9
7.	Chamba	5393	30458	17.7	1564	5726	27.3	8
8.	Kangra	29085	170225	17.1	7484	37336	20.0	10
9.	Kinnaur	1228	7281	16.9	467	1256	37.2	3
10.	Una	8644	55270	15.6	3490	12736	27.4	7
11.	Hamirpur	7638	59853	12.8	2060	13468	15.3	12
12.	Lahaul and Spiti	536	4607	11.6	159	809	19.7	11
	Himachal Pradesh	**151787**	**698275**	**21.7**	**51101**	**153056**	**33.4**	

Source: Different issues of *Statistical Abstract of Himachal Pradesh*, Directorate of Economic and Statistics, Himachal Pradesh.

TABLE 1.18

Coefficient of Variability of Credit-Deposit Ratio, 1990-91 and 1999-2000

Year	*Coefficient of Variability*	*Regional Disparity*
1990-1991	57.14	↓
1999-2000	53.82	

Industrial Workers

The number of industrial workers per thousand of population has been used as an indicator to measure the level of industrial development. At the state level, almost 13 persons per thousand of population were working in factories in 2000, as against seven in 1991 (Table 1.19). Solan district ranked at the top and Lahaul and Spiti at the bottom at both points of time. In fact, the ranking of every district at both points of time remained almost the same, indicating hardly any dispersal of industrial activity in the state. These have been concentrating in Solan district.

TABLE 1.19

District-wise Number of Industrial Workers per 1000 of Population in Himachal Pradesh, 1991 and 2000

Districts/State	*No. of Industrial Workers Per 1,000 of Population, 2000*	*Rank 2000*	*No. of Industrial Workers Per 1,000 of Population, 1991*	*Rank 1991*
Solan	88.12	1	33.77	1
Sirmaur	17.32	2	14.01	2
Kinnaur	9.04	3	7.84	3
Una	7.86	4	6.51	4
Kangra	6.77	5	6.08	5
Shimla	5.31	6	3.77	7
Mandi	4.74	7	4.98	6
Bilaspur	3.09	8	2.16	8
Chamba	2.04	9	1.62	9
Kullu	1.60	10	1.56	10
Hamirpur	0.84	11	0.93	11
Lahaul and Spiti	0.00	12	0.00	12
Himachal Pradesh	**12.56**		**7.09**	

Source: Computed from different issues of *Statistical Abstract of Himachal Pradesh*, Directorate of Economic and Statistics, Himachal Pradesh, and *Census of India*.

Further, a comparison of the values of the coefficient of variability at both points of time indicates an increase in regional disparities (Table 1.20). The districts are moving towards heterogeneity.

TABLE 1.20

Coefficient of Variability of Number of Industrial Workers, 1991 and 2000

Year	*Coefficient of Variability*	*Regional Disparity*
1991	134.05	↑
2000	199.18	

Infrastructure

Such indicators as the percentage of villages with primary health centres, sub-centres, post-offices and banks within a distance of one kilometre, have been used to measure the level of infrastructure essential for social development. A combined picture of these indicates that almost one-fourth of the villages had at least one of these facilities available within a distance of one kilometre in 1999-2000. Kullu, with 45.93 per cent villages with these facilities within a distance of one kilometre, ranked at the top in 1999-2000, followed by Kangra (37.30%) and Bilaspur (35.37%), and Sirmaur with 11 per cent such villages, ranked at the bottom (Table 1.21). These districts had the same rankings in 1990-91. The corresponding figures were 41 per cent and 9 per cent.

The growth of medical and public health facilities reflects one dimension essential for development. The distance at which primary health centres and sub-centres are available in the village has been analysed for this purpose. By and large, medical and public health facilities in the state, as well as in the districts have improved. In all, 5.22 per cent of the villages in the state had primary health centres within a distance of one kilometre in 1999-2000 as against 3.41 per cent in 1991. Kullu with 13 per cent of such villages, ranked at the top in 1999-2000 and Chamba with 0.09 per cent ranked at the bottom. These districts have remained in the same position, the corresponding figures being 10.47 per cent and 0.05 per cent in 1990-91.

As regards access to health sub-centres, 36.3 per cent of the villages had such access within a distance of one kilometre in 1999-2000 as against 30.7 per cent in 1991. Kullu with 62 per cent of such villages ranked at the top in 1999-2000 and Kinnaur with 14 per cent was ranked at the bottom. There has been no change in their ranking since 1990-91, when the corresponding figures had been 58 per cent and 5 per cent.

Availability of postal services at a short distance has been taken as an indicator of the growth of means of communication. Kullu district, with almost 90 per cent of the villages with a post office within one kilometre in 1999-2000 stood at the top and Una with 11 per cent of such villages was at the bottom. The two districts had the same ranking in 1990-91.

TABLE 1.21

District-wise Ranking of Villages with Infrastructure in Himachal Pradesh, 1990-91 and 1998-99

Districts/State	*Villages (in per cent)*	*Rank in 1999-2000*	*Villages (in per cent)*	*Rank in 1990-91*
Kullu	45.93	1	41.28	1
Kangra	37.30	2	33.76	2
Bilaspur	35.37	3	31.37	3
Chamba	31.02	4	27.01	4
Shimla	25.57	5	23.68	5
Lahaul and Spiti	23.07	6	17.67	7
Solan	22.52	7	20.18	6
Una	17.19	8	15.53	8
Kinnaur	15.25	9	9.00	11
Hamirpur	13.58	10	12.33	9
Mandi	12.22	11	10.65	10
Sirmaur	10.67	12	8.99	12
Himachal Pradesh	**24.14**		**20.76**	

Source: Computed from data provided in *Human Development Report of Himachal Pradesh, 2002.*

Banking facilities are an important catalyst of economic growth. The presence of banks in particular areas can give a boost to the process of development. Bilaspur district, with 24 per cent of its villages with a bank within a distance of one kilometre, ranked at the top in 1999-2000 and Chamba, with three per cent of such villages was at the bottom. These districts had the same ranking in 1990-91 with corresponding figures of 24 per cent and two per cent.

TABLE 1.22

Coefficient of Variability of Infrastructure, 1991 and 2000

Year	*Coefficient of Variability*	*Regional Disparity*
1990-1991	50.60	↓
1999-2000	46.42	

A comparison of the combined value of the coefficient of variability at both points of time indicates a decrease in regional disparities (Table 1.22). The districts are moving towards homogeneity but at a very slow pace.

On the whole, regional disparities in the state have decreased during the nineties. This has laid the foundation of socio-economic development. However, the pace at which regional disparities are decreasing is quite slow, with the exception of female literacy. This could be attributed to the varying topography in the districts, which makes creation of every type of infrastructure difficult.

Conclusion

The growth behaviour of the economy of Himachal Pradesh and that of India during 1971-2001 invites an interesting comparison with each other. For the first half, that is during 1971-85, the state's economy grew slower than that of the national economy while during the latter half, the trend reversed when the state's economy grew faster. During the Ninth Plan the annual rate of growth of Himachal's economy was 6.2 per cent as compared to 5.4 per cent of the national economy. The economy of the state, which had been growing at a slower pace than that of the neighbouring states of Punjab and Haryana during the 1980s marked a distinct departure from the previous trend during the 1990s, with a faster rate of growth. Per capita income of Himachal Pradesh in the seventies was higher than the national average; in the eighties it was lower; and in the nineties it was again consistently higher than the national average.

Taking a long-term view, the share of the primary sector decreased significantly from 56.3 per cent in 1970-71 to 25.5 per cent in 2000-2001. By contrast, the share of the secondary sector moved from 18 per cent to 32 per cent. The tertiary sector also got enlarged from 24.8 per cent to 42.5 per cent.

The state has been successful in alleviating poverty. The percentage of population below the poverty line declined from 26.4 in 1973-74 to 7.6 in 1999-2000. The corresponding figures at the national level were 54.88 per cent and 26.1 per cent. Reduction in poverty has been of a high order since 1993-94.

Agriculture and transport were the priorities during the earlier plans. The thrust gradually shifted to social services. Now power generation is receiving prime attention. There has been a drastic decline in the proportion of development expenditure in the state. In 1970-71, it was 83 per cent of the budgetary expenditure. This has come down to 52 per cent in 2000-01. This decline of 30 per cent points is highly worrisome.

An encouraging feature is that regional disparities in terms of per capita income, female literacy, credit-deposit ratio and access to infrastructure declined during the nineties. A greater spatial equity is being generated. Regional disparities in the proportion of industrial workers, however, have widened over time.

This signifies that industry is getting attracted to a few locations offering certain advantages.

Himachal Pradesh is distinguished by a higher level of social development than economic development. The emerging problems of the state, particularly unemployment, are distinctly economic in nature. A major challenge before the state is to deploy its human resources effectively for furtherance of economic well-being.

References

Ahluwalia, M.S. (1988), *History of Himachal Pradesh*, Intellectual Publishing House, New Delhi.

Balokhra, J.M. (2002), *The Wonderland, Himachal Pradesh: An Encyclopedia*, H. G. Publication, New Delhi.

Directorate of Census Operations: Himachal Pradesn, *Census of India (2001)*, "Provisional Population Totals, Paper 1".

Directorate of Census Operations: Himachal Pradesh, *Census of India (2001)*: "Provisional Population Totals, Paper 2 of 2001, Rural-Urban Distribution of Population".

Department of Planning, *Annual Plans* (different issues), Government of Himachal Pradesh.

Department of Planning (1994), *An Overview of Planning in Himachal Pradesh*, Government of Himachal Pradesh.

Directorate of Economic and Statistics, *Statistical Abstracts* of Himachal Pradesh (different issues).

Directorate of Economics and Statistics, *Economic Surveys* (different volumes), Himachal Pradesh.

Khan, A.R. (1996), *Man, Environment and Development in Himachal Pradesh*, Indus Publishing Company, New Delhi.

Krishan, G. (1999), "Regional Variations in Poverty Alleviation Performance in India", *Population Geography*, Vol. 21, Numbers 1 & 2, June-December 1999.

Ministry of Information and Broadcasting (2002): *India 2002: A Reference Annual*, Publication Division, Government of India, New Delhi.

Negi, S.S. (1993) *Himachal Pradesh, The Land and the People*, Indus Publishing Company, New Delhi

Planning Commission: *Five-Year Plan Documents*, Government of India (various plans).

Sharma, L.R. (1987), *The Economy of Himachal Pradesh: Growth and Structure (A Study in Development Performance)*, Mittal Publications, Delhi.

Singh, M.G. (1985), *Social Cultural Economic Survey of Himachal Pradesh*, Minerva Book House, Shimla.

Chapter 2

Natural Resources

Natural resources provide the base on which the edifice of development is raised. Its use depends upon the type of economy, the level of technology and preferences of the culture of a given society. The importance of natural resources is more critical to societies which are at a relatively low level of development. People have to conform their livelihood and life style to the settings of nature. The sustainable use of natural resources to attain high levels of human development has become imperative. Natural resources of Himachal Pradesh have a direct relationship with its physiographic conditions including relief, drainage, climate and geology. These in turn influence the type of soils and the kind of vegetation cover.

Physiographic Zones

Himachal Pradesh has been divided physiographically into four distinctly identifiable zones based on variations in altitude, climate, geology, soil, flora, fauna and topography as follows:

Shivalik Hills

These are the outermost foothills of the state and mark its southern boundary from east to west. Stretching for about 70 km, their average elevation is about 1000 meters. To the north of Shivalik hills lie longitudinal valleys, locally known as duns. These valleys are drained by a network of streams, which deposit vast quantities of sediments that make them highly fertile and support dense populations. Kangra valley, Chakki dun valley and Paonta valley are among the important duns. A small plain tract lying south of the Shivalik Hills falls in Himachal Pradesh. Many seasonal streams known as choes cause flash floods in the rainy season. Markanda and Ghaggar rivers originate in the Shivalik Hills.

Lesser Himalayas

This zone extends to 65 to 85 km with an average elevation of about 3300 mts above the mean sea level, and forms the central part of state. The important ranges here are the Pir Panjal and Dhauladhar Ranges. The Pir Panjal range form the water divide between Chenab river on the one side and the Ravi and Beas on the other. The Dhauladhar is a majestic snow clad range cut across by rivers like the Ravi, Beas and Sutluj. Both north and south facing slopes support luxuriant forests, except in tracts above the snowline. It is marked by several glaciers. The Giri and the Gambhar rivers have their origin in this physiographic zone.

Greater Himalayas

Lying north of the Pir Panjal and Dhauladhar ranges, this zone is marked by lofty snow-capped peaks, glaciers and old U-shaped valleys. Most of the peaks have an elevation of about 5500 meters. Some of the famous passes through the ranges are the Rohtang Pass, the Bara lacha Pass, the Kangla Pass, the Parang Pass and the Pin Parbati Pass. The presence of glaciers, moraines, and U-shaped valleys, indicates that a major part of the state was once under the influence of glaciation. There are several hot springs indicative of geothermal energy. This towering range acts as a barrier for the southwest monsoon, thereby causing a rain-shadow effect in tracts lying to the north.

Trans-Himalayas

This zone lying to the north of Greater Himalayas with an average elevation of 3000 meters is marked by cold desert-like conditions. The Zanskar range is the most important range in the region. It separates Spiti and Kinnaur from Tibet. The Sutluj cuts a deep gorge across the range at Shipki Pass. Leo Parigial (6791 meters) is the highest peak. The zone is devoid of vegetation.

Drainage Network

The state is drained by nine major river systems, and thereby has nine catchment areas. Some of these are the Satluj (30.69%), the Beas (24.5%) the Chenab (14.2%), the Yamuna (10.6%), the Ravi (9.9%) and the Indus (2.6%). These catchment areas are further subdivided by several water divides. The major rivers are glacial-snow fed and perennial in nature. The seasonal streams of the Shivalik foothills depend on rainwater.

Soil Types

The soil of Himachal Pradesh varies from thin and bare soil of high mountains to rich deep alluvial soil of the valleys and to snow-covered soil. These soils can be classified as follows.

1. **UDalfs-Ochrepts soils:** Shallow in veneer and brown in colour, these are high base status soils of humid regions covering parts of Chamba, Lahaul and Spiti, Kinnaur, Sirmaur, Mandi and Bilaspur.
2. **Othents-Ochrepts soils:** A combination of shallow black, brown and alluvial soils, these are found in Lesser Himalayas, including parts of Sirmaur, Solan, Una, Hamirpur, Kangra and Chamba districts. These are also red loamy and red sandy in nature in parts of Kullu, Kinnaur, and are ideally suited for horticulture.
3. **Udolls soils:** There represent the characteristics of a cold desert and are found in Lahaul and Spiti.
4. **Glaciers and snowcap soils:** are spread in part of Kullu, Lahaul and Spiti and Kinnaur where glaciers and snow cover is present throughout the year.

   The soil of Himachal Pradesh is under gully and sheet erosion. About two-fifths of the state's area is under the impact of very high intensity erosion.

Land Resources

The total area of Himachal Pradesh is 55,673 sq. km. This would give less than one hectare of land to every one among the 6.1 million people recorded in the state in 2001 census. Hardly 10 per cent of the total area is cultivated and the actual forest cover extends to 22.5 per cent of the total area. Permanent pastures and other grasslands account for about 24 per cent of the total area. Barren and unculturable land covers about 14 per cent of the area of the state. About 23 per cent of the total area remains unsurveyed.

Himachal Pradesh can be divided into the following five zones on the basis of geographic and socio-cultural patterns:

i. North-eastern region

ii. Northern region

iii. Central region

iv. South-eastern region

v. South-western region

The north-eastern region spreads over an area of 23,695 sq. km., which is around two-fifths of the total area of the state. It comprises the districts of Kinnaur, and Lahaul and Spiti, and Pangi and Bharmaur blocks of Chamba district. The entire region is sparsely populated and has no urban centre. Population density is hardly 7 persons per sq. km. More than 70 per cent of the population belong to the category of Scheduled Tribes. The entire territory has been declared a scheduled area.

The northern region has an area of 3497 sq. km. It has a population density of about 100 persons per sq. km. The development blocks of Tira, Saluni, Chamba, Bhattiyat and Mehla, all in Chamba district, belong to this region. Its economy combines agriculture with pastoral activities. Chamba, Bakhloh, Chauri Khas and Dalhousie are the only urban centres of any significance.

The central region comprises the districts of Kullu and Mandi as well as the Baijnath development block of Kangra district. It covers an area of 10,751 sq. km. Population density is around 125. Agriculture is the main avocation of the people, and the region is predominantly rural. Mandi, Sundernagar, Kullu and Jogindernagar are the important towns.

The south-eastern region comprises Shimla, Sirmaur and Solan districts. Apart from agriculture, horticulture, tourism, trade and commerce and industry have emerged as notable activities. Industrial centres include Paonta Sahib, Nahan, Kala Amb, Solan, Nalagarh, Baddi, Barotiwala, Parwanoo, Dharampur and Chambaghat.

The south-western region largely covers areas which were transferred to Himachal Pradesh after the linguistic reorganisation of Punjab in 1966. It comprises Kangra, Bilaspur and Una districts. Hills, mountains and wide valleys intermingle here. Population density is around 300. This region suffers from serious ecological problems, such as soil erosion, deforestation, land degradation and depletion of the water table.

On the basis of land use, Himachal Pradesh can be subdivided into three broad regions:

i. Intensively cultivated, moderately forested southern region with marginal presence of pastures and other grazing lands;
ii. Moderately cultivated, highly forested central region with a considerable proportion of pastures and other grazing lands; and
iii. Poorly cultivated, and sparsely forested northern region with a high proportion of pastures and other grazing lands.

From the above description, it is clear that considerable improvements are required for an optimum utilisation of land. First, the forest cover needs to be extended to more areas, as it is much below the target of the national forest policy, according to which a hill state should have 60 per cent of its area under forests. The state government may also frame policies for sedentarising the migratory *gujjar* graziers. They may be encouraged to change their traditional mode of livelihood. They may adopt new agro-economic activities, combining livestock rearing, with cottage industry and vegetable cultivation.

Secondly, there is need for proper management of extensive wastelands, culturable fallow or other lands. A co-ordinated and regularly monitored intervention is required.

Thirdly, the policy of shifting the management of common lands from the community to the state has not proved beneficial, as it has reduced the scope of the people's participation in resource management. This process should be reversed.

Above all, the unsurveyed parts of the state need to be studied and mapped by the Remote Sensing Cell using satellite data.

Water Resources

Water is one of the most vital natural resources of Himachal Pradesh. The state is richly endowed with a hilly terrain having an enormous volume of water from the catchment areas of Satluj, Beas, Ravi and Chenab rivers. These rivers form part of the Indus system. As such, the state has enormous potential of water resources in the form of glaciers and rivers but ground water resource is limited.

Inspite of the fact that there is a large volume of water available in the state, only one-third of its cultivated area is irrigated because of physiographic constraints. It is ironical that this water rich state is also not free from drought at times. The normal monsoon rainfall (June-Sept) in the state varies from 17 to 120 cm. Mandi, Bilaspur, Sirmaur, Una, Hamirpur and Kangra are high rainfall districts where the annual rainfall exceeds 100 cm. Lahaul and Spiti and Kinnaur districts receive a low annual rainfall of about 20 cm.

Availability of Water Resources

Surface Water Resource

Most of the surface water resources of Himachal Pradesh flow from perennial rivers which originate from glaciers. The flow in these rivers is further augmented by run-off from the catchment areas.

Glaciers: Glaciers are located in higher Himalayan reaches (above 4000 meters) in Pir Panjal, Dhuladhar, Zanskar and Great Himalyan ranges. There are 601 glaciers in the state and a majority of them are small in size with accumulation zone of 2 to 4 sq. km. These are linear in form, varying in length from 2 to 25 km, and lie on mountain slopes and in depressions. Almost all these glaciers are in a state of constant recession. The glaciers in these mountains are the relics of an older and more extensive series of ice flow. The recent phenomenon of global warming is hastening the process. Glaciers like Bara, Shingri, Gaglu and Sonapani have a yearly recession of 10 meters to 20 meters. The snowmelt contribution to the river systems in the state is as follows (Table 2.1):

TABLE 2.1

Snowmelt Contribution to the River Systems in Himachal Pradcsh

Name of basin	*Name of Tributary*	*Location*	*Snow Melt Area Km. Sq.*	*Total Average Snowfall Considered cubic km.*	*Computed Snow Melt run-off (90% of col 6) cubic km.*
Indus	Beas	Mandi	3128	0.405	0.365
	Sutlej	Plain		1.083	
		Ropar	46882	0.0161	0.975
Ganga	Yamuna	Tejewala	1980		0.145

Source: Water Resources of India, CWC Publication No 30/88.

Rivers: 90 per cent of Himachal's drainage forms part of the Indus river system. The rivers that actually have their origin in the state and flow through it are the Chenab, the Beas, and the Ravi. The Satluj has its origin in Tibet and flows through Himachal Pradesh forming the largest river catchment area in the state. The Yamuna river crosses only the south-eastern border but has some catchment area in Himachal Pradesh. The

Giri, Jalal, Tons Bata are its tributaries originating in the state.

Lakes: There are a number of lakes in Himachal Pradesh, such as Manimahesh and Khajiar lakes in Chamba district, Chandratal and Surajtal lakes in Lahaul and Spiti district, Rawalsar, Prashel and Kamrunag lakes in Mandi district.

Reservoirs: These water bodies are man-made, raised for specific purposes, such as irrigation, hydro power generation, flood control etc. These are tabulated below: (Table 2.2).

TABLE 2.2

Water Bodies

Reservoir	*Location*	*Remarks*
Pandoh	15 Km from Mandi Town	Created by Pandoh to divert Beas water to Satluj
Sundernagar project.	Sundernagar	Balancing reservoir of BSL
Gobind Sagar	Bilaspur & Mandi	Reservoir of Bhakra Dam of 618 sq. km.
Pong	Kangra	Reservoir of Beas Dam

Source: State of Environment Report, H.P. (March, 2000).

Groundwater Resources

The groundwater resource occurs mainly in unconsolidated sediments of intermontane valleys and in the submontane tract. Kangra, Una, Hamirpur, Bilaspur, Mandi, Solan and Sirmaur districts, particularly their valley areas depend upon groundwater. The exploitation is done through open wells, tubewells, infiltration galleries and wells. The status of development of ground water resources in the state is given below (Table 2.3).

TABLE 2.3

Status of Groundwater Resources in Himachal Pradesh

Total replenishable groundwater resources	0.036 m ham/yr
Provision for domestic, industrial and other uses	0.007 m ham/yr
Available net groundwater resources for irrigation	0.029 m ham/yr
Net utilisable groundwater resources for irrigation	0.026 m ham/yr
Net draft	0.005 m ham/yr
Balance groundwater resources for future use	0.024 m ham/yr
Level of groundwater development	18.18%
Utilisable irrigation potential by groundwater development	68,500 ha

Source: CGWB, Ministry of Water Resources; Seminar on Artificial Recharge of Ground Water, December 1998.

Traditional Sources of Water

As there is an imbalance between the supply and consumption of water, particularly by the poor and weaker sections of society, the traditional sources of water play a significant role. These include springs, *kuhls, baories, ponds, khaties* and ditches. These systems supplement the water requirements of the rural and urban areas. There are 10512 traditional sources of water in the state for drinking water in rural habitations (1991-93).

Development of Water Resources

(i) Irrigation Schemes: See chapter on 'Agriculture'

(ii) Drinking Water Supply Schemes

A variety of sources are used in Himachal Pradesh to obtain domestic water supply. Details in respect of rural water supply are given below (Table 2.4).

TABLE 2.4

Water Source Details of Himachal Pradesh (1991-93)

Name of District	*Ground Water*	*Surface Water*	*Rain Water*	*Traditional Source*	*Others*	*Total*
Bilaspur	827	786	0	461	0	2074
Chamba	1717	2433	3	2598	836	7587
Hamirpur	1057	485	0	231	1	1774
Kangra	1602	1317	11	1369	466	4765
Kinnaur	76	217	0	24	2	319
Kullu	0	3392	0	0	0	3392
Lahaul Spiti	1	290	0	57	0	348
Mandi	833	3924	0	1483	840	7080
Shimla	233	3917	5	2518	9	6682
Sirmaur	644	2249	0	535	9	3457
Solan	344	1090	0	1215	316	2965
Una	832	123	1	21	116	1093
Total	**8186**	**20223**	**20**	**10512**	**2595**	**41536**

Source: Survey of Status of Drinking Water in Rural Habitations 1991-93.

The status of drinking water supply to rural habitations in the state given by the Public Health Department till October 2002, is as follows:

	Not Covered (NC)	*Partially Covered (PC)*	*Fully Covered (FC)*	*Total*
No. of rural habitation	921	9613	34,833	45,367

Under the Accelerated Rural Water Supply Programme, special efforts were made by the state government for water supply to rural habitations. During the period 1998 to Sept. 2002, 8103 habitations were covered.

As per the Public Health Department, there are 7130 water supply schemes in the state, 1238 lift, 214 tubewells, and 5678 gravity.

Under urban water supply schemes, augmentation of water supply schemes has been completed in 30 towns. Work is in progress on 21 urban water supply schemes. Further augmentation of water supply has been planned for 15 towns.

Although handpumps do not cover habitations, these are supplementing the existing piped water supply. These have been installed in drought prone acute water scarcity, and other problematic areas. The number of handpumps installed in the state till September 2002, was 11065.

The demand of water in the rural and urban areas based on population projections till 2021 is given in the Table 2.5.

The demand for water in the urban area has been projected by following the norm of 140 lpcd whereas the norm of 70 lpcd has been followed for rural area. By 2021, the urban areas of the state will require 150.49 mld. of water, out of which over one third will be required by Shimla alone. The demand for the water in the rural areas is much higher than in urban areas as a majority of the population of the state lives in the rural areas. Thus, greater thrust is needed for providing drinking water in the rural areas.

Water Quality: Under the National Drinking Water Mission programme, the IPH Department has set up water quality testing laboratories at Dharamsala, Una, Peo and Kandaghat.

The State Pollution Control Board has been monitoring the quality of surface water only. Surface water pollution is on the rise. During the period from 1993-94 to 1996-97, an increase in total coliform has been observed at some places. Dissolved oxygen is lower in deep water. This may prove detrimental to the development of aquatic life.

Groundwater pollution has been observed in the industrial towns of Parwanoo and Kala Amb as per the report of the Central Pollution Control Board, Government of India (1995).

***In situ* Rainwater Harvesting:** Village habitations and towns, which are located at low to high altitude areas of the mountain ranges of Himachal Pradesh, are in dire need of water for domestic as well as irrigation purposes. The only *in situ* water resource available to them is rain water. The most feasible option is to harvest it along the streams as *nallahs*, or the catchment area of watershed and on rooftops etc., and prevent run-off, evaporation and seepage. Fortunately, Himachal Pradesh has abundant rainfall, except at few places and therefore there is a big scope for tapping this resource for drinking and irrigation.

In the towns, rooftop water harvesting in government office buildings, school and *panchayat* buildings and houses should be done on a war footing for *in situ* collection and storage of high quality

TABLE 2.5

Water Demand in Himachal Pradesh (mld.)

District/State	*1999*		*2001*		*2011*		*2021*	
	Urban	*Rural*	*Urban*	*Rural*	*Urban*	*Rural*	*Urban*	*Rural*
Bilaspur	2.69	22.84	2.90	23.76	4.18	28.90	6.04	35.06
Chamba	4.70	30.18	5.03	31.5	7.06	38.96	9.92	48.12
Hamirpur	3.63	27.39	3.90	23.23	5.58	32.75	7.99	37.85
Kangra	8.30	90.9	8.63	94.44	10.46	114.43	12.67	138.37
Kinnaur	—	5.75	—	5.96	—	7.13	—	8.53
Kullu	2.99	23.61	3.13	24.71	3.88	31	4.82	38.89
Lahaul & Spiti	—	2.47	—	2.55	—	2.96	—	3.46
Mandi	7.64	59.57	7.89	62.1	9.31	76.45	10.98	94.12
Shimla	21.75	37.7	23.81	38.47	37.45	41.6	58.91	42.52
Sirmaur	6.05	28.14	6.48	29.3	9.20	35.81	13.06	43.65
Solan	7.63	27.19	8.22	29.15	11.92	36.12	17.27	44.57
Una	4.83	27.86	5.10	28.84	6.71	34.33	8.83	40.82
Himachal Pradesh	**70.21**	**384.32**	**75.04**	**399.01**	**105.76**	**480.44**	**150.49**	**575.97**

Source: Himachal Pradesh Human Development Report, 2002.

rainwater to meet urgent requirements, after necessary purification measures.

Hot Springs: There are a number of hot springs in the districts of Chamba, Kangra, Kinnaur, Kullu, Shimla and Jaoni. Some of these have therapeutic significance. These could be developed as tourist health spots. Important hot springs, with their location and attributes are given in Table 2.6.

Mineral Resources

Himachal Pradesh is rich in mineral resources such as limestone, gypsum, rock salt, magnesite, silica sand and quartzite etc. In addition, building material such as slate, granite, clay and sandstone is also available. Other minerals reported are iron, beryl, copper, lead, silver, kyanite, uranium etc.

TABLE 2.6

Hot Springs in Himachal Pradesh

District	*Locality*	*Potentiality*
Kangra	Jwalamukhi	Six springs.Average salt content from 20 to 26%
	Lausa	Temp. 22°C. Water sulphurous
	Tatwani	Temp. 49°C
	Tira	Temp. 42°C
Kinnaur	Changrizang	Temp. 46.5° C Strong H_2S
Kullu	Vashisht	Temp. 59° C. Strong H_2S
	Manikaran	14 Spring. Temp. 71.4 to 94.4oC. H_2S Low Saline content
Shimla	Suni	Temp. 57°C Strongly sulphurous Highly saline
Solan	Jaoni	Temp. 55°C Highly saline

Source: State of Environment Report, HP, March, 2000.

TABLE 2.7

Mineral Resources of Himachal Pradesh

Mineral	*District*	*Locality*	*Potential*
Limestone	Bilaspur	Gagal-Barmana	117.1 million tonnes
	Kangra	Dharamkot	17.6 million tonnes – 42.52%
	Mandi	Alsinid and Jaunrog	550 million tonnes CaO – 34.4 to 52% MgO – 9.8%
	Shimla	Drawal Kariali Block Jalog-Thench Block	80.43 million tonnes CaO – 4.50% 3.185 million tonnes
		Chamga Nala Shali	224 million tonnes CaO – 44.8% 146 million tonnes CaO – 45.25%
	Sirmaur	Datwardi	101.36 million tonnes CaO – 53.93%
		Hathana	29.87 million tonnes CaO – 53.9%
		Dida	34.65 million tonnes CaO – 53.22%
		Nohra	6.26 million tonnes (Upto 60 m depth) CaO – 53.95%
		Bulain Dhar	1.94 million tonnes (Upto 60 m depth) CaO – 53.60%
Magnesite	Chamba	Muchetar Nala	55,620 tonnes MgO – 39%
Rock Salt	Mandi	Guma	7.55 million tonnes Grade NaCl – 70.40%, KCl – 3% Impurities – 21%
		Darang	-Do-
Slate	Chamba	Rupaina	518400 tonnes
		Bhora	1360800 tonnes
		Chaunda Devi	6480 tonnes
		Renda	172800 tonnes
		Between Kalam Nadi and Sapri	115500 tonnes
	Kangra	Dharamkot	992250 tonnes
		GOT	21600 tonnes
		Bhatti	Impurities – 21%, 162000 tonnes
Stibnite	Lahaul & Spiti	Bara Singri	105682 tonnes 1.65%
Barytes	Kinnaur	Arsomang	3 veins 20 to 60 m long and 15 to 40 cm width. Another vein as 30 m long 97.70% $BaSO_4$
Clay	Kangra	Kothar	15000 tonnes
		Hatli	5076 tonnes
	Sirmaur	Kalidhang	Reserve of clay around Kalidhang, 2.63 million tonnes upto a depth of 20.
Silica sand	Una	Jaijoan Dil Khad	Total reserve for Grade A 50309 tonnes, 97.44% SiO_2
		Bathri	Total reserve for, Grade A, B & C upto a depth of 2m 842570 tonnes
Gypsum	Kinnaur	Shalkar	1.25 million tonnes upto a depth 25 m. Grade not given. Total *in situ* reserve in this belt may be 100 million tonnes
Kyanite	Lahaul & Spiti		Kyanite 40 m in thickness and traceable for 1 km

Source: State of the Environment Report- H.P.-State Council for Science, Technology and Environment, March 2000

The district-wise occurrence and potential of mineral resources (other than Atomic minerals and oil) are given in Table 2.7.

Status of Mineral Production and Value

The mineral-wise production and its value during the year 2002-03 is given below in Table 2.8.

TABLE 2.8

Mineral-wise Production (Tonnes) and Value (in lakh) of Himachal Pradesh During 2002-2003

Mineral	*Production in Tonne*	*Value in Lakh*
Major Minerals		
1. Limestone cement grade	5901346	3914.27
2. Limestone fine grade	78656	1022.00
3. Shale	347302	42.26
4. Baryte	929	1.58
5. Rock Salt	1056	10.56
6. Silica Sand used in glass industries/ Sand stone used as raw mix in cement	12643	5.04
Minor Minerals		
1. Bajri	1406552	617.40
2. Sand	1326263	528.16
3. Building stone	627136	146.38
4. Boulder	824086	316.04
5. Quartzite	31484	9.44
6. Slate	7137	104.29
7. Limestone Kiln grade	4496	5.45
8. Aggregate	525170	74.20

Source: State Geologist, Industry Department, Himachal Pradesh.

At present, there are three cement plants in operation. Of these, two are in Bilaspur and Solan each of 2 million tonnes per annum capacity. The third one of 0.2 million tonne per annum capacity is in Paonta Sahib Tehsil, Sirmaur District. Two more cement plants in Solan and Shimla districts each with 2 million tonnes per annum capacity are in the pipeline.

Marketing Strategies of Major and Minor Minerals

- Limestone extracted from the mines of major cement plant is used by them in their own plants.
- Other major minerals mainly limestone and very rare silica sand and Baryte are marketed by the lessee themselves in the open market.
- Minor minerals are also marketed by the lessees/ contractors in the open market.

Recommendations

Water Resources

- In order to meet the demands of drinking water and life saving crop irrigation for the people living on mountain slopes of the state, it is essential that work on *in situ*-water harvesting is taken up on a war footing to maximise the utilisation of rain water by the habitations instead of allowing the water to flow down into the rivers.
- All micro watersheds/watersheds should be identified in each river basin/sub-basin. Watershed development plans should be prepared for execution on priority basis.
- A Traditional Water Sources Cell may be created in the IPH Department for the development of traditional sources of water in the state. The Cell should have professionals like hydrologists, geologists for scientific development of the resources keeping in view the geological formations, groundwater occurrence and movement in the area.
- To lift part of the flow of hillside kuhls or springs to irrigate adjacent slopy lands or to provide drinking water in the villages, the use of hydraulic rams is strongly recommended. Hydraulic rams do not involve any running cost as no fuel or electricity is required. Installation of hydraulic rams or hydrams in the rural areas should be promoted on a large scale and the government should provide subsidy to the needy habitations of hilly areas.
- An extensive programme of installation of deep tubewells may be drawn up for utilisation of 80 per cent of the available untapped groundwater potential to create irrigation potential of 68,500 ha.
- Construction of sump wells with infiltration galleries in river beds should be promoted to irrigate the cultivated land near the river by the lift system.
- The state should exploit the non-committed river water resources for irrigation purposes wherever cultivable land is available to maximise the irrigation potential.
- River basin/sub basin-wise estimation of water resources should be carried out in the state. An Institute of Mountain Hydrology may be set up to collect and generate hydrological data base.

- There should be scientific assessment and development of groundwater resources of all the valleys of Himachal Pradesh *viz.* Nurpur, Una, Nalagarh, Paonta etc.
- The concept of Water User Association and Participatory Irrigation Management may be introduced in the state.

Mineral Resources

- Keeping in view the vast limestone resources of good quality in Himachal Pradesh, it is recommended that additional cement plants be installed besides increasing the capacity of the existing ones for domestic consumption and export of cement.
- Scientific and systematic extraction of sand, boulders and grit from nallah and river beds should be made.
- An assessment of the impact of mining on associated ecosystems of the existing projects should be carried out.
- The emission levels at every stage of the cement plants should be kept below the permissible level in order to avoid environmental problems.

Chapter 3

Natural Disaster Management

Himachal Pradesh is exposed to various concrete realities. Frequent natural disasters of various intensity and their impact on society and land is one of such problems, which hamper the development of the state. Earthquakes, landslides, cloudbursts, flash floods, avalanches, forest fires, droughts, etc. have caused tremendous loss to the state. Besides loss of life, these disasters also strain the state exchequer.

Landslide is the most common disaster in Himachal Pradesh which causes immense loss of life and property. The Luggar Bhatti landslide on 12 September, 1995, buried 65 persons in the Kullu valley. The state is also avalanche prone. In March 1978, about 30 persons lost their lives in Lahaul and Spiti district. Another avalanche in March 1979, besides causing widespread damage to roads and property, also buried 237 persons.

Frequent flash floods in the last few years have baffled both the meteorologist and the common man equally. The flash flood of 1 August, 2000, in the Satluj left a trail of destruction in Shimla and Kinnaur districts killing more than 150 persons and washing away 14 bridges. The estimated loss to public and private property in this calamity was Rs. 1000 crore. The water level rose suddenly from 12 to 20 metres, damaging a 320 km stretch of the National Highway and the 1500 MW Nathpa Jhakri power project.

In 1995, 114 lives were lost and public property worth Rs. 7552 lakh was damaged in various disasters. Loss to agriculture and horticulture was Rs. 13,251 lakh and Rs. 10,108.29 lakh respectively. Similarly in 1997, 223 lives were lost and private property worth Rs. 8146 lakh was damaged.

On the basis of the damage caused by disasters and their widespread nature, Himachal Pradesh can be called one of the most unstable and disaster-prone states of the country. Although the state is endowed with rich natural resources, the geology, the general topography, the physical features, the climate and active geographic changes have made the area vulnerable to various natural disasters. In addition to the natural causes, various anthropogenic activities have had a multiplier effect and created an imbalance in the overall ecology of the area. All these factors have combined to turn this state into a unique region affected by almost all types of natural disasters. A brief description of the common disasters and their impact is discussed in the succeeding paragraphs.

Earthquakes

Earthquake, quite devastating and sudden in nature, is one of the most common type of disasters that hits the State. This natural disaster has caused immense loss to the state. Lying in the sensitive Himalayan belt, at the juncture of two active tectonic plates, the state is prone to severe seismic activity. Seismologists have categorised Himachal Pradesh in seismic zones IV & V, highly prone to earthquakes. Statistically, more than 250 earthquakes of magnitude above 4.0 on the Richter scale, including 51 with magnitude above 5.0 have rocked the state during the last century. (Table 3.1)

TABLE 3.1

Earthquake (M>5.0) Occurrence in the Region (1897-1991)

Return Period	*No. of Earthquake having Magnitude*			
	5.0-5.9	6.0-6.9	7.0-7.9	>8.0
2.5-3.0 years	25	7	2	1

Source: National Centre for Disaster Management, New Delhi.

Scientific investigations reveal that most of the earthquakes in the region are the result of movement along thrusts/faults and are located along three major thrust zones i.e.:

1. The Main Boundary Thrust (MBT), demarcating the Shivalik Foothills from the rest of the Himalayas.
2. The Main Central Thrust (MCT), demarcating the Lesser and Central Himalayas.
3. The Central Counter Thrust (CCT), separating the Central Himalayas from the Tibetan Himalayas.

As far as geographic distribution of earthquakes is concerned, the area falling in the districts of Kangra, Bilaspur, Chamba, Kullu and Manali falls in the highest seismic zone i.e. Zone V and is most prone to disastrous earthquakes. Blockwise, the Kangra block is most sensitive to earthquakes, followed by Garhwal, Chamba and Shimla blocks. The Kangra earthquake of 4 April, 1904 measuring 8.0 on the Richter scale, the Kinnaur earthquake of Jan 19, 1975 measuring 6.7 on the Richter scale and the Dharamshala earthquake of 26 April, 1986 measuring of 5.7 on the Ritcher scale indicate that the Kangra block is the most sensitive, as far as seismicity is concerned (Table 3.2). The existence of major active thrust sheets is the probable cause of this high vulnerability of the area to earthquakes. The movement of large rock blocks along the thrust planes resulting in the release of stored energy is the basic cause of the earthquakes in this region.

TABLE 3.2

Major Earthquakes in Himachal Pradesh

Date	*Intensity*	*Place*
4th April, 1905	8.0	Kangra
19th January, 1975	6.7	Kinnaur, Lahaul and Spiti
26th April, 1986	5.7	Dharamshala
15th June, 1978	5.0	Dharamshala
1991		Uttaranchal

Source: National Centre for Disaster Management, New Delhi

Kangra Earthquake-1905 (brief description)

Magnitude: 8.0

Time: 06.20 hrs

Epicentre: Near Kangra-Dharamshala

MM intensity observed: X

Lives lost: 20,000

- The earthquake was felt over an area of four lakh square km.
- Kangra town was completely razed to the ground.
- Many houses, buildings, bridges, and roads were damaged.

Landslides

The fragile nature of the rocks forming the mountains, along with climatic condition and various anthropogenic activities have made the state vulnerable to the vagaries of nature. Besides earthquakes, landslides are the other geological hazards that are common and peculiar to this state.

Landslides are the downslide movement of soil, debris or rocks, resulting from natural causes, vibrations, overburden of rock material, removal of lateral supports, change in the water content of rock or soil bodies, blocked drainage etc. In Himachal Pradesh, the mass movement varies in magnitude from soil creep to landslides. Solifluction (form of creep in which snow or water saturated rocks move down the slope) is another type of mass movement that is common on the higher snow covered ranges of the state.

The problem of landslides is common and frequent in Himachal Pradesh. Almost every year the state is affected by one or more major landslides affecting society in many ways. Loss of life, damage to houses, roads, means of communication, agricultural land, and floods are some of the the major consequences of landslides in the region.

Flash floods, particularly in narrow river gorges are the cause of some of the major landslides in Himachal Pradesh. These flash floods trigger landslides in the region, eventually jeopardising the stability of the hill as a whole. Some of these landslides have often created landslide-dams in various river gorges.

The vulnerability of the geologically young, unstable and fragile rocks of the state has increased many times in the recent past due to various unscientific developmental activities. Deforestation, unscientific road construction, terracing and water intensive agricultural practices, encroachment on steep hill slopes are the anthropogenic activities which have increased the intensity and frequency of landslides.

Among the man-induced causes, road construction in the hilly terrain is more responsible for landslides. The quantum of the damage by unscientific road construction may be judged by scientific research, which states that one kilometer of road construction in the Himalayas needs removal of 60,000 cubic meters of debris. Due to this and other anthropogenic activities, landslides have become a regular occurrence in the state, specially during the rainy season. Malling, Nathpa, Powai in the Spiti and Sutluj valleys in Kinnaur district and Marlu, Bhang, Chhayal and Mandh in the Beas catchment are the areas where landslides occur almost every year.

At present, according to gross yet reliable estimates, landslides occupy about 1 per cent of the land surface in five central districts of Himachal Pradesh. They have a total volume of more than 2.2×10^6 m^3 and a mean age of 6.5 years. This helps to evaluate the denudation rate, which is about 12 mm/year (all erosive processes). Landslides have about 2.5 mm/year denudation rate.

Flash Floods and Cloud Bursts

Flash floods, short-lived extreme events, which usually occur under slowly moving or stationary thunderstorms, lasting less than 24 hours are a common disaster in the state. As a result of the high velocity of the current which can wash away all obstacles in its way, this phenomenon has resulted in enormous loss of life and property in various parts of the region. Recent flash flood of 1 August, 2000, in the Sutlej is one such example in which more than 150 persons were killed and enormous loss was caused to various infrastructure like roads, bridges and power plants so the estimated loss to property due to this flash flood was above Rs. 1000 crore.

Glacial melting due to global warming is another major cause of flash floods in Himachal Pradesh. The major glaciers in the higher hill tops are receding at an alarming rate due to anthropogenic activities. Intensive industrialisation is one of such major causes of global warming. As per the Defence Research Development Organisation (DRDO) estimates, the receding rate of famous Himalyan glaciers has been as follows (Table 3.3).

TABLE 3.3

Receding Rate of Glacier

S. No.	*Name of Glacier*	*State*	*Receding Rate (m/year)*
1.	Barashingri	Himachal Pradesh	44.3
2.	Gangotri	Uttaranchal	17.5
3.	Milam	Uttaranchal	13.3
4.	Pindar	Uttaranchal	23.5
5.	Dokriani	Uttaranchal	17.0
6.	Zemu	Sikkim	13.2

Source: DRDO

Along with glacial receding, the bursting of natural or man-made dams, and cloudbursts are other main causes of flash floods. "Cloudbursts, very common in Himachal Pradesh, are basically excessive rain in a short period, resulting in flash floods that wash away every obstacle in the way.

Avalanches

Avalanches, river-like flow of snow or ice descending from mountain tops are common in the high ranges of the Himalayas. Lahaul & Spiti, Drass, Badrinath are areas which are frequently hit by this phenomenon. As per the Snow and Avalanches Study Establishment (SASE) of the DRDO, on an average 30 persons are killed every year due to this disaster in the Himalayas. Beside claiming lives, avalanches also damage roads and other property falling in their way.

Some specific features associated with avalanches are:-

- They are common in elevation of more than 3500 m.
- Very frequent on slopes of 30-45°
- Convex slopes are more prone to this form of disaster
- North-facing slopes have avalanches in winter and south facing during summer
- Slopes covered with grass are also more prone to avalanches

The high ranges of Himachal Pradesh are frequently hit by this snow-related disaster. The major avalanches that hit the area in last two decades are:

TABLE 3.4

Major Avalanches

Time	*Area*	*Loss*
March, 1978	Lahaul & Spiti	30 people killed
March 1979	Lahaul & Spiti	237 people killed
1988	Shimla	Blocking of Districts of Kinnaur, Lahaul & Spiti and Solan
March 1991	Himachal Pradesh	Road blockage for 40 days
September 1995	Himachal Pradesh	Devastating Floods

Source: DRDO

Like floods, avalanches also cause great damage to life and property. The villages at high altitudes and army and para-military camps are frequently hit by this form of natural calamity.

Soil Erosion

Soil erosion is a slow phenomenon, causing extensive loss to soil fertility and damage to the land basin. Though the process of soil erosion is natural and has been continuing on the surface of the earth since its origin, recently, due to various human induced activities, its rate has accelerated to dangerous proportions.

In Himachal Pradesh which is drained by a large network of river systems, soil erosion by water has become a serious problem. Besides causing great loss to soil fertility, the huge quantity of eroded material carried by water channels causes floods in downstream regions.

The problem becomes alarming, considering the average sediment delivery ratio of 525, and an annual silt yield of 11.2 million tonnes. The siltation rate of the reservoirs is higher, by almost 180 per cent, than the originally projected rates of 4.29 million t/year.

Along with other development activities, deforestation, road construction, forest fires etc. are the basic reasons for the high soil erosion rate in the state.

Forest Fires

Forest fires are not new to forests. They have raged across the earth for millions of years. But in the recent past, forest fires have increased enormously due to human-induced factors.

In comparison with other parts of the country, the forests of the Himalayan region, due to various biotic and geographic reasons are more prone to forest fires. Being ecologically very sensitive, the impact of fire on the forests of the Himalayas is more serious and beyond repair. The severity of the problem may be judged from the forest fire of 1995 in two states–Uttaranchal and Himachal Pradesh in which along with direct loss of Rs.1750 million worth of forests, the impact of the fire and its scars on the local environment are still visible prominently.

Approximately, 90 per cent of the forest fires are human-induced, both intentional or unintentional. Most of the forest fires are caused by negligence and poor knowledge of the people. Collection of forest produce, shifting cultivation, throwing smouldering *bidis*, cooking food in the forest etc. are the basic anthropogenic causes that ignite forest fires.

The adverse ecological, economic and social impact of forest fires may be summarised as follows:

- Loss of valuable timber and minor forest produce resources.
- Loss of livelihood for tribal population living within or near the forest.
- Loss of human life (Four women grass cutters were killed in February, 2001 in Gwar village of Uttaranchal)
- Depletion of carbon sinks, deteriorating the environmental conditions.
- Loss of bio-diversity and extinction of plant and animal species.
- Soil erosion resulting in loss of soil productivity and flooding of downstream valleys.
- Loss of agricultural land due to erosion and landslides.
- Degradation of watersheds resulting in low rainfall and fall in the water table.
- Damage to wild life habitat and their death.
- Damage to natural regeneration and reduction in forest vegetation.
- Increase in the percentage of carbon dioxide in the atmosphere.
- Degradation of the microclimate of the area making it unhealthy for living.
- Increase in the incidence of respiratory diseases.

Recommendations

General

- To envisage development by a holistic approach designed to manage disasters on a more proactive basis, the state should have a comprehensive policy on all phases of disaster management that addresses the entire gamut of disasters arising from natural and man-made causes. This policy should take full cognizance of other related policies and initiatives at both the national and state level.
- Himachal Pradesh should develop advance, specific hazard mitigation plans and should provide a strong and stable administrative set-up for disaster mitigation, prepareness and relief.
- All development projects in vulnerable areas should be formulated carefully to minimise the adverse effects of natural disasters and should be linked with disaster mitigation.

- The economic impact of a natural disaster should receive adequate attention and cost-benefit analysis should incorporate the probable disaster events and mitigation programmes to undertake work in disaster prone areas.
- Linkages between environment, natural disasters and development need to be clearly established to mitigate disasters and to improve the environment.

Floods/Landslide Mitigation

- Deforestation/clear felling of trees on mountain slopes and river catchments should be stopped or kept to the minimum.
- Afforestation/vegetation cover on hilly regions and flood prone areas should be given priority.
- Area flood mapping should be prepared to make future preparedness plans.
- Forecast and warning systems should be improved.
- There should be proper river bank protection by constructing embankments and using anti-erosion measures.
- In flood prone areas, evacuation capabilities should be enhanced.

Earthquakes

- Public buildings should be earthquake resistant by using the code of Bureau of Indian Standards (BIS) for earthquake-resistant design.
- Measures should be taken to make houses using gasoline, oil and gas stoves houses resistant to earthquakes.
- In city planning, the load bearing capacity studies of the ground should be undertaken and risk zones should be identified.
- For important transport and communication segments, standby facilities should be provided in earthquake prone areas.

Forest Fires

- Fire prevention may be done by education, enforcement and by reducing the hazard.
- Fire prevention education can be given by training, signs and poster display, exhibition, circulation of literature and visual aids etc.
- Restrictive regulations such as prohibiting smoking in forests, regulation of visitors to certain forest areas and on certain activities may be imposed.
- Agricultural practices including weeding, cleaning, removal of dead leaves, use of chemicals as weed killers and by constructing firebreaks to work as a barrier for preventing fires crossing from one area to another may be adopted.

Soil Erosion

- Afforestation and soil conservation measures should be undertaken on micro-watershed basis in the catchment areas of all the rivers in the state.

Chapter 4

Forestry

Introduction

Himachal Pradesh is a predominantly mountainous state. Consequently, its climate is more congenial to forests. It comprises four forest zones—sub-tropical, sub-temperate, wet-temperate and dry-temperate.

Sub-tropical forests: This zone consists of foothills and valleys up to an elevation of about 915 metres above mean sea level with a sub-tropical climate and an annual rainfall of 70-100 cm, of which 75 per cent falls during the monsoon season. The maximum temperature goes up to 40^{0}C. It comprises dry deciduous, chir pine, sal (2140 sq. km.) and thorny forests (43 sq. km.) mostly of *xerophytic* species.

Sub-temperate forests: These forests extend from 916 metres to about 1523 metres above mean sea level, has a mild climate and an annual rainfall of 90 to 120 cm, nearly 70 per cent of which is received during the monsoon season. Some upper hills get mild snowfall during winter, which does not stay for long. The maximum temperature in summer remains around 30^{0}C. Various species of pines, oaks and broad-leafed species grow in this zone. There are good pasturelands in this area.

Wet-temperate forests: These extend from 1524 to 2472 metres above mean sea level, and have some major forests and pasturelands. The annual rainfall varies from 100 to 250 cm, with snowfall during winter, when the temperature falls to minus 10^{0}C. During summer, the maximum temperature ranges between 15 and 20^{0}C. These forests have been categorised as (a) lower western Himalayan temperate forests consisting of conifers, oaks and various deciduous trees and (b) western Himalayan temperate forests, which consist of firs, oaks and rhododendron species found in alpine zones.

Dry-temperate forests: These extend to above 2472 metres. The mean annual temperature is around 10° C and the mean annual precipitation about 25 cm, most of which is received as snow. The area contains scattered trees and bushes such as *chilgoza*, willow, *robinia*, *ailanthus*, poplars and alpine pastures interspersed with bushes such as *ephedra*.

The flora and fauna of varied natural ecosystems constitute the forest wealth of the state. The forest varieties range from soft-wood conifers to hard-wood deciduous flowering plants. Of the 45,000 species of plants found in the country as many as 3,295 are reported in the state. The status of land utilisation for the state is given in Table 4.1.

TABLE 4.1

Land utilisation in Himachal Pradesh (1999–2000)

Category	*Area (sq. km.)*
Geographical area	55673
Forest area (Forest records)	37033
Permanent pastures and other grazing lands including alpine pastures, barren and uncultivable wastes etc.	7549
Fallow lands (current & other fallows)	719
Net area sown	5514
Cultivable wastes	1194
Land under miscellaneous tree crops not included in cultivation	642
Land put to non-agricultural uses	3022

Source: Himachal Forests, 2002, Forest Department, Himachal Pradesh.

Relevance of Forests

Forests in Himachal Pradesh have a very productive ecological niche. Latitudinally, the state falls in the tropical zone, but its geographical location and good forest cover have enriched it, both biologically and economically. During the immediate post-independence period, planners identified the forests of the state only as a source of timber and other products. This led to large-scale felling and clearing of forest areas. Deforestation, to meet the timber needs of industries set up in the plains and of the flourishing horticulture industry in the state, ultimately created consciousness about the need to protect the forests.

A vast majority of the population of the state is rural and depends mainly for its livelihood either directly on forest products or on those, which are produced by using the resources, conserved or protected by the forests. Unsustainable exploitation of dense forests ultimately led to the gradual loss of the ecological environment suitable for producing different crops, both traditional as well as improved commercial fruit, vegetable and medicinal plants. The damage to the environment and the land is so heavy that certain areas in the mid-hills which 20 years ago were suitable for growing fruit crops, are no longer able to sustain the fruit plants and the farmers are losing interest in growing these fruit crops. This condition of the forests adversely affects the economy of the hill people.

The forests of Himachal Pradesh are not only of importance for the state, but have also a strong influence on the ecology, climate and bio-resources of the neighbouring states of Punjab, Haryana and Rajasthan. Glaciers flowing from the Tibetan hills (China) and the melting snows feed the rivers originating in the state and provide water to other states. The forest cover of Himachal not only regulates the rainfall in the neighbouring areas but also ensures snowfall in the high mountains. A reduction in the forest cover of the state will prevent the formation of glaciers and snow, resulting in less water in the rivers. The summer heat will easily melt the glaciers and the snow and cause flash floods both in the hills and the plains of the neighbouring states.

Status of Forests in Himachal Pradesh

The strategy for the Ninth Five Year Plan of Himachal Pradesh states: "the degraded forest lands, the village common lands and wastelands will be rehabilitated through various state plans/centrally sponsored and externally aided projects/schemes so that a forest cover of 50 per cent by 2000 AD as per policy of the state government is arrived at". The National Forest Policy, 1988, also has recommended that at least two-third of the total geographical area of Himachal Pradesh should be under forests. This comes to about 37,115 sq. km. However, according to statistics provided by the Department of Forests, Himachal Pradesh, the recorded forest area was 37,033 sq. km. in 2000-01. This amounted to 66.5 per cent of the total geographical area. Nearly 16,376 sq. km., or 29.41 per cent of the total geographical area is under alpine pastures and perpetual snow cover. This leaves only 20,657 sq. km., or 37.10 per cent under some kind of forest cover.

Satellite imagery places the forest cover of the state at 13,082 sq. km., or 23.5 per cent of the total geographical area in 1999, an increase of 561 sq. km., from 12,521 sq. km. in 1997 (Table 4.2). According to the latest data, the forest cover is 14,360 sq. km., which is 25.79 per cent of the geographical area. This includes area under orchards and natural regenerated area.

TABLE 4.2

Forest Cover Assessment in Himachal Pradesh Based on Imagery

Year	*Area (sq. km.)*
1997	12521
1999	13082
Change	**+561**

Source: *Himachal Forests, 2002*, Forest Department, Himachal Pradesh.

The difference between the recorded and actual cover is because the actual forest cover takes into account only areas that bear a tree cover and ignores areas which may legally have the status of forests but have no tree cover.

Reserved forests:	An area so constituted under the Indian Forest or other state Forest Acts.
Protected forests:	A legal term for an area subject to limited degree of protection under the provisions of the Indian Forest Act or other state Forest Acts.
Unclassed forests:	Forest land owned by government but non-constituted into a reserved or protected forest.
Dense forests:	All land with a forest cover of trees with canopy - density of 40 per cent and above.
Open forests:	All land with a forest cover of trees with canopy - density between 10 and 40 per cent.
Scrub forests:	All land with poor tree growth, chiefly of small or stunted trees with canopy - density less than 10 per cent.

Table 4.2 shows the classification of forests by legal and ownership status. Nearly 94.3 per cent of the forest area of the state has been classified as reserved and protected forests. The remaining 5.7 per cent falls in other categories. Within the protected forests, 34.3 per cent of the area has been demarcated. Private individuals own only 2.9 per cent of the total forest area, the rest is state-owned and only 0.1 per cent belongs to cantonments and municipalities. However, a part (about 30%) of private individual forests is looked after by the Forest Department and 748 sq.km. are managed by municipalities, cantonment boards or other organisations including private individuals (Table 4.3).

TABLE 4.3

Classification of Forests in Himachal Pradesh (2000–01)

Category	*Area (sq. km.)*	*Percentage*
Legal Status		
Reserved forests	1896	5.1
Demarcated protected forests	11341	30.6
Undemarcated protected forests	21702	58.6
Unclassed forests	977	2.7
Managed by Forest Department	369	1.0
Not Managed by Forest Department	748	2.0
Ownership Status		
State-owned forests	35916	97.0
Cantonment and municipal forests	42	0.1
Private individual forests	1075	2.9
Total	**37033**	**100.0**

Source: Himachal Forests, 2002, Forest Department, Himachal Pradesh.

According to the distribution of forests by crown density (Table 4.4), 24.6 per cent of the forest area is under dense forests, with a crown density of 40 per cent or more. Another 10.7 per cent is termed as open forests with a crown density ranging from 10 to 40 per cent and 20.5 per cent of the total forest area falls in the category of scrub forests. Afforestation work is possible on the scrubs, with low-density forests and the rest of the area where no forests exist. As on 31 March 2003, afforestation has been carried out in an area of 8798 sq.km. and only about 3739 sq. km. is available for raising new plantations under open and scrub forests.

Forest classification shows a decline in the total forest area during 1995-96 over 1990-91. This is because of a decrease in unclassed forest area and protected forest area. Nevertheless, in 2000-01, the total forest area exceeded that of 1995-96 but still remained below what it was in 1990-91. This increase/decrease has occurred because of the change in the needs of the State Forest Department, which enjoys the legal power to alter and notify a particular forest area as protected or unclassed (Table 4.5).

TABLE 4.4

Distribution of Forests by Crown Density (CD): 2000-01

Category	*Area (Sq. km.)*	*Percentage to Forest Area*
Recorded forest area	37033	**100**
Actual forest cover	13082	**35.3**
Dense forest (CD above 40%)	9120	24.6
Open forest (CD 10-40%)	3962	10.7
Scrub forest (CD below 10%)	7575	**20.5**
Uncultivable barren land (alpine pasture, snow area etc.)	16376	**44.2**

Source: Himachal Forests, 2002, Forest Department, Himachal Pradesh.

TABLE 4.5

Changes in Various Classes of Forests in Himachal Pradesh (1990-91 to 2000-01)

Particulars	*Area in sq. km.*		
	1990-91	*1995-96*	*2000-01*
Reserved forests	1896	1896	1896
Protected forests	33448	31453	33043
Unclassed forests	868	680	977
Total	**37591**	**35427**	**37033**

Source: Forest Statistics (different issues), Forest Department, Himachal Pradesh.

The actual forest cover of Himachal Pradesh shows an increasing trend over the years. This is the result of the ban on green felling in the state and inclusion of horticulture trees into the forest cover. Despite this, the decadal rate of increase in forest cover is slow and shall need a long time to achieve the target. (Table 4.6).

TABLE 4.6

Change in Actual Forest Cover of Himachal Pradesh (1991 to 2001)

Forest Composition	*Area in sq. km.*			
	1991	*1995*	*1999*	*2001*
Dense forest (CD above 40%)	8911	9565	9120	10429
Open forest (CD 10 to 40%)	2869	2936	3962	3931
Total	**1178C**	**12501**	**13082**	**14360**
As a per cent of geographical area	**21.16**	**22.45**	**23.50**	**25.79**

Source: Himachal Forests (different issues), Forest Department, Himachal Pradesh.

Table 4.7 shows the percentage of forest area and cover in selected states of India in 1991 and 1999. The percentage of forest cover to recorded forest area is 133.6 in Arunanchal Pradesh and 101.3 in Jammu & Kashmir. In Himachal Pradesh it is only 35.3 per cent, the lowest among all the Indian states, barring the Union Territory of Chandigarh, and much lower than the national average of 83.1 per cent. The per capita availability of forests in Himachal at 0.24 hectare is, however, higher than the national average and the highest in the country (Table 4.8).

TABLE 4.7

Forest Area and Cover in Selected States of India (1991 and 1999 Assessment)

State	*Percentage of Forest Cover to*			
	Geographical Area		*Forest Area*	
	1991	*1999*	*1991*	*1999*
Arunanchal Pradesh	82.1	82.2	133.4	133.6
Assam	31.6	30.2	80.6	77.1
Manipur	79.2	77.9	116.7	114.7
Jammu & Kashmir	9.0	9.2	99.5	101.3
Himachal Pradesh	**21.2**	**23.5**	**31.3**	**35.3**
India	**19.4**	**19.4**	**83.0**	**83.1**

Source: State of Forest Reports (FSI), 1991 and 1999.

The data on annual prescribed yield and growing stock of commercially important species (Table 4.9) reveal that fir/spruce, followed by deodar, are the important species which the state government exploits for different purposes. *Sal* is the least prescribed species for harvesting because of its lowest commercially available growing stock.

TABLE 4.8

Per Capita Availability of Forests in Selected States of India (1997)

Name of the State	*Forest Area (sq. km.)*	*Per Capita (ha.)*
Arunanchal Pradesh	68602	7.93
Assam	23824	0.11
Manipur	17418	0.95
Jammu & Kashmir	20440	0.26
Himachal Pradesh	**12521**	**0.24**
India	**633397**	**0.07**

Source: Statistical Outline of India, 2000-2001, Tata Services Limited, Department of Economics and Statistics, Mumbai.

TABLE 4.9

Growing Stock of Commercially Important Species

(Standing Volume in 000 cu. m.)

Name of Species	*Annual Prescribed Yield*			*Growing Stock of Commercially Important Species*		
	1990	*1995*	*2001*	*1990*	*1995*	*2001*
Deodar	1100	1100	1255	13288	14215	15219
Kail	940	1122	1122	12996	13616	12964
Fir/Spruce	2300	4083	2316	39026	41012	38700
Chil	960	1011	993	8644	10053	12080
Sal	190	190	190	2563	2563	2563
Others			N.P.	20312	12052	13736
Total	**5490**	**7516**	**6120**	**96839**	**102511**	**95262**

Source: Himachal Forests, various issues, Forest Department, Himachal Pradesh.

Note: N.P.- not prescribed.

TABLE 4.10

District-wise Forest Cover of Himachal Pradesh (1999 assessment)

District	*Geographical Area (sq. km.)*	*Forest Area (sq. km.)*	*Forest Cover (sq. km.)*	*Change Compared to 1997 (sq. km.)*	*% of Forest Cover to Geographical Area*	*% of Forest Cover to its Area*
Bilaspur	1167	428	235	+77	20.1	54.9
Chamba	6528	4917	2301	+240	35.2	46.8
Hamirpur	1118	219	188	-35	16.8	85.8
Kangra	5739	2842	1639	-105	28.6	57.7
Kinnaur	6401	5093	649	+17	10.1	12.7
Kullu	5503	5065	1974	-70	35.9	39.0
Lahaul & Spiti	13835	10133	150	+67	1.1	1.5
Mandi	3950	1860	1539	+224	38.9	82.7
Shimla	5131	3418	2390	-35	46.6	67.7
Sirmaur	2825	1843	1108	+84	39.2	60.1
Solan	1936	728	492	+70	25.4	67.6
Una	1540	487	417	+27	27.1	85.6
Himachal Pradesh	**55673**	**37033**	**13082**	**+561**	**23.5**	**35.3**

Source: H.P. Forest Statistics, 2000, Forest Department, Himachal Pradesh.

District-wise percentage of the forest cover to the total geographical area of Himachal Pradesh in 1999 varies from as low as 1.1 per cent in Lahaul & Spiti to 46.6 per cent in Shimla (Table 4.10). The low percentage in Lahaul & Spiti is because of the extreme climate of the region, i.e., snow-bound area. There are four districts, namely, Kangra, Kullu, Hamirpur and Shimla, where the forest area has declined since 1997. This could be because of the expansion of towns, road network, infrastructural development, housing and tourism.

Natural Regeneration and Afforestation

Regeneration of forests becomes essential as more and more forest areas become degraded because of social and economic causes, besides forest fires and other natural phenomena. Currently, the forests of Himachal Pradesh need scientific management. Large-scale afforestation programmes undertaken by the state Forest Department in selected areas in the recent past, also involving such institutions as Joint Forest Management, have yielded good results. If such small-scale efforts are earnestly made throughout the state, one can be assured of an increase in the forest cover in Himachal Pradesh, to achieve the prescribed limit of 66 per cent. The equation between forest degradation and forest regeneration should be maintained, to ensure that the forest cover does not get depleted.

Methods for Regeneration

Natural

Local factors are important for natural regeneration of forest species. Natural regeneration of khair, chil, shisham, eucalyptus and bamboos has been going on in the state. Natural regeneration of shisham is being encouraged, as it helps soil conservation. Eucalyptus regenerates naturally through coppice. In 1998-99, an area of 14.74 sq. km. was regenerated through this method. Natural regeneration is not the only way of afforestation and should be supplemented with artificial regeneration.

Artificial

Artificial regeneration is the main method adopted to increase the forest cover of the state. Plants of economically as well as ecologically important species, *viz.*, chil, khair, deodar, robinia, poplar, fir/spruce, kail, etc., are being planted. Seeds of some of these species are also being developed by the state. In 1998-99, an area of 137.33 sq. km. was regenerated mainly through artificial methods, as compared to only 14.74 sq. km. mainly through natural methods.

Afforestation

Artificial regeneration can also be employed for afforestation. Progress in this regard has been indicated separately in Table 4.11. During 1998-99, the Department of Forests carried out afforestation in an area of 297.96 sq. km., under different schemes. In all, an area of 450.03 sq. km. was regenerated and afforested during 1998-99. The area covered has declined from 524.62 sq. km. in 1990-91.

Plantation

Himachal has so far (as on 31 March 2001) carried out plantation activities in a total area of 8,799 sq. km. as part of its afforestation programme. Trees are planted

TABLE 4.11

Progress of Regeneration and Afforestation (1990-91 to 1998-99)

(Sq. km.)

Name of the Circle	*Regenerated Area*						*Afforested Area*			*Total Area*		
	Mainly Natural			*Mainly Artificial*								
	1990-91	*1995-96*	*1998-99*	*1990-91*	*1995-96*	*1998-99*	*1990-91*	*1995-96*	*1998-99*	*1990-91*	*1995-96*	*1998-99*
CCF Wildlife	—	—	—	—	2.16	2.07	—	2.76	5.60	—	4.92	7.67
Bilaspur	4.24	—	—	67.01	—	30.21	59.82	23.49	31.59	131.07	23.49	61.80
Chamba	4.53	0.77	6.31	10.10	3.67	—	24.78	53.27	43.36	39.41	57.71	49.67
Dharamshala	0.45	0.45	1.10	54.39	19.23	41.59	17.27	27.34	22.99	72.11	47.02	65.68
Kullu	—	1.16	1.60	15.61	28.88	28.62	12.67	27.60	30.37	28.28	57.64	60.59
Mandi	6.03	7.24	1.27	25.25	7.57	1.28	90.62	43.98	41.06	121.90	58.79	43.61
Nahan	—	—	—	—	—	24.45	46.24	44.14	46.69	46.24	44.14	71.14
Rampur	—	1.08	2.54	1.50	4.69	—	34.53	24.85	22.40	36.03	30.62	24.94
Shimla	6.42	1.52	1.92	19.94	6.00	9.11	23.22	26.33	25.20	49.58	33.85	36.23
Total	**21.67**	**12.22**	**14.74**	**193.80**	**72.20**	**137.33**	**309.15**	**302.29**	**297.96**	**524.62**	**386.71**	**450.03**

Source: Annual Administrative Report (different years), Forest Department, Himachal Pradesh.

mostly on forest land and on community lands to supplement regeneration efforts and to increase the forest cover. Both the government and foreign donor institutions fund this activity. As the framework of a particular project being carried out determines plantation, it may sometimes result in heavy planting of the same species, ignoring its cost-benefit to society. It also causes concentration of plantation in selected areas at the cost of other areas and priorities.

The planting activities of selected species are often undertaken on specified targeted areas. Due to lack of adequate fencing and indiscriminate visits of scrub animals in the planted areas, the damage often is large and is rarely recorded. Even the community participation in newer plantings and their conservation is lacking which often results in patchy growth of trees. In fact, the entire planting process including the choice of tree species be worked out in consultation and help of the local community, so that they are fully involved in the management of planting.

Table 4.12 shows the plantation achievements in Himachal Pradesh from 1950-51 to 2000-01. On an average, an area of 172.5 sq. km. was planted every year. Recent trends show a continuous decline in the area planted each year, because of paucity of funds and a ban on silviculture and working plan operations in the state under an order of the Supreme Court dated 12 December 1996, except for the right-holders. However, dry and fallen trees (salvage) can be removed through the HP State Forest Corporation. Chil is the single largest species with about 30 per cent of the area planted by the department. Deodar forms only 12 per cent of the total area planted during this period. Recently, a large number of broad-leafed species, including walnut, poplar, shisham, etc., were planted under different projects. Cultivation of Bamboo has a great potential for the state as it is highly versatile, lending itself to distinct and unique furniture designs, to new generation building materials, and to a vast range of items, thereby generating countless jobs. Since the state has a lot of degraded soils, bamboo holds the promise for their regeneration. At present, two bamboo species namely, *Bambusa bambos* and *Dendrocalamus strictus*, are widely found in the state, whereas new fast growing species suitable to specific agro-climatic regions could be introduced based on the requirement of end objectives such as, making paper pulp, furniture, building material etc. The National Mission on Bamboo Technology and Trade Development has elaborated upon the use of bamboo for cultivation in different regions of the country and has given suggestions for its commercial and environmental benefits.

TABLE 4.12

Plantation Achievements in Himachal Pradesh (1950-51 to 2000-01)

(Hectare)

Species	*Area Planted From 1950-51 to 1998-99*	*Plantations Raised During*		*Total Area of Plantation as on 31.3.2001*
		1999-2000	*2000-01*	
Deodar	101011	6218	3631	110860
Kail	11065	210	168	11443
Fir/spruce	16361	289	151	16801
Chil	261105	4394	3871	269370
Other Conifers	113	—	—	113
Walnut	3612	63	88	3763
Willow	8789	331	204	9324
Khair	147745	3769	3728	155242
Shisham	12560	1264	1592	15416
Bamboos	3230	293	702	4225
Mulbery	1378	—	—	1378
Poplar	12730	722	344	13796
Robinia	41068	1770	1206	44044
Other B L Species	204755	10123	9237	224115
Total	**825522**	**29446**	**24922**	**879890**

Source: Himachal Forests, 2002, Forest Department, Himachal Pradesh.

Forest Produce

Timber

Most of the villages in the state are situated on steep slopes and are connected by tracks rather than concrete roads. Moreover, the villages are either adjacent to or enclosed by forests, which are thus deeply integrated with the livelihood of the local people. They depend on the forests for timber for the construction of houses, firewood, agricultural implements, fodder and a variety of other products and services, including certain medicinal herbs. Some of the users of forest products feel equally responsible for their conservation and ensure proper protection and regular regeneration of forests.

The government of Himachal Pradesh constituted the Forest Corporation in 1974, the only agency responsible for the harvesting and exploitation of forests, including resin extraction. Earlier, private contractors carried out all activities related to forests. This resulted in unscientific harvesting and over-exploitation of the forest resources.

Timber distribution (TD) allows local people to harvest timber legally in forests near their place of habitation, for constructing their own houses. It currently accounts for, on an average, an annual harvest of timber of over 1,00,000 cubic metres. In terms of value it amounted to about Rs. 56 crore in 1998-99. The current market value of this timber is more than one thousand times the nominal price paid by the villagers under TD. The state exchequer's share is negligible.

TD scheme dates back to 1880's which has been widely exploited by a large number of influential people at the cost of needy, for personal economic gains. The regulations need to be updated to plug the economic losses and to identify the genuine and needy users of timber. The communities and groups involved in forest management and conservation may be actively involved in identifying the genuineness of the needs of the local people.

Timber distribution is more of a harvesting policy. In 1999-2000, the share of right-holders in the total timber production of the state was 31 per cent, and if timber distribution to the free grantees is added, it comes to about 33 per cent. Thus, one-third of the total timber produced in the state is consumed under timber distribution. The major effect of timber distribution of forests is the selective harvesting of certain species. Deodar and kail are best suited for the construction of houses because of their durability. But the main focus of the government in the past has been on harvesting fir/spruce to meet the fruit growers' demand for boxes. In 1999-2000, more than 45 per cent of the total wood extracted by the right-holders was deodar and about 25 per cent kail. The Himachal Pradesh State Forest Corporation concentrated on chil (39%) and fir/spruce (30%) (see Table 4.13).

TABLE 4.13

Forest Produce (1991-2000)

Year	*Government Extraction*	*Forest Corporation*	*Right Holders*	*Free Grantees*	*Other Agencies*	*Total*
Timber (M^3)						
1991-1992	2521	227699	113735	7693	4731	**356379**
1995-1996	907	325220	96274	2981	402	**425784**
1998-1999	824	244842	100310	9316	161	**355453**
1999-2000	1779	206750	96572	7181	149	**312433**
Firewood (qtl.)						
1991-1992	49	1346	152	91	490	**2128**
1995-1996	27	834	6	350	5	**1222**
1998-1999	12	281	118	—	—	**411**
1999-2000	11	506	313	122	121	**1073**
Charcoal (qtl.)						
1991-1992	176	295	—	350	—	**821**
1995-1996	605	364	—	—	—	**969**
1998-1999	96	8	—	—	—	**104**
1999-2000	66	8	—	—	—	**74**

Source: Forest Statistics (different issues), Forest Department, Himachal Pradesh.

The most valued forest product in 2000-01 was timber, followed by medicinal plants and herbs and resin. The total forest produce was worth Rs. 231.30 crore (Table 4.14). It would be interesting to have a look at the revenue of the state from these products. Until 1970, timber removal from the forests was more than the annual prescribed yield, which was unsustainable. To overcome this shortcoming, the government of Himachal Pradesh established the Himachal Pradesh State Forest Corporation which was entrusted with all harvesting operations in the forests. As a result, since 1975, the annual removal from the forests has always remained below the prescribed yield (Table 4.15). Timber measuring 4,70,000 cubic metres were extracted annually from the forests of the state during the last five decades of the previous century (1950-2000). The average timber removal was the highest in the decade 1980-90.

TABLE 4.14

Value of Forest Produce in Himachal Pradesh (2000-01)

Name of Produce	*Unit of Measurement*	*Quantity*	*Estimated Value (Rs. in lakh)*
Timber	'000 cu. M.	341766	21791.5
Firewood	Tonnes	2696	76.9
Charcoal	Tonnes	60	3.4
Resin	Qtls.	73567	475.0
Bhabbar Grass	Qtls.	400	0.2
Grazing Fodder	Qtls.	—	13.4
Medicinal Plants	Qtls.	19719	667.2
Other minor products	Qtls.	2150	70.6
Khair	Qtls.	21630	31.5
Total	—	—	**23129.7**

Source: Himachal Forests, 2002, Forest Department, Himachal Pradesh.

TABLE 4.15

Timber Removal from the Forests of Himachal Pradesh

(Standing volume in '000 cu.m.)

Year	*Growing Stock*	*Annual Prescribed Yield*	*Removal from Forests*
1970	82076	5410	6806
1975	98861	7500	4706
1980	99458	7220	4637
1985	95843	4860	4602
1990	96839	5490	4356
1995	102511	7516	4500
1998	103344	7767	3555

Source: State Environment Report, Himachal Pradesh.

Other Forest Products

Besides timber, the forests of Himachal Pradesh are rich in fodder, grass and other grazing plants, organic manure and fibre, gum, resins, medicinal plants/herbs and other products including fruits. The Himachal Pradesh State Forest Corporation is the only agency responsible for extracting resins from the state forests. The state Forest Department issues permits for the collection of other non-timber products. Medicinal and aromatic plants are of special value. Table 4.16 details various non-timber products. Such produce was worth Rs. 12.29 crore in 1999-2000, of which medicinal herbs alone accounted for 57.43 per cent, i.e., Rs. 7.06 crore. Some of these herbs are found only in Himachal Pradesh and many might still have remained undiscovered. The main concern at present is the unscientific harvesting and excessive and ruthless exploitation of these resources by private pharmaceutical companies, whose sole motive is to maximise their profits. These companies have no or very little interest in the regeneration and management of the forest. This has resulted in several species of medicinal and aromatic plants either becoming extinct or being listed as endangered species. *Pinus Gerardiana*, which yields chilgoza nuts, is facing extinction and has already been listed as endangered species.

In fact, medicinal and aromatic plants, wild fruits and spices have not been suitably utilised. To preserve the therophytic value of these plants, such packaging practices are to be adopted, as would help retain their potency, fragrance, smell, aroma and efficacy for making by-products.

Medicinal and aromatic plants have the potential of earning foreign currency and these need to be exploited scientifically using modern management methods. A total of 21,982 quintals were exported outside the state in 1998-99. The main products were *muskbala/nihani*, *patlain*, *rakhal*, *dorighas* and *neoza*.

Recently, the state has introduced Lavender which yields high value aromatic oil at Salooni in Chamba district along with setting up of an oil extraction unit. A Lavender bush remains productive for 15 years and starts yielding flowers for oil extraction in the second year of its cultivation. The processing of Lavender oil and its consequent use in production of agarbati, dhoop, cosmetic creams, etc. could earn additional income, as current Indian demand for Lavender oil is 40 tonnes annually. Seabuck thorn is another wild plant, which is of immense medicinal and environmental value that can be grown in abundance in Lahaul & Spiti, Pangi and Kinnaur. China has successfully utilised its Seabuck thorn treasure.

Other medicinal plants of value which can be propagated in the state are *Chirata* and *Katki* (used for liver disorders), *Jatamani* (used for nervous ailments), and *Indian Barbery* (used for digestive disorders), for which the climate and topography is suitable. However, the state has to work hard to conserve their germ plasm, develop economic package for cultivation and their processing and marketing. As such, some of the medicinal plants, which are not regularly cultivated are being collected from the wild and are becoming scarce in availability besides being threatened with extinction.

TABLE 4.16

Minor Forest Produce from 1995-96 to 1999-2000

(Quantity in Tonnes and Value in '000 Rs.)

Name of Forest Produce	1995-96		1998-99		1999-2000	
	Quantity	*Value*	*Quantity*	*Value*	*Quantity*	*Value*
1. Resin	8733	62644	7201	53739	8725	49024
2. Bamboo	—	—	—	—	—	—
3. Bhabbar grass	536	1988	511	343	671	337
4. Fodder/Grazing	—	908	—	1590	—	709
5. Medicinal Herbs:						
a. Dhoop	202.5		69.2		78.0	
b. Muskbala/Nihani	148.7		162.4		93.9	
c. Chukri/ Rewardchini	83.2		49.1		40.9	
d. T/Patters	59.2		15.3		27.4	
e. Dorighas	56.1		100.8		142.3	
f. Brahmi	50.0		—		6.3	
g. Kaur/Karu	43.0		12.0		4.6	
h. Guchhie	36.3		16.0		10.6	
i. Tej Patra	30.8		53.4		45.9	
j. Thuth	25.9		10.9		13.6	
k. Bankakri	22.4	59621	1.1	89823	0.9	70579
l. Kuth/Diascorea	26.4		0.1		14.2	
m. Efdra	12.7		60.2		—	
n. Barberries roots	11.1		7.0		—	
o. Birch/Bhoj Patra	6.5		5.3		15.6	
p. Banafsha	3.9		0.9		0.5	
q. Kakarsingi	2.6		0.4		2.4	
r. Chora	1.2		12.3		43.0	
s. Baryan	8.0		11.0		3.0	
t. Mithi Patties	5.2		14.3		16.9	
u. Bhutkesi	3.2		8.0		5.9	
v. Others	646.9		1588.3		835.6	
6. Other Produce	—	94	—	113	—	2245
TOTAL	—	**125255**	—	**145608**		**122894**

Source: *Forest Statistics, 2000*, Forest Department, H.P.

Natural Hazards

Forest Fires

Forest fires are the main cause of degradation. Very often these fires are natural, accidental and sometimes intentional. In all cases they destroy valuable timber, grazing ground, bio-diversity and wild life. Forest fires are of three kinds, of which crown fires are the most dangerous, followed by ground and surface fires. The most harmful effect of forest fires is on the ecology of the area concerned. Characteristics of the soil are greatly altered and there is erosion. The microclimate and the flora and fauna are also adversely affected. During 1994-95, 1706 forest fires were recorded, involving about six hectares per fire. In 1997-98, there were 67 reported fires, and each fire damaged more than 32 hectares. Forest officials can reduce the loss per fire with the help of good management practices. Intentional fires are a source of fraudulent gains by the local mafia or communities. Alertness of forest rangers and good intelligence can minimise the number of these fires. At the same time, the genuine needs of the communities and tribes living in or around the forests should be taken note of and alternatives suggested to them for better conservation of forests. Prevention of forest fires should obviously be an important task of the Forest Department, which should act as an enforcement agency to control the sources of fires and to educate the communities living in and around the forests. The Forest Department staff should also be provided with necessary equipment and orientation in forest-fire prevention.

There are other hazards, which include landslides and flashfloods mostly during the monsoon season, avalanches, unauthorised mining and encroachments, etc.

Revenue and Expenditure

The economic value of the forest stock of the state has been estimated at over Rs. 1,00,000 crore, taking into account both direct and indirect benefits. The value of growing stock is about 38 per cent of the total economic value of the forests. In contrast, the revenue realised by the Forest Department is very meagre (Rs. 29 crore in 2001-02). On the other hand, the expenditure on forestry in the same year was Rs. 219 crore. In fact, the expenditure on forests has been increasing since 1971, the year Himachal Pradesh acquired statehood.

The contribution of the Forest Department to the total revenue of the state has also been declining since 1993-94. This was about 37 per cent in 1999-2000, when money was raised through capital bonds.

TABLE 4.17

State Revenue from Expenditure on Forests

(Rs. in lakh)

Year	*Revenue*	*Expenditure*	*Difference (3-2)*
(1)	(2)	(3)	(4)
1990-91	1451.30	5569.06	4117.76
1991-92	2430.16	6724.88	4294.72
1992-93	2343.47	7599.77	5256.30
1993-94	6535.61	7567.31	1031.70
1994-95	4711.37	8524.17	3812.80
1995-96	4493.87	9606.94	5113.07
1996-97	4119.33	10928.11	6808.78
1997-98	4114.61	11588.05	7473.44
1998-99	998.01	18299.43	17301.42
1999-00	66936.66	20632.27	(-) 46304.39

Source: Himachal Pradesh Forest Statistics, 2000, Forest Department, Himachal Pradesh.

TABLE 4.18

Per cent Contribution of Forest Revenue to the State Revenue Excluding Grants-in-aid from Central Government

Year	*State Revenue*	*Per cent Contribution of Forest Revenue*
1990-91	24263.77	5.98
1991-92	29946.31	8.11
1992-93	32458.12	7.22
1993-94	42231.66	15.80
1994-95	48349.51	9.74
1995-96	53775.17	8.36
1996-97	62647.60	6.57
1997-98	79336.93	5.19
1998-99	87814.33	1.14
1999-00	179447.65	37.30

Source: Himachal Pradesh Forest Statistics, 2000, Forest Department, Himachal Pradesh.

In the light of the increasing pressure on forests through multiple stakeholders, and the national policy of conserving the forests for maintaining ecological balance and development, allocation to this sector should have been increasing in successive five-year plans. On the contrary, it has been declining continuously. In the Seventh Plan, allocation for this sector was 7.44 per cent which came down to 6.47 per cent in the Eighth Plan. It further declined to 5.12 per cent in the Ninth Plan. This has affected the pace of afforestation in the state.

According to the work plan of the Forest Department, the state government can earn about Rs. 250 crore annually by felling trees under silviculture. The state has put a ban on green felling in view of conserving and increasing its forest cover in accordance with the national policy. The Finance Commission should duly compensate the state in this regard.

The impact of forests, besides providing economic gains to the owners (state and other individuals) has several indirect benefits through the users of forest-related activities at far-off places. For instance, a 10 to 20 per cent reduction in the forest cover of the Himalayas will cause climatic aberrations in the neighbouring states of Punjab, Haryana, Rajasthan and parts of Uttar Pradesh. Agriculture being the mainstay of these four states, any change in the soil and water resource would affect their economic base. It is therefore imperative that the states that control the Himalayan forests should conserve them for the sake of the neighbouring states, which in turn should contribute economically to sustainable forest management in the hill states. This visible interdependence and interconnectivity between the user and producer states will go a long way in developing a sustainable environmental relationship and mutual economic benefits. A long-term view will have to be taken by state and central finance commissions to develop this concept of interdependence and interconnectivity.

Joint Forest Management

Joint forest management which aims at involving local communities and voluntary agencies in regeneration of degraded forests was initiated by Government of India in 1990. In Himachal Pradesh also, this concept has been adopted by formulating village level forest development committees. With the introduction of the new legislation empowering Panchayati Raj Institutions for forest management, the task of village level committees has been now entrusted to PRIs.

One of the essential components of forest management and conservation is active participation of the stakeholders living in or around the forests. The communities generally oppose imposition of rules and regulations for the development of the forests. But, when development programmes for the forests are planned with their participation, it will result in their involvement and co-operation in the management of the forests. Such participatory/joint involvement has yielded excellent results in the Kandi areas of the state and needs to be extended to all forest management activities of the state.

A study conducted by the Centre for Research in Rural and Industrial Development (CRRID), Chandigarh, in 30 villages of Kangra district analysed the pattern of forest fuel-wood consumption in the households. Based on this study, the project encouraged the housewives to undertake such economic activities as weaving of carpets, foot-mats and other related activities, which generated enough income to enable them to use such alternative fuel as kerosene. Secondly, as these women were kept busy during the day in economic activity, they had no time to collect fuel-wood from the forests. Consequently, illegal forests felling had stopped due to economic empowerment of the housewives.

The Forest Department has adopted the approach of 'participatory forest management' and is building further on the experience gained in this respect from the implementation of externally-aided projects. It has launched a participatory forest management scheme named 'Sanjhi Van Yojana' aimed at empowering local institutions to plan, execute and further maintain forestry operations on their own, with the department only playing the role of a facilitator. The scheme is designed to be a tool of social engineering to empower communities to plan and execute various activities for the conservation and development of these resources through Village Forest Development Societies (VFDSs) consisting of local residents. Under the scheme, funds are placed with a society and utilised according to the approved micro-plan prepared by the society itself. The scheme was launched on 25 December 1998, and is a big step forward in empowering the local communities and ensuring sustainable management of forest resources in the vicinity of the villages.

Women being the primary gatherers of forest produce, their participation is crucial to the success of any forestry programme. The government has taken a policy decision to recruit women forest guards so that the outreach of the Forest Department to this important stakeholders' group is increased. This will not only rectify the gender imbalance in the Forest Department but also facilitate their active interaction with the forest staff.

However, this scheme needs to be reviewed to gauge its success for its replication to other areas of the state.

Wildlife

Wildlife is a heritage of the state. Some species are found only in the western Himalayas. There are 32 wildlife sanctuaries and two national parks in the state, covering an area of about 7002 sq. km., which is about

12.5 per cent of the geographical area. A large variety of wildlife is found in the state, including 64 species of mammals, 463 species of birds, 44 species of reptiles and 516 species of aquatic fauna. A category-wise detail of the protected and threatened species is given below:

Protected Wildlife

Mammals: Himalayan black bear, brown bear, musk deer, ghoral, ibex, thar, snow leopard, lynx, spotted deer, flying fox, leopard, barking deer, Indian wild boar, sambhar, serrow, Kashmir stag, etc.

Birds: Cheer pheasant, monal, snow cock, tragopan, koklas, khaleej, chukor, red jungle fowl, hornbill, siberian white crane, whistling teal, mountain quail, white spoonbill, partridges, martins, pea-fowl, mallards, pochards.

Reptiles: Common indian monitor lizard, yellow monitor lizard, indian python, etc.

Threatened Wildlife

Himalayan brown bear, cheer pheasant, mountain quail, western tragopan, monal pheasant, snow-cock, snow leopard, leopard cat etc.

As a result of various measures taken by the Forest Department for wildlife protection and conservation, the population of leopards has increased.

To attract wildlife enthusiasts, the sanctuaries and parks in the state need improved internal management on scientific lines.

Mixed sanctuaries and animal/bird-specific sanctuaries for endangered species should be encouraged for wildlife protection, conservation and their multiplication.

The state government has already taken a policy decision to develop the parks, sanctuaries, zoos and other water bodies by facilitating both private and public sector investments. This is a bold step taken by the government for the first time in the country, which will reduce the pressure on the wild life. Further, in order to reduce the social tensions because of the wild life, the state intends to re-demarcate the boundaries of various parks, sanctuaries etc.

Suggestions and Recommendations

Till recently, commercial objectives had determined the management of forests, as commercial exploitation of timber had been the main concern. In contrast, conservation and regeneration dominate modern management of forests. Involvement of the communities and others living in and around the forests has become important from the point of view of modern forest management.

A holistic approach is required to reduce the dependence of communities on forests, by providing them with direct and indirect opportunities; directly, by encouraging the use of locally available and renewable energy sources to fuel-wood and timber, e.g., solar, wind and hydel energy sources. Currently biomass is extensively used because of its ready availability and cheapness. Communities, however, may be encouraged to help produce more biomass per unit area so that their production exceeds requirement. Indirectly, by increasing their economic status though skill-oriented vocational training, so as to give them an opportunity to join either the mainstream economy or forest-related activities, such as afforestation, nurseries, fodder cultivation, etc.

Monoculture should give way to multiple species culture so as to encourage biodiversity at different levels of forest regeneration. For instance, monoculture of chil or eucalyptus is less economical and destructive to regeneration of ground vegetation, whereas, mixed plantations of willow, poplar, oak, fir, bamboo, wild fruit species and others are both economically viable and allow ground vegetation. In other words, a policy framework has to be developed to encourage mixed plantations of adaptable species, which are economically useful.

Traditionally, the *Gujjar* communities migrate along with their cattle to the high alpine pastures during summer and return to the lower hills during winter. Their perennial movement leads to degradation and destruction of pasturelands and forests, which have a great impact on soil erosion. Efforts were made by the government to rehabilitate them in permanent settlements, by providing them with free houses, opening schools and dispensaries for them and stall-feeding arrangement for their cattle. Unfortunately, the mindset of the *Gujjars* could not be transformed. There is need for an attitudinal change, through training, exposure and vocational skill-upgradation. Residential, health and educational services for their women and children, coupled with a collection mechanism for their produce, such as milk, milk products, meat and handicrafts, should be developed, so that they are motivated to settle down permanently. Inter-sectoral approaches, with forward and backward linkages with forests, should be adopted for making the economy vibrant, so as to provide rich economic dividends to the local communities.

In Himachal Pradesh's biodiversity, medicinal and aromatic plants are of special value, since these are localised and very few of them are available elsewhere. Conservation of such plants through a detailed inventory would be the first step towards determining the plant wealth of the state. Medicinal and aromatic plants in common use need to be listed and their multiplication techniques perfected, so that their exploitation does not lead to their extinction. Naturally-growing morels and slow-growing plant species should be protected with care so that they can regenerate naturally.

The role of the Forest Department should be more in preserving and conserving the rich biodiversity of such a resource, and private and community lands should be allowed to grow this on scientific lines for multiplication and mass propagation for commercial exploitation.

Primary processing units at the local level are a must, not only from the point of view of employment, but also for preserving their inherent values.

However, a strong modern research-based organisational support is necessary to extend the forests, preserve the dwindling plant and animal species and develop quick regeneration and multiplication technologies for medicinal and aromatic plants etc., with support from extension agencies, laced with modern information and communication technologies for making all concerned aware of the wealth that the forests represent.

In the changing conditions of global trade, timber assumes special importance, as efficient forest management alone can assure leadership in timber export to other countries. India already faces such a challenge, as timber imported from Malaysia and Thailand is of better quality and is priced lower than the indigenous product. This has serious implications for the forest policy of Indian states.

The Central Finance Commission should take cognizance of the concept of interdependence and interconnectivity of the forest-producer states and the user states in developing a sustainable environmental relationship and mutual economic benefits.

All the schemes and projects should have inter-sectoral linkages for better results.

The *Panchayats* need to be strengthened so that they can monitor forest development, check illegal encroachment and destruction, and remove bottlenecks and defects of a centralised administrative system.

Forest development activities are dependent upon management planning and efficient administration with the support of well trained executives and field workers. The research component is essential in developing suitable technologies in forest development and forest produce utilisation. Participatory involvement of juniors and field staff along with local communities is a must for increasing managing the forest cover on a sustainable basis.

References

Bhardwaj, S.D., S. Narkhede (1997), *Guide for Management of Forest Fires*, Dr. Y.S. Parmar University of Horticulture and Forestry, Solan.

Centre for Research in Rural and Industrial Development, (1992-93), Three Reports, *Integrated Resource Management Plan-district Kangra, Himachal Pradesh*, Chandigarh.

Chaudhari, B., A.K. Maiti (eds.) (1986), *Forest and Forest Development in India*, Inter-India Publications, New Delhi.

Chauhan, N.S., Atul Gupta (eds.), *Important Medicinal Plants of Lahaul & Spiti*, Krishi Vigyan Kendra, Kinnaur, Dr. Y.S. Parmar University of Horticulture and Forestry, Solan.

Department of Science and Technology, Government of Himachal Pradesh, *State of Environment Report – Himachal Pradesh*, Shimla.

Forest Department, Government of Himachal Pradesh, Various Issues, *Annual Administration Report*, Shimla.

Forest Department, Government of Himachal Pradesh, Various Issues, *Himachal Forests*, Shimla.

Forest Department, Government of Himachal Pradesh, Various Issues, *H.P. Forest Statistics*, Shimla.

Government of Himachal Pradesh, *H.P. Forest Department Website*.

Government of Himachal Pradesh, (2002), *Himachal Pradesh Human Development Report*, Shimla.

H.P. Institute of Public Administration, *Revival of Cooperative Forest Societies in District Kangra and Cho, Reclamation and Soil Conservation Societies of Una District, Himachal Pradesh*, Shimla.

Jayanarayanan, T., "Forest Degradation in Kerala: Causes and Consequences: A Case Study of Peechi-Vazhani Area", Discussion Paper No. 27, *Kerala Research Programme on Local Level Development*, Centre for Development Studies, Thiruvananthapuram.

Planning Commission, Government of India, (March 2000), *Report of the Task Force on Conservation and Sustainable Use of Medicinal Plants*.

Planning Department, Government of Himachal Pradesh, (1997-2002), *Ninth Five Year Plan and Annual Plan*, Shimla.

Planning Commission, Government of India, (April 2003), *National Mission on Bamboo Technology and Trade Development*.

Sagwal, S.S., "Silviculture in the Service of Mankind", *Kurukshetra*, May 2003.

Soundarapandian, M., "Role of Forests in Tribal Development—A Case Study of Paliyan Tribe in Tamil Nadu", *Kurukshetra*, June 2003.

Vasan, Sudha, "Exploring the Policy-Implementation Interface: Timber Rights in Himachal Pradesh, India", *Occasional Papers in Sociology*, No. 11, March 2003, Institute of Economic Growth, New Delhi.

Chapter 5

Population

Introduction

Among all resources available in any society, 'people' or human resources are valued as the most fundamental. Human resource is critical because utilisation of other resources, such as land, capital and organisation depends, *inter alia,* to a large extent on the nature of human beings. The current paradigm of development focusing on 'quality of life' puts people at the core of planning for reasons of equity, efficiency and dignity. Human development, defined as an expansion of human capabilities, widening of choices, enhancement of freedom and fulfillment of human rights, has come to be accepted as the new model of development, instead of a mere rise in incomes and growth in outputs (Fukuda-Parr and Kumar 2003). Hence, the essence of human resource development involves broadening the horizons of quality, so as to transform 'population' to 'people'. A nation is its people, and in the ultimate analysis, all development must benefit people, individually as well as collectively.

Human resource development is intimately tied to population dynamics, more so in South Asia, where high fertility, rapid population growth and high dependency ratios make economic growth and human resource development relatively more difficult (Jones 1992). Population growth and distribution patterns are also essential to understand the human resource assets, their values and potential use. In addition, demographic changes have direct as well as indirect implications for human resource development, which are complex and synergic (Jones 1992). To elaborate, higher infant mortality means more requirements of health care services; larger working age population cause pressures to create gainful employment; and increasing life expectancy may induce more social security measures. Implications, goals and strategies of human development in any state are direct functions of its population dynamics. Public expenditure on provision of health, education, employment, energy, environment, transport, technology, communication and social security services are largely determined by the quality and quantity of human population. Besides, in the era of liberalisation, demographic dynamics of the population of a nation also affects the process of globalisation. Favourable changes in the population structure boost economic growth and influence the movement of people, products, and investment capital among countries (La Croix *et al.* 2003).

The development of national human resources in India is contingent upon the population stabilisation goals at a sustainable level (National Commission on Population 2001, Planning Commission). In India, three broad themes of the Tenth Five Year Plan, namely, a) growth, poverty and employment, b) social development, and c) sustainability of growth and development revolve around the human resource component. The final assessment of the development process, or for that matter any plan, lies in the way it alleviates deprivation and enhances the well-being of human beings. Appraisal of existing human resources in Himachal Pradesh in a demographic perspective not only helps in understanding the assets and liabilities in launching plan efforts but also in setting targets for achievements and deciding priorities in policy formulation and programme implementation. Examination of demographic dimensions is essential because development cannot be assessed in terms of generation of economic growth alone. In order to be more meaningful, it has to address the key objective of reduced population growth, social integration, removal of disparities, economic empowerment and also protection of environment. Profiling of population in the state helps to identify areas that need policy and programme interventions, to set near- and far-term goals, and to decide priorities, besides understanding them in an integrated structure.

This chapter deals with the overall demographic situation in Himachal Pradesh, the scope being confined to salient features in demographic development in a framework of inter-state comparison, elements of population change and focus on future population perspectives. Based on data from several sources, within and outside government, it covers a range of issues, such as population structure, fertility, mortality, family planning, ageing, sex preference, sex-ratio imbalances and others. It summarises the population dynamics in the state since its creation till the beginning of the twenty-first century and highlights the demographic dimensions of development through an independent review.

Population Change

States in India are experiencing demographic transition, the routes of transition being determined largely by local living conditions. Changes in the natural increase of population, brought about primarily by declining fertility and mortality, suggest that Himachal Pradesh is no exception to this demographic transition. Such transition, along with forces of migration, is affecting population size, age structure, sex composition and distribution patterns that are important indicators of human resources in the state. According to the 2001 Census, the state accounted for a meagre share of the total population of India (0.59%), the same as its share in 1991. The total population in the state grew from 1.9 million in 1901 to 6.1 million in 2001, making a net addition of 4.2 million in the twentieth century. In three decades, since Himachal Pradesh attained full statehood, a little more than a quarter million (2.6) was added to its population. The average annual population growth rate crossed the two per cent mark and peaked at 2.37 per cent during 1971-1981. The last decade of the twentieth century recorded definite signs of deceleration in the momentum of population growth in Himachal Pradesh, with the mean annual growth rate (1.75%) falling not only below the 'standard' two per cent mark but also to pre-1951 level. Much of this population expansion in the state has been indigenous, as the contribution of in-migration from other states in India and from countries outside India was insignificant. To quantify, the share of such international and interstate migrants in total population of the state in 1991 varied between 2.7-5.2 per cent depending on the definition of migration adopted in the census, and it is unlikely that this component will alter substantially in the 2001 census. In the inter-censal period 1991-2001, the households in Himachal Pradesh enlarged from 0.969 million to 1.241 million growing by 28 per cent and the average size of households reduced to 4.9 persons from 5.4 persons, recording the impact of declining population growth rate.

Population size is one of the key determinants of the labour force and its participation rates. With young-age population declining due to fertility reduction and the old-age population not rising commensurately to offset this fall, it is often said that the countries enjoy 'Demographic Bonus' during the course of demographic transition. In a free market, greater size of workforce released from transitional population can make production cost-effective and the economy more competitive, provided appropriate and timely education, health and skill investments are undertaken to effect better capability.

The age structure of the population, on the one hand expresses demographic dimensions of development, and on the other delineates the challenges for development. On the basis of selected age and sex structures, Table 5.1 outlines some planning imperatives

TABLE 5.1

Human Resources, Himachal Pradesh (1971-2001)

Year	*Total Population*		*Reproductive Age Women (15-44 years)*		*Working Age Population (15-59 years)*		*Aged Population (60 plus)*		*Population (7-14 years)*		*Child Population (0-6 years)*	
	Male (in '000)	*Female (in '000)*	*(in '000)*	*% Share in Total Female Pop.*	*(in '000)*	*% Share in Total Pop.*	*(in '000)*	*% Share in Total Pop.*	*(in '000)*	*% Share in Total Pop.*	*(in '000)*	*% Share in Total Pop.*
1971	1767	1693	725	42.8	1786	51.6	248	7.2	725	21.0	701	20.3
1981	2170	2111	920	43.6	2264	52.9	321	7.5	892	20.8	802	18.7
1991	2617	2553	1176	46.0	2898	56.0	421	8.1	998	19.3	840	16.2
2001	3085	2992	1418	47.4*	3519	57.9*	607	10.0	1118	18.4	769	12.7

Source: 1. *Socio-cultural Tables, Census of India 1971, 1981, 1991*, Himachal Pradesh.
2. *Population Totals, Paper 1 of 2001, Census of India 2001*, Himachal Pradesh.

Note: * Indicates that the figures are estimated.

in human development that emanate from demographic effects in Himachal Pradesh. The growth of female population in the reproductive age group (15-44 years) in both absolute and relative senses reinforces the need for levels of investment in health, nutrition and related areas. In the same way, the growth in the workforce from 1.79 million (52% of total population) in 1971 to 3.52 million (58% of total population) in 2001, raises questions on provisions for productive employment and opportunities for gainful participation in economic activity. The result of fertility decline is manifested in the shrinking child population in the age group 0-6 years. The drastic decline in the number of such young age groups (by 8.5%) from 0.84 to 0.77 million in the last decade is attributed to fall in fertility and may initiate the need for rethinking on resource allocation for education and other factors for the needs of the younger generation. Additionally, the implications of life cycle and changing age structure for consumption, saving, investment, etc., as indicated above, need to be factored into planning perspectives in Himachal Pradesh.

Fertility Transition

Limiting population growth in India is at the top of the national agenda and the goals set in the *National Population Policy 2000* (NPP 2000) mirrors this to a large extent. As a result of socio-economic development and family planning intervention, India recorded significant fall in fertility, fairly widespread across the states, in the post-independence period. Yet, regional variations have continued in the onset and speed of fertility transition in the country. In the north, Himachal Pradesh has undergone substantial transformations in its fertility profile during the last three decades of the twentieth century.

Levels and Trends

Fertility has been consistently falling in Himachal Pradesh, as indicated by trends in total fertility rates (TFRs) since the beginning of the 1970s for major Indian States (Table 5.2, Figure 5.1). Though the southern states are ahead in fertility transition and have total fertility rates lower than the northern counterparts, Himachal is a classic case that blurs this north-south divide. The decline in fertility seems to have accentuated in the 1980s as compared to the 1970s, and remained consistent till the end of the 1990s.

The decline in fertility is reasonably widespread in the state and is not confined to any specific region or community. Individual districts along with rural and urban areas are experiencing transition in fertility in different ways, depending on changes in local

TABLE 5.2

Fertility Decline in Major States, India (1970-72 to 1997-1999)

State	*Total Fertility Rate (TFR)*				*Per cent Decline in TFR*				
	1970-72	*1980-82*	*1990-92*	*1997-99*	*1971-81*	*1981-91*	*1971-91*	*1991-98*	*1971-98*
A.P.	4.7	3.9	3.0	2.4	17.0	23.1	36.2	20.0	48.9
Assam	5.5	4.1	3.4	3.2	25.5	17.1	38.2	5.9	41.8
Bihar	—	5.7	4.6	4.4	—	19.3	—	4.3	—
Gujarat	5.7	4.4	3.2	3.0	22.8	27.3	43.9	6.3	47.4
Haryana	6.4	5.0	3.9	3.3	21.9	22.0	39.1	15.8	48.4
H.P.	**4.7**	**4.0**	**3.1**	**2.4**	**14.9**	**22.5**	**34.0**	**22.6**	**48.9**
J & K	4.8	4.4	3.3	—	8.3	25.0	31.3	—	—
Karnataka	4.4	3.6	3.1	2.5	18.2	13.9	29.5	19.4	43.2
Kerala	4.1	2.9	1.8	1.8	29.3	37.9	56.1	0.0	56.1
M.P.	5.7	5.2	4.6	3.9	8.8	11.5	19.3	15.2	31.6
Maharashtra	4.5	3.7	3.0	2.6	17.8	18.9	33.3	13.3	42.2
Orissa	4.8	4.2	3.3	2.9	12.5	21.4	31.2	12.1	39.6
Punjab	5.3	4.0	3.1	2.6	24.5	22.5	41.5	16.1	50.9
Rajasthan	6.3	5.4	4.5	4.2	14.3	16.7	28.6	6.7	33.3
Tamil Nadu	3.9	3.4	2.2	2.0	12.8	35.3	41.0	9.1	48.7
Uttar Pradesh	6.7	5.8	5.2	4.7	13.4	10.3	22.4	9.6	29.9
West Bengal	—	4.2	3.2	2.5	—	23.8	—	21.9	—
INDIA	**5.2**	**4.5**	**3.7**	**3.2**	**13.5**	**17.8**	**28.8**	**13.5**	**38.5**

Source: Statistical Report (different volumes), *Sample Registration System (SRS)*, Registrar General, India.

Note: — Indicates data not available.

conditions, which often act as important inducements for the determination of family size. Substantial fertility reduction in Himachal Pradesh, despite some of the key social indicators, such as emerging son preference, sizeable presence of socially backward population and relatively higher infant mortality being against the decline, is a manifestation of the primacy of intervention by selected development factors, namely, the family planning programme, female literacy, health care delivery and financial prosperity at the household level. Studies to assess the role of economic aspirations, family systems and social status indicators in the fertility transformations, are virtually non-existent.

TABLE 5.3

Crude Birth Rate (CBR) and Total Fertility Rate (TFR), India and Himachal Pradesh (1971-73 to 1999-2001)

Period	*India*		*Himachal Pradesh*					
	CBR Total	*TFR Total*	*CBR*			*TFR*		
			Total	*Rural*	*Urban*	*Total*	*Rural*	*Urban*
1971-1973	36.3	5.1	36.0	36.8	23.5	4.9	5.0	2.9
1972-1974	35.3	5.0	35.2	36.0	23.3	4.7	4.8	2.8
1973-1975	34.8	4.9	35.0	35.9	22.2	4.7	4.8	2.6
1974-1976	34.4	4.8	33.3	34.1	21.9	4.4	4.5	2.6
1975-1977	34.2	4.7	32.5	33.3	20.8	4.3	4.4	2.5
1976-1978	33.3	4.6	30.7	31.4	21.8	4.0	4.1	2.5
1977-1979	33.1	4.5	30.5	31.2	21.2	3.8	3.9	2.4
1978-1980	33.3	4.4	30.2	30.6	21.2	3.7	3.8	2.4
1979-1981	33.8	4.4	31.6	32.2	19.2	3.8	3.9	2.2
1980-1982	33.8	4.5	32.0	32.8	20.0	4.0	4.1	2.3
1981-1983	33.8	4.5	32.3	33.1	20.8	4.0	4.1	2.4
1982-1984	33.8	4.5	32.1	32.7	22.9	4.0	4.1	2.6
1983-1985	33.6	4.4	31.3	31.9	23.2	3.9	4.0	2.6
1984-1986	33.2	4.3	30.5	31.1	22.4	3.7	3.8	2.5
1985-1987	32.6	4.2	30.5	31.1	22.2	3.6	3.7	2.4
1986-1988	32.1	4.1	31.2	31.9	21.8	3.6	3.7	2.4
1987-1989	31.5	4.0	30.2	30.8	22.0	3.5	3.6	2.4
1988-1990	30.8	3.9	29.1	29.7	21.0	3.3	3.4	2.3
1989-1991	30.1	3.8	27.9	28.5	19.6	3.1	3.2	2.1
1990-1992	29.6	3.7	28.0	28.6	19.5	3.1	3.2	2.1
1991-1993	29.1	3.6	27.8	28.5	19.6	3.0	3.1	2.1
1992-1994	30.4	3.5	27.0	27.6	19.6	2.9	3.0	2.1
1993-1995	29.9	3.5	26.0	26.6	18.8	2.8	2.9	2.0
1994-1996	27.4	3.3	24.8	25.4	17.7	2.7	2.8	1.9
1995-1997	27.7	3.4	23.6	24.1	17.3	2.5	2.6	1.8
1996-1998	27.1	3.3	22.7	23.2	17.0	2.4	2.4	1.8
1997-1999	26.6	3.2	23.0	23.5	16.9	2.4	2.4	1.8
1998-2000	26.1	—	22.8	23.3	16.9	—	—	—
1999-2001	25.7	—	22.3	22.7	16.8	—	—	—

Source: Statistical Report (different volumes), *Sample Registration System* (SRS), Registrar General, India.

Note: 1. Rates for India exclude Mizoram till 1995, and Jammu and Kashmir from 1991 onwards.

2. — Indicates data not available.

FIGURE 5.1

Total Fertility Rate, India and Himachal Pradesh (1971-73 to 1997-99)

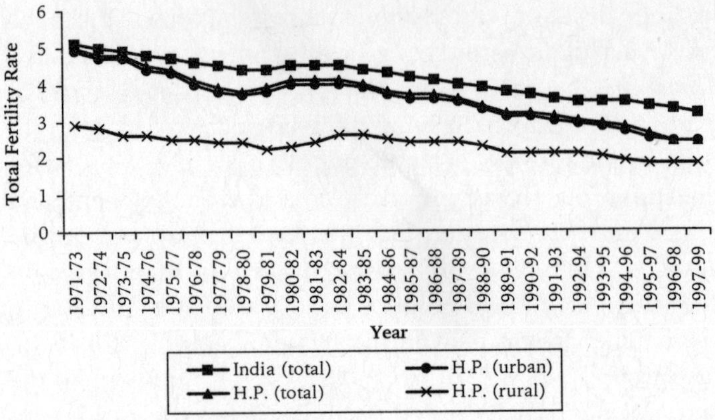

Source: Statistical Report (different volumes), *Sample Registration System*, Registrar General, India.

Replacement Level of Fertility

With fertility falling significantly in Himachal Pradesh during the last three decades of the twentieth century, it is appropriate to look at the far-term prospects of reaching the replacement level. Since achievement of replacement-level fertility is crucial for the long-term objective of 'Stable Population' by 2045 in India, and the medium-term objective of reducing the total fertility rate (TFR) to replacement level by 2010, as laid down in the *National Population Policy 2000* (NPP 2000), it is pertinent to examine the position of Himachal Pradesh in relation to the national target. Recent indications do signal the possibility of the state reaching the replacement level by the year 2010. Himachal Pradesh is yet to attain the replacement level of fertility. National Family Health Survey (NFHS) estimates the state's fertility to be two per cent above the replacement level as against the SRS (1999) estimate of 13 per cent and MICS (2000) estimate of 25 per cent. According to NFHS, urban areas have fertility 20 per cent below the replacement (TFR being 1.74), whereas in the rural areas fertility (TFR being 2.18) remains four per cent higher than the replacement level. With nearly nine-tenths of the population still living in villages that are very much scattered and remote, the prospects of stabilising the population in Himachal Pradesh in near future depends on the success of the efforts in rural areas. This foreseeable task is worth undertaking given volume of unwanted fertility in the state, estimated to be 30 per cent of total fertility (NFHS 2002).

Age Pattern of Fertility

The age pattern of childbearing in Himachal Pradesh has undergone a change during the closing decades of the twentieth century, with fertility limitation being increasingly common at relatively old ages. Though fall in fertility has been observed among women in all ages between 1981 and 1999, the contribution to the fertility decline has been mostly from women in very early (age 15-19) as well as late reproductive years (age 30-34), according to the SRS (Table 5.4, Figure 5.2). Two successive rounds of NFHS, recording a rapid fall in fertility in Himachal Pradesh during the 1990s, higher than the national decline, also document lesser contribution by younger women (age 15-29) than by older women (age 30-44) to overall decline in fertility. Both the SRS and NFHS report almost no childbearing among women in the age group 44-49 years. Relatively less enthusiasm by women in the age group (20-29 years) in limiting fertility can be attributed to social and cultural reasons that stress the need for child-bearing immediately after marriage to establish fertility potential. Child-bearing, coming shortly after marriage, is mainly concentrated in 20-24 and 25-29 age groups, which account for 47 and 30 per cent of the births respectively, in the entire reproductive period of women (NFHS 2002). Such concentration of births is more severe among rural than urban women in Himachal Pradesh: 78 per cent in rural areas as against 71 per cent in urban areas. Interestingly, between 1990-92 and 1996-98, the contribution of women aged 20-29 years to overall fertility increased from 73 per cent to 78 per cent (NFHS), and is a pointer to changing reproductive strategies of Himachali couples, who do not want to prolong childbearing and finish it as quickly as possible in response to larger social and economic changes.

TABLE 5.4

Age-Specific Fertility Rates (ASFRs), Himachal Pradesh (1991-1999)

Age group (in completed years)	*1981*	*1991*	*1995*	*1999*	*Per cent decline in ASFR(1981-99)*
15-19	68.6	69.2	28.4	24.8	63.8
20-24	301.8	271.9	245.9	236.6	21.6
25-29	193.3	169.0	180.9	161.2	16.6
30-34	133.0	69.8	59.6	49.9	62.5
35-39	55.2	34.6	20.6	14.0	74.6
40-44	9.4	8.5	6.9	1.4	85.1
45-49	0.0	1.5	1.4	0.0	0.0

Source: Statistical Report (different volumes), *Sample Registration System (SRS)*, Registrar General, India.

Fertility Differentials

Social and economic conditions considerably determine the course of fertility transition, as fertility varies most according to economic and social backgrounds. In Himachal Pradesh, fertility differentials are sharp when groups are compared in terms of selected economic and social background characteristics. As seen from the recent round of NFHS, variations in fertility (measured in terms of differences in total fertility rates, current pregnancy rates, and mean number of children ever born to women in 40-49 age group) according to the standard of living in the household, educational attainment of women, place of residence of the family, religion and caste-status of the household, are striking. For instance, the TFR of women in households with a low standard of living (2.49) is nearly 1.3 times higher than their counterparts with a high standard of living (1.89); for illiterate women (2.85) it is 1.4 times higher than that of women with education of high school and above (2.04). Women in urban areas also report 40 per cent lower TFR (1.74) than women in villages (2.18). Since there exists a great degree of concurrence between caste status and economic well-being, inequality in the economic sphere often gets translated into demographic outcomes. In Himachal Pradesh, women from Scheduled Caste, and other backward caste women, including the Scheduled Tribe women, record higher levels of TFR (2.15 and 2.37 respectively) as against the women from other castes (2.05). The pregnancy rate is substantially higher among Scheduled Caste women (5.1) than among women from other backward caste (4.2) and non-backward populations (4.0). Variations in fertility due to religious beliefs are of less consequence in Himachal Pradesh, as Hindus alone account for approximately 96 per cent of the total population, according to the 1991 Census. According to the NFHS, demographic reflections of social inequalities are clear

FIGURE 5.2

Age-specific Fertility Rate, Himachal Pradesh (1981-1999)

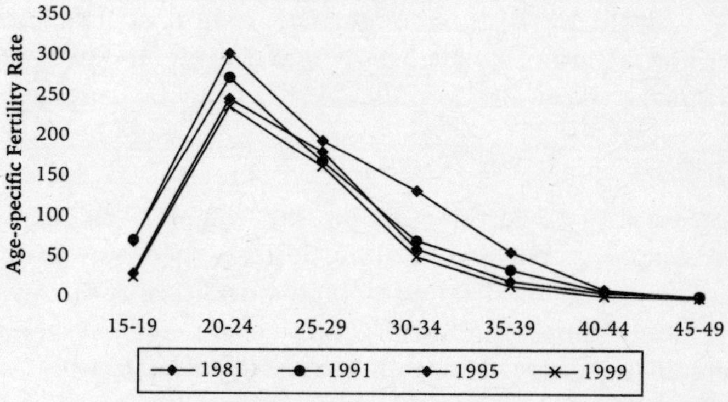

Source: Statistical Reports (different volumes), *Sample Registration System (SRS)*, Registrar General, India.

and still persist. Also, over time, there has been little change in relative positions of communities by social or economic class in terms of the respective contribution to overall fertility, though the major social and economic groups have shown a decline in current pregnancy rates and fertility.

Prospects for Further Decline

Pathways to fertility decline are complex, changing and non-universal. As fertility declines in a variety of situations, generalisations about social, cultural and economic causes of fertility decline are not easy and seldom necessary. However, routes to lower fertility in different settings have been historically documented and have extensively improved the understanding of reproduction patterns. In the absence of systematic explorations of receding fertility in Himachal Pradesh with a focus on dimensions of development and mechanisms of influence, existing evidence point to overall effects of sustained economic prosperity, relatively less gender disparity, impact of a strong family planning programme, greater access to health care services, superior infrastructure in terms of housing and basic amenities, improved exposure to education and communication, better literacy among males and females, and more recently termination of pregnancies, etc.

While it is important to acknowledge the fact that fertility has fallen considerably since the early seventies, despite the constraints of a mountainous state, it is more useful to explore the prospects of further decline in the near future. The key to this lies in eradicating the existing strong son preference, in lengthening the interval between two successive births, spreading out childbearing among women aged 20-29, raising the female median age at marriage beyond the current level of 18.6 years, wiping out early marriage, reduction in the current level of infant mortality, augmenting contribution by socially and economically poor sections of the society, progress in eliminating the unmet needs for contraception, change in reproductive strategies among younger couples and finally overall advance in living conditions.

Mortality Change

Reduction in overall mortality is an important objective of planning since the First Five Year Plan. Continued commitment to essential primary health care, provision of emergency and other life services in the public domain during the Tenth Five Year Plan (2002-2007) are pointers towards this (Planning Commission 2001). The *National Population Policy 2000* (NPP 2000) and the *National Health Policy 2002* (NHP 2002) have also simultaneously reinforced the need for mortality decline. Programmes are afoot at the national as well as state levels to improve overall survival conditions, as a result of which mortality decline is visible among segments of population in most of India. A dramatic fall in mortality has been also recorded in Himachal Pradesh during the last three decades of the twentieth century.

Levels and Trends

In Himachal Pradesh, data show that the crude death rate (CDR) declined from around 15 deaths per 1,000 population in the early seventies, to seven deaths per 1,000 population at the beginning of twenty-first century (Table 5.5). This reduced mortality is an integral part of the demographic transition in the state (Figure 5.3), and has extensively contributed to increase in life expectancy at birth and at other ages. Though overall mortality in Himachal Pradesh has been consistently lower than the national average, yet, over time, the advantage that the state initially had, in terms of lower probability of death, has remained substantially unchanged, except for some fluctuations in the late seventies and eighties. For example, in little less than three decades, the advantage of Himachal Pradesh over the national mortality situation remained almost same, from 14.0 per cent in 1972-74 to 15.3 per cent in 1999-2001. Both rural and urban areas gained consistently from the onset of mortality decline, even if rural death rates continue to exceed urban death rates for a variety of reasons in Himachal Pradesh, as elsewhere in India. Comparison of NFHS results between 1991-92 and 1997-98 also supports the declining trend in overall death rates in Himachal Pradesh.

Age-specific and Sex-specific Death Rate

In addition to the rural and urban variations, the mortality situation is also better understood through its sex composition and age pattern. Over the years, notwithstanding the early-age vulnerability to death, gains from mortality decline are distinct among males and females in Himachal Pradesh (Table 5.6), with net gain to males surpassing that to females in the process of mortality transition. In fact, a notable feature of mortality transition in Himachal Pradesh between 1981 and 1999 has been larger gains for the males than for females in general, as evident from the overall gap in CDR between males and females. The narrowing down of sex differentials in mortality in 1999, as against 1971, seems to have been the result of comparatively slower gain to females both in rural and urban areas.

TABLE 5.5

Crude Death Rates (CDR), India and Himachal Pradesh (1971-73 to 1999-2001)

Years	*India Total*	*Himachal Pradesh*			*Total Comparative Mortality Advantage of H.P (in per cent)*
		Total	*Rural*	*Urban*	
1971-1973	15.9	14.6	15.1	6.9	8.2
1972-1974	15.7	13.5	13.9	6.9	14.0
1973-1975	15.3	12.6	13.0	7.3	17.6
1974-1976	15.0	13.0	13.4	7.1	13.3
1975-1977	15.2	12.8	13.2	6.5	15.8
1976-1978	14.5	12.3	12.7	6.3	15.2
1977-1979	13.9	11.3	11.5	5.9	18.7
1978-1980	13.1	10.9	11.2	6.1	16.8
1979-1981	12.7	10.6	11.0	5.6	16.5
1980-1982	12.3	10.3	10.7	5.2	16.3
1981-1983	12.1	10.3	10.6	5.3	14.9
1982-1984	12.1	10.0	10.3	5.7	17.4
1983-1985	12.1	10.4	10.6	6.4	14.0
1984-1986	11.8	9.8	10.0	6.7	16.9
1985-1987	11.3	9.2	9.4	6.3	18.6
1986-1988	11.0	8.9	9.1	5.9	19.1
1987-1989	10.7	8.9	9.2	5.5	16.8
1988-1990	10.3	8.9	9.1	6.0	13.6
1989-1991	9.9	8.7	8.9	6.1	12.1
1990-1992	9.9	8.7	9.0	5.6	12.1
1991-1993	9.7	8.8	9.1	5.2	9.3
1992-1994	9.5	8.7	9.0	5.3	8.4
1993-1995	9.2	8.6	8.9	5.8	6.5
1994-1996	9.1	8.4	8.6	5.9	7.7
1995-1997	9.0	8.3	8.5	6.0	7.8
1996-1998	9.0	7.9	8.1	5.8	12.2
1997-1999	8.9	7.7	7.9	5.5	13.5
1998-2000	8.7	7.4	7.6	5.4	14.9
1999-2001	8.5	7.2	7.3	5.3	15.3

Source: Statistical Report (different volumes), *Sample Registration System* (SRS), Registrar General, India.

FIGURE 5.3

Demographic Transition in Himachal Pradesh (1971-1973 to 1998-2000)

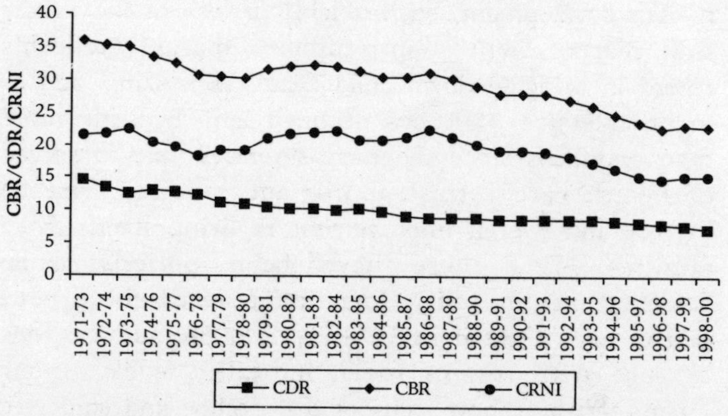

Source: Statistical Reports (different volumes), *Sample Registration System* (SRS), Registrar General, India.

The age-specific mortality curve for Himachal Pradesh was the usual 'U'-shaped in 1981 and 1998, due to relatively higher mortality rates at young and old ages. Though, for nearly two decades, the mortality pattern by age remains broadly the same, significant changes seem to have taken place in the death of different segments of the population. For most of the age groups, a drop in mortality is reported by SRS between 1981 and 1999, irrespective of sex, with some exceptions (Table 5.6). Mortality rate at the early age (0-4 years) of life has strikingly plummeted down for males in urban and rural areas, unlike that for female children in the same age group, for whom mortality conditions have improved more slowly. This change between 1981 and 1999 in the state has significant policy and programme implications. In the reproductive age group (15-44 years) too, where the risks of child-bearing decisively enhance female exposure to death, the gains have been recorded in Himachal Pradesh, particularly in rural areas. The NFHS findings also broadly support the SRS pattern in Himachal Pradesh. Comparison of first (1992) and second round (1999) results indicates a halt to improvement in child mortality, and decline in mortality among women in the reproductive age group in the state.

Notwithstanding annual fluctuations in age-specific death rates as reported by the SRS, it is apparent from Table 5.6 that at some specified ages, the sex of the individual is one of the important indicators of exposure to death. While female mortality-disadvantage is likely during childhood (>5 years), male vulnerability begins to mount from the age of 35 onwards.

Infant, Child and Under-five Mortality

Infant mortality is a significant indicator of human development as it indicates whether development has really trickled down. In view of the fact that children below five years typically have higher probability of death in Indian circumstances, infant and childhood mortality-reduction goals have continued to be a national priority since the First Five Year Plan (Planning Commission, 1952). The Tenth Five Year Plan is also committed to strategies to ensure better survival of children and bridging gender differences in early age mortality (Planning Commission 2003). The *Millennium Development Goals (1990-2015)* also emphasises the urgency of reducing the under-five mortality rate by two-thirds. The *National Population Policy 2000* (NPP 2000) and the *National Health Policy 2002* (NHP 2002) also address the issues of child health and survival and have set the IMR reduction goal of 30 per 1000 live births by 2010.

TABLE 5.6

Age-specific Death Rates (ASDR) by Sex, Himachal Pradesh (1981 and 1999)

Age (in completed years)	1981						1999					
	Male			*Female*			*Male*			*Female*		
	Rural	*Urban*	*Total*	*Rural*	*Urban*	*Total*	*Rural*	*Urban*	*Total*	*Rural*	*Urban*	*Total*
0-4	21.6	15.9	21.4	17.5	11.3	17.2	13.7	8.0	13.4	12.9	7.7	12.6
5-9	0.8	1.2	0.9	0.4	0.0	0.4	0.7	0.0	0.7	1.3	1.5	1.4
10-14	0.0	0.0	0.0	0.0	0.0	0.0	0.6	0.0	0.6	0.3	0.0	0.3
15-19	0.0	0.0	0.0	0.0	0.0	0.0	0.1	1.3	0.2	0.8	0.7	0.8
20-24	0.0	3.3	0.3	4.8	2.2	4.7	0.9	1.5	0.9	1.0	0.0	1.0
25-29	1.0	0.0	0.9	5.0	0.0	4.6	3.3	0.7	3.0	2.0	0.7	1.9
30-34	7.3	0.9	6.6	11.0	0.0	10.3	3.0	0.0	2.7	1.0	1.7	1.1
35-39	9.1	0.0	8.3	7.2	2.6	6.9	4.5	1.7	4.2	1.4	1.0	1.4
40-44	8.2	0.6	7.5	7.5	3.4	7.3	2.4	2.8	2.5	1.8	3.1	1.9
45-49	30.2	4.5	28.2	3.1	3.6	3.2	10.7	4.6	10.0	6.1	1.5	5.8
50-54	0.0	9.6	0.8	3.1	0.0	2.9	8.2	10.0	8.4	7.2	7.4	7.2
55-59	27.1	22.6	26.8	34.8	11.7	33.6	22.6	13.5	21.7	12.6	8.9	12.3
60-64	18.0	41.1	19.1	5.6	24.1	6.5	19.2	20.6	19.3	24.0	22.4	23.9
65-69	83.2	27.6	80.2	66.3	11.0	62.8	23.8	52.1	25.3	24.6	30.9	25.0
70+*	200.2	70.0	194.4	64.3	65.8	64.4	90.4	133.2	91.2	82.6	80.3	82.8
All	14.7	5.8	14.1	8.3	4.2	8.1	8.5	5.6	8.2	6.6	4.8	6.5

Source: Statistical Reports (1981 and 1999), *Sample Registration System* (SRS), Registrar General, India.

Note: * Indicates that the rate is estimated on the basis of rates for 70-74, 75-79, 80-84, and 85 plus age groups.

The situation in Himachal Pradesh, as regards the infant, child and under-five (U_5) mortality, may compare favourably with the national scene, but the overall economic prosperity and social development of the state is not reflected in its levels of infant and child survival (Table 5.7). In spite of the lower incidence of poverty, greater infrastructure facility in terms of irrigation, road density and market density, electrification of villages, types of communication, educational centres, medical centres and provision of drinking water (NIRD 1999), lower share of casual labourers to all workers in rural areas (NIRD 1999), rapid rise in agricultural wages for male workers (NIRD 1999), use of banking services at the household level, attainment of better living standards and access to basic amenities in terms of housing, electricity, fuel for cooking, mobility, communication (*Census of India 2001*), higher female literacy, increasing private participation in health care services and women's exposure to mass media (NFHS 2002), mortality has continued to be high for infants and children in Himachal Pradesh. If development means elimination of preventable deaths for human welfare, then relatively higher mortality trends for children below five years of age should cause rethinking on the nature of development in Himachal Pradesh. Since 71 per cent of the total population in the state is dependent on subsistence agriculture, which contributes only 22 per cent to the net state domestic product (Directorate of Economics and Statistics), the living conditions of the population cannot be improved unless agriculture is given serious attention for improvement in terms of productivity or creation of alternate livelihood options.

Recent estimates of IMR vary in Himachal Pradesh; NFHS measures infant mortality at 34 per 1000 live births during 1994-98 while the SRS mortality rate is 54 per 1000 births in 2001. Higher vulnerability of infants is visible from the data that the share of infant deaths in total deaths was 18 per cent in Himachal Pradesh, as against 4 per cent in Kerala (SRS 1999). For a state known to have a good record in the provision of social infrastructure and overall index of human development, such a level of loss of life in the first year of birth is intriguing. Himachal Pradesh's record in bringing down child deaths is striking, and as in other states, IMR has declined here by little more than two-fifths since the early seventies, due to spread of health care infrastructure and services, rise in literacy and overall improvement in living standards of families. Yet, there have been periods when achievements in controlling infant deaths have been patchy, as witnessed in 1974-78, 1983-88, and 1995-99. In tune with rest of India, mortality levels among infants did not show signs of real decline and stagnated in Himachal Pradesh in the nineties, as indicated by the time-trend (Table 5.8, Figure 5.4). Reasons for this

TABLE 5.7

Infant Mortality Rate (IMR) by Selected Background Characteristics in Selected States, India

State	*IMR [1] (2001)*	*Percentage of Births in Medical Institutions [2] (1998-99)*	*Percentage of Population Poor [3] (2000)*	*Percentage of Females Literate [4] (2001)*	*Percentage of Population Living in Urban Areas [5] (2001)*	*Percentage of Females Participating in Workforce [6] (2001)*	*Percentage of Households Using Electricity for Lighting [7] (2001)*	*Annual Rate of Growth of SDP in per cent [8] (1991-92 to 1997-98)*
A.P.	66	49.8	15.8	51.2	27.1	34.9	67.2	5.0
Assam	74	17.6	36.1	56.0	12.7	20.8	24.9	—
Bihar	62	14.6	42.6	33.6	10.5	18.8	10.3	2.7
Gujarat	60	46.3	14.1	58.6	37.4	28.0	80.4	9.6
Haryana	66	22.4	8.7	56.3	29.0	27.3	82.9	5.0
H.P.	**54**	**28.9**	**7.6**	**68.1**	**9.8**	**43.7**	**94.8**	**6.3$**
J&K	48	35.6	3.5	41.8	24.9	22.0	80.6	—
Karnataka	58	51.1	20.0	57.5	34.0	31.9	78.5	5.3
Kerala	11	93.0	12.7	87.9	26.0	15.3	70.2	5.8
M.P.	86	20.1	37.4	50.3	26.7	33.1	70.2	6.2
Maharashtra	45	52.6	25.0	67.5	42.4	32.6	77.5	8.0
Orissa	91	22.6	47.2	51.0	15.0	24.6	26.9	3.3
Punjab	52	37.5	6.2	63.6	34.0	18.7	91.9	4.7
Rajasthan	80	21.5	15.3	44.3	23.4	33.5	54.7	6.5
Tamil Nadu	49	79.3	21.1	64.6	43.9	31.3	78.2	6.2
U.P.	83	15.5	31.2	43.0	20.8	16.3	31.9	3.6
W.B.	51	40.1	27.0	60.2	28.0	18.1	37.5	6.9
INDIA	**66**	**33.6**	**26.1**	**54.2**	**27.8**	**25.7**	**55.8**	**6.9**

Source: 1. *SRS Bulletin*, Registrar General, India, April 2003.
2. *National Family Heath Survey 2 (1998-99)*, India.
3. *Poverty Estimates for 1999-2000*, Planning Commission, India.
4. 5. & 6. *Provisional Population Totals, Papers 1, 2 and 3, Census of India 2001, Himachal Pradesh.*
7. *Series 1, Tables on Houses, Household Amenities and Assets, Census of India 2001, Himachal Pradesh.*
8. Ahluwalia (2000).
$. *Annual Plan (2001-2002)*, Planning Department, Government of Himachal Pradesh.

Note: 1. The estimates of poverty (percentage of population below poverty line) are based on a 30-day recall period and the states-specific poverty lines of 1999-2000.
2. '–' Indicates data not available.
3. For Himachal Pradesh, the annual growth rate of SDP is based on the period 1992-97.

merit some investigation, in the context of the link between overall economic growth in Himachal Pradesh and living standards of households (Table 5.7).

The underbelly of infant mortality in many Indian states has been the neonatal deaths. In Himachal Pradesh, these deaths constitute a whopping proportion of total infant deaths, accounting for as high as 93 per cent in 1999 (SRS). Unless neonatal deaths are significantly brought down, the scope for reducing infant mortality in the state is extremely limited. Reducing neonatal deaths is extremely complicated, as it would presuppose wider changes in maternal well-being and creation of sophisticated infrastructure in general, as well as in the existing hospitals to handle neonates for infections. Data show that infants have greater probability of death in rural areas than in urban locations; share of infant deaths to total deaths being much higher in villages (17.9%) than in towns and cities (11.9%) in the state.

Hence, for larger success in infant mortality reduction in Himachal Pradesh, there is a need to accord greater priority to rural areas, where nine-tenths of the total population reside. The major states (Kerala, Maharashtra, Tamil Nadu and West Bengal), with mortality among infants before first birthday lower than in Himachal Pradesh, are those, which have been able to reduce infant mortality substantially by focusing on rural areas consistently. The fact that rural areas in Himachal Pradesh require critical attention in this regard is clear from the latest early-life mortality statistics (SRS 1999). Neonatal and post-neonatal infant mortality rates are shown as 39 per cent and 12 per cent higher respectively in villages than in cities and towns. Lack of rural bias is one of the reasons for Himachal Pradesh having a much slower decline in mortality during one and half decades of the last century, as indicated by the percentage change in the IMR. Any innovative programme-formulation and management must recognise this and factor-in this rural-urban dichotomy.

TABLE 5.8

Infant Mortality, India and Himachal Pradesh (1971-73 to 1999-2001)

Year	*Infant Mortality Rate*			
	India	*Himachal Pradesh*		
	Total	*Total*	*Rural*	*Urban*
1971-1973	134	105	107	59
1972-1974	133	100	102	60
1973-1975	133	100	101	65
1974-1976	132	114	116	60
1975-1977	133	114	116	55
1976-1978	129	110	112	57
1977-1979	126	96	98	56
1978-1980	120	92	93	59
1979-1981	115	82	83	60
1980-1982	110	75	77	56
1981-1983	107	73	74	52
1982-1984	105	79	81	45
1983-1985	102	85	87	42
1984-1986	99	87	90	40
1985-1987	96	85	87	39
1986-1988	94	83	85	42
1987-1989	93	79	81	39
1988-1990	88	75	77	38
1989-1991	84	73	75	37
1990-1992	80	70	72	37
1991-1993	78	68	70	35
1992-1994	76	63	64	37
1993-1995	74	61	63	39
1994-1996	72	61	62	39
1995-1997	72	63	64	38
1996-1998	72	63	65	38
1997-1999	71	63	64	38
1998-2000	70	62	64	38
1999-2001	68	59	60	36

Source: Statistical Report (different volumes), Sample Registration System (SRS), Registrar General, India.

Mortality, at all stages of childhood, has declined considerably in most states including Himachal Pradesh since the early eighties (Table 5.9). In India, the slowest decline in child mortality was recorded in Himachal between the early eighties and nineties. Kerala, Tamil Nadu, and Gujarat have done well in all fronts of fighting early age mortality during these decades and have been able to lessen substantially and uniformly components of such mortality, namely, neonatal, post-neonatal, infant, and child deaths. This needs to be emulated in Himachal Pradesh, which records a substantial loss of lives during childhood (0-4 years); 19 per cent of total deaths occur in childhood in Himachal Pradesh as against five per cent in Kerala, 15 per cent in Tamil Nadu and 17 per cent in Maharashtra (SRS 1999). This indicates that with the right kind of

FIGURE 5.4

Infant Mortality, India and Himachal Pradesh (1971-73 to 1999-2001)

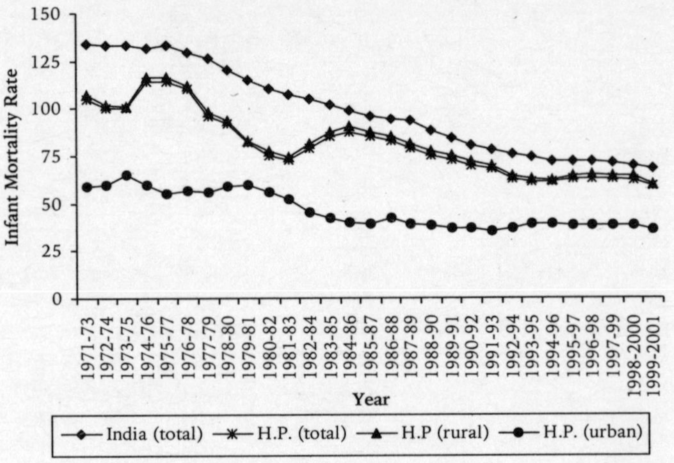

intervention, the scope to reduce deaths during childhood is enormous in Himachal Pradesh. The deaths before fifth birthday (U_5) in the state (42 per 1000 live births) is second lowest in the country after Kerala (19), yet, far away from what can be done in Indian situation, according to the recent NFHS.

Gender Bias in Infant and Child Mortality

Adjusting for data discrepancies, infant and childhood mortality in Himachal Pradesh can be associated with sex-differentials. SRS occasionally establish that relatively higher female early-age mortality in Himachal Pradesh is declining over time (Figure 5.5). In view of considerable gains to both sexes from the onset of mortality decline during last three decades, such male-female divergence, as observed during late eighties, is possible when female children benefit either equally or less in relation to their male counterparts. In spite of improvements in literacy, expansions in outreach of health care services and advances in overall standards of living in recent times, the sex composition of infant mortality trends in Himachal Pradesh suggest that vulnerability of the girl child is not a long-run issue. More recent data from NFHS between 1992-93 and 1998-99 indicate decline in the gender disparity in mortality that existed in Himachal Pradesh at every stage of childhood, particularly before the fifth birthday (Table 5.10).

Stillbirths

The trend in the rate of stillbirths is a good indicator of foetal health in particular and maternal as well as child health in general. It also reflects complications during pregnancy caused by a variety of

TABLE 5.9

Mortality at Different Stages of Childhood, India and Major States

State	Neonatal Mortality Rate			Post-neonatal Mortality Rate			Infant Mortality Rate			Child Mortality		
	1981	1999	Per cent decline during 1981-99	1981	1999	Per cent decline during 1981-99	1981	2000	Per cent decline during 1981-2000	1981	1999	Per cent decline during 1981-99
A.P.	60	46	23.3	26	20	23.1	86	65	24.4	30	17	43.3
Assam	67	53	20.9	39	23	41.0	106	75	29.2	40	24	40.0
Bihar	74	41	44.6	44	22	50.0	118	62	47.5	43	21	51.2
Gujarat	75	43	42.7	41	20	51.2	116	62	46.6	41	20	51.2
Haryana	58	39	32.8	44	28	36.4	101	67	33.7	37	20	45.9
H.P.	**15**	**50**	**-233.3**	**57**	**4**	**93.0**	**71**	**60**	**15.5**	**19**	**13**	**31.6**
J&K	44	—	—	28	—	—	72	50	30.6	26	—	—
Karnataka	49	43	12.2	21	15	28.6	69	57	17.4	24	15	37.5
Kerala	26	11	57.7	12	3	75.0	37	14	62.2	12	4	66.7
M.P.	81	61	24.7	62	28	54.8	142	87	38.0	61	30	50.8
Maharashtra	54	29	46.3	25	19	24.0	79	48	39.2	26	12	53.8
Orissa	80	61	23.8	55	36	34.5	135	95	28.9	42	27	35.7
Punjab	49	34	30.6	32	19	40.6	81	52	35.8	26	15	42.3
Rajasthan	60	50	16.7	49	31	36.7	108	79	26.9	50	25	50.0
Tamil Nadu	63	36	42.9	29	17	41.4	91	51	44.0	35	13	62.9
U.P.	96	52	45.8	54	32	40.7	150	83	44.7	60	28	53.3
West Bengal	64	31	51.6	27	21	22.2	91	51	44.0	34	14	58.8
INDIA	**70**	**45**	**35.7**	**41**	**24**	**41.5**	**110**	**68**	**38.2**	**41**	**20**	**51.2**

Source: Statistical Report (1981 and 1999) and SRS Bulletin, Vol. 36 (1), 2002, *Sample Registration System* (SRS), Registrar General, India.

TABLE 5.10

Neonatal, Post-neonatal, Infant, Child and Under-five Mortality Rate by Sex, India and Himachal Pradesh (1992-93 to 1998-99)

	Type of Mortality									
	Neonatal Mortality		Post Neonatal Mortality		Infant Mortality		Child Mortality		Under-five Mortality	
	1992-93	1998-99	1992-93	1998-99	1992-93	1998-99	1992-93	1998-99	1992-93	1998-99
Himachal Pradesh										
Male	41.6	27.9	25.6	16.9	67.2	44.8	17.6	9.0	83.6	53.4
Female	34.4	21.4	28.5	12.4	62.9	33.6	25.3	9.3	86.6	42.8
Female disadvantage(f/m)	0.8	0.8	1.1	0.7	0.9	0.8	1.4	1.0	1.0	0.8
India										
Male	57.0	50.7	31.7	24.2	88.6	74.8	29.4	24.9	115.4	97.9
Female	48.1	44.6	35.8	26.6	83.9	71.1	42.0	36.7	122.4	105.2
Female disadvantage (f/m)	0.8	0.9	1.1	1.1	0.9	1.0	1.4	1.5	1.1	1.1

Source: National Family Health Survey (1992-93 and 1998-99), India.

factors, such as lack of proper nutrition, low level of maternal care, infections, delivery by unqualified personnel, and delayed referral, which aggravate the problem. Stillbirth happens when a growing foetus suddenly dies either due to nutritional deprivation or owing to some defect with the placenta or the umbilical cord that disrupts oxygen supply to the child. Stillbirths may also happen if the uterus starts contracting more than required but cannot push the foetus out due to its size or abnormal position, leading to non-delivery. Trauma during pregnancy or delay in reaching the health centre can also cause stillbirth.

The stillborn figures inherently reflect bias and are not stable, as seen in Table 5.11. Yet, high rates of stillborns indicate poor quality of obstetric care and health in Himachal Pradesh. Data on pregnancy-outcome indicate greater incidence of stillbirths in the state (2.6%) as compared to the national average (2.0%). Stillbirths are unfortunate, and are regrettably overlooked by the policymakers and programme implementers in the din and bustle of infant mortality. The surest ways to deal with the problem of stillbirths would demand covering smaller and remote localities with facility of antenatal care, safe delivery, faster

FIGURE 5.5

Female Disadvantage in Infant Mortality, India and Himachal Pradesh (1984-86 to 1998-2000)

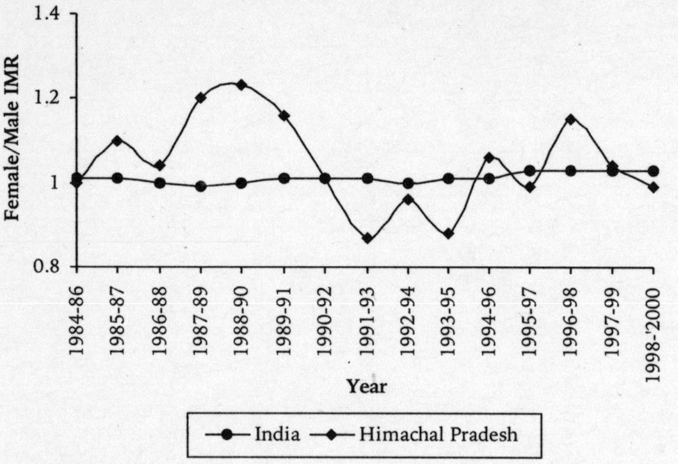

Source: Statistical Reports (different volumes), *Sample Registration System*, Registrar General, India.

transport, as well as referral to emergency obstetric units, provision of blood transfusion services, promotion of iodised salt consumption, better community awareness, etc.

TABLE 5.11

Incidence of Stillbirths, India and Himachal Pradesh (1985-99)

Year	*India*			*Himachal Pradesh*		
	Rural	*Urban*	*Total*	*Rural*	*Urban*	*Total*
1985	10.8	8.9	10.4	6.1	2.5	5.9
1989	13.1	11.2	12.7	10.0	5.2	10.6
1991	10.9	9.6	10.7	14.1	3.6	13.7
1994	7.3	15.2	8.9	6.2	11.4	6.5
1995	9.3	8.8	9.2	6.0	10.0	6.0
1996	9.0	9.0	9.0	6.0	8.0	7.0
1997	8.6	9.0	8.7	6.0	9.0	6.0
1998	9.0	8.0	9.0	12.0	7.0	12.0
1999	11.0	8.0	10.0	14.0	18.0	14.0

Source: Statistical Report (different volumes), *Sample Registration System* (SRS), Registrar General, India.

Causes of Death in Infancy and Childhood

Though reliable data on direct causes of death are vital for its assessment in early childhood, such information is rarely available in a format useful for initiating health-assessment and intervention programmes. The problem is much more compounded for smaller states, for which the *Survey of Causes of Death in Rural Areas* (Registrar General, India 1998) does not identify the top killer diseases during infancy, childhood, and reproductive life of females, unlike the major states in the country. This is a major constraint in health planning and performance.

Investigation of circumstances responsible for higher levels of infant and child mortality in general, and excess female mortality in particular, leads to a set of factors that are deeply embedded in the socio-economic and living conditions of the households. For instance, a study by Pandey *et al.* (1998) on Himachal Pradesh has indicated that mother's literacy, exposure to mass media, access to flush or pit toilet, ownership of household goods, and standard of living and pattern of differential care based on the sex of the child in households, affect the chances of survival of the children below five years of age at various stages. When controlled for the effects of other variables, the rural-urban difference in child mortality disappears. Similarly, caste- and tribe-status intrinsically enhances mortality risks significantly. Overall poverty in the family is also identified as a significant predictor of child mortality in the state. This often gets reflected in the maternal work-status (Krishnaji 2002). Demographic determinants, such as order of birth, sex of the child, mother's age at birth, length of the previous birth interval, etc., are also found to be crucial in the prevalence of neonatal, post-neonatal, infant, child and under-five mortality levels in the state (NFHS 1995 and NFHS 2002). In Himachal Pradesh, during the neonatal period, mortality is high for first order births and in the post-neonatal period for second and higher order births, indicating the relative importance of biological and behaviourial factors. Longer birth interval (duration of previous birth interval being at least 24 months and above) also significantly reduces mortality during neonatal, post-neonatal period and infancy by 36 per cent, 49 per cent and 43 per cent respectively. Likewise, the death of an older sibling at a comparatively young age also raises the post-neonatal mortality by 88 per cent. Antenatal visits also significantly reduce the neo-natal mortality (by 43%) in Himachal Pradesh, as seen from the NFHS analysis (Pandey *et al.* 1998). Research is required to ascertain the role of a dominant backward population, gender preference, access to and utilisation of health care services particularly during natal and post-natal periods, slowing down of economic growth and the impact of the structural adjustment programme, on recent trends in infant and childhood mortality in the state.

Further reduction in mortality, due to the above causes, will certainly depend not only on the state of public health programmes in Himachal Pradesh, but also on overall levels of economic and social development in terms of health, hygiene, environmental sanitation, levels of living, financial capacity to pay for health care and socio-cultural barriers in accessing it. The enormity of the tasks ahead, in relation to infant mortality, can well be visualised from the fact that Himachal Pradesh has to go a long way to achieve the national goal of bringing down the IMR to 45 by 2007, 30 by 2010, and 28 by 2012, as laid down in the *National Population Policy 2000* (NPP 2000) and the Tenth Five Year Plan (2002-2007). This appears to be difficult to achieve as, for some time in the recent past, the infant mortality level has been stagnating in the state, with the rates hovering around 60 per 1000 and not falling in tandem with economic and social development, as normally expected.

Ways to fight infant mortality would include removal of gender bias, strengthening of the Child Survival and Safe Motherhood (CSSM) Programmes under the RCH umbrella, introduction of nutritional programmes especially for anaemic mothers, proper immunisation, baby-friendly infant-feeding practices and nourishment for the newborn, screening mothers-to-be for antenatal check-up and nutritional intake, reduction in the share of non-institutional births, adequate provision for emergency obstetrics services, strengthening the sub-centres, subsidiary health centres and primary health centres, and making women doctors widely available for female clients, particularly in remote rural areas, and wider community involvement.

Maternal Mortality

Childbearing being central to womanhood, the state of maternal mortality shows how effectively women benefit from development in education, health, nutrition and medical care. Safe motherhood is high on the national agenda and maternal deaths are viewed seriously. The successive plans in India, starting from the First Five Year Plan (1951-56) to the Tenth Five Year Plan (2002-2007) recognise maternal mortality as an important indicator of socio-economic development, women's empowerment and access to basic health care in the society (Planning Commission 1952, 2001). The *National Population Policy 2000* (NPP 2000) and the *National Health Policy 2002* (NHP 2002) also reinforce this concern to policy priorities and aim to reduce the existing levels of maternal mortality to 100 maternal deaths per 1,00,000 live births by the year 2010. In India, despite policy statements, health planning and medical advancement, more than 1,00,000 women die every year from causes connected with pregnancy, childbirth and related complications (NFHS 2000). These maternal deaths have strong implications for infant survival, family ties and generational well-being, as they not only devastate the families concerned but also create situations unfavourable to social and economic harmony between generations.

Even if maternal deaths are substantial in India, reliable data on these are yet to be available for the individual states. The SRS figures (1998) on maternal mortality are far from reality and elude the smaller states including Himachal Pradesh, as do the available indirect estimates. The available data put the figures in Himachal Pradesh at a higher level, with 408 per 1,00,000 live births in 1992 (Himachal Health Vision 2020). Lack of studies on different dimensions of maternal mortality, particularly in Himachal Pradesh, hamper efforts to address the problem. However, existing evidence suggests that the state is still far from the National Socio-Demographic Goal for 2010, which aims to bring the MMR below 100 deaths per 1,00,000 live births, as enunciated in the *National Population Policy 2000* (NPP 2000).

Variations in maternal mortality can be directly related to rural and urban residence, availability and use of health infrastructure for antenatal, natal and post-natal requirement, conditions of hygiene and birth-assistance for home deliveries, health awareness and overall levels of living, according to some hospital- and community-based studies. Direct and indirect causes of maternal deaths have to be widely assessed in Himachal Pradesh, for maternal death reduction programmes. While the broad direct causes usually consist of haemorrhage, oedema, proteinuria and hypertensive disorders, obstructed labour due to malposition and mal presentation of foetus, and complications predominantly related to puerperium, the indirect causes range from tuberculosis, viral hepatitis, malaria and anaemia.

As one of the priority areas, the WHO has recommended measures for promoting policy action, society and community intervention along with health sector activation, to reduce maternal mortality. In the context of Himachal Pradesh, this would mean increasing access of women to health-care centres particularly during odd hours, eliminating unsafe practices during delivery and sensitising the community on its importance, regularly training and equipping female health workers including *dais*, and making the community respond effectively to the needs of socially and economically backward pregnant women. Revitalising primary and subsidiary health centres and the designation of certain health centres as nodal units depending on their respective infrastructure, habitation, connectivity and availability of health staff, can be of immense help.

Recent initiative of the Government of India in declaring 11 April as *Rashtriya Janani Suraksha Diwas* and launching a new beneficiary-friendly scheme for poor women to encourage deliveries in hospitals and health centres and supporting nutritional food intake of pregnant women is regarded as a step forward. Since most of the maternal deaths are preventable, the state government can achieve good results by implementing schemes which ensure at least three antenatal check-ups at a health facility, one extra meal a day, iron and folic acid supplementation for 100 days, delivery in a health facility, recognition of danger signs of complicated pregnancies and rush them to the nearest health centre, and finally three check-ups after the delivery.

In addition to putting in place an effective demographic surveillance system, which includes registration and monitoring of pregnancies by local paramedics, measures to meet emergency situations with regard to childbirth and pregnancy complications can also be helpful. One of the various ways of improving assessment of maternal mortality is to upgrade the data on such deaths through advances in vital registration system, reporting of the exact cause of death, and inclusion of some basic background characteristics.

Prospects for Further Decline

Prospects for further drop in mortality is high in Himachal Pradesh. Reducing under-five mortality, which has been inordinately high at different stages, can ensure a decline in overall mortality; focus on the survival of female children can also tremendously contribute to reduction in overall mortality rates.

Similarly, maternal mortality is another area where substantial reductions can be attempted to create a dent in the general mortality level. Tracking down and supporting groups, who, in a given situation, are more vulnerable to infant, child and maternal mortality, can yield direct results. Rural crude death rate in Himachal Pradesh being close to the rural CDR in Kerala, the state with the lowest mortality in India, the best way will be to concentrate on infants and children in rural areas so as to get quick results. As one among select states in India poised for demographic ageing, rise in the proportion of the elderly in Himachal Pradesh is likely to inflate the total mortality level as, with rising age (from 60 years onwards), the death-rate starts rising progressively. Moreover, development-linked epidemiological transition, lifestyles and medical and non-medical intervention programmes are likely to have a decisive impact on future mortality regimes. Some basic reflections on the causes of death are essential in this context. Unfortunately, no reliable and disaggregated statistics are available about these on a wider scale.

The timing of infant death has also far-reaching importance for framing measures that enhance the chances of survival of the newborns. Since biological factors are largely decisive in determining chances of survival in the neonatal period, and environmental and behavioural factors in the post-neonatal period, interventions must recognise this classification. Since infant deaths are out of proportion according to the 'two-thirds rule', deaths occurring in first 24 hours of life, then in the first week of life, and subsequently in the first month of life, need to be tracked down for remedial measures. As deaths in the first four weeks of life are determined by sets of proximate determinants, namely maternal factors, environmental contamination, nutritional deficiency, injury, and personal illness control (James *et al.* 2000), reduction in infant mortality by bringing down neonatal deaths will significantly depend on substantial progress in containing these risk factors. For instance, nutritionists argue that removal of iodine deficiency during pregnancy, which retards the growth and development of the foetus, will result in a substantial reduction in stillbirths and neonatal mortality (Dodd and Madan 1993). The nutritional rehabilitation of expectant women also reduces the chances of birth of low birth-weight babies, who are more susceptible to death in neonatal period. But, the scope for nutritional improvement depends very much on the extent to which the economic standards of living of the families are upgraded and opportunities for livelihood are provided. Since premature births, another source of high neonatal death, are difficult to avoid because of inability to control infections and birth asphyxia without proper and equipped neonatal centres in the existing hospitals, the best way in the short run will be to stick to nutritional programmes. For this, Himachal Pradesh has to place nutrition high on the development agenda, as already done in Tamil Nadu in the south.

Contraceptive Use

The First Five Year Plan in India laid the foundation of a state-sponsored family planning programme to reduce the growth of population, so as to stabilize it at a level consistent with the requirements of the national economy (Planning Commission 1952). Since then, successive Five Year Plans have been providing funding assistance to upgrade the infrastructures and to improve quality, coverage and efficiency of family welfare programmes all over the country. The Tenth Five Year Plan, like the previous ones, also makes an unequivocal commitment to free essential family welfare services. It also highlights the need to make a dent on the fertility profile of the country, through the removal of unmet needs of contraception (Planning Commission 2003). Notwithstanding policy rigidities, socio-cultural barriers, programme deficiencies, etc., contraception today is at the core of demographic changes that are widely sought, both officially and privately.

Levels and Trends in Use

In the past more than 55 years, the use of modern contraceptives in Himachal Pradesh has reached a significant proportion from virtually nil at the time of independence. It is a leader in northwestern India in family planning practice. The state is widely recognised for its good performance in family planning programme, like Maharashtra and Gujarat in the west, Andhra Pradesh, Karnataka, Kerala, and Tamil Nadu in the south, besides Punjab in its neighbourhood. Since the inception of the programme, the contraceptive prevalence rate (CPR) has consistently remained high in Himachal Pradesh, as compared to the national average, notwithstanding the controversies that had dogged the programme during the 'national emergency' and due to institution of incentives. Apart from couples' awareness about method-use and availability, the phenomenal growth in CPR can be attributed to vigorous programme implementation strategies, active involvement of the government health sector, centring on 'target' fixation and achievement mainly tagged to incentives and disincentives to programme-staff and clients. Both official service statistics and independent contraceptive prevalence surveys have consistently established the edge of Himachal Pradesh over others in making contraception reach the eligible population widely (Table 5.12, Figure 5.6). In addition to a real difference in use of methods, the differences between official and non-official figures can also be attributed to methodological differences in the estimation.

TABLE 5.12

Current Contraceptive Prevalence Rate (CPR) due to All Modern Methods, India and Himachal Pradesh (1973-99)

Year	*All Methods*[1]		*NFHS*[2]		*Levels and Trends in Method Composition*[1]							
					Sterilisation		*IUD*		*Condom*		*Oral Pill*	
	India	*H.P.*	*India*	*H.P.*	*India*	*H.P.*	*India*	*H.P.*	*India*	*H.P.*	*India*	*H.P.*
1973	15.0	8.2	12.2	—	11.3	5.9	1.4	1.8	2.3*	0.5	—	—
1975	16.3	9.5	—	—	12.4	7.6	1.4	1.4	2.5*	0.5	—	—
1976	18.9	13.5	—	—	14.1	9.5	1.5	1.5	3.4*	2.4*	—	—
1977	26.1	32.8	—	—	21.1	24.9	1.6	2.3	3.5*	5.6*	—	—
1978	24.4	27.1	—	—	20.4	22.2	0.9	1.4	3.0*	3.5*	—	—
1979	24.4	24.8	—	—	20.2	21.8	1.0	1.4	3.3*	1.6*	—	—
1980	23.9	24.5	—	—	20.2	21.7	1.1	1.6	2.7*	1.2*	—	—
1981	24.3	26.1	—	—	20.0	22.1	1.1	1.7	3.2*	2.2*	—	—
1982	25.6	27.0	—	—	20.7	23.3	1.2	1.9	3.8*	1.8*	—	—
1983	28.4	29.6	—	—	22.0	25.5	1.4	2.1	4.9*	2.0*	—	—
1984	32.4	32.4	—	—	23.7	27.7	2.3	2.6	6.2*	2.1*	—	—
1985	35.8	36.1	—	—	25.0	29.1	3.0	3.6	7.8*	3.4*	—	—
1986	38.7	42.6	—	—	26.5	32.0	3.9	5.0	8.3*	5.6*	—	
1987	46.7	45.9	—	—	27.9	33.5	4.8	6.2	7.4	5.1	1.3	1.1
1988	44.2	47.5	39.9	—	28.9	34.5	5.5	6.9	8.3	5.2	1.5	0.9
1989	46.7	51.7	—	—	29.8	35.8	6.2	7.7	8.9	7.0	1.7	1.1
1990	48.6	54.6	—	—	30.1	36.8	6.6	8.4	10.0	8.2	1.9	1.2
1991	49.6	56.9	—	—	30.3	37.5	7.0	9.1	10.1	8.7	2.1	1.5
1992	48.6	58.8	36.3	54.4	30.3	38.6	6.6	10.0	9.4	8.4	2.2	1.7
1993	48.7	60.3	—	—	30.3	38.7	6.6	10.8	9.9	9.0	2.0	1.7
1994	51.3	61.5	—	—	30.3	39.6	7.2	10.7	11.2	9.1	2.7	2.2
1995	51.6	57.9	—	—	30.2	40.5	7.6	10.3	10.8	4.8	3.0	2.4
1996	52.2	62.1	—	—	30.2	40.7	8.2	10.7	10.7	8.2	3.2	2.5
1997	51.0	59.3	—	—	29.6	40.3	7.8	9.8	10.4	7.0	3.1	2.3
1998	50.8	53.8	—	—	29.3	36.9	7.6	8.6	10.1	6.1	3.8	2.2
1999	—		42.8	60.8	—		—		—		—	

Source: 1. Ministry of Health and Family Welfare (MoHFW), Government of India, *Year Books* (different volumes).
2. *National Family Health Survey* (NFHS), India, 1992-93 and 1998-99.

Note: 1. '*' includes use of oral pills also 2. '—' Indicates data not available 3. Figures are in percentages

FIGURE 5.6

Couple Protection Rate, India and Himachal Pradesh (1973-1998)

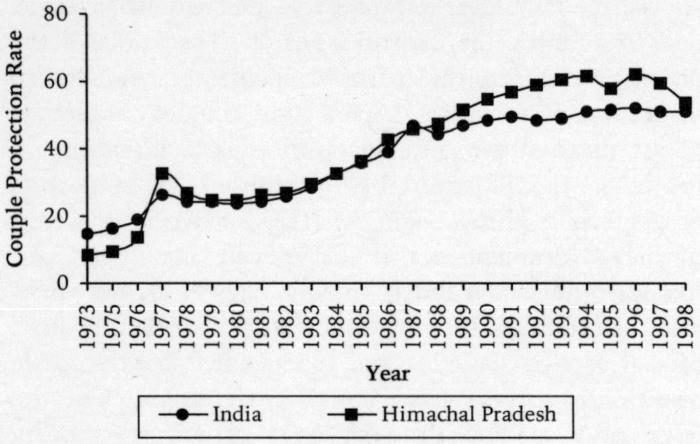

Source: *Year Books* (different issues) Ministry of Health and Family Welfare, Government of India.

TABLE 5.13

Time Lag in Contraception, Himachal Pradesh (1999-2000)

Age/Time Lag (in years)	*Type of Contraceptive Method*		
	IUD	*Vasectomy*	*Tubectomy*
Mean age (of wife) at acceptance[1]	27.5	29.7	28.1
Female mean age at first marriage[2]	18.6	18.6	18.6
Time lag in contraception	8.9	11.1	9.5

Source: 1. Directorate of Health and Family Welfare, Himachal Pradesh.
2. Multiple Indicator Survey (MICS), UNICEF 2000.

Age Pattern of Use

The age pattern of contraception in Himachal Pradesh (Figure 5.7) is interesting. According to NFHS, among the currently married women, in 1998-99, the use peaked in the ages 35-39 followed by 30-34 with 67 per cent and 69 per cent respectively using some modern method of family planning. The younger age couples (aged 20-24 years) report low use, the rate being 27 per cent. Contraception among younger women is more popular in urban than in rural areas. Official statistics on contraception in Himachal Pradesh show that the mean age at acceptance has risen by one year between 1986-87 and 1999-2000 for the acceptors of IUD, and declined by one year for the acceptors of tubectomy, and remained nearly stagnant for the wives of vasectomy acceptors. These are not healthy demographic signs. When linked to the age pattern of fertility, it is observed that women basically resort to contraception on a wider scale after their own contribution to fertility at ages 20-24 and 25-29. If contraception is to have a higher impact on fertility, then ways must be found to make it more popular among younger women, and make spacing methods, other than the IUD, more accessible during the time lag between marriage and acceptance of a terminal method (Table 5.13).

Son-preference influences family planning acceptance in Himachal Pradesh. Whether the couples will opt for contraception or not depends to a large extent not only on the total number of living children they have but also on the number of living son(s). According to NFHS, family planning is mostly accepted after two children; 23 per cent of couples currently use any modern method after one child as against 65 per cent after two children and 80 per cent after three children. Among one-child families, 27 per cent go for family planning just after having a son as against 18 per cent just after a daughter. Similarly, among two-child families, 80 per cent of currently married women resort to family planning after two sons as opposed to 31 per cent after two daughters. A strong correlation also exists between the sex composition of the surviving children and methods preference. Comparison between spacing and terminal methods shows that the acceptance of terminal methods is largely dependent on the needed number of male children in the family. Even such methods as condom and IUD, which do not give finality to termination of child-bearing, are used by couples after meeting the targets of family-composition and size in terms of the required number of sons. If the family planning programme in the state has to make further inroads and be sustainable, it must address the gender dimensions confronting it.

FIGURE 5.7

Age-specific Fertility Rate and Age-specific Couple Protection Rate, Himachal Pradesh (1999)

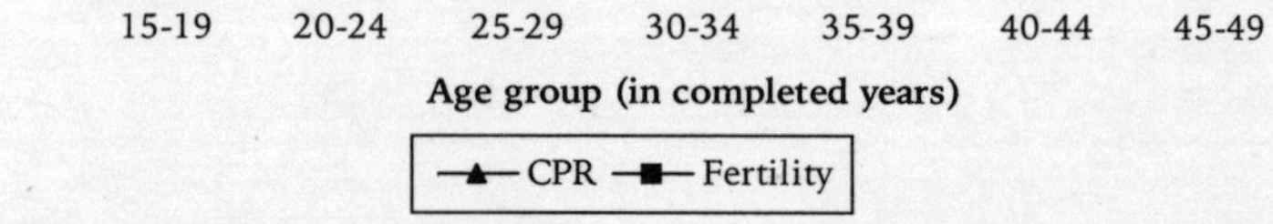

Source: *National Family Health Survey.*

In Himachal Pradesh, the 'Two Child Norm' is strongly rooted in the fertility planning of the couples and determines the choice of method. The idea that contraceptives are only meant for use after the birth of at least one child is highly ingrained in the minds of the couples and needs to be changed. It also confirms that there exists vast scope in the state for expanding family planning practices among couples. At least, spacing methods, such as the IUD and condom, can be more vigorously promoted in the state, particularly among women with no child, one child and two children. If specific concerns relating to pills are dealt with properly, it could also be reasonably promoted among women.

Prospects for Future

The family planning programme in Himachal Pradesh like everywhere else has a dual responsibility. Besides making couples empowered in the process of childbearing through reproductive choices, the programme has also to help in the attainment of replacement level of fertility through universal access to quality contraceptives and prevention of unwanted pregnancies. This would presuppose creation and addition of proper infrastructure at the village level given the fact that 90 per cent of the population in the state resides in villages, that are generally scattered and remote. Upgradation of existing hospitals, PHCs and sub-centres, training of personnel and uninterrupted supply of contraceptives, tubal rings, laproscopes, vaccines and RCH drugs, etc., need to be undertaken widely. Active involvement of the non-governmental sector is essential and social marketing of contraceptives also needs to be extensively promoted.

At another level, family planning cannot be boosted unless child mortality is brought down and couples are reassured about the survival of their children. Ante-natal, natal and post-natal services have to be streamlined and home deliveries, already high, have to be drastically reduced. Better birth attendance and nursing care will promote, in the absence of target setting, provider-client relationship to the advantage of family planning. This is exclusively in the hands of government health workers. Covering the inter-district disparity in determinants of family planning acceptance will also deliver good result in future.

Sex Ratios, Sex Preference, and Sex Selective Abortions

The sex composition of the population is an important indicator of social development. In most populations, females exceed males numerically but, in contrast the Indian sex-ratio (defined as number of females per 1,000 males) has been consistently low for a long time. In the northwestern region, namely Himachal Pradesh, Uttaranchal, Punjab, Chandigarh, Haryana, Delhi, Rajasthan, Gujarat and Maharashtra, low sex ratio continues to be a demographic enigma and cause for concern. In Himachal Pradesh, the recent census shows declining sex ratios for total as well as the child population (0-6 age group) unlike the earlier ones since 1901, which had been consistently indicating a rise in the sex-ratio for the total population, except for a break in 1941. During 1991-2001, while a moderate increase in the femininity of the total population, simultaneously with rising masculinity of the child population, was the situation in India, in Himachal Pradesh it was increasing masculinity for both the groups. In the northwest, the numerical shortfall of females is intense in Punjab and its neighbourhood, both in child (0-6 years) and non-child populations (seven years and above).

Himachal Pradesh is noticeable in the northwest for greater masculinity of the child population as compared to the national average (Table 5.14). Examination of sex-ratio trends indicates that throughout the twentieth century, Himachal Pradesh experienced a deficit of females and the problem of a sex-ratio imbalance is not a recent one. The concern is that instead of getting corrected with time, the situation is deteriorating, as evident in the 1980s and 1990s.

The dynamics of sex ratio are complex and broadly explained in terms of variations in sex composition of births, sex differences in mortality, sex discrepancies in enumeration and the sex pattern of net migration. Being proximate, these factors are responses to some ultimate social, economic, cultural and technological changes in the society. In the absence of more recent data on sex-specific coverage in the census, migration trends for both the sexes in the inter-censal period, and detailed age and sex composition of the population, it is difficult to attribute the part played by each of the above factors. However, the emerging pattern of sex-ratio imbalances in Himachal Pradesh can be comprehended to a large extent by concentrating on trends in the child sex ratio.

Masculinity in child sex-ratio has been observed in Himachal Pradesh since its statehood and male-female imbalance continuously sliding since 1971 from which year direct data are available on child sex composition. However, the situation seems to have worsened faster after 1981, with the femininity level in child population dropping to 897 females per 1,000 males for the state in

2001. Census-based sex ratio indicates substantial rise in the already masculine child population between 1981 and 2001 (Table 5.14). The origin of the current imbalance seems to have been in the late eighties and the early nineties with deficits culminating in 2001. This can be directly related to the emergence and popularity of sex-determination tests in North India in general, and Punjab and its adjoining areas in particular, which receive large and regular inflow from Himachal Pradesh in search of livelihood.

TABLE 5.14

Changes in Sex Ratio, India and Himachal Pradesh (1971-2001)

Year	*India*		*Himachal Pradesh*	
	All ages	*Children (0-6)*	*All ages*	*Children (0-6)*
1971	930	964	958	981
1981	934	962	973	971
1991	927	945	976	951
2001	933	927	970	897

Source: 1. *Provisional Population Totals, Paper 1 of 2001, Census of India 2001, India and Himachal Pradesh.*
2. *Social and Cultural Tables, Census of India, Himachal Pradesh*, 1971 and 1981.

There is no evidence of large-scale selective migration in favour of male children in Himachal Pradesh, and the gender difference in enumeration is also not considered a significant explanation of child sex ratio imbalance here, like elsewhere (Visaria 1971, Miller 1981, Krishnaji 2001), even if the census-recorded sex ratios often under-report females (Natarajan 1972, Premi 1991), specifically in early age. This leaves the sex ratio at birth (SRB) and excess female childhood mortality as the two main factors influencing child sex ratio in the state, their relative contribution varying from one place to the other depending on the local situation. In addition to the sex ratio at birth, the other distortion in child sex ratio comes from excess female child mortality discussed earlier. Shortages of females, at birth and at early age, create numerical disparity in the childhood for each cohort, difficult to alter subsequently. Young-age children from both the sexes have gained in chances of survival in Himachal Pradesh, especially during past two decades. Improvements in mortality conditions have been able to wipe out, to a large extent, the excess female disadvantage that had existed in mortality for some time. Hence, higher female mortality in the young age as a significant determinant of sex ratio among children (0-6 years) in the state seems to be less than expected.

FIGURE 5.8

Changing Sex Ratio, India and Himachal Pradesh

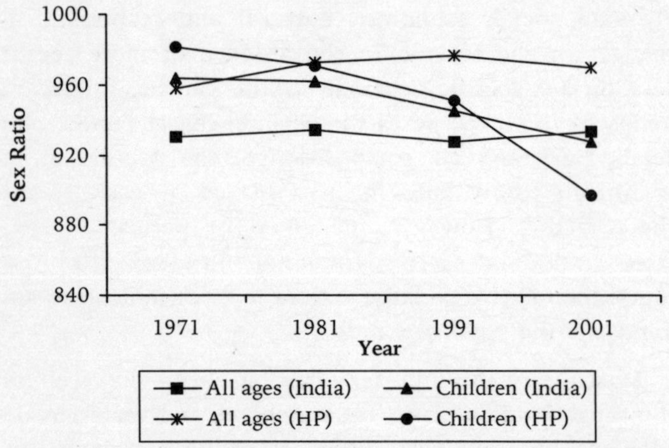

Source: 1. *Provisional Population Totals, Paper 1 of 2001, Himachal Pradesh, Census of India 2001,*
2. *Provisional Population Totals, Paper 1 of 2001, India, Census of India 2001.*
3. *Socio-cultural Tables, Himachal Pradesh, Census of India* 1971, 1981 and 1991.

Sex Ratio at Birth

Data on sex ratio at birth, from more than one source, with all the shortcomings, indicate an overall tilt in favour of males that is rising faster in the recent period in Himachal Pradesh (Table 5.15). In Himachal, a study recorded a SRB of 105, 107 and 117 during 15 years period before 1984-98 (Retherford and Roy 2003). It concluded that SRB gets further distorted in the absence of any living sons, which provides strong indirect evidence of sex-selective abortions, after first births. Data on annual births, culled from different registration units, indicate state of affairs to be still more serious, as the male births exceeded the female births overwhelmingly in the state. Between 1996 and 2001, the number of male births per 100 female births, hovering mostly around 115, indicate a substantial surplus of male babies at birth. In spite of the reservations one may have on the quality of such registrations in a state that has 90 per cent of the population living in villages, which are small, scattered and remote, this is an indication of the extent of the problem. Based on these indications, there is need to reflect, in the first place, on as to why the sex ratio at birth is so much biased in favour of males in Himachal Pradesh, and what are the reasons for it being increasingly so in the recent past?

In Himachal Pradesh, the male advantage is more than 'normal' at the time of birth. This gives currency to the argument that a significant share of females are lost either at the time of conception or during

TABLE 5.15

Sex Ratio at Birth, India and Himachal Pradesh (1978-2001)

State	Sample Registration System (SRS)		National Family Health Survey (NFHS)		Civil Registration System (CRS)					
	1981-90	1996-98	1978-92	1984-98	1996	1997	1998	1999	2000	2001
H.P.	—	—	107	108	114	116	118	115	117	117
India	110	111	106	108	—		—	—	—	—

Source: 1. *Sample Registration System* (SRS), Registrar General, India.
2. *National Family Health Survey* (NFHS) 1992-93: India and different states.
2. *National Family Heath Survey* (NFHS 2) 1998-99: India and different states.
3. *CRS*: Directorate of Health and Family Welfare, Government of Himachal Pradesh.

Note: 1. Sex Ratio at Birth (SRB) is defined as number of males per 100 females.
2. '—' Indicates data not available.

pregnancy. Widely available sex-selection technologies, at affordable prices, with little social or legal hurdles till recently, seem to have made intervention possible for couples, either at conception or during early pregnancy.

Sex Preference

Changes in juvenile (0-6) sex ratio can be linked to the overall preference for the male child in many areas of Himachal Pradesh. Strong male dominance in property transfer, focus on male-centric rituals and kinship system, inadequate appreciation of women's economic contribution, absence of strong social reform movements, etc., have contributed to higher value of the male child among many communities in Himachali society. In modern Himachal Pradesh, in spite of the rise in female education and legal support, there are many reasons, in popular perception, for not having a female child. Here, the position of the daughter-in-law in the family is defined, on her arrival, to the culturally sanctioned urgency of producing a child, preferably a son.

In spite of economic progress, institutional arrangements, constitutional support and educational campaigns, preference for a male child among the couples still persists in Himachal Pradesh. As indicated in NFHS, the fall in mean ideal number of children between 1992 and 1999 for ever-married couples in the state from 2.4 (1.3 sons, 0.8 daughters and 0.3 children of either sex) to 2.2 (1.1 sons, 0.8 daughters and 0.3 children of either sex) can be associated with decline in son preference. This welcome sign is mixed, as it also comes with a virtual stagnation in the desire for daughters among the couples during the same period. The fact that among ever-married women in 1999, 88 per cent of the couples wanted at least a son and 79 per cent at least a daughter, 26 per cent wanted more sons than daughters and 0.6 per cent more daughters than the sons, highlights how the desire for a male child is entrenched in Himachal Pradesh.

Sex-Selective Abortions

Theoretically, in the absence of significant disparity in net migration, age reporting, and gender differences in mortality for the males and females in the under-five age group, the strong desire for a male child makes the sex ratio at birth increasingly masculine either through the adoption of 'stopping rule' or sex-selective abortions. In Himachal Pradesh, it is likely that a sizeable share of female foetuses are terminated during pregnancy. Data on the nature and scale of abortions in the state do not indicate such a scale of pregnancy terminations as to result in a highly masculine sex ratio at birth. Recent large-scale surveys do not establish a somewhat higher incidence of such abortions in Himachal Pradesh than the national average. Direct data too do not suggest acceleration in induced abortions between 1992-93 and 1998-99 in Himachal Pradesh (Table 5.16), in line with the expected impact of the proliferation of sex-determination clinics and their users in the 1990s. Since most of the MTPs are done in the private sector, the number of MTPs indicated by official statistics, fluctuating between the lowest of 4905 (in 1995-96) and the highest of 5938 (in 1996-97) during 1994-95 and 1999-2000 do not reflect the reality. Interestingly, much of these MTPs are attributed to failure of contraception by the couples.

Notwithstanding the above statistics, most likely underestimates, induced abortion is well accepted in many parts of Himachal Pradesh, transcending communities, castes and economic groups. A recent survey in Bhawarna Block (Kangra) shows that among

238 currently married women, a total of 8.4 per cent had induced abortions (CRRID, 2000). Illiterate women and women in socially backward communities, landless and poor households have been observed resorting to voluntary termination of pregnancy in this survey. The motives, methods and consequences of such sex-selective abortions need to be examined in detail. The popularity of sex determination tests is clear from the fact that in Himachal Pradesh among mothers who received antenatal check-ups, 15 per cent received ultrasound or amniocentesis three years before 1999 (Arnold *et al.* 2002).

TABLE 5.16

Pregnancy Outcomes for Ever-married Women, India and Himachal Pradesh (1992-93 to 1998-99)

	Last Pregnancy after 1.1.95		*Himachal Pradesh*		*India*	
Nature of Outcome	*H.P.*	*India*	*1992*	*1998-99*	*1992*	*1998-99*
Spontaneous abortion	1.9	1.9	6.0	4.5	4.5	4.4
Induced abortion	0.7	1.1	1.3	1.6	1.3	1.7
Still birth	1.3	0.8	2.7	2.6	2.3	2.0
Live birth	96.0	96.2	90.0	91.3	92.0	91.9
All	**100.0**	**100.0**	**100.0**	**100.0**	**100.0**	**100.0**

Source: 1. *National Family Health Survey* (NFHS) 1992-93 and 1998-99: India and Himachal Pradesh.
2. *Rapid Household Survey* (RHS), Phase I, India, 1998.

Effects of sex imbalances are manifold in terms of social, cultural and economic consequences. It is widely believed that deficit of females lead to rise in spousal age gap through 'marriage squeeze', replacements of intra-family female discrimination by inter-family female discrimination, change in dynamics of household economy, besides crime against women and others. Sex selection cannot be contained unless son preference is dismantled, unabated commercialisation of health services are checked, the government health sector improves services dramatically to offset attraction by the private sector, the Pre-natal Diagnostic Technique (Regulation and Prevention of Misuse) Act, 1994 is implemented and more couples are sensitised through social movements. But the final blow to female foeticide may come from the rejection of social practices like dowry and true economic empowerment of females in society. The Government of Himachal Pradesh has initiated some steps to counter the trend, which include greater focus on districts bordering Punjab, awareness campaigns, co-ordination with the departments of Education, Social Welfare, and *Panchayati Raj*, motivation of heath workers at the district and below, following up of pregnant women while giving antenatal care till the end of child bearing, etc. The results of such exercises are yet to be assessed.

Demographic Ageing

When a society, with a sizeable share of younger population, is transformed into another with a sizeable share of older population, the average age of the entire population rises. In the absence of substantial in-migration of younger population, falling mortality and fertility inevitably lead to population ageing during the course of demographic transition. In India, high fertility has maintained, for long, youthfulness of the population. With the onset of fertility and adult mortality decline, the percentage share of the aged, 60 years and above, in the total population increased from 5.63 in 1961 to 6.70 in 1991 and to 7.90 in 1998-99. After Kerala (8.82%), Himachal Pradesh has a higher share of the aged in its population (8.12%), followed by Punjab (7.84%) among the major states in India according to the 1991 Census. The most recent estimate from NFHS puts the proportion of population in the age group 60 and above in Himachal Pradesh at 10.0 per cent in 1998-99. Existing projections also indicate a consistent and long-term rise in the proportion of elderly population in most of the Indian States, including Himachal Pradesh (RGI 1996). Notwithstanding the low percentage of the elderly in India at present, the issue of ageing assumes added significance due to their sheer numbers in absolute terms, greater incidence of poverty, wider vulnerability and lack of social security in old age in a fast changing economic and social structure and extensive disparity among the regions.

Expectation of Life

Improvements in living conditions and health have continuously led to reduction in overall mortality levels across sections of the society and this has led to, on an average, a longer life span for individuals in Himachal Pradesh. The fact that mortality declines in the state have immensely contributed to population-ageing is clear from the data on rising expectation of life at birth and at ages 60, 65 and 70 and above, between 1970-75 and 1991-95 (Table 5.17). In the backdrop of national gains in longevity for both sexes, increments in life expectancy have been much higher in Himachal Pradesh.

Females in the state benefited more than males from the increase in life expectancy in tune with the national trend between 1970-75 and 1991-95. In approximately 21 years, increment in female life expectancy has exceeded the increment in male life expectancy at birth and at selected ages. Males and females in Himachal Pradesh have had their longevity at birth increased by 17 per cent and 27 per cent respectively as against 12 per cent and 20 per cent respectively, at the all-India level during this period, making gains of 9.3 and 13.8 years, respectively.

TABLE 5.17

Life Expectancy at Selected Ages, India and Himachal Pradesh (1970-75 to 1991-95)

At age (in years)	*Period*	*India*		*Himachal Pradesh*	
		Male	*Female*	*Male*	*Female*
0 (At birth)	1970-75	50.5	49.0	54.8	50.9
	1976-80	52.5	52.1	58.1	54.9
	1981-85	55.4	55.7	58.5	62.9
	1986-90	57.7	58.1	62.4	62.8
	1991-95	59.7	60.9	64.1	64.7
Increase*		9.2	11.9	9.3	13.8
60	1970-75	13.4	14.3	15.1	13.1
	1976-80	14.1	15.9	15.8	15.2
	1981-85	14.6	16.4	15.1	18.2
	1986-90	14.7	16.1	16.8	17.5
	1991-95	15.3	17.1	18.6	16.2
Increase*		1.9	2.8	3.5	3.1
65	1970-75	10.9	11.6	12.9	10.1
	1976-80	11.7	13.2	12.8	12.6
	1981-85	12.0	13.6	11.8	14.8
	1986-90	11.9	12.9	13.9	14.0
	1991-95	12.5	13.9	15.9	12.5
Increase*		1.6	2.3	3.0	2.4
70+	1970-75	8.6	9.2	9.6	7.6
	1976-80	9.6	10.9	10.5	10.4
	1981-85	9.7	11.0	9.3	12.8
	1986-90	9.4	10.0	11.2	10.9
	1991-95	10.0	11.0	13.3	9.4
Increase*		1.4	1.8	3.7	1.8

Source: *Ageing Population of India: An Analysis of 1991 Census Data*, Registrar General, India.

Note: * Increase between 1970-75 and 1991-95.

With gains in the average life expectancy being substantial in the state as observed, survival to a higher age is increasing, and causing a continuous rise in the numbers and percentages of persons aged 60 and above in both rural and urban areas (Table 5.18). Rise in the share of male and female elderly in Himachal Pradesh, when considered against the national context, is on the higher side. The old age population in this tiny state increased from 0.25 million in 1971 to 0.42 million in 1991 and seems to have touched 0.6 million mark at the turn of the century, thus causing a gigantic 145 per cent rise in 30 years. The female aged population multiplied by 2.68 times (from 0.105 million to 0.281 million) in three decades as opposed to 2.24 times rise (from 0.143 million to 0.321 million) in male elderly numbers between 1971 and 2001.

TABLE 5.18

Share of Aged (60 and above) in Total Population, India and Himachal Pradesh (1971 to 1998-99)

Year	*India*			*Himachal Pradesh*		
	Rural	*Urban*	*Total*	*Rural*	*Urban*	*Total*
1971	6.21	4.98	5.97	7.4	4.3	7.2
1981	6.84	5.36	6.49	7.7	5.1	7.5
1991	7.11	5.75	6.70	8.4	5.4	8.1
1998-99*	8.10	7.30	7.90	10.0	8.4	10.0

Source: 1. *Ageing Population of India: An Analysis of 1991 Census Data*, Registrar General, India.

2. * *National Family Health Survey* (1998-99).

In two decades since 1971, for which the census data on ageing is available directly, one gets some impression of how fast Himachal Pradesh is moving towards 'demographic' ageing. For each sex, males and females separately, the fact that average growth in the number of those aged 60 and above is higher than the average growth of population in all ages in respective categories, is a strong pointer to the foundations of ageing. Himachal Pradesh is not an isolated case as the scene here corresponds broadly with the national scene. The average annual growth rate among the elderly in Himachal Pradesh varied considerably by sex and age. Between 1971 and 1991, the population of elderly women rose from 0.10 to 0.20 million and that of elderly men from 0.14 to 0.22 million; the growth rate of the former exceeding the growth rate of the latter, indicating a faster pace of ageing among the females as against males in the state (Table 5.19). Among both male and female elderly population, growth rates of the 'young-old' population (aged 60-79) exceeded those of the 'old-old' (aged 80 and above).

Condition of the Aged

Unfortunately, not much is known about the old-age population in Himachal Pradesh, except their basic conditions of living. As the 1991 Census summarises, the elderly (aged 60 and more) in the state are primarily rural based (94%), literate with education up to primarily level (62%), source of substantial workforce

TABLE 5.19

Average Annual Growth Rate of Aged Population, India and Himachal Pradesh (1971-91)

Age (in completed years)	*Himachal Pradesh*		*India*	
	Male	*Female*	*Male*	*Female*
60+	2.77	4.42	3.70	3.63
All ages	2.41	2.54	2.73	2.70
60-69	2.40	3.64	3.27	3.40
70-79	3.24	6.04	4.12	3.97
80-89	3.85	6.00	5.93	4.54
90-99	3.20	5.01	5.39	4.16
100+	1.04	0.22	1.25	0.47

Source: *Ageing Population of India: An Analysis of 1991 Census Data*, Registrar General, India.

Note: Figures are in per cent.

(participation rates for total workers being 65 per cent for males and 28 per cent for females) and are cultivators (85% of total male and 95% female workers in main category).

The 52nd round of survey of National Sample Survey (NSS) also brings out the socio-economic profile of the aged in Himachal Pradesh. With regard to marital status, the aged males are primarily currently married (79% in rural areas and 77% in urban areas) and aged females are mostly widowed (64% in rural areas and 66% in urban areas). Living arrangements of the elderly vary on the basis of their sex rather on the basis of place of residence. Less than one per cent of the elderly in the state live alone, either as an inmate of an old age home or outside such a home. In rural areas, a majority of aged males (63%) stay with spouse and other members of family, as against aged females who stay with children but without spouse (54%).

Data on the state of economic independence of the aged indicate that the males (57% in rural areas and 61% in urban areas) are financially independent for livelihood, unlike the females who were fully dependent on others (49% each in rural and urban areas). Among those elderly who are fully dependent on others for economic reasons, 43 per cent in rural areas and 49 per cent in urban areas have to depend on more than one person to eke out a living, at times as many as nine. In old age, own children are the most reliable and important sources of financial support, both for males (87% in rural areas and 82% in urban areas) and females (79% in rural areas and 64% in urban areas). Self-employed agriculture is the usual activity for the elderly (54% male and 36% female) in rural areas, whereas self-employment in non-agricultural activity and domestic chores are the commonly reported activities in old age by males (24%) and females (51%) respectively. The ownership of property and financial assets among the elderly is higher for males than for females, though such female-male disparity is lower in urban areas (0.951 and 0.821) than in rural areas (0.712 and 0.777) of the state. The same pattern is also observed with regard to management of property and financial assets in the state. In the social sphere, the elderly make significant contribution. Irrespective of sex, they are overwhelmingly involved in activities and participate fully in social and religious matters and participate in the household chores. The participation rates for aged persons being as high as 85 per cent in social matters, 89 per cent in religious matters, and 81 per cent in household chores in rural areas, and 95 per cent, 98 per cent and 88 per cent household respectively in urban areas.

Morbidity figures indicate that during old age, women tend to report more ailments than men, and those residing in towns and cities more than those living in villages. Reported health problems are broadly similar between the sexes in old age. Men mostly report problem of joints, followed by cough, high/low blood pressure, urinary problem and heart disease, and women chiefly complain of problems in the joints, high/low blood pressure, cough and heart disease in Himachal Pradesh when they cross the age of 60. Besides these, old men mostly report visual, hearing and locomotor disabilities and old women visual, hearing, locomotor and amnesia or senility disabilities.

Implications of Ageing

Rise in the proportion of the elderly in the scale observed and expected in Himachal Pradesh, has multifaceted consequences that need to be addressed seriously. These broadly relate to continuing social, economic, cultural, technological and health transformations in the society. Specifically, these implications can be elaborated as changes in marital status, newer living arrangements, widespread age and gender discrimination, ongoing epidemiological transition, frequent loneliness and depression, impairment of functional status leading to disability, lowering of socio-economic status, decline in family support, non-availability of social security, lack of care-giving, vulnerability to natural disasters, restructuring of economy, etc. One such implication in financial terms relates to the burden of pension and retirement benefits. The committed expenditure of the state on wages and pension and retirement benefits grew in

Himachal Pradesh from Rs. 118.4 crore in 1995-96 to 494.9 crore in 2002-03 (Budget estimate). There is need for more research and documentation in these areas for effective intervention.

Need for Suitable Measures

At the national level, the *National Policy on Older Persons* (NPOP), announced in 1999, recommends a series of steps that help to deal with issues related to ageing. Similarly, the Action Plan outlined in the *National Population Policy 2000* emphasises the need for greater care for older persons. In Himachal Pradesh, there is need to assess the progress that has been made till date under NPOP and encourage continuing support to the elderly at various levels. For instance, the Social Old Age Pension Scheme (for social security to helpless older persons aged 60 and above) and National Old Age Pension Scheme (social security to persons above 65 years of age) are two direct interventions aimed at restoring the financial stability of individuals with an aid of Rs. 200 per month to deserving cases. Need for 'Old Age Homes' and 'Day Care Centres' for the aged in Himachal Pradesh are also to be assessed in the state. Besides these schemes, the Department of Welfare for Social, Women and Scheduled Castes and Scheduled Tribes also has a number of other programmes in tandem that can indirectly help the aged in the state. It is essential to take a fresh look at these programmes.

For the welfare of individuals during their twilight days, some complementary measures are needed. These include motivation of individuals to make provision for their own as well as their spouse's old age, and other old family members; ensuring primacy of non-institutional care; added protection for vulnerable elderly such as widows, frail, handicapped, abused and destitute; promotion of geriatric health care and services, monitoring, evaluation and upgradation of services for the elderly; fostering inter-sectoral partnership and spread of awareness for the elderly. Involvement of the district administration, local self-government, NGOs and *Panchayati Raj* institutions and self-help groups in devising integrated programmes, also need to be initiated and examined. The actions for a regime of productive ageing must move beyond progress in the establishment of old age homes to a broad system of social security, which incorporate equity concerns for caste, gender, resources and other disadvantages. Such an attempt will make the current and future initiatives and measures more meaningful and relevant to the needs and welfare of the aged.

While dealing with ageing in Himachal Pradesh, lessons have to be drawn from other ageing societies, so that the mistakes of treating the problem primarily as an issue of health care and economic empowerment, is repeated in policy planning for the elderly. In addition to these two aspects, the social and emotional dimension of ageing must be addressed, if its onslaught is to be effectively dealt with. For a regime of 'productive ageing', foundations for a new philosophy of ageing is essential, where older persons are active contributors to society rather than mere consumers.

Civil Registration

Civil Registration System (CRS) is a continuous, permanent and compulsory recording of occurrences and characteristics of vital events (birth, death, marriage, separation, pregnancy, etc.) as defined in and provided through decree or regulation in accordance with the legal requirements of the country. Registration of vital events in any population is of paramount importance for the individual and the state. With the state increasingly assuming a greater role in the life of an individual, the need for registration of such events is progressively felt for legal, protective, administrative and statistical uses. Admission to the school, exercise of voting rights, ownership and transfer of property, insurance entitlements, social security benefit, employment provisions, emigration, foreign visits, etc. are few of such uses. An efficient registration system is an asset in micro-planning for the health sector, particularly in serving the underserved population groups. For example, registration of pregnancies and births can boost the immunisation impact. In view of this, the *National Population Policy 2000* stresses the need to achieve 100 per cent registration of births, deaths, marriages and pregnancies in the country by 2010.

Registration of Births and Deaths Act 1969, which enables the Central Government to regulate registration and compilation of vital statistics in the country so as to ensure uniformity and comparability, leaving enough scope to the states to develop efficient system of registration suited to regional conditions and events, was implemented in the state on 1st April 1978. Himachal Pradesh Births and Deaths Registration Rules 2003 also extend the provisions of this Act. Currently, the births and deaths occurring anywhere in the state are required to be registered within 21 days of the events taking place at the usual residence. If events are not registered within this stipulated period, late registration can be allowed with payment of a late fee and following a predefined procedure. Besides registering births and deaths, information is also collected on some key social and economic aspects in the specified form. There are 3,037 rural and 57 urban registration units in the state. The Director of Health Services in the state is the Chief Registrar (Births and Deaths). The Chief Medical Officer and District Health Officer of the district are his subordinates as District Registrar (Births and Deaths) and Additional District Registrar (Births and Deaths), respectively.

Himachal Pradesh has relatively a better civil registration system as compared to other states in India. Considerable improvement in the CRS seems to have been achieved during late 1990s in spite of the constraints of remoteness of villages in the state. Though nearly 100 per cent registration of births is claimed in the state, some would urge independent verification of reported efficiency (Table 5.20). Vital statistics, as recorded in the CRS, are regularly published and available for the lower administrative units such as the developmental blocks and *Panchayats*. This can largely be attributed to initiatives that the state has adopted in making registration 'People centred'. *Panchayats* in the rural areas are assigned the tasks of registration. Regular campaigns are conducted all over the state to sensitise the public on the importance of such registration and educational materials are widely distributed to educate the public. The campaigns launched by the Department of Health and Family Welfare have the patronage at the highest level in the state and leading public dignitaries, including the Chief Minister and other Ministers, often appeal to the public on importance of registration. Regular orientation courses are also conducted for the 'Local Registrars' for training on the subject. A state-level 'Coordination Committee' under the chairmanship of Secretary to Government (Health and Family Welfare) is also constituted to look into the reported shortcomings of the CRS.

In spite of the strides that Himachal Pradesh has made in streamlining the CRS, there are some areas that need greater attention. For example, registration deaths are lower than the registration of births. Particularly, the deaths during neonatal period are a matter of concern as they are not registered. Such under-reporting of deaths

TABLE 5.20

Efficiency of the CRS, Himachal Pradesh (1991-2001)

Year	*CBR*		*CDR*		*Level of Efficiency of the CRS*	
	CRS	*SRS*	*CRS*	*SRS*	*CBR*	*CDR*
1991	13.2	28.5	2.9	8.9	47.1	33.3
1992	14.7	28.1	3.3	8.8	52.8	37.4
1993	13.8	26.7	3.3	8.6	51.3	37.8
1994	15.1	26.3	3.7	8.6	57.9	42.5
1995	17.6	25.2	4.2	8.7	70.8	49.6
1996	19.6	23.0	4.9	8.0	85.4	61.0
1997	20.2	22.6	5.0	8.1	89.3	61.8
1998	19.8	22.6	5.1	7.7	87.7	66.3
1999	20.4	23.8	5.3	7.3	86.6	72.7
2000	22.9	22.1	5.4	7.2	94.7	74.8
2001	21.8	21.2	5.7	7.1	98.9	79.4

Source: 1. *Civil Registration System* (CRS), *Annual Report 2002*, Chief Registrar of Births and Deaths and Director of Heath Services, Himachal Pradesh.

2. Statistical Report (different issues) and *SRS Bulletin*, April 2003, Registrar General, India.

FIGURE 5.9

CBR as Reported by CRS and SRS, Himachal Pradesh (1991-2001)

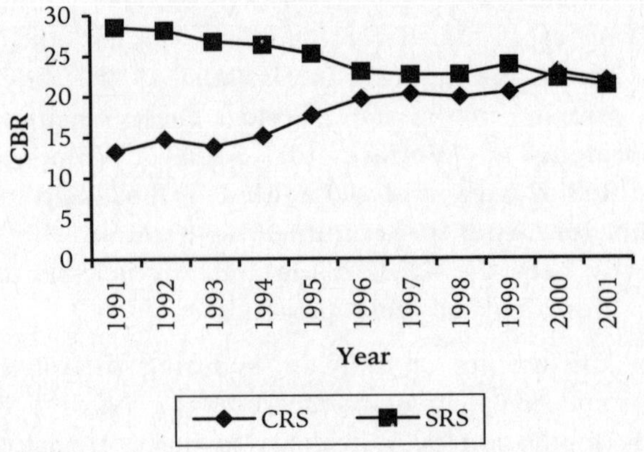

FIGURE 5.10

CDR as Reported by CRS and SRS, Himachal Pradesh (1991-2001)

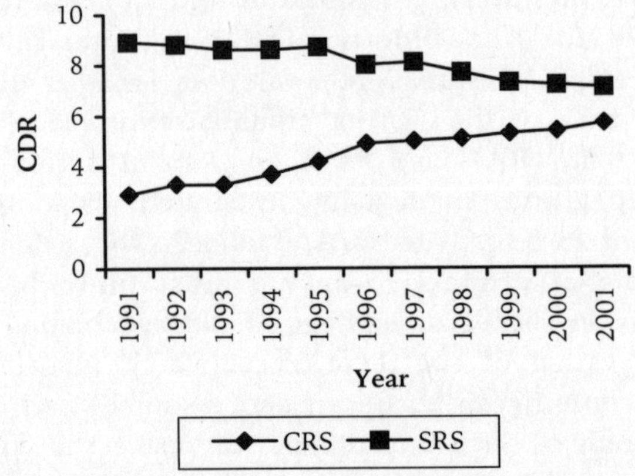

Source: *Civil Registration System* (CRS), *Annual Report 2002*, Chief Registrar of Births and Deaths and Director of Heath Services, Himachal Pradesh.

needs to be corrected by policy measures, and if need be through local and temporary incentives. Regional variations in the registration of demographic events also merits extra inputs and the districts and blocks consistently showing relatively poor performance be closely monitored. Awareness needs to be increased for registering the marriages. Though in villages and towns the marriages are registered with the same authority as births and deaths, yet the marriage statistics are forwarded to the Department of Social Welfare and not to the Department of Health and Family Welfare. Not much is known about the marriage registration, as the data on marriage statistics are neither readily available nor published by the Department of Social Welfare. Some argue that marriages are widely registered because of the need to obtain the ration cards, while many attribute poor registration of marriages to selective necessity, namely the emigration or marriage against the wishes of parents. More training and monitoring camps need to be organised in far-off areas. Uninterrupted supply of forms and other stationeries to local units required for record keeping also need to be addressed. There is a need to educate the migrant groups more. Moreover, greater functional coordination between the Joint Registrar General, local representative of Registrar General, India and Chief Registrar (Births and Deaths) is desired for meaningfully training the concerned staff and collecting, utilising and disseminating the data on vital statistics. This is more relevant in the context of long-term goal of replacing the Sample Registration System (SRS) with the Civil Registration System (CRS). Involvement of the data users at some stage may also add to the benefits of gathering information on births and deaths. There needs to be micro-filming of old records for preservation or computer storage of early registration figures in those units, which have data before and immediately after independence for protection for better understanding of historical demography in the state. Measures to protect such historical data from hazards like fire, etc, are also recommended.

Demographic Challenges and Opportunities: Perspectives For Future

Himachal Pradesh has done exceedingly well in expanding basic amenities and infrastructure. Attempts at further economic and social development must also include focus on demographic dynamics. The demographic challenges the state faces today are manifold and steps are needed to address these concerns. Demographic goals may be easily articulated, quantified and enunciated in policy documents, but translating them into reality is difficult and time-enduring. This is why demographic programmes have long gestation periods before yielding results. Anchored strongly in the economic and social conditions of the people, the fate of human resources in the state is going to be tied to progress in other areas. Bringing about desired behaviourial changes in the target population and influencing demographic development is complex and profoundly influenced by the strategies of economic development and overall improvement in living standards. Moreover, unlike other areas, the externalities are crucial to demographic attainments and there is a great deal of interdependence between population dynamics in the state and events outside, in-migration being a case in point.

The contours of population planning in Himachal Pradesh must go beyond the elementary goals set in the National Population Policy or outlined in *Health Vision 2020*. Demographic priorities need to go beyond the domain of health and cover grounds that are central to larger issues of human development. Some of the direct and foreseeable demographic challenges that Himachal faces today can be listed as attainment of replacement level of fertility, elimination of early-age marriage and child-bearing, investment in health care of the new-born through low cost ventures to further reduce infant mortality including neonatal deaths, getting rid of sex-selection and practice of female foeticide, balancing a skewed sex ratio that is highly masculine among children, eliminating extensive son-preference, raising low hospital delivery rates, curtailing the birth of low-weight babies, bringing down undesirable maternal deaths, changing the unfavourable demographic regime among socially and economically weaker sections, mainstreaming the marginal migrants groups, meeting the unmet need for contraception, promoting men's participation in family planning, removal of demographic disparity among the districts and preparations for dealing with an ageing population. In an ecologically-sensitive state like Himachal Pradesh, population and development linkages envelop environmental concerns that need to be addressed satisfactorily. At one level, these thematic areas must be at the core of a series of actions by the state, whereas at the other, some critical areas should be simultaneously considered to make the thematic outcomes successful.

Increasing private sector participation to supplement government's effort in the health sector is a daunting task in view of low levels of urbanisation and extensive spread of rural population over 20,000 villages in a difficult terrain. This also has implications for the achievement of demographic goals in the state. In rural areas, General Hospitals, Civil Dispensaries, Community Health Centres, Primary Health Centres, and Sub-Centres are not fully equipped to respond to people's needs, which are mounting due to better literacy and awareness. These centres are known to have constraints that prevent optimum utilisation of their services. Since family planning is largely seen as a government's initiative and implemented mainly through the health department, public health sector performance is critical to the success of the family planning programme.

Another area, which merits attention, is the need for greater public participation. Broad-basing community participation implies not only greater involvement in programme-implementation but in policy formulation as well. Often schemes fall short because they do not reflect the needs and concerns of the people with changing times. With the 73rd and 74th Constitutional Amendments providing a framework for grassroots devolution and local participation, efforts to stabilise population can only succeed if the functions, functionaries and funds are used in tune with expectations of the public at all levels. Related with this is the identification of fringe and vulnerable groups and ensuring that their legitimate interests are well represented in programme formulation and implementation. Scheduled Caste and Scheduled Tribe population, migrant groups, landless households, etc., constitute such marginalised sections whose demographic profiles may need more attention. Creating adequate opportunities for these groups, and safeguarding their interests is another major task in the future for achieving demographic goals. The current programme interventions do not address gender disparities adequately. Much of the success in population and related programmes depends on how the issues that confront women and children are reflected in the policy and programme priorities. Since women are at the centre of demographic change, creating a mechanism that is sensitised towards their position in society, will also determine the success of initiatives by the government.

Reliable, long-term and cross-sectional data, aid demographic assessments and make policy formulations and programme interventions accurate as well as focused. In Himachal, there is need to encourage indigenous data generation, particularly in the course of programme intervention in areas such as birth statistics, neonatal mortality, birth weights, termination of pregnancies, etc. Upgradation of the registration system at the village level, side by side with overhauling present data collection, compilation, management and use-systems, are called for, as the current information management system is unable to keep pace with the rapid and ongoing changes in the society. Useful data, thematically oriented and geared to shifting priorities, have to be regularly collected and whatever is collected has to be rigorously tested, systematically compiled, and made accessible to the public through regular and priced publications. The focus on segregation at various levels is lacking, with maintenance of records in most of the health institutions deficient and unreliable. Utility of data management is yet to be fully understood and the meagre networking with nodal centres yields fewer inputs to field staff. There is need to examine the constraints and strong support to such endeavor, in terms of allocation of funds, qualified personnel and infrastructure.

Can the superiority of Himachal Pradesh in social development be retained for long, without taking a view of economic costs of such development? Spending on social development programmes in the state, it is often argued, have added to its current financial problems. Since sufficient enterprise is not available locally in Himachal Pradesh, and outside entrepreneurship is very nearly discouraged, the need is to augment the speed of, rather than turning, the demographic tide in Himachal Pradesh. This is possible, with the current higher ranking in human development being its great asset. Additionally, the state has some inherent healthy features that are the source of enormous advantage in population planning and weigh heavily in favour of attempts to define and shape demographic attributes. Relatively small population, low incidence of poverty, high accessibility and use of banking services, good ownership of motor vehicles for mobility and telephones for outside communication, wider access to basic amenities in terms of provision of tap water, larger share of households living in permanent houses and lower share of one-room dwelling units, modernisation of households with electricity as the source of lighting and separate kitchens and LPG use, less rural-and-urban gap in the provision of health services, household prosperity, regular media exposure through highly diffused television and radio possession, greater female literacy and participation in labour-force, greater community participation in public life, better women empowerment, etc., act as force-multipliers in intervention activities and hold out great promise for any effort to change the population profile.

References

Ahluwalia, M.S. (2000), "Economic Performance of States in Post Reform Period", *Economic and Political Weekly*, XXXV(19), pp. 1637-1648.

Arnold, Fred, Sunita Kishor and T.K. Roy (2002), "Sex Selective Abortions in India", *Population and Development Review*, 28(4).

Department of Women and Child Development, Government of India and United Nations Children's Fund, India (2001), *Multiple Indicator Cluster Survey (MICS 2000): India Summary Report*, New Delhi.

Directorate of Economics and Statistics, *Statistical Outline of Himachal Pradesh 2000-2001*, Government of Himachal Pradesh, Shimla.

Directorate of Health and Family Welfare, *Health Vision 2000*, Government of Himachal Pradesh, Shimla.

Directorate of Health and Family Welfare, *Family Welfare Programme Year Book 1999-2000*, Demographic and Evaluation Cell, Government of Himachal Pradesh, Shimla.

Dodd, Nina S. and Jagmeet Madan (1993), "Iodine Status in Pregnancy", *Asia Pacific Journal of Clinical Nutrition*, No. 2, 119-123.

Fukuda-Parr, Sakiko and A.K. Shiv Kumar (2003), *Readings in Human Development: Concepts, Measures and Policies for a Development Paradigm*, Oxford University Press, New Delhi

Government of India, *National Population Policy 2000*, New Delhi.

International Institute for Population Sciences (1995), *National Family Health Survey, India 1992-93*, Bombay.

International Institute for Population Sciences, Mumbai and ORC Macro, Maryland (2000), *National Family Health Survey 2, India* 1998-99: India.

————. (2002), *National Family Health Survey 2, India 1998-99*: Himachal Pradesh.

James, K.S., Ian Aitken and S.V. Subramanian (2000), "Neonatal Mortality in India: Emerging Paradoxes", *Working Paper Series*, 10(13) Harvard Center for Population and Development Studies.

Jones, Gavin W. (1992), "Population and Human Resource Development", *Asia–Pacific Population Journal*, 7(2), pp. 23-48.

Klassen, Stephan (1994), "Missing Women Reconsidered", *World Development*, 22(7), pp. 1061-1071.

Krishnaji, N. (2001), *India's Sex Ratio Conundrum*, (ed.), Rainbow Publishers, New Delhi.

————. (2002), 'Working Mothers, Poverty and Child Loss' in *Thinking Social Science in India: Essays in Honour of Alice Thorner*, (ed.), Patel Sujata, Jasodhara Bagchi, Krishna Raj, Sage Publications, New Delhi, pp. 187-191.

La Croix, Sumner J., Andrew Mason and Shigeyuki Abe (2003), "Population and Globalisation", *Asia Pacific Population and Policy*, No 64, Hawaii.

Miller, B.D. (1981), *The Endangered Sex: Neglect of Female Children in Rural North India*, Ithaca, New York.

Nanda, A.K. (2000), "Transferring Successful Programme Experience from Bangladesh: Building Sustainability Through Better Management", *Base Line Report for Management Sciences for Health (MSH)*, Centre for Research in Rural and Industrial Development (CRRID), Chandigarh

Natarajan, D. (1972), "The Change in Sex Ratio", *A Census Centenary Monograph, Number 6*, Office of the Registrar General, India, New Delhi.

National Commission on Population (2001), *District-wise Social, Economic and Demographic Indicators*, Government of India, New Delhi.

National Council of Applied Economic Research (2003), *North India Human Development Report*, Oxford University Press: New Delhi.

National Institute of Rural Development (NIRD) (1999), *India Rural Development Report*, Hyderabad.

Pandey, Arvind, Minaja Kim Choe, Norman Y. Luther, Damodar Sahu and Jagdish Chand (1998), "Infant and Mortality in India", *National Family Health Survey Subject Reports*, No. 11. International Institute for Population Sciences, Mumbai and East-West Centre Programme on Population, Hawaii.

Population Research Centre, Himachal Pradesh University, Shimla and International Institute of Population Sciences, Mumbai (1995), *National Family Health Survey: MCH and Family Planning, Himachal Pradesh 1993*.

Planning Commission (1952), *First Five Year Plan*, pp. 489-524, Government of India, New Delhi.

————. (2001), *Approach Paper to the Tenth Five Year Plan (2002-2007)*, p. 6, Government of India, New Delhi.

————. (2003), *Five Year Plan (2002-2007): Sectoral Policies and Programmes, Volume III*, Government of India, New Delhi.

Premi, M.K. (1991), *India's Population: Heading Towards A Billion—An Analysis of 1991 Provisional Results*, B.R. Publishing Corporation, New Delhi.

Retherford, D. and T.K. Roy (2003), "Factors Affecting Sex Selective Abortion in India and 17 Major States", *National Family Health Survey Subject Reports* Number 21, Internal Institute for Population Sciences, Mumbai and East-west Programme on Population, Hawaii.

Registrar General, India (1996), *Population Projections for India and States (1996-2016)*, Census of India 1991, New Delhi.

————. (2000), *Survey of Causes of Death (Rural), India, Annual Report 1997*, Series-3, New Delhi.

————. *Sample Registration System: Statistical Report*, various volumes, New Delhi.

————. *Birth Interval Differentials in India 1984*, Vital Statistics Division, New Delhi.

Sharma, Satish K. and Niranjana (2001), *Social Structure and Fertility Behaviour*, Rawat Publications, Jaipur.

Visaria, P. (1971), "The Sex Ratio of the Population of India", *Monograph No 10, Census of India 1961*, Office of Registrar General, New Delhi.

Chapter 6

Fiscal and Financial Management

Macro Economic Glimpse of Himachal Pradesh

Cradled in the lap of the snow-clad Himalayas, Himachal Pradesh has been designated 'a special category state'. This categorisation, apart from its financial implication, is well deserved in more ways than one. The diversity of its topography and climate and flora and fauna, the four major river basins and traditional methods of water harvesting and use, scattered habitats in the hills, low density of population, rich heritage of arts and crafts, extensive forest coverage and low availability of land for cultivation, all add up to give Himachal Pradesh a distinctive character of its own. These features account for both its strength and weakness. These, in turn, determine its specific development perspective and the resources required for its realisation. This is the fundamental challenge of fiscal and financial management of Himachal Pradesh.

The vast majority of the people of this state live in villages and agriculture is their main occupation. Along with horticulture, it constitutes the base of the economy of Himachal Pradesh. Protecting the interests of lakhs of its farmers, mostly small and marginal, is a major concern of the state. A considerable portion of the agricultural land is under horticulture. There is low level of irrigation and use of power in agriculture, as most of it is rain-fed. Milk production and animal husbandry provide additional cash support to the farmers. Animal husbandry is particularly important as a source of sustainable employment to the hill folk at their very doorsteps. Agriculture contributes about 22.5 per cent of the State GDP.

Small scale industry dominates the industrial sector which contributes 32 per cent of the GDP. The forest wealth of Himachal has yet to be properly utilised, particularly in the areas of medicines and raw materials for the aromatic industry. Tourism is another area of immense potential, demanding development of new destinations and suitable infrastructure, particularly in terms of transport and hotels. Himachal is rightly known as the hydro-power state. This is another area of development and a major potential source of revenue.

Apart from financial resources, Himachal faces the major challenge of converting its people into human resource, which can effectively contribute to the development of the state, and in the process open up new avenues of employment. To achieve this, the major thrust has to be on education and health care. Himachal has the advantage of high literacy, even among women. The need is to raise the level of education to the kind of technical expertise required by industries. Greater empowerment of the local bodies and the Panchayati Raj Institution, particularly through devolution of financial power, has to be another thrust area to ensure people's participation in the development process.

People's participation is one of the instruments to meet the specific challenges facing Himachal's development and fiscal and financial management is the other. Although, as a special category state, it has assured financial support from the Central Government, its magnitude is now dependent on the state's own efforts to put its domestic housekeeping in order.

The Government of Himachal Pradesh is conscious of the precarious financial situation of the state *inter alia* the debt stock, which is about Rs 12,000 crore. The government will have to take effective steps to reduce unproductive expenditure, generate new resources, impose financial discipline, accelerate development through promotion of tourism and horticulture and enhance the income of the state through sale of hydro

TABLE 6.1

Overall Financial Position of the State

(Rs. in crore)

Item	*1991-92*	*1995-96*	*1996-97*	*1997-98*	*1998-99*	*1999-00*	*2000-01*	*2001-02*	*2002-03 (RE)*	*2003-04 (BE)*
Total Revenue Receipts	992.42	1754.02	1992.02	2105.45	2311.93	3715.28	3045.57	3615.78	3880.72	4031.97
a) State's Own Resources	257.86	457.98	544.99	624.87	722.48	1627.62	863.24	1089.04	1159.46	1248.68
b) Central Transfers	635.08	1244.58	1391.30	1346.10	1429.19	1897.92	1946.12	2399.07	2507.61	2654.46
c) CSS Grants	99.48	51.46	55.73	134.48	160.26	189.74	236.21	227.67	213.65	128.83
Total Revenue Expenditure	982.56	1904.35	2146.88	2699.14	3334.26	3821.54	4328.75	4576.26	5624.49	5820.24
NET	9.86	-150.33	-154.86	-593.69	-1022.33	-106.26	-1283.18	-860.46	-1743.77	-1788.27
Total Capital Receipts	177.10	411.26	558.12	1034.32	1785.99	1782.99	1421.22	1672.58	2042.81	1835.86
Total Capital Expenditure	260.76	463.43	515.52	773.37	668.49	614.14	588.98	680.15	629.00	742.67
NET	-83.66	-52.17	42.60	260.95	1117.50	1168.85	832.24	992.43	1413.81	1093.19
Total Rev & Capital (NET)	-73.80	-202.50	-112.26	-332.74	95.17	1062.59	-450.94	131.95	-329.96	-695.08

Source: Finance Commission's Documents.

power, for which power projects have to be executed expeditiously. The latest budget does indicate some bold steps in this direction.

Financial Position of Himachal Pradesh

Himachal Pradesh a 'special category state' ever since it was conferred statehood in 1971, it has been dependent for financial viability on transfers from the Government of India. The overall financial position of the state from 1991-92 to 2003-04 (BE) is shown in Table 6.1.

The total revenue receipt (state's own revenue, central transfers and grants) increased about four times from Rs. 992.42 crore in 1991-92 to Rs. 4031.97 crore in 2003-04 (BE).

The corresponding revenue expenditure in 2003-04 (BE) increased nearly six times to Rs.5820.24 crore, leaving a deficit of Rs. 1788.27 crore on revenue account. The growth of revenue expenditure has been faster than the growth in revenue receipts.

The total capital receipt increased from Rs. 177.10 crore in 1991-92 to Rs. 1835.86 crore in 2003-04 (BE). The projected capital expenditure in 2003-04 is Rs. 742.67 crore, leaving a surplus of Rs. 1093.19 crore on the capital account. A net revenue and capital deficit of Rs. 695.08 crore is estimated in 2003-04.

Capital receipts over capital expenditure have shown a net surplus from 1996-97 (Rs. 42.6 crore) rising to Rs. 1093 crore in 2003-04 (BE). The capital receipts include market borrowings and negotiated loans. Normally, capital receipts are utilised to meet capital expenditure for the creation of assets and for development purposes. However, the surplus of capital receipts over the capital expenditure has been used to meet revenue deficits. The capital receipts (borrowings), have been utilised to meet the revenue deficit on committed liabilities.

Revenue Fiscal Deficit (1990-91 to 2003-04)

Despite the status of a special category state and consequently high central transfers, the financial picture of the state depicts a disturbing trend of revenue and fiscal deficit during the period 1990-91 to 2003-04 (BE) as shown in Table 6.2. The revenue balance of the state has been consistently in deficit.

TABLE 6.2

Revenue and Fiscal Deficit (1990-91 to 2003-04)

(Rs. in crore)

	(In Rupees Crore)			*(As % of GSDP)*	
Years	*Revenue Deficit (+/-)*	*Fiscal Deficit (-)*	*Gross State Domestic Product (GSDP)*	*Revenue Surplus/ Deficit (+/-)*	*Fiscal Deficit (-)*
1990-91	-94.84	-338.61	2815	-3.26	-12.03
1991-92	9.86	-99.21	3317	0.30	-2.99
1992-93	-93.08	-361.95	3824	-2.43	-9.47
1993-94	113.63	-240.90	4782	2.38	-5.04
1994-95	-307.92	-696.32	5825	-5.29	-11.95
1995-96	-150.33	-587.87	6698	-2.24	-8.78
1996-97	-154.86	-654.36	7755	-2.00	-8.44
1997-98	-593.69	-1348.79	8837	-6.72	-15.26
1998-99	-1,022.33	-1661.53	10696	- 9.56	-15.53
1999-00	-106.26	- 189.63	12229	-0.87	- 1.55
2000-01	-1,283.17	-1844.79	13329	- 9.63	-13.84
2001-02	-860.46	-1511.34	14717	-5.85	-10.27
2002-03 (RE)	-1,743.76	-2346.18	16041.8	-10.87	-14.63
2003-04 (BE)	-1,788.27	-2502.02	17806.46	-10.04	-14.05

Source: Finance Commission's Documents.

TABLE 6.3

Debt of the State

(Rs. in crore)

Years	*Small Savings*	*Plan Loans*	*CSS including NCDC*	*Market Borrowings*	*Negotiated Loans*	*GPF/GIS*	*Non-SLR Loans (PSUs)*	*Total*	*Principal Repayment*	*Cumulative Total*
1993-94	75.61	33.57	5.90	23.99	1.84	116.53	0	257.44	62.51	1870.14
1994-95	266.04	33.21	9.20	34.44	1.14	118.03	219.08	681.14	63.41	2487.87
1995-96	134.20	47.72	10.22	40.01	7.57	145.65	84.38	469.75	44.99	2912.63
1996-97	276.09	54.12	15.10	44.00	23.27	129.52	304.34	846.44	52.90	3706.17
1997-98	648.88	64.53	14.13	50.88	41.04	196.59	305.30	1321.35	60.60	4966.92
1998-99	279.29	79.94	21.00	146.02	197.53	270.12	0	993.90	75.62	5885.20
1999-00	68.88	103.99	25.49	229.17	420.31	278.33	767.20	1893.37	95.34	7683.23
2000-01	110.64	104.93	9.21	233.11	422.32	255.20	567.00	1702.41	130.48	9255.16
2001-02	294.15	104.52	12.46	376.21	222.59	206.97	391.00	1607.90	413.08	10449.98
2002-03 (RE)	350.00	139.15	3.90	440.09	331.86	258.98	779.31	2303.29	308.82	12444.45
2003-04 (BE)	324.10	144.53	6.70	340.00	342.00	300.00	1084.00	2541.33	754.94	14230.84

Source: Finance Commission's Documents.

The revenue deficit reached its peak of -10.87 per cent of GSDP in 2002-03(RE) and the fiscal deficit reached an alarming figure of –15.53 per cent of the GSDP in 1998-99. The increasing deficit from 1998 onwards is attributed to the impact of revision of pay and pensions, regularisation of a large number of daily wage workers and higher interest burden on expensive borrowings.

The chronic revenue deficit and fiscal deficit continue to be high at 10.04 per cent and 14.05 per cent of GSDP in the budget estimates of 2003-04. This is unsustainable and requires strategic fiscal restructuring of tax and non-tax base for attracting non-budgetary resources from national and international financial institutions for the development of the state.

Debt of the State

The debt of the state increased to Rs.14230.84 crore in 2003-04 compared to Rs. 12444.45 crore in 2002-03. The growth of the debt of the state from 1993-94 to 2003-04 (BE) is given in Table 6.3.

Interest Expenditure (1991-92 to 2003-04)

The committed expenditure on interest payment, has increased from Rs. 148 crore in 1991-92 to Rs. 1876 crore in 2003-04 (BE). The interest payment as percentage of the state revenue receipts has steadily increased as shown in Table 6.4.

Tax and Non-tax Revenue

Tax and non-tax and total tax revenue as the percentage of GSDP is shown in Table 6.5.

TABLE 6.4

Interest Expenditure

Years	*Rupees in Crore*		
	Interest Payments	*Revenue Receipts*	*Interest as a Proportion of Revenue Receipts (%)*
1991-92	147.85	992.42	14.90
1992-93	177.12	1052.49	16.83
1993-94	209.65	1465.13	14.31
1994-95	222.60	1306.36	17.04
1995-96	285.25	1754.02	16.26
1996-97	312.98	1992.02	15.71
1997-98	372.07	2105.45	17.67
1998-99	498.02	2311.93	21.54
1999-00	597.34	3715.28	16.08
2000-01	798.29	3045.58	26.21
2001-02	1014.59	3715.80	28.03
2002-03 (RE)	1669.20	3880.73	43.01
2003-04 (BE)	1875.74	4031.97	46.52

Source: Financial Documents of Himachal Pradesh 2002-03.

The tax revenue of the state increased from Rs.192.44 crore in 1991-92 to Rs. 1007.60 crore in 2003-04. Table 6.5 shows the growth of tax, non-tax and total revenue from 1991-92 to 2003-04(BE).

Tax and Non-tax Revenue as Percentage of GSDP

Table 6.6 shows the break-up of tax revenue and non-tax revenue of HP as percentage of its GDP and comparison with the corresponding figures of Punjab and Haryana.

TABLE 6.5

Tax and Non-tax Revenue

(Rs. in crore)

Years	*Tax Revenue*	*Non-tax Revenue*	*Total*	*As % of GSDP*
1991-92	192.44	65.42	257.86	7.77
1992-93	221.67	64.38	286.05	7.48
1993-94	255.74	113.06	368.80	7.71
1994-95	299.45	103.57	403.02	6.92
1995-96	341.52	116.46	457.98	6.84
1996-97	412.11	132.88	544.99	7.03
1997-98	476.16	148.71	624.87	7.07
1998-99	572.03	150.45	722.48	6.75
1999-00	620.26	1007.36	1627.62	13.31
2000-01	728.41	134.83	863.24	6.48
2001-02	915.56	173.48	1089.04	7.40
2002-03 (RE)	921.99	237.48	1159.47	7.23
2003-04 (BE)	1007.60	241.07	1248.67	7.01

Source: Finance Commission's Documents.

TABLE 6.6

Tax and Non-tax Revenue as Percentage of GSDP

(Rs. in crore)

	Tax Revenue			*Non-tax Revenue*		
States	*1999-00*	*2000-01*	*2001-02*	*1999-00*	*2000-01*	*2001-02*
Punjab	7.40	8.44	8.38	5.29	7.22	6.89
Haryana	8.27	8.51	9.07	3.52	3.50	3.64
Himachal Pradesh	**5.07**	**5.46**	**6.22**	**8.24**	**1.01**	**1.18**

Source: Planning Department.

Table 6.6 brings out the fact that the tax effort of Himachal Pradesh, in respect of both tax revenue and non-tax revenue is lower than that of Punjab and Haryana. Himachal Pradesh, as one of the high per capita income states, has the potential to mobilise higher tax revenue and particularly non-tax revenue as the percentage of its GSDP.

Committed Expenditure on Major Items

The committed expenditure of the state is 123.54 per cent of its revenue receipts in 2003-04 (BE). It comprises salaries, pensions, grants in aid and interest payment. The percentage of committed expenditure has increased from 116.10 per cent in 2002-03 to 123.54 per cent in 2003-04 (BE). Table 6.7 shows the committed expenditure and Revenue Receipt and percentage of committed expenditure to Revenue Receipt.

The present pension scheme for government employees puts an open-ended financial burden on the consolidated fund of the state. An expert group set up by the Government of India on reducing the financial burden on account of pensions has submitted its report. A hybrid scheme which combines contributions from the employees and the state government on a matching basis assuring the employees of defined benefits as pension has been formulated. A pension scheme based on these parameters could reduce the mounting burden on the consolidated fund of the state and release funds for development.

Himachal Pradesh Government Employees

The expenditure on salaries has been increasing consistently. The highest recruitment was witnessed in 1999, which in a single year was 5.66 per cent. This aggravated the precarious financial position of the state and led to borrowings at uneconomical rates of interest. The increase in expenditure on the employees in this year was due to the liberal policy of regularising daily wage workers after eight years of service.

TABLE 6.7

Committed Expenditure on Major Items

(Rs. in crore)

Item	*1995-96*	*1996-97*	*1997-98*	*1998-99*	*1999-00*	*2000-01*	*2001-02*	*2002-03 (RE)*	*2003-04 (BE)*
Salaries and Wages	769.10	879.14	1053.00	1412.00	1501.70	1683.00	1877.00	1987.05	2275.71
Pensions and Retirement Benefits	103.20	126.50	165.50	222.40	445.11	391.20	442.80	570.00	580.00
Grants-in-aid	214.00	226.20	283.70	222.00	182.01	292.20	201.60	279.27	249.58
Interest Payments	285.30	313.00	372.10	498.00	597.34	798.30	1041.00	1669.20	1875.70
Total above	**1372.00**	**1545.00**	**1874.00**	**2354.00**	**2726.20**	**3165.00**	**3562.00**	**4505.52**	**4980.99**
Revenue Receipts	1754.00	1992.00	2105.00	2312.00	3715.30	3046.00	3716.00	3880.73	4031.97
% of Committed Expenditure to Revenue Receipts	78.20	77.55	89.03	101.83	73.38	103.92	95.86	116.10	123.54

Source: Budget Documents of the State.

TABLE 6.8

Himachal Pradesh Government Employees

Years	Regular	Part Time Employees	Work Charged	Daily Paid Workers	Total	Annual Growth Rate
1990	1,11,700	4,217	6,098	58,617	180632	—
1991	1,13,851	4,613	5,434	58,024	181922	0.71
1992	1,14,831	4,866	6,126	65,042	190865	4.92
1993	1,12,717	5,404	6,624	59,570	184315	-3.55
1994	1,13,039	5,426	6,455	60,124	185044	0.39
1995	1,15,493	5,704	12,023	56,725	189945	2.65
1996	1,17,944	5,667	17,716	58,607	199934	5.25
1997	1,20,703	6,308	19,294	56,318	202623	1.34
1998	1,23,626	7,242	21,039	54,983	206890	2.10
1999	1,31,919	8,718	23,778	54,190	218605	5.66
2000	1,36,085	9,000	27,827	52,430	225342	3.08
2001	1,39,882	9,794	31,001	46,455	227152	0.80

Source: Planning Department of the Himachal Pradesh Government.

The wage bill of government employees in 1995-96 increased from Rs.769.10 crore per year to Rs.1566.17 crore in 1999-2000 mainly because of fresh recruitment and implementation of new scales of pay on the pattern of the Punjab Government employees consequent upon the acceptance of the recommendations of the Fourth Central Pay Commission. The yearly increase in number of employees of the Himachal Pradesh Government is shown in Table 6.8.

Revenue from State Taxes

A critical review of different state taxes is important. The taxes falling in the domain of the state are sales tax, state excise duty, tax on vehicles, tax on goods and passengers, stamp duty and estate duty. Table 6.9 gives the details of income from state taxes from 1991-92 to 2003-04 (BE).

Revenue from different state taxes will touch Rs. 1008 crore in 2003-04 as compared to Rs. 192.43 crore in 1991-92. This growth is not adequate. Income from sales tax, excise duty, stamp registration and estate duty, tax on goods and passengers have good potential to grow and a compound growth of 15 per cent should be achieved like other states with high per capita income. An increase in its own revenue income will have a multiplier effect. Besides, it will attract investment from financial institutions for development.

Income from the state's own revenue, transfers and grants from the Government of India is not enough to meet the mounting pressure of revenue expenditure. Public debt has been a convenient means of raising resources and the state continues to rely on borrowings to cover its mounting deficit.

There is consensus among the states on the need to reduce deficit, but so far very few have addressed the problem comprehensively. Most of them are using piecemeal measures to reduce the deficit. The electorate usually finds reduced spending more tolerable than increased taxes. The cuts in expenditure are painful but can be strategically aimed at unpopular programmes. Cutting expenditure has also its limits. Therefore, increasing the tax base remains the option. Although tax increases are politically unpopular, the state government will have to raise its tax rates to cover the cost of social security, education and health-care and also as a way to transfer wealth from the rich to the poor.

TABLE 6.9

Revenue from the State Taxes

(Rs. in crore)

Years	Land Revenue	Stamp and Registration & Estate Duty	Sales Tax	State Excise	Taxes on Vehicles	Taxes on Goods and Passengers	Taxes & Duty on Electricity	Other Taxes & Duties on Commodities & Services	Total
1991-92	0.89	7.98	66.90	66.25	8.78	26.98	2.77	11.88	192.43
1992-93	1.59	9.52	75.20	75.78	9.87	28.63	5.27	15.80	221.66
1993-94	1.00	10.19	93.88	83.52	11.56	35.22	2.11	18.25	255.73
1994-95	1.15	12.00	107.18	94.54	11.17	39.77	9.88	23.75	299.45
1995-96	0.87	13.78	122.83	105.50	12.31	45.80	17.92	22.50	341.51
1996-97	5.95	15.44	146.26	132.46	14.46	65.26	18.64	13.63	412.10
1997-98	1.67	18.77	171.18	159.54	15.83	96.80	7.05	5.32	476.16
1998-99	1.04	21.62	196.56	185.55	17.48	115.11	28.03	6.64	572.03
1999-00	6.47	24.68	233.06	198.70	28.37	104.84	0.20	23.93	620.25
2000-01	3.38	29.22	302.05	209.17	61.04	43.05	27.39	52.60	728.40
2001-02	51.84	34.27	355.08	236.28	132.70	34.26	8.32	62.79	915.54
2002-03 (RE)	4.30	33.57	383.00	273.00	81.98	34.49	37.00	74.65	921.99
2003-04 (BE)	3.81	37.40	448.00	291.00	82.80	32.43	32.16	80.00	1007.60

Source: Statistical Outline of Himachal Pradesh 2000-01 and *Budget in Brief of Himachal Pradesh, 2002-03.*

The financial position of other states of India also deteriorated over the year, particularly after the implementation of the Fourth Pay Commission report in 1997, but the gross fiscal deficit of Himachal Pradesh remained persistently the highest as is clear from Table 6.10.

TABLE 6.10

Gross Fiscal Deficit as a Ratio of NSDP in Ten States

(in per cent)

States	*1990-91*	*1995-96*	*1997-98*	*1998-99*	*1999-00*
Orrisa	6.4	5.8	6.3	9.4	11.4
Rajasthan	3.0	6.3	4.9	8.6	9.1
Uttar Pradesh	6.2	4.3	5.7	7.6	6.7
Punjab	7.4	4.0	5.6	7.4	5.8
Goa	9.4	3.5	3.5	6.6	—
Gujarat	7.4	2.7	4.0	6.3	—
Haryana	3.2	3.8	3.4	5.8	5.1
Kerala	6.6	3.7	5.0	5.3	—
Bihar	7.0	3.9	1.9	4.1	9.7
Himachal Pradesh	**12.03**	**8.78**	**15.26**	**15.53**	**1.55**

Source: State Finances, published by RBI – 2002.

Reforms should broaden the resource base of the state, enhance the tax and non-tax revenue, visibly decrease unproductive and wasteful expenditure, reduce the debt stock of the state and control the spiralling revenue and fiscal deficit.

Planning and Tenth Five Year Plan

A review of the financial resources of the state indicates that non-plan revenue receipts fell short of the non-plan revenue expenditure. This is because of the state's high committed expenditure on salaries, pensions, grants-in-aid, and interest payments. Therefore, the plan was financed by borrowed funds and central assistance from the Planning Commission.

The balance of the current revenue in each year of the Ninth Plan and 2002-2003 has been consistently showing a deficit. Each annual plan of the Ninth Plan has been financed by non-SLR borrowings, institutional borrowings from HUDCO, LIC and NABARD, market borrowings, small savings and central assistance from the Planning Commission. Plan assistance increased from Rs. 546 crore in 1997-98 to Rs. 1251 crore in 2001-2002. Resources for financing the Ninth Plan are shown in Table 6.11.

TABLE 6.11

Financing of Ninth Plan and Estimates of Annual Plan 2002-03

(Rs. in crore at current prices)

Sources of financing	*1997-98 (Actuals)*	*1998-99 (Actuals)*	*1999-00 (Actuals)*	*2000-01 (Actuals)*	*2001-02 (L.E.)*	*2002-03 (Est.)*
1990	1,11,700	4,217	6,098	58,617	180632	—
1991	1,13,851	4,613	5,434	58,024	181922	0.71
State's Own Resources	928	802	678	752	552	668
Balance from Current Revenue	-458	-832	-1044	-969	-935	-1079
Contribution of State PSUs	0	-49	0	0	0	0
Plan Grants under TFC/EFC	33	18	67	30	42	42
Miscellaneous Capital Receipts (net)	-62	-58	-68	-109	-243	-392
Provident Fund	197	270	278	255	254	245
Mobilisation of Small Saving	649	279	69	111	150	158
Gross SLR based Market Borrowings	51	146	229	233	345	355
Negotiated Loans	62	228	447	454	331	320
a) LIC	5	73	315	186	100	110
b) GIC	0	0	0	0	0	0
c) IDBI	0	0	0	0	0	0
d) NABARD	33	44	44	120	100	110
e) REC	21	31	27	30	31	0
Other (specify) HUDCO	3	80	61	118	100	100
Non-SLR Borrowings	305	0	640	567	508	1017
Debentures/Bonds (HPSEB)	85	38	142	180	100	0
Adjustment of Opening Balance	65	762	-82	0	0	0
Central Assistance	546	765	946	968	1168	1234
Aggregate Plan Resource	1474	1567	1624	1720	1720	1900
State Plan Outlay	1474	1567	1624	1720	1720	1900

Source: Plan Documents of Himachal Pradesh Government.

Resources and Plan Performance during Ninth Plan

The actual resource mobilisation and plan performance during the Ninth Plan is shown in Table 6.12.

TABLE 6.12

Resources and Plan Performance During the Ninth Plan

(Rs. in crore)

Years	Resource Mobilisations			Plan Performance in %
	State's Own Resources	Central Assistance	Total	
Annual Plan 1997-98	788.36	546.31	1334.67	106.07
Annual Plan 1998-99	836.67	764.71	1601.38	106.62
Annual Plan 1999-00	664.32	1013.88	1678.20	104.52
Annual Plan 2000-01	752.11	967.89	1720.00	100.00
Annual Plan 2001-02	468.92	1251.08	1720.00	100.00

Source: Plan Documents of Himachal Pradesh Government upto 2002-03.

Table 6.12 indicates the efforts of the state government to mobilise resources more than the original outlay.

Against the approved outlay of Rs. 5700 crore, the revised outlay of the Ninth plan was Rs. 7488 crore. Ultimately the state exceeded the revised outlay and the actual expenditure was Rs. 7896.72 crore.

Growth of Economy in Eighth, Ninth and Tenth Plan

During the Eighth Plan, the national economy grew at a rate of 6.7 per cent and Himachal Pradesh registered a growth rate of 6.3 per cent per annum. Growth in the Ninth Plan at the national level averaged 5.35 per cent and economy of Himachal Pradesh grew at the rate of 6.2 per cent. The National Development Council resolved that the growth target of the Tenth Plan (2002-07) should be 8 per cent per annum. For Himachal Pradesh, the state government has fixed a growth target of 8.9 per cent per annum.

The Council of Ministers of Himachal Pradesh, taking into account a higher growth achieved in the Ninth Plan, has fixed the growth target for Tenth Plan at 8.9 per cent. The additional resources are in sight due to likely sale of free power from the country's largest Hydro Electric Power Project at Nathpa-Jhakri on account of progressive commissioning of its six 250 MW Units. There are ready buyers for this power including neighbouring states of Punjab and Haryana. It will yield additional income from the year 2003-04 onwards, which is likely to reach Rs. 400 crore per year in 2006-07.

The revenue collection from Sales Tax, Excise Duty, Stamp Duty, Motor Vehicle Tax, which has stagnated, should grow at 15 per cent to 20 per cent per year. The swapping of expensive debt with cheaper debt, targeted reduction in current expenditure level, minimum reliance on borrowings are the other measures to generate resources for projected rate of growth in the Tenth Plan.

Tenth Plan Objectives

The important areas which need to be addressed during the Tenth Plan are:

i. acceleration of hydro power generation
ii. substantial increase in agricultural and horticultural production
iii. creation of infrastructure facilities for tourism to generate employment emerging from a high level of literacy.
iv. introduction of IT courses in colleges and technical education institutions.
v. connectivity to all villages.
vi. access to drinking water, particularly in difficult hilly areas.
vii. bringing fiscal and financial discipline to progressively reduce the mounting revenue and fiscal deficits and a sharp reduction in the interest liability on account of debt of the state.

Resources for Financing the Tenth Plan

Resources of the state for financing the Tenth Plan – 2002-07 have been projected in Table 6.13

TABLE 6.13

Resources for Financing the Tenth Plan 2002-07

(Rs. in crore at current prices)

Source of Financing	2001-02 L.E.	2002-03	2003-04	2004-05	2005-06	2006-07
State's Own Resources	552	666	587	621	662	700
Balance from Current Revenue	-935	-1079	-1206	-1083	-1101	-1288
Contribution of State PSUs	0	0	0	0	0	0
Plan Grants under TFC/EFC	42	42	42	0	0	0
Miscellaneous Capital Receipts (Net)	-243	-392	-637	-708	-788	-878
Provident Fund (Net)	254	245	200	200	200	200
Mobilisation of Small Savings	150	158	166	175	184	192
Gross SLR based Market Borrowings	345	355	365	376	387	398
Negotiated Loans	100	110	121	133	146	160
Non-SLR Borrowings	508	1017	1315	1295	1388	1656
Debentures/Bonds	100	-	-	-	-	-

Source: Plan Documents of Himachal Pradesh Government 2002-03.

The balance of the current revenue is consistently negative in the five years of the Tenth Plan and it increases every year. Therefore, there is no surplus for the Plan from the revenues of the state. Market borrowings, negotiated loans, institutional loans from LIC, NABARD, HUDCO including substantial non-SLR borrowings, Rs. 1656 crore in 2006-07 are the projected resources for the Tenth Plan. These figures will change depending on the borrowings permitted by the Government of India and the Planning Commission.

Essential Features of the Tenth Plan

Essential features of the Tenth Plan, approved by the Government of India, include:

i. creation of additional jobs

ii. aggressive disinvestment of public sector undertakings, notwithstanding the stiff resistance.

iii. increase in the tax-GDP ratio by about two per cent by 2007.

iv. cut in Non-plan expenditure by two per cent of the GDP

v. enhanced tax collection through strict enforcement of tax laws.

vi. withdrawal of unmerited incentives and concessions and introducing an integrated VAT.

vii. right-sizing the government and cut in administrative overheads.

Projected Outlay During the Tenth Plan

Sector-wise Tenth Plan outlay of Himachal Pradesh is given in Table 6.14.

The Planning Commission has approved the size of state's Tenth Plan at Rs. 10300 crores and the breakup of the sector-wise outlay as per Table 6.14. The additional resource mobilisation has been assessed by the Planning Commission, while approving the plan size. This includes enhancing tax collection by strict enforcement, increase in tax GDP ratio by two per cent and cut in non-plan expenditure by two per cent of GDP, right sizing the government, enhancing revenue through sale of free power falling to the share of Himachal Pradesh Government during the plan period and swapping of the expensive debt with cheaper debt. These measures will provide additional resources for implementing the Tenth Plan to achieve targeted growth of 8.9 per cent.

TABLE 6.14

Tenth Plan 2002-07 Projected Outlay Himachal Pradesh

(Rs. in crore)

	Major Heads of Development	*Amount*
1.	Agriculture & Allied Activities	1201.69
2.	Rural Development	438.16
3.	Special Area Programmes	20.80
4.	Irrigation & Flood Control	453.18
5.	Energy	1235.00
6.	Industry & Minerals	104.73
7.	Transport	1635.94
8.	Communications	2.11
9.	Science & Technology	6.42
10.	General Economic Services	223.74
11.	Social Service including Education	4893.48
12.	General Services	8.475
	Grand Total	**10300.00**

Source: *Concerns and Strategies*, Planning Commission of India 2002-03.

Himachal Pradesh, a special category state, receives funds as its share of taxes from the central pool, grants to meet the revenue gaps and grants-in-aid from the Planning Commission as contribution for implementing the five year plans. Transfers from the Government of India from 1995-96 to 2001-02 have been compiled in Table 6.15.

TABLE 6.15

Transfers to Himachal Pradesh by the Government of India

(Rs. in crore)

Items	*1995-96*	*1996-97*	*1997-98*	*1998-99*	*1999-00*	*2000-01*	*2001-02*
Share in Central Taxes	400.68	539.14	705.13	763.74	921.39	330.54	325.07
Non-Plan Grant in Aid	323.98	208.57	77.23	36.82	2.89	842.05	1013.00
Natural Calamity Grants	31.57	31.44	46.13	22.42	23.37	32.61	95.72
Plan Grants including Upgradation/Spl Prob	444.71	565.54	561.12	642.78	950.26	740.92	965.20
C.S.S. Grants	51.46	55.73	134.48	163.18	189.75	235.05	227.68
Total	**1252.40**	**1400.42**	**1524.09**	**1628.94**	**2087.66**	**2181.17**	**2626.67**

Source: *Planning Department Documents* of Himachal Pradesh Government.

TABLE 6.16

Plan Performance of the Himachal Pradesh, Punjab and Haryana

(Rs. in crore)

States	*Ninth Plan Actuals versus Tenth Plan Outlay*		*Central Assistance*						
	Ninth Plan Expenditure	*Tenth Plan Projected Outlay*	*Sixth Plan (1980-85)*	*Seventh Plan (1985-90)*	*Eighth Plan (1992-97)*	*Ninth Plan (1997-02)*	*Tenth Plan (2002-07)*	*State's Own Resources*	*Total of State's Own Resources and Tenth Plan Central Assistance*
Haryana	8035.41	10285.00	280.58	431.31	1932.22	3884.95	3180.00	7105.00	10285.00
Himachal Pradesh	**7922.00**	**10300.00**	**459.16**	**951.39**	**2103.99**	**4426.79**	**5540.00**	**4760.00**	**10300.00**
Punjab	10666.01	18657.00	261.65	285.34	6182.59	4188.73	3979.00	14678.00	18657.00

Source: Compiled from *Concerns and Strategies*, Planning Commission of India.

Central assistance and own resources of Punjab, Haryana and Himachal Pradesh have been compiled in Table 6.16. Central assistance to Himachal Pradesh has been consistently higher than the assistance to Punjab and Haryana.

The plan performance of Himachal Pradesh in financial terms is better than that of its neighbouring states of Punjab and Haryana.

Himachal Pradesh is likely to get the largest central assistance during the Tenth Plan period and per capita plan expenditure in Himachal Pradesh is the highest as compared to Punjab and Haryana. However, the common denominator of the structure of plan resources is that there is no surplus from revenue balance in each of the states and the contribution of the states is from borrowings and negotiated loans.

Growth Targets of the State in the Tenth Plan

Growth targets of Punjab, Haryana and Himachal Pradesh are shown in Table 6.17.

TABLE 6.17

Growth Targets of the States of Punjab, Haryana and Himachal Pradesh Tenth Five Year Plan (2002-07)

(Annual average in %)

States	*Sector-wise Growth Targets*			
	Agricultural	*Industry*	*Services*	*GSDP Growth*
Himachal Pradesh	**4.55**	**12.49**	**8.26**	**8.92**
Haryana	4.07	9.56	10.33	7.93
Punjab	4.07	8.06	8.00	6.42

Source: Compiled from *Concerns and Strategies*, Planning Commission of India.

It is evident that Himachal Pradesh is ahead of the neighbouring states in the matter of planned growth of agriculture, industry and the services sector.

Sectoral State Domestic Product

The percentage of the contribution of the secondary and tertiary sectors to the sectoral state domestic product over the plan periods has been steadily rising at the expense of the primary sector as is evident from Table 6.18.

Table 6.18 indicates that the primary sector in 2001 contributed 22.5 per cent, secondary and tertiary sector contributed 32.9 per cent and 44.6 per cent respectively. There is a clear shift from primary to secondary and tertiary sectors, which is a sign of growth and increase in employment opportunities.

Targeted Sectoral Contribution in the Tenth Plan

In the Tenth Plan period, the secondary sector is expected to grow from 35 to 40 per cent with growth in the manufacturing sector, construction activity and the contribution of electricity, gas and water supply sectors. This is because large power projects will come up in the Tenth Plan and the state will make a quantum leap due to its 'free share' in new power generation. The manufacturing sector will receive a boost as the package recently announced by the Government of India for Himachal Pradesh is attractive for setting up new industries. The tertiary sector is expected to change from 43 per cent to 42 per cent. This is evident from the last column of Table 6.18.

Growth in the Tenth Plan should be a landmark development in the state as the projection of 8.9 per cent is higher than the national target of eight per cent.

TABLE 6.18

Percentage Contribution in Sectoral State Domestic Product at Current Prices

(Rs. in crore)

Sector	*1980-1981*	*1990-1991*	*1996-1997*	*1997-1998*	*1998-1999*	*1999-2000*	*2000-2001*	*2001-2002*	*2006-2007*
Primary	50.35	37.82	32.62	31.92	27.58	26.41	22.5	22	18
Secondary	18.69	25.03	30.17	30.40	32.34	33.01	32.9	35	40
Tertiary	30.96	37.15	37.21	37.68	40.08	40.58	44.6	43	42

Source: *Tenth Five Year Plan (2002-2007)* and *Economic Survey 2002.*

Core Areas of Growth in the Primary Sector

In the primary sector, the prominent areas of growth are horticulture, vegetables, maize, forestry and logging. The contribution to GSDP by core activities in the primary sector is shown in Table 6.19.

The contribution of agriculture and horticulture has been erratic due to wide variations in weather conditions. In horticulture, significant improvement in production cannot be expected in a period of five year as root stock change and replant programmes cannot yield visible results within this time frame. Significant improvement in productivity in horticulture, in the existing orchards is possible through improvement in the techniques of orchard management.

TABLE 6.19

Contribution to GSDP by Core Activities in the Primary Sector

Years	*Contribution to GSDP (Rs. in crore)*					
	Agr.	*A.H.*	*Hort.*	*Fly. & Logging*	*Fishing*	*Mining*
1993-94	568	447	172	331	19	29
1994-95	643	442	98	354	15	39
1995-96	626	444	168	324	17	48
1996-97	616	448	184	334	18	47
1997-98	655	442	144	341	19	63
1998-99	612	454	224	316	19	67
1999-2000	679	456	55	314	19	76
2000-01	649	480	215	315	20	76
2001-02(P)	762	476	142	319	20	85

Source: Data supplied by Planning Department of Himachal Pradesh Government

On the other hand, vegetables and maize are expected to be the major contributors to incremental growth. The supply of quality seed, technology and extension services will help in increasing the output of vegetables in the Tenth Plan period. The increased output of maize will require to be linked with its absorption as a raw material by the industry for value addition.

Priority Sectors

The size of the Tenth Plan has been kept at Rs.10,300 crore. The allocation for the social service and economic service sectors are: -

i. Social Service Sector - 44.4 per cent

ii. Economic Service Sector - 53.6 per cent

The priority sectors are (a) infrastructure development and (b) commissioning of power projects.

The social service sector lays emphasis on developing the tribal areas in particular. This includes construction of new roads, culverts, bridges, and other means of communication. Irrigation facilities have to be extended to ensure higher agricultural production to improve the economic condition of tribal farmers.

Capital Receipts and Capital Expenditure of Himachal Pradesh

Capital receipts and capital expenditure of the state have shown a net surplus in the four years data which are compiled in Table 6.20.

TABLE 6.20

Capital Expenditure and Capital Receipts of Himachal Pradesh

(Rs. in crore)

Years	*1999-2000*	*2000-2001*	*2001-2002*	*2002-2003*
Capital Receipts	1139.21	1729.76	1711.58	2255.54
Capital Expenditure	722.02	672.02	933.27	1114.61
Net	417.19	1057.73	778.30	114.93

Source: Compiled from Budget Documents of Himachal Pradesh Government.

Capital receipts of the state include market borrowings and negotiated loans. Normally, capital receipts are utilised essentially to meet the capital expenditure for the creation of assets and development. However, surplus of capital receipts over the capital expenditure has been diverted to meet revenue deficits. Borrowings have been utilised to meet the revenue deficit on committed liabilities. This has resulted in a high unsustainable debt-GDP ratio. This requires to be corrected for the sake of financial prudence and stability.

Himachal Pradesh has initiated a programme of restructuring the Plan and centrally sponsored schemes so that unproductive schemes are either eliminated or merged to bring rationalisation and achieve results commensurate with the investment.

Himachal Pradesh government is controlling Plan expenditure through 'quarterly expenditure authorisations'. Expenditure on Plan schemes is restricted to 25 per cent of the annual provision for each quarter. Planning Department obtains reports on physical and financial achievement from each department to exercise control and make an assessment. This has led to more than 100 per cent performance of annual plans, which is a distinctive achievement of the state in the northern region.

Hydro Power Potential as a Resource

Hydro Power Potential of Himachal Pradesh

Himachal Pradesh is endowed with a big hydro power potential. Power undisputedly is a critical input and it will be the principal and perennial source of revenue for the state. Its identified power potential is 20376 MW, which is almost 25 per cent of the hydro potential of the entire country. The state is harnessing its power potential through the Himachal Pradesh State Electricity Board (HPSEB), central power sector PSUs, public-private sector ventures or through the private sector. At present only 3942 MW has been harnessed. Projects for generating 6847 MW of power, including several micro hydel projects, are at various stages of execution.

Share of Himachal Pradesh as Royalty

According to a policy decision, Himachal Pradesh is to get as royalty 12 per cent of all non-HPSEB power generated in the state. This is to compensate the state for the environmental degradation and consequent stress caused by these projects. This free power, which in 2001-02 was 322.62 million units worth Rs.74.17 crore will increase to 3923.50 million units worth Rs.1646.17 crore in 2011-12. The estimated long-term income from royalty will increase to Rs. 2968.23 crore in 2021-22. This is net of the transmission and distribution losses. The expected revenue from power project has been taken from Para-iii of letter no. FIN-2-C(5)-4/97-1 dated 4th January, 2002 from the F.C.-cum-Secretary (Finance), Government of Himachal Pradesh to the Chairman, LIC of India, Bombay and Annexure 'B' attached to it. This is supported by a note supplied by Planning Department.

Hydro Power Generation

The trial run of the country's largest hydro electric power project at Nathpa and Jhakri is under way with the commissioning of one of its six 250 MW units. All the six units of this project are expected to be progressively commissioned to produce 1500 MW of power. This should increase the revenue income of the state on account of its share of free power as royalty and its share of 25 per cent of the balance power as 'partner state'. This will work out 34 per cent of the total generation from Nathpa-Jhakri.

There are ready buyers for this power including neighbouring states of Punjab and Haryana. It will yield an additional income of Rs.300 crore at Rs. 1.50 ps per unit and Rs. 400 crore at Rs. 2.00 per unit by 2006-07. Possibly Himachal Pradesh will be able to obtain/settle the latter rate because of the power shortage in the northern states of the region.

Income and Expenditure of HPSEB

The income and expenditure of the HPSEB in the year 2000-01 is shown in Table 6.21.

TABLE 6.21

Sources of Income and Expenditure in 2000-2001 (HPSEB)

Description	*Income Generated (paise)*	*Description*	*Utilisation of Income (paise)*
Domestic	9.94	Purchase of Power	43.82
Commercial	8.03	Repair & Maintenance	3.27
Industrial	44.18	Employees Cost	36.42
Bulk Supply	4.37	Administrative & General Expenditure	2.20
Irrigation and Others	9.00	Depreciation	3.59
Inter States	21.50	Interest & Financial Expenses	9.09
Misc. Income	2.32	Others	.48
Public Lighting	0.66	Prior Period Expenditure	1.13
Total	**100.00**	**Total**	**100.00**

Source: 29th and 30th Annual Administrative Report, Himachal Pradesh State Electricity Board 1999-00 and 2000-01.

Over 44 per cent of the income of HPSEB comes from power consumed by the industry. Farm and allied consumption of power in Himachal Pradesh is low, only nine per cent, because 80 per cent of the agriculture in the state is rainfed. On the expenditure side, 44 per cent of the income goes into purchase of power to meet domestic demand on account of reduced generation in winter months.

The expenditure on employees and administrative expenses is high i.e. 38.62 per cent of the total income. Interest and financial charges of the board are also high, almost Rs.100 crore per year. This is because of borrowings at highly uneconomic rates of interest. The swapping of high-cost loans will substantially reduce the interest and financial charges.

A put and call option should be incorporated as a matter of abundant prudence for enhancing or postponing the payment of loans.

Transmission and Distribution Losses

Transmission and distribution losses of the HPSEB have been increasing over the years. Yet these are lower than several other states as shown in the Table 6.22.

There is need for upgrading the transmission and distribution system. Line losses are due to long-distance distribution networking in hilly terrain. There is little theft of energy in Himachal Pradesh.

The Electricity Bill which Parliament passed in May 2003, seeks to provide legal framework for reforms, restructure the power sector and simplify the administration of this public utility. Emphasis on continuous reduction of transmission-distribution losses will become incumbent on the State Electricity Board as its working is open to critical examination by State Electricity Regulatory Body. Stringent measures have been suggested to contain theft of power.

For evacuating power from inter-state and central projects, World Bank loan for reinforcing and strengthening the transmission system should be availed of by overcoming internal bottlenecks. It may not be possible for the HPSEB to implement this vital task, as funds of this order will not be available from internal or other sources.

Incentives for Upgradation of the System

The Government of India has recently launched an Accelerated Power Development Reforms Programme (APDRP) of reforms including reduction of transmission and distribution losses. Financial assistance from this scheme should be availed of for improving the financial position of the Board.

It is extremely expedient that the state government ensures completion of the projects in hand on schedule, as this will provide support to the state's economy and also the much needed power to the northern states. This is a very promising feature to improve its financial position as the state will sell its surplus power to the adjoining states or to other deficit states through the national grid. Income of the state on account of the sale of power should touch Rs. 400 crore by the end of the Tenth Plan i.e. 2007.

Himachal Pradesh Hydro Electric Power State

The income of the state will progressively increase as hydro power projects are completed and Himachal Pradesh will emerge as an important exporter of power to other states of the country.

In Himachal Pradesh the cost of generation is the lowest and consequently the tariff is also the lowest. Rural electrification is almost complete with 99.83 per cent of its 16997 villages electrified. Himachal Pradesh

TABLE 6.22

Transmission and Distribution Losses of HPSEB

(Rs. in crore)

States	*1990-91*	*1991-92*	*1992-93*	*1993-94*	*1994-95*	*1995-96*	*1996-97*	*1997-98*	*1998-99*
Himachal Pradesh	**17.51**	**18.07**	**18.51**	**17.31**	**17.41**	**17.25**	**17.89**	**19.20**	**20.13**
Haryana	27.49	26.79	25.40	25.50	28.50	31.40	31.70	32.20	31.10
Punjab	18.97	21.52	18.07	18.50	18.30	18.20	18.00	18.00	17.80
Tamil Nadu	18.74	18.63	17.50	17.30	16.90	17.00	17.00	17.00	17.00
Karnataka	20.11	19.88	18.70	18.60	18.90	18.50	18.50	18.40	17.40
Kerala	21.67	21.67	21.00	20.20	20.10	20.10	20.00	19.00	18.00
Maharashtra	18.06	18.40	16.40	15.80	15.30	15.40	15.30	15.20	15.20

Source: Documents of Himachal Pradesh State Electricity Board.

a "Hydro power state", is in a position to supply uninterrupted electricity to its consumers, 365 days in a year.

Performance and Rating of HPSEB

The HPSEB is one of the well-performing boards and was at No.5 in the all India grading. It is overstaffed and could break, even if one-third of its staff is re-deployed or opts for VRS. It could then be one of the best performing boards of the country and a contributor of resources to the state.

The assessment of the HPSEB carried out by the Union Ministry of Power, has worked out its transmission and distribution losses to be about 20 per cent over the past three years. It has been pointed out that the HPSEB is yet to undertake an energy audit and implement other reforms.

The board has a high proportion of in-house hydel energy available at a low cost. The cost of purchase of energy is also low and the tariff levels are adequate in relation to the cost of energy purchased and generated. Despite these positive factors, the board is suffering losses because of overstaffing as reflected in the exceptionally high employee costs.

There was an increase in the cost of purchased power during 2001-02 but a proportionate increase in the tariff was not effected. This affected profitability and the financial performance of the board depends upon its ability to reduce its cost and increase the tariff. The advice of the State Government to roll-back the increase in tariffs for domestic consumers should not be acted upon unless approved by the State Electricity Regulatory Commission as a legal compulsion.

The rating of the HPSEB in the power sector has slipped from No. 5 to No. 8 and strict measures should be taken to retrieve the lost ground. The financial position of the HPSEB has an impact on the finances of the state and visibly affects the state's budgetary resources. Himachal Pradesh Government is entitled to a 12 per cent share in the power generated in the state according to a decision of the Union Cabinet in 1989-90. In addition, Himachal Pradesh claims a tax of 5 paise per unit on power generated, under Item 288 of the state list.

The state has claimed a share up to 7.5 per cent of the power generated in the Bhakhra, SYL and Pong Dam system as a successor state under the Punjab Reorganisation Act. This is a compensation for the stress and environmental degradation consequent upon the building of dams and reservoirs affecting ecology of Himachal Pradesh.

The claim of compensation from Bhakhra Dam and SYL, Pong Dam system in accordance with the provisions of the Punjab Reorganisation Act, has been persistently pursued by Himachal Pradesh government for the last 20 years and at present it is before the Supreme Court of India for adjudication.

Even though the state government has sought intervention of the Supreme Court, the state expects the Government of India to intervene for an out of court settlement in accordance with the provisions of the Punjab Reorganisation Act.

Public Sector Reforms in Himachal Pradesh

In an era of liberalisation, the role of government has considerably changed to that of a facilitator for the creation of infrastructure for economic growth and the consensus is that it should withdraw its role as a 'participator', because doing business is not the government's business. It is conceded that disinvestment is not merely for mobilising resources for the government it is mainly for unlocking the productive potential of the undertakings and taking the government away from business, towards business of governance.

PSU Reforms through Disinvestment/Mergers

Schematic parameters for the reform of Public Sector Undertakings (PSUs) have been outlined by the Himachal Pradesh government in its order dated 20 October, 2000. It provides for the continuance of the Himachal Pradesh State Electricity Board (HPSEB), Himachal Pradesh Road Transport Corporation, Himachal Pradesh State Forest Corporation, Himachal Pradesh Civil Supply Corporation, Himachal Pradesh Khadi Board, Himachal Pradesh Financial Corporation, two development financial corporations under the welfare department (instead of four) and the merger of Himachal Pradesh Housing Board and Himachal Pradesh Nagar Vikas Pradhikaran. These organisations are to be restructured for cost effectiveness. The remaining PSUs should be phased out through disinvestment or mergers/amalgamation. Action in this behalf is at various stages of implementation. It is necessary that this policy decision is implemented expeditiously to reduce avoidable losses to the state.

Considering the poor financial health of the state, disinvestment or even closing down of loss-making PSUs will reduce the deficit, raise resources for investment and help in repaying the mounting debt of the state arising from high-cost loans. It is important that the fast-track disinvestment policy, as chalked out, should be implemented by the state.

High-cost Loans Swapping with Low-cost Loans

It has been noticed that the PSUs of Himachal Pradesh have taken loans from the market from 1994-95 to 2001-02 at uneconomically high rates of interest as shown in Table 6.23.

TABLE 6.23

Highlights of Market Loans Taken from 1994-95 to 2001-02

(Rs. in crore)

Years	*Interest on Loans*	*Loans Taken*	*Arranger Fee*
1994-95 to 1997-98	15.30%	913.08	13.69
	18.26%		
1998-99 to 2001-02	11.45%	1835.17	3.84
	13.75%		

Source: Documents of Himachal Pradesh Government.

It is understood that large borrowings by the government through the PSUs were necessitated by the increased liabilities of revenue expenditure including salaries, wages, grants-in-aid, pensions and other items of committed expenditure which in 2002-03 are estimated at 110.38 per cent of the revenue receipts. It is time that these loans are paid or swapped with low-cost debt to reduce the interest liability.

One Time Settlement (OTS) of NPAs and Asset Management Authority

There is adequate justification and also need for 'one time settlement' (OTS) of non-performing assets and similar investments and re-scheduling of the loans advanced by state sector financing agencies. Receipts from disinvestment should be placed in a 'Disinvestment Fund' managed by an 'asset management authority'. This fund should be utilised for financing, restructuring, implementing the voluntary retirement scheme (VRS) and for re-training and re-deployment of the employees of PSUs. VRS disbursement or retrenchment compensation should be the first charge on the 'disinvestment fund'. Additional resources if required should be raised from financial institutions against the assets of the PSUs transferred to the asset management authority to provide the employees of PSUs a safety net. The employees of PSUs rendered surplus on account of reforms, restructuring, zero-based budgeting, transfer of an activity from one company to another or discontinuation of on-going activities of PSU should be offered VRS.

Himachal Pradesh Infrastructure Development Board

Himachal Pradesh infrastructure development board (HPIDB) was established in January 2002 to develop and finance infrastructure projects in the state. It is a sort of 'special purpose vehicle' to raise resources for development. HPIDB has already raised Rs. 575 crore by the end of 2002 through bonds by private placement. The board has a defined role of raising funds through market borrowings against government guarantee and making these funds available for infrastructure development projects. According to the policy of the state, funds raised by the board are deposited in the account of the Himachal Pradesh Government. Repayment of loans raised through bonds and interest thereon is through budgetary transfers by the state government. This is an innovative measure to bring in non-budgetary resources for enlarging the kitty of the government through market borrowings for infrastructure development within overall approval of Government of India including Planning Commission. The policy of raising resources outside the budget through a 'Special Purpose Vehicle' is likely to undergo a change because of a change in the policy of Government of India.

The policy of raising funds through 'Special Purpose Vehicle' should be given a second look by the state government as this only adds to the debt of the state. Instead, HPIDB should prepare projects relying on the concept of 'user pays' and progressively introduce Public Private Partnership for raising non-budgetary resources for development purposes.

Measures for Stabilising the Financial Position of Himachal Pradesh

The economy of Himachal Pradesh has not recorded growth commensurate with the financial inputs during the Eighth and Ninth Plans. Factors which adversely affected the state's fiscal position over the past ten years are high salaries, a sharp growth in the pension bill, mounting debt, highly subsidised social and economic services, slow growth of revenue income and loss making PSUs.

The quality of governance and also of expenditure over these years have suffered. Excessive recruitment of daily wagers and their regularisation after eight years, now reduced to seven years, deterioration of the quality of education, ill-equipped and ill-supported primary health centres have considerably affected the quality of two vital social services.

There is a need for restructuring the tax collection mechanism, plugging leakages in revenue collection from sales tax, excise duty, stamp duty and motor vehicle tax which have stagnated, with a low rate of buoyancy. It is time to take effective measures to increase revenue from the existing base of taxation, as these taxes can grow 15 to 20 per cent per year over the next four-five years.

It is a sad commentary that the state has been liberally raising loans through the expensive route of small savings and other non-traditional sectors at rates of interest much higher than the nationally accepted norms for government borrowings.

The swapping of expensive debt with cheaper debt, a targeted reduction in the current expenditure level, minimum reliance on borrowings are measures that can reduce the fiscal stress of the state. At present, more than 100 per cent of the state's own revenue is spent on paying the yearly interest on borrowings.

The composition of public expenditure has undergone a significant change in the last decade. A major percentage of the borrowings of the state government have been used to fill the revenue gap. Capital expenditure of the state is down to 6.96 per cent of the GDP. Even about 60 per cent of the plan expenditure is accounted for by revenue expenditure.

After a detailed and intensive review, the state government should gradually withdraw from several unproductive sectors including unmerited subsidies. Primary health care, school education and other social sector activities that enrich the human capital should continue to receive priority for budgetary support.

Himachal Pradesh, a special category state, receives budgetary support which is statutory in nature and is based on the recommendations of the Central Finance Commission. In addition, Plan transfers comprise grants and loans component. These transfers act as a disincentive for the state to enhance its revenue effort.

Unsustainable Macro Fiscal Situation

The Himachal Pradesh government is faced with an unsustainable macro fiscal situation which is evident from the following financial data for 2002-2003 (RE):

- revenue deficit of Rs.1793.77 crore; 10.87 per cent of the GDP.
- gross fiscal deficit of Rs. 2346.18 crore; 14.63 per cent of the GDP.
- public debt of Rs. 14230 crore; 86.4 per cent of the GDP.
- annual interest liability of Rs. 1669.20 crore is 43.01 per cent of the total revenue. It comprises own revenue, grants and transfers from the Government of India.
- salaries, pensions, interest payments and grants-in-aid of Rs. 4505.52 crore is 116.10 per cent of the total revenue of Rs. 3880.73 crore.
- revenue receipts, including transfers, are not enough to pay the salaries, pensions, interest and other committed expenditure.
- PSUs face a still worse unsustainable fiscal situation.

In such circumstances, it is not possible to approach multilateral funding agencies, financial institutions and capital markets for non-budgetary funds, unless backed by state guarantees which in turn increase the contingent liability of the state disproportionately.

The corrective measures to be taken should not only be effective, but also need to be put in place without any loss of time. These measures should result in cutting down and compressing the expenditure with no cut on services like water supply, health, primary education, sanitation and power.

In short, the finances of the Himachal Pradesh government have been showing considerable deterioration since 1991. A very high debt stock revenue deficit and fiscal deficit to the GDP are the marked features of this period. This calls for urgent fiscal reforms.

One of the terms of reference of the Eleventh Finance Commission (EFC) was to review "the state of finances of the Union and the states and suggest ways and means by which the governments collectively and severally, may bring about a restructuring of public finances so as to restore budgetary balance and maintain macro-economic stability".

Based on its examination, the Commission recommended revenue grants for 15 states recognised as revenue-deficit states during 2000-05. The remaining ten states were assessed to be surplus in revenue. The commission, after careful consideration, recommended a monitorable fiscal reforms programme for all the 25 states. It recommended that 15 per cent of the revenue deficit grants meant for 15 states and a matching contribution by the Central Government be credited into an 'incentive fund' from which fiscal-performance based grants should be made available to all 25 states. It was suggested that the total 'incentive fund' should grow to Rs. 10607.72 crore by the end of 2005.

It was decided that 85 per cent of the revenue-deficit grants recommended by the Commission may be released to Himachal Pradesh without linking these to performance under the monitorable fiscal reforms programme. Only 15 per cent of the revenue-deficit grant may be held back and linked with progress and performance as identified below.

Starting with the base year 1999-2000, the state should take effective measures for revenue augmentation and expenditure compression over the five years to achieve the following objectives:

- gross fiscal deficit of the state should be reduced to 2.5 per cent of the GSDP.
- revenue deficit of the state should fall to zero.
- interest payments as a percentage of revenue receipts of the state should be 18 to 20 per cent.
- increase in wages and salaries should not exceed five per cent or increase in the consumer price index whichever is higher.
- increase in interest payments may be limited to ten per cent per year.
- subsidies to be brought down by 50 per cent in next five years and eliminated by 2009-10.

To achieve the above objectives, the Government of India has decided that the state should draw up a medium term fiscal restructuring policy (MTFRP) to achieve 'fiscal objectives and reforms' and 'power sector reforms' as follows:

Fiscal Objectives and Reforms

- widening the tax base.
- increase tax rates on a year-to-year basis.
- pricing services such as irrigation, water charges, bus fares, identifying the subsidy element and preparing a schedule to reduce the subsidy element.
- indexing price/user-charges to major input costs such as POL, wages, etc.
- abolition of vacant posts, except primary school teachers and health workers.
- new teachers to be appointed on contract basis as in Rajasthan and Madhya Pradesh.
- work-charged establishment to be redeployed for new capital works. Practice of engaging new work-charge staff and daily wage workers to be dispensed with immediately.
- tapering grants to institutions.

Power Sector Reforms

Power sector reforms should aim at reducing the negative contribution of the HPSEB to state revenues. The other ingredients are:

- achieving an average tariff equal to the cost of power in two years.
- setting up of a State Regulatory Electricity Commission (SREC).
- implementing the awards of the SREC.
- unbundling of basic services, i.e. generation, transmission and distribution or setting up of separate profit centres.
- reducing T&D losses by five per cent every year.
- metering up to 11 KV substation level.

Public Sector Restructuring Programme (PSRP)

The roadmap of PSRP should be:

- comprehensive VRS package should be drawn-up for loss-making PSUs.
- time bound schedule for winding up such PSUs.
- further infusion of funds either as equity or loans be phased out in five years, unless such PSUs are socially desirable.

Budgetary Reforms

The other budgetary reforms should include:

- separate schedule in the budget, giving total expenditure on salaries and wages.
- separate schedule on pensions and terminal benefits.
- scheme-wise, sector-wise schedule of subsidies.
- schedule of guarantees outstanding, year wise and project wise.

In addition, the revenue deficit should include:

- contingent liabilities such as guarantees and letters of comfort.

- subsidies payable to PSUs including the HPSEB.

These are very hard conditions and cannot be complied with in their entirety by the Himachal Pradesh government and accordingly the state has not entered into a Memorandum of Understanding with the Government of India for implementing this programme.

The year-wise break-up of grants withheld from the incentive fund is given in Table 6.24.

TABLE 6.24

Break-up of Grant Withheld from the Incentive Fund

(Rs. in Crore)

2000-01	*2001-02*	*2002-03*	*2003-04*	*2004-05*	*Total*
161.23	156.96	149.16	133.91	114.92	716.18

Source: *State Financial Reforms Facility 2000-01 to 2004-05*, Ministry of Finance, Government of India, Annexure-III.

Since the state has not complied with the conditions for implementing fiscal reforms, it has not received 15 per cent of the deficit grant recommended by the Eleventh Finance Commission, amounting to Rs. 467.35 crore for 2000-01, 2001-02 and 2002-03. There is no chance of the state's getting 15 per cent of the deficit grants for 2003-04 and 2004-05. Thus the state will be deprived of its due share of deficit grants amounting to Rs. 716.18 crore by the end of 2004-05.

Himachal Pradesh cannot implement the 'fiscal policy objectives' set forth by the Eleventh Finance Commission, which *inter alia* include reducing the fiscal and revenue deficit to 2.5 per cent and zero per cent of the GDP respectively, reducing interest payment to 18 to 20 per cent of the revenue receipts and other harsh parameters. The state, therefore, has not signed a Memorandum of Understanding with the Government of India and the latter has withheld Rs. 467 crore which is 15 per cent of its share of grant.

Measures for Correcting Revenue and Fiscal Deficits

Keeping in view its precarious financial position over the years, the state must take measures for correcting its revenue and fiscal deficits, as listed below:

- revenue deficit be reduced to 2.5 per cent of the GDP by 2006-07 with 2002-03 as the base year.
- gross fiscal deficit as percentage of the GDP be reduced from 14.63 per cent to five per cent by the end of 2007.
- public debt as percentage of the GDP be reduced from 86 per cent to 50 per cent by 2007.
- committed expenditure as percentage of revenue of the state be reduced from 116 per cent to 60 per cent by 2007.
- reasonable caps be fixed on public debt and outstanding guarantees for effective management of the huge public debt burden and contingent liabilities of the state.
- sinking fund and guarantee redemption fund should be created to ensure timely repayment of debts and contingent devolvement of outstanding guarantees.
- the state should take steps to implement 'fiscal objectives and reforms' and power sector reforms, public sector restructuring programme and budgetary reforms as stated above.

These measures are within the reach of the state and should be accepted, for incorporation in the Memorandum of Understanding with the Government of India.

The Fiscal Responsibility and Financial Management Act

The Fiscal Responsibility and Financial Management Act should be enacted for long–term financial stability of the state by controlling in particular revenue and fiscal deficits. The Fiscal Responsibility and Financial Management Act is an important measure as it fixes ceilings on fiscal deficit, revenue deficit and the debt of the state as ratio of the GSDP. This also prescribes a limit on the guarantees issued by the state government involving contingent liability of the state.

The Fiscal Responsibility and Financial Management Act, 2003 was passed by Parliament in May 2003, enforcing fiscal corrective measures in the financial management of the Government of India. It follows that Himachal, a special category state, dependent on transfers from the Centre, adopts a similar measure to control its revenue and fiscal deficits.

Raising Loans Through Special Purpose Vehicle

The route of raising funds from the capital market through bonds by the HP Infrastructure Development Board - a 'Special Purpose Vehicle' - should be given a second look as this adds to the debt of the state. As at present, the instalments of principal and interest on borrowings raised by the Special Purpose Vehicle are a burden on the state revenues and make the financial position of the state vulnerable. The HP Infrastructure Development Board should prepare bankable schemes for infrastructure projects, comprising road upgradation, widening of roads and other urban and rural infrastructure. The concept of 'users pay' should be progressively introduced for promoting public-private partnership through the HP Infrastructure Development Board.

Availing Assistance Through Development

There is a provision in the Central budget offering assistance to the states in areas like 'acceleration of power development reforms programme', 'urban reforms incentive fund', 'rural infrastructural development fund'. The state should avail itself of the assistance by resorting to development measures in specified areas which have chronic deficiencies. This can be achieved only through improving the quality of expenditure and the quality of governance.

Medium Term Fiscal Programme

The state has to play its role in strengthening the physical infrastructure and human development to make it the favoured destination of private investment.

The challenge of fiscal management in Himachal Pradesh is serious. Measures have to be taken to reduce non-plan expenditure to divert funds to development. The share of transfers from the Centre on the recommendations of the Central Finance Commission and grants by the Planning Commission for Plan implementation has grown steadily in Himachal Pradesh - a Special Category State. However, the low growth of the state's own tax revenue, its mounting debt and guarantees for loans raised by the public sector undertakings and high Government expenditure, suggest need for the development of medium-term reforms framework also. A medium-term fiscal reforms programme should be drawn up by the Government and a three-year rolling budget presented with the budget, as a measure of the fiscal responsibility of the state government.

The medium-term fiscal policy provides institutional framework focused on the need for bringing down the fiscal deficit, containing the growth of public debt and improving the effectiveness of the government in the delivery of social and economic services. In such a situation, the government should define the parameters of its fiscal policy in the annual budget stating that the current policies are in conformity with the objectives of the medium-term fiscal plan. The object of the medium-term fiscal plan should include progressive reduction of the revenue deficit as a percentage of the total revenue receipts, reduction in the fiscal deficit as a percentage to the GDP and a projected growth in the yield from major taxes such as sales tax, excise duty, stamp and registration duty, motor vehicle tax, growth in the yield from non-tax revenue and through savings or expenditure compression. The key fiscal measures should explain the rationale for major deviations and measures pertaining to taxation, subsidies, expenditure, borrowings and administered prices. This document should provide a road-map for monitoring the progress of fiscal reforms.

Action Taken Report (ATR)

The preparation of Action Taken Report (ATR) is an important component of fiscal reforms. It is a report on the action taken on the policy decisions announced in the previous budget. This also helps to review and control trends in receipts and expenditure. The quarterly statement of receipts and expenditure of the state should be part of the budget. It is gratifying to note that the state is already taking action on both these measures. These financial controls are essential for fiscal reforms and budgetary management of the state.

Additional Resource Mobilisation

Himachal Pradesh, although a special category state, has a high per capita income of Rs. 18,920 (2001-02), yet it has not been able to enhance its income proportionately through effective enforcement of tax laws and by plugging leakages or doing away with or reducing unmerited subsidies. This situation calls for additional resource mobilisation in the Tenth Plan 2002-07. The nominal growth of revenue projected in the Tenth Plan resources by the state is inadequate. The revenue of this high per-capita income state, has the potential to go up between 15 per cent and 20 per cent per year to fulfil its aspiration of growth in the Tenth Plan.

It has, however, been contended by the representatives of the state that in recent years the growth in the yield from sales tax and state excise duty has been satisfactory and receipts from these two sources have reached a plateau.

The state has justifiably represented to the Central Government for the levy of power generation tax on hydropower generated in the state as a compensation for ecological and social stress on the state. This tax is expected to yield an income of Rs. 160 crore per year.

Income from the sale of the state's share of free power after completion of power projects is expected to yield about Rs. 400 crore per year by the end of the Tenth Plan 2002-07.

User Charges

User charges for drinking water, sewerage, higher education, medical education, technical education and secondary health service etc. will improve the quality and delivery of the services. Any free service ultimately degenerates into no-service.

The additional revenue generated from user charges should exclusively be earmarked for improving the quality of the service for which statutory rules should be framed. However, it should be ensured that minimum burden is cast on the poorer sections of society and steps taken to improve operating efficiency to reduce the cost, so that the consumer does not have to pay for the inefficiencies of the system.

Debt and Cash Management

The state is in a debt trap with a total debt of Rs. 14230 crore and every year interest payment takes away one third of its own revenue and grants from the Government of India. The debt stock of the Himachal Pradesh Government carries an interest liability which exceeds the total annual revenue income of the state. Therefore, a judicious restructuring of its debt is a pressing need to enable the State to come out of the severe debt trap.

The 'debt swap' scheme announced by the Government of India will enable the Himachal Pradesh Government to repay the high-cost debt and substitute it with the current low coupon rate small savings and open market loans. According to the scheme all state loans from the Government of India bearing coupon rates in excess of 13 per cent can be swapped with current average interest rate of 9.3 per cent. The state will thus save a substantial sum in interest over the residual maturity period of the loans. This will also restrain the future debt build-up of the states, particularly through small saving schemes, which are usually contracted at higher rates of interest.

Interest Payment for the Next Five Years

Interest payment in the next five years has been projected by the state as shown in Table 6.25.

These figures can undergo a change, as the rate of interest on borrowings is likely to be reduced to 9.3 per cent resulting in savings in interest payments on the debt of the state. In the memorandum to be submitted by the state to the Twelfth Finance Commission, a strong case should be made for rescheduling and reducing the debt burden of the state, as the projected interest payments are unsustainable.

TABLE 6.25

Interest Payment in the Next Five Years

(Rs. in crore at current prices)

2002-03	*2003-04*	*2004-05*	*2005-06*	*2006-07*
1391	1552	1778	1913	2244

Source: Tenth Plan Projections of Resources – HP Plan Documents.

Cash Management

As in the private sector, cash management is integral to expenditure management. Cash becomes available to the departments of the state from the budgetary ceiling on the passage of the Appropriation Bill by the legislature. The release of budgetary allocations in a phased manner to match the inflow of resources is important. This will avoid a mis-match between expenditure and receipts and substantially reduce temporary withdrawals from the Ways and Means cash facility provided by the RBI.

Surplus Staff and its Re-deployment

The Himachal Pradesh government should prepare a plan to rationalise the staff strength in the public sector undertakings (PSUs) as well as in government departments, as a part of fiscal reforms. Rules should be framed to regulate redeployment/readjustment of the surplus staff. The state should have a master 'manpower register' separately for its Departments and PSUs, which should comprise identified surplus staff. This will enable some staff to be shifted to a surplus pool for redeployment and will help the government in making a proper appraisal of the runaway wages and salaries bill of the state. As a fair estimate, about 20 per cent of the present staff strength including the HPSEB and other PSUs is likely to find place in the 'surplus pool'. Rules for re-deployment or re-adjustment should remain in force for five years. All employees still left in the surplus pool should be retired with compensatory pension under the amended civil services rules. It should follow that all future essential and unavoidable appointments are made on contract basis. With the cutting of the unwanted flab, a new pension scheme, based on defined contributions by the employees and the government, should be introduced so that the direct burden on the Consolidated Fund is progressively reduced. Pensions have already grown four times. This burden will progressively increase on the retirement of employees who have benefited from the revision of pay scales recommended by the Pay Commission. This restructuring is intended to achieve good fiscal housekeeping by eliminating and reducing the excessive expenditure on salaries and pensions on government and public sector employees. This will be justifiable only if the savings are directed towards development for the benefit of the community.

Summing up

The factors, which have adversely affected the state's financial scenario over the last ten years, are:

- high salaries and wage bill, mounting debt burden, heavily subsidised social and economic services, slow growth of revenue and loss-making public sector undertakings
- the state continues to rely on borrowings to finance its deficit and pubic debt is a convenient tool for raising resources
- the tax base in HP continues to be narrow and tax compliance is poor
- the ratio of own tax percentage to the GDP is consistently lower than that of the neighbouring states of Punjab and Haryana and six fast growing states
- high revenue expenditure with low resource mobilisation indicates the need for improving the tax ratio to the GDP

Immediate attention needs to be paid to correct the revenue/fiscal deficits and substantially reduce the public debt. Structural fiscal measures to achieve these goals are required to be taken without delay. These include:

- a three-year rolling budget for the sake of consistency and continuity
- the HP Fiscal Responsibility and Financial Management Act should be enacted to ensure long-term financial stability with caps on state borrowing, state guarantees and deficits
- Sinking Fund and Contingency Fund to cover loans and guarantees
- revision of 'user charges' for services like transport, drinking water, technical, medical, higher education and secondary and tertiary health care to improve the quality of the services

Other measures for improving fiscal health of the state include:

- strict enforcement of tax laws for higher yield from sales tax, excise duty, registration and stamp duty and motor vehicles tax.
- compression of non-plan and non-tax expenditure.
- enhancing the quality of public expenditure and governance.
- aggressive disinvestment in public sector undertakings.
- power sector reforms and improving the finances of the HPSEB by implementing fully the recommendations of the State Electricity Regulatory Commission.
- prudent sale of its 'share of free power' to enhance the revenue of the state.
- accessing the capital market for infrastructure development for tapping non-budgetary resources through bankable schemes.

• The budget for the year 2003-04 that the Chief Minister of Himachal Pradesh presented on 26 June 2003, has notable features aimed at reversing the trend of fiscal deterioration, improving rural infrastructure, strengthening the social sector and power sector reforms targeting better services and reducing commercial losses of the Himachal Pradesh State Electricity Board (HPSEB).

The government has made bold to take some tough measures including imposing fresh taxes amounting to Rs. 50 crore, though this does not make a large dent in the yawning deficit. It has also agreed to sign the MoU with the Centre to pave the way for economic reforms and fiscal restructuring. This will necessitate right-sizing of the administration and compressing expenditure, putting in place training programmes to improve skills of daily-wage workers and other employees rendered surplus for redeployment. The proposed VRS scheme is designed to downsize the government machinery.

The revenue deficit for 2003-04 is Rs. 1788.27 crore. The committed expenditure on salaries, interest payments and pensions has gone up by 33 per cent in a single year. Interest payments have been projected at Rs. 1669.20 crore during 2002-03. The Plan size has been reduced to Rs. 1335 crore by transferring about Rs. 800 crore to the Revenue Account. Transferring committed liabilities from Plan to Non-Plan and curtailing unproductive expenditure will reverse the trend of fiscal deterioration. The signing of MoU for economic reforms will result in the Government of India releasing Rs.750 crore it had blocked so-far for non-compliance with this requirement. Measures will, however, have to be taken to bring down the revenue and fiscal deficits and also the debt burden of the state.

References

29th and 30th Annual Administrative Report of Himachal Pradesh State Electricity Board 1999-00 & 2000-01.

Concerns and Strategies, Planning Commission of India 2002.

Explanatory Memorandum on the Budget of the Himachal Pradesh Government for the Year 2003-2004.

Finance Accounts of the Himachal Pradesh Government and Budget Documents of the State Government.

Financial Documents of Himachal Pradesh 2002-03.

Plan Documents of Himachal Pradesh Government up to 2002-03.

State Finances, Factual Position and *Budget Documents* from 1991-92 to 2002-03.

State Finances, published by RBI-2002.

State Financial Reforms Facility 2000-01 to 2004-05, Ministry of Finance, Government of India.

Statistical Outline of Himachal Pradesh 2000-01 and *Budget in Brief of Himachal Pradesh, 2002-03*.

Tenth Plan of Himachal Pradesh Government, 2002.

Tenth Plan Projections of Resources, HP Plan Documents.

Tenth Five Year Plan (2002-2007) and *Economic Survey 2002 of Himachal Pradesh Government*.

Vision 2020 Document, Planning Commission of India 2002-03.

Compiled from Budget Documents of HP Government.

Compiled from documents of Himachal Pradesh State Electricity Board.

Compiled from documents of Himachal Pradesh Government.

Data supplied by Planning Department of Himachal Pradesh Government.

Chapter 7

Education

Human Resource Development is an essential input for promoting the economic growth and development. Education and training, by imparting knowledge and skills, constitute the most significant factor in raising the level of the quality of human resources. They are the core sectors for generating the proficiencies required for employment and bringing about much needed change in the social environment, leading to overall progress through efficient use of resources. An appropriate education system also cultivates knowledge, a positive attitude, awareness and sense of responsibility towards rights and duties and imparts inner strength to overcome oppression and inequality.

Education being a vast subject, the present chapter has been divided into three parts. The first section is on literacy followed by an overview of school and higher education in the second section. Technical education is the focus of discussion in the third section. Effort has, however, been made to retain the linkages between the different sections wherever possible.

Literacy

Literacy has made remarkable progress in Himachal Pradesh. At the time of independence, with only eight per cent literates, Himachal Pradesh had the lowest literacy level in India. The state was in fact classified as a "backward" region in North India. The literacy rate however improved steadily and today it ranks 11th among all the states and UTs in India which is a remarkable achievement.

The proportion of total literates in the state (77.13%) is higher than the all-India average of 65.38 per cent, according to the 2001 census. As Table 7.1 shows, the literacy rate in Himachal increased by 21.38 per cent points from 1981 to 1991 and by 13.37 per cent points during the last 10 years.

TABLE 7.1

Literacy Rate, 1951-2001

(in per cent)

Year	*Persons*	*Males*	*Females*
1951	7.98	—	—
1961	21.3	—	—
1971	31.96	43.19	20.23
1981	42.48	53.19	31.46
1991*	63.86	75.36	52.13
2001*	77.13	86.02	68.08

Source: *Census of India, Provisional Population Totals, Paper 1 of 2001*, Himachal Pradesh.

Note: * Excludes 0-6 population.

Female literacy increased by 15.95 per cent points and the male literacy by only 10.66 per cent points during the last decade. Despite the relatively faster rate of growth of female literacy, the gap between male and female literacy continues to be very high at 17.94 per cent.

TABLE 7.2

Literacy among Scheduled Castes and Scheduled Tribes (1991)

(in per cent)

District	*Scheduled Castes*	*Scheduled Tribes*
Bilaspur	59.10	48.40
Chamba	36.88	36.70
Hamirpur	68.51	96.19
Kangra	60.53	78.88
Kinnaur	45.67	59.03
Kullu	42.39	68.21
Lahaul & Spiti	54.91	55.30
Mandi	51.83	58.53
Shimla	50.11	61.22
Sirmaur	40.69	33.45
Solan	53.22	57.63
Una	62.99	90.57
Himachal Pradesh	**53.20**	**47.09**

Source: Human Development Report, Himachal Pradesh, 2002.

In Himachal Pradesh 47 per cent of the Scheduled Castes (SC) and 53 per cent of the Scheduled Tribes (ST) are illiterate as per the 1991 data. Hamirpur and Una are the only districts with near total literacy among STs. Illiteracy among the SCs is as high as 63 per cent in Chamba, 60 per cent in Sirmaur, 58 per cent in Kullu and 54 per cent in Kinnaur. Among STs, illiteracy is as high as 63 per cent in Chamba, 67 per cent in Sirmaur and 52 per cent in Bilaspur.

Table 7.3 shows that Chamba district has the lowest literacy rate, followed by Sirmaur and Hamirpur district the highest, and closely followed by Una and Kangra districts. The other districts with literacy rates above the state average of 77.13 per cent are Shimla, Bilaspur and Solan.

The rural-urban literacy gap, which exists in all the districts, is the highest in Chamba, Sirmaur and Kullu. It is also very high among females. 34 per cent rural women are illiterate as compared to only 14 per cent urban women. Literacy of rural women in the districts of Chamba, Lahaul & Spiti, Sirmaur and Kullu calls for special interventions, as nearly 40-50 per cent of them in these districts are illiterate.

In brief, Himachal Pradesh has tremendously improved its literacy percentage. However, the literacy of females and SCs, especially in few pockets, needs particular government attention.

Education Policy and Plans

The Government of India's National Policy on Education, 1986 (modified in the year 1992) is a forthright statement on education as an empowering agent. The Directive Principles of State Policy in the Constitution provide for free and compulsory education for all children till the age of 14 years.

The famous Unnikrishnan Case declared primary education as a fundamental right. The 93rd Amendment has added a new clause to make elementary education a fundamental right. A state subject so far, education has been brought on the Concurrent List. Himachal Pradesh does not have any policy of its own and adheres to the national policy. In order to achieve universalisation of education, the Government of Himachal Pradesh has already made primary education compulsory by promulgating the Himachal Pradesh Compulsory Primary Education Act, 1997. Launching of Sarva Shiksha Abhiyan by the Government of India further reflects its commitment towards the universalisation of elementary education. It is an effort to improve the performance of schools and provide community owned quality education. Its specific aims are to enroll and retain children and bridge gender disparities at elementary level of education.

Perusal of the Five Year Plans of Himachal Pradesh show that during the first six plans, most of the development expenditure was consumed in expansion, i.e., opening new schools, and provision of facilities for free and universal primary education. It was only during the Seventh Plan that the emphasis shifted to qualitative improvement and acceleration of the process of modernisation, besides increasing access. During the Eighth Plan, emphasis was on technical and vocational education in place of general education. During the

TABLE 7.3

Literacy Rates by Residence, Sex, 2001

State/district	*Total*			*Rural*			*Urban*		
	Person	*Male*	*Female*	*Person*	*Male*	*Female*	*Person*	*Male*	*Female*
Himachal*	77.13	86.02	68.08	75.71	85.20	66.30	89.59	92.49	85.91
Chamba	63.73	77.22	49.70	61.50	75.73	46.81	89.84	93.74	85.37
Kangra	80.68	88.19	73.57	80.31	88.05	73.04	87.11	90.46	83.45
Lahaul & Spiti	73.17	82.76	60.94	73.17	82.76	60.94	—	—	—
Kullu	73.36	84.55	61.24	72.02	83.81	59.43	88.31	92.05	83.49
Mandi	75.86	86.67	65.36	74.71	86.06	63.80	91.08	94.26	87.55
Hamirpur	83.16	90.86	76.41	82.62	90.70	75.68	89.97	92.66	86.86
Una	81.09	88.49	73.85	80.93	88.65	73.48	82.71	86.99	77.99
Bilaspur	78.80	87.13	70.53	77.97	86.68	69.42	90.66	93.11	87.84
Solan	77.16	85.35	67.48	74.50	83.66	64.49	88.67	91.44	84.05
Sirmaur	70.85	79.73	60.93	68.69	78.19	58.14	88.89	92.33	84.87
Shimla	79.68	87.72	70.68	75.76	85.46	65.50	92.34	34.25	89.77
Kinnaur	N.A	N.A	N.A	N.A	N.A	N.A	N.A	N.A	N.A

Source: Census of India, Provisional Population Totals, Paper 2 of 2001, Himachal Pradesh. N.A. – Not available * Excludes Kinnaur district

TABLE 7.4

Outlay and Expenditure (Rs. in lakh)

Plans	*Approved Outlay*				*Expenditure*			
	Gen. Edu	*Tech. Edu*	*Others*	*Total*	*Gen. Edu*	*Tech. Edu*	*Others*	*Total*
First Plan (1951-56)	—	—	—	50.00 *8.86*	—	—	—	45.14 *8.56*
Second Plan (1956-61)	—	—	—	114.00 *7.74*	—	—	—	72.7 *34.54*
Third Plan (1961-66)	—	—	—	223.00 *7.98*	—	—	—	282.11 *8.33*
Fourth Plan (1969-74)	661.00 [92.97]	50.00 [7.03]	—	711.00 [100.00] *7.01*	695.96 [94.07]	43.85 [5.93]	—	739.81 [100.00] 6.52
Fifth Plan (1974-79)	1200.00 [96.77]	40.00 [3.23]	—	1240.00 [100.00] *5.19*	1082.04 [96.92]	34.38 [3.80]	—	1116.42 [100.00] 6.89
Sixth Plan (1980-85)	2371.00 [81.13]	179.00 [6.12]	372.52 [12.75]	922.50 [100.00] *5.22*	2629.69 [83.17]	200.51 [6.34]	331.8 [10.49]	3162.00 [100.00] 4.76
Seventh Plan (1985-90)	6717.00 [75.21]	1137.00 [12.73]	1077 [12.06]	8931.00 [100.00] *8.51*	7585.10 [77.22]	1168.61 [11.90]	1069.03 [10.88]	9822.74 [100.00] 7.68
Eighth Plan (1992-97)	22705.5 [79.88]	4200.00 [14.78]	1519.5 [5.35]	28425.00 [100.00] *11.36*	39530.75 [85.99]	4312.96 [9.38]	2127.35 [4.63]	45971.06 [100.00] 13.20
Ninth Plan (1997-2002)	74971.52 [91.74]	3880.00 [4.75]	2869.22 [3.51]	81720.74 [100.00] *14.31*	144509.22 [93.92]	6814.67 [4.42]	2533.29 [1.65]	153857.18 [100.00] 21.61
Tenth Plan (2002-2007)	263310.8 [96.36]	5183.91 [1.90]	4771 [1.75]	273265.71 [100.00] *21.83*	—	—	—	—

Source: Different issues of *Five-Year Plan Documents.*

Ninth Plan, the main focus was on both qualitative improvement and expansion of schools to meet the target of making primary education compulsory by 1997-98. Government embarked upon an expansion programme based on detailed mapping of existing schools and identification of the unserved areas.

Percentage of the outlay and expenditure in different five-year plans on education is given in Table 7.4 and Figure 7.1.

FIGURE 7.1

Outlay and Expenditure

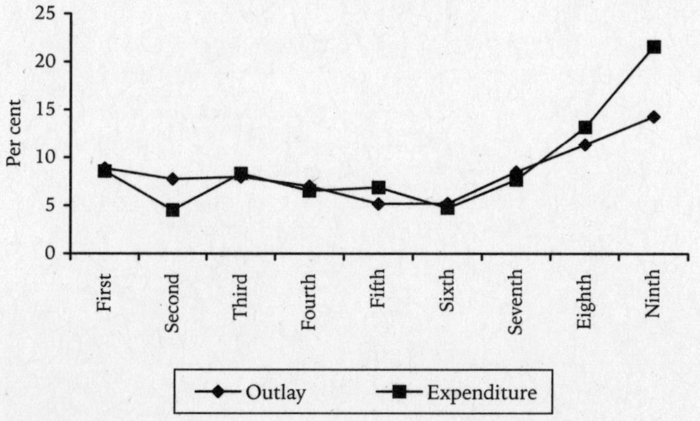

Source: Different issues of *Five-Year Plan Documents*

The data reveal an increase in the outlay and expenditure from 8.8 per cent and 8.6 per cent respectively in the First Plan to 14 per cent and 21.6 per cent in the Ninth Plan, although they had decreased during the Fifth and Sixth Five Year Plan periods.

TABLE 7.5

Expenditure on Education as Percentage of GSDP

State	*Per cent of GSDP on Education*
Himachal Pradesh	**7.08**
Haryana	2.57
Kerala	3.25
Punjab	2.87
All India	3.60

Source: National Human Development Report, Planning Commission, 2000.

It is gratifying to note that the Himachal Government is giving priority to the education sector. It was spending 7.08 per cent of the GSDP on education in comparison to only 2.87 per cent by Punjab, 3.25 per cent by Kerala, 2.6 per cent by Haryana and 3.6 per cent at the national level till the year 2000. The expenditure on education as percentage of GSDP in Himachal Pradesh has further significantly risen to 15.70 per cent in 2002. The budget allocation in the social sector has increased in Himachal Pradesh. The DPEP programme and also the implementation of the Fifth Pay Commission have contributed to the increase in the allocation to education in Himachal Pradesh.

School and Higher Education

The overall educational profile of the population in Himachal, is indicated in Table 7.6.

TABLE 7.6

Educational Attainment in Himachal Pradesh, 1991

Educational Attainment	*Population (%age)*
Total Population	4330456 (100.00)
Illiterate	1565047 (36.14)
Literate	2765409 (63.8)
Literate without formal schooling	5485 (0.13)
Below primary	728996 (26.36)
Primary	913587 (33.0)
Middle	485637 (17.6)
Matriculation/Secondary	400178 (14.5)
Higher Sec./Intermediate	100844 (3.6)
Non-technical diploma or certificate not equivalent to degree	4740 (0.17)
Technical dip./certificate not equal to degree	24285 (0.88)
Graduate and above	101657 (3.7)

Source: Socio-cultural Tables, Census of India (HP), 1991.

FIGURE 7.2

Educational Attainment of Literates

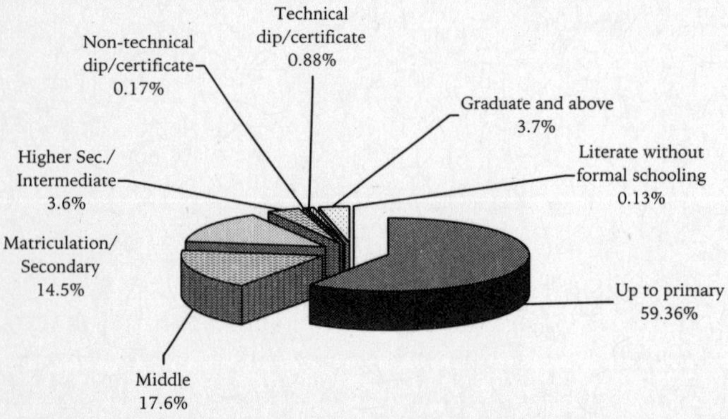

Source: Socio-cultural Tables, Census of India (HP), 1991.

According to the 1991 Census, amongst the literate, nearly 60 per cent of the population had studied only up to the primary level or below, 18 per cent up to the middle and 15 per cent up to the matriculation level. Only 3.7 per cent of the total population had studied up to the graduate level or above. These figures are alarming. Himachal Pradesh has achieved the target of high literacy, so the main focus should now be to make the literate population study beyond the primary level. Another fact revealed is the failure of the education system at the secondary level, as the desired dispersal to the various streams has not taken place. This is obvious from the low figures of diploma holders. The main focus of the government should now be on secondary and higher education.

TABLE 7.7

Number of Educational Institutions in Himachal Pradesh

Schools		
Primary schools	10634	
Middle schools	1709	
High/Sr. Sec. schools	1832	
Universities	3	
Art/Science/Comm. Colleges	64	
Number of Recognised Institutions for Higher Education		
Medical colleges	2	Indira Gandhi Medical College, Shimla; Dr. Rajendra Prasad Government Medical College Tanda, Kangra.
Colleges of education	1	
Colleges of agriculture/horticulture	3	
Sanskrit institutions	17	
District Institutes of Education and Training	12	
Law colleges	1	
Polytechnic institutions	5	
Dental colleges	4	Govt. Dental College, Shimla; DAV Dental College, Solan; Bhojia Dental College & Hospital Dental College Sundernagar (HP).
Number of Universities		
	3	HP Uni., Summer Hill, Shimla; Dr. Y.S. Paramour Uni. of Horticulture & Forestry, Nauni, Solan & C.S.K. HP Krishi Vishva Vidhalaya, Palampur.

Source: Education Department, Himachal Pradesh, 2001.

TABLE 7.8

Expansion in Number of Educational Institutions

Year	Primary/Junior Basic	Middle	High	Colleges of General Education
1970-71	3768	742	435	15
1980-81	6093	1032	665	27
1990-91	7471	1066	1125	44
1992-93	7713	1067	1140	45
1993-94	7617	1108	1266	50
1994-95	7693	1101	1231	55
1995-96	8393	1086	1250	55
1996-97	9142	1037	1278	63
1997-98	10484	1056	1339	52
1998-99	10633	1189*	1525*	57
1999-00	10633	1484*	1563*	64
2000-01	10634	1709*	1832*	64

Source: Education Department, Himachal Pradesh, 2001.

Note: Figures Inclusive of Pvt./Unaided Schools.

TABLE 7.9

District-wise Accessibility to Primary and Middle Schools

District	Average Radial Distance Per Primary School (km.)	Average Radial Distance Per Middle School (km.)
Bilaspur	0.79	1.48
Chamba	1.39	2.69
Hamirpur	0.84	1.28
Kangra	1.01	1.73
Kinnaur	3.28	5.39
Kullu	1.59	3.30
Lahaul & Spiti	4.59	8.87
Mandi	0.86	1.63
Shimla	1.01	1.85
Sirmaur	0.97	1.96
Solan	0.90	1.66
Una	0.97	1.57
Himachal Pradesh	**1.29**	**2.36**

Source: Department of Education, Government of Himachal Pradesh. *Cf Human Development Report, HP, 2002.*

The available data in Table 7.8 reveal a quantitative increase in the number of schools. In this respect the state is progressing well.

Accessibility to Schools

The state has almost achieved the prescribed norm of having a primary school at the distance of one km in almost all the districts barring areas with scattered habitations like Kullu, Chamba, Kinnaur and Lahaul and Spiti. The average distance from middle schools was 2.36 km, which was less than the government norm of three km. However, it is felt that the distance norm prescribed by the Government of India does not reflect the actual picture in the hilly terrain, as the real distance covered in hilly areas is much more, as the habitations are scattered. Unlike in the plains, one to three km in a hilly terrain often means climbing down one ridge and climbing up another and/or crossing a rivulet. All this twice a day is not easy for elementary school-going children. Hence, it is felt that the government of Himachal Pradesh should formulate its own policy of providing accessibility to schools keeping its hilly terrain in mind. The government is, however, trying hard to provide universal accessibility to primary schools and in 2000-2001 the number of schools touched 10,634.

Enrolment in Schools

The data in Table 7.10 show that most of the children of school going age are already on the rolls in schools of the state. Himachal has a much higher enrollment rate than the national average and Punjab and Haryana. The percentage of 6-11 and 11-14 age groups in Himachal Pradesh has in fact increased even more in

TABLE 7.10

Age-specific Enrolment Ratios in Select States

States	6 to below 11			11 to 14			6 to 14		
	Boys	Girls	Total	Boys	Girls	Total	Boys	Girls	Total
Punjab	74.99	72.91	74.01	72.18	65.82	69.19	73.96	70.31	72.24
Haryana	71.07	67.24	69.27	63.56	52.82	58.65	68.33	62.13	65.45
Himachal Pradesh	**86.96**	**82.87**	**84.95**	**87.10**	**76.74**	**82.05**	**81.02**	**80.52**	**83.84**
Kerala	84.74	82.12	83.44	94.98	93.67	94.33	88.75	86.63	87.70
India	**73.20**	**59.13**	**66.40**	**65.02**	**48.20**	**57.06**	**70.33**	**55.40**	**63.17**

Source: Sixth All India Education Survey, 1999.

2002 to 95.77 and 86.18 respectively. DPEP has also acted as a catalytic agent in speeding up the enrolment rates in Himachal Pradesh. Mid-day meal scheme also seems to have created a real impact in terms of children attending schools.

Under the SSA programme, the household survey revealed only 6356 out of school children and steps are being taken to bring these children also in the mainstream of education. EGS schemes have been launched for this purpose. As per status of 2000-01 in DPEP districts (Chamba, Kullu and Sirmaur), there were 160 out of schools children. The state has thus nearly achieved universalisation of primary education in terms of accessibility and enrolment. The *Public Report on Basic Education* (PROBE) 1998 which examined the state of primary schooling in India has singled out HP among the northern states for its remarkable progress towards achieving the goal of universal elementary education. The report suggests that the state has done better than Kerala and Goa and the main reason reported is the HP Compulsory Primary Education Act. This Act makes it mandatory for parents to ensure that their children attend schools. Fines on parents, who do not comply, are imposed under this Act. Parental motivation and monitoring by the community have been reported as the major factors for the success story in HP.

Table 7.11 shows that the enrolment of girls at the primary level is nearly as high as that of boys. The state has achieved gender equity in terms of enrolment of students at the primary level. The gap between male and female enrolment, however, keeps increasing as they move towards higher levels of education. It increases from two per cent at the primary level to four per cent at the middle, six per cent at the high level and 17 per cent at the higher secondary level. Although there is no consistent pattern among the STs, there is a consistent decline in the enrolment of SCs, as they move to higher education, especially after Class X. Such, then is the plight of girls and SCs in Himachal Pradesh in spite of the numerous incentives and schemes initiated by the government for them at various levels, such as free uniforms, attendance scholarships, free education for girls at all levels, mid-day meal programme, free text-books, IRDP scholarships and merit scholarships. Even at the secondary level there are pre-matric scholarship and post-matric scholarship schemes.

TABLE 7.11

Enrolment in Schools, Himachal Pradesh

	Boys			*Girls*			*Boys+Girls*		
	Total	*SCs*	*STs*	*Total*	*SCs*	*STs*	*Total*	*SCs*	*STs*
High Sec (IX-XII)	55721 (58.85)	8639 (15.50)	2211 (3.97)	38955 (41.1)	5659 (14.01)	1343 (3.45)	94676	14098 (14.89)	3554 (3.75)
High (IX-X)	98165 (53.51)	21480 (21.88)	7243 (7.38)	85276 (46.5)	14580 (21.06)	4559 (5.35)	183441	39060 (21.29)	11802 (6.43)
Middle(VI-VIII)	184065 (52.4)	46843 (25.45)	5666 (3.08)	167408 (47.6)	41113 (24.56)	4884 (2.92)	351473	87959 (25.03)	10550 (3.00)
Primary* (I-V)	339172 (51.17)	107656 (31.74)	15875 (4.68)	323601 (48.8)	103123 (31.87)	15680 (4.85)	662773	210779 (31.8)	31555 (4.76)

Source: *Selected Educational Statistics*, GoI, 1998-99.

Note: * Data Pertains to 2001-02.

TABLE 7.12

Drop-out Rates, Himachal Pradesh

Category	*I to V*			*VI to VIII*			*IX to X*		
	Boys	*Girls*	*Total*	*Boys*	*Girls*	*Total*	*Boys*	*Girls*	*Total*
All	1.96	1.54	1.39	4.4	6.2	5.3	13.45	18.03	15.50
SCs	2.00	1.90	1.95	10.5	10.1	10.3	21.54	25.23	23.53
STs	3.79	1.71	2.34	7.9	5.3	6.3	11.69	13.34	12.93

Source: Directorate of Education, HP, 1999-2000.

Retention in Schools

The above data reveal that Himachal Pradesh has reduced its drop-out rates tremendously up to the elementary level. It has attained nearly 99 per cent retention rate at the primary level, which is a real achievement. DPEP has played a major role in this regard. But the drop-out rates are still very high in Classes IX and X. The increase is almost three times for all students from the elementary to the high level. The dropout rate is also very high among SCs and girls.

Poverty, child labour, distance from schools and the quantum of homework are the most important reasons for drop-outs at the secondary level in Himachal Pradesh. Uninteresting and often irrelevant school curriculum and unattractive methods of teaching are the other reasons. The drop-out rate among girls increases at higher levels of education, as parents are reluctant to send their daughters to high schools because of the distance. Girls are often not able to do their homework because of their domestic chores. This is another reason for their dropping out of schools (Cranney, 2001).

Quality of School Education

Access, enrolment and retention in schools have improved considerably, especially at the primary level. Hence, the main target of the government should now be on improving the quality of school education.

Teacher-pupil ratio: It is an important indicator of the quality of school education.

TABLE 7.13

Teacher-pupil Ratio in 1997-98

State	*Primary*	*Upper Primary*	*Secondary*
Haryana	47	34	23
Himachal Pradesh	**30**	**18**	**30**
Kerala	30	29	29
Punjab	40	18	28
India	**42**	**37**	**29**

Source: *National Human Development Report*, Planning Commission, GoI, 2002.

The teacher-pupil ratio at all levels in educational institution in Himachal is fairly adequate, but regional variations exist. The ratio was worst in Kullu (I:39), followed by Una (1:38) at the primary level and worst in Bilaspur and Una at the secondary level. Lahaul & Spiti, however, claims the highest number of teachers. The state has a better pupil-teacher ratio than at the all-India level and Punjab and Haryana at the primary and the upper primary level. The number of teachers in Himachal Pradesh is adequate, however, redistribution and rationalisation of teachers is a must to make them available in the remote areas as well. Accepting the geographic reality, multi-grade and multi-level teaching continues to pose a challenge to the quality of learning. There are at present 28,829 sanctioned posts of JBTs, HTs and CHTs teachers in the primary schools of the state, out of which 25,783 posts have been filled and the rest are lying vacant.

As per the data of the year 2000, there were 1336 single-teacher primary schools. Efforts are being made to provide required number of at least two teachers in every primary school of the Pradesh by the way of para/contract teachers in these schools (Directorate of Education, 2003). The teacher in the single-teacher school teaches Classes I and II without grading them in separate classes and similarly Classes III to V are not graded and they learn collectively. In some single-teacher school, the students of Classes IV or V are given the responsibility of teaching the lower Classes I and II.

Untrained teachers: Further, to impart quality education, it is essential that the teachers should be well qualified and trained.

TABLE 7.14

Percentage of the Trained Teachers, Himachal Pradesh

Level	*Trained*	*Untrained*	*Total*
Primary	18804 (75.84)	5990 (24.15)	24794 (100.0)
Upper Primary	5774 (96.65)	200 (3.34)	5974 (100.0)
High	10180 (96.83)	333 (3.16)	10513 (100.0)

Source: SCERT, Government of HP, 2001.

Table 7.14 reveals that although the number of trained teachers is adequate at the upper primary and high levels, at the primary level nearly one-fourth of them are not adequately trained and do not have the requisite qualifications to meet the educational needs of the children. This is adversely affecting the quality of school education.

It is, however, important to mention that the state government has taken a number of steps to raise the number of teachers in the understaffed schools, especially in the remote and inaccessible areas. Himachal recruited teachers locally under the scheme of

Vidya Upasak Yojna during 2001, 1,681 posts of para teachers (*vidya upasaks*) and 1,398 *Gram Vidya Upasaks* were appointed in the primary schools. These para teachers are provided 21 days teachers' training course under DIET.

The problem of teachers' absenteeism: Absenteeism of the teachers has been further reported as the single most important factor affecting quality of education in Himachal Pradesh.

Lack of infrastructural facilities in schools: For the child, the school is one of the main agencies of socialisation and the first pre-requisite of schooling is availability of good quality infrastructure for imparting education. Hence, a school must have an attractive environment. The data in Tables 7.15 and 7.16 do not present a very positive picture of the infrastructure facilities available in the schools of Himachal Pradesh. A significant percentage of the students at all levels, except higher secondary, study in *kutcha* buildings, thatched huts, tents and open spaces. Special efforts are needed to improve the conditions of these buildings in view of the vagaries of the climate in Himachal Pradesh.

TABLE 7.15

Type of Buildings in Schools, Himachal Pradesh

Level	*Pucca*	*Partly Pucca*	*Kutcha*	*Thatched Huts*	*Tents*	*Open Space*	*Total*
Primary*	5135 (48.8)	2483 (23.6)	2512 (23.9)	—	7 (0.07)	392 (3.72)	10529
Upper Primary	397 (35.8)	262 (23.6)	366 (33.03)	5 (0.45)	1 (0.09)	77 (6.9)	1108
Secondary	447 (43.6)	369 (36.0)	200 (19.5)	0	0	9 (0.87)	1025
Higher Secondary	158 (65.6)	74 (30.7)	9 (3.7)	0	0	0	241

Source: Sixth All India Educational Survey, 1999, * DISE-2000.

TABLE 7.16

Schools Having Ancillary Facilities, Himachal Pradesh

Level	*Drinking Water (%)*	*Urinals*	*Separate Urinals for Girls (%)*	*Lavatory (%)*	*Separate Lavatory for Girls (%)*
Primary	78.0*	15.7*	6.27*	4.46	2.56
Upper Primary	74.01	28.88	19.86	10.92	5.42
Secondary	88.20	61.56	50.93	42.63	23.22
Higher Secondary	98.34	90.87	83.82	71.78	53.53

Source: Sixth All India Educational Survey, 1999, * DISE-2000.

Although the health of the pupils depends to a large extent upon the supply of clean and potable drinking water and neat and clean toilets to keep the flies and mosquitoes away from the schools premise, the data on ancillary facilities reveal that 22 per cent of the schools at the primary level and one-fourth of the schools at the upper primary level in Himachal do not have potable drinking water facilities. Very few schools at the primary and upper primary levels have urinals. The number of primary and middle schools with lavatories are few. Even at the secondary and the higher secondary levels, where girls need privacy, 77 per cent and 47 per cent of the schools respectively do not have separate lavatories for girls. In a nutshell, infrastructure facilities available in the schools of Himachal are poor. The government, however, claims that it is installing drinking water tanks and toilets in primary schools under the Tenth Finance Commission.

Heavy, obsolete syllabus, outmoded teaching methods and inappropriate examination system: Overall improvement of curriculum, teaching practices and examination methods was the core target for secondary education in the National Policy on Education (1986). However, at present, the heavy syllabus prescribed is adversely affecting the quality of school education and the creativity of the students. Although the Himachal Pradesh Government claims that it is striving to make the curriculum more relevant to local specificities, many studies reveal that what the children learn in schools are not relevant in everyday life. It is felt that the curriculum framework should be based on both compulsory and flexible subjects. Except languages, arithmetic and general science, all other subjects, such as algebra, geometry, geography and even history are not of much practical value in day-to-day life and hence could be listed as optional subjects. It is important that the curriculum should be made more relevant and flexible.

Quite often, the teachers encourage memorising the contents of books and rote learning. There is also very little stress on social and ethical values in the curriculum. Methods of teaching and the curriculum have been reported as uninspiring. This has been a major reason for school drop-outs.

Poor examination results: The present mode of teaching/learning is a matter of concern, when one considers that in Himachal Pradesh the pass percentage in the matriculation examination is only 46 and in +2 is only 40. There were only six per cent first divisions at the matriculation level and nine per cent at the +2 level. Nearly one-fourth of the students at both the levels scored second division and the majority were third divisioners.

As no weightage is given to the marks attained in 10+2, students in these classes are busy preparing for various entrance exams, which explains to some extent the poor results at this level.

TABLE 7.17

Pass Percentage in Matriculation and +2 Examination, 1996-2001, Himachal Pradesh

Year	*Matriculation*	*10+2*
1996-97	44.50	33.40
1997-98	67.30	28.30
1998-99	45.70	31.10
2000-01	46.42	40.00

Source: Education Department, HP, 2001

Low examination results at grades 10 and +2, however, clearly indicate the weakness in the knowledge and understanding of the subjects among the students. It is a direct indicator of the low quality of teaching in schools. Otherwise, how could one explain more than a 50 per cent failure rate in the Board Examinations at the matriculation level? Since the parents and the state have invested such huge amounts for a period of 10 to 12 years in the education of children, is not this an expression of the failure of the entire education system?

In fact the traditional methods of teaching, such as the lecture method is still dominant in schools. Teaching continues to be teacher centred. There is need to re-orient the teaching–learning process so as to make it learner- and activity-centered. It is suggested that while classroom learning is important, what the children learn through self-observation, outside the classroom, is equally important. They must become active participants in the process of learning through observations, field studies, experiments and discussions. Their individuality and creativity must be given due importance. Innovations in curriculum, which should be based on the needs of the learners and related to the local environment, are necessary. Priority also needs to be given to a reorientation in the outlook of the teachers, which at present is getting highly commercialised, as reflected in the number of tuitions being encouraged by them. The examination system, too, has to be changed so that it recognises and evaluates creativity and independent thinking, rather than mere memorisation.

Today, the teachers have to play possibly the most important role in enabling the coming generations to develop capabilities to cope with a profoundly change-oriented world. But this demands the education and training of teachers as the first area of intervention.

At higher levels of education, such problems as imbalanced and unplanned institutional growth and gap between general and professional courses exist.

There are three universities and 64 Art and Science colleges in the state (40 government and 24 private). These include one B.Ed. College at Dharmashala and one SCERT Education Institute at Solan. There are six medical colleges including four dental colleges (See table 7.7). The number of disciplines/courses and seats are limited and inadequate at the postgraduate level. Himachal is, however, the first state in the country to announce free education for girls from the academic year 1995-96 at all levels, i.e., from the time of enrolment in a government school till university education, including professional and technical courses.

TABLE 7.18

District-wise Distribution of Degree Colleges in Rural and Urban Areas of Himachal Pradesh

Districts	*Degree College*		
	Rural	*Urban*	*Total*
Bilaspur	01	03	04
Chamba	01	02	03
Hamirpur	01	06	07
Kangra	05	09	14
Kinnaur	01	—	01
Kullu	—	02	02
Lahaul & Spiti	01	—	01
Mandi	02	05	07
Shimla	03	07	10
Sirmaur	—	04	04
Solan	—	04	04
Una	02	05	07
Himachal Pradesh	**17**	**47**	**64**

Source: Education Department, Himachal Pradesh, 2001.

Note: An area having the corporation or committee has been defined as 'urban' and an area having a panchayat is defined as 'rural'.

Table 7.18 shows that out of 64 colleges in 2001, only 17 degree colleges catered to the needs of 90.21 per cent of the rural population, while there were 47 such colleges for the urban population, which constitutes only 9.79 per cent of the total. This is an expression of imbalanced institutional growth at the higher level. Government intervention is, therefore, necessary to bring education to the door-steps even in the rural areas.

TABLE 7.19

Enrolment According to Faculty and Stage at Higher Level

	Total	Female	Male
General Education			
(B.A, B.Sc. B.Com/M.A/M.Sc/M.Com/ M.Com/ Research/ Diploma/Certificate)	32309 (88.4)	9237	23072
Professional/Technical Courses			
Engineering	960	—	—
Medicine	1153	282	871
Agriculture	1019	61	958
Vet Science	—	—	—
Law	577	92	485
Others	544	323	221
Sub-total	**4253 (11.6)**	—	—
Grand Total	**36562 (100.0)**	—	—

Source: *CSO, Ministry of Statistics and Programme Implementation*, GoI, 2002

FIGURE 7.3

Enrolment According to Courses

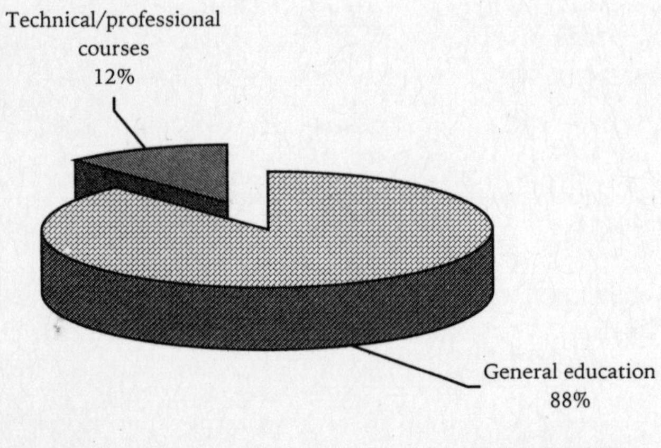

Source: *CSO, Ministry of Statistics and Programme Implementation*, GoI, 2002.

The available data reveal an imbalance between the development of general and technical/professional education, as evident from the majority of the students taking admission at the higher level in general courses and only a minuscule number going in for professional education. At the 10+2 level, only two per cent opted for vocational courses, 14 per cent for science, 5.57 per cent for commerce and the remaining 78 per cent joined art courses, according to the Sixth All-India Educational Survey, 1999. In March 2003, the number of persons registered with employment exchanges was nearing 9.5 lakh out of which 29,000 were postgraduates and 80,000 were graduates.

It is, therefore, important that vocational courses are enriched and diversified. It is extremely important to lay stress on enrolment in the vocational stream at the 10+2 level itself, to enable the students find gainful employment or be self-employed at the later stage of life. A survey should be undertaken in order to identify region-specific courses, so as to diversify the options for students for vocational stream, such as tourism, hotel management, horticulture, adventure sports, etc.

Technical Education

The major conclusions that emerge from the overview of general education are the high drop-out rate and low enrolment at higher levels of education, and also the tendency to opt for general courses at the higher education stage. There is very low dispersal of students to different streams of education. In the development perspective specific to Himachal Pradesh, suitable human resources have to be created to harness the available natural resources, the vast hydel potential and to manage the industries in the state. Manpower has to be converted into human resource. Hence the importance of having a critical look at technical education in Himachal Pradesh.

Table 7.20 indicates the existence of a gap between the skill-types being produced and the demand for them in the market. The market is flooded with persons trained in unwanted skills. There is considerable

TABLE 7.20

Annual Absorption of Engineers in Relation to Total Availability (Diploma)

Year	Automobile		Civil		Electrical		Mechanical	
	Availability	Demand	Availability	Demand	Availability	Demand	Availability	Demand
1991	17	9 (52.9)	122	49 (40.16)	154	42 (27.3)	66	23 (34.8)
1992	18	10 (55.5)	123	50 (40.6)	167	47 (28.1)	58	21 (36.2)
1993	13	8 (61.5)	116	49 (42.2)	169	50 (29.6)	51	22 (43.1)

Source: *Technical Manpower Profile*, 1995.

TABLE 7.21

Number of Institutions and Intake Capacity of Technical Institutions

Level of Programme	*Institutions*		*Sanctioned Annual Intake*		*Student Enrolment in the Year 2002-03*		*No. of Courses*
	Govt.	*Self-financing*	*Govt.*	*Self-financing*	*Govt.*	*Self-financing*	
Degree	—	3	—	460	—	400	7
Diploma	7	—	820	—	560	—	11
Certificate Course	52	5	4000	276	3310	—	36

Source: Department of Technical Education, H.P, 2002.

surplus of engineers in the market. It is necessary to bridge the gap between the demand and supply by training manpower in courses required by the industry and suitable to the local requirement. Education should form an integral part of planning, in which the development of human resources is related to the overall strategy of economic and social transformation.

Besides reflecting on the present status of technical education, an effort has, therefore, been made in the present section, to suggest ways and means to expand technical education in the state, both quantitatively and qualitatively, so that the courses are tuned to local requirements, thus encouraging more students to join technical education to become self-reliant and have wider options for jobs. Both secondary and empirical data have been used to write this section on technical education. Primary data were collected from the principals, teachers, students and other technical personnel in the various engineering colleges, polytechnics, ITIs and the Directorate of Technical Education.

The data reveal that the outlay on technical education increased the maximum during the Seventh Five Year Plan (12.7%) and the Eighth Plan (14.78%) and decreased during the Ninth Plan to only 4.75 per cent.

At present, the state imparts technical education at all levels — degree, technician and craftsman — through different institutions. The details are given in Table 7.21.

Engineering (Degree level)

In Himachal, there are three degree-level institutions. Recently, the centre has upgraded the Regional Engineering College at Hamirpur to National Institute of Technology under the Ministry of Human Resource Development. All those engaged in the developmental process of the new digital economy are building up information technology in Himachal, for integrated participation. The Jai Prakash Institution is a world-class institute of IT at Vakanaghat in Solan district, about 22 km from Shimla.

TABLE 7.22

Details of Courses Offered

Name of the Institutions	*Courses Offered*
N.I.T. Hamirpur	Civil, Electrical, Mechanical, Electronics & Communication, Computer Science and Architecture
I.I.T.T. College of Engg. Kala Amb	Electrical, Electronics & Communication, Computer Science and Engineering
Institute of Engineering and Emerging Technology, Baddi (2002)	Electrical, Electronics & Communication, Mechanical, Computer Science and Information Technology
Green Hill Engineering College,	Electronics and Communication,
Kumar Hatti, Solan, H.P.	Electrical, Mechanical, Computer Science and Engineering

Source: Department of Technical Education, H.P, 2002.

The field survey revealed that at the degree level, the number of institutes is adequate.

Courses are offered in seven disciplines at the degree level — civil, electrical and mechanical engineering, electronics and communication engineering, architecture, computer science engineering and information technology. Electrical, electronics and communication, computer science and engineering are taught in all colleges. The field survey shows that the majority of the respondents feel that the number of courses offered is not only inadequate but also of low relevance. This policy calls for review or reframing of courses to meet the demands of the present-day world so that more and more children could be diverted towards technical education. The data in Table 7.23 give details of the courses to be given priority and added as demanded by the technical department authorities, teachers and students.

TABLE 7.23

Branches to be Given Priority and Added at the Degree Level

Branch/Course to be given Priority	*Branch/Course to be Added*
Electronics and Communication	Instrumentation Engineering
Computer Engineering	Chemical Engineering
Mechanical	Environmental Engineering
	Production Engineering
	Automobile Engineering
	Bio-technology
	Textile Technology

Source: Field Survey, CRRID, 2002.

The majority of the respondents in the field survey wanted the focus at the degree level to be on mechanical, electronics and communication and computer engineering.

The empirical data also revealed that majority of the respondents wanted civil engineering to be completely scrapped off. However, keeping in view the needs of the development of the vast hydro potential available in the state, it is felt that civil engineers would be required. Hence, the course should not be scrapped off but its intake should be limited. Hydrology as a part of civil and electrical engineering should be retained and encouraged, particularly to meet the needs of the power projects. Also courses in civil engineering should be modified to consist of construction in earthquake-prone areas.

The respondents further felt that the scope for diversification was very wide, keeping the local demand in view. According to them additional courses, such as instrumentation engineering, chemical engineering, production engineering, environmental engineering, automobile engineering, textile technology and biotechnology should also be introduced at the degree level.

People in Himachal still have a craze for government jobs for security reasons and fear to venture out to start their own enterprise. The scope for government jobs has, however, narrowed. Industry has not flourished in Himachal Pradesh. Also the market does not require the kind of industrial training they are given. This mismatch inhibits self-employment. They are also afraid of being unable to repay the loans. It is necessary to take urgent steps to harness the vast human potential which Himachal has, by reducing the gap between demand and supply of trained manpower and changing the mindset of the people so that they feel more confident to start their own enterprise.

Because of its wealth of plants and a neat and clean environment, Himachal has good scope for the development of biotechnology industries. It can focus on the optimal management of its forest vegetation, along with diversification of farming for value addition to fruits, vegetables, and flowers. There is a large potential for biotech products and trade in biopharmaceuticals and agriculture-based food products, both for the domestic market and export. Hence, there is full justification for a biotechnology course to be added to the engineering syllabus, to train the manpower for tapping the potential of this industry. The majority of the respondents in the field survey specifically suggested that this particular branch of study should be added.

Similarly, the state has 21,000 MW of hydel power potential and only 30 per cent of it has been harnessed so far. Exploitation of the huge unutilised potential would require setting up many large, mini and micro hydel power plants. This would call for a large human resource with skills to use new knowledge-based tools in the power sector.

Environmental engineering courses should also be introduced. There is a good potential for non-polluting and environment-friendly industries in Himachal. Its realisation calls for training of technical manpower in precision engineering at both degree and diploma level, involving such courses as watch making, perfume making and winery. Industries and courses dealing with herbal medicines and herbal cosmetics could also be encouraged. Tourism, horticulture, sheep and goat rearing are the other potential areas, which need to be tapped. There should be orientation towards hill topography and so a course on Hill Architecture should be started. There is of course a need for studies and surveys to determine the actual potential of the courses identified so that they could be introduced as per their priority in the state of Himachal.

Polytechnics

There are seven diploma institutions, all run by government, providing technical education in the state.

The courses offered in the polytechnics cover 11 disciplines at the diploma level — civil, electrical, mechanical, and instrumentation engineering, information technology, automobile, architecture assistantship, computer engineering, pharmacy, electronics and communication engineering and modern office practice.

The maximum number of polytechnics provide courses in computer engineering (5) and electronics and communication engineering (3). Two polytechnics provide courses in civil, electrical and mechanical engineering, pharmacy and modern office practice. Only the Government Polytechnic College, Sundernagar, conducts a course in automobile engineering. Further, there is provision for instrumentation engineering in only one polytechnic.

TABLE 7.24

Details of Courses being Offered

Name of the Institutions	*Courses being Offered*
Govt. Polytechnic College Sundernagar (1959)	Civil, Electrical, Mechanical, Automobile and Architecture Assistantship
Govt. Poly. College Hamirpur (1963)	Civil, Electrical, Mechanical, Information Technology and Computer Engineering
Govt. Poly. College for Women Kandaghat (1984)	Electronics & Communication, Computer, Pharmacy and Modern Office Practice
Govt. Poly. College Kangra (1992)	Electronics & Communication, Computer and Instrumentation Engineering
Govt. Poly. College Rohroo (1984)	Electronics & Communication, Pharmacy and Modern Office Practice
Govt. Poly. College Ambota (1999)	Computer Engineering and Architecture Assistantship
Govt. Poly. College Talwar (2001)	Computer Engineering

Source: Department of Technical Education, H.P, 2002.

The Government Polytechnic Colleges at Hamirpur and Kandaghat have introduced a diploma course in information technology and computer science and engineering. Government Polytechnic, Sundernagar has been upgraded as Institute for Physically Disabled persons. Polytechnic College Sundernagar has the capacity of running diploma and degree courses keeping in view their infrastructure strengthened with the World Bank Assistance.

Table 7.25, based on the empirical data collected, shows the type of courses to be given priority/added in polytechnics.

Majority of the polytechnic Officers/Principals/Students strongly recommended that the main focus should continue to be on branches such as mechanical, information technology, electronics and computer engineering, instrumentation, electronics and communication, pharmacy and automobile engineering. The new areas they recommended were fashion designing, chemical engineering, biotech courses, repair and maintenance, hotel management, textile technology, production engineering, garment technology, food products and processing, precision engineering, interior decoration, plastic technology, metallurgy, paper technology (including waste-paper recycling), rain-water utilisation and advanced course in refrigeration and airconditioning.

TABLE 7.25

Branches to the Given Priority/Added in Polytechnics

Branch/Course to be Given Priority	*Branch/Course to be Added*
Mechanical Engineering	Fashion Designing
IT	Chemical Engineering
Electronics	Biotech Courses
Computer Engineering	Textile Technology
Instrumentation Technology	Repair and Maintenance–Advance Course
Electronics and Communication	Production Engineering
Pharmacy	Hotel Management
Automobile Engineering	Garment Technology
	Food Processing
	Food Products
	Precision Engineering
	Interior Decoration
	Plastic Technology
	CNC Training
	Metallurgy
	Hybrid AC/DC High Voltage Transmission Courses
	Rain Water Utilisation
	Paper Technology
	Advanced Course in Ref. & AC

Source: *Field Study*, CRRID, 2002.

Note: The courses have been listed as per the priority indicated by the respondents.

The respondents wanted civil engineering and modern office practice to be scrapped off, because according to them these branches offered no employment opportunities in either the public or the private sector. However, it is felt that the civil engineering diploma course should not be completely scrapped off, but its intake capacity limited. It is further recommended that in the near future, the course on modern office practice, at present with seven teachers and one student should be closed.

Industrial Training Institutes (ITIs)

At present, there are 52 industrial training institutes in the state, including one for the physically handicapped, which has been established in Sundernagar, and 16 ITIs for women, apart from four in the private sector and one for motor drivers in the Heavy Earth Moving Machinery Operators School in Amb.

Out of the 100 ITIs selected by the Government of India for information technology and the electronics system maintenance trade, three are in Himachal, at Shahpur, Mandi and Nahan.

The ITIs are being equipped with the latest equipment and technical infrastructure under the World Bank aided Skill Development project at a cost of Rs. 8.13 crore, as a centrally sponsored scheme. The World Bank assisted project for strengthening technical education amounting to Rs. 45.75 crore has been completed successfully.

A Rs. 23.75 crore project has been submitted to the Government of India for seeking assistance from the World Bank under the Vocational Training Programme (Phase-II). So far, the National Open School has given accreditation to 15 ITIs and one polytechnic college to help provide vocational training through distant education.

Craftsmen Training Schemes involve training in:

1. Industrial Training Institutes
2. Industrial Training Institutes for Women
3. Industrial Training Institutes for Physically Handicapped

TABLE 7.26

Details of ITIs

ITI – Co-educational	33	Bilaspur, Chamba, Jubbal, Mandi, Nahan, Nalagarh, Nadaun, Rampur, Neharnpukhar, Paonta Sahib, Reckongpeo, Shimla, Solan, Shamshi, Shahpur, Una, Nurpur
		Jogindernagar, Paplog, Bagsaid, Rajgarh, Berthi, Bhoranj
		Karsog, Udaipur & Saliana
		Shilai, Sainj, Bani, Dhameta, Kuamrsain, Bangana
ITI for Physically Handicapped	1	Sundarnagar
ITI for Women	16	Dharamshala, Palampur, Shimla, Nahan, Reckongpeo, Bilaspur, Nalagarh, Mandi, Kullu, Una, Hamirur, Chamba, Deegal, Kausali, Chopal & Jawali.
Motor Drawing and Heavy Earth Moving Machine Operator Training Scheme	1	Amb
ITCs Under Private Sector	4	Pragpur, Luhari, Parwanoo, & J.P. ITC Samirpur
VTC under SCVT Scheme	1	Matu Private UTC Nurpur
Food Craft Centre under SCVT Scheme	1	Hamirpur

Source: Department of Technical Education, HP, 2002.

Note: Five Food Craft Institutions and 15 Para Medical Training Centres have also started working in the year 2003.

Available data indicate that the most common trades taught at most of the ITIs in Himachal were electrician, motor vehicle mechanic, welder, fitter, COPA, draftsman, carpenter and electronic mechanic. Trades which were found in only one or two ITIs were mason, bleach dye and printing, stenography, tractor mechanic, fruit and vegetable processing, pump mechanic, instrument mechanic, weaving of woollen fabrics, watch and clock repairer, upholstery, diesel mechanic, plastic processing operator and sheet metal, refrigerator and airconditioner.

All women's ITIs, except one, provide training in embroidery and needlework and cutting and tailoring. It might be worthwhile considering a wider range of courses for women including interior decoration, beautician, music and dance, handloom and handicrafts, herbal cosmetics, sculpture-making and weaving of woollen fabrics.

Most of the ITIs in the private sector conduct courses for electrician, COPA, cutting and tailoring, embroidery and needlework.

The primary data collected revealed that the majority of the respondents felt that the number of courses offered at the ITIs were not only inadequate but also of low relevance. Table 7.27 provides information on the branches that could be added/given priority.

TABLE 7.27

Branches to be given Priority/Added in ITIs

Branch/Course to be given Priority	*Branch/Course to be Added*
IT Based Courses - Computer Application and Data Processing, Programming, Computer Operator	Garment Manufacturing/Textile
Mechanical Motor Mechanic	Fashion Designing
Electrician	Maintenance of Electrical and Electronic Machinery and Appliances
Motor Driving Trade	Beautician
Welder	Floriculture
Fitter, Tractor Mechanic	Horticulture
Diesel Mechanic	Painting and Polishing
Dress Making and Cutting/Embroidery	Agricultural Equipment
Mechanical and Construction Engineering	Fabric Printing
Carpenter	Electro Plating
Turner	Woodwork/Wood Carving
Refrigeration and AC	Cinematography
Plumber	Hosiery
Electronic Mechanic	Leather Trade
Para Medical Courses	Cement
Foods Craftsman	
Cutting & Tailoring	

Source: *Field Study*, CRRID, 2002.

Note: The courses have been listed according to the priority indicated by the respondents.

The empirical data revealed that the majority of the respondents felt that courses as information technology, motor mechanic, electrician, motor driving, welder, computer trades, computer education and data processing, fitter, tractor mechanic, diesel mechanic, dress making and cutting/embroidery, mechanical and construction engineering, carpenter, turner, refrigeration and AC, plumber, etc., should be given priority and further expanded.

The empirical data also suggest the need to introduce such new craftsman trades as garment manufacturing/textile, fashion designing, maintenance of machinery, beautician, floriculture, horticulture, painting and polishing, fabric painting, hosiery, wood-work and leather trade. The respondents felt that such training would help them run their own private workshops. All trades are very useful for self-employment.

The respondents were rather doubtful about the value of training in such trades as stenography, in both English and Hindi, and secretarial practice, as they were outdated and had no job opportunities. The respondents felt that the number of seats in these courses should be reduced and eventually they should be totally scrapped off or if these courses have to retained then they should be modified and their scope widened to include computer training. It is also pointed that even the trade Hair and Skin Care is also not very popular.

Majority of the Small-Scale Units and Tiny Industries in Himachal Pradesh (75%) relate to food and allied products, hosiery, mechanical, wood and wood products, chemical, leather and leather products. 85 per cent of the Large and Medium Scale Industry relate to food products, textiles, chemical, paper and paper products, steel, plastic, electronics, precision and mechanical engineering. Hence there is full justification for the manpower to be trained in the new courses identified by the field study. If need be, the potential of these courses could be again determined by undertaking a detailed study or survey in the State of Himachal Pradesh.

Achievements in Education

- The literacy rate of Himachal Pradesh has increased tremendously in the past.
- Himachal Pradesh ranks 11th when compared to other states and UTs in India.
- Female literacy has grown rapidly in the last decade.
- There has been a quantitative expansion of educational institutions in Himachal Pradesh. The state has almost achieved the prescribed norm of having a primary school at a distance of one kilometer in all the districts except for some scattered habitations in some districts.
- The state has also achieved gender equity in terms of enrolment of students at primary level.
- The age-specific enrolment ratio in Himachal Pradesh is quite high. In fact it is much higher than the national figure and those in Punjab and Haryana.
- Himachal Pradesh has achieved nearly 99 per cent retention rate at the primary level.
- The state is spending a very high proportion of GSDP on education. Allocation of resources in education in Himachal Pradesh is much higher than in Punjab, Haryana, Kerala and at the all-India level.
- The teacher-pupil ratio in educational institutions in Himachal Pradesh is fairly adequate.
- The field survey revealed that at the degree and diploma levels of technical education, the number of institutes is adequate.

Areas of Concern

- In spite of relatively faster attainment of female literacy, the gap between male and female literacy is still very high.
- The rural-urban differences are very high among females. The literacy rate of rural women in the districts of Chamba, Sirmaur and Kullu needs special intervention, as nearly half the women in these districts are totally illiterate.
- Though the literacy rate is quite high, most of the literates have studied up to primary or lower levels. Very few children go in for higher education.
- Though there is gender equity in enrolment at primary level, the gap between male and female enrolment is quite high at higher secondary level.
- There are 1336 single-teacher primary schools and nearly 25 per cent of the primary school teachers are untrained. This is adversely affecting the quality of education.
- The drop-out rate among Scheduled Castes and girls is very high, as they move to higher levels of education.

- The pass percentage of students at the matriculation and the 10+2 levels is very low.
- There is total lack of infrastructure facilities in the schools of Himachal Pradesh.
- Quality of education imparted in schools is poor. There is need for revamping curriculum, teaching methods and examination system.
- The number of courses offered in technical institutions is not only inadequate but their relevance is also low.
- At higher levels of education, problems like imbalanced and unplanned institutional growth in rural and urban areas and gap between general and professional courses have affected the quality of higher education resulting in a gap between human resources being produced and the demand for them in the market.

Recommendations

- **Increase retention among Scheduled Castes and girls at higher levels:** The economic incentives being provided should be used to ensure the arrest of the social and cultural handicaps of enrolment and retention of SCs/girls. NGOs and Panchayati Raj Institutions need to be associated with an effective effort to initiate an attitudinal change in parents of girl children and SCs (especially in rural areas) in the districts of Chamba, Sirmaur and Kullu, to let their children continue with their studies up to the higher levels. The role of MTAs, especially for creating awareness among girls should be strengthened.
- **Focus on pre-service/in-service teachers' training:** Efforts should be made to ensure that there are adequate trained, qualified teachers who are deployed rationally at all levels. Although orientation courses for teachers have already started, there should be more emphasis on these, so that the teachers are themselves trained with the most modern teaching methods. Such teachers should also be given post-recruitment training. Further, the in-service teachers' programme should be organised and teachers should be compulsorily deputed for refresher courses. In fact, teachers' training should be linked to their promotion. In-service teachers training programmes should be constantly reviewed and strengthened. There should be co-ordination between DIETs and SCERTs. It is essential that SCERT should act as a key agency in the state for the professional development of teachers at school level and DIET teachers. In fact DIET and all research and training should be brought under the umbrella of SCERT.

  Although the Department of Education provides for in-service training to technical/vocational teachers and the teachers are sent on short-term and long-term training programmes in their respective disciplines, it is felt that such programmes should be strengthened for updating the knowledge and skills of the teachers to keep pace with developments and change in the IT sector. The faculty should be strengthened through modernised workshops and advanced courses. The Technical Teachers Training Institute should draw up programmes for training polytechnic teachers in the new diversified areas.

  Instructors do not have adequate knowledge to operate modern equipment, wherever they might have been introduced. Hence, it is important to upgrade their working knowledge in this area.
- **Revamp the curriculum:** A special thrust is necessary to make education at elementary level useful and relevant for the children. At present, it is highly regimented with uniform courses. The state has been blindly following the national curriculum without considering the special conditions at the grassroot level of Himachal Pradesh. Hence modernisation of the syllabus with more flexibility in the choice of subjects is recommended. The curriculum framework should be based on a combination of compulsory and flexible subjects, giving the children a choice to opt for subjects of their interest. It is recommended that subjects that do not have practical value in day-to-day life should be made optional. There should really be a continuing review of the utility of the curriculum. Further, there is need to emphasise moral values and iterate their importance in everyday life.

  The curriculum should be framed at the state-level, taking into consideration the state-specific requirements, their vocational needs, opportunities for self-employment and the requirements of the employing agencies. Vocational education and training has to be strengthened. It is imperative that the students are trained in only such occupational areas wherein self- or wage-employment opportunities are assured.

Government should conduct labour market surveys from time to time, to work out need-based programmes and remove obsolete courses.

While redesigning the syllabus, it is important that due priority is given to the 29 items clubbed in five clusters in the 73rd Amendment Act, i.e. agriculture, rural industrialisation, infrastructure development, human development and social welfare/gender development.

- **Training of the trainers:** The government has decided to devolve powers and responsibilities to the PRIs. At present there are 26,532 elected representatives of PRIs and about 430 of ULBs in Himachal Pradesh.

  Education is one of the 29 subjects specified in the 73rd amendment to be shifted to PRIs. In this context it is very important to initiate training of the trainers and elected representatives. In fact there should be ongoing training of the *sarpanches* and *panches* so that the trained representatives link the system of education with management and move from training to implementation.

- **Provision of infrastructure:** Efforts must be made to bridge infrastructure gaps. Schools should also raise resources from voluntary organisations and *Panchayats*, with the state government contributing matching grants. A low-cost strategy has to be evolved for providing toilet facilities in educational institutions at all levels. The local community, in co-ordination with the government and the PRIs, should raise resources to provide all local schools with potable drinking water.

- **Ban homework** till the Kindergarten level and reduce it at the elementary level.

- **Decentralisation and community participation:** The state government should take effective steps to encourage transfer of elementary educational institutions to the PRIs and urban local bodies, in order to empower the community and other stakeholders. It is essential that the control of schools and teachers should be transferred to local bodies. Efforts should be made to involve the community in the development of education. In Himachal Pradesh, some powers have been devolved to PRIs, since 1996, for the inspection of primary schools, maintenance/repair of primary school buildings and monitoring the various incentive schemes. *Gram Vidya Upasaks* in primary schools have been made employees of *Gram Panchayats*. By ensuring the appointment of para teachers by *Gram Panchayats*, the state can move towards a situation where the local community appoints all teachers. Decentralisation will, however, be actually achieved only when the *panchayats*, VEDCs and UEDCs become fully autonomous to plan, manage and control school affairs, with full financial powers. It is also important to enlarge and strengthen the role and participation of PTAs/MTAs, especially for girls in schools. MTAs are already operative in the State. Their role should be widened to counselling and adolescent education, etc.

- **Motivate students to continue education up to higher levels and join technical/professional courses:** More boys and girls should be encouraged to continue up to higher levels and join technical and professional courses. Guidance cells, awareness and motivation programmes should be organised in schools/colleges to provide them with information about various opportunities and branches available, which could open up very satisfying careers for them in future in areas of their interest.

- **Introduction of new courses in existing engineering colleges/polytechnics/ITIs and the removal of the obsolete ones:** In order to bring about an improvement in job opportunities for vocational and technical students, it is essential that a prior assessment of locally available and emerging occupations should be made and such courses should be offered to students as will come under the purview of these occupations. The new courses, suggested by the empirical data in the present chapter should be studied and rationalised and then introduced and the obsolete ones should be removed.

- **To make technical education more effective, syllabus should be redesigned with more emphasis on practical work than theory.**

- **Promote interaction between industry and institutions**: There is a need for closer industry-institute interface to improve quality and productivity of industry and increase employability of the students passing out from the Industrial Training Institutes. Although government is taking steps to promote interaction between industry and institutions, through good representation of industry in the managing committees of educational institutions, the empirical data reveal that so far there has only been formal paper correspondence between industry and technical training institutions. The interaction is limited only to factory visits during training.

To reduce the mismatch between the demand and supply of skilled manpower, it is imperative that there is participation of industry in curriculum designing itself so that courses are framed according to the local need and requirement of the industry. Technical training institutes should have a cell, where people are guided to set up their own enterprises. For this, instructors should be invited from the industry to participate in such programmes. Experts should be invited from industry to deliver special lectures on selected topics in ITIs/polytechnics. At least three-month in-plant industrial training should be provided for all the engineering trades, to make the trainees familiar with the industrial environment. Seminars should be regularly organised to create awareness of modern technology among students. Educational tours and training in industries should be made compulsory and the period for such training increased. Experts from industries could be involved for maintenance of machinery and equipment at technical training institutes. Educational institutions could also arrange courses to update the knowledge of practising engineers.

These objectives will be facilitated if the Institute Managing Committees (IMCs) are empowered. Such initiative was undertaken by DGET and CII, which proposed to constitute a separate IMC for each ITI having representation of Industry, State Directorates, Principal of ITI, senior faculty member of ITI, student representatives, District Employment officer etc. ITI Solan from Himachal Pradesh was also selected as part of pilot project. The role and responsibility of IMCs included generation and utilisation of resources, students selection, examination supervision, faculty evaluation, teaching aids, MIS system, placement, faculty and staff development, equipment maintenance, curriculum revamping, transfer of faculty etc. The steering committee was also formed to monitor the performance of IMCs. Formation of such IMCs needs to be strengthened in Himachal Pradesh.

- **Monitoring placement of students:** Placement cells should be opened and strengthened in every institute and tracer studies should be carried out regularly on placement of students passing out of the training institutes.
- **Guidance:** A cell or guidance bureau should be set up for the proper guidance and counselling of the students about the various subjects/trades, so that they can seek admissions in courses suited to their aptitude and interests. Final year trainees should also be provided proper guidance about job opportunities and guidelines for higher studies. The teachers should also be made aware of the various options available during their refresher/ orientation courses, so that they pass the information on to the students in class.
- **Upgradation of polytechnics and ITIs:** The empirical data clearly bring out the fact that the present number of technical institutions is adequate. The respondents stressed the importance of improving the quality of the existing institutes and upgrading a few of them where trades/ courses/disciplines as per the need of hour could be introduced so that the low percentage of admission seekers in technical/professional education could be increased. Government should upgrade the Government Polytechnics at Sunder Nagar pending any future plan to open a new engineering college in the state as it has the capacity of running both degree and diploma courses.

The major drawback of technical education in Himachal Pradesh, as pointed out by majority of the respondents, is the lack of industries. Polytechnics and ITIs are far away from the industrial belt. If ever government proposes to open more Institutes, then they should be in industrial hub. Paonta Sahib in Sirmaur district or Baddi in Solan district were suggested for polytechnics.

- **Provision of funds for maintenance and repair of machinery:** The current government allocation for technical education is Rs. 1,786.01 lakh. Funds provided under the World Bank assisted project are being utilised to meet the shortage of equipment in the technical institutions. There is, however, no money demarcated for repair and maintenance. It is suggested that five per cent of the cost of machinery be made available for their maintenance and repair. There is a very strong recommendation for starting new courses on maintenance of machinery in the polytechnics and ITIs.
- **Pooling of resources**: AICTE should be approached to consider allowing pooling of resources-faculty, library, and lab by technical institutions situated at the station.

- **Change procedure for admissions in professional and technical institutions:** No weightage is given to marks obtained in 10+2 examination. During the 10+1 and 10+2 stages students hardly attend any classes in their colleges/schools. On the other hand, almost all of them take tuitions and prepare for various entrance tests. Students have lost the habit of attending classes, or doing practicals, etc. A very strong recommendation has emerged from the empirical data that some kind of weightage should be given to the marks attained at 10+2 level, for admission to professional, technical and other institutes
- **Monitoring and evaluation:** An institutionalised mechanism for regular inspection and monitoring and follow-up needs to be established. An appraisal of teachers and heads must be initiated. At least one inspection per year from the Directorate of Technical Education in the Training Institutes is a must.

Conclusion

It is gratifying to note that Himachal Government is giving priority to the education sector and is spending a very high proportion of GSDP on education. Literacy and enrolment have improved considerably. At the time of independence, with only eight per cent literates, Himachal Pradesh had the lowest literacy level in India. The literacy rate however improved steadily and increased to 77 per cent in 2001 and today H.P. ranks 11th among all the states and UTs in India. Himachal Pradesh has also reduced its drop-out rates tremendously up to the elementary level which is a remarkable achievement.

Himachal Pradesh government should however frame an education policy of its own to target improving the quality of education imparted in the state which is directly linked to the teaching community, which needs to be made more accountable and effectively trained. The curriculum should be framed taking into consideration the state specific requirements, their vocational needs, opportunities for self-employment and the requirements of the employing agencies. The state has to broadly follow the syllabi prepared by the NCERT but it should revamp the curriculum to increase its local content/context. An earnest endeavor has also to be made by the state of Himachal Pradesh to provide adequate buildings and necessary infrastructure to all government educational institutions. The state government needs to take effective steps to encourage transfer of elementary educational institutes to PRIs and urban local bodies, in order to empower the community. The state government should also give priority to providing accessibility to educational institutions keeping its own hilly terrain in mind. To curb the problem of high drop-outs at the higher levels of education and to reduce the gap in enrolment between general and technical courses, there is need to diversify students to different streams of education. So stress has to be laid on vocational education at the 10+2 level itself and the courses need to be enriched and diversified so that students find gainful employment at later stages of life. In the development perspective specific to Himachal Pradesh, suitable human resource has to be created to harness the available natural resources, the vast hydel potential, tourism and to manage industries in the State. There is also a need for training technical manpower in non-polluting and eco-friendly industries, herbal medicines and herbal cosmetics. There is also need to promote interaction between industry and technical institutes in Himachal Pradesh.

Himachal Pradesh has been adhering till date to the National Policy of Education. Although Himachal Pradesh has taken the initiative to provide free education to girls at all levels, it now needs to move ahead to formulate its own 'Education Policy' with priority to its specificities highlighted above.

References

Cranney Brenda (2001), *Livelihood and Environment, Local Environment and Lived Experience, The Mountain Women of Himachal Pradesh,* Sage Publications, New Delhi.

Department of Planning, *Five Year Plans,* Government of Himachal Pradesh, Himachal Pradesh.

Directorate of Census Operations (2001), *Census of India, Provisional Population Totals,* Paper 1 & 2, Series 4, Himachal Pradesh.

Directorate of Economic and Statistics (1997), *Statistical Abstract of Himachal Pradesh,* Himachal Pradesh.

Directorate of Economic and Statistics (2002), *Economic Survey of Himachal Pradesh,* Himachal Pradesh.

Directorate of Economic and Statistics (2002), *Statistical Abstract of India,* Government of India.

Directorate of Technical Education (2002), Vocational and Industrial Training, *Concept Paper For Technical Education Quality Improvement Project,* Himachal Pradesh, Sundarnagar, 2002.

Directorate of Technical Education (2002), Vocational and Industrial Training, *Perspective Plan for Improvement of Technical Education in Himachal Pradesh,* Himachal Pradesh, Sundarnagar.

Directorate of Technical Education (2002), Vocational and Industrial Training, *Status of Technical Education, in the State of Himachal Pradesh,* Himachal Pradesh, Sunder Nagar.

Himachal Pradesh, *Human Development Report, 2001.*

ICDEOL, Lohumi, Manju (1996), *Development of Tertiary Education in Himachal Pradesh,* Himachal Pradesh University.

Institute of Applied Manpower Research (1995), *Technical Manpower Profile,* New Delhi.

Ministry of Education (1985), *Challenge of Education 1985, A Policy Perspective*, Government of India, New Delhi.

Ministry of Human Resource Development (1986), Government of India, *National Policy on Education, Programme of Action*, New Delhi.

Ministry of Human Resource Development (2001), *Manpower Profile*, India Year Book.

Ministry of Human Resource Development (1998), *Selected Educational Statistics*, Government of India, New Delhi.

National Council of Applied Economic Research (NCAER) (1999), *India Human Development Report*, New Delhi.

National Council of Educational Research and Training (NCERT) *(1999), Sixth All India Education Survey, Main Report.*

Planning Commission (2001), *National Human Development Report*, Government of India.

State Council for Educational Research and Training (SCERT) (2001), *Status, Issues and Future Perspectives*, Government of Himachal Pradesh, Solan.

Chapter 8

Health

Introduction

This chapter opens with a brief summary of health planning in Himachal Pradesh, and analyses various issues, such as trends in outlays and expenditure during the different five year plans; availability of infrastructure facilities and other health services in Himachal Pradesh; morbidity and treatment pattern; health-seeking behaviour and utilisation patterns of available health care facilities and services including cost of treatment. The last section tries to present a vision of the state of health of the people of Himachal Pradesh and work out some operational strategies to achieve the same.

At the time of the formation of Himachal Pradesh on 15 April 1948, medical and health care facilities were virtually primitive. Since the First Five-Year Plan, the government of Himachal Pradesh has been making continuing efforts to provide medical care of a reasonable standard. During the initial years of planning, it attempted to provide access to health care services to the people by increasing the number of health care institutions and diagnostic facilities. The programme to control venereal diseases, implementation of the national programmes, providing quality education, and training programmes were assigned top priority. Later, measures were taken to strengthen rural health care and reduce the existing regional disparities in this area. The previous three plans had laid emphasis on strengthening the existing infrastructure, dental health care, food and drug laboratory, audit planning and legal cell besides implementation of different national health programmes. The Tenth Plan, for the first time, aims at improving the quality of the health services. In recent years, the state government has focused more on the development of the Indian system of medicines and Homoeopathy (ISM&H), particularly *Ayurveda*, involving members of the Panchayati Raj Institutions (PRIs), and ensuring greater community participation through hospital welfare societies, etc. However, providing tertiary health care services in the form of super specialised hospitals, both in the public and private sectors, establishing a strong health management information system (HMIS), proper referral linkages, management of lifestyle diseases, and involvement of the voluntary sector in different health programmes are some areas which are still lagging behind in the state.

Resource Allocation and Expenditure

There has been a massive increase in the outlay and expenditure on medical and public health services since the First Five-Year Plan (Table 8.1). At present, this sector comprises Allopathic, *Ayurveda* or other systems of medicine, medical education, dental department and Director, Medical Education and Research (DMER). Table 8.1 shows that during the First Five-Year Plan, the outlay and expenditure on social services was 3.1 times and 3.4 times as that on medical and public health. In the Ninth Plan, the proportions became 6.6 times and 5.6 times for outlay and expenditure respectively. This implies that even though the outlay and expenditure on medical and public health sector has risen in absolute terms, it has not kept pace with the rise in expenditure on social services as a whole.

Table 8.2 and Figure 8.1 shows that the percentage share of medical and public health (MPH) to the total outlay and total expenditure has fluctuated during various five year and annual plans. It has declined sharply from the Third Plan and fluctuated between two and four per cent of the total allocations up to the Seventh Plan. After the Eighth Plan, the share has started increasing but has remained less than the

TABLE 8.1

Plan-wise Outlay and Expenditure on Medical and Public Health, Social Services in Himachal Pradesh

(in Rs. lakh)

Name of the Plan	*Medical and Public Health*		*Social Services*[1]		*Total Plan*	
	Outlay	*Expenditure*	*Outlay*	*Expenditure*	*Outlay*	*Expenditure*
First Plan (1951-56)	35.96	30.86	112.66	104.85	564.40	527.25
Second Plan (1956-61)	79.65	81.78	341.05	308.36	1472.53	1602.60
Third Plan (1961-66)	171.00	116.23	632.00	716.27	2793.00	3384.47
Annual Plans						
1966-67	30.44	18.38	144.98	112.22	900.00	946.05
1967-68	55.00	24.91	219.24	157.33	1572.00	1443.94
1968-69	50.00	33.70	209.00	190.12	1550.00	1595.19
Fourth Plan (1969-74)	415.00	338.15	1692.00	2042.49	10140.00	11342.97
Fifth Plan (1974-78)**	750.00	414.24	4335.00	2709.78	23895.00	16714.10
Annual plans						
1978-79	190.47	189.76	1460.96	1477.09	7329.11	6810.17
1979-80	219.50	168.04	1297.00	1654.91	7877.00	7877.00
Sixth Plan (1980-85)	1608.00	2338.68	10750.00	15854.29	62217.00	66471.00
Seventh Plan (1985-90)	3721.00	4346.86	28162.75	30099.36	117800.00	132474.75
Annual plans						
1990-91	1265.00	1473.14	11265.00	11729.69	36000.00	37762.93
1991-92	1550.00	1962.00	11718.00	12546.00	41000.00	40482.00
Eighth Plan (1992-1997)	12100.00	16280.00	74815.00	121310.00	250200.00	349905.00
Ninth Plan (1997-2002)	31765.00	51885.12*	210644.00	293966.34*	570000.00	712117.67*
Tenth Plan (2002-07)	78772.28	N.A.	488248.04	N.A.	1252057.50	N.A.

Source: Five Year Plans and *Statistical Abstract of Himachal Pradesh* (different issues).

Notes: '*' includes anticipated expenditure for FY 2001-02.

'**' Plan was implemented only up to March 1978. As a result, expenditure figures are up to March 1978 only.

allocations made during the initial Five Year Plans. On the other hand, a review of expenditure patterns during the plans indicate that the expenditure on MPH was less than the allocations up to the Sixth Plan and started increasing thereafter. Less than five per cent of the total expenditure was incurred on MPH services during the Eighth Plan, while the estimates for the Ninth Plan projects this to be nearly seven per cent. From this, it can be inferred that health in Himachal Pradesh started getting priority after the Seventh Plan. One of the reasons for increased expenditure and allocations after the Seventh Plan is the increased expenditure on the Indian system of medicines and Homoeopathy (ISM&H), after a separate department of ISM&H was created in November 1984. There has been a steady increase in the budget outlay of the Department of ISM&H. The total budget outlay has increased to Rs. 5,348 lakh during 2002-03, which is 17.1 times of the outlay in 1983-84, when the department was not working as an independent entity. The Tenth Five Year Plan proposes a total outlay of Rs. 78,772.28 lakh for Health and Family Welfare. The distribution of this outlay among different departments is 21.3 per cent for *Ayurveda*, 60 per cent for Allopathy, 17.8 per cent for medical education, 0.6 per cent for dental department and 0.15 per cent for DMER.

However, a comparison of expenditure on MPH with the overall expenditure on social services during the different five-year and annual plans reveals an entirely different picture. Whereas the percentage expenditure on MPH remained around five per cent or less during the different plans, on social services other than MPH it rose rapidly during these plans, clearly indicating that medical and public health was accorded a lower priority among the social services (Table 8.2 and Figure 8.2). Figure 8.2 shows that up to the Eighth Plan, the percentage expenditure on MPH mostly remained less than five, on social services other than MPH it rose to 30 per cent of the total plan performance.

Health Services in Himachal Pradesh

It is well known that Himachal Pradesh, like most other states, has made significant progress in bringing

1. The 10th FYP classification of social services include education, sports, arts and culture; health and family welfare; water supply, sanitation, housing and urban development; information and publicity; welfare of SCs, STs and OBCs; labour and labour welfare; and social welfare and nutrition.

TABLE 8.2

Total Percentage Share in Outlay and Expenditure on MPH, Social Services including MPH and Social Services Excluding MPH

Name of the Plan	*Medical and Public Health*		*Social Services including MPH*		*Social Services excluding MPH*	
	Outlay	*Expenditure*	*Outlay*	*Expenditure*	*Outlay*	*Expenditure*
First Plan (1951-56)	6.37	5.85	19.96	19.89	13.59	14.03
Second Plan (1956-61)	5.41	5.10	23.16	19.24	17.75	14.14
Third Plan (1961-66)	6.12	3.43	22.63	21.16	16.51	17.73
Annual Plans						
1966-67	3.38	1.94	16.11	11.86	12.73	9.92
1967-68	3.50	1.73	13.95	10.90	10.45	9.17
1968-69	3.23	2.11	13.48	11.92	10.26	9.81
Fourth Plan (1969-74)	4.09	2.98	16.69	18.01	12.59	15.03
Fifth Plan (1974-78)**	3.14	2.48	18.14	16.21	15.00	13.73
Annual Plans						
1978-79	2.60	2.79	19.93	21.69	17.33	18.90
1979-80	2.79	2.13	16.47	21.01	13.68	18.88
Sixth Plan (1980-85)	2.58	3.52	17.28	23.85	14.69	20.33
Seventh Plan (1985-90)	3.16	3.28	23.91	22.72	20.75	19.44
Annual Plans						
1990-91	3.51	3.90	31.29	31.06	27.78	27.16
1991-92	3.78	4.85	28.58	30.99	24.80	26.14
Eighth Plan (1992-1997)	4.84	4.65	29.90	34.67	25.07	30.02
Ninth Plan (1997-2002)	5.57	7.29*	36.96	41.28	31.38	33.99
Tenth Plan (2002-2007)	6.29	N.A.	39.00	N.A.	32.70	N.A.

Source: Five Year Plans and *Statistical Abstract of Himachal Pradesh* (different issues).
Notes: * includes anticipated expenditure for FY 2001-02.
** Plan was implemented only up to March 1978. Therefore, the expenditure figures are up to March 1978 only.

FIGURE 8.1

Outlay and Expenditure during Five Year and Annual Plans (as per cent of total), (1951-56 to 2002-07)

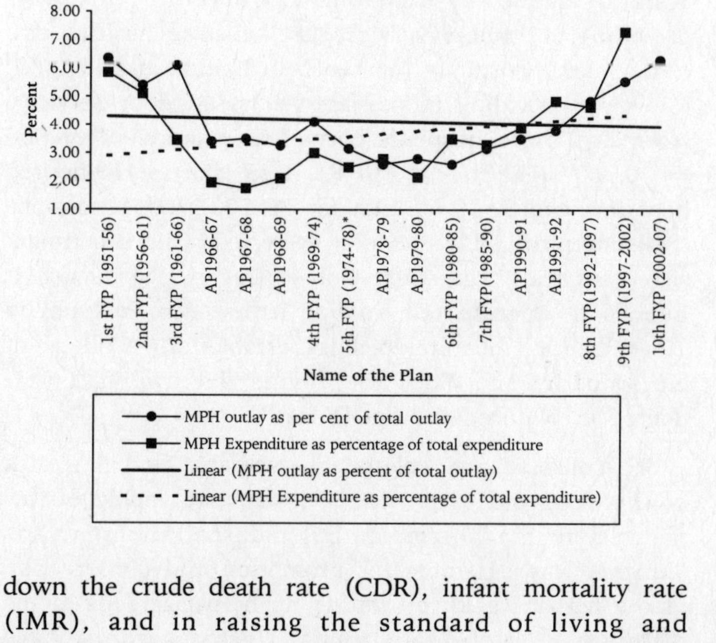

FIGURE 8.2

Variations in Expenditure on MPH and Social Services other than MPH during Different Plans (1951-56 to 1997-2002)

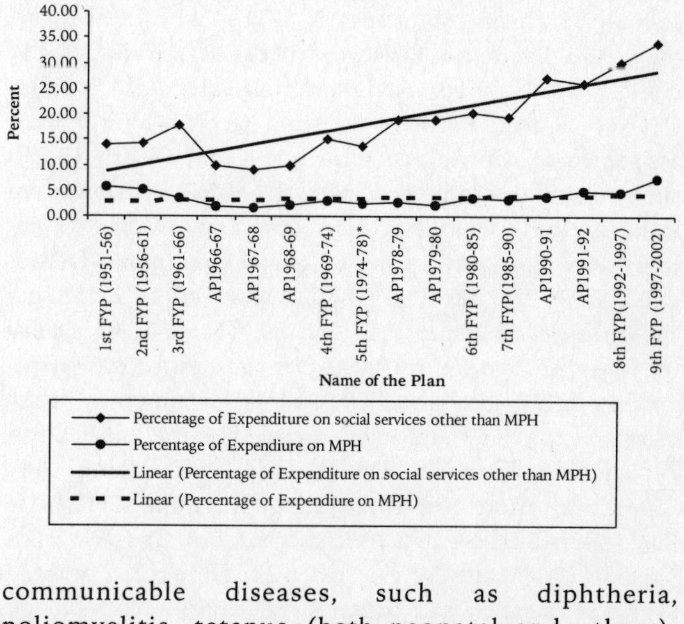

down the crude death rate (CDR), infant mortality rate (IMR), and in raising the standard of living and expectancy of life at birth. This is also true of the control of different communicable and non-communicable diseases, such as diphtheria, poliomyelitis, tetanus (both neonatal and others), whooping cough, measles, leprosy, malaria, goitre, blindness, etc. Although the state has made remarkable achievements in controlling the spread of venereal diseases through family health awareness campaigns, tuberculosis remains the major killer in the state.

In Himachal Pradesh, health services (preventive, promotive and curative) are provided through the Department of Health and Family Welfare and the Department of Indian System of Medicines and Homoeopathy (ISM&H). Since primary health care is the first and the nearest contact between the individual and the health care services, the state has made good provision for primary health care services through a network of sub-centres (SC), primary health centres (PHCs) and community health centres (CHCs). To support the primary health care services, provision has been made for secondary-level health care facilities through sub-divisional and zonal/district hospitals. Further, tertiary-level health care has been catered for through specialised hospitals and those attached to the state medical colleges. These institutions, besides extending support to the secondary-level health care systems, are expected to carry out research and manpower development for the health services of the state.

Health services under the Allopathic System of Medicines

The state has a number of medical, public health and Ayurvedic institutions (Table 8.3). The table shows that the state also has a number of specialised institutions for treating tuberculosis, leprosy, and sexually transmitted diseases (STDs). Besides these, there are adequate facilities of dental clinics, X-ray clinics, ENT clinics, and maternal and child welfare (MCW) centres. Further, the state receives World Bank assistance to the Reproductive and Child Health (RCH) sub-project in Kinnaur district, UNICEF assistance for Kangra and Chamba districts and World Bank assistance for prevention of gastrointestinal diseases and AIDS. The rural population covered is 2,738 per sub-centre, 12,832 per PHC and 85,745 per CHC against the stipulated norms of 3,000 per sub-centre, 20,000 per primary health centre and 80,000 per community health centre in the hilly and tribal areas[2]. For the tribal areas, comprising Kinnaur, Lahaul and Spiti, Pangi and Bharmour, there are three hospitals, nine CHCs, 36 PHCs, 100 SCs, 84 ayurvedic dispensaries, and two state special hospitals. There are 422 allopathic and 58 ayurvedic beds in the region.

2. Department of Health and Family Welfare, Government of Himachal Pradesh, *Health at a Glance (2002)*, pamphlet

As on 31 March 2003, the total number of beds available under the modern system of medicine is 8,872. Of these, 5,558 beds are in general hospitals, 1,202 in CHCs, and 966 in PHC grade-2 and 124 in PHC grade-1. In addition, 35 beds are reserved for cancer, 751 for tuberculosis, 232 for leprosy, four for sexually transmitted diseases.

Health Services under the Indian Systems of Medicines and Homeopathy

In recent years, the state has been attaching greater importance to institutions related to the Indian system of Medicines and Homoeopathy (ISM&H). A separate department of ISM&H was created on 7 November, 1984. As on 31 March, 2003, there were 724 beds under the ISM&H. There has been tremendous increase in the number of institutions and the amount of budget for Indian systems of medicines and homeopathy since then. Ever since its inception as a separate department, there has been an independent minister in-charge of the Department and senior I.A.S./H.A.S. officers have held the charge of Director. The department has a large network of primary and secondary level institutions. The basic primary unit is Ayurvedic Health Centre (AHC). It covers a population of 3000 to 5000 and caters to outdoor patients only. This centre also functions as a referring unit in case of any emergency after providing first aid treatment. Normally, medicines worth Rs. 15,000 to 20,000 are provided free of cost every year to each AHC. In addition, there are 22 district level/sub-divisional ayurvedic hospitals providing secondary services in the state besides two tertiary level hospitals (one each in Shimla and Kangra). They are providing indoor as well as outdoor services. Normally, these hospitals cover a population of 15,000 to 20,000. Medicines worth Rs. 1.25 lakh for 10-bedded hospitals and Rs. 2.50 lakh for 80/100-bedded hospitals are being provided free of cost every year. The department also started a Nature Cure Unit at Oel in Una district. It intends to upgrade the existing nature cure hospital to 10-50 bedded hospital besides establishing College of Naturopathy and Yoga to provide five and half year degree in Naturopathy and Yoga.

To conserve and enlarge the valuable herbal wealth of the state and to provide a sustainable supply of raw material to the pharmaceutical industry, the state has launched a programme for promotion and conservation of the herbal wealth by setting up herbal gardens in the different agro-climatic zones. Herbal gardens have already been established in Jogindernagar (district Mandi), Neri (District Hamirpur), Dhumrehra (Rohru,

TABLE 8.3

Number of Health Institutions as on 31.3.2003

S. No.	Type of Hospital	Rural	Urban	Total	Remarks/Observations
1.	General hospitals (GHs)	17	33	50	No GH in rural areas in Bilaspur, Kullu district
2.	Community health centres (CHCs)	56	10	66	No primary health care facilities to be set up in urban areas. The institutions shown in urban were earlier in rural areas
3.	Primary health centres (PHCs)	437	4	441	
4.	Civil dispensaries (CDs)	3	18	21	Available in rural areas of Solan, Sirmaur and Kangra district. No urban CD in Chamba, Hamirpur, Kullu, Mandi and Una district. **Maximum 8 Urban CDs in Shimla district**
5.	Sub-centres	2067	-	2067	
	Tuberculosis Institutions				
1.	Hospitals	2	0	2	One in Kangra and another in Solan
2.	District TB clinics/centres	2	10	12	
3.	TB sub-clinics	4	3	7	Two each in rural areas of Chamba and Kinnaur. All three urban Sub-Clinics in Shimla
	Leprosy Institutions				
1.	Hospitals/wards	4	2	6	Chamba, Kangra, Kullu and Solan in rural areas. Mandi and Sirmaur in urban areas
2.	District nucleus	2	10	12	One at each district
3.	State survey assessment units (SSAU)	-	1	1	At Shimla
4.	Leprosy training centers	2	4	6	Rural areas of Solan and Kangra district. Urban areas of Shimla, Sirmaur, Kullu and Chamba district
	STD Institutions				
1.	Clinics/sub-clinics	11	15	26	No STD clinic in rural areas of Bilaspur, Hamirpur, Kangra, Kullu and Una district
2.	Units	34	11	45	No STD unit in rural areas of Hamirpur, Kangra and Una districts. No STD unit in urban areas of Chamba, Hamirpur, Kangra, Solan and Una district
	Indian System of Medicines and Homoeopathy (ISM&H)				
1.	Ayurvedic college	1	0	1	Kangra district
2.	Ayurvedic hospitals	10	13	23	No rural ayurvedic hospital in Mandi, Shimla, Sirmaur and Solan districts. No urban ayurvedic hospital in Kullu district
3.	Ayurvedic dispensaries	1092	20	1112	No urban ayurvedic dispensary in Chamba, Hamirpur, Sirmaur and Una districts
4.	Unani dispensaries	2	1	3	Available only in Kangra, Shimla and Solan districts
5.	Homoeopathic dispensaries	4	10	14	Available at all district headquarters and two in rural areas of Bilaspur and Chamba districts
6.	Nature cure unit	1	0	1	Una district
7.	Ayurvedic pharmacy	1	1	2	Available in rural areas of Sirmaur and urban areas of Mandi district
8.	Ayurvedic research institute	0	1	1	Available in Mandi district
9	Panchkarma centres	1	1	2	One at Paprola in Kangra district, and another in Bilaspur district (urban)
10.	Amchi clinics	4	0	4	Two in each district (Kinnaur and Lahaul and Spiti)
	Other Clinics and Centres				
1.	Dental clinics	67	41	108	Maximum 20 in Kangra followed by 15 in Mandi
2.	X-ray clinics	98	44	142	Maximum 26 in Shimla followed by 20 in Mandi
3.	Eye-ENT clinics	0	11	11	None in rural areas
4.	Maternal and child welfare (M&CW) centres	19	27	46	None in rural areas of Hamirpur, Kullu and Una district. None in urban areas of Hamirpur district

Source: Information provided by the Department of Health and Family Welfare and the Department of ISM&H, Government of Himachal Pradesh.

Note: There is no urban area in Kinnaur and Lahaul and Spiti districts.

All SHCs were converted into PHCs in the year 1986-87.

district Shimla), and Jungal-Jhalera (district Bilaspur). In addition, proposals are to set up herbal gardens at Rakcham/Chitkul (district Kinnaur) and Paprola (district Kangra). Besides a Herbarium has been established at Jogindernagar to keep the specimens of medicinal plants systematically and scientifically. Separate counters are maintained for Root drugs, Bark drugs, Flower drugs, Fruit/Seed drugs, Leaf drugs and Whole plant drugs, etc. During the year 2002-03, the department also organised 33 farmers training camps and three department exhibitions in different districts to create awareness among the farmers/participants with respect to identification, conservation, propagation, cultivation and utilisation of the medicinal flora existing in the State of Himachal Pradesh. A total of 960 farmers were trained/participated. Tenth Plan (2002-07) proposes to strengthen the health care facilities of the ayurvedic system by strengthening the infrastructure and introducing specialised services like *Panchkaram* and *Kshar Sutra*. The Plan also lays stress on the conservation, development, cultivation and utilisation of medicinal plants to improve the quality of raw herbs, material for herbal medicines, and to develop Himachal Pradesh into a herbal state of India. It also recognises the need for modern facilities for drug testing, research, and development of drugs. It contemplates the introduction of modern technology and management techniques to improve the quality and competitiveness of medicines produced in government and private pharmacies of the state. The Plan also proposes to expand the Ayurveda tourism activities in close collaboration with public and private sector hotel industry/health institutions in all parts of the state. Two such centres (one in Joginder Nagar and another at Kullu) has already been started.

Regarding the homoeopathic systems of medicines, the state opened 12 homoeopathic dispensaries (one at each district headquarters) in 1995-96. During the Tenth Five Year Plan, provisions have been made for opening 10 more homoeopathic centres (two each year). There are only three Unani dispensaries in the State functioning since very long. No new unani institution was opened after bifurcation of the department since the department feels absence of public demand for this system of medicine from other parts of the state.

Himachal Health Vision 2020 lists some problems related to the infrastructure. Some of these are uneven distribution of primary health care facilities (400 *panchayats* are still without primary health care facilities, whereas a number of them have two primary health care institutions including ayurvedic health centres) and uneven distribution of health manpower (better staffing in comfortable areas than those in rural and remote areas). Further, the lack of well-defined service norms and standards (absence of hospital manual), poor referral system resulting in under-utilisation of health services and overburdening of the secondary and tertiary health care centres too make a negative contribution. Buildings are poorly maintained and there is absence of residential accommodation. Information, education and communication (IEC) and health management information system (HMIS) are lacking in many respects and are still at a rudimentary stage.[3]

Training Facilities

Adequate training facilities exist for different categories of staff in the state through various training centres and schools. For imparting in-service training to medical officers and para-medical staff, there are two health and family welfare training centres, one at Shimla and the other at Kangra. Further, there are five general nursing training schools with a total capacity of 230 per batch, seven female health workers' training schools with a total capacity of 420 per batch, and six male health workers training schools with a total capacity of 360 per batch. Moreover, Indira Gandhi Medical College, Shimla, and the Zonal Office at Dharamshala also train operation theatre assistants (20), lab technicians (75), radiographers (20) and para medical ophthalmic assistants (20). Training in these hospitals is given only when there is a need to fill departmental vacancies. In addition, there are six leprosy training centres in the state (Table 8.3).

For the ISM&H Department, there are two training institutions, Ayurvedic College at Paprola (Kangra) with an yearly intake of 50, for Bachelor of Ayurvedic Medicines and Surgery (BAMS), and an intake of 14 for M.S./M.D. (Ayurveda) course, and a pharmacy training school at Jogindernagar, which provides a two-year course for ayurvedic pharmacists to meet the needs of the department.

Private Sector, NGOs and Voluntary Health Institutions

The private sector is growing fast in the state with private clinics, nursing homes, and other diagnostic centres. However, with a total bed capacity of approximately 500, the private sector has grown mainly

3. Department of Health and Family Welfare, Himachal Pradesh, *Himachal Health Vision 2020*, p. 21-23.

at Shimla and other district towns.[4] NGOs and other voluntary sectors have not been providing curative services in the state so far. However, one free hospital is being set up in Hamirpur district by a charitable organisation.[5] It seems that NGOs/voluntary sector institutions are not inclined to venture into difficult and far-flung areas of the state, which need their services the most.

Availability of Staff

An examination of the staff position of the Department of Health and Family Welfare (as on 31 March 2003) shows that 21 per cent of its sanctioned 16,743 posts, are vacant. The major vacancies among the medical staff include doctors (9%), nursing superintendents (55%), staff nurses (28%), public health nurses (30%), ANMs designated as staff nurse (21%), female health workers (18%), dais (35%), pharmacists (13%), male health workers (28%), health supervisors (20%), health educators (28%) and computors (25%).[6] Vacancies among the support staff include drivers (14%), class IV servants (22%), sweepers (15%), and cleaners (77%). Besides, vacancies exist in such administrative posts as District Family Welfare Officer (NM), senior assistants, steno-typists, projectionists, housekeepers, etc.

The Department of ISM&H has a total staff strength of 6,359 as on 31.6.2003. They include *ayurveda* medical officers (18%), ayurvedic pharmacists (18%), ANMs (3%), trained *dais* (14%), junior assistants (2%), and Class IV (regular or otherwise) (39%). The department of homoeopathy and Unani system has less staff. For example, there are only 14 homoeopathic doctors and three unani medical officers who constitute an insignificant proportion of the staff strength of the Department of ISM&H. Regarding the vacancies, 26% of total sanctioned posts are vacant in the Department as on 31.6.2003. The major vacancies include teaching staff including professors, readers, lecturers (41%), senior *ayurvedic chikitsak* (56%), *ayurvedic* medical officers (13%), *ayurvedic* pharmacists (46%), staff nurses (33%), ANMs (17%), dais (39%), laboratory technicians (53%), and class IV staff including drivers (19%).

4. *Ibid*, p. 5
5. *Ibid*, p. 21-22.
6. The total sanctioned positions of medical staff include doctors (1498), nursing superintendents (9), staff nurses (1540), public health nurses (30), ANMs designated as staff nurse (258), female health workers (2210), dais (467), pharmacist (854), male health workers (2005), health supervisors (413), health educators (81) and computors (101). The total positions of support staff include drivers (363), class IV servants (2247), sweepers (915), and cleaners (30).

Recent Reforms in Health Sector

Re-classification of Health Institutions

Recently, the government of Himachal Pradesh re-classified the existing health institutions in the rural areas, and rationalised them as under:

TABLE 8.4

Re-classification of Institutions

Sr. No.	*Existing Institutions*	*New Classifications*
1.	Civil dispensaries (except urban) and all PHCs with no facility for indoor treatment	PHC-I
2.	All PHCs with 6 beds and above	PHC-II
3.	All CHCs having only 10 beds in Indoor patients	CHC-I
4.	All CHCs having 11-30 beds	CHC-II

Source: Vide notification No. Health-A-B(1)/5/98-II dated, Shimla-2, the 24th November 2001 by Government of Himachal Pradesh, Department of Health and Family Welfare.

It was further notified that all CDs and PHCs would have the same kind of staff. All PHC-II and CHC-I shall have the same kind of staff. The circular also fixed the staff norms for these institutions, which are as under:

TABLE 8.5

Staff Norms for Health Institutions

Post	*PHC-I*	*PHC-II*	*CHC-I*	*CHC-II*
Medical Officer	1	2	2	4
Ward Sister	-	-	-	1
Staff Nurse	-	1	1	4
Senior Lab Technician	-	-	-	1
Laboratory Technician	-	1	1	-
Radiographer	-	-	-	1
Ophthalmic Assistance	-	-	-	1
O.T. Assistant	-	-	-	1
Pharmacist	1	1	1	2
Clerk	-	1	1	1
Driver	-	1	1	1
Class-IV*	1	1	1	5
Sweeper*	1	1	1	3
Total	**4**	**9**	**9**	**25**

Source: Vide notification No. Health-A-B(1)/5/98-II dated, Shimla-2, the 24th November 2001 by Government of Himachal Pradesh, Department of Health and Family Welfare.

Note: *: It was decided that in future all posts of sweepers/cooks and cleaners would be contractual in nature and on vacation by existing incumbents, these posts will stand abolished and will not be a part of norms for calculating future staff requirements.

Hospital Welfare Societies

Himachal Pradesh is the only state in this region to have started a community financial management

TABLE 8.6

Composition of PARIKAS at Panchayat, Block and District Level

Composition/Level	*Panchayat Level*	*Block Level*	*District Level*
Adhyaksh or Chairman	Pradhan of the gram panchayat	Adhyaksh of panchayat samiti	Chairperson of zila parishad
Sachiv or Secretary	Either male or female health worker	Block Medical Officer	Chief Medical Officer
Sadasya or Members	Ward Panches (not more than four, at least one woman elected Panch); Representatives of NGOs; Social Workers; Opinion Builders: President and Secretary of Mahila Mandal; ayurvedic Chikitsa Adhikari (if an AHC in village); forest guard; One teacher from each of the school in the Panchayat; Anganwadi workers; Trained Traditional Birth Attendants; the other Health Workers. If there are two in the Panchayat shall be the co-opted members.	All the members of the Panchayat Samiti; Representative of the NGOs (if any), Opinion builders, social workers, known active female workers; Ayurvedic Chikitsa Adhikaris; Medical Officer incharge of PHC in the block; Male and Female Health supervisors; Block Primary and Secondary Education Officers; Assistant Engineer (Roads and Buildings); Representative of Social Welfare Department looking after the block.	All members of Zila Parishad; Active Female workers of the District; District Primary/ Secondary Officer; Executive Engineer (B& R); representatives of NGOs (if any); Social Workers; Representative of Deputy Commissioner to be nominated by DC; District Panchayat Officer, District Social Welfare Officer

Source: Vide notification no. HFW-B (F) 7-2/2001 dated 10.12.2001 of Department of Medical Education, Department of Health and Family Welfare, Government of Himachal Pradesh and orders of Commissioner-cum-Secretary (Health) to the Government of Himachal Pradesh.

programme. It has set up hospital welfare societies at zonal/district hospitals to collect user charges and utilise these for fulfilling the needs of these hospitals. Earlier these societies were known as *Rogi Kalyan Samitis* (patient welfare committees). These committees were autonomous in nature and were capable of improving the hospitals by collecting finances from the community and levying user charges. By 2001-2002, these were set up in all the 12 zonal/district hospitals and 21 sub-divisional hospitals. Since these committees were fixing user charges for diagnostic and other services differently in different parts of the state, there was resentment among the population. As a result, the state government recently changed the name of these committees to Hospital Welfare Societies and rationalised the user charges. Now uniform user charges (as prevailing before 1998) would be applicable throughout the state in all hospitals for diagnostic and other services.

c. Involvement of Panchayati Raj Institutions (PRIs)

Himachal Pradesh has set up health and family welfare advisory committees known as Parivar Kalyan Salahkar Samiti (PARIKAS) at the *panchayat*, block and district levels[7] for the involvement of the PRIs. The functions of the *panchayat* PARIKAS include supervision and monitoring; implementation of national health programmes; ensuring cleanliness of the villages; checking pollution of water, air and noise; making people aware of dog and snake bites and their first aid treatment; cleaning and using bleaching powder, etc., for traditional water sources; disseminating information about reproductive and child health (RCH) care; checking regular opening of sub-centres and ensuring that immunisation and other necessary facilities are being provided to the newborn by the health functionaries; helping in updating the records of births, deaths and marriages; and preparing health micro plans every year. The functions of the block and district PARIKAS are to provide effective leadership and able guidance; hold periodic inspection of health institutions through sub-committees (with each sub-committee having an elected representative and a medical officer nominated by PARIKAS); appropriate counselling, whenever required; and disseminating information, education and communication (IEC). It is also envisaged that the PARIKAS at the three levels will be broad based and shall function as interdepartmental co-ordination committees. The composition of the PARIKAS at the *panchayat* level will be as under:

Morbidity Patterns in Himachal Pradesh

Himachal Pradesh has a generally healthy population. The NSS 52nd round gives information on morbidity patterns in the state. It indicates that the state has a high morbidity rate compared to India and the neighbouring states of Haryana and Punjab (Table 8.7). The table further indicates that morbidity is high in the rural areas of Himachal Pradesh compared to Haryana and Punjab, and the all-India position. This is because Himachal is primarily a rural state. Morbidity is

7. Vide Notification No. HFW-B (F) 7-2/2001 dated 10.12.2001 of Department of Medical Education, Department of Health and Family Welfare, Government of Himachal Pradesh and orders of Commissioner-cum-Secretary (Health) to the Government of Himachal Pradesh.

TABLE 8.7

Number of Persons Reporting Ailments during the Last 15 Days Prior to Survey per 1000 Persons by Age and Sex (Type of Ailments: Any)

Characteristics	*Rural Areas*				*Urban Areas*			
	H.P.	*Punjab*	*Haryana*	*India*	*H.P.*	*Punjab*	*Haryana*	*India*
Males								
0-14	57	76	64	50	53	85	38	54
15-39	60	54	36	35	63	75	46	35
40-59	94	66	60	64	88	77	56	61
60 and above	295	171	139	178	241	194	101	148
All	84	71	57	54	71	84	47	51
Females								
0-14	45	50	47	45	41	64	47	49
15-39	79	69	51	45	46	72	66	45
40-59	136	126	123	75	80	120	117	73
60 and above	305	181	136	161	244	242	260	166
All	96	81	65	57	59	86	80	58

Source: 'NSS, 52nd Round (July 1995-June 1996)', *Morbidity and Treatment of Ailments*, NSSO, Department of Statistics, Government of India, November 1998.

particularly high among elderly persons (aged 60 and above) in both the sexes. This may be due to the higher life expectancy in the state.

Table 8.8 compares prevalence of acute[8] and chronic[9] illnesses in respect of age, sex, caste, and residential status. In Himachal Pradesh, there is a higher prevalence of acute and chronic illnesses in rural as well as urban areas. Although chronic diseases among males appear usually after the age of 60 years (169 in rural areas and 90 in urban areas), the prevalence of such illnesses is also on the higher side among young males (age 40-59) in urban areas. Females show a similar trend except that chronic illness among the rural women starts at an early age compared to urban women. The prevalence level of acute illness has a direct relationship with increase in age. Higher the age, higher the prevalence of acute illness. In all, long duration illnesses are less prevalent than short duration illnesses at most ages, but for 60 plus. No substantial caste differentials in morbidity have been noticed.

Since mostly the elderly (Table 8.8) suffer from chronic or long duration illnesses, an attempt has been made to understand the types of diseases involved. Table 8.9 shows that major chronic illnesses suffered by rural elderly persons include problems of joints, cough, high/low BP while the major illnesses among the urban elderly persons include high/low BP and problem of joints. The table further reveals that urinary problems are more prevalent among males than females in both rural and urban areas. The incidence of high/low BP and heart diseases is much higher in urban areas. Prevalence of piles is relatively higher among males in the urban areas. Diabetes is more prevalent in urban areas.

Disease Prevalence (Based on Inpatient and Outpatient Records)

The Department of Health and Family Welfare maintains and compiles records of all inpatients and outpatients in the state. Examination of data for five years (1997-2001) surprisingly reveals that the department did not classify 67-70 per cent of outdoor patients, and 77-82 per cent of the indoor patients by the type of diseases they suffered from and simply marked them under other diseases. Among the classified diseases, acute respiratory infections (ARIs)

8. Acute or short duration ailments include diarrhoea and gastroenteritis dysentery (including cholera); tetanus; diphtheria; whooping cough; meningitis and viral encephalitis; fever of short duration; chicken pox; measles/German measles; mumps; disease of eye; acute disease of ear; heart failure; cerebral stroke; cough and acute bronchitis; acute respiratory infection (including pneumonia); diseases of mouth, teeth and gum; injury due to accident and violence; other diagnosed ailments (up to 30 days); and undiagnosed ailments (up to 30 days).
9. Chronic or long duration ailments include chronic amebiosis; pulmonary tuberculosis; STDs; leprosy; jaundice; guinea worm; filaria (elephantiasis); cancer; other tumours; (general debility) anaemia; goitre and thyroid disorders; diabetes; beri beri; ricket; other malnutrition diseases; mental and behavioural disorders; epilepsy; other diseases of nerves; cataract; other visual disabilities; other diseases of the eye; hearing disability; other diseases of the ear; diseases of the heart; high/low blood pressure; piles; speech disability; diseases of mouth, teeth and gum; gastritis hyper-acidity/gastric/peptic/duodenal ulcer; diseases of kidney/urinary system; prostrate disorders; pain in joints; other disorders of bones and joints; locomotor disability; other congenital deformities (excluding disability); other diagnosed diseases (more than 30 days); and undiagnosed ailments (more than 30 days). It is pertinent to mention here that chronic illnesses are long duration illnesses involving very slow change. It does not imply anything about the severity of the disease.

TABLE 8.8

Acute and Chronic Ailments Classified by Age, Sex, Caste, and Residential Status (per 1000 persons)

	Rural Areas				*Urban Areas*			
	H.P.		*All India*		*H.P.*		*All India*	
	Acute	*Chronic*	*Acute*	*Chronic*	*Acute*	*Chronic*	*Acute*	*Chronic*
Males classified by age								
0-14	52	4	46	3	49	4	51	3
15-39	49	12	27	8	49	14	28	7
40-59	80	14	42	22	67	31	36	24
60+	153	169	95	86	163	90	65	85
All	64	23	41	13	56	17	39	13
Females classified by age								
0-14	38	7	43	3	41	-	47	3
15-39	57	23	36	9	41	5	37	9
40-59	94	47	48	27	65	16	42	31
60+	132	186	90	73	104	140	73	94
All	63	35	44	14	48	11	43	15
Males classified by caste								
Scheduled Castes	75	13	41	12	50	6	39	10
Scheduled Tribes	19	10	37	5	-	-	35	7
Others	61	28	42	14	58	20	39	13
Females classified by caste								
Scheduled Castes	79	49	43	12	27	-	45	12
Scheduled Tribes	49	16	38	5	-	-	37	10
Others	56	29	45	16	52	13	43	16

Source: 'NSS, 52nd Round (July 1995-June 1996)', *Morbidity and Treatment of Ailments*, NSSO, Department of Statistics, Government of India, November 1998.

including influenza but excluding pneumonia accounted for 21 per cent to 24 per cent of the outdoor patients during 1997-2001, followed by acute diarrhoreal diseases including gastroenteritis and cholera (7%). Pneumonia, pulmonary tuberculosis and enteric fever patients together constituted about one per cent of the outdoor patients. Very few patients were suffering from whooping cough and syphilis. The state reported almost complete absence of diphtheria, whooping cough, acute poliomyelitis, tetanus (neonatal or otherwise), Japanese encephalitis, meningococcal meningitis and rabies. On the other hand, classification of the records of indoor patients shows that ARIs accounted for seven to ten per cent of the indoor patients, followed by acute diarrhoreal diseases including gastroenteritis and cholera (5 to 7%). Pneumonia, enteric fever and pulmonary tuberculosis together accounted for about five per cent of the indoor patients in different hospitals. Among the indoor patients, the major causes of death were pulmonary tuberculosis, pneumonia, ARIs, and acute diarrhoreal diseases.

The Directorate of Health and Family Welfare, Government of Himachal Pradesh, entrusted a special study to the Department of Community Medicine, Post Graduate Institute of Medical Education and Research (PGIMER), Chandigarh, to assess the burden of disease in Himachal Pradesh. The findings of the draft estimation report are shown in Table 8.10. It shows the top ten causes of the burden of diseases (DALYs) in Himachal Pradesh classified by age and sex. According to it, the disease pattern vary with age and sex in

TABLE 8.9

Number of Elderly Population Reporting Chronic Diseases per 100,000 Aged Persons by Type of Chronic Disease Suffered, Sex and Residential Status

Name of Chronic Disease	*Rural Areas*		*Urban Areas*	
	Male	*Female*	*Male*	*Female*
Cough	14449	12139	17330	11814
Piles	1794	2764	5111	1789
Problem of joints	31169	38350	19124	50178
High/Low B.P.	10402	19838	39490	27250
Heart disease	2412	5908	14925	5252
Urinary problems	8186	1475	4820	2199
Diabetics	-	967	3172	2269
Cancer	764	1368	-	-
Any	43896	45882	54592	68914
Sample	391	374	50	46

Source: 'NSS 52nd round, July 1995-June 1996,' *Socio-economic Conditions of Ageing*, *Sarvekshana*, Vol. XXIII, No. 3, 82nd Issue, January-March 2000, p. S-414-416.

TABLE 8.10

Top 10 Causes of Burden of Diseases (DALYs) in Himachal Pradesh Classified by Age and Sex

Rank	Males					Females				
	0-4	5-14	15-44	45-59	60+	0-4	5-14	15-44	45-59	60+
1	Lower respiratory infections	Iron-deficiency anaemia	Road accidents	Chronic obstructive ,Pulmonary disease	Chronic obstructive Pulmonary disease	Lower respiratory infections	Iron-deficiency anaemia	Iron-deficiency anaemia	Chronic obstructive Pulmonary disease	Chronic obstructive Pulmonary disease
2	Diarrhoreal diseases	Asthma	Other unintentional injuries	Tuberculosis	Ischaemic heart disease	Diarrhoreal diseases	Diarrhoreal diseases	Other maternal conditions	Other maternal conditions	Asthma
3	Other maternal conditions[10]	Other unintentional injuries	Iron-deficiency Anaemia	Other unintentional injuries	Asthma	Other infectious diseases	Other unintentional injuries	Other unintentional injuries	Iron-deficiency anaemia	Ischaemic heart disease
4	Perinatal conditions	Diarrhoeal diseases	Chronic obstructive Pulmonary disease	Ischaemic heart disease	Tuberculosis	Other maternal conditions	Otitis Media	Maternal haemorrhage	Other unintentional injuries	Other infectious diseases
5	Other	Otitis media infectious diseases	Self-inflicted injury	Iron deficiency anaemia	Other unintentional injuries	Perinatal conditions	Asthma	Chronic obstructive Pulmonary disease	Tuberculosis	Tuberculosis
6	Road accidents	Dental caries	Ischaemic heart disease	Asthma	Other infectious diseases	Birth asphyxia and birth trauma	Dental caries	Asthma	Dental caries	Cataract
7	Iron deficiency anaemia	Lower respiratory infections	Asthma	Dental caries	Iron-deficiency anaemia	Iron deficiency anaemia	Lower respiratory infections	Road accidents	Ischaemic heart disease	Iron-deficiency anaemia
8	Birth asphyxia and birth trauma	Upper respiratory infections	Upper respiratory infections	Road accidents	Diarrhoeal diseases	Measles	Upper respiratory infections	Dental caries	Other cardiac diseases	Diarrhoeal diseases
9	Dental caries	Other infectious diseases	Dental caries	Peptic ulcer	Cataracts	Falls	Falls	Upper respiratory infections	Diarrhoeal diseases	Other unintentional injuries
10.	Falls	Falls	Diarrhoreal diseases	Cataracts	Dental caries	Low birth weight	Other infectious diseases	Abortion	Other infectious diseases	Dental caries

Source: Department of Community Medicine, Post Graduate Institute of Medical Education and Research, (2003) *Himachal Burden of Disease Study Draft Estimation Report 2003.*

Himachal Pradesh. Lower respiratory infections and diarrhoreal diseases are the most frequent causes of the disease burden among children aged 0-4 years irrespective of sex. While iron-deficiency anaemia is the most frequent among the children in the age group of 5-14, diarrhoreal diseases, asthma and other unintentional injuries are also widely prevalent in this age group. Whereas road accidents and other unintentional injuries are most common among males in the age group of 15-44, it is iron-deficiency anaemia and other maternal conditions that account for most of the burden of disease among females in this age group. From the age 45 and above, chronic obstructive pulmonary disease constitute the largest burden of disease among both sexes. Further, tuberculosis, ischaemic heart disease, other unintentional injuries and asthma are widely prevalent among the males aged 45 and above, while other maternal conditions, asthma, iron-deficiency anaemia and ischaemic heart disease are prevalent among the females of the same age group.

Status of Maternal, Child and Reproductive Health

Two recent surveys, namely, National Family Health Survey (NFHS-II, 1998-99) and Multiple Indicator Survey (MICS 2000), collected information on the status of maternal and child health (comprising antenatal, natal and postnatal care), management of reproductive track infections and nutritional deficiencies

10. Includes maternal sepsis, maternal haemorrhage, hypertensive disorders of pregnancy and abortions.

in the state. A few findings where immediate intervention is required are listed below:

Deficiencies: Anaemia[11] is widely prevalent among women (41%) and children (70%) in Himachal Pradesh with nine per cent of women and 41 per cent of children being severely anaemic[12]. 41 per cent of the children are chronically undernourished (stunted), 17 per cent wasted and 44 per cent underweight.[13] In Himachal Pradesh, 68 per cent of the babies (31% in urban areas and 71% in rural areas), born in the three years preceding the survey, were not weighed at birth.[14]

Antenatal care: NFHS-2 points out that 13 per cent women (mostly rural) had no antenatal check-up at the time of first child birth, 6 per cent had only one antenatal checkup and 19 per cent (10% in urban areas and 20% in rural areas) had only two antenatal check-ups, against the Ministry of Health and Family Welfare (MOHFW), Government of India's guidelines of having at least three antenatal care visits for pregnant women. Among those who received at least one antenatal check-up, only 55 per cent received it during the first trimester, 40 per cent during the second trimester and five per cent during the third trimester. Moreover, among them, 67 per cent received antenatal check-up from a medical officer outside their homes and 33 per cent from other health professionals at home or outside. Regarding the administration of tetanus toxoid injection to prevent neonatal deaths, 34 per cent of the women did not receive the two desired doses of TT injections during their recent pregnancy, 23 per cent received only one injection and 11 per cent none. Fourteen per cent of the women did not receive any iron and folic acid tablets or syrup to provide additional nutrient requirements of foetal growth.[15] The *Multiple Indicator Survey* (MICS-2000) also points out that in Himachal Pradesh only 81 per cent of the women (80% in rural areas and 89% in urban areas), who delivered during the year preceeding the survey, received antenatal check-up. The position with regard to TT doses was much worse. For instance, only 54 per cent of the women received two or more doses. Similarly, only 57 per cent women (55% in rural areas and 79% in urban areas) had their blood pressure checked.

Natal care: The place of delivery and assistance during delivery constitute two essential ingredients of natal care. NFHS-2 indicates that most (71%) of the births in the state are home deliveries, and only 29 per cent are institutional deliveries, out of which 80 per cent are in the public sector. Mostly people with a high standard of living visit private institutions for delivery. Women who received more than three antenatal check-ups constitute the major chunk of institutional deliveries (49%). The survey points out that 57 per cent of the births in the three years preceding the survey were attended by traditional birth attendants (TBAs), three per cent by friends, relatives and other persons, and only 40 per cent by a health professional, including 31 per cent by a doctor and nine per cent by an ANM, nurse, midwife or LHV. According to MICS-2000, only 32.5 per cent of the deliveries (30% in rural areas and 61% in urban areas) were institutional deliveries. But, deliveries assisted by a health professional were 44 per cent (41% in rural areas and 71% in urban areas). Some of the reasons for fewer institutional deliveries in Himachal Pradesh are absence of health workers from the place of posting, and poor connectivity (road transport) particularly in rural areas.

Postnatal care: Postnatal care requires a minimum three postpartum visits by the field worker according to the RCH manual. During these visits, abdominal examination, advice on breast-feeding, baby care and family planning is provided. According to NFHS-II, only 21 per cent of the women received a postpartum check-up within two months of childbirth. One of the reasons for less post-natal care is the lesser number of home visits by health workers. NFHS-II indicates that only 3.7 per cent of the women received at least one visit by a health or family planning worker in the 12 months preceding the survey.[16] Further, the proportion of non-institutional births that receive post-partum check-up is very low (4-14%) largely depending upon whether the woman has received the antenatal check-up and the standard of living of the household.[17] During the check-up, abdominal examination was carried out on 50 per cent of the women, and advice on breastfeeding, baby care and family planning was given to 60 per cent, 53 per cent and 27 per cent of the women respectively. According to MICS-2000, only 16 per cent of the women (15% in the rural areas and 30% in the urban areas) received postnatal care.

Immunisation: People in Himachal Pradesh are aware of child immunisation. NFHS-II figures for the state

11. With haemoglobin level < 11.0 grams/decilitre for children and pregnant women, and < 12 grams for non-pregnant women.
12. With haemoglobin level < 10.0 grams/decilitre.
13. Stunting assessed by height-for-age, wasting assessed by weight for height, underweight assessed weight-for-age.
14. *National Family Health Survey-II, Himachal Pradesh*, p. 184.
15. *National Family Health Survey –II, Himachal Pradesh*, p. 176-179.
16. National Family Health Survey-II, (NFHS-II), Himachal Pradesh, p. 198.
17. *Ibid.*, p. 185.

show that 83 per cent of the children aged 12-23 received all vaccinations. The vaccination coverage rates are higher for the boys (87%) than the girls (79%). Literacy of the mother is important for the immunisation drive to be successful since the coverage rates ranged from 67 per cent for illiterate women to more than 90 per cent for women who were educated at least up to middle school level.

Reproductive Health: NFHS-II points out that reproductive health problems are widely prevalent in Himachal Pradesh with 34 per cent of the currently married women reporting some such problem. Among them, 27 per cent related to vaginal discharge, 14 per cent symptoms of urinary track infection, nine per cent complained of painful intercourse and one per cent reported bleeding after intercourse. These reproductive health problems are indicative of some serious reproductive track infection (RTI). The worrisome factor is that 47 per cent of these women have not sought advice or treatment for these infections.

HIV/AIDS: HIV/AIDS emerged in the state only in the early 90s, when the first AIDS case was detected in 1992. During the period March 2000-March 2003, the number of HIV-positive persons have increased from 201 to 531, and the number of AIDS patients from 72 to 143[18]. By 2001, HIV/AIDS cases were reported from every district except the tribal district of Lahaul and Spiti. HIV-positive cases are concentrated in the five districts of Shimla, Bilaspur, Hamirpur, Mandi and Kangra.[19] Thus, a majority of the HIV/AIDS infections are reported along the national highways, i.e., from Shimla to Kangra and from Anandpur Sahib to Manali. MICS-2000 focuses on awareness about HIV/AIDS. Sixty-four per cent of the women aged 15-49 in Himachal Pradesh (61% in rural areas and 85% in the urban areas) have heard about HIV/AIDS. Awareness about AIDS was higher among the never married women (78%) than among the ever-married women (59%). Given the socio-economic status of the state, and the recent spurt in HIV-positive/AIDS cases, the problem needs thorough investigation. Voluntary counselling and testing facilities should be extended to all zonal/district hospitals with immediate effect.

Health-Seeking Behaviour/ Utilisation of Health Care Services

Health-seeking behaviour or utilisation of health care services is influenced largely by access to health facilities, individual and family beliefs and attitudes related to illness and the system of medicine, cost of treatment and individual capacity to pay. The following section is an attempt to analyse the health-seeking behaviour of the population for preventive and curative health care services during non-hospitalised (outdoor) and hospitalised (indoor) illnesses. An attempt has also been made to find out the influence of socio-economic, and other behavioral factors such as the type of treatment preferred, choice of public/private or voluntary sector and the cost of treatment.

Preventive and Curative Services by Source of Treatment

Table 8.11 gives a picture of the role of the public and the private sectors in providing contraceptives, preventive and curative services in Himachal Pradesh, as pointed out by NFHS-II. The table shows that the public sector plays a crucial role in all spheres of health including preventive, contraceptive, immunisation, and curative services in the state. The public sector caters more to the rural population than to the urban. The table shows that 98 per cent of all children received vaccination from the public sector. Ninety-four per cent of the contraceptive users in rural areas and 68 per cent in urban areas obtain contraceptives from the public medical sector. The survey has revealed that the share of the private health sector in immunisation has a direct relationship with urbanisation, mother's education (at least high school), and households with a

TABLE 8.11

Share of Public and Private Sector in Contraceptive, Preventive, Curative Services

Type of Service	*Share of Public Sector*			*Share of Private Sector Including Shops*		
	Rural	*Urban*	*Total*	*Rural*	*Urban*	*Total*
All modern contraception	94.2	68.4	91.7	4.8	29.3	7.1
Male sterilisation	100.0	(100.0)	100.0	0.0	0.0	0.0
Female sterilisation	99.2	97.8	99.1	0.7	1.8	0.8
IUD	(85.3)	56.0	77.2	(14.7)	44.0	22.8
Oral Pills	(59.3)	*	(53.1)	(37.0)	*	(42.6)
Condoms	36.1	14.8	29.2	48.2	78.3	57.9
Childhood vaccination	98.3	94.9	98.0	1.0	4.6	1.3
Per cent share in institutional delivery	20.6	55.6	23.2	4.8	16.4	5.7
Usual source of health care	58.6	60.5	58.8	41.3	39.5	41.1

Source: *National Family Health Survey (NFHS)-II, Himachal Pradesh*, India 1998-99.

Note: The totals will not add up to 100 due to the presence of other categories such as missing and source unknown.

( ) Based on 25-49 unweighted cases.

* Percentage not shown: based on fewer than 25 unweighted cases.

18. Director, State AIDS Control Society, Himachal Pradesh.
19. Government of Himachal Pradesh (2002), *Himachal Pradesh Human Development Report 2002*, p. 139

high standard of living. As for the curative services, the table shows that 59 per cent of the households in Himachal Pradesh normally visit the public medical sector. In fact, the utilisation of public health services is much higher in Himachal Pradesh than in the country as a whole (29%). Overall, three types of health providers are generally used as a source of treatment by almost all the households. Thirty per cent of the households prefer treatment from private doctors, 55 per cent from the government/municipal hospital, government dispensary, CHC/PHC, and 10 per cent from private hospitals. Moreover, the pattern of service utilisation is almost similar in rural and urban areas. As for institutional deliveries, more people visit public health institutions than private nursing homes (23.2% as against 5.7% of the total deliveries).

Type of Treatment Preferred for Non-hospitalised Illnesses Episodes

Different household sample surveys (NSSO 1986-87 and NCAER 1993) conducted in the state point out that the allopathic treatment remains the most preferred form of treatment among the households. For instance, Table 8.12 (based on the sample survey conducted by NSSO through 42nd round) shows that a large majority of the state's population (93% in rural areas and 97% in urban areas) relies on allopathic medicines for treatment of non-hospitalised illnesses.

Likewise, the household survey of health care utilisation and expenditure (NCAER, 1993) reaffirms that allopathic treatment remains the most preferred form in both rural and urban areas of Himachal Pradesh for non-hospitalised illnesses. Despite the tremendous efforts made by the state government to promote the Indian system of medicines and Homoeopathy, nine out of ten households still prefer treatment by allopathic sources. According to the survey, no household in Himachal Pradesh received treatment from Unani or Homoeopathic sources. Ironically, more households in Haryana preferred treatment from sources other than allopathic (Table 8.13).

TABLE 8.12

Non-hospitalised Illness Episodes by Type of Treatment

System of Medicines	*Rural Areas*				*Urban Areas*			
	H.P.	*Punjab*	*Haryana*	*India*	*H.P.*	*Punjab*	*Haryana*	*India*
Allopathic	93.0	97.8	97.4	95.9	97.4	97.8	98.2	96.3
Homoeopathic	1.9	0.2	0.0	1.8	0.4	0.9	0.7	2.1
Ayurvedic	4.3	1.1	1.9	1.5	0.4	0.6	0.6	1.0
Unani/Hakimi	0.1	0.4	0.4	0.3	1.4	0.4	0.1	0.3
Any combination	0.4	0.1	0.0	0.1	0.0	0.0	0.3	0.1
Others	0.3	0.4	0.3	0.4	0.4	0.2	0.0	0.2
Total	100.0	100.0	100.0	100.0	100.0	100.0	100.0	100.0

Source: 'NSS 42nd round (July 1986-June 1987), *Morbidity and Utilisation of Medical Services*, *Sarvekshana*, *Vol.* XV, No. 4, Issue no. 51, April-June 1992, p. 71-72.

TABLE 8.13

Non-hospitalised Illness Episodes by Type of Treatment

System of Medicines	*Rural Areas*				*Urban Areas*			
	H.P.	*Punjab*	*Haryana*	*India*	*H.P.*	*Punjab*	*Haryana*	*India*
Allopathic	93.5	97.3	86.2	90.9	97.2	94.9	89.9	93.2
Homoeopathic	0.0	1.4	0.0	2.0	0.0	0.7	0.0	2.9
Ayurveda/Siddha	3.1	0.0	8.3	3.8	2.8	2.3	4.1	2.2
Unani	0.0	0.0	0.0	0.2	0.0	0.0	0.0	0.1
Any combination	3.4	1.4	5.2	2.0	0.0	2.	6.1	1.2
Rituals	0.0	0.0	0.3	0.6	0.0	0.0	0.0	0.3
Others	0.0	0.0	0.0	0.5	0.0	0.0	0.0	0.2
Total	100.0	100.0	100.0	100.0	100.0	100.0	100.0	100.0

Source: NCAER, *Household Survey of Health Care Utilisation and Expenditure*, March 1995.

Recent Trends

An examination of indoor and outdoor patients seeking treatment from the two departments (Department of Health and Family Welfare and the Department of ISM&H) indicates that ISM&H enjoys a share of 24 to 30 per cent among the total patients treated during the period 1994-95 to 1999-2000.[20] This state of affairs calls for introspection of the government.

Source of Treatment and Payment Mechanism for Non-hospitalised Illness Episodes

This section describes the findings of some all-India surveys on preferred source of treatment and payment mechanism in Himachal Pradesh. For a non-hospitalised illness episode, NSS 42nd round points out that more people have obtained no-payment treatment or free treatment in both rural and urban areas of Himachal Pradesh than in India (Table 8.14). Payment was made to government or private institutions by 30 per cent of the households in rural areas of Himachal Pradesh as compared to 46 per cent in India, and by 16 per cent households in urban areas of Himachal Pradesh compared to 44 per cent in India. Very few households (4%) in rural and urban areas made payment to private institutions in the state as compared to the rest of India (above 30%). From this, it can be inferred that in Himachal Pradesh very few people are willing to pay for the treatment received. This is different from the attitude in some of the neighbouring states of Punjab and Haryana, where more people are willing to pay for treatment, and also more people obtain health services from the private sector.

Another survey (NCAER 1993) reveals that the distribution of non-hospitalised illness-episodes by the type of treatment is slightly favourable to the private sector for males in rural areas. Otherwise a higher percentage prefer treatment from a public source. Only few females in rural areas of Himachal Pradesh reported receiving treatment from a medical shop or store, which is the usual practice in other parts of India. Moreover, households in Himachal Pradesh do not believe in going to faith healers or religious persons for treatment, according to this survey. Only three per cent of the women preferred home remedies, that too in rural areas.

The 52nd round (1995-96) of NSSO also collected data on the treatment of ailments. Table 8.16 shows that more households preferred treatment (including medicines and tests) from government sources in Himachal Pradesh than in the neighbouring states of Punjab and Haryana, and the rest of India.

TABLE 8.14

Percentage Distribution of Treatments (not as an in-patient) by Payment Category

Payment Category/ Institution	*Rural*		*Urban*	
	H.P.	*All-India*	*H.P.*	*All-India*
Payment category				
No payment	65.78	49.14	49.19	42.26
Under employer's medical welfare scheme	4.49	5.21	15.63	13.74
Per cent reportedly made payment to institutions				
Government institutions	25.91	12.42	31.62	12.65
Private institutions	3.82	33.23	3.56	31.35
All (Government and Private)	29.73	45.65	16.25	44.00
Total	100.0	100.0	100.0	100.0

Source: 'NSS 42nd round (July 1986-June 1987)', *Morbidity and Utilisation of Medical Services, Sarvekshana*, Vol. XV, No. 4, Issue no. 51, April-June 1992, p. 71-72.

TABLE 8.15

Percent Distribution of Non-hospitalised Illness Episodes by Type of Treatment

Type of Facility	*Rural Areas*				*Urban Areas*			
	H.P.		*India*		*H.P.*		*India*	
	Male	*Female*	*Male*	*Female*	*Male*	*Female*	*Male*	*Female*
Public facility	43.6	56.5	40.2	43.3	60.8	63.6	34.7	33.2
Private facility	56.4	40.0	54.5	50.8	39.2	36.5	58.9	60.9
Medical shop	0.0	0.8	2.6	3.7	0.0	0.0	5.5	5.0
Faith/healer/ religious person	0.0	0.0	0.7	0.3	0.0	0.0	0.3	0.2
Home remedies	0.0	2.7	2.0	2.0	0.0	0.0	0.7	0.8
Total	**100.0**	**100.0**	**100.0**	**100.0**	**100.0**	**100.0**	**100.0**	**100.0**

Source: NCAER, *Household Survey of Health Care Utilisation and Expenditure*, March 1995.

20. Government of Himachal Pradesh (1999), *Statistical Abstract of Himachal Pradesh*.

TABLE 8.16

Percentage of Ailments Receiving Non-hospitalised Treatment from Government Sources Classified by Type of Service

Type of Treatment	*H.P.*		*Punjab*		*Haryana*		*India*	
	Rural	*Urban*	*Rural*	*Urban*	*Rural*	*Urban*	*Rural*	*Urban*
Medicine	38.7	48.1	7.0	7.2	13.4	17.3	25.2	17.4
X-Ray, ECG, Scan etc.	33.2	(*)	6.7	26.8	(*)	22.5	18.5	24.7
Other diagnostic tests	10.1	(*)	6.3	10.8	51.5	23.1	20.2	21.1
Surgery	(*)	(-)	(*)	(*)	(-)	(*)	14.8	18.3
Other treatment	(*)	(-)	18.3	(*)	(*)	40.7	27.6	22.1

Source: 'NSS, 52nd Round (July 1995-June 1996)', *Morbidity and Treatment of Ailments*, NSSO, Department of Statistics, Government of India, Report No. 441, November 1998.

Note: (-) indicates no sampled household.

(*) indicates the results were ignored since the sample size was too small (n=<20).

Table 8.17 illustrates the distribution of non-hospitalised cases by the type of treatment and type of medical service (medicines, X-ray, ECG, other diagnostic test, surgery and other treatment). It reveals that even though people utilised paid medical services in the private sector, yet the percentage of people visiting the private sector is much less in Himachal Pradesh than in the whole of India. 38 per cent of the rural population and 48 per cent of the urban population in Himachal Pradesh continue to visit the public sector services for medicines. The sample size is very small to arrive at conclusions with respect to other services comprising X-ray, ECG, diagnostic tests, surgery and other treatment.

TABLE 8.17

Per Thousand Distribution of Non-hospitalised Cases (not treated as in-patients of hospitals) During Last 15 Days by Type of Ward of Government and Other Hospital

Type of Medical Service	*Government*				*Other*				*No. of Cases Treated*
	Free	*Partly Free*	*Paying*	*All*	*Free*	*Partly Free*	*Paying*	*All*	
Medicines									
H.P. (rural)	42	56	289	387	3	6	606	615	757
India (rural)	60	26	96	182	17	6	796	819	15949
H.P. (urban)	32	23	426	481	36	-	483	519	109
India (urban)	73	20	81	174	20	7	799	826	11472
X-ray, ECG, Scan etc.									
H.P. (rural)	57	78	197	332	57	-	612	669	21
India (rural)	48	9	128	185	39	6	770	815	654
H.P. (urban)	312	-	623	935	-	28	36	64	8
India (urban)	137	11	99	247	42	11	699	752	777
Other diagnostic tests									
H.P. (rural)	32	13	56	101	278	-	621	899	20
India (rural)	129	7	66	202	56	38	705	799	1606
H.P. (urban)	362	-	354	716	-	-	284	284	11
India (urban)	138	7	66	211	55	4	731	790	1704
Surgery									
H.P. (rural)	180	-	-	180	12	-	808	820	9
India (rural)	75	1	72	148	77	3	772	852	225
H.P. (urban)	-	-	-	-	-	-	-	-	0
India (urban)	128	4	51	181	126	6	685	817	211
Other treatments									
H.P. (rural)	45	-	-	45	214	-	742	956	9
India (rural)	165	9	102	276	64	26	635	725	1237
H.P. (urban)	-	-	-	-	-	-	-	-	0
India (urban)	136	11	74	221	72	14	694	780	1041

Source: 'NSS, 52nd Round (July 1995-June 1996)', *Morbidity and Treatment of Ailments*, NSSO, Department of Statistics, Government of India, November 1998.

TABLE 8.18

Per Thousand Distribution of Hospitalised Cases During Last 365 Days Classified by Type of Ward of Government and Other Hospitals and Residential Status of the Household

Area	*Government*				*Other*				*No. of Cases Treated*
	Free	*Paying General*	*Paying Special*	*All*	*Free*	*Paying General*	*Paying Special*	*All*	
H.P. (rural)	772	79	14	865	18	56	40	115	393
Punjab (rural)	235	135	7	377	33	529	17	579	542
India (rural)	388	41	8	438	28	411	91	529	14029
H.P. (urban)	705	175	33	913	5	23	53	80	107
Punjab (urban)	159	102	5	265	28	608	61	696	504
India (urban)	347	55	16	419	35	372	146	553	12497

Source: 'NSS, 52nd Round (July 1995-June 1996)', *Morbidity and Treatment of Ailments*, NSSO, Department of Statistics, Government of India, November 1998.

Source of Treatment and Payment Mechanism for Hospitalised Illness Episodes

Table 8.18 shows the division of hospitalised cases by the type of treatment and payment category. It is evident that Himachal Pradesh is one state where more people (86% in rural areas and 91% in urban areas) visit a public sector facility for indoor treatment. The respective figures for the neighbouring state of Punjab and all-India are 38 per cent and 44 per cent for rural areas and 26 per cent and 42 per cent for urban areas respectively.

Cost of Treatment

It is well established that the cost of treatment is an important factor in the choice of health care. The following section is an attempt to highlight the differences in the cost of treatment considering the type of illness (non-hospitalised or hospitalised), system of treatment (modern or Indian) and the socio-economic characteristics of the households.

For Non-hospitalised Illness Episodes

NSSO 42nd round (1986-87) points out that the cost of treatment of non-hospitalised illnesses is much less in the private sector than in the public sector in the rural areas of Himachal Pradesh, Punjab and all-India and the urban areas of Punjab and India. Similarly, the cost of treatment and average duration of the illness is much higher in Himachal Pradesh than in Punjab and India (Table 8.19). Outdoor treatment being cheaper and the average duration being higher in the private sector than in the public sector in the rural areas of Himachal Pradesh, one is inclined to conclude that the private sector in these areas is not sufficiently qualified and therefore competing with the public sector by providing services at a lower cost. Elsewhere, for example, in Punjab the private sector is competing with the public sector to provide services on a par.

TABLE 8.19

Average Total Expenditure/Duration of Sickness Per Illness Episode by Source of Treatment

Expenditure/Duration	*Rural Areas*			*Urban Areas*		
	H.P.	*Punjab*	*India*	*H.P.*	*Punjab*	*India*
Average Total Expenditure (in rupees)						
Government	162.89	99.09	114.75	116.25	92.90	103.39
Private	113.80	83.05	84.93	132.37	76.61	91.30
Average Duration of Sickness (in days)						
Government	15.0	11.9	13.2	15.0	11.8	13.3
Private	16.4	10.1	12.2	14.2	9.3	11.5

Source: 'NSS 42nd Round (July 1986-June 1987)', *Morbidity and Utilisation of Medical Services*, July 1986-June 1987

NCAER (1990) has pointed out that the cost of medical treatment in Himachal Pradesh is much higher for homoeopathic treatment (Rs. 247 per episode in rural areas and Rs. 175 in urban areas), and a little higher for ayurvedic treatment (Rs. 69 per episode in the rural areas) than for allopathic treatment (Rs. 68 per episode in the rural areas and Rs. 45 in urban areas). The all-India picture shows a reverse trend with higher medical cost for allopathic treatment. In case of Himachal Pradesh, the cost of treatment is much lower than in Punjab and at the all-India level. The cost of treatment usually has a direct relationship with the distance covered by the patient from home to the health facility. Approximately 75 per cent of the total cost in the rural areas and 80 per cent of the total cost in the urban areas goes into fees and medicines (NCAER 1990 & 1993). NCAER (1993) further reveals that the average expenditure per non-hospitalised illness episode is less for female adults compared to male adults, and female children compared to male children in the rural areas of Himachal Pradesh. On the other hand, in urban Himachal Pradesh, the expenditure per illness episode for female adults is twice as much as for male adults. For children in the urban areas, the trend is similar to the rural areas. The cost of treatment is slightly higher in a private facility in the urban areas and in a public facility in the rural areas. The survey has also pointed out that transportation is a major factor in the high cost of medical treatment.

Table 8.20 shows the average total medical expenditure required for treatment of one non-hospitalised illness episode according to NSS 52nd round. The table shows that the treatment cost per illness episode, particularly in the rural areas of Himachal Pradesh, is definitely less than the cost of treatment in Punjab, Haryana and the rest of India. The table also shows that the cost of treatment per episode of non-hospitalised illness is higher for females than for males in Himachal Pradesh, irrespective of their residential status. The treatment is expensive for the Scheduled Castes than the non-Scheduled Castes. Contrary to the findings of the previous surveys, the table shows that treatment is less expensive in Himachal Pradesh compared to all-India and neighbouring states of Haryana and Punjab.

For Hospitalised Illness Episodes

Table 8.21 indicates that the share of the private sector among hospitalized cases in both rural and urban areas of Himachal Pradesh is much less than in India (9% as against 32% in the rural areas and 19% as against 30% in the urban areas). 88 per cent and 81 per cent of the hospitalised cases in Himachal Pradesh are treated by the government sector. Charitable institutions, nursing homes and other non-specified institutions provide treatment to a very small section of the population. Fewer people are willing to pay for the treatment of hospitalised illness episodes in Himachal Pradesh than in India. Even among those who are willing to pay, fewer households prefer to pay special rates. A large majority of the population (98% in the rural areas and 99% in the urban areas) receive allopathic treatment for hospitalised illnesses. This points to the need for further strengthening the awareness of people about alternative systems of medical treatment, namely, ISM&H.

TABLE 8.20

Average Total Medical Expenditure (for treatment) Per Ailment (not treated as inpatient of hospital) During Last 15 Days Classified by Age, Sex, Caste and Residential Status

(in Rupees)

Sex/Caste	*H.P.*		*Punjab*		*Haryana*		*All India*	
	Rural	*Urban*	*Rural*	*Urban*	*Rural*	*Urban*	*Rural*	*Urban*
Males	**79**	**139**	**160**	**143**	**189**	**487**	**151**	**187**
0-14	51	63	93	112	117	483	97	146
15-39	142	163	143	140	194	676	196	203
40-59	92	138	312	172	424	189	180	220
60+	51	202	189	206	168	355	163	198
Females	**112**	**148**	**187**	**169**	**177**	**345**	**137**	**164**
0-14	62	124	151	94	122	119	101	113
15-39	124	270	221	220	296	332	170	193
40-59	188	117	178	162	153	523	166	187
60+	55	34	339	168	78	367	101	153
Persons	**97**	**143**	**173**	**155**	**183**	**402**	**144**	**175**
0-14	56	83	114	105	119	303	99	131
15-39	131	207	186	176	251	480	181	198
40-59	154	132	226	167	247	403	173	203
60+	53	99	179	185	123	364	133	174
Castes								
Scheduled Castes	96	176	160	138	160	107	117	137
Scheduled Tribes	85	-	12	198	-	-	68	108
Others	83	127	165	151	171	437	138	166

Source: 'NSS 52nd Round (July 1995-June 1996)', *Morbidity and Treatment of Ailments*, Department of Statistics, NSSO, Government of India, November 1998.

TABLE 8.21

Percentage Distribution of Hospitalised Cases by Type of Hospital, Type of Ward for Himachal Pradesh, All-India

Characteristics	*Rural*		*Urban*	
	H.P.	*All-India*	*H.P.*	*All-India*
Type of Hospital				
Public hospital	80.09	55.40	77.13	59.51
PHC	7.84	4.34	3.85	0.75
Private hospital	8.89	31.99	19.02	29.55
Charitable institutions run by public trusts	—	1.71	—	1.91
Nursing home	1.20	4.86	—	7.04
Others	1.98	1.70	—	1.24
Type of Ward				
Free	83.56	60.71	76.76	55.22
Paying general	10.40	32.46	13.09	31.79
Paying special	3.06	6.83	10.15	12.99
System of Medicine				
Allopathic	97.70	98.50	99.32	98.52
Homoeopathic	0.43	0.30	—	0.25
Ayurvedic	0.77	0.51	0.68	0.42
Unani/Hakimi	0.09	0.22	—	0.28
Any combination of these	—	0.11	—	0.10
Others	1.01	0.36	—	0.43
Payment Category				
No payment	45.80	23.16	16.85	19.61
Employer's medical welfare scheme	10.62	6.18	18.48	12.95
Reporting payment to institutions	43.58	70.66	64.66	67.44
Total	**100.0**	**100.0**		**100.0**

Source: 'NSS 42nd round (July 1986-June 1987)', *Morbidity and Utilisation of Medical Services, Sarvekshana*, Vol. XV, No. 4, Issue no. 51, April-June 1992, p. 53-58.

Table 8.22 indicates that more hospitalised illness episodes occurred in H.P. (12 per thousand in rural areas and 22 per thousand in urban areas) than in the rest of India (seven per thousand in the rural areas and nine per thousand in urban areas). In fact, according to this survey, the urban areas of Himachal Pradesh have reported the largest number of hospitalised illness episodes per thousand population among all other states and union territories in India (Table 8.21). While all rural hospitalised illness episodes were treated in a public facility, only 70 per cent of the urban illness episodes were so treated. Distance covered for seeking hospitalised treatment is much longer in the rural areas of Himachal Pradesh than in most of the neighbouring states and the rest of India.

According to the above survey, the average expenditure on hospitalised illness episode is higher in Himachal Pradesh than in Punjab and at all-India in public sector in both the rural and urban areas. The hospitalisation expenditure in private facility in urban areas is higher than Punjab, but lower than in Haryana and all-India level (Table 8.23). The cost of treatment in the private facility in urban areas is higher by 3.7 times in Himachal Pradesh as compared to 3.6, 4.1 and 5.1 times in Punjab, Haryana and all-India levels respectively compared to public facility.

NSSO 52nd round survey points out that the cost of treatment per episode of hospitalised illness in government hospitals is much higher in Punjab than in the rest of India. In Himachal Pradesh, the cost of private sector treatment is substantially higher in urban

TABLE 8.22

Per cent Distribution of Hospitalised Illness Episodes by Type of Treatment

Number of Cases, Type of Treatment and Distance	*Rural Areas*				*Urban Areas*			
	H.P.	*Punjab*	*Haryana*	*All-India*	*H.P.*	*Punjab*	*Haryana*	*All-India*
Reported Number of Hospitalised Cases by Sex (per '000 persons)								
Male	14.3	22.2	9.5	8.4	31.6	12.4	9.5	10.9
Female	9.8	5.7	2.1	5.5	11.5	16.6	10.5	8.4
Total	12.2	14.2	6.3	7.1	22.1	14.3	10.0	9.7
Distribution of Hospitalised Cases by Type of Treatment								
Public facility	100.0	95.3	73.5	62.0	69.7	68.7	65.9	60.1
Private facility	0.0	4.7	26.5	38.0	30.3	31.3	34.1	39.9
Total	100.0	100.0	100.0	100.0	100.0	100.0	100.0	100.0
Average Distance Travelled for Seeking In-patients (in kilometers)								
Public sector facility	35.0	9.0	15.2	18.6	3.3	3.5	2.7	5.7
Private sector facility	0.0	15.0	22.2	18.7	5.6	5.4	2.2	6.2
All	35.0	9.3	17.1	18.7	4.0	4.1	2.5	5.9

Source: NCAER, *Household Survey of Health Care Utilisation and Expenditure*, March 1995.

TABLE 8.23

Average Cost of Treatment Per Illness Episode for Hospitalised Illness Classified by Ownership of Service Provider

Type of Treatment	*Rural Areas*				*Urban Areas*			
	H.P.	*Punjab*	*Haryana*	*All India*	*H.P.*	*Punjab*	*Haryana*	*All India*
Public	659.01	434.21	690.31	535.20	460.64	372.81	579.34	452.55
Private	—	762.50	2257.55	1877.21	1730.38	1357.31	2392.14	2318.84
Total	**659.01**	**449.62**	**1105.86**	**1044.49**	**845.10**	**696.03**	**1197.70**	**1196.87**

Source: NCAER, *Household Survey of Health Care Utilisation and Expenditure*, March 1995.

areas. As a result, more people prefer to visit government hospitals in Himachal Pradesh. (Table 8.24)

Vision and Strategies for the Future

Himachal Pradesh provides health services of a reasonable standard in the public sector, with an adequate choice of allopathic and ayurvedic treatment. The vision of the state of health in Himachal Pradesh for the immediate future includes the provision of primary, secondary and tertiary health care services, both in the public and private sectors on par with the neighbouring states of Punjab and Haryana. Such a vision looks forward to a picture of a generally healthy population, free from communicable and non-communicable diseases, and a client-friendly manpower in the health and family welfare centres. Besides the continuation of the usual preventive health care measures, the state must ensure the availability of quality health care services (including secondary and tertiary health care services) to everyone. The health care system of the future should be more scientific and technologically advanced. Better health care services in the future are envisaged, with the introduction of selected health sector reforms, such as integration of the public and private sectors, framing of rules to regulate the private sector, introduction of sustainable approaches towards treatment and cure of communicable diseases, particularly HIV/AIDS, and a viable health insurance policy. We also look forward to immediate state interventions, such as setting up special clinics for the vulnerable sections (children, adolescents, women, and the elderly), and also bringing about an attitudinal and behavioural change in the removal of existing socio-cultural practices, particularly related to the reproductive health of women. Revitalising the existing health care institutions through reforms in governance (with greater involvement of the Panchayati Raj Institutions), and provision of additional funding on a self-sustainable basis (levying of user charges in consultation with the PRIs) would help the state come out of the administrative problems and resource crunch. We also foresee greater inter-sectoral and inter-departmental co-ordination, which would not only ensure effective and optimal utilisation of the existing and future health care programmes, but also result in increased public awareness towards healthy practices. Periodic assessment of health problems and needs of the state is an essential prerequisite for assessing the future requirements. To achieve the above, the following policy interventions are suggested:

1. For efficient and smooth functioning of health institutions, adequate monitoring and supervision

TABLE 8.24

Average Total Expenditure Per Hospitalised Illness Episode During Last 365 Days by Source of Treatment

(in Rupees)

Type of Treatment	*H.P.*		*Punjab*		*Haryana*		*All India*	
	Rural	*Urban*	*Rural*	*Urban*	*Rural*	*Urban*	*Rural*	*Urban*
Government hospitals	2542	2250	3645	5436	2667	8888	2080	2195
Other hospitals	2889	7293	6171	6130	3496	5087	4300	5344
Total	**2530**	**2643**	**4988**	**5712**	**3224**	**6537**	**3202**	**3921**

Source: 'NSS 52nd Round (July 1995-June 1996)', *Morbidity and Treatment of Ailments*, Department of Statistics, NSSO, Government of India, November 1998.

is necessary. The performance of various health indicators would improve to a large extent if there is regular monitoring and supervision. All officials of the Directorate, Chief Medical Officers (CMOs) and Block Medical Officers (BMOs) must make periodic field visits to different health institutions under their jurisdiction. Adequate POL expenses should be provided for regular monitoring and supervision work. Induction training and regular refresher courses are necessary for updating the knowledge of healthcare providers.

2. During the last few annual and five year plans, the government of Himachal Pradesh has advocated rapid expansion of ISM&H. It is time to integrate its functioning with the Department of Health and Family Welfare. To effectively achieve the national goals and objectives of health, both modern and Indian systems of medicine must work as harmonious units rather than in two separate compartments. Though some work has already been started in this direction and the necessary notification has been issued by the state government to implement various national health programmes jointly by the two departments, much needs to be done. Further, inter-departmental co-ordination between the Department of Health and Family Welfare and the Departments of Education, Public Health, Women and Social Welfare, Public Relations, etc., is needed for effective health intervention programmes.

3. The state has a *Health Vision 2020* document. Besides, some policy objectives have been highlighted in the Tenth Plan document. Considering the fact that, with the changing composition of the population, changing life-styles, urbanisation and industrialisation, Himachal Pradesh would have newer morbidity challenges in the future, it should work on a state health policy with a proper time schedule for the different activities. The policy should clearly spell out the future health care requirements of the state in the field of preventive, promotive, curative and rehabilitative health care. Adequate research through primary surveys should be conducted before fixing the goals and advocating policy prescriptions.

4. The primary health care facilities in the rural areas and the existing number of medical institutions in the state are sufficient to meet the needs of the people, but they have to be brought to a higher level of efficient functioning. Shortcomings, such as inadequate para-medical staff, buildings and equipment, must be overcome. The inconsistency in the distribution of primary health care facilities and health manpower (more staffing in comfortable areas than in the rural and remote areas) must be rectified immediately. The buildings of health institutions have to be maintained properly with adequate residential accommodation for the staff. Separate wings have to be established in each hospital in the urban areas for proper implementation of primary health care such as updating of records, undertaking survey work, etc. Further, implementation of service norms and standards (through hospital manual), and a proper referral system would contribute to reducing the burden of the secondary and tertiary health care services. The same applies to institutions under the ISM&H wherein all institutions require restructuring for delivering proper health care services and very often these institutions are lacking in proper infrastructure/ amenities. Sufficient funds are required to provide specialised treatments at these Centres.

5. Special emphasis needs to be given to preventive measures, such as vaccination against communicable diseases and identification of high-risk pregnancies to detect deformities and disabilities. Special clinics should also be established in each district to deal with problems related to infertility, reproductive health, and menopause.

6. Focused attention needs to be given to curative aspects of health care, particularly in a hilly state like Himachal Pradesh where the share of the private sector in the number of illness episodes treated is almost negligible. Strengthening the existing public health services and widening their network through the involvement of private practitioners, voluntary non-government organisations and research institutions will improve the health care services in the state.

7. It is important that professional medical bodies and the government of Himachal Pradesh evolve rules and regulations and develop appropriate strategies to regulate the private sector. It is important to have directives on the manufacture, sale and prescription of pharmaceutical drugs on the one hand, and medical and clinical practices,

including licence to practice, basic code of conduct, negligence and consumer complaints on the other. The rating of private clinics, nursing homes and hospitals based on physical facilities, manpower, equipment and technology will be useful.

8. Rising medical costs raises the question of available financing options. Hospitalised treatment in both the public and private sectors is very expensive and leads to loss of lifetime's savings, leaving no money for future social security. It is suggested that the state government should work out the modalities for a viable health insurance policy to meet the rising health costs in both public and private sectors. It is also an essential ingredient of social security measures.

9. Urbanisation brings with it mental stresses and strains. Efficient strategies need to be evolved to combat such stresses leading to accidents and other eventualities. More trauma wards need to be established to handle such cases.

10. In tune with the objectives of NHP-2002, convergence of all national programmes of health, such as malaria, tuberculosis, HIV/AIDS, RCH and universal immunisation programme, under the management of autonomous bodies for overall implementation, is desirable. Effective implementation by such bodies would not only reduce the incidence of communicable and non-communicable diseases in the state but also reduce the burden of the state government, enabling it to plan and implement alternative strategies for health care.

11. Special strategies need to be planned for HIV positive cases in the state. The present voluntary counselling and testing centres (VCTC) for HIV/AIDS testing in Indira Gandhi Medical College, Shimla, is grossly inadequate. Such testing facilities should be made available at all zonal/district hospitals.

12. Although the Panchayati Raj Institutions have been involved through the formation of health and family welfare advisory committees known as PARIKAS at the *panchayat*, block and district levels, yet effective decentralisation of powers, according to the 73rd Amendment of the Constitution is still to take place. Its implementation will help PRIs to identify their area-specific priorities, develop programmes and mobilise resources. Sensitisation and training of the elected PRI representatives on different health issues is important.

13. Introduction of telemedicine for appropriate consultation for the treatment of illnesses in the far-flung areas of the state through connectivity with the state headquarters would be useful in reducing people's hardship and the number of patients in specialised health institutions.

14. A number of primary studies should also be undertaken through autonomous research institutions, to assess the health needs of the state.

15. Last but not least, a proper computerised health-management information system should be developed from the block level to provide immediate access to information on health and other indicators. An effective Health Management Information System will help in planning area-specific and need-based policies and programmes in the future.

A few concerns which are outside the domain of this chapter, but constitute an integral part of the healthy growth of the human mind and body are environment and occupational health, adequate availability of drinking water, hygienic living conditions, nutritious food, removal of drug addiction and other health hazards. Excessive use of alcohol is a deterrent to growth. The state has to design the future of the next generation by ensuring minimisation of alcoholism and drug addiction. We visualise the need for extending the scope of interconnectivity and interdependence of the state within the region to ensure a disease-free, and an environmentally clean society.

References

Aggarwal, Rajesh Kumar and Komila Parthi (2002), "Chapter on Health" in '*Punjab Development Report 2002*' prepared by the Centre for Research in Rural and Industrial Development, Chandigarh and published by Planning Commission, Government of India.

Bir, T. (2000), "User Charges: A Policy Option for Health Service Development in Developing Countries like India", *Health and Population: Perspectives and Issues*, 23(2): 71-84, 2000.

Brugha, Ruairi and Anthony Zwi (1998), "Improving the Quality of Private Sector Delivery of Public Health Services: Challenges and Strategies", *Health Policy and Planning*, 13 (2), 107-120.

Caldwell, *et al.*, "What We Know about Health Transition, the Cultural, Social and Behavioural Determinants of Health", *Health Transition Series*, Vol 1 and 2, The Australian National University Printing Service for the Health Transition Centre, National Centre for Epidemiology and Population Health, The Australian National University, Canberra, Australia.

Central Bureau of Health Intelligence, Directorate General of Health Services, Ministry of Health and Family Welfare, Government of India, New Delhi, *Health Information of India* (various issues),

————. *Health Map of India, 1998.*

Department of Planning, Government of Himachal Pradesh, *Annual Plan* (different issues).

————. *Five Year Plan Documents* (various issues).

Department of Health and Family Welfare, Government of Himachal Pradesh, *Directory of Medical, Public Health and Ayurvedic Institutions in Himachal Pradesh* (As on 31 March 2001, updated manually up to March 2002).

————. *Drug Policy of Himachal Pradesh*, June 1999.

————. *Family Welfare Programme Yearbook 2000-01.*

————. *Himachal Health Vision 2020.*

————. *Himachal Pradesh Ke Karyakaram Aur Panchayati Raj Sansthayain*, booklet on involvement of PRIs in Health and Family Welfare Programme.

————. *List of Essential Drugs*, 1999.

————. *Standard Treatment Guidelines*, June 2000.

Department of Women and Child Development, Government of India and United Nations Children's Fund, New Delhi, *Multiple Indicator Survey (MICS-2000), India, Summary Report*, December 2001.

Directorate General of Health Services, Ministry of Health and Family Welfare, Government of India, *Bulletin on Rural Health Statistics in India, March 2002.*

Economic and Statistical Organisation, Government of Himachal Pradesh, *Statistical Abstracts of Himachal Pradesh* (various issues)

Government of Himachal Pradesh (2002) *Himachal Pradesh, Human Development Report 2002.*

International Institute for Population Sciences and Macro ORC, *National Family Health Survey-II*, India 1998-99.

————. *National Family Health Survey-II*, Himachal Pradesh, India 1998-99.

Kumar, Rajesh, J.S. Thakur and A.K. Srivastava *Himachal Burden of Disease Study Draft Estimation Report, 2003*, Department of Community Medicines, Post Graduate Institute of Medical Education and Research, Chandigarh sponsored by Directorate of Health and Family Welfare, Himachal Pradesh.

Ministry of Health and Family Welfare, Government of India, New Delhi *Family Welfare Programme in India, Year Book* (different issues).

————. *Annual Reports* (different issues)

————. *National Health Policy* 2002.

National Council of Applied Economic Research (NCAER), New Delhi, *Household Survey of Medical Care (May-June 1990)*, June 1992, 52 p.

————. *Household Survey of Health Care Utilization and Expenditure*, March 1995, 95 p.

National Institute of Health and Family Welfare, New Delhi (December 2000), *Development of Health Insurance in India: Current Status and Future Directions*, Report of Seminar held on 29-30 December 2000, 46 p.

National Sample Survey Organisation, Department of Statistics, Government of India *Sarvekshana*, Volume IV, No. 1& 2, 1980.

————. *Morbidity and Utilisation of Medical Services* (42nd Round), July 1986-June 1987, Sarvekshana, Vol. XV, No. 4, Issue No. 51, April-June 1992.

————. *Morbidity and Treatment of Ailments (52nd Round)*, July 1995-June 1996, Report No. 441, November 1998.

————. Morbidity and Treatment of Ailments (52nd Round), July 1995-June 1996, *Sarvekshana*, Vol. XXIII, No. 3, 82nd Issue, January-March 2000.

Planning Commission, Government of India, *Five Year Plan Documents* (various documents).

World Bank, *A Vision for India's Health System*, Report of Conference held on 15-16 November 2001, New Delhi, downloaded from Internet.

David H. Peters, *et al.* (2002), *Better Health System for India's Poor: Findings, Analysis and Options*, World Bank, Human Development Network, Health Nutrition and Population Series.

World Health Organisation (1978), *Primary Health Care*, Report of the International Conference on Primary Health Care, Alma Ata, USSR, 6-12 September 1978.

————. *The World Health Reports* (various issues).

Chapter 9

Nutrition

Nutrition is to a human being what development is to a state. Article 47 of the Constitution of India, says "State shall regard the raising of the level of the nutrition and the standard of living of its people and the improvement of public health among its primary duties....." *The National Nutrition Policy (NNP) 1993* further iterates, "Nutrition affects development as much as development affects nutrition". The state of malnutrition has a direct bearing on social and economic progress. This section is geared to the task of understanding vital issues pertaining to nutrition in Himachal Pradesh. It is divided into sub-sections namely, government initiatives, current nutritional status of children, adolescents, adults, women and the elderly; food consumption patterns; the status of micronutrient deficiencies and the role of the private sector in the state. The recommendations and strategies are based on field reports.

Government Initiatives

The existing budgetary allocations for nutrition in the state in various plans indicate the interest that is evoked in alleviating the nutritional status of its human resource. Even though nutrition was part of earlier plans, real emphasis on the nutrition budget became evident in the Fifth Plan, when the Union Department of Women and Child Development introduced Integrated Child Development Scheme in the country, as well as in the states. Since the Seventh Plan, nutritional programmes have been receiving priority. Expenditure on these programmes have exceeded the outlay. The expenditure on nutrition-related programmes and schemes was 1.16 times the outlay in the Seventh Plan, 1.63 times that of the Eighth Plan and 1.18 times in the Ninth Plan. To combat malnutrition and micronutrient deficiencies, the state is implementing centrally-sponsored schemes as well as certain self-initiated ones. Some of these are:

Initiatives

Central Government Initiatives	*Aims/Objectives*
The Applied Nutrition Programme (1963-64)	The objective was to arrange nutritious food for pre-school children, expectant and nursing mothers. It was initiated in three blocks. Subsequent to the trifurcation of Punjab and reorganisation of Himachal Pradesh, another four blocks were added.
The Special Nutrition Programme (1970)	The objective was to provide high protein and nutritious diet to children below six years and pregnant and nursing mothers. It was initiated in three tribal blocks on an experimental basis in addition to some slum areas of Shimla. In 1970-71; the programme benefited 4,032 tribal and 440 urban children. The feeding programme was run for 300 days in a year. Initially, the target group was children below three years, but by 1971-72 the programme was extended to children up to six years of age and pregnant and nursing mothers.
Integrated Child Development Scheme (ICDS)	ICDS aims at reaching all needy children below six years (to improve their health and nutritional status), expectant and nursing mothers and women (to enhance their capability to look after their health and the nutritional needs of their children) covering the age group of 15-45 years with basic services to alleviate conditions of deprivation. At present, there is a wide network of workers to implement the programme. There are 72 ICDS projects, with 7,354 *Anganwari* centres, in different districts of the state. The beneficiaries' list includes 2,70,741 children below six years and 60,008 pregnant and nursing mothers.
Public Distribution System (PDS)	A network of 3,955 fair price shops has been set up to streamline the functioning of the PDS. The earlier policy of 1997 was amended in 2001 dividing the PDS into four categories, *viz.*, above poverty level (ABL), below poverty level (BPL), *antodaya* (poorest) and *annapurna* (indigient).

Contd...

...Contd...

Central Government Initiatives	*Aims/Objectives*
National Programme of Nutritional Support to Primary Education (1995)	The basic objective is to promote universalisation of primary education and also to improve the nutrition of children in primary classes. Foodgrains (wheat/rice) at the rate of three kg. per student per month is distributed, subject to a minimum of 80 per cent attendance in primary classes. The Ministry of Human Resource Development, Department of Education is implementing this scheme.
Udisha Project (1998)	Udisha is a nationwide training component of the World Bank-assisted Women and Child Development Project. The aim of Udisha is to develop all functionaries into agents of social change, people who can act positively at all times. The functionaries trained in the programme include Anganwari workers, supervisors, Additional Child Development Project Officers (ACDPO), Child Development Project Officers (CDPO), medical officers and para- medical staff. Under this project, 2500 Anganwari workers (AWWs) were trained by the year 2002-03. A batch of 35 Anganwari workers is being trained at four training centres at Suni and Theog in Shimla district, Rasmai in Sundernagar (Mandi) district and at Gaggal in Kangra district.
Kishori Shakti Yojana (11-18 years) (2000)	The basic objective of this scheme is to prepare adolescent girls to understand and learn the significance of personal hygienic environment, sanitation, nutrition, first aid, health and nutrition education, family life, child care and development etc. and to prepare healthy future mothers. At the All-India level, 2000 blocks were selected for implementation of the scheme; 15 of these blocks are in Himachal Pradesh.
Administration of Vitamin-A	The objective is to prevent blindness. Vitamin-A drops are orally administered to children every six months. This programme is implemented through the Department of Health and Family Welfare.
Distribution of iron and folic acid tablets	The objective is to prevent nutritional anaemia among women and children; the Department of Health and Family Welfare distribute IFA tablets.
National Iodine Deficiency Disorders Control Programme (NIDDCP)	The focus is on popularising the use of iodized salt consumption.
The National Nutrition Mission (2001)	The objective is to address the problems of malnutrition in a holistic manner and to review and implement the National Nutrition Policy and the National Plan of Action on Nutrition
Mobile Anganwari Centres (2000)	The objective is to cover the left-out children and mothers in rugged and inaccessible areas. The *Anganwari* worker organises a Mobile *Anganwari* Centre once in two weeks. The activities undertaken are to distribute food (nutrition), monitor growth of children and organise immunisation camps with the assistance of health functionaries. Of the total 7,123 *Anganwari* centres, 3,693 have mobile Centres (Department of Social, Women and Scheduled Castes, Government of Himachal Pradesh, February 2003).
Him Viyanjan (2000)	The Department of Social, Women and Scheduled Castes Welfare, Himachal Pradesh has collected from different districts of the state recipes along with their nutritive values. It is a compilation of information on improving the nutritional status of the people. This book is circulated among the functionaries of the department to disseminate the required information among the people.
Panchayati Raj Institutions	In view of the implementation of the 73rd and 74th Constitutional Amendment, the Welfare Department has handed over to the PRIs the task of appointing and ensuring smooth functioning of *Anganwari* workers and helpers. To ensure their effective and efficient functioning the department has produced a document outlining the functions of the PRIs in relation to ICDS.

Despite the strong efforts of the state to ensure food security to its people, there is need for an innovative and creative approach to uplift the nutritional status of the people. This calls for an intensive planning strategy.

Nutrition Planning in Himachal Pradesh

Planning at the national and state level has had the aim of achieving balanced growth. The process has moved from a sectoral to an integrated approach. Himachal Pradesh's emphasis on nutrition has been evident from the First Plan onwards, when for combating nutritional deficiencies such as goitre, rickets and tuberculosis, a doctor was specially trained in the science of nutrition. In the subsequent plans, the state formulated and implemented a number of schemes to enhance the nutritional level of its people. The national Tenth Plan marks a paradigm shift from food security at the state level to nutrition security at the individual level.

Over a period, the state has reached close to ensuring food security for its people. The monthly per capita expenditure (availability of two square meals a day) indicates that almost all households (rural 99.7 per cent and urban 99.8 per cent) receive two square meals a day. While according to the latest survey by ORG MARG done in 1999, six per cent of the families still do not get two square meals in Himachal Pradesh as against 14 per cent at the all-India level. It is important that mere availability of adequate foodgrains in a state is not sufficient. What is required is to ensure the quality of the food available and the awareness to convert it into a balanced diet.

The National Nutrition Policy has outlined certain short-term and long-term interventions. It is imperative for the state to streamline the policy and integrate it with its own agenda.

Assessing Nutritional Status: Children, Adolescents, Adults, Women and the Elderly

Nutritional Status of Children

Low Birth-weight Children

It is pertinent to plan eradication of nutritional discrepancies among children. Infants born underweight (less than 2.5 kg) indicate a number of maternal complications such as malnutrition, anaemia, hypertension and infections. The percentage of underweight children in Himachal Pradesh has gone up in the last five years from 28.2 in 1992-93 to 35.1, even when 87 per cent of the mothers received antenatal care during pregnancy. Other states of the region, such as Punjab, Haryana and Jammu and Kashmir have experienced a decrease in the proportion of underweight births during the same period. This is the position at the national level too (Table 9.1). It appears that high-risk pregnancies are not being identified and an effective referral system does not exist. The state's goal of reducing the proportion of low birth-weight babies from the existing 30 per cent (2000) to 10 by 2020 (*Himachal Health Vision, 2020*), seems to be a far-fetched idea until the Departments of Welfare and Health work together to provide quality service to pregnant women.

The micro level situation indicates variations in the proportion of underweight children; Hamirpur had the highest (65.9 per cent) whereas Mandi had the lowest proportion (2.7 per cent) of low birth-weight babies (*Reproductive Health Survey, 1998*). The state is well placed in the matter of neonatal (22.1 per cent), post-neonatal (12.3 per cent), infant (34.4 per cent) and under five mortality rate (42.4 per cent) (NFHS-India, 1998-99). The state needs to take up urgently the health care of women and children, in addition to their survival, so that morbidities and other deficiencies due to lack of nutrition among adolescent girls and women is effectively taken care of. This would, in the long run, enhance the quality of the workforce of the state.

Malnutrition among Children

Malnutrition in Himachal Pradesh is a silently creeping crisis under the cover of an emerging developed state in terms of a decline in its infant mortality rate. At 60 per 1000 live births, it was lower than the national average of 68 per 1000 (SRS, 2000), but the problem of under-nutrition persists. An undernourished child is prone to morbidity and has longer periods of illness as compared to a well-fed child. Its impact is evident from late school entry, slow learning abilities and eventually becoming an under productive adult. A reduction in child malnutrition in Himachal Pradesh is evident during 1992-93 to 1998-99, but it was not as noteworthy as its neighbouring states (Table 9.2). The state government proposes to reduce malnutrition by less than five percent (*Himachal Health Vision, 2020*). It would be relevant for the state to replicate the Tamil Nadu Integrated Nutrition Programme, which is a success story as far as decreasing the proportion of underweight children is concerned.

TABLE 9.1

Underweight Children at Birth as per cent of Total Deliveries in Himachal Pradesh, Neighbouring States and India: 1992-93 and 1998-99

States	*Weight less than 2.5 kg*					
	1992-93			*1998-99*		
	Total	*Rural*	*Urban*	*Total*	*Rural*	*Urban*
Himachal Pradesh	**28.2**	**30.8**	**18.7**	**35.1**	**35.8**	**31.7**
Punjab	28.6	31.0	25.4	23.8	25.3	21.6
Haryana	26.0	26.5	25.5	24.3	29.1	18.5
Jammu & Kashmir	32.4	38.0	23.2	28.2	24.0	33.8
India	**26.0**	**24.7**	**26.3**	**22.7**	**23.9**	**21.1**

Source: Computed from the *National Family Health Survey, India* 1992-93 and 1998-99.

TABLE 9.2

Child Malnutrition in Himachal Pradesh, Neighbouring States and India : 1992-93 to 1998-99

States	*Percentage of Malnourished Children*	
	1992-93	*1998-99*
Himachal Pradesh	**47.0**	**43.6**
Punjab	45.9	28.7
Haryana	37.9	34.6
Jammu & Kashmir	44.5	34.5
India	**53.4**	**47.0**

Source: *National Family Health Survey, India,* 1992-93 and 1998-99.

Note: Age of children (under 4 years), 1992-93; Age of children (under 3 years), 1998-99.

The nutritional status of children (0-36 months) in Himachal Pradesh indicates that more than two-fifths are underweight and stunted. Twelve per cent of the children are severely underweight. The corresponding figures at the national level are 47 per cent, 45.5 per

TABLE 9.3

Nutritional Status of Children in Himachal Pradesh, Neighbouring States and India

State	Weight for Age				Height for Age				Weight for Height			
	% below-3SD		% below-2SD		% below-3SD		% below-2SD		% below-3SD		% below-2SD	
	1992-93	1998-99	1992-93	1998-99	1992-93	1998-99	1992-93	1998-99	1992-93	1998-99	1992-93	1998-99
H.P.	**12.9**	**12.1**	**47.0**	**43.6**	**—**	**18.1**	**—**	**41.3**	**—**	**3.3**	**—**	**16.9**
India	**20.6**	**18.0**	**53.4**	**47.0**	**28.9**	**23.0**	**52.0**	**45.5**	**3.2**	**2.8**	**17.5**	**15.5**

Source: National Family Health Survey-India, IIPS, Mumbai (1992-93 and 1998-99).

Note: — Not available because children's height/length was not measured.

cent and 18 per cent. Himachal Pradesh has a higher proportion of underweight children than the neighbouring states of Punjab, Haryana and Jammu and Kashmir. Apparently, the proportion of underweight males is higher than females. The standard of living has an impact on the nutritional status of the child. Nearly one-third of the children with a higher standard of living are undernourished (33.1 per cent) and stunted (29.0 per cent), as against nearly three-fifths (57.7 per cent) of children with a lower standard of living. The literacy level of the mother has a deep impact on the nutritional status of the child; the higher the education level of the mother, the lower the under-nutrition level of the children (NFHS 1998-99). This makes a case for focusing on children belonging to lower income groups and imparting education to women.

At the district level, more than three-fifths of the children (1-5 years) in the rural areas of Bilaspur, Sirmaur, Solan, Mandi and Kullu are underweight. While, more than half the children in the districts of Kangra and Hamirpur and more than two-fifths of the children in Shimla, Kinnaur and Una are underweight. The low proportion of underweight children in Shimla can be attributed to the impact of urbanisation (23.12 per cent), increased awareness and access to quality health services. In the tribal areas of the state, data are available only for Kinnaur, which also has the lowest proportion of underweight children among the 10 districts (Table 9.4). The better nutritional status of the tribals can be attributed to their consumption of local cereals, such as amaranthus, which has a high nutritive content. Non-availability of vegetables and fruits round the year increases the consumption of non-vegetarian food, which provides them with adequate nutrients.

The present nutritional status of children below six years is evident from the data provided by the Department of Social, Women and Scheduled Castes Welfare, which indicates trends similar to the ones

TABLE 9.4

Prevalence of Underweight, Stunting and Wasting at District Level (Rural) Children (1-5 years) in Himachal Pradesh

(in per cent)

Districts/State	Underweight			Stunting			Wasting		
	Male	Female	Total	Male	Female	Total	Male	Female	Total
Bilaspur	73.6	70.1	72.1	73.5	82.1	77.3	11.5	10.4	11.0
Hamirpur	59.8	50.7	56.0	67.6	60.6	64.7	2.9	1.4	2.3
Kangra	65.9	51.2	58.8	71.6	69.1	70.3	6.8	4.8	5.8
Kinnaur	45.9	43.5	44.5	52.4	56.6	54.9	11.5	14.1	13.1
Kullu	67.3	54.9	61.0	61.6	70.2	66.1	17.7	9.0	13.3
Mandi	58.3	64.9	61.2	71.8	77.0	74.1	10.4	10.9	10.6
Shimla	43.9	51.4	47.4	52.4	69.5	60.4	1.2	4.2	2.5
Sirmaur	63.7	63.4	63.5	79.6	75.6	77.7	4.5	4.9	4.7
Solan	52.3	69.8	61.7	61.6	63.2	62.5	10.7	13.1	12.0
Una	42.1	47.0	44.4	72.7	67.7	70.4	2.5	2.0	2.2
Himachal Pradesh	**57.6**	**55.9**	**56.8**	**67.3**	**68.8**	**68.0**	**7.8**	**7.4**	**7.7**

Source: India Nutrition Profile, Department of Women and Child Development, Ministry of Human Resource Development, Government of India (1998).

reported by the *India Nutrition Profile (1998)*. During 2000-03, the proportion of underweight children in the state marginally increased by 1.6 per cent points. In the four districts of Chamba, Bilaspur, Mandi and Kangra, the proportion of underweight children has increased during this period. In Chamba, the number of such children increased by 16.1 per cent points and in Bilaspur by 13.5 per cent points. On the other hand, in Solan this proportion decreased by 12.2 per cent points and in Kinnaur by 11.2 per cent points (Table 9.5). The reasons for this position in these districts need to be investigated.

TABLE 9.5

Underweight Children (0-6 years) in Himachal Pradesh (in %), 2000 to 2003

Districts/State	2000	2001	2002	2003	Change in Per cent Points 2000 to 2003
Lahaul & Spiti	51.41	54.76	42.35	51.42	0.01
Kangra	49.23	50.72	53.22	50.75	1.52
Sirmaur	49.24	49.10	47.89	49.29	-0.95
Bilaspur	32.59	39.77	39.04	46.13	13.54
Solan	57.83	46.59	44.59	45.58	-12.24
Chamba	26.21	25.62	27.49	42.28	16.07
Hamirpur	43.58	42.45	44.45	42.09	-1.49
Mandi	33.49	37.14	37.33	38.44	4.95
Kullu	37.68	36.64	34.56	37.12	-0.57
Shimla	38.13	39.34	38.37	36.60	-1.54
Una	35.72	38.10	42.17	31.59	-4.12
Kinnaur	37.24	33.52	25.07	26.04	-11.20
Himachal Pradesh	**40.47**	**41.22**	**40.85**	**42.05**	**1.58**

Source: Department of Social, Women and Scheduled Caste Welfare, Government of Himachal Pradesh, Shimla.

Overall, it is important to ensure nutritional and health care coverage of all children below six. Children up to three years can be covered by imparting awareness and healthy diet to the mother, and children in the 3-6 years age group should be encouraged to regularly attend the Anganwari Centre and eat the food supplied for them.

Adolescent Health and Nutritional Care

Adolescence is a period of tremendous stress, strain and turmoil and it is imperative to anticipate their problems and formulate suitable strategies for implementation. The National Population Policy 2000 has identified this age to be of great significance and has stressed on the need for prioritising it.

TABLE 9.6

Adolescent (15-19 years) Nutritional Status Based on Height, Weight for Height and Anaemia Levels in Himachal Pradesh, Neighbouring States and India

States/India	Mean Height	Percentage below 145 cm	Weight for Height (% with BMI below 18.5 kg/m^2)	Percentage of Women with any Anaemia
Himachal Pradesh	**153.2**	**9.9**	**43.4**	**43.2**
Punjab	154.6	3.8	29.1	53.1
Haryana	153.3	6.9	27.0	49.8
Jammu& Kashmir	153.6	6.3	34.2	58.2
India	150.6	14.7	38.8	56.0

Source: National Family Health Survey 1998-99.

The NFHS 1998-99 reveals that ten per cent of the adolescent girls (15-19 years) in Himachal Pradesh were below the height of 145 cm. This is a clear indication of a high-risk pregnancy, particularly problems associated with labour. Anaemia levels during 15-19 years were also the highest when compared to other age groups. A comparison with other states reveals that a smaller proportion of girls in Himachal Pradesh are suffering from anaemia (Table 9.6). This problem will continue in the reproductive years of the girls. Due to their ill health, they will give birth to anaemic and underweight children. In the age group of 12-18 years, a higher percentage of girls (3.79 per cent) suffered from goitre while a higher proportion of boys (1.00 per cent) suffered from Angular Stomatitis (INP, 1998). Further, at 16 years of age, three-fourths of the children (74.6 per cent) were being immunised against tetanus toxoid in the state (*Family Welfare Year Book, 1997-98*), which reveals the lack of initiative among the medical staff as well as the community towards this vulnerable section of society, particularly girls who are getting ready for motherhood. Information pertaining to counselling services being provided to unmarried adolescent girls by the ANM, is available only in half the districts of Himachal; one out of every ten adolescents is getting counselling in Kangra (12.0 per cent), Chamba (11.7 per cent), Una (11.7 per cent) and Mandi (11.0 per cent) districts in comparison with one out of every 20 in Kinnaur (6.8 per cent) and Sirmaur (4.1 per cent) (*District Household Survey, Phase-II, 1999*).

A specific programme under which they can be given access to information and counselling services pertaining to their health, nutritional and reproductive needs and problems cannot be overlooked. Age at menarche is a less researched area and a major determinant of the nutritional status of adolescents and needs to be studied in-depth.

In this era of competitiveness, adolescents aspire to get admission to professional colleges or other institutions of repute. This implies that the adolescent moves out of parental care to acquire professional guidance and tuition. Under these circumstances, the adolescent's nutritional requirements need to be redefined. The challenge is to devise a diet plan for these aspiring achievers, which embraces a healthy cuisine and discourages excesses. Being out of parental care or under the stress of unforeseen events, such as rejection by professional courses, leads these adolescents into habits of smoking and drinking. A higher proportion of boys in the age group of 10-14 years in the state (9 per 1000 persons) take to smoking regularly in the urban areas, while in the rural areas the figure is two per 1000 persons (*Sarvekshana, 1998*). Strict law should be enforced against smoking by youths below 18 years of age. School authorities, both in rural and urban areas, need to be alerted on these matters. Where counselling is accessible at the primary health centres, it should be adequate to ensure dissemination and optimal utilisation.

Nutritional Status of Adults

The nutritional status of adults in Himachal Pradesh reveals that nearly two-fifths of the population in rural areas suffer from chronic energy deficiency, and nearly seven per cent of them from severe forms of chronic energy deficiency. Nearly three-fifths of the adults are normal, while less than five per cent are obese (Table 9.7), as against the national average of one-third chronically energy deficient and less than five per cent obese.

A district-wise nutritional status of the adults (Table 9.8) reveals a prevalence of both extremes in the state, i.e., chronically energy deficient as well as obese adults. More than two-fifths of the chronic energy deficient adults live in the rural areas of the districts of Solan, Bilaspur, Kangra, Shimla and Sirmaur. While, obesity patterns at the district level reveal a higher percentage of obese adults in the rural areas of the districts of Hamirpur, Bilaspur, Una and Shimla.

TABLE 9.7

Per cent Distribution of Adults According to Body Mass Index in Himachal Pradesh and India

(Prevalence %)

State	*Area*	*CED III*	*CED II*	*CED I*	*CED Total*	*Low Normal*	*Normal*	*Normal Total*	*Obese I*	*Obese II*	*Obese Total*
H.P.	**Rural**	**6.7**	**8.3**	**22.9**	**37.9**	**26.0**	**32.3**	**57.3**	**3.3**	**0.5**	**3.8**
India	Rural	8.6	7.8	18.2	34.6	20.9	40.5	61.4	4.1	0.7	4.1
	Urban	6.8	6.1	14.7	27.7	18.4	47.9	66.3	5.4	0.6	6.0
	Total	8.2	7.4	17.3	32.9	20.4	42.1	62.5	3.8	0.7	4.5

Source: India Nutrition Profile, 1998, Department of Women and Child Development, Ministry of Human Resource Development, Government of India.

Note: CED Stands for Chronic Energy Deficiency.

TABLE 9.8

Prevalence of CED, Normal and Obese at District Level (Himachal Pradesh-Rural)

(in per cent)

Districts/State	*CED III*	*CED II*	*CED I*	*CED (T)*	*Low Normal*	*Normal*	*Normal (T)*	*Obese I*	*Obese II*	*Obese (T)*
Bilaspur	10.1	10.5	27.2	47.8	20.4	26.8	47.2	4.8	0.3	5.1
Hamirpur	6.6	10.2	21.4	38.2	20.5	35.4	55.9	5.2	0.8	6.0
Kangra	9.3	10.5	25.6	45.4	24.9	26.3	51.2	3.0	0.4	3.4
Kinnaur	3.5	5.2	25.5	34.2	32.5	31.5	64.0	1.6	0.2	1.8
Kullu	3.5	6.8	20.0	30.3	32.8	34.1	66.9	2.6	0.2	2.8
Shimla	6.2	9.1	25.6	40.9	24.6	30.3	54.9	3.7	0.6	4.3
Mandi	5.7	5.9	17.2	28.8	26.4	42.5	68.9	2.0	0.3	2.3
Sirmaur	8.4	9.0	22.8	40.2	27.1	30.6	57.7	1.8	0.3	2.1
Solan	9.6	12.8	25.5	47.9	22.3	25.5	47.8	3.9	0.4	4.3
Una	4.9	4.4	22.7	32.0	28.5	34.3	62.8	4.0	1.1	5.1
Himachal Pradesh	**6.7**	**8.3**	**22.9**	**37.9**	**26.0**	**32.3**	**57.3**	**3.3**	**0.5**	**3.8**

Source: India Nutrition Profile, 1998, Ministry of Human Resource Development, Department of Women and Child Development, Government of India, New Delhi.

Note: CED – Chronic Energy Deficiency.

Lack of awareness and faulty dietary intakes could be the possible reasons for adults suffering from these extremes. An in-depth study is necessary to ascertain the underlying factors.

Nutritional Status of Women

The needs of pregnant, sick and disabled women have to be addressed more systematically. One of the vital indicators of women's health is the maternal mortality rate (MMR). The MMR of Himachal Pradesh is 456 per 1,00,000 against the all-India figure of 453 and Kerala's 87. This reflects the unhealthy status of women in the state.

Besides, more than one-fourth of the women suffer from chronic energy deficiency (30 per cent), i.e., they have a body mass index below 18.5 kg/m^2. These figures are higher than those of Punjab (16.9 per cent), Haryana (25.9 per cent) and Jammu and Kashmir (26.4 per cent). The all-India figure is 35.8 per cent. A higher proportion of women in the younger age group (15-19 years) are energy deficient and belong to families with a low standard of living. A higher percentage of children born to deficient mothers are malnourished (53.7 per cent), stunted (45.3 per cent) and wasted (22.7 per cent) (*NFHS-II*). The proportion of obese women is higher in Himachal Pradesh (13.1 per cent) than the national average of 10.6 per cent, although the state's terrain forces the women to consume more energy, which should mean a lower fat accumulation. Six per cent of the women in Himachal Pradesh are short with height below 145 cm. Stunted women have problems during labour and also have adverse affect on the nutritional status of their children. Severe stunting (40.4 per cent) is evident among children whose mother's height is below 145 cms. Special care needs to be given to stunted women during their medical check-up, particularly during antenatal care.

Sexually transmitted infections cause infertility, chronic pelvic inflammatory disease and ectopic pregnancy, which seriously affect child survival, by causing pre-term delivery of low birth-weight and immature infants (*Pachauri, 1996*). The status of women as regards the reproductive health problems in Himachal Pradesh is not favourable as more than one-third of them suffer from reproductive health problems (33.7 per cent). Morbidity and mortality among women in their reproductive period (15-49 years) can be reduced by providing quality antenatal care during pregnancy, increasing institutional deliveries and providing prompt postpartum services for all women (*NFHS-II*).

The Auxiliary Nurse Midwives, the Village Health Guides, the Mahila Mandals and the PARIKAS (Parivar Kalyan Salahkar Samiti) need to join hands with ICDS teams to evolve strategies in the rural areas. The young girls in the state need to be targeted for imparting education related to importance of physical fitness, the appropriate consumption of vitamins and dietary modification, since they are the future mothers. It is vital that the average woman of Himachal Pradesh is made aware of 'balanced diet', so that she addresses her own needs directly and those of her family indirectly.

Nutritional Status of the Elderly

Improved health care facilities have enhanced life expectancy levels from 63.2 years in 1987-91 to 64.5 years in 1991-95 (*Statistical Abstract, Himachal Pradesh, 1999*). The rising number of the elderly requires special attention towards their nutritional needs too. Their nutritional care, in view of their decreasing energy levels and micronutrient deficiencies, needs to be highlighted and monitored effectively. 15 per cent of the currently married women (30-49 years) in Himachal are in the menopause stage (*NFHS 1998-99*). Cessation of menstruation results in nutritional deficiencies, which eventually lead to major health problems.

There is need to establish geriatric and menopause clinics. No fresh investment on staff or infrastructure is required. The existing staff can be trained and utilised and the medical officer at the primary health centre can devote one day in a week to imparting guidance and medical care to the elderly.

Food Consumption Patterns in Himachal Pradesh

Calorie, Protein and Fat Consumption

To ascertain the nutritional status of the community, it is imperative to study its food consumption patterns. An assessment of the food consumption level also includes an analysis of traditional diets and gender equality in food distribution. The National Sample Survey Organisation carried out sample surveys in 1971-73 (27th round), 1981 (38th round) and 1991-94 (50th round) to assess the consumption of calories, proteins and fats. In Himachal Pradesh, the people were reported to be consuming calories and proteins as per the required dietary allocations i.e. calories 2425 Kcal and proteins 60g. Though an overall decline in the calorie and protein intake is evident in the 1971 to 1993-94 period, a significant decline in the calorie consumption in the rural areas of the state is seen in 1993-94. Fat consumption has remained nearly constant in rural areas in the three survey periods, while in the urban areas a sudden decrease in the consumption is seen between 1971-73 and 1986. Thereafter a consistency is evident in 1993-94. A comparison with its neighbouring states of Punjab, Haryana and the all-India level reveals a decrease in the consumption of calories and proteins with an increase in fat intake (Table 9.9). A strong positive correlation between per capita expenditure and per capita per diem intake of calories, protein and fats is seen in the rural as well as urban Himachal Pradesh (*NSSO 50th Round, 1993-94*).

The overall change in dietary patterns is the result of increased literacy, awareness and preference for sedentary jobs. Facilities such as telephones (the number of subscribers has increased from 58,697 in 1994 to 2,25,103 in 1999) and other means of transport (the number of registered motor vehicles has gone up from 9,275 in 1994 to 20,485 in 1999), which reduce the need for walking have an indirect impact on the amount of food consumed.

Micro-level Variations in Food Consumption

Distinct inter-district variations are evident because of extreme climatic conditions, people's tastes and food habits. Consumption of wheat, rice and potatoes is dominant in the districts of Lahaul and Spiti, Kinnaur, Shimla, Solan and Sirmaur. In winter, an increase in the consumption of meat is reported in the districts of Lahaul and Spiti and Kinnaur. Chamba district also records a higher consumption of meat. An inter-state impact on food habits also emerges in districts touching Punjab such as, Kangra, Una, Kullu, Mandi, Bilaspur and Hamirpur, where, the consumption of maize flour, milk and milk products and green leafy vegetables is high. The consumption of milk and milk products in the state shows a gender bias against the females (1-18 years). A similar bias is also evident in the neighbouring state of Punjab. Caste-wise variation in the consumption of sugar and milk and milk products reveals that the consumption of these items is the lowest among the Scheduled Tribes although the consumption of fruits and flesh foods is the highest among them (*India Nutrition Profile, 1998*).

In 1995, under the Prevention of Food Adulteration Act (1954), 28 per cent of adulteration was found in various food products that were examined. Half the milk samples were found adulterated. Adulteration was also found in butter, ghee and ice cream, fruit products, edible oils, fats and vanaspati.

The state has the advantage of being able to grow a wide variety of fruits. Higher availability and consumption of fruits will enhance the nutritional level of its people. Milk production in the state has also increased, though per capita availability of milk has remained at 343 grams/day (*Economic Survey, 2002, Himachal Pradesh*). The contribution of major livestock

TABLE 9.9

Per Capita Intake of Calories, Protein and Fat Per Diem in Himachal Pradesh, Neighbouring States and India

States	*Per capita per Diem Intake of* Calories according to			Protein according to			Fat according to		
	1971-73 (Kcal)	*1981 (Kcal)*	*1993-94 (Kcal)*	*1971-73 (Kcal)*	*1981 (Kcal)*	*1993-94 (Kcal)*	*1971-73 (Kcal)*	*1981 (Kcal)*	*1993-94 (Kcal)*
Himachal Pradesh									
Rural	**2954**	**2636**	**2324**	**86.0**	**80.0**	**70.5**	**45.0**	**46.0**	**44.6**
Urban	**2961**	**2429**	**2416**	**85.0**	**70.0**	**70.0**	**69.0**	**56.0**	**56.2**
Punjab									
Rural	3493	2677	2418	85.0	79.0	74.7	50.0	52.0	59.8
Urban	2783	2100	2089	70.0	63.0	61.8	52.0	49.0	53.7
Haryana									
Rural	3215	2554	2491	90.0	78.0	78.4	47.0	47.0	53.6
Urban	2404	2242	2140	67.0	67.0	63.6	42.0	49.0	49.4
Jammu & Kashmir									
Rural	3151	2569	2507	80.0	71.0	75.4	34.0	36.0	46.0
Urban	2467	2234	2392	62.0	60.0	69.1	33.0	41.0	58.6
India									
Rural	**2266**	**2221**	**2153**	**62**	**62**	**60.2**	**24**	**27**	**31.4**
Urban	**2107**	**2089**	**2071**	**56**	**57**	**57.2**	**36**	**37**	**42**

Source: Sarvekshana, October-December, 1997, National Sample Survey, 50th Round.

products during 2000-01 was 7.60 lakh tonnes, 81.56 million eggs and 3434 tonnes of meat.

Food Consumption by Women

Low food consumption levels of women have led to late menarche and early menopause. There is a higher probability of miscarriage and stillbirth among inadequately-fed pregnant women. In case such a women delivers a live baby, her lactational amenorrhea after parturition may be longer than that of a well-nourished woman (*Chen, Ahmed, Gesche and Mosley, 1974; Frisch, 1975; Frisch, 1977*).

Above 90 per cent of the women consume pulses or beans, green leafy vegetables, and other vegetables. Above four-fifths of them consume milk or curd (87 per cent) and nearly three-fourths of them consume fruits. The consumption of eggs and chicken, meat or fish is a little low. In spite of a rich dietary pattern and adequate iron and folic acid supplementation, more than two-fifths of the women in Himachal Pradesh (40.5 per cent) suffer from anaemia. The Scheduled Caste and other backward caste women consume relatively less milk or curd and fruits. A high standard of living is indicated by increased consumption of pulses, leafy vegetables and other vegetables, roots and tubers, fruits, milk and milk products and sugar (*NFHS II, Himachal Pradesh*). Intra-familial disparities in food consumption, with particular reference to the left-over food available to the woman, after all at home have been fed, calls for immediate intervention to create awareness about her health needs. Further, an empowerment of women with education related to income-generation activities, which will enable her to buy food, will ensure a healthy woman and a healthy family.

Infant Feeding Practices in Himachal Pradesh

Infant feeding practices are mutually supporting for the mother and the child. The child gets life-saving colostrums from the mother and fertility level is controlled. To monitor nutritional deficiencies in children and to improve the nutritional status of children, mothers need to be made aware of the importance of breast-feeding. UNICEF recommends breast-feeding immediately after birth. In Himachal Pradesh, the situation in this respect is dismal. One out of every ten women (12.2 per cent) in 1992-93 followed the appropriate breast-feeding practices. By 1998-99 the number increased to two out of every ten women. Even this is quite low, though the proportion of infants being breast-fed within one hour of birth was higher than in the neighbouring states of Punjab (6.1 per cent) and Haryana (11.7 per cent) or even at the national level (15.8 per cent). We need to look at the better performing states such as Tamil Nadu (50.3 per cent) and Kerala (42.9 per cent). Immense scope for improvement in breast-feeding practices exists in Himachal Pradesh. A higher literacy level of the mother and delivery in public hospital has enhanced the proportion of mothers who initiate breastfeeding within one hour of birth. Lack of awareness makes more than four-fifths of the mothers (86.2 per cent) squeeze out the first milk from their breasts, thus underestimating the importance of colustrum in the first milk. In Himachal Pradesh, exclusive breast-feeding of infants (0-3 months) came down from 36.4 per cent to 17.5 per cent during the period 1992-93 to 1998-99.

It is imperative to understand the reasons for the decline in breast-feeding practices. The change could be attributed to the impact of urbanisation, i.e., availability of infant feeds, increase in the work burden of women and inadequate awareness. A strategy needs to be evolved to encourage breast-feeding in the urban areas and improve it further in the rural areas.

Overall, the most cost-effective way to achieve a healthy population is to create awareness about locally available nutritious food products and to overcome beliefs against the consumption of non-vegetarian food. The state needs to ensure the availability of unadulterated, nutritionally balanced and hygienically prepared food.

Micronutrient Deficiencies

Anaemia

Anaemia in a child leads to impaired cognitive performance, behavioural and motor development, and ultimately affects academic performance (*Seshadri, 1997*). It is one of the micronutrient deficiencies, which needs constant vigil. Its consequences are very far reaching as it could lead to reduced immunity and increased morbidity. Seven out of every ten children (6-35 months) in Himachal Pradesh are anaemic, 2.2 per cent of them severely anaemic, while the corresponding all-India figures are 74.3 and 5.4 per cent. A comparison with Kerala (44 per cent) indicates scope for improvement in Himachal (Figure 9.1). Children in the age group of 24-35 months are more prone to anaemia (71.3 per cent). Anaemia is also high among rural (70.3 per cent) and other backward class (77.9 per cent) children in the state.

Anaemia among pregnant women leads to maternal mortality, risk of premature delivery and low birth-weight. Himachal Pradesh (40.5 per cent) has almost double the number of anaemic women than Kerala (22.7 per cent). The all-India figure is 51.8 per cent. The percentage of anaemic women in the age group of 15-19 years (43.2 per cent) is higher. A large percentage of anaemic women are illiterate (40.9 per cent) and live in rural areas (40.7 per cent). Severe anaemia is reported among women with height <145 cm (1.4 per cent) and body mass index <18.5 kg/m^2 (1.1 per cent). Of them, only 0.6 per cent consume fruits and vegetables. Anaemia level is higher among non-pregnant and non breast-feeding women. Iron supplements are being supplied to pregnant and nursing mothers, while due care is not being provided to women under normal conditions.

FIGURE 9.1

Anaemia Amongst Women and Children in Selected States, 1988-99

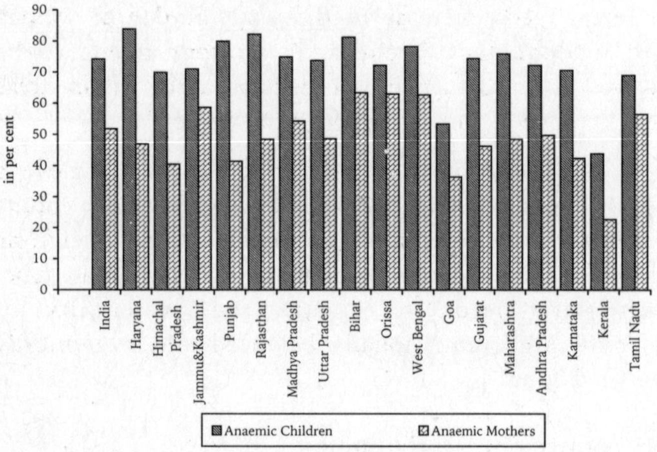

Source: National Family Health Survey, India 1998-99.

Detection of the actual cause of anaemia is important. It could be due to worm infestation, malaria or inadequate absorption of dietary iron. A high incidence of malaria has been reported from the districts of Solan, Sirmaur, Bilaspur, Kangra and Una. Worm infestation is also widely prevalent in the state (*Directorate of Health and Family Welfare, Himachal Pradesh 1993-95*). Rich sources of dietary iron include fish and poultry, but their intake may be inadequate because of their high cost and also religious and cultural inhibitions. To combat nutritional anaemia, the Department of Health and Family Welfare and the Department of Social, Women and Scheduled Castes, have included distribution of iron and folic acid tablets (IFA) to pregnant women. In 1999-2000, 97.5 per cent of the mothers received iron and folic acid (IFA) tablets from the department. The question of actual consumption of iron and folic acid tablets, and deworming medicines being distributed among anaemic women and children needs to be addressed.

Iodine Deficiency

Iodine is a vital micronutrient. Iodine deficiency disorders have been identified as a public health issue and have been accorded importance since the mid-twenties. The National Goitre Control Programme (NGCP) was launched in 1962, after a successful trial of iodized salt in Kangra valley. Initially it was aimed at the well-recognised sub-Himalayan 'goitre belt'. But the sale of non-iodised salt did not decline, and the problem remained. Subsequently in 1992 the NGCP was renamed National Iodine Deficiency Disorders Control Programme, which has concentrated on iodisation of salt before use.

UNICEF's goal was to achieve virtual elimination of iodine deficiency disorders. However, 2.47 per cent of the rural inhabitants still suffer from goitre, which is higher than the all-India figure of 0.74 per cent (INP, 1998). The prevalence rate of goitre in Mandi district was 34.5 per cent in 1981 and came down to 13.9 per cent in 1998 (*Health Information, 1997-98*). Over 90 per cent of the households in Himachal Pradesh use iodized salt (*NFHS, 1998-99*). Households not using iodized salt belong to the Scheduled Castes (4.1 per cent), other backward castes (3.4 per cent), persons living in rural areas (3.5 per cent) and persons with a low standard of living (5.3 per cent) (*NFHS, 1998-99*). Kapil *et al.* (1997) conducted a study in Kullu district and found that 9.5 per cent of the women had iodine excretion less than 10 ug/dl, indicating that pregnant women were suffering from iodine deficiency disorders in this area. A study conducted on school-aged children (6-11 years) in Kangra revealed a goitre prevalence rate of 12.1 per cent. If more than five per cent of school-aged children in an area suffer from goitre, it should be declared as endemic. Overall, Kangra district was found to be in a transition phase from an iodine deficient district to an iodine sufficient district (Kapil *et al., 2000*). Under the Iodine Deficiency Disorder Control Programme, testing of salt is a regular activity and the proportion of samples of salt tested and found to have zero iodine content doubled in the last one year (*Department of Health and Family Welfare, 2001*). A drive to promote the use of iodized salt by the below poverty level families is feasible, if provided through the public distribution system.

Vitamin-A Deficiency

Vitamin-A deficiency can lead to blindness. It causes increased morbidity and mortality among infants, children and pregnant women. Prevention and control of Vitamin-A deficiency by administering the Vitamin-A solution to children below three years of age is a shared responsibility of the Health Department and the ICDS team. Eradication of Vitamin-A deficiency as visualised by the state government is possible by strengthening interlinkages between the two departments. Seven out of every ten children aged 12-35 months received at least one dose of Vitamin-A. A higher proportion of male children as compared to female children was administered Vitamin-A solution (*NFHS, 1998-99*). The achievement of Himachal Pradesh's Department of Health and Family Welfare in administering Vitamin-A drops to children in 1999-2000 was 91.09 per cent.

Thus, nutritional deficiencies can be attributed to inadequate purchasing power, wrong dietary patterns, inadequate availability of preventive (testing facilities against anaemia, Vitamin-A deficiency during pregnancy, supplementary medication) and curative (de-worming) services and lack of adequate knowledge regarding right eating habits.

Role of the Private Sector

The emergence of concepts such as privatisation, liberalisation and open market economy, will redefine the role of the public sector in enhancing the nutritional status of the people. As in other development sectors, we also need to strike a balance between the public and private sectors in nutrition. The state has a progressive juice processing industry and this can be the stepping-stone for the creation of a state food fortification authority, which forms rules and regulations keeping in view the nutritional health of the people. The people of the state will be ready to pay if the nutritional supplements (such as iron supplements and infant formula food or complementary food) are quality controlled, fairly priced and have the government's stamp. This would serve as the entry point for private corporations through the public window, with an assurance to the private sector about economic returns and to the public about freedom from the malnourishment trauma.

State level officials' views on private sector involvement is in terms of involving the NGOs, who can set up nutrition counselling units in every *panchayat* and intensive research can be conducted to identify the causes of malnutrition.

Glimpses from the Field

The Centre for Research in Rural and Industrial Development (CRRID), Chandigarh conducted a district level primary survey to evolve a strategy to cope with the problem of malnutrition in the state. A questionnaire was prepared in English and Hindi and sent to the Secretary, Department of Planning, and the Secretary, Department of Social, Women and Scheduled Castes, Government of Himachal Pradesh. They sent it to all 12 district level officers and subsequently to Child Development Project Officers (CDPOs) and *Anganwari* workers in their area. Of the total 72 CDPOs and 7,354 *Anganwari* workers in the state, responses was received from 49 CDPO's and 6278 *Anganwari* workers. All questionnaires were processed and tabulated. All CDPOs and five per cent of the total *Anganwari* workers formed the sample for the study.

The CDPOs stressed the continuing role of the government in providing services related to nutrition and also on co-ordination with the Health Department to reduce the proportion of low birth-weight babies. The need to generate awareness among the people regarding health and nutritional care (Table 9.10) was also considered important. One CDPO has put forth a SMART (Sustainable, Manageable, Actionable, Reliable and Time bound) Action Plan for enhancing the nutritional status of the people.

The response of the Anganwari workers matched those of the CDPOs as far as strengthening the linkage with the Health Department and also on generating awareness among the people were concerned. In addition, they also felt that creating employment avenues, reducing poverty and increasing the intake of locally available seasonal fruits, vegetables and non-vegetarian food could enhance the level of nutrition in the state (Table 9.11). Besides giving their opinions, they also drew attention to certain strategies to make the functioning of the *Anganwari* centres more effective. Training of the Panchyati Raj Institutions on health and nutritional aspects was emphasised.

The views of state level officials on controlling malnutrition also reinforced the importance of generating awareness among the masses besides expanding the ICDS programme to all villages, introducing health and nutrition education as a compulsory subject in all schools (government or private) and integrating and strengthening the nutrition module in the training of the staff of the sectors concerned, *viz.*, Agriculture, Health, Education and Rural Development, who in turn would strengthen communication on malnutrition through the existing infrastructure.

Strategy for Nutrition-energised Growth

Nutrition enhancement is not the task of the Department of Welfare alone or of the centrally

TABLE 9.10

Opinions of the CDPOs to Enhance the Nutritional Status of People of Himachal Pradesh

Task	*Strategy*	*Sample (N)*
Reduction in the proportion of low birth-weight babies	Provide adequate and timely antenatal care.	27(55.1)
	Impart health and nutrition education through camps and village level meetings.	27 (55.1)
	Check age at marriage, which will ensure that the woman conceives after the age of 20 years, control frequent childbirths and increase spacing between children.	8 (16.3)
	Emphasis on adolescent health and nutrition education and provision of services/ counselling to them.	5 (10.2)
	Others	8 (16.3)
Reduction in the proportion of malnutrition in Himachal Pradesh	Provide health services, i.e., preventive (immunisation, antenatal care, iron and folic acid tablets, Vitamin-A solution, calcium tablets) and curative (safe deliveries, de-worming tablets).	42(85.7)
	Organise seminars and camps to impart nutrition and health education pertaining particularly to the kind, quantity and timing of consuming diet.	40 (81.6)
	Increase literacy and generate awareness.	18 (36.7)
	Alleviate poverty.	12 (24.4)
	Improve environmental sanitation, hygiene and provide safe drinking water.	9 (19.5)
	Improve breast feeding practices and weigh children every month.	8 (16.3)
	Check age at marriage and counsel on spacing between children.	6 (12.2)

Source: *CRRID Field Survey*, 2003.

Note: (i) The figures in parentheses are in per cent.
(ii) Multiple responses permitted.

sponsored scheme of ICDS. It needs proper inter-departmental co-ordination, disciplined execution and systematic implementation. The state has to play the role of a facilitator. Here are some steps it should take:

- Establish a nutrition surveillance system under state authorities, so as to identify and regularly monitor nutritional deficiencies at the grassroot level. It should co-ordinate closely with the Health Department to enforce a mandatory anaemia-testing facility in rural and urban areas. Consumption of IFA tablets and worm infestation tablets should be ensured. The use of iodized salt can be promoted by organising awareness campaigns.
- Set up a Therapeutic Nutritive Care Unit under the paediatrician posted at every primary health centre to help malnourished children, referred by the ICDS project area and to monitor their growth.
- Ensure effective co-ordination with the agriculture/horticulture universities at Nauni and Palampur to carry out regular research projects to identify local foods rich in iron, Vitamin-A, proteins and calcium and how their productivity can be increased.
- Enhance co-ordination with the Health Department to provide adequate antenatal care to pregnant women and provide facilities to make institutional deliveries more functional.
- Involve the community, through self-help groups and provide them with training to bring about a behavioural change among the people towards their health and nutritional needs.
- Make the *Anganwari* Leaving Certificate mandatory for admission to a primary school. This will improve attendance at the *Anganwari* centre and also ensure that growth patterns of all children are monitored.
- Generate purchasing power of the people to obtain nutritive food by creating employment opportunities.
- Ensure sustained nutrition security of the families by making the woman the central figure, with educational and economic empowerment.
- Network with the school authorities in the state to enhance the nutrition level of the children. School canteens should provide milk and milk products, fruits and other high protein food. Monthly talks on health and nutrition should be held in the schools. The school authorities can finalise a diet plan age-wise with the state authorities and have it circulated among the

TABLE 9.11

Opinions of the Anganwari Workers to Enhance the Nutritional Status of the people of Himachal Pradesh

Task	*Strategies*	*Sample (N)*
Reduction in the proportion of low birth-weight babies at birth	Impart health and nutrition education through camps and village level meetings.	221(68.2)
	Provide adequate and timely antenatal care.	202(62.3)
	Consumption of locally available fruits, vegetables and non-vegetarian food, such as eggs and meat to be encouraged.	31(9.5)
	Check age at marriage. Special care to adolescent girls and promote institutional deliveries.	19(5.8)
Reduction in the proportion of malnutrition in Himachal Pradesh	Organise seminars and camps to impart nutrition and health education pertaining particularly to the kind, quantity and timing of consuming diet.	234(72.2)
	Alleviate poverty.	115(35.4)
	Provide health services, i.e., preventive (immunisation, antenatal care, iron and folic acid tablets, vitamin-A solution, calcium tablets) and curative (safe deliveries, deworming tablets).	112(34.5)
	Improve environmental sanitation, hygiene and provide safe drinking water.	73(22.5)
	Increase literacy.	62(19.1)
	Promote breast feeding practices and weigh children every month.	32(9.8)
	Check age at marriage and counsel on spacing between children.	20(6.1)
	Special attention to be paid to adolescent girls and women's nutritional needs.	17(5.2)
	Ensure provision of Hyderabad Mix and double diet to all undernourished women and children.	16(4.9)

Source: *CRRID Field Survey*, 2003.

Note: (i) The figures in parentheses are in per cent.

(ii) Multiple responses permitted.

parents for effective implementation. Regular health check-ups in school is essential.

- *Him Viyanjan* is a book with tips on nutrition, compiled by the state to promote low-cost nutritious food and recipes from locally available raw material. It must be ensured that it is optimally utilised, periodically upgraded and duly promoted by the functionaries, particularly in the rural and tribal belts of the state.
- Popularise a more cost-effective strategy to make the public distribution system more effective. A wider variety of nutritious products, such as pulses, millets, coarse grains and iodized salt should be introduced to increase their consumption.
- Formulate a state plan of action for the elderly to help them cope with problems related to their health and nutritional needs.
- Enforce the Prevention of Food Adulteration Act, 1954, to ensure the sale of unadulterated, nutritionally balanced and hygienically prepared food in the market not only for local inhabitants but also for tourists. Wayside food stalls and sale of cut fruit need to be checked.
- Seasonality of nutrition plays a vital role in the state, particularly in the higher reaches. Assured supply round the year will help the people cope with their nutritional problems.
- A public-private initiative towards social marketing of iron supplements, infant formula foods and complementary food at affordable prices needs to be worked out.
- Form a state food fortification authority, which could be made responsible for the supply of fortified food to reduce micronutrient deficiencies in the state.
- Enforce nutrition enhancement as a movement, as it is the most cost-effective measure towards promising a healthy and productive human resource.

Conclusions

Nutritional planning for Himachal Pradesh is a challenging task since the diverse structure and composition of its population leads to differences in its food habits as well. Besides implementing the centrally sponsored schemes effectively, the state has formulated certain state-specific approaches towards ensuring food security and working towards the well-being of its people. It provides integrated services through various departments such as Agriculture, Health and Family Welfare, Food and Supply, Rural Development, and the Social, Women and Scheduled Caste Welfare Department.

The increase in the proportion of underweight children at birth and the slow decline in the percentage of underweight children under three years of age is a matter of concern for the state. Chronic energy deficiency is high among the adults, particularly among women and this needs immediate intervention. Though the proportion of children being breastfed within one hour of birth is higher than in the neighbouring states of Punjab and Haryana, and the proportion of anaemic children is lower, yet, there is scope for improvement. Enhancing the socio-economic status of the people, their awareness regarding a balanced diet and the positive impact of timely-health seeking behaviour will result in favourable nutritional outcomes.

Apart from focusing on inadequate food consumption, there is need for identifying causes of anaemia, high incidence of gastrointestinal and respiratory infections, lack of safe drinking water and poor access to health care and such behavioural factors as faulty breast-feeding and weaning practices, which contribute to low absorption of nutrients from the food consumed and result in malnourished individuals.

References

Chen, L. C., S. Ahmed, M. Gesche, and W.H. Mosley (1974), "A Prospective Study of Birth Interval Dynamics in Rural Bangladesh", *Population Studies*, 28: 277.

David H. Peters, *et al.* (2002), *Better Health System for India's Poor: Findings, Analysis and Options*, World Bank, Human Development Network, Health Nutrition and Population Series.

Department of Economics and Statistics, *Economic Survey (2002)*, Government of Himachal Pradesh, Shimla

Department of Health and Family Welfare, *Himachal Health Vision, 2020*, Himachal Pradesh, pp. 26 and 27.

Department of Health and Family Welfare, *Year Book, 1997-98, Family Welfare Programme in India*, Government of India.

Department of Women and Child Development (1998), *India Nutrition Profile*, Ministry of Human Resource Development, Government of India.

Department of Women and Child Development, Government of India and United Nations Children's Fund, New Delhi, *Multiple Indicator Survey (MICS-2000), India, Summary Report*, December 2001.

Directorate General of Health Services, Ministry of Health and Family Welfare, Government of India, *Bulletin on Rural Health Statistics in India, March 2002*.

Economic and Statistical Organisation, Government of Himachal Pradesh, *Statistical Abstracts of Himachal Pradesh* (different issues)

Frisch, R.E. (1975), "Demographic Implications of the Biological Determinants of Female Fecundity", *Social Biology*, 22: 17.

————. (1977), *Population Food Intake and Fertility: Historical Evidence for a Direct Effect of Nutrition on Reproductive Ability*, Science in Press.

Government of Himachal Pradesh (2002), *Himachal Pradesh Human Development Report 2002*.

International Institute of Population Sciences (1995), *National Family Health Survey: Himachal Pradesh - 1992-93*, Mumbai

————. (2000), *National Family Health Survey: Himachal Pradesh -1998-99*, Mumbai

————. (1995), *National Family Health Survey: India, 1992-93*, Mumbai

————. (2002), *National Family Health Survey: India, 1998-99*, Mumbai

International Institute for Population Sciences and Macro ORC, *National Family Health Survey-II*, India 1998-99.

————. *National Family Health Survey-II*, Himachal Pradesh, India 1998-99.

Kapil, U., K.S. Sohal, M. Tandon, and P. Pathak (2000), "Assessment of Iodine Deficiency Disorders Using the 30 Cluster Approach in District Kangra, Himachal Pradesh, India", *Journal of Tropical Pediatrics*, Volume 46, Issue, 5, pp. 264-266

Kapil, U., N. Saxena, S. Ramachandran, and D. Nayar (1997) "Iodine Status of Pregnant Mothers Residing in a District of Endemic Iodine Deficiency in the State of Himachal Pradesh, India", *Asia Pacific J. Clin Nutr*, 6(3): 224-225

Kumar, Rajesh, J.S. Thakur and A.K. Srivastava. *Himachal Burden of Disease Study Draft Estimation Report, 2003*, Department of Community Medicines, Post Graduate Institute of Medical Education and Research, Chandigarh Sponsored by Directorate of Health and Family Welfare, Himachal Pradesh.

McLaren, D.S. (1974), *The Great Protein Fiasco*. Lancet; 2: 93-96.

Ministry of Health and Family Welfare, Government of India, New Delhi, *Family Welfare Programme in India, Year Book* (different issues).

————. *Annual Reports* (different issues)

————. *National Health Policy* 2002.

National Sample Survey, *Sarvekshana*, Volume XXI, No. 3, Issue No. 74. January-March 1998

National Sample Survey 50th Round, 1997, *5th Quinquennial Survey of Consumer Expenditure*, July 1993-June 1994

National Council of Applied Economic Research (NCAER), New Delhi, *Household Survey of Medical Care (May-June 1990)*, June 1992, 52 p.

————. *Household Survey of Health Care Utilisation and Expenditure*, March 1995, 95 p.

National Institute of Health and Family Welfare, New Delhi (December 2000), *Development of Health Insurance in India: Current Status and Future Directions*, Report of Seminar held on 29-30 December 2000, 46 p.

National Sample Survey Organisation, Department of Statistics, Government of India *Sarvekshana*, Volume IV, No. 1& 2, 1980.

————. "Morbidity and Utilisation of Medical Services" (42nd Round), July 1986-June 1987, *Sarvekshana*, Vol. XV, No. 4, Issue No. 51, April-June 1992.

————. "Morbidity and Treatment of Ailments" *(52nd round)*, July 1995-June 1996, Report No. 441, November 1998.

————. "Morbidity and Treatment of Ailments" (52nd round), July 1995-June 1996, *Sarvekshana*, Vol. XXIII, No. 3, 82nd Issue, January-March 2000.

ORG, MARG, (1999) Quoted from Brij K. Taimni, *Food Security in 21st Century: Perspective and Vision, 2001*.

Pachauri, S. (1996) "NGO Efforts to Prevent Maternal and Infant Mortality in India", *Social Change*, Volume 26, Nos. 3-4, September-December, 1996, pp. 30-44).

Planning Commission, Government of India, *Five Year Plan Documents* (different documents).

Shekar, M., 1991. *The Tamil Nadu Integrated Nutrition Project: A review of the project with special emphasis on the monitoring and information system*. Cornell Food and Nutrition Policy Program, Working Paper No. 14. Cornell University Press. Ithaca, New york.

Srivastava, M., U. Kapil, V. Kumar, A.B. Dubey, K.M. Nagarkar and G. Sekaran (1996). "Knowledge, Attitude and Practice Regarding Nutrition in Patients Attending Geriatric Clinics at AIIMS", in V. Kumar (ed.), *Ageing: Indian Perspective and Global Scenario*, AIIMS, New Delhi, 1996. pp. 407-409.

UNICEF. *The Progress of Indian States, 1995*, India Country Office, New Delhi, p 42

————. *List of Essential Drugs*, 1999.

————. *Standard Treatment Guidelines*, June 2000.

World Bank, *A Vision for India's Health System*, Report of Conference held on 15-16 November 2001, New Delhi, downloaded from Internet.

World Health Organisation (1978), *Primary Health Care*, Report of the International Conference on Primary Health Care, Alma Ata, USSR, 6-12 September 1978.

————. *The World Health Reports* (different issues).

Chapter 10

Gender Empowerment

Introduction

Gender empowerment is conceived as a process by which women can overcome many of the hurdles that they face such as education, work status, employment opportunities, health care, social security, position in decision making by virtue of their gender. Thus gender empowerment veritably implies empowerment of women to do away with "subordination" or "discrimination" and "injustices" done to them in male dominated society.

The Government of India as well as various state governments have taken numerous measures and are continuing in their endeavors to raise the status of women in the society. The constitutional obligations and different plans, programmes and policies have laid emphasis on women's empowerment, to make them active participants in the process of development.

Measures taken by the Government of India include the establishment of the National Commission for Women (NCW); Rashtriya Mahila Kosh (RMK); launching of Indira Mahila Yojana (IMY), Balika Samridhi Yojana (BSY); and Rural Women's Development and Empowerment Project (RWDEP). Formulating a National Policy for Empowerment of Women and setting up a National Resource Centre for Women are other efforts of the context undertaken by government in the interests of women.

The government of Himachal Pradesh has also undertaken many gender empowerment initiatives to upgrade the status of women. Monthly pension scheme for widow and destitute women and Mantri Shakti Bima Yojana for women living below poverty line and belonging to IRDP families are aimed at economic empowerment of women. Moreover, Support to Training

Women Empowerment Measures Undertaken in Different Five Year Plans by Government of India and Himachal Pradesh Government

Five Year Plans of Govt. of India	*Women Welfare Measures Formulated by Govt. of India*	*Women Welfare Measures Formulated by H.P. Govt.*
First Five Year Plan	Central Social Welfare Board was set up, 1953	—
Second Five Year Plan	Mahila Mandals were organised	—
Third Five Year Plan	Priority for education of women	Women Welfare Extension Centres and State Homes for women
Fourth Five Year Plan	Supplementary nutrition for women and children	Bal/Balika Ashram
Fifth Five Year Plan	Shift from women's welfare to women's development	Working Women's Hostels
Sixth Five Year Plan	Separate chapter on women and adoption of a multidisciplinary approach with thrust on health, education and employment	Pension to Widows
Seventh Five Year Plan	Raise social and economic status of women. A separate department for women and child development under HRD Ministry created	Marriage Grant to Destitute Girls and Women
Eighth Five Year Plan	Shift from women's development to women's empowerment	Setting up Women's Development Corporation
Ninth Five Year Plan	Vigorous steps on economic empowerment of women by launching DWACRA, STEP etc.	Setting up Women's Commission
Tenth Five Year Plan (Approach Paper)	Promote access of women to information, resources and services	Mahila Protsahan Yojana, Womens' Cell

and Employment Programme (STEP); setting up of employment and income generating training-cum-production units for women; establishment of Rastriya Mahila Kosh; setting up Women Development Corporation; launching Indira Mahila Yojana are other steps aimed particularly at rural women. Reservations for women in Panchayati Raj Institutions have encouraged their participation in decision-making process at the grassroots. The 'Women Commission' constituted by the state government is actively engaged in checking crime against women and ensuring equal wages and opportunities for them. Such social security measures, as construction of state homes, marriage grants to destitute girls, construction and expansion of hostel buildings for working women, short stay homes for women and girls, and Swadhar Yojana for women in difficult situations and widows have been effective in raising the social status of women in this hilly and mountainous state. Three Nari Sewa Sadans are functioning at Chamba, Mandi and Mashobra to provide shelter to destitute and lonely women. The Mahila Mandals Protsahan Yojana launched by the Rural Development Department during 1998-99, provides incentives to Mahila Mandals on the basis of their performance in family planning and child welfare, promotion of small savings, education about social evils and participation in literacy campaigns. During 2001-2002, Rs. 156.58 lakh was sanctioned in favour of 18 women entrepreneurs. Unfortunately, both the financial and physical achievements which had increased during the year 1998-99 to 2000-2001 have declined during 2001-2002. This seems to indicate that during 2001-2002 women empowerment measures were not vigorously pursued (Table 10.1).

TABLE 10.1

Financial and Physical Achievement in Welfare, Himachal Pradesh

Year	*Financial Achievement (Rs. in lakh)*	*Physical Achievement*
1998-1999	53.14	741
1999-2000	72.02	742
2000-2001	94.43	993
2001-2002	78.84	824

Source: Department of Social, Women and Scheduled Caste Welfare, Government of Himachal Pradesh.

Women and Economic Empowerment

The economic empowerment of women means their participation in economically productive activities; their access to savings and credits and their control over income and other productive assets such as land, business and industries. Despite legislation on equal pay for equal work, women continue to be paid considerably less than men, even when the occupational category and actual hours of employment are virtually same. It is encouraging that of total women employed in organised sectors in Himachal, 94.95 per cent are in the public sector. But this is mainly in lower-cadre jobs. The number of men employed in the gazetted posts are ten times higher than women. Of the total employed women only 3.1 per cent are in gazetted posts and the rest 97 per cent in non-gazetted posts. A study on urban female labour participation in Himachal Pradesh reveals that women are found in such activities as teaching, clerks, assistants, peons, etc., which are of lower status and carry lower remuneration (Sharma, 1994).

In the agricultural sector too women are engaged in low-skill activities, such as seed application, post-threshing, storing and, looking after crops in the slack season, and are engaged in livestock farming (Raj Kumari, 1989). According to the census, wages of

TABLE 10.2

Government Employees: A Gender Description, Himachal Pradesh

Types of Employees of all Depts/Offices	*SC*		*ST*		*Others*		*Total*		*Grand Total*
	Male	*Female*	*Male*	*Female*	*Male*	*Female*	*Male*	*Female*	
Gazetted	647 (93.36)	46 (6.64)	281 (89.21)	34 (10.79)	5633 (89.71)	646 (10.29)	6561 (90.04)	726 (9.90)	7287
Non-Gazetted	17296 (82.38)	3699 (17.62)	4181 (80.90)	987 (19.10)	69375 (79.51)	17878 (20.49)	90852 (80.11)	22564 (19.89)	113416
Total	**17943 (82.73)**	**3745 (17.27)**	**4462 (81.38)**	**1021 (18.62)**	**75008 (80.20)**	**18524 (19.80)**	**97413 (80.71)**	**23290 (19.29)**	**120703**

Source: Abridged Table-8, Page No. 14, Census of H.P Employees as on 31 March 1997, Government of Himachal Pradesh.

marginal workers increased from 1.56 per cent to 11.40 per cent, during 1991-2000, but wages of female workers increased from 15.45 per cent to 22.61 per cent. (Director of Census, H.P. 2002). This indicates that women, a large number of whom are marginal workers, are being further concentrated in the same level. The quality of women employment is poor in the state. This supports the finding that the effective per day wage rate for all wage-work (agricultural and non-agricultural work) for females is Rs. 18.6, at least 40 per cent lower than that of male workers (Rs. 31.2). The wage rate of women in Haryana is Rs. 38.3; Kerala, Rs. 30.3 and Punjab, Rs. 26.2. The lower wage rate means greater exploitation of women by the employers. Considering the geographical situation, the women are supposed to get more than their counterparts in other non-hilly states. Higher work burden and lower wage rate have affected the health and well-being of women and their dependent families in the state.

TABLE 10.3

Women Employment in Organised Sector

State	*Public*	*Private*	*Total*
Andhra Pradesh	219.90 (51.38)	208.10 (48.62)	428.00
Assam	83.70 (19.61)	343.10 (80.39)	426.80
Bihar	95.50 (84.28)	17.80 (15.72)	113.30
Gujarat	141.80 (84.55)	25.90 (15.45)	167.70
Haryana	62.80 (91.95)	5.50 (8.05)	68.30
Himachal Pradesh	**39.50 (94.95)**	**2.10 (5.05)**	**41.60**
Karnataka	245.60 (46.29)	284.90 (53.71)	530.50
Kerala	192.30 (88.29)	25.50 (11.71)	217.80
Madhya Pradesh	153.40 (42.65)	206.30 (57.35)	359.70
Maharashtra	352.00 (99.77)	0.80 (0.23)	352.80
Orissa	85.70 (71.36)	34.40 (28.64)	120.10
Punjab	102.60 (71.50)	409.00 (28.50)	143.50
Rajasthan	132.90 (28.98)	325.60 (71.02)	458.50
Tamil Nadu	419.70 (98.64)	5.80 (1.36)	425.50
Uttar Pradesh	186.80 (58.28)	133.70 (41.72)	320.50
West Bengal	113.90 (99.82)	0.20 (0.18)	114.10

Source: National Sample Survey Organisation, Report No. 455, *Employment and Unemployment in India, 1999-2000, Key Results.*

Note: Figures in parenthesis show percentages to total.

FIGURE 10.1

Female Work Participation Rate, 1999

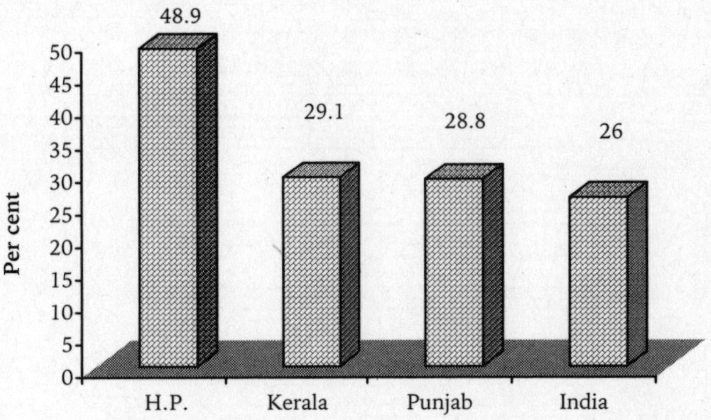

Source: Same as in Table No. A–10.1, Annexure-II.

Female workforce participation in the state is 48.9 per cent, higher than other major states and much higher than that of India's average (26.0%).

There were over 6000 registered Mahila Mandals in the state. Cash awards are given to those who perform well. They work in the villages to eradicate liquor shops and to promote women's economic empowerment. The Mahila Mandals in Kangra districts are performing well. Moreover, Himachal Pradesh has a good record of the status and functioning of Mahila Mandals for employment generation for women through the formation of Self-Help Groups in rural areas, for raising the per capita income of women. SHGs are emerging as a success story in Himachal Pradesh. Against a target of setting up 3000 SHGs during 2000-01, a total of 1038 SHGs have been established until December 2000. An important achievement is that loan repayment of 95 per cent of those SHGs is 100 per cent. Moreover, a group of members of SHGs (Kathur, Solan district) travelled to one of the South Indian states in 1995-96 on a field trip and are now implementing the lessons learnt from the experience of their counterparts. The SHGs are involved in a wide range of economic activities, such as agro-business; handicraft; floriculture; sheep, goat and pig farming; *papad* making; tailoring and carpentry; running of fair price shops, etc., in order to be gainfully employed and augment household incomes. The higher percentage of work participation of women and the effective functioning of Mahila Mandals and SHGs have raised the level of women's involvement in household decision-making. The NFHS II (1999) report maintains that in Himachal Pradesh, 80.1 per cent of women have access to surplus money as compared to 66.2 per cent in Kerala and 78.3 per cent in Punjab.

FIGURE 10.2

Women Access to Money

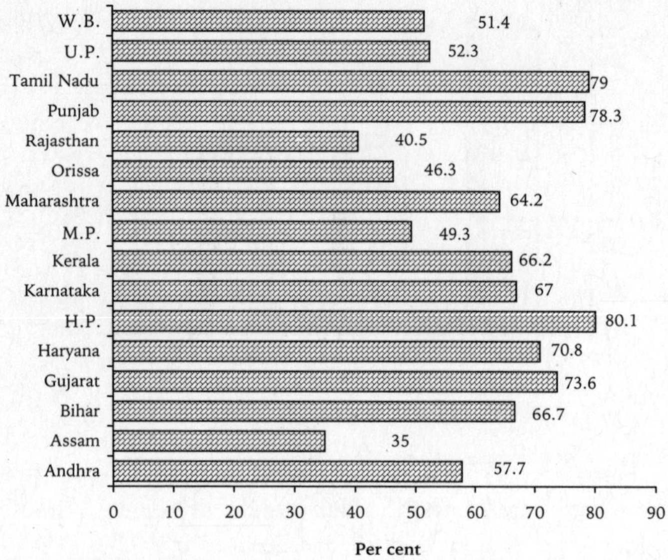

Source: *NFHS II*, India, 1998-99.

Empowering Rural Women through Agro-Business Consortium

The Samridhi Mahila Cooperative, an agro-business consortium, was formed in 1996 in the resource-poor changer areas of Kangra and Chamba districts. The organisation got support from the Indo-German Changer Eco-Development Project (IGCEDP) and also from two NGOs viz. New Hope (Kangra) and Himalaya Bachao Samiti (Chamba). From a modest beginning with 16 women members and 357 kg of processed products in 1995-96, Samridhi has grown into a sizable agro-business consortium with 182 members producing about 23,000 kg of processed pickles, *chutneys*, and candles in 2000-01. These have wide consumer acceptability in various parts of the country (Ashokan and Singh 2002). This example needs to be followed by other women groups.

Women and Education

Education is a source of enlightenment and a means to achieve the goal of faster social development. Even after more than 50 years of Indian independence, gender-disparity in literacy continues and the situation varies from state to state and even within a state from district to district and from one community to another. Cultural prejudices, government apathy, lack of political and community will, illiteracy and the negative attitude of parents towards the education of the girl child, cost of education, etc., are some of the factors which have deprived girls and women of their right to education. Himachal Pradesh has made considerable progress in the matter of universalisation of primary education and has successfully raised the level of literacy. As Jean Dreze (1999) has said "the schooling revolution has raised the literacy status in general and women in particular in Himachal Pradesh. Fifty years ago, educational level in Himachal Pradesh was no higher than Bihar or Uttar Pradesh. Today, Himachal Pradesh is second only to Kerala in terms of school participation and literacy rate in the younger age-groups".

The government of Himachal Pradesh has taken a number of steps in order to raise the educational status of women in the state. Some of these are: (I) formation of Village Education Committees (VECs) with one-third women members, and making them responsible for universal enrolment and retention of children in schools; (II) A girl child scheme was launched on 2 October 1997 involving a gift amount besides a scholarship at the age of six; (III) 2745 Mother-Teacher Associations have been formed till 31 March 2000; (IV) exemption of tuition fee to Himachal domicile girl students in all institutions within the state irrespective of the income of parents; (V) free text books to girls of DPEP districts and free uniform to tribal girls; (VI) girls' attendance scholarship at two rupees per month up to ten months.

TABLE 10.4

Female Literacy Rate (1971-2001)

State	*Literacy Rate*				*Increase 1971-2001*
	*1971**	*1981***	*1991***	*2001***	
Himachal Pradesh	**20.23**	**37.72**	**52.00**	**68.00**	**3.36**
Kerala	54.31	75.65	86.20	88.00	1.62
Punjab	25.90	39.70	50.40	64.00	2.47
India	**18.69**	**29.76**	**39.24**	**54.35**	**2.91**

Source: * Director Publication Division Ministry of Information and Broadcasting GoI. 1976.

** *Census of India* 1981,1991, 2001.

FIGURE 10.3

Female Literacy Rate From 1971-2001

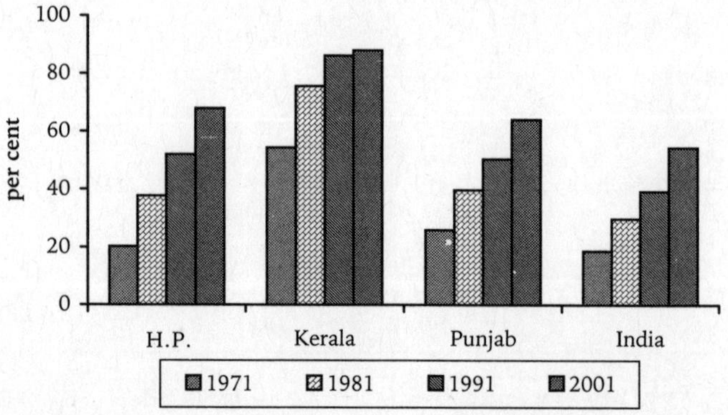

Source: Same as in Table 10.4.

The rate of growth of female literacy in Himachal has been the highest as compared to Kerala, Punjab and the national average between 1971 and 2001 (Table 10.4). This clearly reveals that after becoming full-fledged state, the literacy status of its women has risen considerably.

FIGURE 10.4

Educational Status

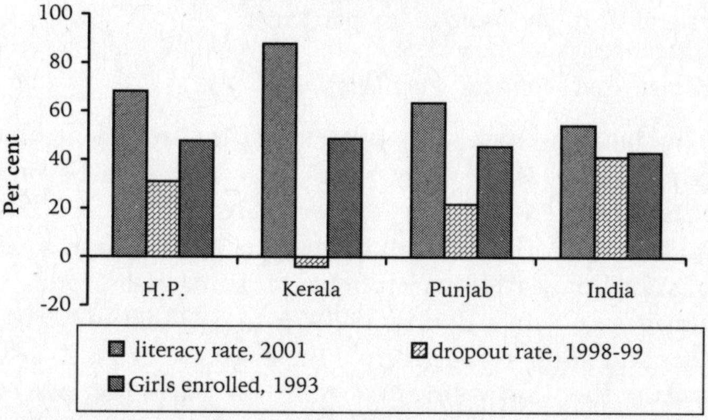

Source: Same as in Table A–10.2, Annexure II.

Notwithstanding all the supporting measures, however, the gap between male and female literacy in Himachal Pradesh is 17.94 per cent, which is three times higher than that of Kerala. Moreover, female drop-out rates of 31.03 per cent, 28.05 per cent and 43.20 per cent at the stages of I-V, VI-VIII and IX-X respectively are a cause of concern (Table A–10.2, Annexure II). The districts which need special attention for the promotion of women's literacy are Chamba, Solan, Kullu, Lahaul and Spiti, and Sirmaur. The poverty of the household, distance of school from the village, girl child labour in rural areas, etc., are a few of the many reasons for a high drop-out rate in the state. Moreover, it is amply revealed that incentive can promote enrolment but cannot effectively raise participation and school attendance unless and until the motivation of pupils and parents is raised and also equally backed up by active community support. Literacy is a necessary but not a sufficient condition for gender empowerment. The higher the level of women's education, the better will be their understanding of and participation in the development process of the society and the nation. Therefore, the level of education of women in general and vocational and technical education in particular needs to be raised in the state.

Women and Health

Health care of women is of paramount importance for the promotion of health care of the children and the family. The health status of women in Himachal Pradesh has not been sufficiently upgraded. The NFHS-II report shows that only 30 per cent women in the state have received three recommended ante-natal care services, such as three ante-natal check-ups, two doses of tetanus injections and IFA tablets, during their pregnancies. This is more than 50 per cent lower than that of Kerala. Deliveries conducted in the health institutions are 29 per cent and only 21 per cent of the women who delivered received post-natal check-up. However, the NFHS-II report points out that women's involvement in the decision-making process to take care of their own health is 80.8 per cent which is higher than the socially advanced Kerala (72.6%), and economically developed Punjab (78.5%). Notwithstanding the status of empowerment of women in health care decision-making, the inaccessibility of health centres, because of the topography, poor infrastructure facilities, and frequent transfer of grassroot health workers may be the reasons for lower maternal health status of women.

FIGURE 10.5

Women's Health Status

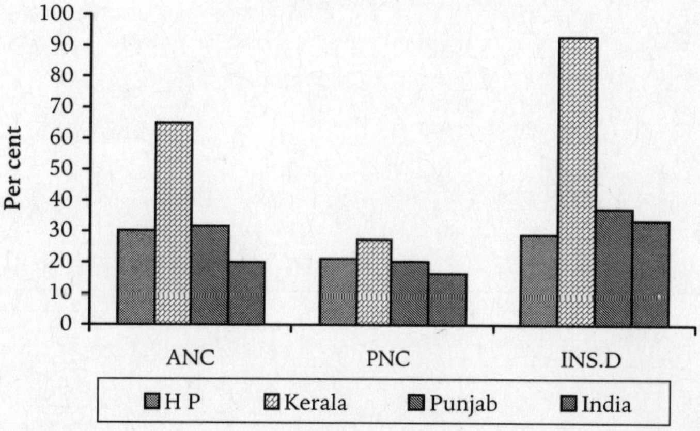

Source: Same as in Table A–10.3, Annexure II.

The NFHS-II also reveals that 34 per cent of currently married women in Himachal Pradesh report some type of reproductive health problems, such as Reproductive Tract Infections. Another gloomy picture of the reproductive health situation in Himachal Pradesh is the declining sex ratio, the overall decline being from 976 to 970 during 1991-2001. What is of major concern is the very heavy decline in sex ratio of children in 0-6 age group from 951 to 897. The NFHS-II (1998-99) points to a strong son preference among women in Himachal Pradesh; 88 per cent of women want at least one son and 62 per cent of those who have no daughter want no more children. Thus, strong male child preference is possibly one of the reasons for the declining sex ratio in the state. This is a process of undermining the status of women and girl children in Himachal Pradesh. In the matter of women literacy Himachal Pradesh is closer to Kerala, while in the matter of health care of women, the state is way behind.

FIGURE 10.6

Women's Decision Making in Health Care

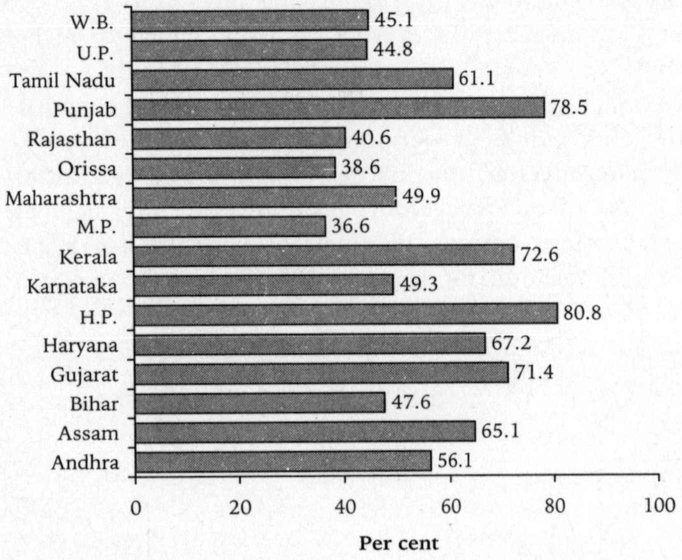

Source: *NFHS II*, India, 1998-99.

The spread of HIV/AIDS is a major concern for India. According to NFHS-II less than two thirds (61%) of women in Himachal Pradesh have heard of AIDS. Awareness of AIDS is particularly low among women who are not regularly exposed to any media, belong to households with a low standard of living, and illiterate and Muslim women. The floating nature of the population in a few districts of tourist attraction poses a threat of the risk of HIV/AIDS to the people in general and the women in particular.

Women and Political Participation

In India, women's representations in Parliament and state assemblies of many states have not gone beyond eight and ten percent respectively (Table A 10.4 Annexure-II). The average percentage of women elected to state legislative assemblies in Himachal Pradesh, Punjab and Kerala during 1970-75 to 1998-99 are 5.04, 4.35 and 4.66 respectively (Table 10.5). This clearly reveals the lower level of political participation of women in state level politics. However, as compared to socially progressive Kerala and economically developed Punjab, Himachal Pradesh has the highest representation. The constitutional amendment, which proposes reservation of one-third seats for women in Parliament and state assemblies, if passed, will be a great advantage for participatory democracy and women's political empowerment.

TABLE 10.5

Women in State Legislature 1975-1999 (per cent of Women MLAs)

State	*1970-75*	*1977-78*	*1979-83*	*1984-88*	*1989-92*	*1993-97*	*1998-99*	*State Averages*
Andhra Pradesh	9.1	3.4	4.1	3.4	3.7	2.7	9.5	5.12
Assam	7.0	0.08	0.08	4.0	4.0	4.8	****	3.33
Bihar	3.8	4.0	3.7	4.6	2.8	3.4	****	3.72
Gujarat	3.2	****	2.7	8.8	2.2	1.1	2.2	3.36
Haryana	6.2	4.4	7.8	5.6	6.7	4.4	****	5.85
Himachal Pradesh	**5.9**	**1.5**	**4.4**	**4.4**	**5.9**	**4.4**	**8.8**	**5.04**
Karnataka	5.1	4.0	0.9	3.6	4.5	3.1	2.3	3.36
Kerala	1.5	0.7	3.2	5.7	5.7	9.3	****	4.35
Madhya Pradesh	5.4	3.1	5.6	9.7	3.4	3.8	8.1	5.58
Maharastra	9.3	2.8	6.6	5.6	2.1	3.8	4.2	4.91
Orissa	1.4*	4.8	3.4	6.1	4.8	5.4	****	4.32
Punjab	5.8	2.6	5.1	3.4	5.1	6.0	****	4.66
Rajasthan	7.1	4.0	5.0	8.0	5.5	4.5	7.0	5.87
Tamil Nadu	2.1	0.9	2.1	3.4	9.0	3.8	****	3.55
Uttar Pradesh	5.9	2.6	5.6	7.3	3.3*	4.0*	****	4.78
West Bengal	1.6*	1.4	2.4	4.4	7.1	6.8	****	3.95

Source: Jayaprakash Narayan Lok Satta Hydrebad, Dhiru Bhai Sheth Lokeyan Delhi, CSDS, Centre for the Study of Development Society, Yogendra Yadav and Madhu Kishwar (Manushi).

Note: % women MLAs elected to state legislature in relevant elections.

* two election held during this period. The given figures are the average of the two.

**** States did not exist/no elections held in that year/ period.

With the reservation of seats, a good number of women have been elected to Panchayati Raj Institutions in Himachal Pradesh (Table 10.6). 40 per cent of them are chairpersons of *zila parishads*, 31.94 per cent chairpersons of *panchayat samitis* and 33.20 per cent chairpersons of *gram panchayats*. However it has been observed that, in Himachal Pradesh, women are still ostracised by political parties and isolated from mainstream democracy on the basis of caste, class and poverty, and the majority of women *panchayat* members are illiterate or educated up to the primary level (PRIA, 2002). At the same time it must be admitted that the greater participation of less educated and more disadvantaged women would not have been possible, but for the reservation of seats for women (Mahapatra, 2002).

Ironically, Himachal Pradesh does not have a single woman MP, in the current Lok Sabha, but the current Rajya Sabha has one. The Ninth *Vidhan Sabha* has only four women members, which constitute only 5.9 per cent of the total Assembly seats. However, the rate of success of women who contested assembly election in 2003 is quite encouraging (60%). The success in Assembly elections clearly shows that, if provided with the opportunity, women can excel in state politics.

Women and Security

Crime against women is a manifestation of social insecurity and of the real lower status of women in the society. Himachal Pradesh falls in the category of higher-ranking states in crime against women. Kangra, Mandi and Shimla districts have recorded high rates of crime against women. The prevalence of drug abuse among male, female-headed households, migrant population, etc., are some of the reasons for this state of affairs.

FIGURE 10.7

Gender and Security

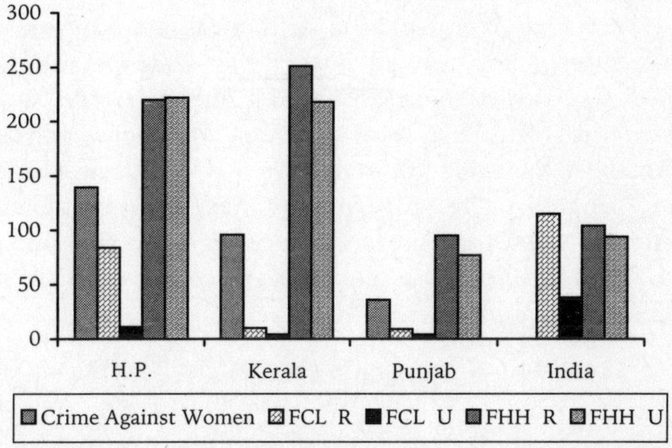

Source: Same as in Table A–10.5, Annexure II.

Another noteworthy feature of social security is the care for female-headed households. The National

TABLE 10.6

Women's Pepresentation in Panchayati Raj Institutions in Himachal Pradesh

Type	*Total Institutions*	*Total Member*	*Members Category-wise*						*Overall*	
			SC		*ST*		*General*			
			M	*F*	*M*	*F*	*M*	*F*	*M*	*F*
Zilla Parishad	12									
Chairpersons of *Zilla Parishad*		12	2 (66.66)	1 (33.34)	1 (50.00)	1 (50.00)	5 (66.66)	2 (33.34)	8 (60.00)	4 (40.00)
Members in *Zilla Parishad*		252	46 (69.70)	20 (30.30)	14 (66.66)	7 (33.34)	108 (65.45)	57 (34.55)	168 (66.67)	84 (33.33)
Panchayat Samiti	72									
Chairpersons of *Panchayat Samiti*		72	14 (70.00)	6 (30.00)	3 (50.00)	3 (50.00)	32 (69.57)	14 (30.43)	49 (68.66)	23 (31.94)
Members in *Panchayat Samitis*		1661	280 (66.04)	144 (33.96)	74 (67.27)	36 (32.73)	749 (66.46)	378 (33.54)	1103 (66.40)	558 (33.59)
Gram Panchayat	2922									
Chairpersons of *Gram Panchayat*		2922	503 (66.62)	252 (33.38)	120 (68.18)	56 (31.82)	1329 (66.75)	662 (33.25)	1952 (66.80)	970 (33.20)
Members of *Gram Panchayats*		18264	3824 (71.81)	1548 (28.82)	672 (66.66)	336 (33.34)	7749 (65.20)	4136 (34.80)	12244 (67.04)	6020 (38.96)

Source: Panchayati Raj Department, Government of H.P. and Himachal Pradesh Human Development Report-2001.

Commission on Self-Employed Women maintains that the number of women-headed households is the maximum among the poor, as a result of widowhood, migration, desertion, unemployment and addictive habits of their husbands. Even the United Nations has noted that the underlying reasons for the greater incidence of female-headed households are two-folds: (a) *de jure* as a result of being single, divorced, or widowed; and (b) *de facto* due to long-term migration, economic crisis, refugee status or abandonment. Next to Kerala, Himachal Pradesh has the highest number of female-headed households. Female-headed households per thousand households in rural areas are 220 and in urban areas 222. Kangra district has 42.28 per cent of widows, the highest among all the districts. Out-migration of male members for jobs and widowhood are mostly responsible for the existence of female-headed households. The government has to pay special attention towards the social security and welfare of these households in general and widows with no children in particular.

TABLE 10.7

District-wise Incidence of Crimes in Himachal Pradesh

District	*1998*	*1999*	*2000*	*2001*
Bilaspur	865	986	1241	1284
Chamba	790	831	759	878
Hamirpur	633	717	754	883
Kangra	2999	2665	2455	2712
Kinnaur	187	226	134	177
Kullu	1036	1053	1069	1104
Lahaul & Spiti	138	146	176	152
Mandi	1970	1970	2262	2254
Shimla	2411	2363	2398	2458
Sirmaur	1128	1252	1160	1063
Solan	1575	1419	1426	1385
Una	1205	1123	1136	1161
Himachal Pradesh	**14983**	**14758**	**14976**	**15516**

Source: *Economic Survey 2002*, Police Department, Himachal Pradesh.

Unlike female-headed households, female child labour is also another dark feature of the status of women in the society. The number of girl child labour in Himachal Pradesh is more than eight times higher than in Kerala and Punjab. Engagement of girl children in petty-income earning activities deprives them of school education. This is one of the contributory factors to high drop-out rates of girls at the primary, middle and secondary levels of education. This also affects the health of young and adolescent girls.

TABLE 10.8

Status of Crime Against Women in 15 Major States of India

(Per million persons)

Major States	*Persons*	*Status of Crime*
Andhra Pradesh	121.97	High
Bihar	38.98	Low
Gujarat	89.27	Lower Middle
Haryana	119.41	High
Himachal Pradesh	**139.42**	**High**
Karnataka	74.51	Lower Middle
Kerala	95.76	Upper Middle
Madhya Pradesh	206.97	High
Maharashtra	173.81	High
Orissa	110.35	Upper Middle
Punjab	35.81	Low
Rajasthan	208.16	High
Tamil Nadu	72.03	Lower Middle
Uttar Pradesh	77.40	Lower Middle
West Bengal	86.77	Lower Middle

Source: National Crime Records Bureau (NCRB) Averages 1995 to 1997 Economic and Political Weekly 27 October, 2001.

TABLE 10.9

District-wise Figures of War-widows in Himachal Pradesh

District	*Number*
Bilaspur	1205 (6.64)
Chamba	606 (3.34)
Hamirpur	4111 (22.64)
Kangra	7646 (42.28)
Kinnaur	30 (0.17)
Kullu	145 (0.80)
Lahaul & Spiti	21 (0.12)
Mandi	1768 (9.74)
Shimla	253 (1.29)
Sirmaur	254 (1.40)
Solan	231 (1.27)
Una	1873 (10.32)
Himachal Pradesh	**18155 (100.00)**

Source: *Statistical Outline Himachal Pradesh*, Economic & Statistical Abstract, 1998.

Note: Figures in parenthesis show percentages to total.

Women and Environment

Women can be best involved in increasing the growth of the flora and fauna and protection of the environment of this beautiful mountainous state. Facilitating such capacity of women in different agro-based and plantation activities would augment income of the household substantially and raise the status of women in the society. One of the capacity building projects entitled *Gender sensitisation of rural women through the introduction of agro-based vocation — A case study of Himachal Pradesh,* conducted by the Mountain Women Development Centre of Dr. Y.S. Parmar University of Horticulture and Forestry, Nauni, Solan, has revealed that as a result of knowledge gained through training, women farmers are taking necessary precautions in using insecticides and pesticides. One of the encouraging findings of the project is that, it has promoted an increasing trend of jointly completing an activity by both males and females of the households and thus promoted equal participation of both. The Directorate of Extension Education (DEE) of Dr. Y.S. Parmar University of Horticulture and Forestry has conducted eight training programmes entitled *Training on Environmental Conservation through the Mahila Mandals under the Indo-Norwegian Project* of four days duration each, during March to August-2002. Moreover, several capacity-building programmes for women have been conducted by the Directorate of Extension Education from time to time, largely aimed at increasing their involvement in horticultural activities and conservation of forests.

Women can be oriented and motivated to be engaged in social forestry activities, which would provide them sustainable income. Care should be taken that under the social forestry programme, only such socially accepted trees should be considered for plantation, as would be helpful in generating employment for female labour on the one hand and promoting the ecology on the other. It will have dual benefit of forestation and also economic earning by women. A NORAD-aided project titled Environmental Conservation through Mahila Mandals, is to be launched in three districts, *viz.*, Hamirpur, Kullu and Solan: (i) to create awareness among selected Mahila Mandals in environmental conservation and the concept of Self Help Groups; (ii) conservation of the environment to be undertaken by the Mahila Mandals in the following (a) afforestation and protection of forests; (b) conservation of traditional water resources; (c) solid waste management and promotion of organic farming; (d) alternate fuel and fodder; and (iii) to activate and empower Mahila Mandals to form Self Help Groups and, with the help of Micro-credit, help them in income generating activities. Himachal Pradesh can adopt SEWA's model of *Feminise our Forests* campaign, (1998). As the women workforce participation is quite high in Himachal Pradesh, this could be an added opportunity to canalise their energies and efforts to the management of natural resources, environment and forest.

Feminise our Forests

The Self Employed Women's Association (SEWA) in Gujarat launched a campaign to Feminise our Forests. The campaign had three major goals: (i) to highlight the critical role women play in forests; (ii) to call attention to the ways current policies have failed to support women and their activities; and (iii) to advocate for changes in state and national forest policy to benefit women. The campaign began with a workshop that brought to shelter women tree nursery growers from nine states to share experiences and discuss common issues. SEWA's experience successfully demonstrated that it was possible and potentiality profitable to Feminise forest.

Conclusion

Himachal Pradesh is ranked third in the Women Empowerment Index, calculated by using following 14 variables i.e. (1) female literacy rate, (2) girl enrolment rate, (3) girl drop-out rate, (I-V), (4) antenatal care, (5) post-natal care, (6) institutional deliveries, (7) nutritional anaemia in women, (8) women life expectancy, (9) crime against women, (10) female child labour (average of rural and urban percentages) (11) women members in Lok Sabha, (12) women members in Rajya Sabha, (13) female work participation rate, usual and subsidiary status, and (14) effective wage rate for all wage work for females. However, the state should not be complacent about its high position in the Women Empowerment Index among 16 major states. Rather it should think of taking appropriate steps to overcome the shortcomings in different areas of women's empowerment. Himachal must augment its efforts to elevate the status of women by formulating appropriate strategies to deal with some of the existing weaknesses: (i) to reduce gender gap in literacy below five per cent and female drop-out rate at the primary level of education below five per cent. Districts requiring specific attention are Chamba, Solan, Kullu, Lahaul and Spiti and Sirmaur; (ii) reduce discrepancies in effective wage rates between male and female workforce and raise the effective wage rate for women, at par with men, if not, at least to Rs. 25; (iii) more percentage of women need to be positioned in gazetted posts; (iv) reduce girl child labour to less than 10 per thousand female children in rural areas; (v) 100 per cent female-headed households living below poverty line need to be covered under social security schemes; (vi) in order to prevent maternal and child mortality and for raising the health status of women, at least 50 per cent of deliveries need to be conducted in health institutions; and (vii) reduce crimes against women such as rape, molestation, abduction, eve-teasing, dowry deaths, etc. and (viii)

TABLE 10.10

Women Empowerment Index

States	Women Education Empowerment Measure Index (WEMI)	Women Health Empowerment Measure Index (WHEMI)	Women Political Empowerment Measure Index (WPEMI)	Women Economic Empowerment Measure Index (WEEMI)	Women Social Security Measure Index (WSSMI)	Women Empowerment Measure Index (WEMI)
Andhra Pradesh	0.45	0.52	0.47	0.48	0.25	0.43
Assam	0.49	0.15	0.79	0.12	0.67	0.44
Bihar	0.04	0.09	0.33	0.28	0.93	0.33
Gujarat	0.53	0.341	0.34	0.50	0.43	0.41
Haryana	0.63	0.30	0.50	0.58	0.45	0.49
Himachal Pradesh	**0.68 (3)**	**0.41 (7)**	**0.50 (5)**	**0.63 (1)**	**0.61 (9)**	**0.57 (3)**
Karnatka	0.58	0.55	0.22	0.36	0.63	0.47
Kerala	0.99	0.89	0.13	0.59	0.83	0.69
Madhya Pradesh	0.41	0.12	0.36	0.31	0.37	0.31
Maharashtra	0.68	0.48	0.29	0.36	0.52	0.47
Orissa	0.40	0.18	0.51	0.26	0.68	0.41
Punjab	0.64	0.46	0.39	0.52	1.0	0.60
Rajasthan	0.12	0.17	0.55	0.37	0.05	0.25
Tamil Nadu	0.74	0.67	0.21	0.37	0.59	0.52
Uttar Pradesh	0.17	0.11	0.25	0.27	0.82	0.32
West Bengal	0.37	0.34	0.52	0.25	0.75	0.45

Note: Figures in parenthesis show rank of H.P.

considering the success of women in recent assembly elections (2003), one Lok Sabha seat and 33 per cent of State Assembly seats need to be voluntarily left for women until reservation is made through a constitutional amendment.

Suggestions

- The state should launch a special drive for the education of women and girl children belonging to Scheduled Castes and Scheduled Tribes. Adult, non-formal and functional literacy programmes for women would be helpful in reducing the gender gap in literacy. Special emphasis needs to be given to the districts with lower literacy rate and higher gender gap in literacy.
- Participation of women needs to be promoted in decision-making positions. Protective discrimination measures of reservation in government jobs would enable women to occupy gazetted posts. Orissa government has for instance reservations for women in government jobs.
- At least one Lok Sabha seat out of the four should be left for women in Himachal Pradesh. Political parties need to reach a consensus to do so, until the amendment on reservation of seats is passed in Parliament. Moreover, at least 33 per cent of seats in the State Legislative Assembly should be left for women. For example, recently Haryana Government has reserved 33 per cent of seats for women in the state assembly.
- The State Human Rights Commission needs to have a special Cell on Women for the speedy disposal of cases of crime against women and for the proper rehabilitation of war widows.
- Cent per cent enrolment and retention of girl children in primary school would reduce percentage of girl child labour in the state particularly in rural areas. The two main causes of drop-out are the engagement of girl children in household activities and the negative attitude towards education of girl children. The *Panchayat* and the Village Education Committees (VEC) have to play a key role to check drop-out rates and raise the level of education of girl children. The vocational education and technical education need to be promoted among girls.
- For effective participation in grassroot democracy, women members of the Panchayati Raj Institutions need to be given training and encouraged to participate in workshops, seminars and meetings held at the village, block, district and state levels. Confidence building exercises would help them to fulfil their responsibilities on their own. Grassroot functionaries of government

and NGOs need to encourage educated women to contest elections for various positions of Panchayati Raj Institutions.

- The health status of women needs to be improved and ante-natal and post-natal care should be raised to more than 60 per cent and at least 50 per cent of deliveries should be required to be conducted in health institutions. The PRIKAS (Parivar Kalyan Salahkar *Samities*) need to be activised in the respective *panchayats*. The AIDS awareness campaigns need to be vigoriously undertaken in the districts experiencing in and out migration in population such as Hamirpur, Kangra, Manali, Kullu, Shimla. The most volunerable are women population.
- Women need to be involved actively in social forestry and farm forestry activities. Formation of Self Help Groups and economic support to them will not only promote afforestration and environmental conservation but also raise the income of the family. Mahila Mandal Members and SHG members, along with the women *Panchayat* members, need to be given orientation training on environmental conservation and be provided with other necessary inputs to carry out the afforestation and social forestry programmes.
- Himachal should formulate a Women Empowerment Policy (WEP) to integrate women effectively into the process of development. A holistic policy approach is necessary to consider all aspects of women's empowerment, social, economic, education, political, cultural, security and decision-making. Different state governments, for instance Rajasthan, have formulated WEP.
- A separate chapter on women in the State Five Year Plan document should help focus particular attention to women's development.
- Himachal should set up a Women Resource Centre (WRC). It will provide update information regarding women's empowerment in such areas as health, education, politics, economic, cultural and social activities, etc. It will also act as a documentation and information unit. Moreover, it can conduct capacity-building programmes and other activities, aimed at raising the status of women in the society.
- An enabling environment has to be created for Mahila Mandals, SHG members and women *Panchayat* members to act on various gender issues to further improve the status of women in the state. These organisations need to play a key role in natural resources management and poverty alleviation programmes.

References

Ashokan, S.R. and G. Singh, "Socio–economic Empowerment of Rural Women through Agro-Business Consortium – A Success Story of Samridhi Mahila Cooperative in Himachal Pradesh', *Political Economy Journal of India*, January – June, 2002.

Dreze Jean 'A Surprising Exception, Himachal's Success in Promoting Female Education', *Manushi*, No. 112, May-June, 1999.

Hirway, I. and D. Mahadevia, 'Critique of Gender Development Index Towards an Alternative,' *Economic and Political Weekly*, 26 October, 1996.

Kumari Raj 'Female Labour Participation in Agricultural Sector – A Study of Chandpur Panchayat of Bilaspur District", *M.Phil Dissertation*, Himachal Pradesh University, Shimla, 1989

Leach, M. and C. Green, "Gender and Environment History: Moving beyond the Narrative of the Part" *Contemporary Women Environment Policy Debate*, Sussex, 1995.

Manushi, A Journal of Women & Society, No. 116, Jan-Feb. 2000, P.6.

Mohapatra, A.K. and PRIA findings have been downloaded from the website of Himachal Pradesh, *'Issues: Population, Gender, Children, Health, Education, Environment Empowerment, Panchayati Raj Livelihood'*.

National Family Health Survey–II Himachal Pradesh, International Institute for Population Sciences, Bombay, 1998.

Sharma, Aruna, 'Urban Female Workforce Participation in Himachal Pradesh', *Unpublished Thesis*, Department of Economics, Himachal Pradesh University, Shimla, 1994.

Sarkar, D. and N. Das, "Women's Participation in Forestry, Some Theoretical Issues", *Economic & Political Weekly* 26 October 2002, P.4412.

UN, Women Challenges to the Year 2000, United Nations, New York, 1999.

ANNEXURE-I

Method of Construct

The *Women Development Index* for Himachal Pradesh and fifteen major states were constructed by employing, more or less the same method used in the construction of the *Human Development Index*. However, the objective was to construct gender development measures independently for women only (that is without reference to male-female disparity). (Hirway and Mahadevia Method-1996).

The steps followed for the construction of the indices are as follows:

(A) To start with, variable scores were calculated for all variables using the following formula:

$$I = \frac{\text{actual value} - \text{min value}}{\text{max value} - \text{min value}}$$

Where, I is the variable score for the index. Min value is the minimum value observed in the 16 states and max value is the maximum value observed in the 16 states.

(B) The negative variable scores were converted into positive scores by subtracting each of these from one. This was done in order to have all the variable positive variables.

(C) Sector indices were constructed for each of the components by giving equal weightage.

(D) *Women Development Index* (WDI) is the composite indices of the component indices computed for each of the 16 states and by giving equal weightage to each of the component indices. *Women Development Index* is the average of the added-up total scores of compound indices.

ANNEXURE-II

TABLE A–10.1

Women and Economic Empowerment

State	*Work Participation Rate Usual and Subsidiary Status, Female, 1999 (i)*	*Effective Wage Rate for All Wage Work Female 1999 (ii)*
Andhra Pradesh	37.8	18.2
Assam	8.9	17.8
Bihar	19.0	19.9
Gujarat	29.5	19.3
Haryana	14.9	38.3
Himachal Pradesh	**48.9**	**18.6**
Karnataka	32.5	14.0
Kerala	29.1	30.0
Madhya Pradesh	28.3	15.2
Maharashtra	38.3	11.5
Orissa	24.8	14.8
Punjab	28.8	26.2
Rajasthan	25.8	20.5
Tamil Nadu	29.1	18.3
Uttar Pradesh	20.6	18.2
West Bengal	20.4	17.4
India	26.0	16.9

Source: (i) & (ii) Abusaleh Shariff, *India Human Development Report*, Oxford University Press,New Delhi, 1999.

Note: Figures relate to usual status of individual, workforce covers those involved in gainful activity regularly and those involved in gainful activity occasionally. The figures represent size of workforce as per cent of population.

TABLE A–10.2

Women and Education

States	Female Literacy Rate (2001)(i)	Female Dropout Rate (1998-99) (ii)	Girls Enrolled (1999)(iii)
Classes		I-V	I-V
Andhra Pradesh	51.17	47.03	45.64
Assam	56.03	42.43	45.46
Bihar	33.57	62.00	35.66
Gujarat	58.60	33.98	44.61
Haryana	56.31	15.59	45.49
Himachal Pradesh	**68.08**	**31.0**	**47.73**
Karnataka	57.45	33.46	46.68
Kerala	87.86	-6.83	48.67
Madhya Pradesh	50.26	27.89	42.57
Maharashtra	67.51	25.73	46.76
Orissa	50.97	47.90	44.09
Punjab	63.55	21.82	45.63
Rajasthan	44.34	57.99	33.75
Tamil Nadu	64.55	16.18	48.29
Uttar Pradesh	42.98	55.98	37.41
West Bengal	60.22	54.15	45.87
India	**54.28**	**41.34**	**43.16**

Source: (i) *Provisional Population Totals, Paper 1 of 2001 Page 126, Census of India.*

(ii) and (iii) *Sixth All India Educational Survey, NCERT*, 1999, Vol. 4, Table IS132, Pages 127-130.

TABLE A–10.3

Women and Health

States	ANC (i)	PNC (ii)	INS.D (iii)	Nut. A (iv)	Wom.L.Ex (v)
Andhra Pradesh	35.6	44.9	50.0	49.8	62.8
Assam	15.8	25.5	17.6	69.7	NA
Bihar	6.4	10.0	14.7	63.4	58.0
Gujarat	25.0	10.4	46.4	46.3	62.0
Haryana	20.8	15.7	22.3	47.0	64.0
Himachal Pradesh	**30.2**	**21.2**	**29.0**	**40.5**	**64.7**
Karnataka	41.5	35.3	51.1	42.4	63.9
Kerala	64.9	27.4	93.0	22.7	75.6
Madhya Pradesh	10.9	10.0	20.4	54.3	54.6
Maharashtra	31.0	29.8	52.8	48.5	65.8
Orissa	21.4	19.2	22.9	63.0	56.2
Punjab	31.7	20.3	37.5	41.4	68.4
Rajasthan	8.3	6.4	21.7	48.5	59.4
Tamil Nadu	50.8	53.0	79.8	56.5	64.4
Uttar Pradesh	4.4	7.2	15.7	48.7	56.0
West Bengal	19.7	31.6	40.4	62.7	62.8
India	**20.0**	**16.5**	**33.6**	**51.8**	**60.9**

Source: (i), (ii), (iii), (iv) *National Family Health Survey (II) 1998-99.*

(v) *National Human Development Report*, Planning Commission, India, March 2002.

Note: ANC-Ante Natal Check-Up. PNC- Post Natal Check-Up. INS.D- Institutional Delivery.

Wom. L. Ex— Women Life Expectancy, IMR -Infant Mortality Rate. CMR -Child Mortality Rate.

TABLE A–10.4

Women and Political Participation

States	Rajya Sabha (i)	Lok Sabha (ii)
Andhra Pradesh	2 (11.11)	5 (11.90)
Assam	2 (28.57)	2 (14.28)
Bihar	2 (9.09)	3 (7.5)
Gujarat	1 (9.09)	2 (7.69)
Haryana	Nil	2 (20.00)
Himachal Pradesh	**1 (33.33)**	**Nil**
Karnataka	1 (8.33)	1 (3.57)
Kerala	Nil	1 (5.00)
Madhya Pradesh	1 (6.25)	3 (10.34)
Maharashtra	1 (5.26)	4 (8.33)
Orissa	1 (10.00)	3 (14.28)
Punjab	Nil	2 (15.38)
Rajasthan	1 (10.00)	4 (16.00)
Tamil Nadu	1 (5.55)	2 (5.12)
Uttar Pradesh	1 (2.94)	7 (8.15)
West Bengal	3 (18.75)	4 (9.52)

Source: (i) State-wise data is as on 29 August 2000, *(Rajya Sabha) Secretariat Statistical Abstract India, 2000.*

(ii) www.goidirectory.nic.in

TABLE A–10.5

Women and Security

States	Crime Against Women (per million persons) (i)	FCL (ii)		FHH (iii)	
		R (per 1000)	U (per 1000)	R (per 1000)	U (per 1000)
Andhra Pradesh	121.97	359	105	121	100
Assam	118.78	23	78	84	103
Bihar	38.98	46	19	96	83
Gujarat	89.27	51	19	90	79
Haryana	119.41	17	4	81	58
Himachal Pradesh	**139.42**	**84**	**11**	**220**	**222**
Karnatka	74.51	212	34	139	119
Kerala	95.76	10	4	251	218
Madhya Pradesh	206.97	108	25	60	78
Maharashtra	173.81	129	17	98	79
Orissa	110.35	83	28	93	86
Punjab	35.81	9	4	95	77
Rajasthan	208.16	355	65	85	63
Tamil Nadu	72.03	224	70	150	139
Uttar Pradesh	77.40	49	19	97	65
West Bengal	86.77	42	65	78	115
India	**—**	**115**	**38**	**104**	**94**

Source: (i) *Economic and Political Weekly 27 October 2001.* National Crime Records Bureau (NCRB) averages 95 to 97.

(ii) K.P Kannan, *Economics of Child Labour*, Deep & Deep Publication Pvt. Ltd, 2001. (NSS data).

(iii) National Sample Survey Organisation Report No. 458: *Employment and Unemployment* Situation in India 1999-2000.

Note: Number of female-headed households per 1000 households and average household size by sex and states, 1993-94.

FCL- Female Child Labour, FHH- Female-Headed Households.

Chapter 11

Agriculture

Himachal Pradesh, described by the ancients as 'Dev Bhoomi' (abode to the Gods), is situated in the heart of the Himalayas in the northern part of India. It has a geographical area of 55.67 lakh hectares by professional surveys (42.67 lakh hectares by village papers), most of which is under forests, pastures and grazing lands. Less than ten per cent (5.6 lakh hectares) of the state's net area is under cultivation. The state has a large range of mountains and valleys rising from 350 meters to 7000 meters above mean sea level. Its climate ranges from sub-tropical to sub-arctic cold with an annual rainfall of 350 millimeters to 3800 millimeters. Its temperatures vary from –25 C to 42 C. The state has snow-fed perennial rivers and rivulets flowing in almost all its parts. In addition, there are some natural lakes. The topography, soil, climate, rainfall and temperature provide the state with wide opportunities and potential for agriculture and horticulture.

Due to its hilly terrain, the economy of the state is predominantly mixed farming, agro-pastoral, silvi-pastoral and agro-horticultural. Most of the group based farming systems, engaging a majority of the farmers, are found in the valleys of Yamuna, Satluj, Beas, Ravi, Chandera Bhaga and their tributaries. Agriculture accounts for over 30 per cent of the state's net domestic product and provides employment to about 71 per cent of its residents. The annual growth rate of the State during 1999-2000 was 5.8 per cent against India's 6.4 per cent. Earlier, during the Eighth Plan the annual growth rate of the State was 6.3 per cent. The state enjoys the special category status and thus gets special funds from the center for its development activities. Per capita income at the current prices is over Rs. 18000 (1999-2000).

Important crops grown in the state are cereals – maize, wheat, rice and barley; pulses; oilseed; buckwheat; and minor millets; cash crops – potato, ginger, tea, peas, kuth, hops; and a variety of vegetables including out-of-season and exotic vegetables; and fruits, particularly pome, stone and dry fruits like *chilgoza*, walnut, pecan nut, pistachio, etc. Although the state is deficient in foodgrains, it has gained importance in the production of vegetables and fruits such as seed potato, vegetables, ginger, chicory seed, hops, olives, figs, apples and mushrooms, besides certain medicinal and aromatic plants.

Agriculture in the state suffers from certain limitations. Most of the farming is rainfed as only about one lakh hectares of its net sown area has assured irrigation. Operational land-holdings are small and scattered. Fruit cultivation is thriving on old plantations whose bearing is low. Farm mechanisation is scanty. Awareness level of farmers is low and technologies are out of date. A concerted approach has to be made by injecting reforms and designing policy measures which can give a boost to crops and horticulture in the state.

Profile of Agriculture

Himachal Pradesh has 16,997 inhabited villages and over 90 per cent of the state's population lives in rural areas. Some important parameters of its agriculture are given in Table 11.1. Considering the precipitation, altitude and irrigation, the state has been divided into four agro-ecological zones whose characteristics are given in Table 11.2. The texture of the soil, climate and rainfall vary in the four zones and so does the cropping pattern. More than 70 per cent of the rainfall occurs during the monsoon season and for the rest of the year there is water shortage in areas where irrigation is scarce. Most of the crop area lies in Zone II where rainfall and irrigation are the maximum and the least is in Zone IV. Crop intensity is over 177 per cent.

TABLE 11.1

Profile of Agriculture in H.P. (1996-97)

(Area in Lakh ha)

Indicators	*H.P.*	*India*
Reporting area	33.96	3048.80
Net area sown	5.58	1428.19
Area sown more than once	3.59	467.24
Gross cropped area (GCA)	9.47	1895.43
Cropping intensity (%) 1997	176	133
Net irrigated area	1.05	551.43
Gross irrigated area (GIR) (GIR as % of GCA)	1.76 (18.58)	732.75 (38.65)
Average size of operational holding (ha)	1.21	1.55
Fertiliser consumption (kg/ha)	39.43	95.33
No. of Inhabited villages	16997	557137
Poverty		
Total (%)	7.63	26.1
Rural (%)	7.94	27.09
Urban (%)	4.63	23.62

Source: Statistical Outline of H.P., 2001, DTE of E&S.

Operational Land Holdings

More than eight lakh farmers of Himachal Pradesh cultivate about 10 lakh hectares of land with an average operational landholding of 1.2 hectares (Table 11.3). About 84 per cent of the farmers have less than two hectares of land while 16 per cent own between 2 and 10 hectares. In the case of the Scheduled Castes, 93 per cent of the farmers own less than two hectares, and cultivate 70 per cent of the total area. They have an average land-holding of 0.73 hectare. The Scheduled Tribes own an average of 1.16 hectares of land. According to the 1991 census, over 22 per cent of the farmers belong to the Scheduled Castes and four per cent to the Scheduled Tribes. Together, the Scheduled Castes and the Scheduled Tribes own 17.6 per cent of the cultivated area.

TABLE 11.3

Distribution of Operational Land Holdings (1990-91)

Category	*No. of Farmer (lakh)*	*Per cent*	*Area (lakh ha)*	*Per cent*	*Operational Holdings (ha)*
Marginal (1 ha)	5.32	63.8	2.25	21.3	0.40
Small (1-2 ha)	1.66	19.9	2.35	23.3	1.42
Medium (2-4 ha)	0.94	11.3	2.58	25.5	2.74
Large (4-10 ha)	0.36	4.3	2.05	20.3	5.69
Extra large (> 10 ha)	0.06	0.7	0.97	9.6	16.17
Total	**8.34**	**100**	**10.10**	**100**	**1.21**

Source: Annual Administration Report, Department of Agriculture, and H.P., 2001-02.

Due to sub-division and fragmentation, land holdings are becoming uneconomic. Besides, due to the lack of land consolidation, the holdings are scattered and are often unmanageable and are a limiting factor for crop production. Land lease and tenancy regulations do not allow farming on large areas.

Agricultural Production

The Agro Climatic Regional Planning (ACRP) scheme was launched in the state in June 1998. Himachal Pradesh comes under Western Himalayan Agro Climatic Zone No. I, which consists of three distinct sub-zones, namely, Jammu & Kashmir, Himachal Pradesh and Uttar Pradesh. Himachal Pradesh falls under the second sub-zone and is further divided into four zones under the ACRP programme as

TABLE 11.2

Characteristics of Agro-ecological Zones

Character	*Zone I*	*Zone II*	*Zone III*	*Zone IV*
Ecology	Low Hill Sub-tropical	Mid Hill Sub-humid	High Hill Temperate Wet	High Hill Temperate Dry
Geographical Area (0%)	35	32	25	8
Cropped Area (0%)	33	53	11	3
Irrigated Area (0%)	17	18	8	5
Altitude (MASL)	Upto 914	915-1523	1524-2472	2476-7000
Rainfall (cm)	100-150	150-300	100-200	20-50
Area (Districts)	Kangra, Hamirpur, Solan, Sirmaur,	Kangra, Mandi, Solan, Shimla, Sirmaur, Chamba	Kangra, Mandi, Sirmaur, Shimla, Kullu Bilaspur, & Chamba	Lahaul & Spiti, Kinnaur,Chamba, Kullu

Source: Agricultural Statistics at a Glance, H.P., 2001.

described earlier. Rapid strides in agricultural production were planned and various programmes were initiated to increase productivity of foodgrain and other crops.

Since 1998-99, foodgrain production and productivity have been fluctuating over the years whereas the total area under cultivation has remained almost the same (Table 11.4). The year 2000-01 recorded exceptionally low production and productivity because of drought conditions in both *Kharif* and *Rabi* seasons. Production was the highest in 2001-02. The Tenth Plan target aims at an increase of about 10 per cent in production as well as productivity.

TABLE 11.4

Foodgrain Production

Year	*Production (lakh mt tonne)*	*Area ('000 Ha)*	*Productivity (Kg/Ha)*
1998-1999	13.13	8.37	1569
1999-2000	14.46	8.22	1760
2000-2001	11.04	8.12	1360
2001-2002 (Exp.)	17.60	8.43	2080
10th Plan Target	18.75	8.22	2281

Source: Annual Administrative Report, Department of Agriculture H.P., 2001-2002.

TABLE 11.5

Growth Rate in Area, Production and Productivity of Some Crops During VIth to VIIIth Plan

Crop	*Growth Rate (%) Over VIth Plan*		
	Area	*Production*	*Productivity*
Maize	6.44	25.82	18.18
Rice	-14.12	4.25	21.46
Wheat	3.19	40.15	35.33
Pulses	-22.93	-3.82	24.80
Oilseeds	0.33	49.18	48.81
Potato	-5.26	17.36	23.89
Vegetables	74.82	113.05	21.87

Source: Work Plan for Accelerated Growth of Agriculture and Horticulture in H.P., (2002-2003).

Growth rate in area, production and productivity of some important crops of the state during the Sixth Plan to the Eighth Plan are shown in Table 11.5. The area under rice, pulses and potato has decreased during this period, while the maximum increase has been in the area under vegetables. The rate of productivity of different crops has also been increasing, maximum being in oilseeds and wheat and the least in maize. As far as productivity of different crops is concerned, only maize yield has been higher than the all-India average while that of wheat is low - about 46 per cent less. Productivity of rice and barley is also less than the all-India average (Table 11.6). The state, however, has surplus maize and little wheat but is deficient in rice, oilseeds and pulses.

TABLE 11.6

Production Scenario (lakh mt) and Yield (kg/ha) in H.P. and India (1999-2000)

Crop	*Production*		*Yield*		*Surplus/Deficit*	
	H.P.	*India*	*H.P.*	*India*	*1987-88*	*2000-2001*
Foodgrains	13.13	0.64	1597	1697	-	-
Rice (1998-99)	1.25	0.10	1423	1928	-166	-149
Wheat	2.51	0.64	1266	2755	-81	+19
Maize	6.84	5.93	2272	1785	+48	+100

Source: Statistical Outline, H.P., 2001 DTE & E & C.

Since 1997-98, the productivity of rice, maize, millets, pulses and oilseeds (*Kharif*), and chickpea has shown a rising trend but the productivity of wheat, barley, *rabi* pulses and oilseeds has been going down (Table 11.7). The total area under these crops has been decreasing and has yielded place to vegetable crops.

There is a great variation in foodgrain production and productivity in different districts of the state (Table 11.8). During 1997-98, the productivity of foodgrains was the maximum in Bilaspur district followed by the districts of Una and Sirmaur. It was the least in Kinnaur district. However, during 1999-2000, foodgrain productivity was the highest in Sirmaur district. Productivity, in general, showed an increasing trend in almost all districts, though 1998-99 and 2000-01 recorded a poor performance due to drought conditions. Nevertheless, the variation of productivity between different districts is wide.

In the drought prone areas of Zone IV, only rainfed crops such as barley, oats, rapeseed and mustard, etc., are grown while vegetable production is common wherever irrigation is available.

Horticulture

Himachal Pradesh has the advantage of climate and topography in the cultivation of a variety of fruits. Sub-tropical fruits such as mango, litchi, guava, citrus, etc., mature about one month later than in the plains thus fetching better prices.

Temperate fruits cover about 64 per cent of the total cultivated area of the state of which more than 40 per

TABLE 11.7

Crop Production (1997 to 2001)

Crop	1997-98			1998-99			1999-2000			2000-01		
	Area	Production	Productivity	Area	Production	Productivity	Area	Production	Productivity	Area	Production	Productivity
Kharif												
Corn	311.86	620.68	1990	300.98	662.82	2202	299.91	681.42	2272	298.05	683.64	2222
Paddy	86.18	120.44	1398	82.13	117.00	1425	80.22	120.37	1500	81.52	124.90	1532
Millets	11.67	7.38	632	10.53	7.23	686	11.11	7.41	667	10.78	7.07	656
Ragi	4.06	4.29	1056	3.67	4.16	1134	3.96	4.44	1121	4.13	4.16	1007
Pulses & Oilseed	27.85	8.67	315	26.65	10.02	376	24.21	9.67	399	23.22	7.97	343
Total	**441.63**	**761.42**	**1724**	**423.95**	**800.68**	**1889**	**419.40**	**823.32**	**1963**	**417.70**	**827.73**	**1982**
Rabi												
Wheat	377.34	641.31	1700	379.72	481.27	1267	370.59	583.30	1574	362.68	251.32	693
Barley	27.69	41.34	1493	26.75	27.76	1038	25.90	32.50	1255	25.64	21.41	835
Chickpea	2.34	2.50	1068	1.91	1.29	675	1.70	1.53	900	1.35	1.49	1104
Pulses & Oilseed	4.59	1.55	338	4.64	2.02	435	4.84	5.50	1136	4.87	1.62	333
Total	**411.96**	**686.69**	**1667**	**413.02**	**512.33**	**1240**	**103.02**	**622.82**	**1545**	**394.54**	**275.54**	**699**
Grand Total	**853.58**	**1448.11**	**1696**	**836.97**	**1313.02**	**1569**	**827.42**	**1416.14**	**1722**	**812.23**	**1103.58**	**1359**

Source: Annual Administrative Report, Department of Agriculture, and H.P., 2001-02.

Note: Area ('000 ha); Production ('000 mt); Productivity (kg/ha).

TABLE 11.8

District-wise Foodgrain, Area, Production and Productivity

District	1997-98			1998-99			1999-2000		
	Area	Production	Productivity	Area	Production	Productivity	Area	Production	Productivity
Bilaspur	57.23	115.45	2017	54.08	77.55	1434	55.72	101.68	1825
Chamba	59.60	115.96	1946	56.28	103.55	1840	58.02	102.28	1763
Hamirpur	70.82	102.97	1454	73.88	109.23	1478	69.89	106.00	1517
Kangra	196.70	267.36	1359	199.35	266.24	1336	197.42	303.86	1539
Kinnaur	6.75	6.09	902	6.31	6.48	1027	6.09	5.08	834
Kullu	53.48	95.59	1787	48.74	81.82	1679	45.25	87.83	1941
Lahaul & Spiti	0.79	1.20	1519	0.90	1.08	1200	0.80	1.17	1462
Mandi	148.59	282.28	1900	146.58	238.51	1627	145.90	286.86	1966
Shimla	65.82	82.07	1247	62.04	79.15	1276	55.95	78.14	1396
Sirmaur	67.13	131.99	1966	66.70	120.72	1810	65.46	138.93	2122
Solan	57.68	105.32	1826	57.44	111.66	1944	56.76	102.57	1807
Una	68.99	135.82	1969	64.68	117.08	1810	65.17	131.82	2023
Total	**853.58**	**1448.11**	**1697**	**836.97**	**1313.02**	**1569**	**822.42**	**1446.24**	**1759**

Source: Annual Administrative Report, Department of Agriculture, and H.P., 2001-2002.

Note: Area: '000 ha; Production = '000 mt; Productivity=kg/ha.

cent is under apple cultivation. The area under fruits more than doubled in the last two decades. Similarly, the productivity of apples almost doubled to 4500 kg per hectare during 2000-2001, but the productivity of nuts and dry fruits, citrus and other sub-tropical fruits decreased even though the area under these crops increased (Table 11.9). Production of apples was the maximum during 1988-1990.

The districts of Shimla and Kullu are the dominant areas of apple production while in Sirmaur peach is the main fruit crop. Kullu district grows plums and pears. Citrus, mango and litchi are main fruits grown in the district of Kangra (Table 11.10). The area under mango is about 39 per cent of the total area under sub-tropical fruits in the lower hill region and about 6 per cent of the total area under all fruits in the state as compared to 19 per cent under citrus fruits.

TABLE 11.9

Fruit Production

Fruit	*1980-81*			*1990-91*			*2000-01*		
	Area	*Production*	*Productivity*	*Area*	*Production*	*Productivity*	*Area*	*Production*	*Productivity*
Apple	43.3	118.1	2727	62.8	342.1	5447	83.7	376.7	4500
Other Temperate Fruits	17.5	9.3	531	28.5	14.9	523	32.4	20.5	633
Nuts and Dry Fruits	6.9	1.8	261	13.2	3.1	235	16.4	2.7	165
Citrus	14.5	4.4	303	36.0	12.6	350	39.1	11.1	284
Other Sub-Tropical Fruits	10.3	6.4	621	22.9	13.6	594	36.3	17.0	468
Total	**92.5**	**140**	**1574**	**163.4**	**386.3**	**2364**	**207.9**	**428.0**	**2059**

Source: Work Plan for Accelerated Growth of Agriculture and Horticulture in H.P., 2002-2003.

Note: (*Area: 00 ha; Production mt ; Productivity: kg/ha*).

TABLE 11.10

District-wise Area under Different Fruit Crops Bearing Trees (1998-99)

(Hectares)

District	*Apple*	*Peaches*	*Plum*	*Pears*	*Kinnow & Orange*	*Litchi*	*Mango*
Bilaspur	—	—	2	7	28	80	178
Chamba	—	—	—	—	—	—	—
Hamirpur	—	—	—	—	—	—	79
Kangra	—	—	8	—	2139	107	2141
Kinnaur	1591	—	—	—	—	—	—
Kullu	7958	—	740	44	—	2	—
Lahaul & Spiti	19	—	—	—	—	—	—
Mandi	916	—	190	—	—	—	—
Shimla	20028	10	226	—	24	45	4
Sirmaur	649	323	59	24	33	41	286
Solan	80	5	63	30	30	55	49
Una	—	—	—	—	—	—	—
Himachal Pradesh	**31241**	**342**	**1288**	**105**	**2254**	**330**	**2737**

Source: Annual Season and Crop Report (1998-99), Commissioner Revenue, H.P.

About one-seventh of the fresh fruit trees are non-bearing while in case of dry fruits the proportion of non-bearing trees is about one-eighth of the total plantation covering about 16 per cent of the area under fruits. The districts of Shimla and Kinnaur have the largest number of non-bearing trees of fresh as well as dry fruits (Table 11.11). Fruit production, which was 1200 metric tons in 1950-51, increased to 4.3 lakh metric tons in 2000-2001 (about 360-fold increase), but the yields are about 10-12 times below what is produced in the European countries (*H.P. State Plan, 2001-02*).

According to the time series data, the average productivity of apple (kilogram per hectare) has been 5830, other temperate fruits 990, nuts and dry fruits 450, citrus 510 and other sub-tropical fruits 1370 (*Work Plan for Accelerated Growth of Agriculture and Horticulture in H.P. 2002-03*). Punjab produces 10 to 15 tonnes of citrus fruits per hectare whereas the yield of these fruits in Israel is between 43 to 65 tonnes per hectare. In Kashmir, apple production is about seven to eight thousand kg per hectare.

Experiments are under way in the state to grow fruits like strawberry, pomegranate, olive, kiwi, hazelnut, etc., which have been identified as the potential crops of the future. Some high-bearing clones of these fruits have been imported and are being tested for commercial cultivation. Planting material imported during 2001-02 includes apples (six cultivars) 5000, cherry (two cultivars) 3500 and plum (three cultivars) 1500.

TABLE 11.11

District-wise Bearing and Non-bearing Area under Fresh Fruits, Dry Fruits and Vegetables (1998-99)

(Hectares)

District	*Fresh Fruits*		*Dry Fruits*		*Vegetables*		
	Bearing	*Non-bearing*	*Bearing*	*Non-bearing*	*Potato*		*Others*
					Kharif	*Rabi*	
Bilaspur	338	75	2	—	—	13	498
Chamba	2147	—	—	—	533	26	698
Hamirpur	84	—	—	—	—	13	199
Kangra	6092	—	9	—	122	1246	2229
Kinnaur	1597	318	552	57	244	—	921
Kullu	8744	272	58	3	850	139	2308
Lahaul & Spiti	19	40	—	—	874	—	900
Mandi	5757	—	—	—	1635	195	4904
Shimla	20337	6815	308	93	5130	817	13062
Sirmaur	1489	100	33	5	1082	384	3395
Solan	745	137	4	—	18	125	3197
Una	538	—	—	—	89	293	927
Himachal Pradesh	**47887**	**7757**	**966**	**158**	**10577**	**3251**	**33238**

Source: Annual Season and Crop Report 1998-99. Commissioner (Revenue) Himachal Pradesh.

The work plan for the development of horticulture aims at complementing and supplementing the efforts of the state government to bridge the gap between the low level of productivity and the quality of fruit crops resulting from:

- Lack of availability of elite planting material
- Lack of modern production and protection technologies and facilities
- Lack of rapid and efficient transfer of technology
- Poor communication due to hilly terrain
- Inadequate irrigation
- Lack of post-harvest management
- Losses due to the vagaries of nature, etc.
- Inadequate marketing infrastructure and intelligence

Modernisation of horticulture is necessary to improve production and quality in competitive environment. Horticulture industry at present contributes about Rs. 584 crore per annum to the GDP. Gross income from fruits has increased from Rs. 45.74 crore in 1990-91 to about Rs. 584.35 crore in 1998-99.

Vegetables

Like fruits, cultivation of vegetables too covers a wide variety, thanks to varied seasons and topography. Almost all vegetables can be grown. In recent years more area has come under vegetable crops due to availability of irrigation facility and also because of high returns from these crops. Over the last decades, the area under vegetables as well as their production has increased more than 40 per cent. This is exclusive of potato and ginger crops (Table 11.12).

TABLE 11.12

Area, Production and Productivity of Vegetables, Potato and Ginger

Crop	*Index*	*1990-91*	*1995-96*	*2000-01*	*2001-02*
Vegetables	Area	22	25	32	36
	Production	370	425	580	655
	Productivity	16818	17000	18125	18194
Potato	Area	16	14	16	15
	Production	115	135	160	160
	Productivity	7188	9642	1000	1066
Ginger	Area	1.5	3.0	3.1	3.5
	Production	2.9	3.2	3.7	4.2
	Productivity	1933	1066	1194	1200

Source: Annual Plan, H.P., 2001-02.

Note: Area = '000 hectare; production = '000 mt: productivity = kg/ha.

Himachal Pradesh was considered to be the highest producer of quality seed potato during the 70s and 80s but since the end of 1980, a declining trend has been noticed. It is because other states of India have also started producing good quality seed potato besides true potato seed is also being used for cultivation. Potato production has increased nearly by 40 per cent (Annual Plan H.P., 2001-02). The crop is grown both in *Rabi* and *Kharif* seasons. Most of the potato is grown during

Kharif in Shimla district followed by the districts of Mandi and Sirmaur. In the *Rabi* season it is grown mostly in the districts of Kangra, Shimla and Sirmaur (Table 11.11).

Ginger is another commercial crop that has received considerable priority over the years. An area of 1,500 hectares was brought under ginger in 1990-91, which more than doubled by the end of 2001-02. Production saw an upswing all through the 1990s. It was 2.9 thousand metric tonnes in 1990-91 and reached 4.2 thousand metric tonnes by the end of 2001-02 (Table 11.12).

The maximum area under vegetables, apart from potato and ginger, accounts for peas and tomato. Productivity of tomatoes is quite high i.e., 34,645 kg per hectare as against an average of 24,000 kg in Punjab and 15,000 kg in India. Productivity of cauliflower is about the same as the all-India average while Punjab produces about 24,000 kg per hectare (Table 11.13). Fresh peas of the state are of premium quality and fetch a higher price particularly in the plains where it is an off-season variety. Vegetable seed production is a dominant feature of vegetable cultivation in the state as the climate of the central region is very conducive to seed production. Cultivation of exotic vegetables like broccoli, asparagus, leek, parsley, Brussels sprout, and others is catching up because these vegetables are in demand in hotels and by foreign tourists. The advantage of topography enables vegetable cultivators to grow out-of-season crops.

TABLE 11.13

Production of Vegetables (1998-99)

Crop	*Area (ha)*	*Production (mt)*	*Productivity (kg/ha)*
Peas (green)	9400	90000	9574
Tomato	6000	207870	34645
Beans	2170	21310	9912
Cabbage	2150	61820	28753
Cauliflower	1340	24340	14933
Capsicum & chillies	1630	15250	9355
Others Vegetables (Potato excluded)	9310	159410	17122
Total	**32000**	**500000**	**18125**

Source: Administrative Report, Department of Horticulture, and H.P. 2001.

Note: Area = '000 hectare; Production = '000 mt: Productivity = kg/ha.

Other Horticultural Activities

a) ***Flower cultivation*** – Commercial cultivation of flowers in Himachal Pradesh started in 1980 under the guidance of the Department of Horticulture. It was declared a thrust area for economic development. The District Rural Development Agencies (DRDA) in the districts of Kangra, Mandi, Shimla and Solan are engaged in this activity. Several small nurseries have been established for the propagation of floriculture planting material for distribution to the growers. The main crops are gladiolus, carnation, chrysanthemum, tulips, daffodils, etc. The cultivation of some traditional flowers, such as marigold, has also caught up in certain areas like Rajgarh. The area under floriculture in the state has increased from five hectares in 1991 to more than 188 hectares in 2002 and flowers worth about Rs. 6 crore are being produced every year (Table 11.14). These are being exported to Chandigarh, Amritsar, Delhi, Haridwar, Hrishikesh and other places. The floriculture industry of the state is still in a nascent stage and requires to be organised properly so that it becomes a remunerative enterprise.

b) ***Mushroom cultivation*** – Mushroom cultivation technology was first introduced in the state in 1961 on a trial basis under the Technological Co-operation Programme of FAO. Later, commercial application of technology was introduced under FAO and UNDP assisted projects at Chamba Ghat in Solan district during 1977-82. During 1986-1992, a project under Indo-Dutch programme for mushroom production was introduced at Palampur, Kangra district. All these establishments helped in popularising button mushroom (Agaricus bisporus) cultivation and its productivity increased from six kg per square metre in 1992 to 10 to 15 kg per square metre now. During 2001-02 over 3260 metric tonnes of mushrooms were produced in the state (Table 11.14). This is showing an increasing trend. Production of pasteurised compost for distribution to mushroom growers has been taken up by the government at Dharbaggi in Kangra district, and Bajaura in Kullu district, under centrally sponsored scheme.

These units will supply pasteurised compost to about 400 new production units in the districts of Kangra, Kullu, Mandi and Bilaspur. About 20 small units are operating in the private sector in Solan district which produce pasteurised compost. The present capacity to produce pasteurised compost is about 11170 metric tonnes annually. There are nine spawn production laboratories in the state of which six are in the private sector and three are with research institutions. A production of 2495 metric tonnes of mushrooms was recorded in 2000-2001 in the state. An export-oriented mushroom unit, namely, M/s Himalayan International Private Limited, has been set up at Paonta Sahib, Sirmaur district, to export 150 metric tonnes of mushroom and its products in various forms.

TABLE 11.14

Trend and Targets of Horticulture

Item and Unit	*Annual Plan*	*Annual Plan 2001-2002*		
		Target	*Achievement*	*Annual Plan*
Fruit production area ('000 ha)	217.2	225.2	223.2	228.3
Production ('000 mt)	428.1	539.6	263.4	561.0
Floriculture area (ha)	154	155	188	175
Mushroom production (MT)	2945	2500	3261	4000
Bee keeping (maintenance of colonies (No.)	1586	1800	1830	2000
Distribution of bee colonies (No.)	1729	1800	1038	500
Plant nutrition Plant analysed (No.)	11994	12000	13821	15000
Plant protection area apple scab control (ha)	88649	55000	89454	85000
Area other fruit diseases control (ha)	45893	35000	43837	35000
Total area under plant protection (ha)	260782	185000	271092	183000

Source: Work Plan for Accelerated Growth of Agriculture and Horticulture in H.P. 2002-03.

c) ***Bee-keeping*** - The state has a wide diversity in agro-climatic conditions and flora, which provide enormous potential for the development of bee keeping. The British first introduced it in Kullu valley in 1934 and in Kangra valley in 1936. The migratory system of bee keeping was introduced in 1952 when bee flora from the high hills was brought down to lower altitudes during winter months. The state took a lead in the introduction of exotic honey bee, *Apis mellifera* (Italian honey bee) for the first time in 1962-63. Before this honey was produced in the state from *A.acerana* and production was ten metric tons per annum from 2,500 bee colonies maintained by 150 beekeepers. Now there are about 26,000 bee colonies with more than 939 beekeepers producing over 650 metric tonnes of honey of diverse flora every year. Private entrepreneurs have established breeding and multiplication centres under centrally sponsored schemes, which have become quite popular with new beekeepers. Fruit growers also indulge in honey production during the flowering season on rental basis as this facilitates pollination of the fruit trees, which increases fruit productivity, besides yielding honey. Over 1000 bee colonies were distributed by government agencies in 2001-02. One honey processing unit with a capacity to process 120 metric tonnes of honey every year is working at Kandrori in Kangra district, and is managed by the Agro Industry Corporation Limited.

d) ***Medicinal and aromatic plants*** – Himachal Pradesh is a rich repository of medicinal and aromatic plants because of its situational advantage. It is unfortunate that no compendium or systematic inventory about the medicinal and aromatic plants is available. During the last several years the flora of Himachal Pradesh has been under scrutiny and exploitation by various national and multinational pharmaceutical organisations. It is estimated that about 500 medicinal, 150 aromatic and a large number of potent alternative and substitute drug plant species are available in this area. The demand for medicinal and aromatic plants is increasing day by day. There are 70 units/pharmacies in the state, which manufacture Ayurvedic medicines. Two bigger units set up at Joginder Nagar and Majra procure raw material from the market, process them and supply the ingredients to outside agencies. Not many medicinal or aromatic plants have been brought under cultivation. Collection by outside agencies of wild medicinal plants at a rapid rate has threatened some species with extinction. The state government and the universities are attempting to develop package of practices for growing some of the medicinal plants commercially for use both in India and abroad. Table 11.15 shows a few important medicinal and aromatic plants and wild species, which are cultivated in the state for export. To these, many more can be added.

The Department of Ayurveda, Government of Himachal Pradesh, has set up one herbal garden in each of the four agro-climatic zones of the state to raise germplasm nurseries, and has perfected conservation and other agro-techniques for the sustenance and multiplication of such plants in the respective zones. An *Ayurvedic* herbarium has also been set up at Joginder Nagar to keep specimens of medicinal plants in a systematic manner. A lot more needs to be done to preserve the wealth of the Himalayas in the form of medicinal and aromatic plants.

TABLE 11.15

Major Medicinal Herbs Exported from Himachal Pradesh

(Quintal)

Name	*1988-89*	*1989-90*	*1991-92*	*1994-95*
Jurinea sp.	5,884	4,064	4,939	3,260
Dioscorea sp.	1,672	180	380	4
Gentiana kurroo	1,468	199	2,899	343
Valeriana sp.	1,954	1,247	2,014	1,642
Cinnomomum camphora	1,430	849	-	675
Centella asiatica	417	166	335	921
Saussurea lappa	3	648	667	321
Morchella sp.	402	137	2,800	490
Viola sp.	26	195	-	71
Pistacia integerima	129	437	278	17
Aconitum violoceum	60	12	48	-
Aconitum heterophyllum	189	1	2	25
Bunium persicum	70	5	5	-
Berberis sp.	2,981	11,195	12,824	-
Pinus gerardiana	656	568	600	403
Agaricus bisporus	37	15	-	-
Other sp.	4,239	4,913	10,328	684

Source: Biotechnology Policy of Himachal Pradesh, Department of Biotechnology, and Govt. of H.P. Brochures, 2001.

Among the cultivated medicinal plants, *Saussurea lappa* (Kuth), *Bunium persicum* (Kala Zira), *Cichorium itybus* (Chicory), *Crocus sativus* (Kesar) and *Humulus lupulus* (Hops) are important. However, some of the medicinal plants have become endangered. These include *Podophyllum hxandrum* (Bankakri), *Nardostachys grandiflora* (Jatamansi), *Gentiana kurroo* (Indian Gentian), *Aconitum heterophyllum* (Patees), *Onosma bracteatum* (Ratanjot), *Ephedra gerardiana* (Somlata), *Swertia chirata* (Chirayata), *Taxus baccata* (Talispatra), *Atropa acuminata* (Indian belladonna), bamboo, Jatropha etc. It is high time agro-technologies were developed for the domestication of these plants. This will not only help in the diversification of farming and improving the economic condition of the farming community but also help in conserving these endangered species.

Irrigation

Himachal Pradesh has high ranges of the Himalayas some of which contain perennial glaciers and snow-capped peaks. These supply water throughout the year to various rivers that pass through the state. A number of tributaries close to the snow-capped mountains join one another to form these rivers. While there is plenty of water in the hills yet water use for irrigation is limited to over 1.05 lakh hectares out of nearly 6 lakh hectare of cultivated land. More than 50,000 hectares of cultivated land can be brought under irrigation through major and medium irrigation projects, which are underway, and the remaining area can be provided with irrigation through minor and other irrigation schemes. By the end of March 2001, about two lakh hectare of cultivated land is expected to come under irrigation. This accounts for nearly 33 per cent of the cultivable area of the state (Table 11.16). Minor irrigation projects including kuhls and others cover over 1.8 lakh hectares for irrigation. It is evident that the progress of irrigation has been dependent mostly on private organisations as the number of kuhls and tube wells operated and developed by the farmers at their own level are more in number than those provided by government agencies (Table 11.17).

TABLE 11.16

Irrigation in Himachal Pradesh

(hectares)

Item	*End of Eight Plan*	*Achievement*				
		1997-98	*1998-99*	*1999-2000*	*2000-01*	*Cumulative*
Major and Medium irrigation	10936	300	150	150	200	11736
Minor irrigation	82595	2000	2000	2120	1800	90515
Kuhls and Others	92796	NA	NA	NA	NA	92796
Total	**186327**	**2300**	**2150**	**2270**	**2000**	**195047**

Source: Tenth Five-Year Plan, Himachal Pradesh.

Traditional irrigation practices include pond irrigation, terrace bunding and development of *kuhls*. The latter are perennial source of water provided the hill cover has adequate forest cover. Some of the *kuhls* have become seasonal giving water during rainy season or little after because the forest cover has ceased to accumulate water for long. Terrace bunding and continuous flow from one field to another is practiced where the terraces are contiguous and are particularly on flat land. On sloppy lands, ordinary bunding can retain rainwater for short time.

Since irrigation is a crucial input for increasing productivity of crops, many major, medium and minor irrigation projects have been set up after conducting feasibility studies. Some important irrigation projects are:

Major Irrigation Projects

A major irrigation project, with a cultivable command area (CCA) of more than 10,000 hectare is Shah Nahar Project on the Beas in Kangra district. This project ran into problems with the Punjab Government after it was conceived in 1983. It was cleared in April 1996, with the help of the Central Government. This project aims at irrigating 15,287 hectares of CCA benefiting 93 villages. It is likely to become operational by the end of 2003.

Medium Irrigation Projects

Medium irrigation projects cover a CCA of more than 2,000 but less than 10,000 hectares. An area of 11.38 thousand hectares stood irrigated till March 1999. Four projects have been completed and work on two is in progress. The completed projects at a total cost of Rs. 325.71 lakh are:

a) Giri Irrigation project (5263 hectares)

b) Bhabour Sahib Project-Phase I (923 hectares)

c) Bhabour Sahib Project-Phase II (2640 hectares)

d) Balh Valley Project (2410 hectares)

Schemes in hand are Sidhata Project with a CCA of 3,150 hectares, and LIP in Changer area with a CCA of 2,350 hectares. These projects are likely to be completed in five to seven years. Eighteen other medium irrigation projects are under feasibility study and hopefully these will be taken up soon. It is estimated that about 32 thousand hectare of land shall be irrigated by these projects by the end of next Plan period.

Minor Irrigation

Minor irrigation with a CCA of 2,000 hectare or less is operated both by government and privately in the form of tubewells, kuhls and lift irrigation, which are shown in Table 11.17. Several government projects are subsidised and subsidy is also available to farmers to develop their own *kuhls* or to put up tubewells to augment the existing irrigation facilities. Till March 2001, an area of 195 thousand hectares was brought under irrigation by these methods.

TABLE 11.17

Sources of Water Supply and Area Irrigated

(Hectares)

Water Source		*1994-95*	*1996-97*	*1998-99*
Tube wells	Govt.	1275	1629	432
	Private	179	179	1629
	Total	1454	1808	2061
No. of *Kuhls*	Govt.	6420	6420	6412
	Private	10475	10475	10475
	Total	16895	16895	16887
Lift irrigation	Govt.	243	243	243
	Private	246	246	246
	Total	489	489	489

Source: Annual Season and Crop Report 1998-99. Commissioner (Revenue), H.P.

Under the Micro Management of Agriculture projects, there are several schemes, which encourage farmers to develop their own irrigation facilities. These include Irrigation tank scheme, wherein a nine square meter tank can be provided with a subsidy of Rs. 8,000 to a farmer having a minimum of one *bigha* of land. During 2001-2002, 1785 irrigation tanks were set up to irrigate about 143 hectares. Another scheme is the Shallow Well Irrigation Scheme, which carries a subsidy of Rs. 12,000 per well to a farmer who has a minimum of two *bighas* of land. During 2001-02, 267 shallow wells were constructed to irrigate about 43 hectares. The Command Area Project is operative in the catchment areas of the Sutluj, Beas and Ravi covering the districts of Mandi, Kullu, Kangra and Chamba. This aims at reducing soil erosion through planting of grass and trees, construction of bunds, stonewalls, etc. During 2001-02, 204 hectares was saved for cultivation and irrigated.

Despite projected schemes and proposals that are in hand or are under consideration several factors create impediments wherein the targeted approach is jeopardised. Among these, financial crunch, unavailability of funds at required time and quantity and disbursing state's share in Central Government allocation are the major bottlenecks. Besides, land acquisition, deployment of trained staff and terrain factors also govern the progress and implementation.

Watershed Development

Nearly 70 to 75 per cent of the rain occurs during the monsoon season, which flows as run-off without much use or conservation. As a consequence, all areas, which are without assured irrigation, suffer from water stress and low productivity. Development of watersheds has been emphasised for the conservation of water.

TABLE 11.18

List of Watershed Identified for Tenth Five Year Plan

District	*No. Watershed*	*Arable Land (ha)*	*Non-arable (ha)*	*Total (ha)*
Bilaspur	6	2062	1410	3472
Hamirpur	3	1113	840	1953
Kangra	14	5178	5401	10579
Kullu	7	2129	401	2530
Mandi	20	5456	7651	13107
Shimla	2	346	687	1033
Sirmaur	8	2188	3261	5449
Solan	10	2592	3370	5962
Total	**70**	**21064**	**23021**	**44085**

Source: Work Plan for Accelerated Growth; Himachal Pradesh, 2002-03.

During the Ninth Plan, 61 watersheds were proposed to be constructed and for the Tenth Five Year Plan, 70 watersheds have been identified in eight districts of Himachal Pradesh (Table 11.18). These watersheds, when commissioned, will irrigate about 44,000 hectares of cultivated land in the dry season. Watershed projects can become effective and sustainable only when participation of the local community is ensured right from the beginning of planning to execution and maintenance. Panchayati Raj Institutions can play a major role in this and other irrigation programmes. The local communities should be involved in working out immediate plans to manage the scarce water resources in a collective way till proper irrigation systems are developed.

Agricultural Inputs

Seed

Seed is the most important determinant of agricultural potential on which the efficiency of other agricultural inputs depends. Seeds of appropriate character, variety, quality and certification is required to meet the demand of diverse agro-climatic conditions and cropping pattern. The state has no well-defined seed production programmes as there is no Seed Corporation. Further, the private seed organisations are not coming forward to help the state in seed production/distribution programmes. The state government relies greatly on the seed production/ multiplication of the important crop varieties by the farmers within the state, which is rather insufficient, and without any quality determinants.

The Department of Agriculture procures about 60,000 quintals of wheat seed every year from registered growers of the state, out of which 15,000 to 18,000 quintals of seed is procured from the farmers of Una district alone. In this district, however, there is an acute shortage of seed-grader-cum-seed-cleaners. The seed is procured immediately after the harvest in May and properly stored. Similarly, the seed of other crops is produced by designated farmers and procured.

Certified seeds of high-yielding varieties procured for different crops, including vegetables, are distributed among the farmers (Table 11.19). The area under high-yielding varieties of maize, rice and wheat is shown in Tables 11.7 and 11.20. During the Tenth Plan period the estimated coverage with HYV seed will be 280,000 hectare under maize, 79,000 hectare under paddy and 3,61,000 hectares under wheat. There has been considerable increase in the area (about 50%) under corn since 1998-99, while the area under paddy has remained static and there has been some reduction in the area under wheat. Production and use of high quality seed of composite or hybrid maize by the state agencies can have a direct impact on productivity of this crop.

TABLE 11.19

Consumption of Fertilisers, Certified Seed and Pesticides

(*mt.*)

Year	*Fertilisers*	*Certified Seed*	*Pesticides*
1998-1999	38557	378	150
1999-2000	37343	367	196
2000-2001	35552	353	232
2001-2002 (P)	40165	367	222
2002-2007	42500	366	210
(Yearly, P)	**46000**	**361**	**200**

Source: Annual Administrative Report, Department of Agriculture, and Himachal Pradesh, 2001-02.

Note: P= Provisional

Since irrigation is a constraint in the cultivation of food grain crops, the area under high yielding varieties is small (235,000 hectare) as only about 20 per cent of the area is irrigated. The area under rice with assured irrigation is 78.15 per cent, and for other varieties about 50 per cent of the area is irrigated. For wheat, irrigated area under HYV and other varieties is about 18.5 per cent whereas in the case of maize it is 11.7 per cent under HYV and 6.5 per cent under other varieties (Table 11.20). Seeds of food grains and other crops distributed by the Department of Agriculture are supplied with a subsidy of 50 per cent to the SCs, STs, IRDP and other backward areas.

Lot of opportunity exists in developing sound technologies for production of quality seed of vegetables, potato, ginger, some food crops, medicinal plants and herbs for export to other states and even abroad. For this, linkages and cooperation will have to be developed between two state universities, state department of agriculture, floriculture, horticulture and biotechnology, farmers and the government.

TABLE 11.20

Irrigated Area Covered under High Yielding Varieties (HYVs) and Other Cereal Varieties (1995-99)

('000 ha)

Crop	*HYV*			*Others*		
	Area	*Irrigated*	*Per cent*	*Area*	*Irrigated*	*Per cent*
Rice	13.96	10.91	78.15	68.17	39.58	58.12
Maize	88.68	10.34	11.66	221.30	14.44	6.53
Wheat	129.49	23.92	18.47	250.23	46.38	18.53
Barley	3.06	0.85	27.71	23.70	3.34	14.09
Total	235.19	46.02	19.57	563.40	103.74	18.41

Source: Annual Administrative Report, Department of Agriculture, H.P. (2001-02).

Every year about 10,000 quintals of maize, 600 quintals of sorghum, 300 kg of vegetable (tomato, cabbage, cauliflower and cucumber) hybrid seeds are procured from private companies and supplied to farmers. Private seed companies are also allowed to market non-certified seeds directly to the farmers.

Fertilisers

Traditionally, the small farmers of Himachal Pradesh have been using farmyard manure (FYM) as the main fertiliser. For this, cattle, sheep, goats and other animals find place in their farmhouses, even though some of these animals are unproductive. The state government, while trying to popularise the use of chemical fertilisers in crop production, has introduced the element of subsidy on the use of fertilisers by the farmers. The subsidy varies with the type of fertilisers. For instance CAN, urea and ammonium sulphate have a subsidy of Rs. 20.25 per bag of 50 kg while on NPK (12:32:16) it is Rs. 37 per bag and on NPK (15:15:15) it is Rs. 31 per bag. This subsidy is given on three bags per farmer per season. In the case of tea farmers, a subsidy of 50 per cent is given on ammonium sulphate, super phosphate and murate of potash for eight hectares per year. The consumption of fertilizers is estimated to be 42,500 metric tonnes during 2002-03 (Table 11.21).

TABLE 11.21

Consumption of Nitrogen (N), Phosphorus (P) and Potassic (K) Fertilisers

(mt)

Year	*N*	*P*	*K*	*Total NPK*
1998-1999	29140	5219	4198	38557
1999-2000	27593	5762	3988	37343
2000-2001	24418	6540	4594	35552
2001-2002	27615	7320	5230	40165
2002-03 (Target)	29800	7400	5300	42500
Tenth Plan Target	32300	8000	5700	46000

Source: Annual Administrative Report. Dept. of Agriculture, H.P. 2001-02.

The Department of Agriculture is experimenting with bio-fertilisers produced by the bio-fertiliser laboratory at Shimla, which has a capacity of 50 metric tonnes per year. During 2001-02, the department promoted the use of bio-fertilisers in 1,600 acres. However, quality control measures are necessary for which testing facilities should be made available.

Pesticides

The consumption of pesticides has been rather low, i.e., 225 grams per hectare per year. The consumption pattern (Table 11.19) shows that during 2001-2002, 222 metric tonnes of pesticides (technical grade) were used in the state covering about 405,000 hectares. Fruit and vegetable growers use most of the pesticides.

The state is laying great emphasis on strengthening bio-control technology. A state bio-control laboratory has been set up at Palampur with grants-in-aid received from the Government of India. Integrated Pest Management (IPM) has also been adopted at the state level with great enthusiasm with the help of the universities of the state. The area covered under IPM activities like augmentation and conservation of bio-control agents by CIPMC, Solan, is 23,331 hectares till January, 2002 and the crops covered are paddy, tomato, cabbage, peas, cauliflower, beans, apple, plum, pear, etc. The bio-control laboratory has also promoted IPM activities by conservation of bio-control agents in 449 hectares and augmentation in 493 hectares till January 2002, mainly in crops like paddy, cole crops, onion, potato, tomato, etc. Major pests and diseases for which IPM packages have been developed are given in Table 11.22.

Bio-pesticides and *neem*-based pesticides are not readily available in the market. Therefore, their usefulness and application procedures are not known to most of the farmers. Efforts are being made through various extension agencies to make the farmers aware of the benefits of bio-control agents and IPM. Pesticide testing laboratories should be efficient to check the samples quickly and catch the culprits indulging in malpractices before it is too late. Presently, there are limited number of quality control test laboratories for checking fertilisers and pesticides. Their number should be increased.

TABLE 11.22

Integrated Pest Management Packages Used in the State

Crop	*Pest/Disease*
Rice	Rice Sterm Borer, Leaf Folder,
Potato	Tuber Moth
Rapeseed and Mustard	Aphid
Ginger	Rhizome Rot
Brinjal	Fruit and Shoot borer, Hodda Beetle, Jassids, Mites, Bacterial blight, Wilt, Phomopsis blight, Fruit rot and Nematodes
Pea	Leaf minor, Pod borer, White rot, Powdery mildew, *Ascochyta blight*, Bacterial blight, Rust, Root rot and Wilt
Tomato	Bacterial wilt, Fruit rot, Blight, Leaf spot, Damping-off, Fruit Borer, Cut worm, Fruit flies
	Package for White Grub, Cut Worm and *Heliothis armigera*

Source: National Conference on Agriculture (H.P), 2002.

Farm Implements

Farm mechanisation is limited to the southwest submontane region where land is mostly flat and less undulated. In the hilly terrain, small tractors, power tillers and power sprayers are made available to the farmers on subsidy but mechanisation is rather marginal and only some big orchardists use these implements. There is great scope for giving farm equipment on hire. Special small instruments to meet the needs of hill farming have to be developed and popularised.

Developmental Potential, Prospects and Constraints

Crop Production

The increase in the population of Himachal Pradesh from 45 lakh to 61 lakh in the 1980-2000 decades has naturally led to an increasing demand for food. Since the inception of the state, cultivation of foodgrains has been a priority with the farmers as well as with the state. It is a matter of concern that food production has not been able to keep pace with the demand even though there has been a massive increase in the technology input and money for the development of agriculture in the state.

At present, there is a deficit in the state's production of foodgrains, except maize. Despite having missions for increase in the production of pulses and oilseeds the yields are still low. In fact, the average production of wheat, rice, pulses and oilseeds, besides many other crops, is lower than the Indian average.

The main reasons attributed to low production are:

- Cultivation is on the slopes
- The soils are shallow
- Irrigation is limited
- Land holdings are small and scattered
- Use of inputs is limited
- Farm mechanisation is scarce
- Absence of quality and certified seed

However, nowhere management of production and dissemination of technology have been considered as factors responsible for low productivity. In fact, these are the two key reasons of low productivity because the basic physical situation that exists in Himachal Pradesh has a parallel in some hilly South-East Asian and European regions where productivity is much higher. There is tremendous scope for improving the land-use pattern and minor irrigation schemes for giving a boost to production. Dissemination of suitable and practical technologies which are available have not received due emphasis.

The state is trying to improve agricultural production through various policies, projects and schemes. Quality seed production is a great determinant for increase in production. The state depends upon local farmers for its seed production programmes. A large number of private seed growers are also allowed to sell their seed, hybrid or otherwise, to the growers directly. Though it is claimed that the private seed dealers get their seed approved from the designated agencies, yet very often the farmers are cheated because of the poor quality of the seed. Nevertheless, quality certified HYV seed of different crops has yet to reach a large number of farmers. The state agricultural university and state department of agriculture can join hands in developing programmes for seed production and distribution. Private sector can also be encouraged to participate in the programme under proper guidelines so that farmers are not cheated.

The consumption of chemical fertilisers in the state is hardly 40 kg per hectare per year as compared to the Indian average of 95 kg per hectare per year. Chemical fertilisers are available to small and marginal farmers and the Scheduled Castes and Scheduled Tribes on 50 per cent subsidy. Even then fertiliser consumption is very low, indicating that the usefulness of chemical fertilisers is not known to most of the farmers. Farmyard manure obtained from domesticated animals remains the most favoured fertiliser.

The demographic structure of the villages reveal that 2613 villages have more than 50 per cent concentration of the Scheduled Castes and Scheduled Tribes who have an average operational landholding of 0.7 to 1.2 hectares per household. Nearly 64 per cent of the total landholdings are less than one hectare. In the hilly terrain, landholdings are small and scattered and thus unmanageable. This is one of the biggest bottlenecks hampering the development of agriculture. Furthermore, the land lease and tenancy laws are conservative and orthodox with the result that leasing out of farmland becomes difficult. On account of this, the farmers prefer to keep their land fallow than to lease it out to other farmers.

Eighty per cent of the farming in the state is rainfed and about 70 per cent of the rainfall occurs in the three months of the rainy season. Most of the rainwater is lost through *nallah*, streams, and rivulets and as run-off. Although construction of water harvesting structures for conserving rainwater has been taken up by the farmers, yet this process is slow and has not been adopted on a mass scale for want of awareness and appropriate technology.

Similarly, though incentives have been offered to farmers to construct water tanks and shallow wells as subsidy, even these schemes have met with limited success in augmenting irrigation. A state with ample water resources should not have agriculture dependent on rain. At present only one per cent of the cultivated area has assured irrigation, whereas a large potential exists to augment irrigation through major and minor schemes. Watershed development is another convenient method to conserve rainwater, the technology for which has to be disseminated and used extensively to make these support the main irrigation programme.

Soil conservation has to be considered with all seriousness as rapid felling of forest trees and clearing of bushes by rampant grazing is leading to erosion of hills on large scale. Besides, during rains, flash floods also cause enormous damage to the soil. While bringing more land under cultivation is very expensive and difficult, it is necessary that the existing soil resources are well protected and guarded. Besides soil erosion, mineral starvation and disturbances in soil physico-chemical characteristics have to be kept under check. Soil management thus assume great importance.

It is encouraging to note that the state is putting emphasis on the use of bio-fertilisers, bio-pesticides, integrated pest management and integrated nutrient management programmes. In addition the state has set up testing laboratories for pesticides and fertilizers to minimize adulteration. There are very few soil testing laboratories in the state with facilities for micronutrient tests and these need to be augmented.

Apparently, there are a number of projects and schemes for the development of agriculture, yet the action programmes do not seem to have reached the stakeholders because of relatively less emphasis on communication technology and dissemination practices. Emphasis is laid on training of agricultural development officers and a few farmers through a number of courses. However, personal contacts with the farmers and demonstration and adoption of modern cultivation technologies have been the backbenchers. The universities at Palampur and Solan need to have strong and modernised agricultural extension and training programmes for each district and the state Agriculture Department should have mobile teams to train and visit the farmers frequently and lay extensive demonstrations in the farmers' fields. Such an exercise will go a long way in improving the productivity level. Technology, information and communication are the keys to agricultural progress by increasing the receptivity and awareness of the farmers. Added to this, if farmers are organised into farmer interest groups, community groups, using Panchayati Raj Institution as a tool along with NGO's and private sector, a lot can be achieved in short time.

Horticulture

Horticulture is the strength of Himachal Pradesh. Its topography allows the production of all kinds of fruit crops ranging from temperate to sub-tropical species. The gross annual turnover of the state's horticulture industry is over Rs. 600 crore from less than five lakh farming families. Normally 75 to 80 per cent of the horticultural produce is marketable surplus, which can either be processed or exported.

Taking advantage of the variation in climate, the state is producing fruits as well as vegetables, which mature early, or late in the season and this fetches a better price in the markets of the neighbouring states. This competitive advantage has not been fully exploited for want of adequate infrastructure. Similarly, the surplus marketable horticultural produce often languishes in remote markets for want of infrastructure, transport, cold storage, processing facilities and above all suitable marketing outlets and intelligence for disposal of the produce.

Most of the apple orchards are old and have become less productive while the replacement rate of newer hybrid/dwarf cultivars of apples and pears is slow. The urgency of developing planting material is great and the University at Solan should develop technologies for mass production and the horticulture department should energise its resources to distribute and ensure their planting rapidly. In the meantime, suitable package of practices be evolved for the aging orchards where replacement of plant is not immediately due. Increasing productivity of aging orchards is dependent upon proper management and technical input. Proper linkages be established between horticultural scientists of the universities, government and the farmers so that declining trend in productivity is arrested and if possible reversed till new planting material blooms for high production.

The population of non-bearing fruit trees occupies a large, occupying area, which could be used profitably. Encouraging cultivation of olives, kiwi fruit, saffron and similar crops can only have ornamental value since their cultivation has become very professional in other countries and some states of India. In contrast, flower cultivation; exotic vegetables, off-season vegetables and organic farming have tremendous potential and competitive advantage to the state with very little extra effort on the development of infrastructure. Comparatively the best crop productivity average of the state is lower than the best in the world (Table 11.23) thereby showing the productivity gaps, which could be filled with the use of modern technologies. The two state universities can play a significant role in this.

Biotechnology in Agriculture

The state government in 2001 with the objective of harnessing biotech developments for increasing agricultural and industrial production established a Department of Bio-technology. The Department of Biotechnology has a mission for promoting diversified farming of high value cash crops, conservation and commercial exploitation of bio-resources and promoting entrepreneurships in biotechnology based industries in the state. Three state universities at Palampur, Solan and Shimla, the Institute of Himalayan Bio-resource Technology, Palampur, and the Central Potato Research Institute, Shimla, are responsible for research and development besides developing the human resource. Biotechnology parks are also being set up in association with the private sector at Solan and Shahpur. The main emphasis is on improving agriculture through biotechnology and the use of micro-propagation through tissue culture, mass micro-propagation of fruit trees and forestry material, somatic embyogenesis, meristem culture for disease-free material, cell/ protoplast culture, somaclonal variations, genetic transformation, gene manipulations and genetic engineering etc. The biotechnology laboratories require large funding for research and ultimate application of the developed technologies and human resource development for which the state government and other agencies are contributing. It is expected that the lead taken by the state in giving importance to biotechnology will enrich its programmes in agriculture including horticulture, floriculture and other related areas.

TABLE 11.23

Productivity of Different Crops in Himachal Pradesh, India and Best in the World (2000-01)

(Kg/ha)

Crop	*H.P*	*India*	*World's Best*	
Foodgrains				
Rice	1423	2914	12090	Australia
Wheat	1266	2756	8656	Ireland
Maize	2272	1769	10226	New Zealand
Vegetables				
Tomato	34645	15068	377667	Ukraine
Beans (Green)	9921	9600	12471	Israel
Pea (Green)	9574	10000	16010	France
Cabbage	28663	18085	57641	Germany
Cauliflower	18164	15000	45134	New Zealand
Capsicum	9355	9074	49639	Kuwait
Potato	23890	18657	46662	Bosnia

Source: FAO Abstract, 2002.

Statistical Outline of Himachal Pradesh, 2001.

Thrust for Development Initiative

Land Use

Small, scattered and unconsolidated landholdings are a limiting factor for intensive agriculture. Land lease and tenancy regulations do not allow the farmers to acquire cultivable land for commercial cultivation. Even farm mechanisation becomes difficult with small holdings. All these result in low productivity of crops. Land reforms, therefore, assume great importance in the context of low productivity of the crops in the state.

Input-use Efficiency

Among the vital inputs, the use of fertilizers and pesticides is very restricted and limited to a few crops. Even irrigation is scanty and appears to be somewhat misused. Distribution of the seed of high yielding varieties is faulty as it is not being supplied in full in areas where there is assured irrigation (see Table 11.20). There is need for bringing more areas under irrigation at a rapid pace. Programmes of major, medium and minor irrigation projects are moving at a slow speed. Minor irrigation needs to be encouraged in all areas along with watershed development wherever possible. The state policy to develop power through micro hydel projects should be integrated with its major or minor irrigation projects so that its irrigation potential is increased rapidly and the drought prone areas are well served. Conservation of water by the use of drip and sprinkler irrigation for vegetable and fruit crops and rainwater harvesting will add to the irrigation potential. Participation of local communities is essential in appropriate execution of water conservation and management.

Certified seeds of high yielding varieties of vegetables, flowers and other important crops or hybrids with assured germination should either be produced within the state or procured from authorised agencies for distribution in the state. Private seed dealers may be allowed to sell seeds of known and certified varieties only, for which checking agencies need to be installed.

Cropping Pattern

The State has the advantage of its topography and climate where all kinds of crops can be grown. The present scenario of the cropping pattern reveals that most of the foodgrain crops, oilseeds, pulses, millets, etc., are grown by a large number of farmers, even when their productivity is low and economically these do not yield good returns.

Should all crops be grown in the state? Instead, the focus should be on crops like maize, potato, ginger and some high yielding, exotic, off-season and temperate vegetables and other crops which have high productivity and give good economic returns to the farmers. This policy can help the farmers and the state in improving agriculture.

Horticulture

Apple has made the state popular while for other fruits it is yet to gain ground. Productivity of all the fruits is lower than the Indian average. Apple orchards are old, becoming unproductive and the replacement rate with newer and high yielding varieties is three per cent per year. Similarly, no cultivars of mango, citrus and litchi are making any headway in production and productivity. Nearly 16 per cent of the area under temperate and dry fruit trees are non-bearing. Technology for production of fruits, including the use of inputs and farm machinery, is very old and needs to be replaced. At the present rate of introduction of high yielding dwarf cultivars of temperate fruits, it will take about 20 years to gain advantage in their production. While there is marketable surplus of apple in the state, there is no adequate backing for utilising the produce for processing purposes and marketing infrastructure is inadequate.

Introduction of kiwi fruit, olives, hazel nut, pecan nut is attractive, yet these demand an extra degree of technical input to achieve economic productivity. Instead of venturing on newer introductions, it would be worthwhile to pay extra attention to improving the quality and productivity of the existing fruits by developing professional management and through the injection of newer technologies and infrastructure back-up.

Flowers

Economic gains from flower cultivation come with strong infrastructural support for marketing. The state neither has an international airport nor extensive cold storage and road network for this perishable produce. Nevertheless, taking advantage of climatic factors, professional flower cultivation, leading to production of seed and bulbs/rhizomes, can be profitable and safe. Production of cut flowers for nearby markets give of temporary advantage.

Vegetables

The state has the distinct advantage of climate in the production of vegetables, including potato and ginger, as productivity is higher than the national average in many cases. Additional inputs of modern technology, like out-of-season cultivation, cultivation in glass houses and poly houses; research and other modern management inputs can make a serious contribution to boosting the production of vegetables. The state can earn additional revenue by concentrating on growing exotic vegetables like Broccoli, Brussels sprouts, asparagus, leek, horseradish, out-of-season vegetables and vegetable seeds. Tremendous potential exists in these areas when the extension agencies and universities support the cultivators in their efforts for modernisation and upgradation. Value addition to surplus vegetables will be an added economic activity.

Other Crops

Cultivation of tea in Kangra district needs full encouragement. The produce has an acceptable national and international market as the Chinese hybrid tea has both flavour and strength of the brew. Currently, the tea gardens are small, scattered and improperly managed. Concerted effort is required to organise tea plantations on a commercial basis and support the system developed for extensive cultivation of tea and its processing on modern lines.

Medicinal and aromatic plants need special attention as these are not only valuable from the health or cosmetic point of view but are also great foreign exchange earners. Extensive surveys leading to the creation of an exhaustive inventory is required. A full package of practices for the cultivation of commonly used medicinal and aromatic plants should be developed and popularised among the farmers who have assured marketing by government or private agencies. Leaving valuable plants to be exploited by commercial organisations can result in over exploitation and ultimate extinction which must be avoided at all costs.

Commercial and Contract Farming

Commercial and contract farming require relatively large farms. Because of the low yields from small holdings or terraces, contract farming seems a remote possibility. Land reforms and relaxation in land-lease regulations can encourage both contract and commercial farming and give an opportunity to the corporate sector to enter the field of agriculture by providing services and thereby increasing productivity.

Organic Farming

Most of the small and marginal farmers are not using chemical fertilisers or pesticides due to economic reasons. Some such farmers can be lured into organic farming by the technical experts of the agricultural universities and the department of agriculture by providing adequate training and incentives. This can be very profitable particularly in vegetable and fruit cultivation besides tea. Technological and management inputs are necessary for introducing this activity.

Technology and Information Boost

The Agricultural University at Palampur and the Horticulture and Forestry University at Nauni (Solan) are the two organisations mandated to generate technologies for improving crop and horticultural production. While the state has ventured into the cultivation of all kinds of crops, fruits and vegetables, it has lagged in utilising the modern cultivation technologies evolved by local and other leading organisations in the country. Above all, the extension network of the universities and the state Departments of Agriculture and Horticulture have not been able to reach the farmers with modern technology, appropriate seed and other inputs. Technology development and dissemination appears to be a weak link, which should receive full attention for boosting production. Modern training programmes can be introduced at village level for crop cultivation.

Infrastructure

Infrastructure for agriculture is particularly deficient in terms of roads, cold stores, power and irrigation. Valuable agricultural produce does not fetch appropriate returns. Quality control laws are inadequate. Augmenting the infrastructure in the hilly regions in particular will greatly boost agricultural and horticultural productivity as well as profitability to the cultivators. Facilities for quick marketing of perishable produce, supported by market intelligence, a chain of cold stores and processing industry, are necessary to encourage the farmers to accelerate their production capabilities. Procurement of quality and graded produce and direct marketing without the involvement of middlemen will greatly improve the economy of farmers.

References

Annual Administrative Report, Directorate of Agriculture. Government of Himachal Pradesh, Shimla, (various issues in Hindi).

Annual Administrative Report, Horticulture Department. Government of Himachal Pradesh, Shimla, (various issues in Hindi).

Annual Plan, 2000-2001 and 2001-2002. Planning Department, Government of Himachal Pradesh, Shimla.

Annual Seasons and Crop Report, Commissioner Revenue, Government of Himachal Pradesh, Shimla 1996.

Biobusiness for Entrepreneurship and Employment Generation, Department of Biotechnology & H.P. University, Shimla, Conference Proceedings. August 2001.

Biotechnology Policy of Himachal Pradesh, Department of Biotechnology. Government of Himachal Pradesh, Shimla, 2001.

Dahiya, P.S. and Ranveer Singh, "Horticultural Development: Himachal Pradesh: Profitability, Policy and Prospects," *Indian Journal of Agricultural Economics*, 52 (3), 1997.

David H. Peters, *et al.* (2002), *Better Health System for India's Poor: Findings, Analysis and Options*, World Bank, Human Development Network, Health Nutrition and Population Series.

Department of Women and Child Development, Government of India and United Nations Children's Fund, New Delhi, *Multiple Indicator Survey (MICS-2000), India, Summary Report*, December 2001.

Directorate General of Health Services, Ministry of Health and Family Welfare, Government of India, *Bulletin on Rural Health Statistics in India, March 2002*.

Draft Tenth Five Year Plan Document, Government of Himachal Pradesh. Shimla.

Economic and Statistical Organisation, Government of Himachal Pradesh, *Statistical Abstracts of Himachal Pradesh* (different issues)

FAO Bulletin of Statistics, FAO Publication (2), 2001.

Government of Himachal Pradesh (2002) Himachal Pradesh, *Human Development Report 2002*.

Horticultural Development in Himachal Pradesh – At a Glance, Horticulture Department. Government of Himachal Pradesh. Shimla (in Hindi) 1998-99.

HPKV Perspective Plan – Vision 2020, HPKV, Palampur 1999.

International Institute for Population Sciences and Macro ORC, *National Family Health Survey-II*, India 1998-99.

————. *National Family Health Survey-II*, Himachal Pradesh, India 1998-99.

Kumar, Rajesh, J.S. Thakur and A.K. Srivastava, *Himachal Burden of Disease Study Draft Estimation Report, 2003*, Department of Community Medicines, Post Graduate Institute of Medical Education and Research, Chandigarh sponsored by Directorate of Health and Family Welfare, Himachal Pradesh.

Ministry of Health and Family Welfare, Government of India, New Delhi, *Family Welfare Programme in India, Year Book* (different issues).

————. *Annual Reports* (different issues)

————. *National Health Policy* 2002.

National Conference on Agriculture Department of Agriculture, Government of Himachal Pradesh, held at New Delhi, April 2002.

National Council of Applied Economic Research (NCAER), New Delhi, *Household Survey of Medical Care (May-June 1990)*, June 1992, 52 p.

————. *Household Survey of Health Care Utilisation and Expenditure*, March 1995, 95 p.

National Institute of Health and Family Welfare, New Delhi (December 2000), *Development of Health Insurance in India: Current Status and Future Directions*, Report of Seminar held on 29-30 December 2000, 46 p.

National Sample Survey Organisation, Department of Statistics, Government of India, *Sarvekshana*, Volume IV, No. 1& 2, 1980.

————. *Morbidity and Utilisation of Medical Services* (42nd Round), July 1986-June 1987, Sarvekshana, Vol. XV, No. 4, Issue No. 51, April-June 1992.

————. Morbidity and Treatment of Ailments (52nd Round), July 1995-June 1996, Report No. 441, November 1998.

————. Morbidity and Treatment of Ailments (52nd Round), July 1995-June 1996, *Sarvekshana*, Vol. XXIII, No. 3, 82nd Issue, January-March 2000.

Planning Commission, Government of India, *'Five Year Plan Documents'* (various documents).

"Potato in Himachal Pradesh", CPRI (ICAR), Shimla. *Tech. Bulletin* No. 15, 1996.

Salient Research Achievements – An Overview, Director of Research, DYSP University of Forestry and Horticulture, Nauni (Solan), 2003.

Sharma, H.R., Virender Kumar and A.K. Tripathi, 'Horticulture in Himachal Pradesh - Emerging Threat from Globalization, Technological and Climatic Changes', *Man & Development*, 25 (1): 21-34, March 2003.

Statistical Outline of Himachal Pradesh, Directorate of Economics and Statistics. Government of Himachal Pradesh, Shimla.

Work Plan for Accelerated Growth of Agriculture and Horticulture in Himachal Pradesh (2002-2003).

————. *List of Essential Drugs*, 1999.

————. *Standard Treatment Guidelines*, June 2000.

World Bank, *A Vision for India's Health System*, Report of Conference held on 15-16 November 2001, New Delhi, downloaded from Internet.

World Health Organisation (1978), *Primary Health Care*, Report of the International Conference on Primary Health Care, Alma Ata, USSR, 6-12 September 1978.

————. *The World Health Reports* (various issues).

Chapter 12

Livestock

Livestock sector is a major factor in fulfilling the fat and protein requirement of a growing population. Against a world average of 25 grams per person per day of animal protein in diet, the Indian diet contains just 10 gm. As such, the development of livestock is essential for maintaining the nutritional level, particularly of growing children and nursing mothers.

Livestock sector contributes 5.59 per cent of India's GDP. It provides regular employment to about 11 million in principal status and 8 million in subsidiary status. Women constitute 69 per cent of the labour force in livestock section (Economic Survey, India, 2002-03, p. 163).

In India, livestock population is recorded quinquennially, for example in 1992, 1997 and 2002. It does not coincide with human census, which is conducted after every ten years, for example 1981, 1991 and 2001. The first livestock census in Himachal Pradesh, was conducted in 1972. It completed its seventh count in 2002. The available data, as projected, is only up to the year 1997.

A total of 5.2 million livestock was estimated by the livestock census of 1997 (Table 12.1). This number was close to that of human population in the state. It accounted for one per cent of the total livestock population in the country.

Livestock-keeping is very common in Himachal Pradesh. 19 out of every 20 households keep at least one of the species of livestock. Bovine is most common species. Of the total households in the state, 91.39 per cent have bovine. Goat is the next important livestock. Nearly one-fourth of the total households keep goat. Similarly, two out of every five households keep a sheep. Rearing of pigs is rare. However, households keeping poultry accounted for 5.54 per cent of the total households in the state. In 1992, the state accounted for 1.1 per cent of India's livestock population while its human population was 0.6 per cent (Table 12.2).

TABLE 12.1

Himachal Pradesh: Livestock, 1972-1997

Census Years	*Livestock (in million)*
1972	4.7
1977	4.8
1982	5.0
1992	5.1
1997	5.2

Source: Integrated Sample Survey for Estimation of Animal Products, Milk, Eggs, Wool and Meat, 2001-2002, Directorate of Animal Husbandry, Himachal Pradesh, Pasudhan Bhawan, Shimla, pp.9-10.

TABLE 12.2

Comparison of Livestock in India and Himachal Pradesh, 1992

Category	*All India ('000)*	*Himachal Pradesh ('000)*	*Percentage to total of India*
Cattle	204533	2165	1.06
Buffaloes	83499	704	0.84
Sheep	50799	1079	2.12
Goat	115278	1118	0.96
Pigs	12795	-	-
Horses and ponies	826	14	1.70
Others	2415	37	1.54
Total	470145	5117	1.08
Total Poultry	307075	722	0.24

Source: Integrated Sample Survey for Estimation of Animal Products, Milk, Eggs, Wool and Meat, 2001-2002, Directorate of Animal Husbandry, Himachal Pradesh, Pasudhan Bhawan, Shimla, pp.9-10.

The composition of the state's livestock population underwent some change during 1972-97 (Table 12.3). While the percentage share of cattle declined from 46.3 to 41.6, that of buffaloes increased from 11.6 to 14.3. Similarly, while the percentage share of sheep went

TABLE 12.3

Himachal Pradesh: Composition of Livestock, 1972 and 1997

Livestock	*Total*		*Percentage to Total Livestock*		*Trend*
	1972	*1997*	*1972*	*1997*	
Cattle	2175690	2173575	46.26	41.60	Decline
Buffaloes	543887	748246	11.56	14.32	Increase
Sheep	1039946	1080464	22.11	20.68	Decline
Goats	906415	1167992	19.27	22.35	Increase
Horses and ponies	16234	12884	0.34	0.24	Decline
Others	20283	40906	0.43	0.78	Increase
Total	4702455	5224067	100	100	

Source: Integrated Sample Survey for Estimation of Animal Products, Milk, Eggs, Wool and Meat, 2001-2002, Directorate of Animal Husbandry, Himachal Pradesh, Pasudhan Bhawan, Shimla, pp.9-10.

down from 21.1 to 20.7, that of goats experienced a rise from 19.3 to 22.4. The number of horses and ponies had come down by one-fifth. However, poultry recorded a 4.6 times multiplication from 187 thousand in 1972 to 864 thousand in 1997.

Distribution Pattern

While there is a general increase in livestock population of the state during 1982-97 period, five out of twelve districts registered an absolute decline. These are Hamirpur, Kullu, Lahaul & Spiti, Shimla and Una. Nearly 20 per cent of the total livestock was concentrated in Mandi. It was followed very closely by Kangra district (Table 12.4).

TABLE 12.4

Himachal Pradesh: District-wise Concentration of Livestock, 1982-1997

Districts	*1982*		*1997*		
	Total Population of Livestock	*Percentage to Total Livestock in the State*	*Total Population Livestock*	*Percentage to Total Livestock in the State*	*Trend in Proportion to Total Livestock*
Bilaspur	237582	4.76	238448	4.56	Decline
Chamba	727149	14.57	739036	14.14	Decline
Hamirpur	250236	5.01	232521	4.45	Decline
Kangra	809434	16.22	981483	18.78	Increase
Kinnaur	93869	1.88	123179	2.35	Increase
Kullu	332314	6.66	327628	6.27	Decline
Lahaul & Spiti	68023	1.36	62172	1.19	Decline
Mandi	871093	17.46	996565	19.7	Increase
Shimla	630695	12.64	560647	10.7	Decline
Sirmaur	410276	8.22	430083	8.2	Unchanged
Solan	317703	6.36	329953	6.3	Unchanged
Una	240166	4.8	202352	3.87	Decline
Total	**4988540**	**100**	**5224067**	**100**	

Source: Statistical Outline, Himachal Pradesh, 1992, p.85.

Cattle: Table 12.5 reveals that more than half of the total cattle in the state are concentrated in Mandi (21.31), Kangra (18.07) and Shimla (14.92) districts. Kinnaur and Lahaul & Spiti have a small number of cattle. In spite of efforts towards improving the quality of cattle, only about one sixth of them are crossbred and rest indigenous.

Buffaloes: Kangra, Mandi, and Hamirpur districts show the highest concentration of buffaloes (Table 12.5). These districts share half of the buffaloes in the state. The high altitude areas of Lahaul & Spiti, Kinnaur, Kullu, Shimla and Sirmaur have very few of them.

TABLE 12.5

Himachal Pradesh: Major Districts Identified by Concentration of Livestock, 1997

Category	*Dominant Districts in Terms of Proportion of Livestock Population to Total of That Species*
Cattle	Mandi (21.31), Kangra (18.07), Shimla (14.92)
Buffaloes	Kangra (20.4), Mandi (15.77), Hamirpur (13.53)
Sheep	Chamba (23.81), Mandi (18.48), Kangra (17.56)
Goat	Kangra (20.24), Mandi (17.94), Chamba (16.79)
Horse	Kangra (28.67), Mandi (15.34), Shimla (14.84)
Yaks	Chamba (41.41), Lahaul & Spiti (35.48)

Source: Integrated Sample Survey for Estimation of Animal Products, Milk, Eggs, Wool and Meat, 2001-2002, Directorate of Animal Husbandry, Himachal Pradesh, Pasudhan Bhawan, Shimla, pp.11-12.

Note: Figures in parentheses indicate per cent to total animals in the State under respective category.

TABLE 12.6

Himachal Pradesh: District-wise Livestock Combination, 1997

Districts	*Major Species*
Bilaspur	Buffalo, Goat, Cattle
Chamba	Sheep, Cattle, Goat
Hamirpur	Buffalo, Cattle, Sheep
Kangra	Cattle, Goat, Sheep
Kinnaur	Sheep, Goat, Cattle
Kullu	Cattle, Sheep, Goat
Lahaul & Spiti	Sheep, Goat, Cattle
Mandi	Cattle, Goat, Sheep
Shimla	Cattle, Sheep, Goat
Sirmaur	Cattle, Goat, Buffalo
Solan	Cattle, Goat, Buffalo
Una	Buffalo, Cattle, Goat
State	Cattle, Goat, Sheep

Source: Integrated Sample Survey for Estimation of Animal Products, Milk, Eggs, Wool and Meat, 2001-2002, Directorate of Animal Husbandry, Himachal Pradesh, Pasudhan Bhawan, Shimla, pp.9-10.

TABLE 12.7

Himachal Pradesh: Animal Produce, 1987-2002

	1984-85	*1988-89*	*1989-90*	*1990-91*	*1991-92*	*1992-93*	*1993-94*	*1994-95*	*2001-02*
Milk ('000 tonne)									
Cow	166.58	218.13	242.18	257.56	264.75	260.66	292.27	303.55	350.55
Buffalo	227.63	265.88	278.82	300.84	311.67	319.95	355.39	331.35	380.29
Goat	9.62	15.74	8.19	14.20	20.44	29.47	26.19	28.00	32.02
Total	**404.127**	**499.75**	**529.19**	**572.60**	**596.86**	**610.08**	**653.85**	**662.90**	**762.86**
Wool (in tonne)	1270	1351	1405	1452	1567	1510	1532	1533	1586
Egg (Lakh)	338	485	491	532	580	697	714	669	822
Meat ('000 kg.)	3392	3670	4026	4049	4406	4163	4664	3646	3548

Source: (i) Statistical Outline of different years, Himachal Pradesh.

(ii) Integrated Sample Survey for Estimation of Animal Products, Milk, Eggs, Wool and Meat, 2001-2002, Directorate of Animal Husbandry, Himachal Pradesh, Pasudhan Bhawan, Shimla.

Sheep: Chamba, Mandi and Kangra are the districts of major sheep concentration. Both low altitude relatively agriculturally developed and very high altitude pasture-free lands do not attract this animal. The number of sheep in Una, Solan, Bilaspur and Sirmaur districts is small; these together do not have even six per cent of the total sheep in the state.

Goats: Kangra, Mandi, and Chamba districts have the largest concentration. Together, these districts share more than half of the state's goat population. Geographically, the distribution of sheep and goats overlap each other.

Poultry: Kangra is the leading district in poultry, followed by Mandi and Solan. Lahaul & Spiti and Kinnaur districts have few poultry birds. Poultry is more popular in districts which adjoin Punjab.

Livestock combinations: Livestock combinations presented in Table 12.6 reveal that low altitude gentle sloping terrain of districts adjoining Punjab, such as Bilaspur, Hamirpur and Una, have dominance of buffaloes in their livestock. Kangra, Kullu, Mandi, Shimla, Sirmaur and Solan have dominance of cattle and high altitude cold climate districts of Chamba, Lahaul & Spiti and Kinnaur have a dominance of sheep in their total livestock.

Produce

Milk: Milk is the most important produce of cow, buffalo and goat. In 1984-85, the total milk production of the state was 404 thousand tonnes, which increased to 763 thousand tonnes in 2001-02. This represents a nearly two-fold increase (Table 12.7).

Buffaloes are the major milk producing livestock. They contribute nearly half of the state's milk production and cattle make nearly an equal contribution. The average milk produce per cow is only 2 litres and that of a buffalo is 3 litres. Goats contribute hardly 4 per cent of the total milk production. Kangra is the largest milk-producing district in the state. It is followed by Mandi (Table 12.8).

TABLE 12.8

Himachal Pradesh: District-wise Annual Milk Production 2000-2001 and 2001-02

District	*2000-01 ('000 Tonnes)*	*2001-02 ('000 Tonnes)*
Bilaspur	37.35	35.11
Chamba	55.67	61.57
Hamirpur	74.69	60.33
Kangra	145.35	143.94
Kinnaur	5.59	6.38
Kullu	35.40	30.41
Lahaul & Spiti	6.55	6.91
Mandi	124.06	120.63
Shimla	71.69	79.25
Sirmaur	63.41	71.82
Solan	68.82	73.78
Una	71.78	72.68
Total	760.41	762.86

Source: Integrated Sample Survey for Estimation of Animal Products, Milk, Eggs, Wool and Meat, 2001-2002, Directorate of Animal Husbandry, Himachal Pradesh, Pasudhan Bhawan, Shimla, p. 49.

Wool: Chamba, with the largest sheep population, is also the biggest producer of wool in the state. Mandi and Kullu are next important producers (Table 12.9). Wool production increased by about 25 per cent during 1984-85 to 2001-02 period. The annual yield per sheep is only 1.2 kgs.

TABLE 12.9

Himachal Pradesh: District-wise Annual Wool Production 2000-2001 and 2001-02

District	*2000-01 ('000 kg.)*	*2001-02 ('000 kg.)*
Bilaspur	37.34	29.52
Chamba	343.15	381.79
Hamirpur	78.55	65.87
Kangra	224.35	201.63
Kinnaur	93.11	80.58
Kullu	200.23	218.72
Lahaul & Spiti	71.73	60.74
Mandi	261.71	266.92
Shimla	200.38	175.91
Sirmaur	34.78	61.80
Solan	25.93	28.98
Una	7.24	9.96
Total	1578.56	1582.45

Source: Integrated Sample Survey for Estimation of Animal Products, Milk, Eggs, Wool and Meat, 2001-2002, Directorate of Animal Husbandry, Himachal Pradesh, Pasudhan Bhawan, Shimla, p. 55.

Meat: The meat production in the state recorded a marginal increase from 3392 tonnes in 1984-85 to 3548 tons in 2001-02. Goats contribute two-thirds of the total meat produced. Meat of sheep is next in importance. Pigs are relatively insignificant in this respect. Shimla, Kangra and Mandi are the largest producers of goat meat. The largest producer of sheep meat is Kangra. Pork is produced mostly in Solan and Shimla districts (Table 12.10).

TABLE 12.10

Himachal Pradesh: Meat Production by Districts, 2001-02

(in tonnes)

District	*Goat*	*Sheep*	*Pig*	*Total*
Bilaspur	46.95	10.78	1.84	59.57
Chamba	107.72	76.02		183.75
Hamirpur	82.41	36.92	-	119.33
Kangra	415.68	260.51	15.41	691.60
Kinnaur	52.43	40.32	-	92.75
Kullu	179.93	122.85	-	302.78
Lahaul & Spiti	102.00	155.66	-	257.67
Mandi	262.36	122.06	14.00	398.43
Shimla	911.55	113.99	88.86	1114.41
Sirmaur	82.78	19.50	35.80	138.17
Solan	25.03	4.57	115.29	144.90
Una	42.13	2.75	-	44.88
Total	2311.11	965.98	271.20	3548.30

Source: Integrated Sample Survey for Estimation of Animal Products, Milk, Eggs, Wool and Meat, 2001-2002, Directorate of Animal Husbandry, Himachal Pradesh, Pasudhan Bhawan, Shimla, p. 64.

Eggs: Egg production, which was 38 million in 1984-85 increased to 82.2 million by 2001-02. The production as such, multiplied by more than two times. Kangra is the major egg producer. It accounts for about 42 per cent of the total eggs produced in the state. Kinnaur is the smallest egg producer (Table 12.11).

TABLE 12.11

Himachal Pradesh: District-wise Annual Egg Production 2000-2001 and 2001-02

District	*2000-01 (million)*	*2001-02 (million)*
Bilaspur	6.8	7.5
Chamba	9.1	10.4
Hamirpur	3.7	2.9
Kangra	33.8	34.5
Kinnaur	0.6	0.5
Kullu	3.0	2.0
Lahaul & Spiti	0.6	1.8
Mandi	12.4	10.3
Shimla	4.7	4.8
Sirmaur	2.3	2.1
Solan	1.6	2.3
Una	2.9	3.1
Total	81.6	82.2

Source: Integrated Sample Survey for Estimation of Animal Products, Milk, Eggs, Wool and Meat, 2001-2002, Directorate of Animal Husbandry, Himachal Pradesh, Pasudhan Bhawan, Shimla, p. 60.

Veterinary Facilities

Healthy animals, like healthy human beings, are an asset for any state. Better health of livestock denotes qualitative improvement in livestock. It is ensured through provision of veterinary services.

Himachal Pradesh has in all 1927 different centres providing veterinary care. There were only nine veterinary hospitals functioning in 1948. The number of centres has multiplied manifold since then. The distribution is, however, highly uneven. Of the 303 veterinary hospitals in the state, 52 are confined to Kangra district alone (Table 12.12).

Major Thrust Areas

Strengthening of animal health care services: Improved health care facility would ensure not only quality produce but also raise the productivity.

Upgradation of genetic stock of cattle and buffaloes: The state has yet very limited crossbred cattles. Steps to improve the indigenous stock by extension services from veterinary institutions are desired.

TABLE 12.12

District-wise Hospital & Dispensaries, 2001-02

Districts	*Hospitals**	*Dispensary*	*Mobile Dispensary*	*Total*
Bilaspur	20	86	1	107
Chamba	33	143	1	177
Hamirpur	17	104	1	122
Kangra	59	301	2	362
Kinnaur	20	37	1	58
Kullu	16	79	1	96
Lahaul & Spiti	13	39	1	53
Mandi	38	241	1	280
Shimla	44	230	2	276
Sirmaur	29	112	1	142
Solan	22	120	1	143
Una	17	93	1	111
Total	**328**	**1585**	**14**	**1927**

Source: Annual Administrative Report, 2002-03, Animal Husbandry, Himachal Pradesh, p. 10.

* Including those run by the Central Government.

Quality feed and fodder: Animal food in future shall be more in demand to supplement the protein requirement of our diet. Better feed and quality fodder can be ensured by developing locally-grown maize crops and by following a rotational system in pasture management.

The government is keen to augment the existing infrastructure. In particular, it is going to raise the number of the veterinary hospitals from the existing number of 328 to 550 in 2010. This augurs well for the livestock sector, if things materialise as projected.

Dairy Co-operation: Women labour force is the largest in livestock management particularly in cattle and buffaloes. Dairy co-operatives run by women may be promoted.

Credit and marketing support: As mentioned earlier, nearly every household has at least one species of livestock; credit from financial institutions at lower rate of interest and liberal terms may promote this potential sector of the economy.

Disaster management programme: The western districts where buffaloes are mostly concentrated are unfortunately drought prone also. In the event of drought it is pertinent to have a disaster management programme, which can save the poor from destitution.

Some Imperatives

The proceeding discussion brings forth two important messages: (i) Productivity of the livestock in Himachal Pradesh is inordinately low and offers a big scope for its increase, and (ii) livestock sector holds a great promise for the state where landholdings are small, a very high proportion of the population is dependent upon agriculture calling for its diversification, a sizeable number of people are directly linked with livestock through transhumance, and extensive pasture lands are available for grazing of livestock. In that light, livestock cannot be ignored in the scheme of things for this hill state.

As a first step in this direction, it is essential to upgrade the quality of the livestock. This involves two-pronged effort, on the one hand, the indigenous breeds are to be conserved and improved, and on the other hand, crossbreeding is to be propagated on a large scale.

Herein comes the crucial role of the veterinary medical and paramedical staff. Ironically, while considerable veterinary infrastructure has been laid out in the state, there is a gross inadequacy of the professional and technical personnel to manage it. Perhaps veterinary sector is one of the few sectors, which is understaffed and offers vast employment opportunities for the educated youth. It is most desired that intake of students in the veterinary institutions is increased in a big way.

A strategy, which is already being favoured at the government level, calls for reconsideration. The state government is contemplating to arrange veterinary services through private sector. NABARD is being involved to promote this idea. A word of caution is necessary here. Keeping in view the topographic conditions, scatter of habitations and associated livestock, and quite a prominence of transhumance, private sector is not likely to be enthused into entering this area. The proposition is not going to be viable and sustainable for them. Therefore, government will have to continue shouldering this responsibility at their own level.

Feed and fodder management is one of the pre-requisites for improving the quality of livestock. The experience of the Army Dairy Farm of Dagshai is worth quoting here. By mixing the apple peel (which was available free from a nearby government agro-processing plant) with the feed, they could raise the daily milk yield of a cow by two litres. Himachal Pradesh is rich in apples and the use of this byproduct can go a long way in increasing the milk yield. At the same time, scientific research should be geared towards upgradation of the alpine pastures as also of the quality of grass in village common lands. Equally critical here is to clear pasturelands of congress grass and laltana which have been spreading rapidly in many parts of the state.

A point of special note needs to be highlighted here. Provision of extension services for raising and caring of livestock has emerged as a crucial task. This calls for arranging training courses for proper management of livestock, at the household level. Since it is generally the women who look after the livestock, such training courses should target women. The necessary training exercises can be conducted through the local *Panchayati Raj* Institutions.

As such, the upgradation of livestock requires a concerted co-ordination between the Department of Animal Husbandry and several other departments to achieve the goal: with Forest Department for management of pastures; with Agriculture Department for raising quality fodder; with industry for processing the livestock produce of all variety; with Department of Rural Development for organising training courses. Above all, active links with the Department of Biotechnology and veterinary science education institutions are also no less crucial.

Chapter 13

Rural Development

Himachal Pradesh can be classified into two distinctive zones on cultural grounds. The first one is inhabited by tribes or semi-nomadic, semi-agricultural and semi-pastoral people living in the great Himalayas. The districts of Lahaul and Spiti, Kinnaur, Upper Shimla, Upper Kullu, remote areas of Sirmaur, Chamba and Kangra districts fall in this zone. The people of these areas are an admixture of the Indo-Aryan or Mongolian stock. These are Kinnaures, Lahules, Gaddis, Gujars, Lambas, Khampas, Bhots, Pangwalas and Swanglas. The other zone consists of the outer Himalaya or the Shivalik and mid-Himalaya. The people of this zone have much in common with the people of the plains of Punjab and Haryana. The caste patterns, value systems and traditions are also similar to those of Punjab and Haryana. The main caste groups in Himachal Pradesh are Rajputs, Brahmins, Kanets, Kulindas, Girths, Raos, Rathis, Thakurs, Kolis, Holis, Chamars, Darains, Rehars, Chanals, Lohars, Baris, Dagis, Dhakhis, Turis, Batwals and some groups like Jats, Lubanas, Sainis, Nais, Jhiwars, Chimpas, etc. The tribals can be categoriesed as Gaddis, Gujars and Bhots. These castes are further classified as general castes, the Scheduled Castes, Other Backward Castes and the Scheduled Tribes.

The rural society of Himachal Pradesh has its own identity and psyche regarding traditions, culture and heritage. Therefore, within the overall rural development strategies, there has to be an explicit recognition of its identity. At the time of its formation in 1971, Himachal Pradesh was an economically backward rural state (93 per cent rural population in 1971). Its rural population was deprived of basic amenities such as health, education and drinking water. Rural infrastructure, i.e., rural roads, electricity, housing, transport, banking and market network, was also very poor. Almost half the rural households were living below the poverty line.

To accelerate the pace of economic development and significantly improve the standard and quality of living of rural people, the government of Himachal Pradesh took bold steps to improve their socio-economic condition. The government incorporated new policy initiatives and programmes in its budgets. New strategies were evolved to;

a) Raise farm productivity

b) Create the much needed rural infrastructure

c) Empower families below the poverty line by enlarging the scope of the programmes of poverty alleviation and welfare of women, the Scheduled Castes and Scheduled Tribes

d) Expand education and health facilities

e) Promote institutional finance

f) Upgrade technical skills

g) Strengthen rural institutions such as *panchayats*, co-operatives and others.

Successful implementation of various plans made a dent in rural poverty. Much improvement has taken place in the provision of basic amenities and building up rural infrastructure.

The government of Himachal Pradesh has chalked out its planning strategies mostly on the lines followed by the central government. The state government in its document on the Tenth Five Year Plan (2002-07) and the Annual Plan (2002-03) has strategically defined areas, which need to be addressed and require the highest attention. These areas are

- Improvement of financial position of the state
- Proper utilisation of its hydro-power generation potential

- Breaking stagnation of agriculture and horticulture
- Development of tourism
- Provision of safe drinking water
- Connectivity to all villages
- Tackling the unemployment problem
- Introduction of information technology in educational and technological institutions

The contribution of Himachal Pradesh to India's Net Domestic Product (NDP) in 2000-01 (at current prices) was estimated at 0.62 per cent only. According to the census of 2001, while nearly three-fourth of India's population lived in villages, in Himachal Pradesh more than four-fifths of the people live in rural areas. Almost one-fourth of the state's NDP comes from agriculture and allied sectors. It shows the weak position of the primary sector of the economy, since, a majority of the population lives in the rural areas and depends on agriculture. However, agriculture is of a subsistence nature and is unable to shape the level of living of the rural people. In this situation, the non-farm rural sector, with its forward and backward linkages can become an integral part of rural development in the state. But it has not received much attention. As a result, a sizeable number of the people of rural areas, especially the youth, are migrating to urban centres, inside and outside the state, in search of livelihood. To stop the migration of the rural unemployed, it is essential to create better socially acceptable employment opportunities by developing non-farm activities in the rural areas. To stop this trend, the basic facilities are required to be utilised properly, wherever these exist, and to be developed where these are non-existent. There is need for mobilising and involving the community in the proper maintenance of the available facilities at the local level under Panchayati Raj Institutions.

There is need for better co-ordination between government departments, non-government organisations, Panchayati Raj Institutions and private institutions to explore better opportunities of employment. The corporate sector can play a leading role by bringing in resources, new technology, modern management and extension services, which can create employment opportunities in the non-farm sector by training them for the required jobs. For example, Himachal Pradesh was a land of some rare handicrafts, and these goods were exported to overseas markets. In course of time, handicrafts such as *Pattus* (sheep wool shawls), *Thobis* (goat hair items), *Kasida* (embroidery goods) and silver ornaments have almost vanished and the artisans have abandoned this skill-based vocation. In the present era of liberalisation, such distinctive works can be revived through technical and managerial intervention. The people can be trained in these indigenous skills through modern techniques.

Keeping in view the development that has taken place in the past plan periods, much more remains to be done to improve the quality of life in the rural areas. Himachal Pradesh, with 90.2 per cent of its population in the rural areas, according to the 2001 census (Table 13.1), has a sizable deprived population consisting of marginal farmers, landless labourers besides Scheduled Castes, the Scheduled Tribes and other Backward Castes. This component of the population has to be brought into focus for uplift with special emphasis on their skill upgradation, removal of unemployment and vertical growth to acquire productive assets for better living on a sustainable basis. Sector-wise allocation of funds during different plan periods shows that the main stress has been on social services, energy, transport and agriculture (Table 13.2)

TABLE 13.1

Rural Urban Population in Himachal Pradesh

Year	*Total Population (in lakh)*			*Percentage of Total Population*	
	Total	*Rural*	*Urban*	*Rural*	*Urban*
1971	34.60	32.78	2.42	93.0	7.0
1981	42.81	39.55	3.26	92.4	7.6
1991	51.71	47.55	4.49	91.3	8.7
2001	60.77	54.82	5.95	90.2	9.8

Source: Census of India.

For an integrated development of such a rural economy, the development of physical as well as social infrastructure has an important role as it directly contributes to employment generation and asset creation. A better network of physical infrastructure facilities (well-built roads, rail links, irrigation, power and telecommunications, information technology, market-network, processing of horticulture and vegetables produce, cold chain system and social infrastructure support, viz, health and education, water and sanitation, veterinary services and co-operatives) is essential for the development of the rural economy. Tables 13.3, 13.4, 13.5 and 13.6 highlight inter-district disparities with regard to some of the basic development indicators.

Himachal Pradesh has comparatively better rural infrastructure facilities, such as cent per cent rural

TABLE 13.2

Plan-wise Expenditure under Different Heads in Himachal Pradesh (Fifth Plan to Tenth Plan)

(Rs. in lakh)

	Fifth 1974-78	Annual 1978-79	Annual 1979-80	Sixth 1980-85	Seventh 1985-90	Annual 1990-91	Annual 1991-92	Eighth 1992-97	Ninth 1997-2002	Tenth* 2002-07
Agriculture programme	26.02	25.42	27.47	15.81	19.63	18.43	20.98	13.91	11.63	11.67
Co-operation and community development	1.09	1.57	1.87	—	—	—	—	—	—	—
Water, irrigation and power	26.60	21.42	22.68	—	—	—	—	—	—	—
Industry and mining	3.53	3.43	3.28	3.08	3.22	2.93	3.46	2.47	1.47	1.02
Transport and communication	22.73	24.47	21.40	17.81	14.78	13.37	1494	12.56	14.10	15.90
Social services	—	—	—	—	—	—	—	—	40.68	47.51
Misc	—	—	—	—	—	—	—	—	—	—
Rural development	—	—	—	4.67	3.71	3.46	3.81	3.34	3.92	4.03
Irrigation and flood control	—		—	5.85	5.39	6.55	6.39	4.24	4.02	4.40
Spec area programme	—	—	—	0.08	—	—	—	—	0.25	—
Energy	—	—	—	26.97	26.55	18.04	12.92	18.89	16.03	12.21
Social and community services	16.72	21.69	20.82	22.44	—	—	—	—	—	—
Scientific services and research	—	—	—	0.03	0.07	0.10	0.21	0.14	0.09	0.06
Economic services	0.08	0.10	0.06	0.12	—	—	—	—	—	—
General services	2.22	1.89	2.42	3.14	2.13	2.08	1.88	2.40	1.62	1.03
General economic services	—	—	—	—	1.80	3.98	4.41	7.39	6.18	2.17
Edu, sports, art and culture	—	—	—	—	7.41	10.20	11.79	13.00	—	—
Health	—	—	—	—	3.28	3.90	4.85	4.65	—	—
Water supply, housing urban development and sanitation	—	—	—	—	10.61	13.63	12.47	14.91	—	—
Information and publicity	—	—	—	—	0.25	0.27	0.56	—	—	—
Welfare of SCs/STs/OBCs	—	—	—	—	0.42	0.35	0.27	—	—	—
Labour and labour welfare	—	—	—	—	0.08	0.12	0.11	—	—	—
Social welfare	—	—	—	—	0.66	2.58	0.95	2.10	—	—
Total	(100) 16214.10	(100) 6810.17	(100) 7945.36	(100) 66471.40	(100) 132474.75	(100) 37762.92	(100) 40482.00	(100) 34990.05	(100) 789672.00	(100) 1030000.00

Source: Five Year Plans and Annual Plans.

Statistical Abstracts of Himachal Pradesh, various issues.

Note: * - Plan outlay.

TABLE 13.3

District-wise Selected Socio-economic Indicators in Himachal Pradesh

Districts	No. of Inhabited Villages (1995-96)	% of SC Popu. (1991)	% of ST Popu. (1991)	Sex Ratio (2001)	Density of Popu. % sq. km. (2001)	% Age of Main Workers in Total Popu. (2001)	Work Participation Rate (2001)	Male Work Participation Rate (2001)	Female Work Participation Rate (2001)	% Age Workers Engaged in Non-Agri. Activities	% Age of BPL Households, to Total Households (1998-99)
Bilaspur	950	28.82	2.70	992	292	32.52	48.95	52.31	45.56	14.44	26.63
Chamba	1144	19.75	28.35	961	71	27.88	50.04	53.98	45.94	13.12	61.72
Hamirpur	1617	23.68	0.06	1102	369	29.34	49.90	51.06	48.85	14.18	24.17
Kangra	3620	21.17	0.14	1027	233	25.20	44.04	50.84	37.41	16.01	24.07
Kinnaur	228	26.87	55.58	851	13	50.79	60.54	65.62	54.78	18.85	26.57
Kullu	172	29.93	3.61	928	69	43.96	57.05	60.63	53.20	12.11	19.00
Lahaul & Spiti	272	7.11	76.97	804	2	57.88	63.50	68.39	57.43	28.78	37.93
Mandi	2818	28.98	1.21	1014	228	29.89	50.44	52.69	48.23	13.07	24.73
Shimla	2311	27.13	0.71	898	141	42.19	51.19	57.46	44.20	16.81	33.67
Sirmaur	965	30.18	1.61	901	162	38.38	49.30	56.49	41.32	12.73	22.89
Solan	2348	31.27	0.64	853	258	34.57	52.70	61.32	42.60	22.63	27.44
Una	552	22.46	0.01	997	291	26.60	45.03	53.02	37.01	16.74	19.06
H.P.	**16997**	**25.35**	**4.22**	**970**	**109**	**32.36**	**49.28**	**54.70**	**43.69**	-	**27.59**

Source: Statistical Abstract of Himachal Pradesh, various issues.

Census of India, Himachal Pradesh, 2001.

TABLE 13.4

Distribution of Total Rural Workers (2001)

Districts	*Cultivator*	*Agricultural Labour*	*Worker in Household Industry*	*Other Workers*
Bilaspur	71.67	1.77	1.57	24.99
Chamba	76.88	0.66	1.17	21.22
Hamirpur	73.29	1.44	1.23	24.04
Kangra	59.15	6.90	3.25	30.70
Kinnaur	66.67	2.20	1.81	29.32
Kullu	80.58	2.64	1.17	15.61
Lahaul & Spiti	53.11	1.57	0.47	44.85
Mandi	75.92	1.40	1.38	21.30
Shimla	77.75	2.96	1.12	18.17
Sirmaur	76.45	2.57	1.09	19.89
Solan	64.45	3.14	1.22	31.19
Una	60.33	5.82	1.94	31.90
H.P.	**70.43**	**3.29**	**1.71**	**24.57**

Source: *Census of India, Himachal Pradesh, 2001.*

TABLE 13.5

Percentage of Workers and Non-workers in Total Population (2001)

Categories	*Total Workers*	*Main Workers*	*Marginal Workers*	*Non-Workers*
Total	49.28	32.36	16.92	50.72
Male	54.70	43.30	11.40	39.30
Female	43.69	21.08	22.61	56.31

Source: *Census of India, Himachal Pradesh, 2001.*

electrification, public distribution system and households using separate kitchens (Table 13.7). However, there are inter-district disparities in the accessibility of basic facilities.

In the present economic situation, agriculture and rural development, especially agriculture and allied activities, are now poised for a paradigm shift. The core factors that can bring forth tangible transformation are:

(a) Development of rural infrastructure, such as roads, power and communications for generating more employment opportunities at the local level

(b) Development of village and cottage industries and agro-processing industries

(c) Skill upgradation through research and extension and information technology so that the rural people especially the youth can design means for their own betterment

(d) Minimising social differences through collective participation in rural development activities; developing common programmes for village uplift and minimising economic and gender disparities in the rural society

To meet future challenges, It is now felt that rural transformation can be hastened through the effective

TABLE 13.6

District-wise Physical, Social and Economic Indicators in Himachal Pradesh

Districts	*% of Geographical Area (sq. km) of the State (2001)*	*% of Popu. to Total Popu. of State* (2001)*	*% of Holdings in Total no. of Holdings (1991)*	*% age of Area in Total Area (in hec)*	*% of Crime Rate (2001)*	*% of Panchayats in Total Panchayats (2001)*	*% of Backward Panchayats in Total Backward Panchayats (2001)*	*% of Agri Cooperative Societies in Total (2001)*	*% of Telephone Connection in Total (2001)*	*% of Road Length in Total (2001)*	*% of Primary School in Total (2001)*	*% of Govt. Employee in Total (2001)*	*% age of Bank Offices in Total (2001)*	*% of Below Poverty Line Households in Total of State (1998-99)*
Bilaspur	2.10	5.61 (10)	5.63	5.27	8.28	4.48	2.66	3.50	4.21	4.61	5.54	5.09	5.42	6.10
Chamba	11.72	7.58 (5)	7.47	5.67	5.66	8.89	30.47	6.19	3.60	10.14	10.16	6.63	6.97	16.48
Hamirpur	2.01	6.78 (8)	8.01	7.66	5.69	7.08	2.66	10.45	7.21	4.43	4.76	5.96	6.97	7.05
Kangra	10.31	22.02 (1)	26.03	20.97	17.48	24.10	3.48	28.37	17.55	16.05	16.85	19.00	19.61	22.36
Kinnaur	11.50	1.38 (11)	1.12	1.43	1.14	2.04	-	1.65	1.56	3.78	1.78	2.24	2.32	1.01
Kullu	9.88	6.25 (9)	6.61	4.43	7.11	6.32	14.72	5.91	6.94	4.62	6.55	4.98	6.06	4.00
Lahaul & Spiti	24.85	0.55 (12)	0.46	0.64	0.98	1.35	-	2.46	0.12	3.88	1.97	1.59	1.03	0.85
Mandi	7.09	14.82 (2)	15.83	12.98	14.53	13.90	24.13	10.12	13.39	16.12	16.17	12.81	12.77	14.68
Shimla	9.22	11.82 (3)	10.44	12.60	15.84	10.90	14.72	8.09	22.50	13.83	15.20	21.88	15.74	11.10
Sirmaur	5.07	7.54 (6)	5.22	10.26	6.85	7.21	5.32	5.58	5.26	8.88	9.04	6.69	6.32	4.69
Solan	3.48	8.22 (4)	5.74	9.17	8.93	6.52	1.23	7.61	11.84	8.58	7.10	7.02	10.06	6.27
Una	2.77	7.34 (7)	7.44	8.91	7.51	7.21	0.61	10.12	5.82	5.08	4.89	6.16	6.71	5.40
H. P.	**100 (55673)**	**100 (6077248)**	**100 (863437)**	**100 (999099.68)**	**100 (15516)**	**100 (3037)**	**100 (469)**	**100 (2115)**	**100 (225103)**	**100 (26373)**	**100 (10633)**	**100 (123626)**	**100 (775)**	**100 (286112)**

Source: Various Statistical Abstract of Himachal Pradesh.

Note: * Figure in the parenthesis are ranking of the districts according to population

TABLE 13.7

Rural Infrastructure in Himachal Pradesh

	Rank	*States Having Better Ranks*
Percentage of household having *kutcha* houses	8	Bihar, UP, MP, Orissa, North-east, West Bengal and Kerala
Households using separate kitchens	2	Kerala
Using toilets	5	North-East, Kerala, West Bengal and Punjab
Electricity	1	Nil
Piped water	1	Nil
Protected water	9	Eight other states
Households using PDS	3	Tamil Nadu and Kerala
Population below poverty line (rural)	3	Orissa and West Bengal
Proportion of total H.H. income spent on education	1	Nil

Source: India Human Development Report, 1999, NCAER.

TABLE 13.8

Caste-wise Distribution of Male and Female Representatives of *Gram Panchayats* in Total Wards of Twelve Districts of Himachal Pradesh

Districts	*Male*					*Female*					*Grand Total*
	General	*S.C.*	*S.T.*	*B.C.*	*Total*	*General*	*S.C.*	*S.T.*	*B.C.*	*Total*	
Bilaspur	454	115	12	-	581	230	139	12	-	381	**962**
Chamba	472	221	286	-	979	316	72	177	-	565	1544
Hamirpur	676	213	-	-	889	338	106	-	-	444	1333
Kangra	2319	777	-	-	3096	1080	256	-	-	1336	4432
Kinnaur	-	70	152	-	222	-	36	92	-	128	350
Kullu	499	151	28	-	678	262	193	3	-	458	1136
Lahaul & Spiti	-	1	122	-	123	-	23	59	-	82	205
Mandi	1091	354	2	-	1447	780	444	21	-	1245	2692
Shimla	919	255	-	-	1174	466	336	5	-	807	1981
Sirmaur	583	272	10	-	865	304	142	6	-	452	1317
Solan	552	260	5	-	817	265	158	2	-	425	1242
Una	642	215	-	-	857	411	87	-	-	498	1355
H.P.	**8207**	**2904**	**617**	-	**11728**	**4452**	**1992**	**377**	-	**6821**	18549

Source: Panchayati Raj Department, Himachal Pradesh, Shimla.

implementation of the multilevel decentralised system, as envisaged in the New Panchayati Raj System, which has Constitutional authority to plan and implement programmes for rural development.

Rural Development and Panchayati Raj

Panchayats have been in existence since time immemorial. In the ancient period, the *Panchayats* generally functioned as informal institutions to solve intra-village and sometimes inter-village feuds, and organised forums for village-level social development and cultural functions.

In Himachal Pradesh, the *Panchayati* Raj system was established in a statutory form in 1954 under the Himachal Pradesh Panchayati Raj Act-1952. After the reorganisation of the state on 1 November 1966, the 1952 Act was replaced by the Himachal Pradesh Panchayati Raj Act 1968, incorporating the major recommendations of Balwant Rai Mehta Committee and a two-tier system was established in the state.

With the passage of the 73rd Constitutional Amendment Act, 1992, the Himachal Pradesh Panchayati Raj Act, 1994, came into force on 23 April 1994, in place of the Himachal Pradesh Panchayati Raj Act, 1968. New rules were framed under new Act. Simultaneously, the State Election Commission and the State Finance Commission were also constituted. The two-tier *Panchayati Raj* system, namely *Gram Panchayat* and *Panchayat Samiti*, gave way to the three-tier system. First elections to the *Panchayats* were held in December 1995.

The second general elections to the PRIs were held in December 2000, and in the scheduled areas in June 2001. At present there are 3037 *Gram Panchayats*, 75 *Panchayat Samitis* and 12 *Zila Parishads* with 24623, 1658 and 251 members respectively (Tables 13.8 & 13.9).

TABLE 13.9

Panchayati Raj Institutions in Himachal Pradesh - A Glance

Particulars	*Male*					*Female*					*Total Male & Female*
	General Castes	*Schedule Castes*	*Backward Castes*	*Tribal Castes*	*Total*	*General Castes*	*Schedule Castes*	*Backward Castes*	*Tribal Castes*	*Total*	
Ward Members of *Gram Panchayat*	8207	2904	-	617	11728	4452	1992	-	377	6821	18549
Panchayat Samiti Members	663	282	76	72	1098	330	155	42	35	560	1658
Zila Parishad Members	98	41	11	14	164	48	24	8	7	87	251
Pardhans of Panchayat	1233	501	147	130	2011	615	270	77	64	1026	3037
Chairpersons *Panchayat Samitis*	29	12	3	4	48	15	7	2	3	27	75
Zila Parishad Chairpersons	5	2	-	1	8	1	1	1	1	4	12

Source: Panchayati Raj Department, Himachal Pradesh, Shimla.

The 73rd Constitution Amendment Act, 1992, has enabled the PRIs to assume the role of self-governing institutions at the micro level of the administration for decentralised planning and management. It provides an arrangement for the association of rural voters, both men and women, in governance by managing the local affairs in a more meaningful manner that conforms to local wishes and aspirations. This constitutional status of PRIs has also empowered women, the Scheduled Castes and the Scheduled Tribes in the position of chairpersons by providing reservation.

The Himachal Pradesh *Panchayati Raj* Act, 1994 gives greater importance to the *Gram Sabha*. A minimum of four general meetings on the first Sundays of January, April, July and October have been made mandatory and the family has been made the unit for determining the quorum of *Gram Sabha* meetings. For every ward, an *Upgram Sabha* has also been constituted, which must meet twice in a year to discuss local issues and to suggest viable solutions. It will also nominate 15 per cent of the families for the general *Gram Sabha* meeting, and one-third of the participants shall be women. The *Gram Panchayats* and *Panchayat Samitis* shall prepare development plans for their areas, which will be consolidated at the *Zila Parishad* level and submitted to the District Planning Committee (DPC). For efficient functioning of the PRIs, rules have been framed for setting up standing committees at all the three levels. Besides this, administrative and judicial powers have also been delegated to the *panchayats*.

Delegation of Powers and Functions

The state government devolved powers, functions and responsibilities relating to 15 departments, namely Agriculture, Animal Husbandry, Ayurveda, Education, Food and Supply, Forest, Health and Family Welfare, Horticulture, Industries, Irrigation and Public Health, Public Works, Revenue, Rural Development and Social and Women's Welfare, to the PRIs on 31 July 1996. These powers relate mainly to planning and execution and monitoring of schemes.

The government has empowered the *Gram Panchayats* to enquire and give reports on grassroot level government functionaries, such as peon, bailiff, constable, head constable, *chowkidar*, patrol of the irrigation department, forest guard, *patwari*, vaccinator, canal overseer, *gram sewak*, *gram* watcher and *panchayat* secretary. The panchayats are also empowered to hear and decide cases relating to minor offences under the Indian Penal Code (IPC). In reality, the *Gram Panchayats* have been delegated powers only to report on the physical attendance of grassroots level functionaries such as *patwaris*, forest guards, school teachers, water carriers, water guards and *panchayat* secretaries in their assigned areas of work.

The other important delegated functions are:

- *Gram Panchayats* are empowered to hear and decide cases relating to minor offences under the IPC.
- *Gram Sabhas* have been empowered to consider and make recommendations and suggestions to *gram panchayats* in respect of the annual statement of accounts, and other related issues.
- Constitution of vigilance committees of the *Gram Sabha* to supervise the works, schemes and other activities of the *Gram Panchayat*.
- Delegation of powers to the *Gram Panchayats* to execute works up to the value of Rs. 50,000 without any external sanction and development works costing up to Rs. 5 lakh to be executed by the *Gram Panchayat*.

TABLE 13.10

Recommendation of First State Finance Commission

(1996-97 to 2000-01)

Devolved Functions		*Grants*		*Taxes*
I. Delegated functions of:	= 3750.00	1. Honorarium		1) Raise resources through taxes and levies
(1) Agri Deptt		(a) GPs representatives = 788.95	808.40	
(2) Animal Husbandry		(b) PSs representatives = 19.45		
(3) Agurveda & Homeopaths				2) Fix minimum and maximum cash tax to be levied in the rural areas.
(4) Education		2. Office Expenses		
(5) Fishery		(a) GPs = 606.53	650.48	
(6) Forest		(b) PSs = 43.95		
(7) Health & Family Welfare				
(8) Horticulture		3. Construction of Zila Parishad Buildings		
(9) Industry			300.00	
(10) Irrigation & Public Health				
(11) Public Works				
(12) Rural Development				
(13) Social & Women Welfare				
II. Rural Infrastructure Maintenance Corpus	= 1280.00			
(1 per cent of the capital cost of assets)				
Total	**= 5030.00**		**= 1758.88**	

- The *Panchayat Samitis* are supervising the implementation of Indira Awaas Yojana.
- The *Zila Parishads* will evaluate all poverty alleviation programmes and coverage of women, SC, ST and BPL families under these programmes.
- *Gram Panchayats* shall prepare micro-plans proposing development intervention which will be approved by the *Gram Sabha*.
- Formation of seven standing committees, namely Public Works Committee, Health and Welfare Advisory Committee, Village Education Committee, Forest Committee, Agriculture Production Committee, Irrigation and Public Health Committee and Food, Civil Supply and Consumers Committee.

Financial Devolution

The District Planning Committees (DPCs) have been constituted by the state government in all districts and ministers of the state government have been designated as chairpersons of the DPCs. For empowering the PRIs and to make them financially sound, the state government has accepted most of the recommendations of the First Finance Commission. The Commission recommended the devolution of functions involving an expenditure of Rs. 5030 lakh for a period of five years from 1996-97 to 2000-01 (See Table 13.10). In its recommendations, the commission has suggested that the state government should consider fixing the maximum rates for each tax. The state government has allowed the *Gram Panchayats* to levy taxes, fees and duties in their areas subject to the maximum rates of such taxes specified by the government. The Second Finance Commission was constituted on 25 May 1999. According to the recommendations of the First State Finance Commission and the Tenth Finance Commission, Rs 8.05 crore is being released to the PRIs annually to discharge the delegated functions. The Eleventh Finance Commission has awarded Rs 1313.38 lakh annually for the period 2000 to 2005. The state government has earmarked an amount of Rs. 57.00 lakh for the construction of *Zila Parishad Bhawans*, Rs. 193.34 lakh to meet the office expenses of all the three tiers of PRIs and Rs. 689.65 lakh for honorarium to be paid to the elected representatives of PRIs. In addition, the state government is also providing a grant of Rs. 561.17 lakh on account of honorariums to *panchayat chowkidars*, *panchayat sahayaks*, tailoring mistresses and junior engineers of the *Panchayats*.

Himachal Pradesh is one of the states of India, which give a monthly honorarium to the elected representatives of PRIs. It gives an honorarium of Rs. 2700, Rs. 1250 and Rs. 750 to the chairpersons of *Zila Parishads*, *Panchayat Samitis* and *Gram Panchayats* respectively. For the vice-chairpersons of all the three tiers, the monthly honorarium is Rs. 1800, Rs. 1000 and Rs. 650 respectively. Members of *Zila Parishads* and *Panchayati Samitis* are given Rs. 1250 and Rs. 750 each as monthly honorarium. Members of *Panchayats* receive an honorarium of Rs 100 per meeting up to two meetings in a month.

TABLE 13.11

Revenue and Expenditure of *Gram Panchayats*: Comparison

Particulars	*Himachal Pradesh*	*Punjab*
No. of *Gram Panchayats*	3037	12369
Rural Population per *Panchayat*	1800	1320
Average No. of *Panchayat* Members (including *Pardhan* & *Up-Pardhan*)	8	7
Revenue		
i) Revenue of (2001-02) (in lakh)	7958	18732*
ii) Revenue per *Panchayat* (in lakh)	2.62	1.51
iii) Per capita Revenue (in Rs.)	145.00	115.00
iv) Percentage of Revenue Collection		
(a) Taxes	2.19	0.73
(b) Non Taxes	7.57	38.16
(c) Grants-in-aid	9024	61.11
Total	100.00	100.00
Expenditure		
(i) Expenditure (in lakh)	6564	14078
(ii) Expenditure per *Panchayat* (in lakh)	2.13	1.14
(iii) Per Capita Expenditure (in Rs.)	120.00	87.00
(iv) Percentage of Expenditure on		
(a) Office Expenditure	3.50	2.92
(b) Developmental & Other Activities	96.50	97.00
Total	100.00	100.00

Source: Annual Administrative Report (2001-02) Panchayati Raj Department, HP, Shimla.

Report of the Second Punjab State Finance Commission, Feb 2002, Government of Punjab, Chandigarh.

The financial resources of the PRIs are grants-in-aid from the government, house tax, tax on extraction and export of sand, stone, *bajri* and slates, excise cess, land revenue, water charges, one per cent contingency, interest money, *Teh-Bazari* from shopkeepers, service fees and income from own assets. Data show that only 2.09 per cent of the funds are generated by the PRIs through taxes and almost 90 per cent of the revenue comes from grants-in-aid from the centre or the state government and only eight per cent from other sources (Table 13.11).

The first State Finance Commission has done little to review the fiscal relations and to suggest a way to provide finances to the local bodies. The result has been apathy to implementing the recommendations and that has made the *Panchayats* dependent on resource transfers from the state. That is the reason why:

- Administrative support to the District Planning Committees is not forthcoming from the bureaucratic network. Political support too is not very enthusiastic. Untied funds should be given to the *panchayats* on a large scale so that development works could be started according to the needs of the people.
- Only certain functions, not powers, are being devolved to the *Panchayats*. Thus from the very beginning, the *Panchayats* have been treated as executing agencies. Even if powers are given to the PRIs, these cannot be brought into effect without a political will.
- Since the officials deputed to PRIs are not put under the direct administrative control of the *panchayats*, the officials working in a bureaucratic network take it for granted that there is no need to share power with the elected representatives of the PRIs.
- Devolution of administrative responsibility to the PRIs without a commensurate devolution of resources may result in limited reforms. Though, the State Finance Commission puts greater emphasis on internal revenue mobilisation, an effective and appropriate mechanism has not been suggested. However, rapid devolution of financial responsibility may create problems of accountability and resort to corrupt practices. Thus, a gradual approach for financial devolution in phases through proper institutional arrangements is appropriate to ensure proper accountability.
- Expenditure assignments need to be more decentralised than revenue collection. Further, greater local accountability and direct visibility of

benefits at the local level encourage greater resource mobilisation. Often, effective decentralisation also fails to mobilise adequate local resources. Therefore, more than resource mobilisation, strengthening of the *Gram Sabha* to prevent misappropriation at the grassroot level is crucial.

- There are growing apprehensions among the leadership of different political parties about the participation as well as development related role of the elected representatives of the PRIs at the lower level, as the leaders may lose their political authority in rural development programmes. Therefore, the test of democratic decentralisation lies in the extent to which members of the *Gram Sabha* will participate in the political process and self-governance.

Moreover, the objectives of the *Panchayati Raj* System could be revitalised by transferring more funds, functions and functionaries as provided in the 73rd Constitutional Amendment Act-1992 and Himachal Pradesh *Panchayati Raj* Act, 1994. In the changed situation, the PRIs will have to be viewed as institutions of local self-government, not as implementing agencies for central and state government programmes, but as institutions that prepare and implement micro-plans. Active participation of women, the Scheduled Castes and Scheduled Tribes has to be ensured in decision-making so as to build, promote and empower a new leadership of these sections. For this, the PRIs will have to be strengthened with clarity about their role, the system of governance, accountability, transparency and interlinkages. Therefore, to strengthen the *Panchayati Raj* system and its institutions, the state must ensure effective transfer of functions, finances and functionaries to the PRIs, empowerment of the *Gram Sabhas*, and strengthening the District Planning Committees. There is also need to integrate the development funds allotted to members of Parliament with the funds of *Zila Parishads*, and to ensure training of all newly elected representatives within a year of their election and to organise refresher courses periodically. All this will add up to building the capacity of the PRIs and their members without which rural development will be slow and remain incomplete.

Capacity Building

Training

In order to make the representatives aware of their functions, powers and responsibilities, the state government has decided to impart training to all newly elected office-bearers of the PRIs from the first year of their tenure. Accordingly, office-bearers of *Zila Parishads* and Panchayat Samitis are imparted training at the Himachal Institute of Public Administration (HIPA), and members of *Panchayat Samitis* and chairpersons and vice-chairpersons of *Gram Panchayats* at the district level and at the Panchayati Raj Training Institutes at Baijnath and Mashobra. Training to the members of *Gram Panchayats* is provided at the block level. The state government has imparted training to one-fourth of the PRIs representatives since the election of these bodies in 2000. Of the 26,532 representatives, 61 per cent of the *Zila Parishads* members, 96 per cent of the *Panchayat Samiti* members, 26 per cent of the *Pardhans* and *Up-Pardhans* and 89 per cent of the *Panchayat* members are still without training.

Approaches to Training and Development for Capacity Building

The Panchayati Raj System in Himachal Pradesh is working under the guidelines set by the State Panchayati Raj Act. It is imperative to increase and upgrade the knowledge, administrative and technical skills, leadership qualities and governance capabilities of members of PRIs through education, research and training for planning and implementing programmes concerning the 29 subjects mentioned in the Eleventh Schedule. These subjects could further be clubbed into five clusters, viz., *agriculture and allied activities, rural industrialisation, infrastructure development, human development and social welfare; and gender development* (Annexure 1). Once these elected representatives are converted into more effective human resources, they will become the trainers for members of the *Gram Sabhas* (co-ruler in rural governance). This will convert every rural adult into a valuable human resource capable of accelerating the rural development process and its sustainability.

Though, the state government is making efforts to impart training to the representatives of the PRIs, it has not yet developed an integrated or holistic model for rural development. For this there is need for setting up or developing the existing centres for conducting research on issues and problems of the rural society and suggest viable solutions. These centres could impart training and education to representatives of local governance (PRIs), co-operatives (dairy, fishery, forest, floriculture, tourism and processing), *Mahila Mandals, Parivar Kalyan Salahkar Samitis*, Youth Clubs and other

TABLE 13.12

Action Plan for Education, Training and Empowerment of the Elected Representation of PRIs

Particulars	*No. of PRIs*	*Total No. of Elected Representatives*	*Proposed No. of Workshops*	*Expenditure Per Participant (in Rs.)*	*Total Expenditure Required (in Rs.)*
Gram Panchayats	3037	24623	492	1500	3,69,34,500
Panchayats Samiti	75	1658	75	2000	33,16,000
Zila Parishads	12	251	12	2500	6,27,500
Total	**3124**	**26532**	**579**	-	**4,08,78,000**

Note: Based on CRRID's Training Programme.

stakeholders if any, about their role and responsibilities and also promote appropriate rural technologies and skills for human development. At present, Himachal Pradesh needs a long-term policy for the development of human resources, through education, training and empowerment of grassroot level institutions, especially PRIs, and creation of a congenial socio-economic, institutional and political environment. Himachal Pradesh has two training institutes, at Baijnath and at Mashobra, which cater mainly to the training needs of development functionaries of *Panchayats* and the office-bearers of *Zila Parishads, Panchayats Samitis* and *Panchayats*. These are grossly inadequate to meet the training requirements of the elected representatives of *Gram Panchayats*. This conclusion is derived from the experience of CRRID in conducting the training and education workshops for representatives of PRIs in Punjab.

At present, Himachal Pradesh has 24,623, 1658 and 251 members of *Gram Panchayats, Panchayats Samitis* and *Zila Parishads* respectively. An estimated sum of Rs. 4 crore will be needed for a one-time training programme (Table 13.12). It is also necessary to build a reorientation-training programme, for which a separate budget should be worked out every year.

Course Contents of PRI Training

The *Panchayati Raj* system is meant not only for decentralisation of power and the people's participation but also for accelerating rural development and strengthening the planning process at the micro level. The PRIs have been made responsible for promoting development and social activities, which are listed in the 11th Schedule of the 73rd constitutional amendment. This is an integrated model of economic development with social justice, based on a decentralised planning system. Therefore, for rural development and decentralised planning, proper training of the representatives is necessary. This should include:

- *Panchayati Raj* concept, historical perspective, main features of the 73rd Constitutional Amendment and the Himachal Pradesh Panchayati Raj Act.
- *Gram Sabha* and its role.
- *Gram Panchayat*: powers, functions and responsibilities.
- Power and responsibilities of *Pardhans, Up-pardhans* and members of *panchayats*.
- *Gram Panchayat* meetings, quorum, agenda preparation and its circulation, rules and regulations for maintaining discipline and taking decisions.
- Statutary committees and sub-committees.
- Duties and responsibilities of the *panchayat* secretary.
- Rural development, central and state sponsored programmes and schemes.
- Maintenance of records: cashbooks, receipt books and assets created.
- Concern for environmental degradation, especially deforestation.
- Planning, its need and relevance, multilevel decentralised planning process of the village plan, its formulation and implementation.
- Preparation of budget, its approval and execution and resource mobilisation.
- Rules, regulations and procedures for purchases, maintenance of accounts and audit of accounts.
- People's participation in the development process.
- Gender issues.
- Rural leadership: emerging patterns in rural leadership, importance of democratic values and ethics in grassroot level leadership.

- Good governance; role of *panchayat* and village functionaries.
- Computer application in local governance.
- Social and other problems: their management by the *panchayat*.
- Co-ordination with Non-Government Organisations and other bodies.
- Social mobilisation, human resource development through skill formation, promotion of education and health infrastructure/facilities and protection of the interests of those in the grip of grinding poverty and indebtedness.

Some Other Socio-economic Factors

The social factors that dominate the style of living and the working of the state, when compared with Indian standards, are better in some respects but there is need for restructuring the following areas, according to the spirit of decentralisation, and for overall rural development of the state.

Indigenisation of Rural Education

In the light of the 73rd Constitutional Amendment time has come when rural development programmes must take the lead. The National Council of Rural Institutes (NCRI) has started considering introduction of rural higher education programmes, primarily based on the New Education (*Nai Talim*) concept in accordance with local needs. The people have not so for been made part of the mainstream higher education, covering research, teaching, extension and networking. With the introduction of such rural education programmes, the *Panchayai Raj* system will get the required strength for understanding and resolving local problems. Rural problems of Himachal Pradesh, are different from those of other states. In the context of rural development, indigenisation of concepts and theories is essential for understanding and resolving the issues that confront the state government, the PRIs and the stakeholders. This calls for social science research in Indian experience and reality, particularly relating to the rural areas. Such an approach in social science research is likely to bring rural transformation at a faster pace.

Rural Industrialisation

In the present situation, rural development requires a positive change in the rural areas both qualitatively and quantitatively. This is possible only by providing gainful employment utilisation of local resources, introduction of modern-technology industries and micro planning under the *Panchayati Raj* setup with decentralisation of finances and delegation of powers.

To explore employment opportunities in the rural areas, there is need for a study of the potential of rural industrialisation in the context of the 73rd amendment. The demand for encouraging the setting up of rural industrial enterprises is going to be generated with the mandate to plan and implement the work plan on subjects transferred to the PRIs. A close look at the 29 subjects in the Eleventh Schedule provides a clear picture of the potential of setting up all types of industries in the rural areas. Now is the time for the state government to consider it seriously. The state government should also hold dialogue with international organisations like the International Labour Organisation (ILO) and the corporate sector or big industrial houses to work out operational plans for capacity building and clearly designed operational strategies for promoting enterprises for the manufacture of products, demand for which is going to be generated by decentralised activities. The operational strategy is sure to get the support of the central government in view of its plan to have a National Programme for Rural Industrialisation (NPRI) and to set up 100 rural clusters every year to give a boost to rural industrialisation in the context of a rural-urban integrated economic complex. Besides the promotion of cottage industries and handicrafts, a good network of engineering and foundry industries, agro-based and livestock based industries can be created in Una, Hamirpur, Kangra, Bilaspur, Sirmaur and Solan districts. The districts of Kullu, Shimla, Chamba, Mandi, Bilaspur and Solan are suitable for horticulture and forest-based industries. The tribal areas of Kinnaur, Lahaul-Spiti and Chamba, besides Kullu and Shimla, are suitable for handicraft units.

The slow growth of the rural non-farm sector can be attributed to the low CD ratio (24.4 in 2000) in rural Himachal Pradesh (Table 13.13). This sector has the potential of generating more employment. There is need for providing credit to village-based cottage and small-scale industries, agro-processing units, transport and other services.

In the absence of an institutionalised banking system, the rural people especially the marginal farmers and the underprivileged sections, such as the Schedule Castes and Scheduled Tribes approach moneylenders and traders for their credit needs. It has been seen that

TABLE 13.13

Number of Branches, Deposits and Credit Deposit Ratio in All Commercial Banks for the Year 1990 and 2000

(Rs. in lakh)

Name of the State/India	*Nature of Bank Branches*	*No. of Branches*		*Deposits*		*Credits*		*Credit-Deposits Ratio (%)*	
		1990	*2000*	*1990*	*2000*	*1990*	*2000*	*1990*	*2000*
Himachal Pradesh	**Rural**	**626 (88.3)**	**657 (84.5)**	**83916 (69.4)**	**394326 (63.9)**	**29512 (67.4)**	**96285 (68.1)**	**35.2**	**24.40**
	Total	**709**	**778**	**120970**	**617464**	**43810**	**141372**		
Haryana	Rural	736 (57.8)	697 (46.7)	85505 (24.9)	344318 (20.2)	58109 (28.0)	143535 (20.3)	67.95	41.68
	Total	1273	1491	343324	1705250	207801	706137		
Maharastra	Rural	2491 (43.7)	2309 (37.1)	148237 (4.5)	602134 (3.9)	111083 (4.9)	351640 (2.7)	74.93	58.40
	Total	5689	6216	3281284	15299611	2276369	12820100		
All-India	**Rural**	**34184 (56.50)**	**32719 (50.00)**	**2623364 (15.3)**	**12044675 (14.6)**	**1606785 (15.4)**	**4739602 (10.1)**	**61.25**	**39.35**
	Total	**60515**	**65521**	**1719439**	**82213276**	**10431193**	**46903171**		

Source: Banking Statistics, Basic Statistical Returns Volume 19 March 1990. *Banking Statistics, Quarterly Handout* – March 2000.

Note: Figures in parentheses represent the share in rural region to the total of all the regions.

such credit does not help in capital formation and is used for consumption and meeting the daily needs of the rural people, which has not helped the growth of the non-farm sector.

At this stage, micro-credit may become a successful programme to realise the social agenda of the banking sector. Here, the role of the PRIs, co-operatives and NGOs can be acknowledged as a catalyst. These bodies can stand for guarantee for the loans advanced to 'Self Help Groups'. This will ensure timely repayment and reduce the cost through participatory approach.

Rural Informatics

Information technology is an integral part of the future development process, especially for rural development and so are the new concepts and contents of 'Governance Information Technology'. The Seventh Five Year Plan Document (1985-90) has recognised that information technology has a facilitative role to play in providing information about the Intensive Rural Development Programme, development problems and possibilities. All components of rural development, *viz.*, agricultural growth, infrastructure development, human resource development, rural industrialisation and grassroot level rural governance can directly or indirectly benefit from information technology by focusing attention on improvement of production, consumption and social services. Computerised information can be used in decision making at the village, block, and district levels, for maintaining land records, forestation, beneficiary details, development schemes, rural banking, rural environment and other socio-economic indicators; It has become necessary that information technology is made a part of the training of the rural youth.

Rural Poverty Alleviation Programme

The basic objectives of the poverty alleviation programme are to provide income-yielding assets and skills, to ensure employment opportunities; and to improve the quality of rural life. To achieve these objectives, several poverty alleviation schemes have been started from time to time. The emphasis in rural development has progressively shifted from growth to welfare and then from responsive to an integrated approach.

Poverty alleviation has always been the main agenda of the policy planning of successive governments in Himachal Pradesh. Various programmes of the central and state governments have been implemented. Due to these efforts, the poverty figure in the state, according to Planning Commission estimates, has been decreasing. In 1977-78, the percentage of the states population below the poverty line was 32.45, which came down to 16.39 in 1983, 15.46 in 1987-88 and 7.63 in 1999-2000 (Table 13.14). On the basis of a BPL survey, conducted by the state government in 1998-99, the percentage of families living below the poverty line has decreased from 42 in 1981 to 26.69 in 1998-99. The survey shows that of the 2,86,447 identified poor families, 1,06,468 (41.13%) belonged to the Scheduled Castes, 10,801 (4.17%) to the Scheduled Tribes and the remaining 1,41,590 (54.70%) were from other categories. The results indicate that poverty still persists in the state and its prevalence is more among the unprivileged sections of society consisting mainly of marginal and small farmers, agricultural labourers, rural artisans, the Scheduled Castes, the Scheduled Tribes, physically handicapped persons and women. Hence, more serious efforts are required for poverty alleviation and employment generation in the rural areas. The Tenth Five Year Plan of Himachal Pradesh envisages efforts to reduce poverty and provide rural employment to the poor. For this, the involvement of the PRIs in implementation, supervision, monitoring and evaluation shall be ensured. The PRIs and NGOs shall be closely associated in planning and execution of rural development programmes.

TABLE 13.14

Poverty Ratio in Himachal Pradesh and India

Year 1999-2000	*Poverty (Total)*	*Rural*	*Urban*
Himachal Pradesh			
1999-00	7.63	7.94	4.63
1993-94	28.44	30.34	9.18
1987-88	15.46	16.28	6.8
1983-87	16.39	17.00	9.25
1977-78	32.45	33.49	19.47
India			
1999-00	26.10	27.09	23.62
1993-94	35.97	37.27	32.36
1987-88	39.34	39.06	40.12
1983-87	44.76	45.61	42.15
1977-78	51.81	53.07	47.40

Source: Report of the Expert Group on Estimation and No. of Poor, Perspective Planning Division, Planning Commission, Government of India, New Delhi, July 1993. Planning Commission, Government of India.

The financial and physical achievements of some major centrally and state sponsored schemes during the plan periods are briefly discussed below:

Swaranjayanti Gram Swarozgar Yojana (SGSY)

The scheme aims at covering 30 per cent of the BPL families in each block during 1999-2000 to 2003-2004 and envisages that the monthly income of an assisted family will increase by at least Rs. 2,000. SGSY adopts a project approach for key activities. The selection of key activities is based on the cluster approach and resources, occupational skills and availability of markets.

For 2001-2002, a target of credit mobilisation of Rs. 20 crore was earmarked. Till March, 2002, 3588 individual *swarosgaris* were assisted and given Rs. 220.89 lakh and Rs. 966.67 lakh as subsidy and credit respectively. Besides this, 2707 groups were formed since the inception of the programme, of which 563 groups consisting of 5503 BPL members have been given Rs. 377.221 lakh and Rs. 1074.39 lakh as subsidy and credit respectively.

The physical progress of this scheme is shown in Table 13.15. The total number of swarosgaris assisted till to December 2002 was 33393 and the scheme particularly focuses on vulnerable groups among the rural poor. Accordingly, 38 per cent of the beneficiaries belong to the SCs, about 11 per cent to the STs and almost one half are women. The SGSY is being implemented by the DRDA through the *Panchayat Samitis*.

TABLE 13.15

Financial and Physical Achievement under SGSY

	1999-00 to 2002-03 (Rs. in lakh)	*Per cent to Total*
Total Funds Available	3364.54	—
Total Expenditure	2446.152	72.59
Total Beneficiaries/ Swarogaries Assisted (No.)	33393	—
SCs	12715	38.07
STs	3802	11.38
Women	16732	50.11
Handicapped	129	0.38
No. of Groups Formed	4613	—
No. of Women SHGs Formed	390	—
No. of SHGs taken up Economic Activities	1479	—
No. of Women SHGs taken up Economic Activities	158	—

A total of 4613 Self Help Groups have been formed, of which 390 are women's groups. The performance of utilisation of central allocation is satisfactory. The projects/schemes, being taken up by the groups or individual *swarosgaris* have been selected keeping in view the backward and forward linkages.

Sampoorn Grameen Rozgar Yojana (SGRY)

The objectives of the SGRY are to provide additional wage employment and food security, in the rural areas along with the creation of durable community, social and economic assets and infrastructure. The programme is self-targeting and will be available to all the rural poor (BPL/APL) who are in need of wage employment and are willing to engage in it. Preference will be given to the poorest among the poor, women, SCs/STs and parents of child labour withdrawn from hazardous occupations.

Under the scheme, 5 kg of foodgrains (in kind) is to be distributed as part of the wage per manday. The remaining part of the wages is to be paid in cash to ensure the notified minimum wage.

SGRY is Executed in Two Streams

The first stream is being implemented at the district and intermediate *Panchayat* level; 50 per cent of the funds are to be earmarked (out of the total funds available under the SGSY) for distribution between the *Zila Parishads* and intermediate-level *Panchayats* (*Panchayat Samitis*) in the ratio of 40:60. (Of the 50 per cent funds under the first stream, 20 per cent are to be utilised by the *Zila Parishads* and 30 per cent by the intermediate-level *Panchayats*)

The second stream is being implemented at the Village *Panchayat* level; 50 per cent of the funds available under the SGSY are earmarked for the Village *Panchayats* and for distribution among *Gram Panchayats* through the *Zila Parishads* or DRDAs. The funds are so allocated as to ensure that each *Panchayat* receives a minimum of Rs. 50,000/-.

Physical progress under the two streams is shown in Table 13.16. Table 13.17 shows details of food-grains made available and their utilisation.

TABLE 13.16

Physical Progress (Stream I & II) of SGRY

Category	*Steam I*		*Steam II*	
	Lakh Manday Generated	*Percentage*	*Lakh Mandays Generated*	*Percentage*
SC	3.08	41	2.52	42
ST	0.73	10	0.87	14
Other	3.66	49	2.60	44
Total	7.47	-	5.99	-
Women	0.37	5	0.35	6
Landless	-	-	-	-

Source: Department of Rural Development, Himachal Pradesh.

TABLE 13.17

Foodgrain Availability and Utilisation under SGRY (Stream I & II) during 2002-03

(Foodgrains in tonnes)

Stream	*Total Availability of Foodgrains Based on Lifting*	*Foodgrains Utilised*	*% age*
I	7828.65	3809.77	49
II	5446.77	3059.40	56

Source: Department of Rural Development, Himachal Pradesh.

*Reasons for Slow Progress of the Scheme**

- In this hilly state some areas are far-flung and snow bound. Therefore, the working season is very limited.
- Foodgrains allocated under the scheme have often been received two three months after the issue of sanction letter by the Ministry of Rural Development, Government of India.
- The scheme could not pick up in the introductory year of the scheme. Implementing agencies (PRIs) have taken a long time for approval of shelf of work.
- The lifting of foodgrains is slow due to late release by the Food Corporation of India. Hence, the Ministry of Food and Consumer Affairs, Government of India, should ensure quick release of foodgrains so that these are lifted on time.
- Under the directions of the Government of India, 5 kg. of foodgrains per manday are being distributed as part of the wages. The targeted persons in the state are also getting foodgrains under other schemes. Therefore, it is suggested that the state may be permitted to distribute 3 kg. of foodgrains per manday under this scheme.
- The Government of India releases funds under the two streams in two equal instalments. As the funds are not sufficient to start a durable infrastructure, it is suggested that these should be released in one instalment.
- The labourers should be given the option to get foodgrains or wages in cash. If they are forced to accept foodgrains, they may sell these, which will defeat the purpose of the scheme.

Jawahar Gram Samridhi Yojana (JGSY)

JGSY is the restructured, streamlined and comprehensive version of the erstwhile Jawahar Rozgar Yojana (JRY). Designed to improve the quality of life of the poor, JGSY was launched on 1 April 1999.

The primary objective of JGSY was to create a demand-driven community village infrastructure, including durable assets at the village level and, to increase opportunities for sustained employment for the rural poor. The secondary objective was the generation of supplementary employment for the unemployed poor in the rural areas.

* As envisaged by Department of Rural Development, Himachal Pradesh.

TABLE 13.18

District-wise Physical and Financial Progress under SGSY Special Projects Component "Installation of Hydrams"

District	*Target Fixed*	*Sites Selected/ Approved*	*Hydrams Procured*	*Expnd. (Rs. in lakh)*	*Installed in Year 2000-01*	*Installed in 2001-02/ 2002 -03*	*Total Hydrams Installed*	*Under Installation/ Work in Progress*	*Expnd. (Rs. in lakh)*
Bilaspur	30	10	17	16.32	1	9	10		8.142
Chamba	30	5	5	4.80	1	4	5		0.462
Hamirpur	20								
Kangra	30	26	15	14.40		7	7		Nil
Kinnaur	10								
Kullu	50	60	28	26.88					
Lahaul & Spiti	10								
Mandi	80	30	57	54.72		27	27		8.80
Shimla	60	45	45	43.20					
Sirmaur	30	2	5	4.80		1	1		0.23
Solan	30	39	9	8.64		6	6		2.20
Una	20	9	7	6.72		2	2		1.96
H.P.	**400**	**226**	**181**	**180.48**	**2**	**56**	**58**		**21.794**

Source: Department of Rural Development, HP.

This programme is being implemented by village *Panchayats* and executed with the approval of the *Gram Sabha* of the village concerned.

The Government of India had fixed a target of generating 11.74 lakh mandays in 2001-02, against which 13.899 lakh mandays were generated and Rs. 1219.06 lakh was spent on the *yojana*.

Prime Minister's Gramodaya Yojana (PMGY)

PMGY was launched in 2000-01 with the objective of achieving sustainable human development at the village level. Additional central assistance is being received and earmarked for various components of this *yojana*. PMGY aims at consolidating the gains of the earlier BMS programme and further improving and strengthening rural infrastructure facilities. Rs. 70 crore has been approved and earmarked for this *yojana* during the 2002-03 annual plan. The state has been allocated Rs. 60 crore for 2002-03 under PMGY, exclusively for rural roads. Besides this, PMGY funds are used for the development of primary health (18.57%), primary education (8.71%), rural drinking water supply (56.14%), nutrition (15%) and rural electrification (1.57%).

SGSY Special Projects

Installation of HYDRAMS: The Government of India had approved a project for installation of 400 hydrams in 1999-2000 with a total project cost of Rs. 1047.20 lakh, which includes a subsidy of Rs. 770.48 lakh, Rs. 161.40 lakh as loan and Rs. 115.32 lakh as beneficiary share. Till March, 2002, 226 sites had been selected and approved. Only 58 hydrams have been installed and Rs. 202.27 lakh spent on them. The district-wise physical and financial progress of this project is shown in Table 13.18.

Apart from this, there was a programme to install hydrams to develop waste and marginal lands through the application of appropriate technology, extension and training in the districts of Kullu and Shimla, under this programme. A target of 200 hydrams was fixed; 170 sites were selected/approved and 100 hydrams were procured in 2001-02. Only 72 hydrams were installed at an expense of Rs. 88.46 during this period.

Gold mines project: The Government of India approved in 2000-01 a project on gold mines in Bilaspur district as an SGSY special project. Three activities, floriculture, sericulture and mushroom cultivation, are being taken up under this project at a total expense of Rs. 840.35 lakh. The project was to run for two years and had a target of 900 beneficiaries. Till December, 2002, Rs. 152.243 lakh was spent on the development of these activities. The progress made till December, 2002, is shown in Table 13.19.

Marketing of rural goods: The Central Government approved in 2001-02 another project as SGSY special project component with a total project cost of Rs. 914.52 lakh. Under this project 50 Himachal Gramin Bhandars and one Central Gramin Bhandar are being constructed in the state. Till March, 2002, 29 sites of these *Bhandars* were selected and construction on 21 sites was completed. Construction on 12 sites was awarded to contractors. An expenditure of Rs. 20 lakh has been incurred till March, 2002. It is suggested that construction activity under this project should be given to PRIs instead of private contractors.

Milch livestock improvement: To promote dairy farming activities, the Government of India has approved a project on milch livestock improvement in Solan district, the total cost of which is Rs. 886.95 lakh. The project will run for five years and is targeted to benefit 10,000 families. The progress made till December, 2002, is shown in Table 13.20.

TABLE 13.19

Gold Mines Project: Progress Made up to December 2002

Sericulture Production	*Targets of Farmers to be Assisted*	*Cases Sanctioned*	*Subsidy (Rs. in lakhs)*	*Loan (Rs. in lakhs)*
Gladiolus Farming	100	18	3.346	5.544
Carnation Farming	100	16	4.50	7.05
Mushroom Cultivation	200	34	8.50	32.54
Sericulture Production	500	282	53.523	127.59

Source: Department of Rural Development, HP.

TABLE 13.20

Milch Livestock Improvement Project: Progress Made upto December 2002

Name of the Component	*Expenditure Incurred (Rs. in lakh)*	*Physical Progress*
Extension & Training	12.00	6385 cattles treated in 92 field level camps. 448 breeder imparted training. 45 Vet Officials trained
Breeding Efficiency Improvement	4.34	Equipments
Genetic Improvement	7.13	Do
Young Stock Rearing	9.75	—
Improvement of Fodder Production	1.21	Procurement of seeds
Milch Livestock Management	17.64	Mineral mixtures, medicines etc.
Marketing	03.65	Equipment
Monitoring Vehicles	16.04	Advts., tenders, honorarium,
Total	**71.76**	

Source: Department of Rural Development, Himachal Pradesh.

Rural development through diversification of agriculture in Mandi district: The project, started in November, 2001, was to run for four years and its total cost was Rs. 1385.32 lakh. It will benefit 36,365 individuals. An expenditure of Rs. 148.06 lakh has been incurred till March, 2002.

The main activities under this diversification project are:

- Cultivation of medicinal and aromatic plants, flowers and orchards
- Sericulture
- Innovative practices in animal husbandry

The physical and financial progress of this programme is shown in Table 13.21.

Other special component projects under SGSY are Green Gold in Chamba district, Self-reliance through Sericulture and Dairy Development in Hamirpur district, and Intensive Dairy Development Project in Kangra district.

Issues Relating to SGSY Special Project Component

- Hundred per cent subsidy is given under wasteland development project, whereas under SGSY Special Projects, a loan component is also involved. The Government of India has asked the state government to surrender the special project on hydrams, if it is not implemented properly. The state government wants to continue this project and has requested the central government to provide 100 per cent subsidy for this project also.
- Special projects augment the resources and to get the maximum benefit, a period should not be imposed. Rather the quality of the output should be the criterion to judge the success of the projects.

Watershed Development Projects

The objective of these projects is to promote economic development of the village community and to check the adverse effects of drought by restoring the ecological balance and generating employment for the people of watershed area.

Under the Integrated Wastelands Development Project, funds worth 33.32 per cent of the total cost have been released. Of the released funds, 71.11 per cent have been utilised for the improvement of 21.36 per cent of the area targeted under the Desert Development Programme; 36.78 per cent of the total cost of the project has been released and of the released funds, 79.47 per cent have been utilised for treating 25.91 per cent of the total targeted area. Under the Drought Prone Area Programme, 36.52 per cent of the total cost of the project has been released. Of released funds, 65.25 per cent have been utilised for treating 44.55 per cent of the total targeted area.

TABLE 13.21

Physical and Financial Progress

Activity	*Physical Achievement*	*Financial Achievements (Rs. in lakh)*
Cultivation of medicinal plants, aromatic plants and flowers	1. One poly house has been constructed, another one is under construction and the remaining eight are yet to be completed.	32.21
	2. Three demonstration farms have been established for the plantation of medicinal and aromatic plants.	
	3. 2500 orchids have been planted. 9000 chrysanthemums of nine different varieties have been planted and successful rooting and multiplication of these plants have been achieved. About 16,000 chrysanthemums have been sent to Delhi and Chandigarh markets for sale.	
	4. One tissue culture laboratory is under construction for training SHGs in tissue culture.	
	5. A district level society, namely, "The Mandi District Herbs and Flower Promotion Society", has been set up.	
	Total	**32.21**
Sericulture	1. Establishment of three technical service stations has been undertaken by the District industry Centre, Sericulture wing, Mandi.	21.67
	2. Five hundred new families (in SHGs mode) have been identified for taking up this activity.	
	3. Short-term training camps are being organised by the DRDA.	
	Total	**21.67**
Innovative practices in animal husbandry	1. Livestock survey is being carried out.	
	2. All the equipment required under the project for upgradation of 105 artificial insemination centres has been procured.	91.18
	Total	**91.18**
	Grand Total	**145.06**

Source: Department of Rural Development, HP.

TABLE 13.22

Physical and Financial Achievements (till September 2002)

Programme	*Project Cost (in lakh)*	*No. of Watersheds*	*Targeted Area (in Hec.)*	*Total Funds Released (in lakh)*	*Total Expenditure (in lakh)*	*Total Area Treated (in Hec.)*
Integrate Wasteland Dev. Project	13971.79	422	261666	4656.04 (33.32)*	3310.58 (71.11)**	55890.27 (21.36)***
Desert Dev. Programme	10496.00	371	117098	3860.629 (36.78)*	3068.05 (79.47)**	30339.97 (25.91)***
Drought Prone Area Programme	6430.00	238	79866	2348.11 (36.52)*	1532.217 (65.25)**	35579.04 (44.55)***

Source: Department of Rural Development and Panchayat, Himachal Pradesh.

Note: * % taken with total project cost.

** % taken with total funds released.

*** % taken with total targeted area.

Details of physical and financial achievements under these three programmes are given in Table 13.22.

Issues

- The Central government while sanctioning a project, insists that forest land should not be more than 25 per cent and private land not more than 50 per cent. It is suggested that watershed, should cover all types of land, whether forest, private, community or government, because it is a geo-hydrological unit.
- The cost norms should be revised because of hard and peculiar geographical conditions, particularly under the DDP, being executed in the tribal districts of Lahaul & Spiti and Kinnaur. It is also suggested that per hectare cost under IWDP and DPAP should also be increased, considering the geographical conditions of the state.

- Besides other activities relating to water harvesting structures, irrigation schemes should also be allowed to be taken up under the watershed development project, because nothing can be grown in hilly areas without assured irrigation.
- Instead of creating a parallel body i.e. Watershed Association or Watershed Committee, a single *Panchayat* should be given jurisdiction to execute the projects through user groups, SHGs and the village community.
- For the sustainability of the project, the *gram panchayats* and other local level institutions, such as *Mahila Mandals, Yuvak Mandals*, SHGs should be involved in post-project maintenance.
- For capacity building, the DRDA should ensure that relevant time-bound training programmes are organised for all functionaries.
- Desilting should be a continuing activity, as the problem of silting is a perennial problem.

Problems are faced by watershed projects in winter because much of the area remains under snow for three to four months.

Desert Development Project, Pooh, District Kinnaur
A Journey towards success

The watershed guidelines impress upon the implementation of all watershed-based programmes with active participation of the community. However, till I joined the project in May 2000, community participation was nil. Rather, the community was not even aware of the full form of DDP, as a result the community gave several sarcastic names to the project, depending upon the results on the ground, such as ***Dat Ke Dakaro Paisa, Dat ke Daru Piyo,*** etc. No community participation was possible without awareness of the community, organisation of the community into watershed associations/committees, user groups and SHGs, training of the functionaries at all levels. When I joined the project, there were four functionaries at the PIA level, only two Junior Engineers to implement 32 watershed projects, no watershed committees.

One year and 10 months after I took over the project in March 2002, 102 micro watershed projects were in hand with an allocation of Rs. 2900 lakh. (Once the project was streamlined and the desired level of expenditure was achieved, 70 new watershed projects were sanctioned for Pooh) Now, there are 12 official functionaries at the PIA level, three watershed development teams (civil engineer team 12 members), Agri/Horticulture/Forestry team six experts, community organisation team, five community organisers, 35 watershed associations have been organised after generating detailed awareness in the community. The watershed associations have one male and one female member from each household of the watershed area; all watershed committees have been formed by watershed associations unanimously and these committees have appointed watershed chairmen for all watershed committees. Watershed associations have further organised user groups, which are the actual implementing agencies. The community organisers of the project have formed 60 SHGs, which are functioning ideally. These groups hold their monthly meetings regularly. Thrift and credit norms are being followed regularly. 45 groups have been given revolving funds after proper gradation by watershed development team members. This success is due to the seven day training, which was imparted to WDT members, watershed chairmen and secretaries. The Desert Development Project (DDP) now is working on the modalities of taking up some income-generating activities by exploiting the existing potential of the area. The identified activities are traditional handloom cottage industry, potato chips, chulli oil, horticulture-based cottage industry and medicinal herbs.

The community has now understood the concept of a holistic development approach. After the awareness campaign, exposure visits to other successful watershed areas and training of the community as a whole, the community has felt that watershed means not water or installation of tanks as kuhls only, it is more than this. There is need for mass scale plantations in the watershed areas. Technology for raising vegetables during winter has been learnt and the community has decided to adopt trench cultivation during winter for vegetables production. It is hoped that within the project period the entire watershed area can be covered under a modern drip/sprinkler irrigation system.

— CAPT. J.M. PATHANIA
Project Director
DDP, Pooh

Indira Awaas Yojana (IAY)

Under this centrally sponsored scheme an assistance of Rs. 22000 is given to a below- poverty line (BPL) family to construct a house. Earlier, the financial assistance was provided only for construction of a new house but, since 1999-2000, an assistance of Rs. 10,000 is also provided for conversion/upgradation of a *kutcha* house in to a semi-*pucca/pucca* house. The financial and physical performance of the scheme in the state is given in Tables 13.23 and 13.24

- The selection of the beneficiaries is done strictly by the *Gram Sabha*.
- The beneficiaries are motivated to complete the houses on time.
- The findings of the Concurrent Evaluation of IAY have been circulated to all DRDAs for strict compliance.

- Sanitary latrines are constructed in every house under IAY.

TABLE 13.23

Financial Performance (Rs in lakh)

Total Available Funds	Expenditure				
	SC	ST	SC+ST	Other	Total
553-788	161.13	20.02	181.15	181.986	363.136 (82%)

Source: Department of Rural Development, HP.

TABLE 13.24

Physical Achievements

Target	Houses Completed					Houses Upgradated
	SC	ST	SC+ST	Other	Total	
3901	559	74	633	482	1115	2834

Source: Department of Rural Development, HP.

It is suggested that the present limit of Rs. 22,000 should be raised to Rs. 40,000 due to the specific geographical conditions of the state.

Credit-cum Subsidy Housing Scheme

This scheme was launched on 1 April 1999, and it aims financing the construction of houses for the SCs/STs and the freed bonded labourers. The scheme is being implemented in rural areas five km away from the towns. The target groups under the scheme are rural households having an annual income up to Rs. 32,000. However, BPL households are given preference. In 2001-2002, 158 houses were constructed against a target of 155 houses for which Rs. 67.69 lakh was given as credit and Rs. 19.88 lakh as subsidy.

Other housing schemes implemented in the state are:

- Innovative Rural Housing Scheme in Sirmaur district.
- Innovative Rural Housing Project in Kullu district.
- Innovative Housing Project at Solan.
- SAMAGRA Awas Yojana in Sirmaur district.

Restructured Central Rural Sanitation Programme

The Government of India restructured the Central Rural Sanitation Programme in April 1999, and reduced the subsidy from Rs. 2000 to Rs. 500. A total of 353 schools and women complexes and 38 individual latrines were constructed in 2001-02 at a total expenditure of Rs. 55.73 lakh. Under the sanitation campaign in Sirmaur district, 77 sanitary complexes for women and school sanitation and 13 individual latrines were constructed at an expenditure of Rs. 34.27 lakh.

The other important centrally sponsored schemes implemented in the state are:

- National Social Assistance Programme; National Old-Age Pension Scheme, and National Family Benefit Scheme.
- NORAD aided project titled Environmental Conservation through *Mahila Mandals* in the districts of Hamirpur, Kullu and Solan.
- Rural building centres for DRDA, Hamirpur, Kangra, Bilaspur and Mandi.

State Plan Schemes

Besides the Centrally sponsored schemes, the government of Himachal Pradesh has been implementing various welfare schemes for poor families. These are:

- Chief Ministers Gratuity Scheme
- Rural Housing
- Rural Sanitation
- Social Audit Scheme and
- Mahila Mandal Protsahan Yojana

Monitoring and Evaluation

Progress under different rural development programmes is reviewed at various meetings by the Ministry of Rural Development at the Chief Secretary and Secretary levels. The state government has started a process to hold district level review meetings under the chairmanship of the Chief Secretary, where the progress of different rural development programmes is reviewed.

An evaluation study on IRDP was assigned to evaluation division of the Planning Department in the year 2000 for assessment of the implement of this programme in the Eighth Five Year Plan period (1992-97). The main findings were as under;

- The names of the majority of the beneficiaries (99.42%) were approved by *Gram Sabha* which shows that selection of beneficiaries has been done according to the guidelines as poorest of the poor families were given priority in providing assistance.

- Out of the total assisted beneficiaries, 51.66 per cent covered under primary sector activities, 7.44 per cent under secondary sector activities and remaining 40.90 per cent under tertiary sector activities. The more coverage under primary sector was due to the reason that in rural areas people concentrate on dairy farming and other allied agricultural activities.
- Majority of the beneficiaries (98.43%) face no difficulties in obtaining loan.
- Majority of the beneficiaries (93.15%) reported that no training with regard to operational skill/ maintenance of assets was imparted to them.
- Majority of the beneficiaries (72.21%) has fully repaid their loan. Hence recovery position is quite satisfactory.
- Marketing facilities were available in the village for majority of the beneficiaries (84.31%)
- Majority of the beneficiaries (73.19%) were not able to derive annual income of Rs. 11,000 from the assets.
- It was found that none of the family members of the sample beneficiaries were employed under any other poverty alleviation programme.

The observations regarding implementation of various poverty alleviation programmes made during another CRRID project implemented in 88 *panchayats* of two blocks namely Nagrota Bagwan and Punchrukhi of Kangra district are as under:

- Failure to reach the right beneficiaries, pilferages and leakages, procedural difficulties, inadequate assistance, the beneficiaries using the money for other unproductive purposes, the problem of marketing the products, bank loan formalities, lack of proper information about the schemes, lack of training and human resource development.
- For proper identification of BPL families, the role of NGOs, *Panchayats* and the community must be ensured. Transparency can be ensured by the people's participation and proper training of the surveyors.

Sub-plans for the Development of Scheduled Castes, Scheduled Tribes and Backward Areas

Formation of a special component plan for the SCs and Sub-plans for the tribal and backward areas is an extension of the decentralised planning process. The main objective is to ensure the speedy, equitable and rational development of all areas.

Special Component Plan for Scheduled Castes

The Scheduled Castes in Himachal Pradesh account for almost one-fourth of the state's population and they are concentrated mostly in the districts of Bilaspur, Kullu, Mandi, Solan, Shimla and Sirmaur. These six districts have more than 60 per cent of the Scheduled Caste population of the state. Most of the Scheduled Caste families depend on agricultural pursuits and other low-income activities, such as sweeping, shoe-making, basket-making, weaving, blacksmithy, poultry and some similar occupations. A special component plan for the Scheduled Castes was initiated in 1979-80 for improving their living conditions and promoting their skills. Rs. 4.61 crore was earmarked for their development. During the Sixth Plan (1980-85) a thrust was given to this activity by providing 11 per cent of the total state plan outlay for the special component plan. The Tenth Five Year Plan (2002-07) approach paper clearly defines the goals and the strategy for improving the quality of life of the Scheduled Castes in the state. Literacy among the SCs is below the state average. It was 10 per cent less than the state average (only 53.20% in 1990-91). Among the women it was still lower (41.02%) as against the state average of 52.17 per cent. The sex ratio was also low at 967 against the state average of 976 in 1990-91. Since the implementation of the plan, there has been a marked improvement in the infant mortality rate, health services, literacy and skills among the Scheduled Caste families. Much remains to be done to improve their economic and social conditions by conserving their assets, providing them with land for tilling, upgrading their skills for improving productivity, ensuring the minimum agricultural wage, provision of minimum literacy and imparting of technical and entrepreneurial skills, and promoting their capacities in the areas of industrial and service sectors through self-empowerment programmes. Further, there is need for modernising their existing traditional occupations like shoe-making, leather processing, basket-making, carpentry and blacksmithy. On the social side, much more shall have to be done to liberate this section from untouchability, social discrimination and exploitation. There is need for basic amenities, such as safe drinking water, education and health, approachable roads and a better public distribution system in their habitations. There are almost 2613 villages (one-sixth of the total number of villages in the state) where more than 65 per cent of the population consists of the Scheduled Castes.

The outlay for the Scheduled Castes component plan for 2002-03 has worked out to Rs. 187 crore, which is 11 per cent of the total state plan. For the Tenth Five Year Plan, the outlay is Rs. 1046.65 crore.

Sub-Plan for Tribal Areas

Kinnaur and Lahaul and Spiti districts, besides the Pangi and Bharmaur tehsils of Chamba district, have been declared tribal areas. These tribal areas fall in the High Hill Zone having cold and dry weather conditions. More than 40 per cent of the geographical area of the state falls in the tribal belt which has a population of less than two lakh. During the last Plan period, almost one-eleventh of the state's plan outlay was allocated for the development of the tribal areas under the "Tribal Plan". The Tenth Five-Year Plan (2002-07) has envisaged in its approach paper the basic problems of the tribal people and implementation of protective and anti-exploitative measures for safeguarding their rights. The government has accorded the highest priority to education, health, promotion of social and cultural values of the local communities, sustainability of environment, creation of direct and indirect employment opportunities, involvement of PRIs in development activities, implementation of watershed development programmes for irrigation and the revival of handicrafts.

Yet, much remains to be done for protection of their land rights (when their land is acquired for major hydel projects, a feeling of alienation arises among them), promotion of credit facilities (due to non-institutional indebtedness, they pay heavy interest to money lenders), protection of forests (deforestation is creating economic, environmental and social problems in this tribal border zone) and rehabilitation of the displaced people. (A substantial number of the people shall have to be displaced from the catchment areas of major hydel projects). To improve the quality of their life, there is also need for poverty alleviation schemes implemented through tribal *panchayats*.

The outlays for tribal sub-plan for 2002-03 is Rs. 153 crore which is nine per cent of the total state plan. For the Tenth Plan, the outlay is Rs. 856.35 crore.

Sub-Plan for Backward Areas

This sub-plan was introduced by the state government during the Fifth Five Year Plan. The basic criterion for the identification of backward areas was remoteness and inaccessibility, besides the level of socio-economic development and infrastructure backwardness. The state government framed a comprehensive policy for the backward areas in 1995-96, and accorded special weightage to remoteness and inaccessibility (25 points), demographic indicators (35 points), infrastructure indicators (36 points) and agricultural indicators (4 points). The policy clearly elaborates the concept of backward areas, area-based plans, beneficiary-based plans, separate budgetary arrangements, administration of plans and categorisation of areas (three categories i.e. backward blocks (8), contiguous pockets (15) and dispersed *panchayats* (109). Of the 3037 *Gram Panchayats* in the State, 489 have been declared backward. More than four-fifths of the backward *panchayats* (84%) fall in the districts of Chamba, Kullu, Mandi and Shimla. Successful efforts have been made to develop rural infrastructure such as roads, power, irrigation, drinking water and credit facilities in these areas.

Fifteen per cent of sectoral outlay has been earmarked under this sub-plan for the development of agriculture, social conservation, horticulture, minor irrigation, food and civil supplies, animal husbandry, social forestry, rural electrification, education, general education, rural health, ayurveda and rural water supply.

These sub-plans are playing an effective role in modernising the rural economy of Himachal Pradesh and can be treated as an integral part of the development planning. Lastly, it can be said that rural development is a joint venture of the public, private, co-operative and corporate sectors. Any single sector cannot effectively tackle all the problems of rural development. Panchayati Raj Institutions, co-operatives, non-government organisations, private companies and corporations can jointly play an important role in the process of development by complementing and supplementing the functions and activities of the government.

Summary and Recommendations

Himachal Pradesh is a state where 90 per cent of the population lives in rural areas and almost 70 per cent depends on agriculture which contributes only 23 per cent to the Gross State Domestic Product at factor cost at constant prices (1993-94). No development can be successful if it is not built on the foundation of the rural sector. In view of this, there is urgent need for giving high priority to rural development, taking into account the following recommendations.

- Ensure effective dissemination of information, education and impart training to the elected representatives of the PRIs for good governance and management for overall rural development.

- Besides the elected representatives, government officials working with the PRIs too need to be trained. Though the government, non-government organisations and civil society groups are imparting such training, yet there is need for joint training so that the impact is more effective and transparent.
- Ensure co-ordination between *Panchayats*, government and NGOs to upgrade the skills of the rural people and improve the quality of their life by establishing rural enterprises catering to their skills and needs.
- Maintain and upgrade the existing rural infrastructure and promote facilities such as cold chains, marketing intelligence network to facilitate the agro-processing industries.
- The Government of India in certain cases provides funds for the development of rural areas through the agency of NGOs, whereas the PRIs, being the real representative bodies of the people, are not treated as NGOs. The Government of India should abandon this approach and provide funds from all agencies, including international funding, to the PRIs.
- The state government is in the process of adopting the central pattern of devolution of functions, functionaries and funds in respect of 29 items. The Government of India is also required to devolve to the PRIs similar functions in respect of schemes implemented by various ministries of the Government of India in the rural areas.
- To discourage over dependence on funds from outside, the PRIs should be encouraged and empowered to mobilise their own physical and human resources.
- Special efforts should be made to promote and facilitate a network of elected women representatives. Intra-state and inter-state exposure visits of women representatives of PRIs need to be encouraged.
- Agricultural reforms are a key element for improving the economic condition of the small and marginal farmers. The involvement of PRIs in this process has a great scope.
- For better implementation of poverty alleviation programmes, there is need for effective co-ordination between the officials of various departments and the PRIs.
- *Gram Panchayats* should be encouraged to involve themselves actively in planning, implementing, monitoring and evaluating the poverty alleviation programmes for better results.
- All poverty alleviation programmes at the village level should be put at the disposal of the *gram panchayat* and implemented with the help and co-operation of the local-level bureaucracy. Further, the *Gram Panchayats* should be selective in this regard and take into account the needs of the people and the scope of real employment generation, before taking up the programmes for implementation.
- For proper identification of the BPL families, the role of the NGOs, *panchayats* and the community must be ensured.
- An appropriate institutional and organisational structure is a prerequisite for the success of a rural development programme. Appropriate technology skills, equitable access to production inputs, services and credit are other prerequisites for the success of a production-oriented programme: A producer-owned and -controlled integrated system of production, procurement, processing and marketing is necessary to derive full benefits from the backward and forward linkages of these activities.
- Although, the government has been and will continue to be the most important actor in rural development, it alone cannot effectively tackle all problems. The PRIs, co-operatives, voluntary agencies and the private sector can play an important role in the process of development by complementing and supplementing the functions and activities of the government.

Himachal Pradesh has a large deprived population, consisting of marginal and small farmers, Scheduled Castes, Scheduled Tribes and backward classes. This segment of the population has to be brought into focus for their uplift with special emphasis on their skill upgradation, removal of unemployment and poverty and vertical growth, to acquire productive assets for better living on a sustainable basis.

References

Altekar, *State and Government in Ancient India*, Motital Banarsidas, Banaras, 1955.

An Evaluation Study on IRDP in Himachal Pradesh (1992-97), Planning Department, Government of Himachal Pradesh, Shimla, 2002.

Annual Administrative Report, Department of Rural Development Himachal Pradesh, Shimla, 2002.

Annual Plan (2003-2007) Himachal Pradesh, 2003.

India: Human Development Report, National Council for Applied Economic Research, Oxford University Press, New Delhi, 1999.

India Panchayati Raj Report-2001 Volume I & II, National Institute of Rural Development, Hyderabad, January 2002.

Jagmohan, Balokhra, 2002, *The Wonder Land, Himachal Pradesh: An Encyclopedia*, H.G. Publication, New Dehli.

Jain, S.P. (edit), *Emerging Institutions for Decentralised Rural Development, Vol. I & II*, National Institute of Rural Development, Hyderabad, November 2001.

National Human Development Report, 2001, Planning Commission, Government of India, March 2002.

NCAER, *Indian Human Development Report, 1999.*

Riddell, Rogar and Mark C and Robinson, 1995, *Non Government Organizations and Rural Poverty Alleviation*, Clarendon Press, Oxford.

Sarkar, K. Gautam, 1995, *Agriculture and Rural Transformation in India*, Oxford University Press, Delhi.

Satyaketu, Vidyalankar, *Maurya Samrajya Ka Itihas* Indian Press, Allahabad, 1928.

Singh, Katar, 1999, *Rural Development: Principles Policies and Management*, Sage Publication, New Delhi.

State Development Report Punjab, Planning Commission, Government of India, 2003.

Status Note Regarding the Devolution of Powers, Functions and Responsibilities of Panchayati Raj Institutions, Department of Rural Development, Himachal Pradesh, Shimla 2002.

Statistical Abstract India, 2000, CSO, Ministry of Statistics and Programme Implementation, Government of India.

Statistical Abstracts of HP, various issues, Government of Himachal Pradesh.

Tenth Five-Year Plan, Himachal Pradesh, 2003.

Chapter 14

People's Participation

According to UNDP (1993:21), "Participation means that people are closely involved in economic, social, cultural and political process that affect their lives". Therefore, participation is a process by which the beneficiaries influence the direction and execution of a development programme to enhance prosperity in terms of income, personal growth, self-reliance or other values that they cherish.

The Directive Principles of State Policy enshrined in the Constitution, entail two dominant goals of economic policy; (i) increase the national income; and (ii) ensure equitable distribution of the national income among the members of society. The 73rd Constitutional Amendment is based on the same goals; (i) to prepare plans for economic development with social justice; and (ii) to implement schemes of economic development and social justice as may be entrusted to them, including those related to matters listed in the Eleventh Schedule.

These goals are reflected in economic policies enunciated in the Five Year Plans. People's participation is the core factor in the approach paper of the Tenth Plan, where much importance is given to it in the promotion of agriculture, food and nutritional security, providing safe drinking water, primary health care, universal primary education, housing and connectivity to all, containing the growth of population, ensuring environmental sustainability, empowerment of women and the socially disadvantaged groups, promoting participatory institutions like Panchayati Raj Institutions (PRIs), co-operatives and Self-Help Groups (SHGs) and building self-reliance.

Implementation of any development project is not possible without the active and widespread participation of the people. It becomes the responsibility of the administrative authority to spot active persons in the local population, awaken their interest and mobilise their initiative.

The government of Himachal Pradesh has accepted the concept that the top-down model of development may not be successful in the state. The poor and underprivileged sections of society such as the small and marginal farmers, the Scheduled Castes, the Scheduled Tribes and women cannot fully benefit from the poverty alleviation and development programmes under this model of development. Non-participatory bureaucratic approach and non-involvement of the people in the planning process has created an attitude of depending on the government, and a lack of effort on the part of the people. It is realised that there will be no development unless the people are involved in planning and controlling the development process. Therefore, decentralisation of development planning and governance has become a precondition to the mobilisation of the untapped growth potential. Only a decentralised structure of governance can facilitate direct participation of the people, which is based on local socio-traditional knowledge. To make it successful, the government has strengthened the *Panchayati Raj* system. *Gram Sabhas* have been empowered to prepare and implement plans at the local level.

Local level planning with people's participation has the capacity to transform a centralised planning system into a decentralised participatory planning one. It promotes participation of the people at the grassroot level and pays attention to resource mobilisation at the local level for a particular development project. Participatory planning involves the people in the process of problem identification, prioritisation and plan preparation. This process promotes the sense of transparency and accountability of the stakeholders. The government of Himachal Pradesh has taken the initiative to promote the people's participation under the following programmes:

Local District Planning: This scheme was introduced in 1984-85 for the development of infrastructure at the grassroot level. It envisages allocation of untied funds to the districts, based on a formula: 60 per cent on the basis of area. Infrastructural schemes benefiting at least five families with no recurring liability can be taken up under this scheme. Upkeep and maintenance of the assets created is either the responsibility of the user community or the government department concerned. Development works such as construction of school buildings, rural water supply schemes, motorable roads, ropeways, minor irrigation schemes and multipurpose community centres come under this scheme.

***Vikas Mein Jan Sahyog*:** To ensure effective people's participation, the state government in 1991-92 diverted some funds from the Local District Planning allocation to launch a programme '*Gaon Bhi Apna Kam Bhi Apna*'. It was renamed '*Vikas Mein Jan Sahyog*'' in 1994. Under this programme it was ensured that if the people contributed 30 per cent of the cost of a development project, the government would contribute the remaining 70 per cent. The maximum limit of this development scheme to be sanctioned by the Deputy Commissioner was kept at Rs. 70,000/- in 1995. The government's share was raised to 75 per cent and the maximum limit to Rs. 1 lakh. It was further raised to Rs. 3 lakh in 1997 and to Rs. 5 lakh in 1999. However, for tribal areas, backward *panchayats* and areas predominantly inhabited by the SCs, STs and OBCs, the ratio of contribution between the community and the government has been set at 15:85 per cent. Even an individual can get a public asset constructed as a philanthropic activity to commemorate his or her ancestors by contributing 50 per cent of the cost of the work. Works are required to be completed within a specified period under the close monitoring of local committees constituted by the Deputy Commissioner. The community has a leading role in selecting the implementing agency and both the community and the government are liable to contribute 10 per cent additional funds for the maintenance of the assets. Projects such as construction of government schools buildings, multipurpose community halls, motorable roads, ropeways, irrigation schemes, drinking water schemes, public health services and provision of missing links such as three-phase transmission lines, transformers, ambulances and X-ray plants are being sanctioned under this programme.

Sectoral Decentralised Planning Programme: Under this programme, five per cent of the funds from approved outlays under selected heads of development are taken out and allocated to non-tribal areas, 60 per cent on the basis of population and 40 per cent on the basis of area. There are 14 selected heads under this programme which has been in operation since 1993-94. The districts have the discretion to identify projects under this scheme irrespective of sectoral bounds. The only constraint is that no diversion is allowed from outlays earmarked for rural water supply schemes. The Deputy Commissioner is required to get the scheme's approval from District Planning Board.

Member of Parliament Local Area Development Scheme: Introduced in 1993-94, this scheme authorises Members of Parliament (MPs) to recommend small works of capital nature in their constituencies. Each MP has the choice to suggest development works worth Rs. 1 crore every year (the amount was raised to Rs. 2 crore by the Government of India in 1998-99) in his constituency. The cost of each suggested work should not exceed Rs. 10 lakh. The Planning Department has been made the nodal agency for implementing this scheme in co-ordination with the Deputy Commissioner concerned. Development works such as construction of school buildings, drinking water facilities, village roads, bridges, common shelters, buildings for cultural activities and hospitals, social forestry, farm forestry, horticulture, gardens on government and community land, desilting of ponds, irrigation canals, common *gobar* gas plants, non-conventional energy, small irrigation bunds, lift irrigation schemes, reading rooms, crèches and *anganwadis*, public health-care buildings, cremation or burial grounds, public toilets, bathrooms, drains and gutters, footpaths, pathways and foot bridges, civic amenities such as electricity, water, public toilets in slum areas, worksheds for artisans, residential schools in tribal areas, bus stops and veterinary-aid centres are taken up under this scheme.

Forest Development: The state government through its Forest Department has adopted structural empowerment and contribution strategies to promote participation in and operationalize the participatory mechanism. The Forest Department launched 'Sanjhi Van Yojana' (SVY) in 1998-99 for the protection and promotion of the forest cover. Already there were several local village level institutions, directly or indirectly linked with forestation and its protection. Direct linked forest institutions were Village Forest Development Societies (VFDSs), Village Forest

Development Committees (VFDCs), Village Eco-Development Committees (VEDCs) and Village Development Committees (VDCs), set up under externally supported forestry projects and with the support of the Forest Department. Non-forest related village institutions, linked indirectly with forestation, were PRIs, *mahila mandals*, youth groups, *devta* committees, *mela* committees, village committees, parents-teachers associations, village education committees, mothers-teachers associations, self-help groups and co-operative societies. Both types of institutions initiated the process of involvement and collection of people around tangible issues of their interest. However, the multiplicity of committees is confusing the people about their functional role and responsibilities.

Except the *Panchayats*, *devta* committtees and one or two others, most of these committees often become defunct with the passage of time, as they are *ad hoc* in nature and their activities are limited. Money is the binding factor in their working and the leadership usually comprises interested community members.

These participatory programmes involve active, collectively organised and continuing efforts of the people in setting goals, pooling resources and taking action, to improve the living conditions of the people.

Development works, under various people's participation schemes in 2001-02, prove the success of the participatory model. Achievements under various programmes are as under:

(a) Distribution of rural toilets	: 1244
(b) Construction of houses under Indra Awaas Yojana and Gandhi Kuteer Yojana	: 3259
(c) Construction of irrigation tanks	: 365
(d) Construction of school buildings	: 3092
(e) Repair of school buildings	: 937
(f) Construction of *panchayat ghars*	: 79
(g) Construction of *mahila mandal bhawans*	: 466
(h) Repair of *mahila mandal bhawans*	: 155
(i) Construction/repair of other development of streets, kuhl, bowlies water supply schemes, playgrounds, culverts bridges, rain shelter and milk booths, community centre buidings,check dams, boundary walls, health centre buildings, etc.	: 5588

People's Planning in Kerala

Kerala is the state where the government has recognised the planning process with people's participation in the form of "People's Campaign". According to *World Bank Report (2000)*, "The programme was formally inaugurated on August 17, 1996. More than one lakh people turned up for the training programmes and 30 lakh people all over the state participated in the special *gram sabha* and municipal ward meetings to discuss the planning issue. The primary objective of the people's campaign has been to motivate and empower local self-government to take up the new challenges of development planning. It was sought to be achieved by mobilising people regardless of their political affiliations, religion, caste or gender to help the local governments in all stages of development planning, from plan formulation and implementation to maintenance".

For giving meaningful direction to decentralisation process, there was need to transfer an appropriate budgetary outlay to local bodies to help them prepare and implement their need-based plans. The Kerala government has proposed to transfer 35-40 per cent of their budget outlay to these bodies.

The participatory development process goes through a number of stages. These are;

(i) Discussion on the problems of development and identification of needs in *gram sabha*/ward committee meetings.

(ii) Sector-wise discussion on socio-economic indicators shown in "Panchayat Development Report", through development seminars.

(iii) Constitution of task force for all sectors in order to convert into action programmes, the solutions suggested in the development seminars.

(iv) Formulation of plans for the local bodies.

(v) Integration of local plans and formulation of block and district level plans.

(vi) Appraisal of technical feasibility and financial viability of the projects and plans through Voluntary Technical Corps (VTCs).

People's Planning in West Bengal

Having almost the same characteristics, West Bengal has formulated village-based people's planning, with the followings steps;

(i) Identification of a place for discussion.

(ii) Identification of problems and issues for discussion.

(iii) Identification of local resources/assets through planning map.

(iv) Formulation of problem-solving measures through effective and efficient use of local resources.

(v) Prioritisation of these measures.

(vi) Programme formulation.

The 73rd constitutional amendment seems to have generated great expectations from grassroot level democracy in the form of PRIs. Therefore, there is need to review the interlinkages and sustainability of village-level committees with the PRIs. In the given situation, the PRIs have emerged as the common point of intervention, where the possibility of convergence of all local/village level institutions of different nature with the PRIs seems plausible. However, to make this convergence and assimilation meaningful, effective and workable, some basic issues have to be addressed. Standing committees at all the three levels and mechanism to ensure interaction and inter-linkages between various departments can create a developmental atmosphere. The district planning committees shall have to be made more functional. As the state government has transferred some functions of 15 departments to the PRIs and efforts are being made to operationalise the district planning committees (DPCs) and other standing committees, it is felt that the PRIs have not been able to establish their credibility due to procedural and systemic delays. To make the representatives aware of their functions, powers and responsibilities, there is need for building their capacity through training and education.

In the present situation, it is important to have an organic linkage of the village-level institutions with the PRIs regarding the area of operation such as the ward or the *Panchayat*. The micro-plans developed by various institutions/committees should be integrated with the panchayat level micro plans and the *panchayat* vigilance committees should be made responsible for monitoring activities in the panchayat area, irrespective of the project or department.

To promote people's participation, there is also need for effective governance, which relies on accountability and transparency. This form of governance can be possible when there is decentralisation of powers and there are elected bodies at the local level. Now, after the 73rd and 74th constitutional amendments, the local bodies (PRIs and ULBs) have been made constitutional entities to function as the institutions of local self-governance, thus enabling the people at the grassroot level to participate in the democratic process. Local bodies ought to ensure the flow of timely information to the people and enable them to take informed decisions as well as make plans at the grassroot level. Thus, the relevance of information has increased in the context of local self-governance. There is need to set up information centres at the local level to provide timely and relevant information to the people and their elected representatives. These centres can perform the role of catalysts to agents of development.

Panchayat Resource Centres: Agents of Change

In order to empower and enhance women's participation in decision making, Participatory Research in Asia (PRIA) and its partners initiated a joint action programme to strengthen PRIs as institutions of local self-governance in Himachal Pradesh, PRIA has promoted setting up "panchayat resource centres" (PRCs) in the state as a way to bring simplified information within easy reach of local citizens. With a participatory perspective on local self-governance, the organisation facilitated PRCs initially in collaboration with its partner, Samaj Seva Parishad (SSP) a local NGO, in three *gram panchayats* – Tatwani, Ambadi and Dadhamb in Rai Block of Kangra. These PRCs have taken up the task of creating awareness among citizens and enhancing participation of women and marginalized sections in local governance to a large extent. The experience of Tatwani PRC reveals the frequent visits of the local *Mahila Mandal*. This group of 33 members met every Sunday to discuss local problems of the village and pass resolutions to solve the problems. The *Mahila Mandal* took an initiative in April 1999 to construct a *pucca* path (tar road) through a cluster of agricultural fields and passed a resolution, sent it to the *gram panchayat* to undertake the activity. The *gram panchayat* neglected this issue. Frustrated by the *gram panchayat*'s inactivity, the *Mahila Mandal* began to collect money from amongst themselves and the community (who had a stake in the creation of the *pucca* path). All together, the *Mahila Mandal* collected more than Rs. 7000. They deposited this sum with the Deputy Commissioner who, through a matching grant scheme called *Vikas Mein Jan Sahyog*, was able to donate the rest of the funds needed for construction. Finally, they were able to construct the pucca path. Currently, the *Mahila Mandal*, the community and *gram panchayat* together are successfully running the Tatwani PRC.

The community has realised the importance of PRC and its implications towards better local self-governance. The experience and learning in Tatwani was used to set up PRCs at the block level in collaboration with New HOPE, an NGO in Kangra district. Currently, three PRCs are running in three blocks namely Sulaha (Kangra), Sujanpur (Hamirpur) and Bharmour (Chamba) in collaboration with PRIA.

— AJAYA MOHAPATRA
Co-ordinator
PRI Programme in Himachal Pradesh for
Participatory Research in Asia (PRIA)

In accordance with the provisions of the constitutional (73rd and 74th) amendments, multilevel decentralised planning has become the major agenda to promote people's participation in the development process. To promote participatory planning and its implementation, the following steps shall have to be taken:

- *Gram Sabha*/Ward Committee meetings have to be held regularly and with the required quorum for effective participation of the people belonging to all sections of society.
- Pictorial presentation of the *panchayat*/ward plans to be displayed at a central place in the village/ward.
- Collection of essential data through participatory methods from each *panchayat*/ward and its updating from time to time.
- To ensure authenticity and holisticity of the *panchayat*/ward plan, smaller meetings should be organised at ward/*panchayat* levels.
- Concerned data, map list of beneficiaries, plan documents, budget and other related documents should be available to everybody.
- Exposure visits of representatives of local bodies to *panchayats*/organisations where participatory planning initiatives have already been taken.
- Organisation of block- or district-level melas in collaboration with voluntary organisations, government departments for spreading the concept of people's participation in development planning.
- Capacity building of PRIs, NGOs and VLWs on various participatory planning techniques and other relevant methods.
- Government officials should take the initiative to carry out participatory planning in their departments and the assessment of their performance could be linked to the local bodies' plans to promote the concept of accountability.
- Incentives for those who are promoting the concept of people's participation in development and contributing to the preparation of participatory plans.
- Inclusion of participation planning course in the curriculum of training institutes who are imparting training to elected representative of local bodies and government departments.

Reference

Annual Administrative Report, Himachal Pradesh (2001-02), Government of Himachal Pradesh, Shimla.

Jain, S.P. (ed.) 2001, *Emerging Institutions for Decentralized Rural Development*, Volumes I & II, National Institute of Rural Development, Hyderabad.

Mudgal; Gauri and Sushil; "Village-level Institutions and their Linkages with PRIs", *Emerging Institutions for Decentralized Rural Development*, Volume-II, edited by S.P. Jain, NIRD, Hyderabad, November 2001).

Parshad, D.R. "Participation and Empowerment: Rhetorics and Realities, *Kurukshetra*, May 2002, p-11.

Raietall, Manoj (ed.) 2001, *The State of Panchayats - A Participatory Perspective*, PRIA, New Delhi

Singh, Katar, "Co-operative: Emerging Challenges and Coping Strategies", *Kurukshetra*, November 2002, p-21.

Chapter 15

Public Distribution System

Introduction

Poverty alleviation and eradication of hunger are two vital objectives of rural development programmes in India. Amongst various programmes of poverty alleviation and hunger mitigation, the public distribution system (PDS) is one. PDS aims at eradication of rural poverty and inequality by providing justice to the poor (Pattanaik, 1997). It was clubbed with the minimum needs programme (MNP) in the Seventh Five Year Plan. With a network of about 4,51,000 fair price shops (FPS) for the distribution of commodities worth over Rs. 150 billion to about 180 million households throughout the country, the PDS in India is perhaps the largest distribution network of its type in the world (Meenakshisundaram, 2001). PDS, over the years, has become an important instrument of the governments' policy of ensuring availability of foodgrains to the public and providing enhancing food security to the poor. This is also true for Himachal Pradesh.

Need and Importance of PDS in Himachal Pradesh

Agriculture is the mainstay of the people of Himachal Pradesh and 66.71 per cent of the population depends on it. In this hilly and mountainous state, 80 per cent of the landholdings belong to small and marginal farmers. Only one-fifth of the cultivable land is irrigated and the rest continues to depend heavily upon the monsoon. Therefore, achieving foodgrain productivity through planned target is an arduous task. The Ninth Five Year Plan document has rightly pointed out that "having realised the fact that we could not plan for foodgrain self-sufficiency, the future plans of the state concentrated more on (a) diversifying agriculture and (b) raising productivity levels in vegetables and fruit". Nearly 30 per cent of its population comprises the Scheduled Castes and Scheduled Tribes. According to a household survey, 27.62 per cent of the families are living below the poverty line, which varies between the highest of 61.72 per cent in Chamba and lowest of 19.6 per cent in Una. The families identified to be living below the poverty line are 2,86,447 (Annual Administrative Report, 2001-02). From spatial situations, it can be inferred that PDS has or will have an important role in dealing with poverty, hunger and malnutrition in the state.

PDS Schemes in Himachal Pradesh

Various schemes of PDS launched in the state are:

Targeted Public Distribution System (TPDS)

This scheme was introduced in the State on 1 June 1997. Families were divided broadly into two categories such as: (i) Above the Poverty Line (APL) and (ii) Below the Poverty Line (BPL). The number of APL and BPL families in Himachal Pradesh on 01.03.2003 was 10,46,967 and 2,98,181 respectively. However, with the launching of the Antyodaya Anna Yojana, the number of BPL families has come down to 2,19,481.

Antyodaya Anna Yojana (AAY)

The AAY scheme was introduced in the State on 1 March 2001. The numerical ceiling of the poorest of the poor families to be covered under this scheme fixed by the Government of India was 78,700. Under this scheme, wheat and rice are being issued at the scale of 15 kg and 20 kg per family per month at the rate of Rs. 2 and Rs. 3 per kg respectively.

Annapurna Scheme (AS)

This scheme was introduced in the State on 1 April 2000. The numerical ceiling of the beneficiaries to be covered under this scheme set by the Government of

India in the state is 6373. Out of these, 5484 families have been identified to be benefited by the scheme. The beneficiaries are old, destitute, indigent citizens (65 years and above) who are eligible for old age pension under National Old Age Pension Scheme (NOAPS) but have been denied. Under this scheme, foodgrains are issued to them free of cost at the scale of 10 kg per beneficiary per month.

Other Schemes

Sampooran Gramin Rojgar Yojana

This *Yojana* has been operating in the state since 11 January 2002. Under this food-for-work programme, rice and wheat are supplied to the beneficiaries at the rate of Rs. 5 per kg per manday. The Food and Supplies department makes the foodgrains available to the FPS and the scheme is executed by the Rural Development, Department. It is implemented on the analogy of food-for-work programme.

Supply of Foodgrains for Welfare Schemes at Half the Economic Cost

Under this scheme, the Government of India has decided to provide foodgrains to the inmates in the tribal hostels at the rate of 15 kg per head per month at BPL rates. This facility will also be available to the inmates of tribal hostels being run by NGOs and sponsored by the Ministry of Tribal Affairs/State Governments. Under the Government of India's policy, these schemes are to be implemented by the Tribal Development Department. The current position is that the Himachal Pradesh Government has circulated the instructions of the Government of India to all departments concerned for compliance.

Sarvpriya Yojana

The Government of India, under the Sarvpriya Yojana, has proposed to supply essential items such as pulses, salt, tea, toilet soap, detergent cakes, exercise books, mustard oil and toothpaste through the network of FPS under the TPDS. The Government of Himachal Pradesh has issued the necessary instructions to all concerned departments as well as to the field functionaries. However, it is learned that these items are already being distributed through the FPS.

Additional Allocation of Foodgrains for Distribution at BPL Rates in Drought-Affected Areas

Under this scheme, the Government of India has allotted rice and wheat to Himachal Pradesh at BPL rates at the scale of 20 kg of foodgrains per family per month. This is in addition to the foodgrains available to BPL families at the scale of 35 kg per family per month at BPL rates under the TPDS.

Status of FPS and Ration Cards

As far as fair price shops are concerned, 3895 such shops have been operating in the state till 2002, of which 3280, 279 and 336 were operating in the rural, urban and far-off areas (Table 15.1) constituting 84.21

TABLE 15.1

Fair Price Shops in Rural/Urban Areas as on 31.03.2003

District	*Fair Price Shops (Number)*				*Percentage*			
	Urban	*Rural*	*Far Flung*	*Total*	*Urban*	*Rural*	*Far Flung*	*Total*
Bilaspur	8	177	0	185	4.32	95.68	0.00	100.00
Chamba	19	283	74	376	5.05	75.27	19.68	100.00
Hamirpur	29	249	7	285	10.18	87.37	2.46	100.00
Kangra	42	821	5	868	4.84	94.59	0.58	100.00
Kinnaur	0	0	56	56	0.00	0.00	100.00	100.00
Kullu	20	274	67	361	5.54	75.90	18.56	100.00
Lahaul & Spiti	0	0	65	65	0.00	0.00	100.00	100.00
Mandi	34	502	67	603	5.64	83.25	11.11	100.00
Shimla	60	361	5	426	14.08	84.74	1.17	100.00
Sirmaur	19	269	0	288	6.60	93.40	0.00	100.00
Solan	38	227	2	267	14.23	85.02	0.75	100.00
Una	32	231	0	263	12.17	87.83	0.00	100.00
Total	**301**	**3394**	**348**	**4043**	**7.44**	**83.95**	**8.61**	**100.00**

Source: Food and Supplies Department, Government of Himachal Pradesh.

FIGURE 15.1

Status of Fair Price Shop

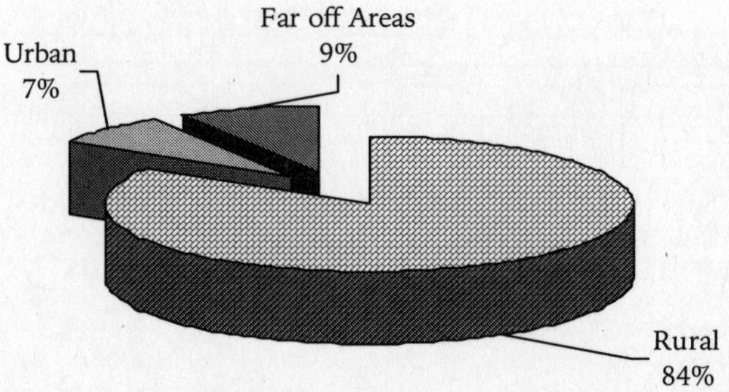

FIGURE 15.2

Categories of Ownership of F.P.S.

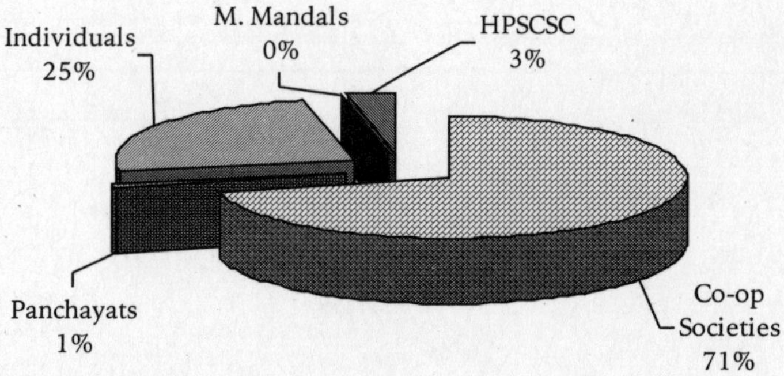

per cent, 7.16 per cent and 8.63 per cent in their respective areas. As far as the concentration of FPS in the rural areas is concerned, 95.83 per cent (the highest) are operating in Bilaspur district. Solan district accounts for the highest number of fair price shops in the urban areas (14.73%), which is higher than Shimla district's 11.79 per cent.

In Kinnaur and Lahaul-Spiti districts all fair price shops are in far-off areas. This indicates that the PDS in Himachal Pradesh has paid adequate attention to the needs of the rural and far-off areas where the vulnerable sections are largely concentrated. The number has increased and in March, 2003, the number was 4043. As far as the ownership of these shops is concerned, of the 4043 shops, 2855 (70.62%), 47 (1.16%), 129 (3.19%), 1008 (24.93%) and 4 (0.10%) are being run by co-operative societies, *panchayats*, Himachal Pradesh State Civil Supply Corporation (HPSCSC), individuals and *Mahila Mandals* respectively (Table 15.2).

There are 13,50,529 ration card holders in the state, of whom 2,19,481 are BPL card holders, 78,700 are AAY card holders and the rest 10,52,348 are APL card holders (Table 15.3). Moreover, 5484 (0.41 per cent) families have been identified under the Annapurna Yojana. It is estimated that the number of ration cards per fair price shop in Himachal Pradesh is 323 (as on May 1998).

The role of community participation is vital for the effective functioning of PDS. However, the meagre percentage of 1.18 shops being run by *panchayats*, clearly indicates that their role in PDS has not been effectively promoted. Women who largely manage the foodgrains

TABLE 15.2

District-wise Ownership of Fair Price Shops as on 30.11.2003

District	*Number*						*Percentage*					
	Co-op	*Panchayat*	*Mahila Mandal*	*HPSCSC*	*Private Individual*	*Total*	*Co-op*	*Panchayat*	*Mahila Mandal*	*HPSCSC*	*Private Individual*	*Total*
Bilaspur	149	1	0	5	30	185	85.54	0.54	0.00	2.70	16.22	100.00
Chamba	233	21	0	16	106	376	61.97	5.59	0.00	4.26	28.19	100.00
Hamirpur	251	3	0	4	27	285	88.07	1.05	0.00	1.40	9.47	100.00
Kangra	664	2	2	16	184	868	76.50	0.23	0.23	1.84	21.20	100.00
Kinnaur	51	0	0	1	4	56	91.07	0.00	0.00	1.79	7.14	100.00
Kullu	186	9	0	2	164	361	51.52	2.49	0.00	0.55	45.43	100.00
Lahaul & Spiti	59	0	0	4	2	65	90.77	0.00	0.00	6.15	3.08	100.00
Mandi	446	0	0	15	142	603	73.96	0.00	0.00	2.49	23.55	100.00
Shimla	266	1	0	51	108	426	62.44	0.23	0.00	11.97	25.35	100.00
Sirmaur	166	0	0	6	116	288	57.64	0.00	0.00	2.08	40.28	100.00
Solan	171	9	2	7	78	267	64.04	3.37	0.75	2.62	29.21	100.00
Una	213	1	0	2	47	263	80.99	0.38	0.00	0.76	17.87	100.00
Total	**2855**	**47**	**4**	**129**	**1008**	**4043**	**70.62**	**1.16**	**0.10**	**3.19**	**24.93**	**100.00**

Source: Food and Supplies Department, Government of Himachal Pradesh.

TABLE 15.3

District-wise Ration Card Status as on 30.11.2003

District	*Number*				*Percentage of Ration Cards*			
	APL	*BPL*	*AAY*	*Total*	*APL*	*BPL*	*AAY*	*Total*
Bilaspur	62099	13676	4791	80566	77.08	16.97	5.95	100.00
Chamba	44222	35100	12959	92281	47.92	38.04	14.04	100.00
Hamirpur	82718	15746	5539	104003	79.53	15.14	5.33	100.00
Kangra	244078	48012	17583	309673	78.82	15.50	5.68	100.00
Kinnaur	16847	2105	791	19743	85.33	10.66	4.01	100.00
Kullu	71811	8641	3137	83589	85.91	10.34	3.75	100.00
Lahaul & Spiti	5231	1773	672	7676	68.15	23.10	8.75	100.00
Mandi	176191	31824	11550	219565	80.25	14.49	5.26	100.00
Shimla	119987	23678	8730	152395	78.73	15.54	5.73	100.00
Sirmaur	64826	11420	3775	80021	81.01	14.27	4.72	100.00
Solan	79266	14032	4933	98231	80.69	14.28	5.02	100.00
Una	85072	13474	4240	102786	82.77	13.11	4.13	100.00
Total	**1052348**	**219481**	**78700**	**1350529**	**77.92**	**16.25**	**5.83**	**100.00**

Source: Food & Civil Supplies Department, Govt. of H.P.

FIGURE 15.3

Categories of Ration Cards

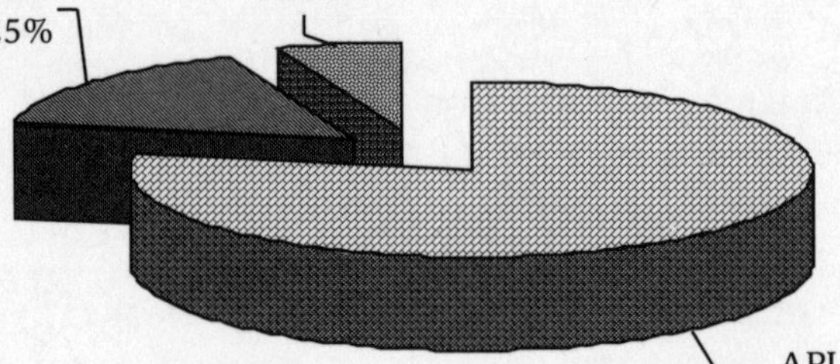

of the households can effectively manage the PDS. But only three fair price shops are owned by *Mahila Mandals*. Under the *Mahila Mandal Protochahlan Yojana*, the ownership of more and more fair price shops need to be given to Mahila Mandals. As *Mahila Mandals* are functioning effectively in Kangra district, more *Mahila Mandals* in that district need to be given ownership of fair price shops.

The highest percentage of APL card holders is in Kullu district (85.91%) and the lowest in Chamba district (47.92%). On the other hand, BPL card holders are 38.04 per cent in Chamba district and the lowest number (10.34%) is in Kullu district. Unlike BPL families, the highest number of AAY card holders are in Chamba district and the lowest in Kullu district (3.75%). This implies that Himachal Pradesh has a greater percentage of vulnerable sections in Chamba as compared to other districts.

Allocation, Lifting, Distribution and Diversion of Foodgrains

The allocation, lifting and distribution of foodgrains in 2001-02 and 2002-03 show that the lifting of wheat and rice from the allocated amount for APL families has gone down from 17.23 per cent to 6.47 per cent and wheat alone has gone down from 6.20 per cent to 5.20 per cent. But the lifting of wheat for BPL families has increased from 44.42 per cent to 45.11 per cent and rice from 38.84 per cent to 57.66 per cent. The lifting of rice and wheat for other categories such as AAY, *Annapurna*, food-for-work, etc., is high as compared to the former two categories. This indicates that the PDS caters to the needs of vulnerable groups. Lifting from the central pool shows that there is genuine dependence on PDS by the vulnerable sections.

Diversion of wheat from PDS to the free market in Himachal Pradesh is 47 per cent (TECS, 1998), which is three times that of Andhra Pradesh (Table 15.5). Diversion of wheat in Himachal Pradesh may be largely done from APL families pool who rarely use their ration cards to purchase wheat largely because of their home production, the poor quality of the wheat supplied through PDS and narrow differences between the PDS price and the free market price. As compared to wheat, there is less diversion of rice and sugar, 18 per cent and eight per cent respectively. Home production is the main reason for less dependence on PDS rice, which leads to diversion. The diversion of sugar is the lowest, mainly because of higher percentage of the use of ration cards by APL families for purchasing sugar from fair price shops.

TABLE 15.4

Status of Allocation, Lifting and Distribution of Wheat & Rice (2001-02 & 2002-03)

Commodities	*Categories of Schemes*	*2001 – 2002*			*2002 – 2003*		
		Allocation	**Lifting*	***Distribution*	*Allocation*	*Lifting**	*Distribution***
Wheat	APL	38400	6615 (17.23)	9041 (136.67)	125268	8110 (6.47)	7593 (93.63)
	BPL	44280	19668 (44.42)	19672 (100.0)	53482	24125 (45.11)	25131 (104.04)
	AAY	9444	9341 (98.91)	9400 (100.63)	12323	13113 (106.41)	13045 (99.48)
	Annapurna	589	473 (80.31)	466 (98.58)	—	99	76 (76.77)
	Food for work	-	-	-	—	-	148
	Drought Relief	30000	11097 (36.99)	7470 (67.32)	—	18903	22530 (119.19)
	SGRY	2970	NA	NA	13788	6486 (47.04)	3511 (54.13)
Rice	APL	62760	3894 (6.20)	4116 (105.71)	204982	10667 (5.20)	13830 (129.65)
	BPL	54705	21248 (38.84)	22671 (106.70)	80234	46259 (57.66)	43455 (93.94)
	AAY	14172	13645 (96.28)	13570 (99.45)	16949	18865 (111.30)	17628 (93.94)
	Annapurna	559	456 (81.57)	456 (100.0)	762.3	744 (97.60)	464 (62.37)
	Food for work	11549	11549 (100.0)	11401 (98.72)	—	—	148
	Drought Relief	119250	80080 (67.15)	80080 (100.0)	—	36670	36670 (100.0)
	SGRY	3300	NA	NA	—	—	—

Note: * Figures in parenthesis show percentages to total allocation.
** Figures in parenthesis show percentages to total lifting.

TABLE 15.5

Average Offtake Per BPL Household and Diversion of PDS Commodities

States	*Offtake (kg)* per BPL Households*	*Estimated Diversion***		
		Wheat	*Rice*	*Sugar*
Rajasthan	1.0	31	36	17
Haryana	1.1	53	44	28
Punjab	4.9	69	40	6
Himachal Pradesh	**23.3**	**47**	**18**	**8**
Bihar	42.4	44	64	47
Uttar Pradesh	54.0	46	49	36
Gujarat	75.4	23	21	18
Maharastra	76.7	26	30	22
West Bengal	85.2	40	34	24
Madhya Pradesh	90.8	20	24	32
Karnataka	210.4	30	18	19
Assam	226.3	61	64	52
Tamil Nadu	253.9	24	33	28
Andhra Pradesh	262.4	15	19	16
Orissa	302.6	39	54	28
Kerala	315.9	28	23	25

Source: *M.D. Asthana and Pedro Medrano (Ed.) Towards Hunger Free India, Agenda and Imperatives, Monohar, 2001, P.486

**Total Economic Consultancy Service (TECs) 'Study to Ascertain the Extent of Diversion of PDS Commodities, study undertaken on behalf of the Ministry of Food & Consumer Affairs, (GoI), New Delhi, February. 1998.

Field Survey

A study of utilisation of PDS and consumer satisfaction with it was conducted in three villages and one urban colony of Shimla (March 2003) by the Centre for Research in Rural and Industrial Development (CRRID). These are Kapaur, Sandholi and Joron villages of Kinnaur, Solan and Sirmaur districts respectively and Krishna Nagar locality of urban Shimla. 150 households comprising 6 Antodaya families, 3 BPL families and 141 APL families were covered.

FIGURE 15.4

Diversion of Wheat

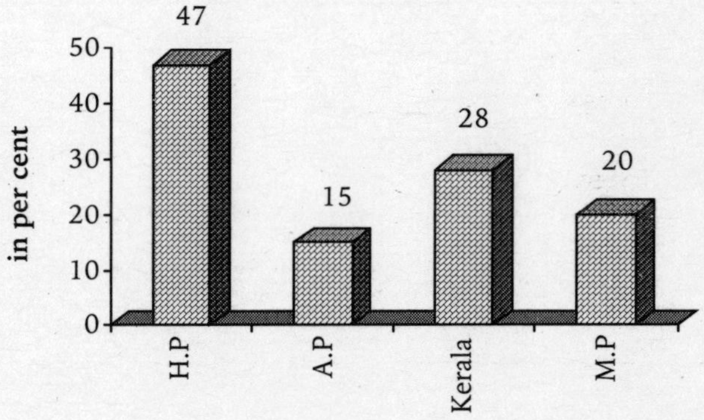

TABLE 15.6

Commodity-wise Users and Non-users

Commodity	*Urban*		*Rural*		*Far-off Areas*		*Total*	
	User	*Non-user*	*User*	*Non-user*	*User*	*Non-user*	*User*	*Non-user*
Sugar	37 (90.24)	4 (9.76)	48 (60.76)	31 (39.24)	25 (83.33)	5 (16.67)	110 (73.33)	40 (26.67)
Wheat	12 (29.27)	29 (70.73)	4 (5.06)	75 (94.94)	10 (33.33)	20 (66.67)	26 (17.33)	124 (82.67)
Rice	20 (48.78)	21 (51.22)	6 (7.59)	73 (92.41)	21 (70.00)	9 (30.00)	47 (31.33)	103 (68.67)
Kerosene Oil	—	41 (100)	24 (30.38)	55 (69.62)	4 (13.33)	26 (86.67)	28 (18.67)	122 (81.33)

Note: Figures in parenthesis show percentages to total users and non-users in respective categories.

Three main objectives of the study were:

- To analyse the use of ration cards by ration card-holders for purchasing rations from fair price shops.
- To assess the satisfaction and reaction of ration card holders towards the quality, supply and prices of foodgrains available in fair price shops; and
- To collect information regarding the prices of commodities available in fair price shops and compare these with the local free market prices.

It was found that 83 per cent of the ration card holders, mostly APL families, were not using the ration cards for the purchase of rice. The use of ration cards for the purpose of sugar and kerosene was 73 per cent and a meagre 18.67 per cent respectively. One of the important findings was that 95 per cent and 92 per cent of the ration card holders belonging to the rural areas had not used their cards for the last one year for the purchase of wheat or rice. This was largely because of the handiness of home grown rice and wheat, the poor quality of foodgrains available in fair price shops and the narrow difference between the PDS price and the free market price. However, the percentage of non-users in the urban and far-off areas is lower than that of the rural areas. The percentages of non-users of ration cards for rice are 96.62, 85.71, 51.28, 66.67 among the Backward Castes, General Castes, Scheduled Castes and Scheduled Tribes respectively (Table 15.7). The Scheduled Castes are the highest utilisers of ration cards for rice. This implies that PDS fulfils the need of the vulnerable sections of society and the poorer sections depend on PDS.

FIGURE 15.5

Status of Non-users of Ration Cards

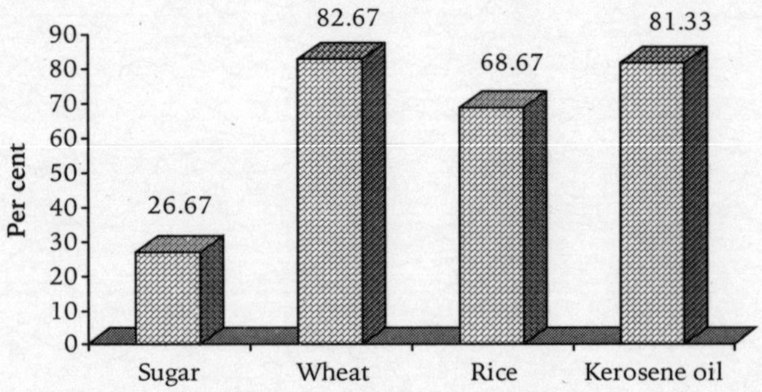

TABLE 15.7

Caste and Item-wise, User and Non-user of Ration Cards

Particular	*General*		*BCs*		*SCs*		*STs*		*Other's*		*Total*	
	User	*Non-user*	*User*	*Non-user*	*User*	*Non-user*	*User*	*Non-user*	*User*	*Non-user*	*User*	*Non-user*
Sugar	5 (35.71)	9 (64.29)	45 (69.23)	20 (30.77)	33 (84.62)	6 (15.38)	25 (83.33)	5 (16.67)	2 (100.0)	—	110 (73.33)	40 (26.67)
Wheat	2 (14.29)	12 (85.71)	2 (3.08)	63 (96.92)	10 (25.64)	29 (74.36)	10 (33.33)	20 (66.67)	2 (100.0)	—	26 (17.33)	124 (82.67)
Rice	1 (7.14)	13 (92.86)	4 (6.15)	61 (93.85)	19 (48.72)	20 (51.28)	21 (70.00)	9 (30.00)	2 (100.0)	—	47 (31.33)	103 (68.67)
Kerosene oil	—	14 (100.0)	22 (33.35)	43 (66.15)	—	39 (100.0)	4 (13.33)	26 (86.67)	2 (100.0)	—	28 (18.67)	122 (81.33)

Note: Figures in parenthesis show percentages to total users and non-user in respective categories.

TABLE 15.8

Occupation-wise User and Non-user of Ration Cards and Items

Particular	*Cultivator*		*Labour*		*Service*		*Domestic Work*		*Business*		*Other's (Retd & old age)*	
	User	*Non-user*	*User*	*Non-user*	*User*	*Non-user*	*User*	*Non-user*	*User*	*Non-user*	*User*	*Non-user*
Sugar	34 (75.56)	11 (24.44)	22 (78.57)	6 (21.43)	39 (81.25)	9 (18.75)	3 (75.00)	1 (25.00)	4 (26.67)	11 (73.33)	8 (80.00)	2 (20.00)
Wheat	4 (8.89)	41 (91.11)	10 (35.71)	18 (64.29)	9 (18.75)	39 (81.25)	1 (25.00)	3 (75.00)	1 (6.67)	14 (93.33)	1 (10.00)	9 (90.00)
Rice	10 (22.22)	35 (77.78)	13 (46.43)	15 (53.57)	18 (37.5)	30 (62.5)	2 (50.00)	2 (50.00)	2 (13.33)	13 (86.67)	2 (20.00)	8 (80.00)
Kerosene Oil	11 (24.44)	34 (75.56)	5 (17.86)	23 (82.14)	4 (8.33)	44 (91.67)	—	4 (100.00)	7 (46.67)	8 (53.33)	1 (100.00)	9 (90.00)

Note: Figures in parenthesis show percentages to total users and non-user in respective categories.

As far as occupation-wise users and non-users of the ration cards for wheat is concerned, the percentages are 91.11 for cultivators, 64.29 for labourers, 81.25 for services classes, 75.0 for domestic workers and 93.33 for business classes. Here again the labourers are the biggest users of ration cards for wheat. PDS provides food security to labourers, either marginal or landless. For rice, the percentages of users are lower in the case of cultivators and business classes (Table 15.8).

90 per cent of the families opined that they were not satisfied with the quality and prices of the foodgrains supplied through fair price shops. As compared to this, 56 per cent of the ration-card holders complained about irregular supply of rations at the fair price shops (Table 15.9). 100 per cent of the ration-card holders in the far-off areas were not satisfied with the quality of the rations. Moreover, the villagers of Joron in Sirmaur district also complained of corruption in these shops and lack of information regarding the date and time of the supply of rations.

One of the important findings as shown in Table 15.10 is that the prices of wheat at the fair price shops in the far-off areas (Kinnaur) meant for BPL families is higher (Rs 5.40) than those in other rural areas. Similarly, for APL families both wheat and rice prices are higher in the far-off areas as compared to other areas. This is mainly because of the cost of transportation. Therefore, most of the consumers belonging to the far-off areas are not satisfied with the prices of foodgrains. Quality being already a constraint, the high price of the foodgrains dissuades the consumer from going to the fair price shops. Ironically, the price variation in wheat for APL families in the far-off areas of Kinnaur district is only 20 paise.

FIGURE 15.6

Consumers not Satisfied Q.S.P.

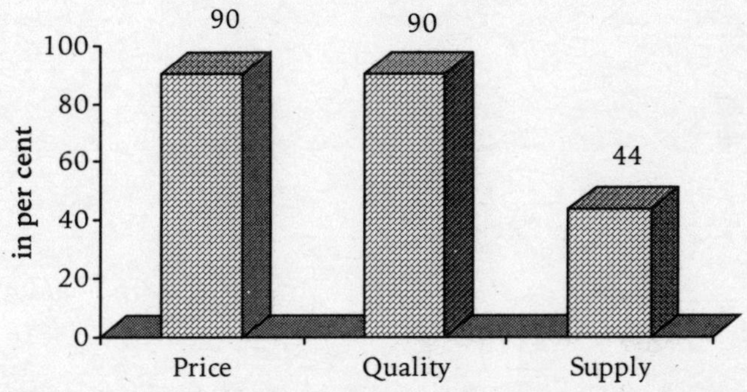

TABLE 15.9

Ration Card Holders Satisfied or Not Satisfied with Price, Quality and Supply

Particular	*Urban*		*Rural*		*Far-off Areas*		*Total*	
	Satisfied	*Non-Satisfied*	*Satisfied*	*Non-Satisfied*	*Satisfied*	*Non-Satisfied*	*Satisfied*	*Non-Satisfied*
Price	6 (14.64)	35 (85.36)	7 (8.86)	72 (91.14)	2 (6.67)	28 (93.33)	15 (10.0)	135 (90.0)
Quality	4 (9.75)	37 (90.25)	11 (13.93)	68 (86.07)	0 (0.00)	30 (100)	15 (10.0)	135 (90.0)
Supply	41 (100)	0 (0.00)	35 (44.30)	44 (55.70)	8 (26.67)	22 (73.33)	84 (56.0)	66 (44.0)

Note: Percentages to total satisfied and not- satisfied in respective categories.

TABLE 15.10

FPS and Free Market Rates of Commodities in Different Districts

Sr. No	Item	Place	Rate Per Kg			Quantity per Member/ Ration Card			Market Rate
			Antodaya	BPL	APL	Antodaya	BPL	APL	
1.	Wheat	Shimla	—	—	7.89***	-	-	12 Kg	9.50
		Kinnaur	2.00	5.40	7.30	12 Kg	12 Kg	12 Kg	7.50
		Solan	2.00	5.30	5.70	15 Kg	20 Kg	12 Kg	7.00
		Sirmaur	2.00	5.25	6.00	15 Kg	20 Kg	12 Kg	7.00
2.	Rice	Shimla	—	—	9.50	-	-	15 Kg	11.00
		Kinnaur	3.00	7.00	10.00	12 Kg	12 Kg	12 Kg	12.00
		Solan	3.00	7.00	7.00	20 Kg	40 Kg	15 Kg	10.00
		Sirmaur	3.00	7.00	7.00	20 Kg	40 Kg	15 Kg	10.00
3.	Kerosene Oil	Shimla	—	—	—	—	—	—	13.00
		Kinnaur	9.44	9.44	9.44	10 Lt.	10 Lt.	10 Lt.	13.50
		Solan	9.40	9.40	9.40	5 Lt.	5 Lt.	5 Lt.	12.00
		Sirmaur	9.64	9.64	9.64	10 Lt.	10 Lt.	10 Lt.	12.00
4.	Sugar	Shimla	—	—	13.50	—	—	1 Kg	14.00
		Kinnaur	13.50	13.50	13.50	700 Gm.	700 Gm.	700 Gm.	15.00
		Solan	13.50	13.50	13.50	500 Gm.	500 Gm.	500 Gm.	14.00
		Sirmaur	13.50	13.50	13.50	1 Kg.	1 Kg.	1 Kg.	14.00

Note: * Figures in parenthesis show percentages to total allocation.
** Figures in parenthesis show percentages to total lifting.
*** Rate of per kg atta.

Findings/Observations

- People desire that the quality of foodgrains needs to be improved.
- The percentage users of ration cards for foodgrains among the APL families is seasonal.
- APL families in the rural and urban areas are largely utilising their ration cards for the purchase of sugar.
- Discrepancy in the opinion of the APL families regarding their lower utilisation of ration cards for purchase of foodgrains and the utilisation status as given by ration-depot holder create apprehensions about the diversion and leakages of foodgrains to the free market.

Suggestions

The following suggestions will be helpful in effective functioning of the PDS for the alleviation of poverty, hunger and malnutrition in the state.

- Three types of cards for different categories of consumers may be prepared for effective identification not only for PDS but also for other security net benefits— yellow for *Antodaya* families; blue for BPL families and white for APL families. It would also be helpful in the prudent allocation of foodgrains quotas to the depot holders and check diversion of foodgrains.
- Inter-state visits of Food and Civil Supplies authorities and fair price shop-owners, preferably to Andhra Pradesh and Kerala, should be organised. The lessons learned from the visits and their few good features can be adopted in Himachal Pradesh.
- A monitoring mechanism through the effective involvement of not only *panchayat* members but also other sections of society, such as members of youth clubs, self-help groups and *Mahila Mandals*, need to be evolved. This would prevent exclusion of genuine beneficiaries; help in proper functioning of the fair price shops; streamlining of PDS and controlling of diversion of foodgrains to the free market.
- Himachal Pradesh has an efficient SHG (Self-Help Group) scheme operating in the state. SHGs with good savings should be provided with an opportunity to run fair price shops. It will fulfill the objective of economic empowerment of women and fortify their role in poverty alleviation.

- The fair price shops needs to be within the village. If it is not possible, it can open an extension counter with fixed dates and timing. Ward or cluster delivery system may be tried.
- Kerosene, sugar and other essential items need to be supplied at subsidised rates to *Antodaya* and BPL families.
- The QQP (Quantity, Quality and Price) management is important for an effective public distribution system. The government should evolve a mechanism to deal with this aspect.
- Political commitment, administrative ingenuity, fairness in the selection of fair price shops owner and effective participation of panchayati raj institutions and society and gender role are *sine–qua-non* for the effective functioning of PDS.
- As many APL households are occasionally using their ration cards for the purchase of food grains, this facility may either be withdrawn or made available seasonally to them to check possible leakage and diversion of foodgrains to the free market.
- Studies of the efficacy of fair price shops run by different organisations and individuals need to be conducted and the system found comparatively effective need to be proliferated in the state.
- Careful attention needs to be paid to 'E' mistakes (exclusion of deserving persons) and 'I' mistakes (inclusion of non-deserving persons) while selecting beneficiaries of BPL, AYY and *Annapurna* schemes, particularly the latter two.
- Last but not the least, the PDS in Himachal Pradesh is well catering to the needs of the poorest of the poor, despite of some short comings.

References

Asthana, M.D. and Medrano, P. (ed.) *Towards Hunger Free India–Agenda and Imperatives*, Manohar, 2001.

Coondoo, D., A. Majumder and K. Bhattacharya, "Employment, Level of Living and Utilization of PDS", in Krishanaji, N. and T.N. Krishnan, (ed), *Public Support for Food Security*, Sage Publication, New Delhi, 2000.

Dutta, B. and Ramaswami B., "Targeting and Efficiency in the Public Distribution System Case of Andhra Pradesh and Maharastra", 5 May, 2001. *Economic & Political Weekly*, May 5, 2001.

Five Year Plan of Government of Himachal Pradesh.

Pattanaik, B.K. "Rural Poverty and Public Distribution System", *Yojana*, November 1997.

Rao, V.M. and Deshpande, R.S., "Food Security in Drought Prone Areas: A Study in Karnataka", *Economic & Political Weekly*, 31 August 2002.

Status of the Topics/Activities Pertaining to Food and Supplies Department, Government of Himachal Pradesh.

Swaminathan, M., and Misra N., "Errors of Targeting, Public Distribution of Food in a Maharastra Village", 1995-2000, 30 June, 2001, *Economic & Political Weekly.*

Vyas, V.S., "New Economic Policy and Vulnerable Sections", *Economic & Political Weekly*, 28 (10); 405-7.

World Bank, *Reducing Poverty in India–Options for More Effective Public Service*, Report No. 17881-IN, Poverty Reduction and Economic Management Unit, South Asia Region, Washington, DC. 1993.

Chapter 16

Industry

The Industrial Sector Over the Years

Industrialisation is a comparatively recent phenomenon in Himachal Pradesh. It gained momentum during the last two decades. Monetary and fiscal benefits as incentives and subsidies to industry, provided by the state as well as the central government, and the availability of quality industrial infrastructure in the form of developed plots, and sheds equipped with basic amenities, have played a key role in the industrial development of the state. Industries in Himachal Pradesh, are now producing from traditional to a wide spectrum of high-tech products like computer monitors, magnetic components, high quality precision components, tele-communication equipment, electronics, drugs and pharmaceuticals, processed food, textiles, and spinning products. The contribution of the industrial or manufacturing sector has grown significantly from Rs. 774 crore in 1995-96 to Rs. 1920 crore in 2001-02. In terms of percentage, the share of the manufacturing sector in the Gross State Domestic Product (GSDP) has increased from 12.18 in 1995-96 to 14.38 in 1999-00. Table 16.1 shows the share of the manufacturing sector in Himachal Pradesh as compared to Punjab and the whole of India over the period 1995-96 to 1999-00.

TABLE 16.1

Percentage Share of Manufacturing Sector in Gross State Domestic Product

(At current prices)

Year	*Himachal*	*Punjab*	*India*
1995-96	12.18 (774)	15.76	18.10
1996-97	13.16 (998)	15.23	17.70
1997-98	13.68 (1118)	15.04	16.70
1998-99	14.24 (1413)	14.04	15.60
1999-00	14.38 (1626)	14.44	15.40

Source: *National Accounts Statistics*, CSO, Government of India Director of Industries of Himachal Pradesh *National Abstract of Punjab*, ESO, Government of Punjab.

Note: Figure shown in brackets are in crore.

By March 2002, the total production was worth Rs. 5000 crore, providing direct employment to 1.56 lakh persons, with an investment of Rs. 3048 crore in the SSI and L&M sectors.

Table 16.2 also shows that investment in the L&M sector accounts for 78 per cent while employment only 19 per cent. On the other hand, in the SSI and tiny sectors investment is only 22 per cent and employment 81 per cent. In the Eighth Plan (1992-97) the number of industrial units increased from 21,630 to 25,777 (19.3%), employment from 1,05,277 to 1,30,560 persons (24%) and investment from Rs. 446.38 crore to Rs. 1634.63 crore (466.6%). On the other hand, in the Ninth Plan (1997-02) industrial units increased 13.1 per cent, employment 16.2 per cent and investment 46.5 per cent.

Growth Pattern of the Industrial Sector

Table 16.2 shows that during 1979-80 to 2001-02, large and medium industries (L&M) have increased 8.7 times. The investment in this sector has gone up 11.5 times between 1990-91 and 2001-02 and employment has doubled.

In the small scale (SSI) sector, between 1980 and 2002, the number of units has multiplied 4.2 times. The investment increased 4.5 times during 1990-91 to 2001-02 and employment 1.5 times.

Concentration of Industry

Industrial development in the state has been uneven. The periphery districts of Solan, Sirmaur, Kangra and

TABLE 16.2

Growth of Industry in Himachal Pradesh

Year	*Units (No.)*			*Employment (No.)*			*Investment (in crore) Current Prices*		
	SSI	*L&M*	*Total*	*SSI*	*L&M*	*Total*	*SSI*	*L&M*	*Total*
1979-80	6969	22	6991						
1990-91	20545	110	20655	86227	15125	101352	150.54	200.84	351.38
1991-92	21518	112	21630	89997	15280	105277	222.38	224.00	446.38
1992-93	22440	114	22554	93577	15747	109324	289.28	265.00	554.28
1993-94	23265	121	23386	96779	17824	114603	350.20	404.33	754.53
1994-95	24121	129	24250	100119	19693	119812	412.40	761.27	1173.67
1995-96	24845	147	24992	103269	22467	125736	465.10	1447.40	1912.50
1996-97	25617	160	25777	106665	23895	130560	485.34	1595.66	2081.01
1997-98	26378	173	26551	110112	25988	136100	518.78	2031.14	2549.92
1998-99	27253	174	27427	114491	26103	140594	564.43	2085.41	2649.84
1999-00	28045	182	28227	119618	28930	148548	613.56	2288.49	2902.05
2000-01	28731	188	28919	122745	29047	151792	643.50	2310.52	2954.03
2001-02	29479	191	29670	126594	29382	155976	685.48	2363.34	3048.82

Source: Director of Industries Himachal Pradesh.

Una are comparatively better developed. About 60 per cent of the total and 95 per cent of the large and medium (L&M) units are concentrated in these districts. On the other hand the inner districts of Bilaspur, Chamba, Hamirpur, Kullu, Kinnaur, Lahaul & Sipiti, Mandi and Shimla have been categorised as backward districts and account for 40 per cent of the total industries. The periphery districts of Solan and Sirmaur are the most developed and have been categorised as developed districts, while Kangra and Una are less developed and come under the category of backward districts. Thus, the state has been classified into two categories, *viz.*, industrially developed and backward areas/districts.

Table 16.3 shows that in the industrially developed areas of Solan and Sirmaur districts, L&M units account for 88 per cent, investment 70 per cent and employment 34 per cent while in the remaining 10 districts categorised as backward areas/districts, SSI and tiny sector units account for 82 per cent, investment 30 per cent and employment 66 per cent. Another feature is that in Solan and Sirmaur districts,

TABLE 16.3

District-wise No. of Industrial Units, Investment and Employment (31 March 2002)

District	*Units (No.)*			*Employment (No.)*			*Investment (in crore) Current Prices*		
	SSI	*L&M*	*Total*	*SSI*	*L&M*	*Total*	*SSI*	*L&M*	*Total*
Bilaspur	1879	3	1882	6876	1221	8097	28.65	384.66	413.32
Chamba	1479	—	1479	5247	—	5247	20.62	—	20.62
Hamirpur	2286	—	2286	8322	—	8322	35.61	—	35.61
Kangra	7844	6	7850	34096	791	34887	143.69	21.35	165.04
Kullu	2000	1	2001	9784	52	9836	33.81	6.25	40.07
Kinnaur	506	—	506	1533	—	1533	2.97	—	2.97
Lahaul & Spiti	542	—	542	1452	—	1452	2.31	—	2.31
Mandi	2904	1	2905	11620	186	11806	63.14	2.70	65.84
Shimla	2723	4	2727	10080	541	10621	43.60	33.29	76.89
Sirmaur	2291	30	2321	10057	4343	14400	85.78	256.14	341.93
Solan	2639	138	2777	17436	21345	38781	161.32	1640.04	1801.36
Una	2386	8	2394	10091	903	10994	63.92	18.90	82.82
Himachal Pradesh	**29479**	**191**	**29670**	**126594**	**29382**	**155976**	**685.42**	**2363.33**	**3048.78**

Source: Director of Industries Himachal Pradesh.

TABLE 16.4

District-wise Group-wise Details of Units in Large and Medium Scale Sector as on 31 March, 2003

Sr. No.	*Total No./Group*	*Solan*	*Sirmaur*	*Kangra*	*Una*	*Shimla*	*Bilaspur*	*Kullu*	*Mandi*	*Total*
1.	Food Products	17	2	6	1	—	1	—	—	27
2.	Beverages	3	1	—	1	—	—	1	—	6
3.	Textiles/Spinning	21	1	—	1	—	—	—	—	23
4.	Chemical & Chemical Products	20	5	—	1	—	—	—	1	27
5.	Engineering	10	—	—	—	—	—	—	—	10
6.	Non-metallic Mineral Products	2	—	—	—	—	—	—	—	2
7.	Electronics	23	2	—	—	3	—	—	—	27
8.	Steel & Steel Products	21	9	—	2	—	—	—	—	31
9.	Paper & Paper Products	11	5	—	2	1	—	—	—	19
10.	Cement	3	3	—	—	—	2	—	—	8
11.	Leather & Leather Products	2	—	—	—	—	—	—	—	2
12.	Ceramic	1	—	—	—	—	—	—	—	1
13.	Plastic Products	7	2	—	—	—	—	—	—	5
	Total	**141**	**30**	**6**	**8**	**4**	**3**	**1**	**1**	**194**

Source: Director of Industries Himachal Pradesh.

investment in the SSI sector per unit is Rs.5 lakh to Rs.6 lakh, while in Kinnaur and Lahaul and Spiti it is as low as Rs. 50,000 per unit and in the remaining districts Rs. 1.5 lakh to Rs. 2 lakh. It also reveals that in the backward districts SSI, tiny and the cottage industry form a major industrial sector and hold the key to large-scale employment and generation of economic activities in remote areas. These industries are based on local raw materials and artisan entrepreneurs.

Table 16.4 shows that L&M industries exist only in eight districts. More than 95 per cent of these industries are in the periphery districts of Solan, Sirmaur, Kangra and Una. In the remaining districts L&M industries are mainly based on local raw material, like the two cement plants in Bilaspur, while the electronics industries have been located in Shimla mainly due to the availability of better infrastructure and manpower. The major industries are food products, textile/spinning, chemical and chemical products, electronics, steel and steel products, paper and paper products and precision and mechanical engineering. They constitute 80 per cent of the total L&M industries.

In the SSI and Tiny sectors of Himachal Pradesh, 65 per cent of the industrial units relate to food and allied products, hosiery, wood and wood products and mechanical items. These, along with chemical and allied products, are major sources of employment. Details of the number of industrial units and the employment provided by different industrial groups with percentages are given in Table 16.5.

TABLE 16.5

Industrial Group-wise, No. of Units and Employment in Small-Scale Industries in the State as on 31 March, 2001

Sr. No.	*Industrial Groups*	*Units*		*Employment*	
		Number	*Percentage*	*Number*	*Percentage*
1.	Food & Allied	7982	27.7	27937	18.9
2.	Hosiery	3916	13.6	11748	8.0
3.	Wood & Wood Products	3562	12.4	16029	10.9
4	Paper & Paper Products	462	1.6	2541	1.7
5.	Leather & Leather Products	1336	4.6	4676	3.2
6.	Glass & Ceramic	577	2.0	6058	4.1
7.	Chemical & Allied	1621	5.6	19452	13.2
8.	Mechanical Items	4136	14.3	31020	21.1
9.	Electric & Electx.	931	3.2	8379	5.7
10.	Misc. & Other	4319	15.0	19435	13.2
	Total	**28842**	**100.0**	**147275**	**100.0**

Source: *State Industrial Profile of Himachal Pradesh (2001-02)*, by Small Industries Service Institute (SISI), Government of India, Solan, Himachal Pradesh.

Exports

Exports from the state have risen from Rs. 40 crore in 1995-96 to Rs. 500.00 crore in 2000-2001. The main items of export include cotton, synthetic and blended yarn, engineering goods like bearings, filters, gears, scientific instruments, electronic goods, leather products, essential oils, medicines, processed food, water dials. There are about 80 export-oriented units and most of them are located in Solan and Sirmaur districts.

Sickness of Industry

A number of industrial units, particularly in the SSI sector are reported to be sick. Of the total member of units financed by Himachal Pradesh Financial Corporation (HPFC), Himachal Pradesh State Industrial Development Corporation (HPSIDC) and 15 banks, 1150 are sick units in the SSI sector. According to the all India Census 2001 of SSI units, the percentage of working units in the state, as on 31st March 2001, is only 61.6. Industrial sickness causes heavy losses in terms of unemployment, non-payment of dues to state and central government, financial institutions and banks and non-utilisation of productive assets. A mechanism should be evolved to assess the real magnitude of sick units and for timely detection of sickness at the initial stages. There is need to determine expeditiously preventive and remedial measures for the revival of the potentially viable sick industrial units. It is necessary to set up a state-level institution, with adequate powers and resources, consisting of the representatives of the Reserve Bank of India, financial institutions, banks, industry and state government, to provide requisite financial support to small scale units suffering from sickness or showing symptoms of sickness.

Overview of Industrial Policies and their Impact

In order to promote effective and systematic industrial growth, the industry department of the state government has been formulating industrial development policies and strategies on a regular and continuing basis, particularly in the last two decades. In this hilly and industrially backward state, the major bottleneck is the possibility of an industrial unit becoming unviable mainly because of the high cost of procuring raw materials and reaching markets outside the state. Therefore, for the utilisation of its natural resources and opening up of new avenues of employment, it is essential to encourage industrial development, supported by a package of incentives to improve their viability.

Since the Sixth Five Year Plan (1980-85) emphasis has been laid on the co-ordinated development of large and medium, small scale, tiny and cottage industries, with a thrust on:

- Package of attractive concessions and subsidies to promote investment.
- High priority to industries that are based on local raw materials and provide major employment opportunities.
- Thrust on rural industrialisation, small-scale, tiny and cottage industries.
- Creation of quality infrastructure through setting up industrial areas/estates. At least one industrial area/estate is to be established in each district of the state.
- Strengthening support institutions and setting up new industrial projects in the public sector.

The Sixth Five Year Plan (1980-85) provided an outlay of Rs. 20.35 crore for the implementation of various promotional schemes and a package of incentives, concessions, and spent Rs. 20.48 crore. The Seventh Plan (1985-90) continued with the same policy but with greater vigour and thrust. The Seventh Five Year Plan provided an enhanced outlay of Rs. 35.45 crore but the actual expenditure was Rs. 42.62 crore. During the Sixth and Seventh Five Year Plans (FYPs) the industry gained a momentum and grew at a faster pace.

During the Eighth Plan (1992-97) an outlay of Rs. 76.2 crore was approved and the expenditure incurred was Rs. 86.46 crore. In this plan, the main emphasis was on providing more infrastructure facilities to the entrepreneurs by establishing industrial areas/estates at the *tehsil* and block levels, thus enabling industrial activity in the rural and far-flung areas of the state.

During this period, new industrial policies were introduced in 1991 and 1996. According to the industrial policy of 1991, the industrial areas were categorised in A, B or C grade, to bring about a balanced industrial development in the state. The categorisation was based on location and the following parameters:

- Distance from the border of the adjoining states of Punjab, Haryana and Uttar Pradesh (except within Shimla district).
- Extent of industrial development/industrial backwardness existing in that block.
- Extent of overall backwardness of the block.
- Extent of potential for generating employment for the local people.

The existing development blocks were categorised accordingly. The Quantum of concessions and subsidies and the duration of their applicability will depend on the category of the industrial block (A, B or C), the type of industry (tiny/khadi & village/small scale/L&M) or whether these were in the priority or general sector. Based on these parameters, the industrial policy of 1996 also continued to provide the package of incentives and subsidies which included:

- Sales tax concessions.
- Electricity duty exemption.
- Capital investment and interest subsidies.
- Special schemes of incentives to specific categories of entrepreneurs like the Schedule Caste, the Schedule Tribes, women, and the physically handicapped.
- Special package of incentives to tiny, cottage and khadi & village industries.
- Up to 15 per cent purchase price preference in government/semi-government organisations to the tiny/SSI sector and up to three per cent to the large and medium sector.
- Additional concessions to priority industries like out-of-turn allotment of plots.
- Special schemes and facilities to NRIs and special support and incentives for export promotion.
- In addition, the Government of India provided 75 per cent transport subsidy to industry.

The beginning of the Ninth Plan (1997-2002), continued with the same concessions and incentives as stated in the industrial policy of 1996, but new policy guidelines in 1999, laid emphasis on expansion and upgradation of the infrastructure and ensuring advantages to investors. The plan also envisages a thrust on the development of the tiny, cottage, khadi & village and small-scale industries by graded incentives. According to these guidelines, the state has been divided into two categories, namely "industrially developed areas" and "industrially backward areas" instead of A, B and C categories. The development blocks of Poanta Sahib and Nahan in Sirmaur district and Nalagarh, Dharampur and Solan in Solan district would fall in the category of "industrially developed areas". The rest of the state will be in the category of "industrially backward areas". The industrial policy of 1999 also incorporates, a special package of incentives for fruit, vegetable and maize based units consuming locally available raw material. The Ninth Plan provided an outlay of Rs. 150 crore but utilised only Rs. 91.90 crore. The Tenth Plan (2002-07) has an approved outlay of Rs. 104.73 crore for the industrial sector. Plan-wise approved outlay and actual expenditure and its percentage to the total plan figures are given in the table below.

TABLE 16.6

Plan Wise Outlay Approved and Actual Expenditure

Plan	*Period*	*Outlay (in crore)*	*Percentage Share to Total Plan*	*Actual Expenditure (in crore)*	*Percentage Share of Total Expenditure*
6th Plan	1980-85	20.35	3.27	20.49	3.08
7th Plan	1985-90	35.45	3.01	42.62	3.22
8th Plan	1992-97	76.20	3.20	86.54	3.05
9th Plan	1997-02	150.00	2.63	91.90	1.29
10th Plan		104.73	0.84		

Source: Different Five Year Plans, Himachal Pradesh.

Table 16.6 reveals that plan expenditure has been increasing in successive plans. However, the share of the total plan expenditure has declined. It is also evident from the industrial policy statement, the package of incentives, the increased utilisation of funds, and enhanced investment in infrastructure in successive Plans, that industry has grown over the years.

To provide further impetus to industry, the Government of India notified on 7 January, 2003 a new industrial policy and other concessions to Himachal Pradesh which can provide a fillip to the industrial development of the state.

1. *Fiscal Incentives to New Industrial Units and to the Existing Units on their Substantial Expansion*

   a) The notified areas are entitled to:

   - Hundred per cent outright excise duty exemption for 10 years from the date of commencement of commercial production.
   - Hundred per cent income tax exemption for an initial period of five years and thereafter 30 per cent for companies and 25 per cent for other than companies for a further period of five years for Himachal Pradesh.
   - A capital investment subsidy at 15 per cent of their investment in plant and machinery, subject to a ceiling of Rs. 30 lakh.

   b) Thrust sector industries, as listed below are entitled to similar concessions as mentioned above in the whole state, of without any area restrictions.

Thrust Sector Industries

Horticulture and agro-based industries such as:

- Sauces, ketchup, fruit, juices and fruit pulp, jams, jellies, vegetable, puree, pickles, preserved fruits and vegetables, processing of fresh fruits and vegetables including packaging; and processing, preservation and packaging of mushrooms
- Floriculture, medicinal herbs and aromatic herbs, honey, food processing industry, sugar and its by products, silk and silk products, wool and wool products, sports goods, paper and paper products, pharma products, bottling of mineral water, industrial gases, handicrafts, non-timber forest-product based industries

2. *Fiscal Incentives to Industrial Infrastructure*

The growth centre scheme, currently envisaging a central assistance of Rs. 10 crore per centre has been raised to Rs. 15 crore per centre.

The financing patterns of Integrated Infrastructure Development Centres (IIDC) between the Government of India and SIDBI will change from 2:3 to 4:1 and funds would be in the nature of grants, so as to provide the required infrastructural support.

Industries in the negative list are not eligible for the above concessions.

Impact of Industrial Policy Announced by the Government of India (Dated 7 January 2003)

- The policy will be most beneficial to excisable and profitable units with production of more than Rs. 1 crore.
- Most entrepreneurs will prefer to set up new units in the periphery districts as these have close proximity to the neighbouring states and Chandigarh, access to raw materials and better connectivity. These periphery districts will have the same incentives and concessions as are applicable to the inner districts.
- Most of the units located in the inner districts (backward areas) are in the small-scale, tiny and cottage sectors and are not excisable (production less than Rs. 1 crore). Therefore, the industrial policy notified by the Government of India would not be of much benefit to most of the units located in the inner districts.

Therefore, new units are likely to be set up in the periphery districts, achieving accelerated growth but may not be sustainable in the long run, as fiscal concessions are available only for a limited period. On the other hand, industrial growth in the inner district will not be encouraged by the new policy.

After the announcement of the new industrial policy for Himachal Pradesh by the Government of India, the pace of registration of industrial units in the large and medium sector has increased tremendously. From 1 April 2003 to 31 May 2003, i.e., in two months, 31 units were registered with an investment of Rs. 385.20 crore and employment for 4201 persons, while only 11 units with an investment of Rs. 149.88 crore and employment for 1388 persons were registered from 1 April 2001 to 31 December 2002. It means that with the announcement of the new industrial policy, the registration of L&M industries has increased eight to nine times.

To achieve accelerated industrial growth and long-term sustainability, two independent strategies, one for the periphery districts and the other for the inner districts, have to be formulated separately, so that all districts of the state reap the benefits of the industrial policy notified by the Government of India.

Industrial Support System

The Government of India and Himachal Pradesh have established a number of institutions/centres/organisations/corporation/boards to provide technological, HRD development and training, financial and other promotional support to industry. A brief overview of this industrial support system follows:

1. *Small Industries Service Institute (SISI), Chambaghat, Solan*

An extension centre of the Small Industries Service Institute of the Government of India was set up at Chambaghat in 1960 and converted into a branch office in 1973. Keeping in view the requirements of industrial development in Himachal Pradesh, it was converted into a full-fledged institute in 1976. It provides the following services to existing and prospective entrepreneurs:

- Economic information and consultancy service
  - Educates entrepreneurs on the incentives and facilities being provided by the central and the state governments to small-scale units.
  - Collects, compiles and disseminates information on small-scale industries.
  - Informs entrepreneurs about the schemes and programmes of various development agencies.

- Conducts studies and surveys about the problems of small-scale units in the state.
- Industrial potential survey report.
- Educates entrepreneurs about the government's single point registration scheme.

• Technical consultancy service/Techno-managerial assistance

- Prepares project profiles on products according to the needs of prospective entrepreneurs.
- Solves technical problems of small-scale industries.
- Helps entrepreneurs in selecting suitable machinery and raw materials and appropriate technology.
- Conducts in-plant studies of small-scale units and suggests modernisation.
- Energy conservation.
- Management courses for existing units.
- Cluster development activity.

• Management and technical training

- Organises intensive industrial motivation campaigns to motivate entrepreneurs.
- Organises entrepreneurship development programmes to promote entrepreneurship among various sections of society.
- Conducts skill-oriented entrepreneurship development programmes.
- Conducts short entrepreneurship development programmes for the benefit of entrepreneurs under self-employment schemes.

2. *Bureau of Indian Standards, Chandigarh*

It is a Central Government department, which specifies quality standards for different products. It helps in selecting appropriate machinery and equipment for installing quality facilities. It also helps in setting up testing laboratories in units and also authorises units that manufacture products of specified standards to use the ISI mark. The Bureau has opened its branch office in Nalagarh, district Solan, Himachal Pradesh.

3. *Reserve Bank of India, Chandigarh*

Its main objective is to provide guidelines to lending institutions such as the IDBI, IFCI, ICICI, SIDBI, financial corporations/banks, on lending money to the industrial sector and control money supply. It is also the convener of the 'state level inter institutional committee' (SLIIC) for Himachal Pradesh, dealing with sickness and financial problems of the SSI sector.

4. *Electronics Test and Development Centre, Chambaghat, Solan*

Its main functions are to provide testing and commercial facilities to units manufacturing electronics products and also to impart training in basic electronic and development of new electronic products.

5. *Himachal Pradesh State Environment and Pollution Control Board, Shimla*

It assists units in installing the necessary pollution control devices and grants the necessary permission.

6. *Small Industries Development Bank of India, Shimla*

It provides finance to small-scale industries through its various refinance schemes. It also provides refinance through state financial corporations and banks at concessional rates.

7. *Directorate of Industries, Shimla*
(with network of district industries centres (DICs) at the district level and extension officer, industry, at the block level).

Its main functions are:

- Registration of SSIs and recommendation of medium and large-scale industries to the appropriate authority.
- Technical consultancy/general consultancy.
- Recommendation of cases for financial assistance to financial Institutions/banks, for margin money and loans.
- Industrial infrastructure development.
- Collection and maintenance of data relating to industrial units.
- Allotment of industrial plots/sheds/shops in the district.
- Liaison and feedback with the central and state governments.
- Administration of all incentives to industries given by both central and state governments.

Besides, two single window clearance agencies have been set up in the industrial areas at Parwanoo and

Baddi, which provide services and facilities required by small-scale industries under a single roof.

8. Himachal Pradesh State Small Industries and Export Corporation, Shimla

It was incorporated on October 20, 1966, to achieve the following objectives:

- To supply raw materials through raw material depots.
- To supply machinery on hire-purchase.
- To provide assistance in export and marketing.

9. Himachal Pradesh Electronics Development Corporation, Shimla

It was set up in 1984 to promote the growth of the electronics industry in Himachal Pradesh.

10. Himachal Pradesh Khadi and Village Industries Board (KVIB), Shimla

It was constituted on January 8, 1968 with the objectives of:

- Promoting, encouraging and assisting the development of khadi and village industries in the state.
- Providing financial assistance and loans at concessional rates to individuals, societies/ institutions.
- Providing marketing assistance by selling products of KVIB through its own showrooms.
- Conducting training courses, to impart necessary skill and training.

11. Himachal Pradesh State Handloom and Handicrafts Corporation Limited, Shimla

The main objectives and targets are:

- To promote and develop handloom and handicrafts industry in the state.
- To impart training to weavers/artisans to improve their skills in weaving and also provide financial and raw materials assistance.
- To assist entrepreneurs in setting up units in their areas.
- To provide marketing assistance by selling handloom and handicraft products of local entrepreneurs through showrooms.

12. Himachal Consultancy Organisation Ltd. (HIMCON), Shimla

Its main functions are:

- To render consultancy to entrepreneurs starting from project identification to marketing.
- Development of entrepreneurship by conducting entrepreneurship development programmes.

13. Himachal Pradesh Financial Corporation, Shimla

It was established on April 1, 1967, as a result of reorganisation of the erstwhile Punjab Financial Corporation with the following objectives:

- To provide medium-and long-term loans as well as working capital loan to small and medium scale units under its various schemes.
- To provide loans for expansion, modernisation and rehabilitation of the existing units.

14. Himachal Pradesh State Industrial Development Corporation Ltd. (HPSIDC)

The Himachal Pradesh State Industrial Development Corporation Ltd. (HPSIDC) was incorporated in November 1966 to promote and develop medium and large-scale industries in the state and act as an institutional entrepreneur. It provides long-term finance, besides equity participation, to industrial units in the L&M sectors. The corporation acts as the state-level financial institution under the refinance scheme of the Industrial Development Bank of India (IDBI) and the Small Industries Development Bank of India (SIDBI). The agency has also been designated as the nodal agency for the administration of the capital investment and subsidy scheme announced by the Government of India. In addition, it is involved in planning and developing industrial estates and industrial areas.

15. Himachal Pradesh Centre for Entrepreneurship Development (HPCED)

It was set up at Parwanoo in Solan district to provide training to prospective entrepreneurs of the state, to enable them set up their own self-employment centres. The main objectives are:

- To promote entrepreneurship by organising programmes and workshops, to motivate and infuse the spirit of entrepreneurship with focus on youth.

- To carry out the message of industrialisation to the unemployed youth, who are unaware of the self-employment outlets provided by the industrial sector.

16. Technical Institutions in Himachal Pradesh

The State has a network of institutions imparting technical education in different disciplines of engineering. There are three institutions offering degree courses in engineering. Besides, there are seven diploma level courses and 57 industrial training institutes for men and women to impart technical training in different trades.

Industrial Infrastructure

Availability of high quality industrial infrastructure with basic amenities and modern facilities in different industrial areas and estates is most essential for sustaining and accelerating industrial growth. The Industry Department of the State had developed by March 31, 2002, 30 industrial areas and 10 industrial estates in different districts (details in Table 16.7) with only such basic amenities as roads, power, sewerage, water and communication. Besides, more industrial areas and estates are proposed to be developed during the Tenth Five Year Plan in different districts. One growth centre, with an estimated cost of Rs. 22 crore has been developed at Sansarpur Terrace in Kangra district. Besides, an export promotion industrial park, with an investment of Rs. 20 crore, is being developed at Baddi as a sponsored project by the Union Ministry of Commerce. In addition, the Department of Industries proposes to set up an apparel park, clusters, agri-export zones (AEZ), and special economic zones (SEZ). Effective implementation of the existing and proposed schemes and programmes, encouragement of private sector participation in infrastructure development, and simplification of procedures are necessary to ensure accelerated industrial growth in the state.

The State government has already developed 30 industrial areas and 10 industrial estates with all basic amenities like roads, power, sewerage, water and communication, etc., as shown below:

TABLE 16.7

Industrial Areas/Industrial Estates in Himachal Pradesh

District	*Industrially Backward Area*		*Industrially Developing Area*	
	Industrial Area	*Industrial Estate*	*Industrial Area*	*Industrial Estate*
Bilaspur	i) Bilaspur ii) Golthai			
Chamba	i) Sultanpur ii) Parel iii) Hatli	Hatli		
Hamirpur	i) Hamirpur ii) Nadaun			
Kangra	i) Nagrota Bagwan ii) Sansarpur Terrace iii) Electronics Complex Nagri iv) Dhaliara v) Bianatarian	i) Kangra ii) Jawali iii) Dehra Gopipur		
Kullu	Shamshi			
Kinnaur	Reckong Peo			
Lahaul & Spiti		Keylong		
Mandi	i) Ner Chowk (Ratti) ii) Bhambla iii) Sulikhad iv) Maigal	Kotli		
Shimla	Electronics Complex, Shoghi	i) Theog ii) Pandranoo		
Sirmaur			i) Kala Amb ii) Paonta Sahib	
Una	i) Mehatpur ii) Tahliwala iii) Amb iv) Gagret			
Solan			i) Baddi ii) Barotiwala iii) Chambaghat Solan iv) Parwanoo	i) Chambaghat-Solan ii) Dharampur

Source: Director of Industries, Himachal Pradesh

The existing industrial areas and estates provide the basic infrastructure, but modern and technological infrastructure is highly inadequate. In the present era of globalisation and WTO agreements, the technological capabilities of the industrial sector have to be enhanced to make it competitive in the international market in terms of quality and price. Therefore, the existing industrial areas and estates must be modernised and upgraded. The broad measures suggested are technological upgradation, product adaptation and development of new products, human resource development through skill upgradation and training and marketing support. This will facilitate building a centralised modern network of infrastructure, including marketing.

Himachal Pradesh comprises diverse terrain ranging from the sub-montane, sub-tropical areas to hills and mountains and thus has varied climatic zones. This diversity has endowed the state with rich natural resources. With diverse agro-climatic conditions and geographical features, horticulture, floriculture, sericulture, forestry, hydro-power generation, handicrafts, handlooms, herbs-based and aromatic, minerals, wool-based industries are comparatively better developed. These industries have been identified as thrust industries. Therefore, to reap the full advantage of local raw materials, coupled with a package of incentives for the growth of these industries, it is essential that a modern and appropriate infrastructure is created at a faster pace by setting up clusters at different locations. This approach will promote industrial development and create a large number of sustainable small-scale and tiny industrial units and increase employment opportunities in the state.

In addition to these industrial areas and estates, small and medium clusters should be set up at different places. A micro-enterprise concept, based on local resources, should be encouraged by setting up small clusters, to overcome the disadvantages of small size and enhance co-operation, to meet the challenges of trade and market reforms and liberalisation. The bulk of the artisan-based industry belongs to the category of home-based, cottage and tiny industries. The small clusters can cover different products, mainly based on local raw material. In addition to basic infrastructure, these clusters should have relevant centralised facilities, like training programmes, design centres, raw material depots, testing facilities, packaging and marketing support and information hubs. Industrial clusters have a high potential for collective efficiency. Although networked, individual units have the flexibility for innovation and experimentation. While successes get quickly multiplied, failures remain limited. Some industrial development agencies, *viz.*, KVIC, NABARD and SIDBI have identified some rural industrial clusters. A bee-keeping cluster has been promoted by KVIB in Kullu; another for steel/wooden furniture in Mandi district and one for bamboo in Kangra district are under consideration. Similarly, NABARD, and SIDBI have identified clusters for metal, woodcraft, wool weaving and Tibetan handicrafts in Kullu district. SIDBI has appointed Him Bunkar as the implementing agency.

Besides these identified clusters, some of the District Industries Centres (DICs) of the Industry Department have recommended activities, which could be viable under the industrial cluster programme. These activities and areas are:

TABLE 16.8

Recommended Clusters, Activity Location-wise

Name of the District	*Name of the Activity*
Kangra	
1) Kandror	Engineering/agriculture implements
2) Nagri	Wood carving
Lahaul & Spiti	
1) Udaipur	Weaving of woollen patti
Kinnaur	
1) Tapri	Metal fabrication
Kullu	Shawl weaving bamboo craft, pattu making etc.
Mandi	
1) Nerchowk	Automobile
2) Ramnagar	Wooden and steel furniture
Sirmaur	
1) Rajgarh	Fruit processing
2) Sangarh	Limestone
3) Shillai	Weaving
Shimla	Food products, pickles, Jam, packaging & potato wrappers (at Theog)
Hamirpur & Nadaun	Shawl making, furniture, hosiery, leather products, card board boxes & herbal processing
Bilaspur	
1) Lethwin	Potters
2) Bhadrog	Weavers

Source: *State Industrial Profile of Himachal Pradesh* (2001-02) by a Small Industries Service Institutes (SISI), Government of India, Solan, Himachal Pradesh.

In addition to these, some herbal-based clusters could be set up in the state as the higher reaches are endowed with a large number of precious herbs. Similarly, sericulture could be taken up through clusters in the districts of Kangra, Mandi and Sirmaur. Thrust should be on promoting more rural industrial clusters under the National Programme of Rural Industrialisation (NPRI).

NABARD has selected Solan as a model district to launch its newly initiated project, "District Rural Industries Project". The purpose of this project is to create rural non-farm sector (RNFS) activities, which will be undertaken in association with different government agencies as well as NGOs.

To create a state-of-art infrastructure, the following aspects need priority;

- Modernisation of industrial areas/estates.
- Cluster development around thrust areas.
- Promotion of maximum participation of the private sector in the development of sustainable industrial infrastructure.
- Government as a facilitator through decentralisation, deregulation and self-certification.
- Thrust on fostering clusters around villages, facilitating rural industrialisation.
- Local educated youths should be trained for each cluster, activity-and location-wise to adopt new designs, testing and marketing techniques for ensuring long-term sustainability of these clusters.

An advisory council should be constituted for each cluster, in addition to an 'Industrial Area Development Authority', for the development and upgradation of industrial areas and estates in the state.

The state government should identify administrators and mangers, with technological and professional background, to work as facilitators and co-ordinators for rapid, non-polluting industrialisation, especially in the interior and rural areas.

Strategy For Industrial Development

The specific climatic and agricultural features and rich natural resources determine the kind of productive economic activities in Himachal Pradesh. The dust-free and cool climate, power supply in abundance at a comparatively low cost, conducive environment of the state are also suitable for the growth of light and precision engineering industry, electronics, horticulture and food processing and power based industries. The pattern of industrial development of the state is based on its division into industrially developed and backward areas. Most of the large and medium industries are located in developed areas, while a small-scale, tiny, khadi and village industries are located in backward areas/districts. Other important aspects of the emerging scenario are discussed below.

In the process of the integration of India's economy with the global economy and the WTO agreements, the industrial sector will have opportunities and also face challenges in terms of access to a wider global market and meeting global competition. To overcome this, the SSI and tiny sector need to be strengthened on a priority basis, as these are major sources of employment and distribution of wealth. At present the SSI and tiny sector uses low-level technology, resulting in low industrial productivity and poor quality of products. This poses for them a competitive disadvantage, both in the domestic and global market. The SSI sector has to acquire capability to produce quality products to become competitive in the international market.

Wide gaps have been observed between the technologies in use in the state and those used in the developed countries. It is necessary to bridge the gap by modernisation and technological upgradation through innovative research, design and development (RD&D). As it is beyond the capabilities of the existing small-scale (SSI) and tiny sector, it is necessary to upgrade and strengthen the existing RD&D centres in the state, which should be set up in the thrust areas of industry, with financial and technical assistance from international agencies and with the participation of the industry. A trained workforce adopting the latest designs, manufacturing, management, marketing and quality control techniques will be able to produce quality products and compete in the international market.

Another important consideration is the credit-deposit ratio of Himachal Pradesh, which is only 25 per cent, as compared to Tamil Nadu's 90.6 per cent and Maharashtra's 85.39 per cent in 2001. It is evidence of poor entrepreneurship in the state. Therefore, emphasis should be put on the development of entrepreneurship to motivate especially the rural educated women and youth. Entrepreneurship development programmes have to be conducted so that the message of industrialisation is carried to the masses who are unaware of the self-employment outlets provided by the industries. These programmes should also inform potential entrepreneurs about the fiscal incentives and facilities offered by the support institutions.

Specific suggestions for achieving accelerated growth in the industrially backward and developed areas/ districts are:

Industrially Backward Areas/Districts

The industries in these districts are SSI, tiny, khadi and village industries. In addition, artisan entrepreneurs also belong to this category. These industries are mainly based on local raw materials and hold the key to large-scale employment and generation of economic activity. The new industrial policy announced by the Government of India has significantly enhanced the financing pattern and grants for the development of industrial infrastructure in the state. Some schemes are:

(i) The financing pattern of integrated infrastructure development centres (IIDC) between the Government of India and SIDBI will change from 2:3 to 4:1, and the GoI funds would be in the nature of grants, so as to provide the required infrastructural support.

(ii) Deen Dayal Hathkargha Protsahan Yojna and other incentives of the Ministry of Textiles: The funding pattern between the Government of India and the state will be changed from 50:40 to 90:10 under these schemes. The Ministry of Textiles will extend to Himachal Pradesh its package of incentives, as notified for the North-Eastern states.

(iii) Pradhan Mantri Rozgar Yojana (PMRY): The Ministry of Agro & Rural Industries will provide to Himachal Pradesh relaxation under PMRY with respect to age (i.e. 18-40 years from 18-53 years) and subsidy at 15 per cent of the project cost subject to a ceiling of Rs. 15,000 per entrepreneur.

The State government should implement these schemes efficiently and speedily. It should encourage private participation to ensure long-term sustainability. These schemes will also enhance the income of the artisans and small entrepreneurs.

Strategy for Industrial Growth in Backward Districts

- Thrust on setting up small and medium sized clusters around the villages, incorporating state-of-the-art infrastructure, facilitating rural industrialisation. This will further facilitate technological and marketing support at affordable cost to small-scale, tiny and cottage industries.
- Set up information hub in each cluster and industrial area to facilitate marketing and product information from international and other related agencies.
- Modernisation of industrial areas and estates.
- Promotion of maximum private participation in the development of sustainable modern industrial infrastructure.
- Appoint a nodal agency to co-ordinate and formulate plans to implement the schemes and programmes of industrial development awarded to state by Government of India so that maximum benefits could be achieved.
- Advisory councils should be constituted for each cluster involving representatives of industries, technical and research and development (R&D) institutions.

Measures should be taken to integrate large industrial establishments with small and tiny industrial clusters, for the flow of technology, marketing and financial support to these clusters on a mutually beneficial basis. The government should assist in bringing about such integration.

Developed Areas and Periphery Districts

Most of L&M industries are located in the developed areas, parts of Solan and Sirmaur districts, categorised as periphery districts. Some of these are also located in Kangra and Una districts. Mostly, these industries have shifted from other states to reap the benefits of incentives and subsidies. The major industries are food products and beverages, textiles and spinning, precision and light engineering, chemical and pharmaceuticals, electronics including magnetic components, paper and paper products, steel and steel products.

The fiscal incentives and measures announced by the Government of India on January 7, 2003, will encourage more industries to set up units in the periphery districts, achieving substantial growth. Sustainability of the migrated industrial units might, however, be limited to the period during which the incentives are applicable. For long-term sustainability, the state government has to provide high grade infrastructure, and responsive, good governance.

To convert the periphery districts into a hub of the industrial sector and for long-term sustainability, a well thought-out, co-ordinated strategy has to be formulated. The suggestions are:

- Industrial clusters and agri-export zones (AEZs) should be set up, activity/product wise. This will facilitate building a centralised modern infrastructure. These facilities will significantly upgrade the technological, marketing and management capabilities of SMEs.

- The private sector should be encouraged to participate effectively in setting up clusters, AEZs and modernisation of the existing industrial areas and estates on a sustainable basis with initial financial assistance from the Government of India and support from Himachal Government.
- New industrial units should develop physical as well as institutional infrastructure i.e., the complete product should be manufactured in the state. A monitoring mechanism may be evolved to ensure this.
- Fostering close interaction between entrepreneurs, associations, R&D institutions, design centres, testing centres and technical institutions.

Brief details of employment-oriented industrial groups mainly located in the backward areas are as under.

Udyog Mitra

Udyog Mitra Committee, a single window clearance system was constituted by Maharashtra in 1984 under the chairmanship of Development Commissioner (Industries) with Chief Executives of the industrial development organisations of the state as its members. Officers have been drawn from organisations like SICOM Ltd., Maharashtra Industrial Board (MIB), Maharashtra State Financial Corporation (MSFC), Maharashtra Pollution Control Board (MPCB), Director of the Industries and other similar organisations. The main function is to liaise, on behalf of the entrepreneurs with the respective organisations to improve co-ordination among them so as to speed up the process of decision-making in respect of grant of various facilities covered under their jurisdiction.

As suggested by the Planning Commission the State government of Himachal Pradesh may study the 'Udyog Mitra' model developed by Maharashtra. Taking into consideration the local conditions and environment, a new model could be developed for the state.

Agro/Food Processing Industry

At present, the food processing Industry is limited mainly to the traditional processing of agricultural and horticultural raw materials using low-grade technology. The number of units in this area is 8,000 in the SSI & Tiny and 27 in L&M sector and employ approximately 30,000 persons.

Due to conducive agro-climatic conditions, the state has tremendous scope for the production of horticulture products as off-season vegetables, tomatoes, peas, cauliflower, cabbage and seasonal fruits like apple, plums, apricots and olive. There is a large scope for expanding and diversifying food processing industries in the state. Understandably, these industries have been declared priority industries and are given special incentives and concessions in the industrial policy of the state. Some fruits and vegetables are processed within the state by public/private sector units such as HPMC, HIMCO, HIMFED, NEFED, located at Kullu, Mandi and Parwanoo. Horticulture-related units are not doing well. Large quantities of fruits go waste in the process of grading and packing.

Besides, the production of all kinds of fruits has decreased sharply during the year 1999-2000. This is evident from the fact that as against the production potential of 4.92 lakh tonnes, the production of fruits during the year 1999-2000 was 0.89 lakh tonnes. As such, the fruit sector in the state is in the throes of a very significant phase of transition with severe challenges. **To overcome these the state government has to take effective steps to raise the quality and productivity of apples and other fruits; simultaneously, an integrated strategy involving fruit farming and food processing industry has to be evolved.**

Horticulture can play a vital role in improving the socio-economic conditions of the state's rural population. Therefore, the growth of value-added horticulture/food processing industry is very important for rural employment. At present the entire emphasis is on producing table-variety fruits. Horticulture-based food processing units can only be viable if fruits of processable varieties are grown.

Large gaps exist in the industry at different stages of operation, such as availability of processable raw material, post-harvest management, cool-chain infrastructure, processing techniques, quality control and packaging. Most of the units in the food processing industry use old, inefficient, uneconomic machinery and technology and they lack in infrastructure. At present the workers do not have the basic idea of food processing and unskilled workers and supervisors are working in the industry. Training of floor-level workers and maintaining their personal hygiene are essential.

The agro/food processing industry has the potential of expansion and growth, if modern tools and techniques are employed. The suggestions are:

- Integration of the farming sector, processing industry and marketing, i.e., vertical integration of different activities across the agro-business chain.
- Agri-parks and clusters should be set up to facilitate centralised, modern infrastructure, latest processing and packaging techniques and to impart training. These facilities should be available to medium and small-scale industries and the farmers, on a shared basis against a reasonable cost.

Textile and Hosiery

Textile/spinning is one of the important industries which accounts for 60 per cent of the total employment offered in the large and medium sector. It has attracted large investments in the state. Today about eight per cent of the country's yarn production is installed in the state. These industries are located in the periphery districts. The new industrial policy is also likely to attract more textile and hosiery units to the state.

The major hosiery industries are in the SSI and Tiny sector located in the backward areas. They number approximately 4,000 and provide employment to 16,000 persons. The main products are shawls, patti, caps, jackets, sweaters and mufflers. **Clusters have been suggested at Kullu, Shillai, Udaipur and Hamirpur. These clusters will facilitate for weavers, artisans and entrepreneurs, introduction of new products and designs, technical and marketing support, skills upgradation and training, and liaison with banks and government departments.** This will greatly enhance the capabilities of the industries resulting in higher production and employment.

Cement

Himachal Pradesh, which has been described as an "apple bowl", and "hydel state", is now on the threshold of becoming the "cement state" of India. Quality limestone which is one of the important ingredients in the manufacture of grey portland cement is available in plenty. At present there are four cement plants in the large and medium (L&M) sector in addition to three mini plants. The present position is shown in Table 16.9.

The domestic requirement of cement is 10 lakh tonnes. The rest is exported to other states. Cement manufacturers were keen that cement clinker should be allowed to be exported to other states, so that finished cement could be manufactured there. A formula was worked out between the state government and the manufacturers that clinker and cement could be exported to other state in the ratio of 50:50. However, in the new industrial policy, clinker has been placed in the negative list, i.e., such incentives as excise duty and income tax exemption are not applicable to clinkers, but applicable to cement. In the changed situation, the manufacturers will prefer to manufacture cement in Himachal Pradesh itself, while clinker export to other states might be limited.

TABLE 16.9

Present Status of Cement Plants in Himachal Pradesh

Name of Company	*Production Date*	*Investment (Rs. in crore)*	*Employment*	*Production Capacity (lakh tonnes)*
M/s A.C.C Ltd.	12.03.84 (i)			
	15.09.94 (ii)	471	918	22
M/s Gujarat Ambuja Cement Ltd	26.09.95	404	453	10
M/s CCI Ltd.	1.04.80	28	473	2
Total production capacity 34 lakh tonnes				

The total production figures for 2001-02 are 39.21 lakh tonnes detailed below against the production capacity of 34 lakh tonnes:

M/s A.C.C Ltd.	: 27.88 lakh tonnes
M/s Gujarat Ambuja Cement Ltd.	: 9.72 lakh tonnes
M/s C.C.I. Ltd.	: 1.61 lakh tonnes
Total	: 39.21 lakh tonnes

Three more large-scale cement plants, based on limestone, have been approved to be set up in Sundarnagar, Alsindi (Mandi district) and Chamba. These plants in the private sector are being set up by:

M/s Larsen Toubro Ltd. Chamba.

M/s Grasim Industries Ltd. at Alsindi (Mandi).

M/s Harish Chandra Ltd. Sundarnagar.

More proposals under consideration are:

M/s Gujarat Ambuja Cement Ltd has proposed to set up new plants near their plant, already in production in Solan district. In addition, two plants one at Koti and another in Gumma in Shimla district, are also under consideration. The installation of these plants may create environmental problems. The emission levels at every stage of the plant should be kept below the permissible level. **A state level "environmental impact assessment and monitoring committee"**

should standardise specifications, tools and equipment to be used compulsorily by all cement manufactures for environmental pollution control.

Details of the environment management system installed in Ambuja Cement plant are given below:

Environment Management in Ambuja Cement Plant at Darlaghat

A glass bag house (GBH) has been installed for the control of emissions from the kiln and raw mill section, the most polluting section in a cement factory. The GBH has an efficiency of 99.9 per cent and maintains emissions even below 50 gm./Nm^3.

Electrostatic Precipitators (ESPs) have been installed at the clinker cooler and cement mill sections, while bag filters have been installed at the coal mill, cement mill and packing plant, for the control of emissions.

The emissions from all the stacks are maintained at much below 100 mg/Nm^3, as against the National Standards of 150 mg/Nm^3 for the cement industry. Bag filters have also been installed at all material handling/loading/unloading points for the control of fugitive emissions. There is no solid waste generation and all the dust collected in the air-pollution control equipment is automatically recycled into the process.

Handloom Industry

Handloom is an important cottage industry of Himachal Pradesh and has the second largest employment potential in the rural sector. The importance of the handloom industry in the economy lies in the artistic designs, low-cost investment and family based skills which is passed on from generation to generation with no formal training. At present, there are about 42,000 handlooms in the state, primarily based on wool and providing gainful employment to about 45,000 weavers. The major products woven on handlooms are woollen ladies' shawls, woollen gents' shawls, woollen tweeds, shirting, dress material and woollen carpets, etc. Weaving activities are mostly undertaken in Kullu, Mandi, Kinnaur, Kangra, Lahaul & Spiti and Chamba districts of the state. There is a vast potential of development of handloom industry in the state. Keeping in view the changing scenario, there is need to diversify the existing products by introducing new designs according to modern trends. A project named "Hill Area Woollen Development Project" has been taken up in co-operation with Government of India. These programmes include setting up training-cum-demonstration centres for training weavers on improved looms and equipment, modernisation of traditional pit looms into fly shuttle looms; setting up production-cum-service centres and improving the designs, quality of products and introducing need-based designs according to modern trends. Manufacturing of readymade garments (woollen) on a large scale in the design-cum-fashion centre would also be undertaken. In addition, for the development of the handloom industry in the state, various centrally sponsored schemes like Deen Dayal Hathkargha Protsahan Yojana, Baba Saheb Ambedkar Hastshilp Vikas Yojana sponsored by the office of Development Commissioner of Handlooms, Ministry of Textiles, Government of India are being implemented.

Sericulture

It is a village oriented, labour-intensive industry in all its phases, from cultivation of silk worms and food plants to silk worm rearing, silk reeling and other processes, such as twisting, dyeing, weaving, printing and finishing. Climatic conditions of the state are most favourable for the growth of this industry. The sericulture industry is an effective tool to develop the rural economy as it supplements the income of the weaker sections of society. To provide more employment to the rural depressed classes, the growth of this industry is most essential. At present, it provides subsidiary occupation to more than 10,000 families, most of whom belong to the poor sections of the society. A congenial environment, coupled with marketing and financial help and training in the use of better methods and tools, will lead to a high growth rate of the industries in the state.

Medicinal and Aromatic Herbs

The state is endowed with nature's treasure like valuable herbs, plants, flowers etc. Some of these herbs and plants available in the states are *guchhi, tej patta, patish, bankakari, dhoop* roots, *bharami, katha, kalajira, karu, banaksha, kesar, hyphopia* and some other species are found in the high reaches. The Himalayan National Park is one of the sources of these medicinal herbs in the state. Besides these, there are many species which remain unidentified due to lack of knowledge and research. This treasure is at present being drained out of the state at a very low price. To avoid this kind of exploitation and to process the available resources within the state, the herb collectors should form a co-operative society and educated professional youths should be motivated to set up industrial units for processing these medicinal and aromatic herbs in the state. At present, the state has one *ayurvedic* college and two ayurvedic pharmacies. These pharmacies are manufacturing some traditional medicines, which are supplied to health institutions of the state. To identify new species and to avoid unscientific ways of extraction, training programmes should be organised in the state. It is evident that there is vast scope for processing these herbs, shrubs and medicine within the state. Setting up of herbal-based clusters has been suggested. These clusters must provide high quality infrastructure in terms of marketing, training, financial and technical support. This approach will greatly boost the growth of medicinal and aromatic based industries in the state and their export.

Sports Equipment

The state offers a variety of opportunities for adventure sports, such as paragliding, ice-skating, mountaineering, hill-sking and river rafting. The mountaineering institute at Manali offers facilities as well as training in various adventure sports in Kullu and Kangra districts. Besides, the Department of Tourism provides training in water sports, paragliding, river rafting and trekking, etc. For these sports, various kinds of equipment and accessories such as anklets, helmets, trekking shoes, tents and other types of equipment are required. At present all these equipment and accessories are imported from outside the state. **So there is scope for setting up units for their manufacture in the state, keeping in view the demand, quality and prices**.

Recommendations

Modernisation and technological upgradation through innovative Research, Design and Development (RD&D), human resource development through skill upgradation and training, adoption of small and medium sized clusters around the villages for systematic infrastructure development, market-oriented policies, simplified procedures and good governance are essential for the industrial growth of the state. Some suggestion and recommendations are:

- Small scale, tiny and cottage industries located in industrially backward districts, are the backbone of the industrial sector and major provider of employment. These industries use local raw material, low-level technology and manual methods. All this results in low industrial productivity and poor quality. For the very survival and growth of these industries, technological upgradation, skill development and training, easy and timely credit facilities at interest rate not more than prime lending rate are the key factors.
- Industrial clusters, agri-export zones (AEZs), export promotion parks with state-of-the-art infrastructure should be set up in the developed areas. In the backward areas, small sized clusters should be set up activity-wise at different locations. These small clusters should have centralised facilities like design centres, testing facilities, preparation of project reports, marketing support, information hub and raw material depots, to boost the growth of local industries and promote employment.
- The private sector, financial institutions, industrial development agencies should be encouraged to participate effectively in modernising and creating high-grade industrial infrastructure. The central and state governments may provide the initial financial assistance. However, in the long run, it should be financially sustainable.
- Multinational and reputed Indian companies should be attracted to set up industrial units in the state. This will facilitate upgradation of the entire infrastructure for achieving the benefits of large-scale integration in different sectors of industry.
- The new industrial policy is likely to attract big investments in large and medium sectors in keeping with the existing trend in the state. The entrepreneurs will prefer to set up their units in the periphery of the adjoining states of Punjab and Haryana. These large and medium industries should be encouraged to set up ancillary units in their areas. To promote the small scale and tiny sector in the vicinity, a conducive ancillarisation policy should be formulated.
- The functioning of the support institutions of the state needs to be reviewed and reoriented, to make them relevant to the emerging requirements of industry in the changed situation. Training/ awareness programmes should be organised to impart knowledge about modern methods and tools relevant to industry.
- The government's role should be that of an effective facilitator, enabler and co-ordinator, providing a transparent and conducive policy framework and an efficient delivery mechanism through responsive and good governance.

- Upgradation of the existing centres of research and development, design, testing, marketing and setting up of more such centres have been suggested, to make available to the industry the latest designs, manufacturing and testing techniques to meet its emerging requirements. Large and medium industries should be encouraged to set up in-house research, design and training cells in their relevant areas.
- Emphasise on human resource development through skill upgradation and training. Foster linkages between industry, R&D and technical institutions and re-orient technical education to meet the requirements of industry in view of recent developments.
- Rationalised, graded merit-and target-group oriented incentives and concessions need to be resorted to for the balanced industrial growth of different regions and for the benefit of weaker sections of society.
- To deal with sickness in the SSI sector, a state level institution, with adequate powers and resources should be set up, consisting of the representatives of the Reserve Bank of India, financial institutions, banks, industry and state government, to provide requisite financial support to small scale and tiny units suffering from sickness or having symptoms of sickness. A system should be evolved for timely detection of sickness at the initial stages.

References

Industrial Policies of 1991, 1996 and 1999 of Government of Himachal Pradesh.

Journal of Rural Development, Vol. 20 No. 4, National Institute of Rural Development, Hyderabad.

National Accounts Statistics 2001, Central Statistical Organisation, Government of India.

Punjab Development Report, Planning Commission, Government of India.

Reports, Notes, and Data on Industrial Sector, Director of Industries, Himachal Pradesh.

Sixth, Seventh, Eighth, Ninth and Tenth Five Year Plans, Government of Punjab.

State Industrial Profile of Himachal Pradesh (2001-02), Small Industries Service Institute (SISI), Solan, Government of India.

State of the Environment Report, Himachal Pradesh (March, 2000), Government of Himachal Pradesh.

Statistical Abstract of Himachal Pradesh 1999-2000.

Chapter 17

Infrastructure

Mountains present a challenge to mankind. Though seen as obstacles to trade, they have been home to remarkable trade activities like the Silk Route in Central Asia, routes built by the Roman Empire across the Alps, and the Incas in the Andes. Hill regions need linkages with surrounding lands because while they remain extremely important for hill residents, open areas for cross-region co-operation, to the mutual benefit of both societies.

Widespread and deep-rooted poverty has been the single biggest challenge for sustainable development of mountain areas in the Himalayas, and India has recorded notable successes in this endeavour. While the hitherto-targeted improvements in agricultural productivity and employment are critical, the rapidly growing labour force in mountain areas cannot be gainfully absorbed by agriculture alone, and substantial efforts are needed to diversify the mountain economy and enhance the living standards of the mountain population.

In order for mountain economies and environments to develop in a sustainable manner, development decisions concerned with their diversification must be based on sound assessment of past experiences, existing constraints, and available opportunities.

The critical issue here is – accessibility. This is both in terms of the local citizens, and for societies outside the region. For residents, infrastructure brings in products and services like energy and raw materials, necessary for survival and economic sustainability. It also brings in the tourist, with possibilities of dramatic rise in societal incomes. For people outside the region, it opens up new markets.

The fundamental role of infrastructure in a hill state like Himachal Pradesh is two fold:

I. To open up the state and improve accessibility, both for the residents and the outside world, including tourists, and

II. To ensure that the demands of energy and communication are put in place concurrently, to cater to sustained economic development, without environmental degradation.

Thomas Kohler *et al.*, have stressed that *"access, communication and energy are key issues in sustainable development of mountain areas. Experience has shown that they are very powerful agents of change, not only, but especially in mountains. Access, communication and energy in mountain regions also involve vital linkages between these regions and adjacent lowlands, centres of population, and industrialised and urbanised areas."*

There is a cruel twist to infrastructure provision in difficult terrains like Himachal Pradesh. While it is more vitally required, it demands higher capital infusion. In a plain area, if there is absence of a road to the district centre, there is possibility of walking to it. In a hill terrain, it would take a day to walk to the next hilltop, where the next district centre may be, and the walk would be through inhospitable terrain.

To overcome these natural obstacles, infrastructure provision ends up demanding a higher cost. The development of modern transport infrastructure, especially of roads and railways is a costly enterprise in general. Costs in mountains are even higher than in lowlands, for both construction and maintenance, due to difficult topography, harsh climate, and the need for protection from hazards, such as avalanches, landslides, and rockfalls, as well as the need to secure road- and railside slopes.

The important sectors of infrastructure in which we propose to concentrate in this chapter are:

1. Energy
2. Transport

In this regard, it is important to distinguish between the infrastructure, which is strictly local in potential, and that which has local and regional/national implications.

Local Infrastructure

This includes transport and communication sectors which, when laid down, present sunk and fixed costs that permit strictly local exploitation. While a road does connect place A to place B, its immediate use, by its very nature, is restricted. Some cross relationship is always established – for example – if Punjab has no road, it is difficult for road vehicles to enter Himachal Pradesh, but roads in Punjab cannot substitute for roads in Himachal Pradesh. Thus, such fixed infrastructure has a largely local context.

Regional/National Infrastructure

Energy falls in this segment. While local distribution networks serve local needs, but this infrastructure can be "wheeled" out of the state, and be used elsewhere too. Thus, the development of this infrastructure sector in Himachal Pradesh has regional/national possibilities. While it can bring in energy for deficient regions, it can also bring in income for Himachal Pradesh through sale.

The Electricity Act, 2003 now enacted and duly notified since June 11, 2003, is a promising framework for Himachal Pradesh to exploit its "mobile" infrastructure of electrical power.

The Tenth Plan document clearly notes the crux of infrastructure as "Good infrastructure raises productivity and lowers production costs". Infrastructure is the mother base for all activities. It is from the band of services within this domain that all other developmental activities draw their sustenance. Inadequately envisioned, or poorly delivered, it can stunt growth for decades. (SDR for Punjab, CRRID, 2002).

The Eleventh Finance Commission Report 2000 mentions an infrastructure index, based on social and economic factors. This rates Goa and Punjab as the highest, with an index of 200.57 and 187.578 respectively. Himachal Pradesh is ranked 13th in India, with an index of 95.03, lowest being Arunachal Pradesh with 69.71. What is worrisome is that Himachal Pradesh is only marginally better than Mizoram (82.13), Bihar (81.33), and Orissa (81.00). The Tenth Plan has noted that the index represents infrastructure facilities, and states with better facilities will attract private sector investment decisions and capital flows.

ENERGY

Current Scenario

One of the most vital inputs, energy is the prime mover, literally fuelling the engine of progress and development. It is now clearly recognised that the level of availability of affordable and reliable power supply can be an important determinant of the overall quality of life.

In India, from an installed capacity of only 1300 MW at the time of independence, power generation has now risen to 100000 MW, with consequent increase in transmission and distribution (T&D) systems. Despite this seemingly impressive increase, overall power generation and availability has not grown at the required pace, and the states have been facing constant shortage. The pace of growth has failed to reach target levels in the Ninth Plan, with a capacity addition of only 19015 MW, against a target of 40,245 MW. For the Tenth Plan, the *Working Report on Power* has laid down a target of addition of 46,939 MW, but the Planning Commission has fixed the following targets:

Ongoing Projects	18659 MW
Central Electricity Authority Cleared Projects	9193 MW
New schemes	13258 MW
Total	**41110 MW**

In this context, Himachal Pradesh with a hydro power potential of 20000 MW, can play an important part, with only 20 per cent of the total potential harnessed so far.

Power can be tapped from both renewable and non-renewable resources. Let us examine the availability of the primary sources of energy in Himachal Pradesh.

Renewable	
Hydro-power	Yes
Biogas	Yes, limited
Solar	Yes
Wind	Negligible potential
Geo-thermal	Yes
Tidal	No
Non-renewable	
Coal	No
Oil	No
Gas	No (not economically viable)

Nuclear energy as an energy source is not considered on account of it being ruled out for strategic reasons, and the government has no plans to set up an atomic power plant in the state.

Geo-thermal energy can be an important component. For India, the potential is as under:

TABLE 17.1

Potential Geothermal Provinces of India

Province	*Surface T°C*	*Reservoir T°C*	*Heat Flow Thermal Gradient*	
Himalaya	>90	260	468	100
Cambay	40-90	150-175	80-93	70
West Coast	46-72	102-137	75-129	47-59
SONATA	60-95	105-217	120-290	60-90
Godavari	50-60	175-215	93-104	60

Source: D. Chandrasekharam, *Geothermal Power Asia 2000*, Indian Institute of Technology, Mumbai, India.

Note: Heat Flow: mW/m²; Thermal Gradient: °C/km.

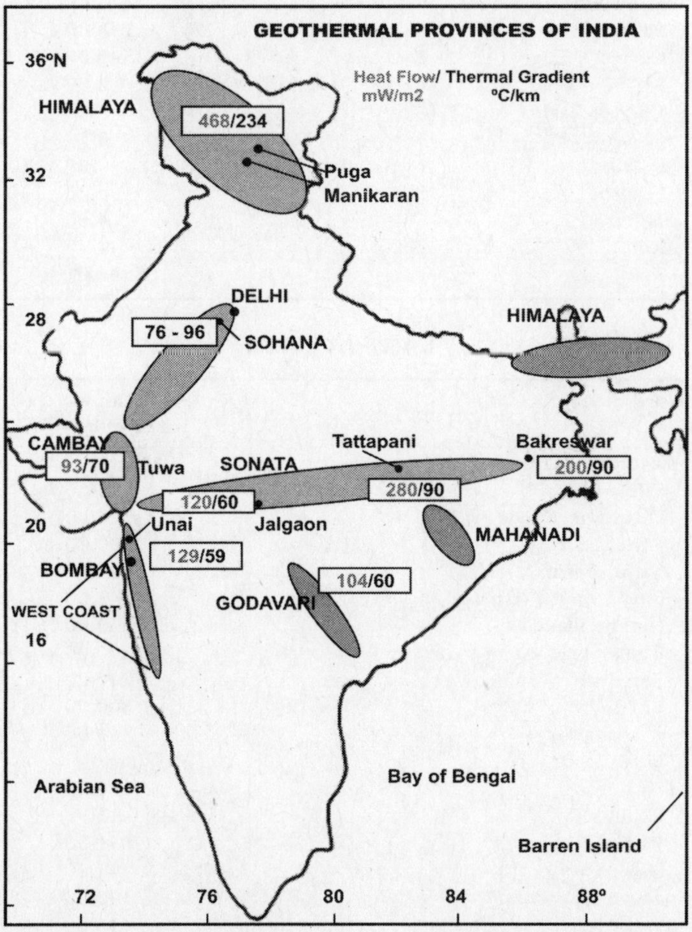

Source: D. Chandrasekharam, *Geothermal Power Asia 2000*, Indian Institute of Technology, Mumbai, India

Himachal Pradesh has the highest heat flow and highest thermal gradient geothermal basin in India. The first pilot binary 5 kW power plant was successfully operated by the Geological Survey of India at Manikaran, which proved the power producing capability of this province. Scientific data from 500 metre drill-holes estimated reservoir temperatures as high as 260° C. Space heating experiments were also successfully conducted using thermal discharge by the Geological Survey of India.

The non-conventional sources of geo-thermal and solar power have potential for rural and hamlet electrification schemes. However, considering the potential and resource base, HP should concentrate on large hydro power projects, mini-and micro-hydel schemes in conventional power.

The major potential in HP remains in the hydro electric sector, and in our analysis, we concentrate on this mode of generation.

For India, the power generation scenario is shown in Table 17.2:

TABLE 17.2

Power Generation

	Change over previous year April-November					
	Billion Kwh				*% growth*	
	1997-98	*1998-99**	*1998*	*1999*	*1998-99*	*1999-2000@*
Power generation	420.6	448.4	291.6	313.8	6.5	7.5
Hydro-electric	74.5	82.7	58.3	57.2	8.8	1.9
Thermal	336.1	353.7	225.8	248.2	4.6	9.9
Nuclear	10.0	12.0	7.5	8.4	14.1	12.8
Plant load factor of thermal plants (%)	64.7	64.6	62.0	62.1	—	—

Source: http://www.ficci.com/ficci/econo-upda/power.htm

Note: *: Provisional @: April-November

It is seen that the major growth in power is being accounted for by the thermal sector on a national level, with 9.9 per cent growth in 1999-2000, over a generation base of 336 billion units in 1997-98.

Himachal Pradesh Becomes Nationally Important in This Context

It is imperative that India must have a cheaper source of electrical power so that the users can cut their "fuel" costs, and Indian products remain globally competitive. It is extremely important for Himachal Pradesh to move ahead and exploit its hydro potential to the full, because this is internationally recognised as the cheapest source.

TABLE 17.3

Decreasing Cost of Power with Hydro Share Rising

Country	*% Hydro Share*	*Selling Price (cents/Kwh)*
India	**24**	**7**
Sweden	48	2
Canada	62	2
Norway	99	1

Source: Himachal Pradesh State Electricity Board (HPSEB).

The detailed power planning studies carried by Central Electricity Authority (CEA) have suggested that the share of hydro-power in the overall installed generated capacity in the country should be at least about 40 per cent to ensure optimum utilisation of natural and financial resources for electric power generation. In spite of large hydro resources being available in India, its share in the total installed capacity has been declining in successive plans. Hydro-power which was 50 per cent of the total installed capacity in 1962-63, has now declined to 25 per cent. Such a dismal share of hydro – thermal mix is adversely affecting optimal utilisation of natural and financial resources. Thus, accelerated hydro-power generation is an unavoidable proposition when about 75 per cent of the hydro potential of 84,000 MW still remains to be harnessed (*Planning Power Development in India – Emphasis on Hydro Projects,* R.N. Srivastava, *et al.*).

Hydro Power Status in Himachal Pradesh

Only 20 per cent of the total available potential of the hydro power in the state has been harnessed up to now, with another 7060 MW projects under various stages of execution. By 2012, only 55 per cent of the potential would be utilised, if all plans go as per target.

TABLE 17.4

Hydro Power in Himachal Pradesh: The Current Status

Total Identified Potential	**20376 MW**
Harnessed so far	3942 MW
Under execution	7060 MW
For which Draft Project Report ready	815 MW
For which Investigations are in progress	2008 MW
For which Investigations yet to be taken up	6551 MW

Source: *www.hpseb.com*

Harnessed

Name of Project	*River/Khad*	*Estimated Installed Capacity (MW)*
Yamuna Basin		
Andhra	Andhra	16.95
Giri	Giri	60.00
Yamuna Projects	Share from HP Catchment	131.57
Gumma SHP	Gumma Khad	3.00
Satluj Basin		
Rongtong	Rongtong	2.00
Rukti	Rukti	1.50
SVP Bhaba	Bhaba	120.00
Nogli Stage – I	Nogli	2.50
Chaba	Nauti	1.75
Bhakra Dam	Satluj	1200.00
Ghanvi	Ghanvi Khad	22.0
Beas Basin		
Beas Satluj Link	Beas	990.00
Uhl Stage – I	Uhl	110.00
Uhl Stage – II	Uhl	60.00
Binwa	Binwa	6.00
Baner	Baner	12.00
Gaj	Gaj	10.50
Pong Dam	Beas	360.00
Malana	Beas	86.00
Ravi Basin		
Gharola	Gharola	0.05
Bhuri Singh P/House		0.45
Baira Suil	Baira & Suil	198.00
Chamera Stage – I	Ravi	540.00
Sal-II	Ravi	2.00
Chenab Basin		
Sissu	Sissu	0.10
Billing	Billing	0.20
Shansha	Shansha	0.20
Thirot	Thirot	4.50
Killar	Mahal	0.30
Total		**3942.07**

Under Execution

Name of Project	*Estimated Installed Capacity (MW)*
Yamuna Basin	
Sainj	5.50
Dhamwari Sunda	70.00
Renuka Dam	40.00
Satluj Basin	
Bhaba Aug. P/House	3.00
Nathpa Jhakri	1500.00
Baspa Stage – II	300.00
Karchham Wangtoo	1000.00
Kol Dam	800.00
Keshang Stage – I	66.00
Beas Basin	
Larji	126.00
Khauli	12.00
Parbati Stage – II	2051.00
Neogal	15.00
Allian Dhugan	192.00
Patkari	16.00
Fozal	6.00

Contd. ...

Contd. ...

Name of Project	*Estimated Installed Capacity (MW)*
Uhl Stage – III	100.00
Ravi Basin	
Holi	3.00
Chamera Stage – II	300.00
Chamera Stage – II	231.00
Budhil	70.00
Bharmour	45.00
Harsar	60.00
Kugti	45.00
Mini Micro (up to 3MW)	101.59
Total	**7059.14**

Draft Project Report Ready

Name of Project	*River/Khad*	*Estimated Installed Capacity (MW)*
Yamuna Basin		
Shalvi	Pabbar River	7.00
Swara Kuddu	Pabbar River	144.00
Satluj Basin		
Keshang	Keshang Khad	160.00
Ravi Basin		
Kutehar	Ravi	260.00
Hibra	Ravi	231.00
Siul	Siul Nallah	13.00
Total		815 MW

Investigation Under Progress

Name of Project	*River/Khad*	*Estimated Installed Capacity (MW)*
Yamuna Basin		
Tangnu Romani	Pabbar River	44.00
Chirgaon Majhgaon	Pabbar River	46.00
Paudital Lassa	Pabbar River	36.00
Satluj Basin		
Thopan Powari	Satluj River	400.00
Shongtong Karcham	Satluj River	225.00
Jangi Thopan	Satluj River	300.00
Sorang	Sorang Khad	100.00
Tidong	Tidong Khad	100.00
Baspa-I	Satluj River	210.00
Beas Basin		
Sainj	Sainj Nallah	100.00
Tirthan	Tirthan Nallah	25.00
Dhaulasidh	Beas River	80.00
Ravi Basin		
Bajoli Holi	Ravi River	200.00
Saikhoti	Baira Nallah	17.00
Chamba	Ravi River	125.00
Total		**2008 MW**

Current Availability in Himachal Pradesh

There are three ways in which HPSEB makes power available in the state:

i. Own generation

ii. Free power from central, joint, and private sector plants

iii. Purchase from other generators

HIMACHAL PRADESH STATE ELECTRICITY BOARD (HPSEB)

Installed Capacity

The current installed capacity of HPSEB from various schemes is 326 MW from its 20 stations of capacities ranging from 120 MW (SVP Bhabha) to 0.05 MW (Gharola). At 60 per cent load factor, this should be able to produce about 1700 million units per year. However, the target for generation from these stations was fixed at 1458 million units, but this has 'not been achieved since 1998-99 (representing a load factor of 50 per cent only).

TABLE 17.5

Generation by HPSEB in Million Units

Year	*HPSEB Total (in Million kwh)*	*Decline*
1998-99	1480.82	
1999-00	1198.26	282.57
2000-01	1150.20	330.57
2001-02	1146.12	334.70

Source: Himachal Pradesh State Electricity Board.

The Board has given the reasons for this shortfall as unfavourable monsoons/snowfalls, and a continuingly declining water flow.

Ongoing Projects

HPSEB proposes to add another 284 MW from projects presently under implementation. The status is shown in Table 17.6:

TABLE 17.6

HPSEB's Proposed Ongoing Projects and Capacity (in MW)

Name of the Project	*Capacity (in MW)*	*Name of the Basin*	*Likely Date of Commissioning*
Bhaba Aug. P/H	3	Satluj	2001-2
Larji	126	Beas	2003-4
Holi	3	Ravi	2001-2
Khauli	12	Beas	2002-3
UHL – III	100	Beas	2005-6
Renuka	40	Yamuna	2007-8
Total	**284**		

Source: Himachal Pradesh State Electricity Board.

By 2008, another 284 MW capacity will be added to the existing 326 MW through these schemes.

Proposed HPSEB Projects

HPSEB has also proposed to put up further projects as shown in Table 17.7:

TABLE 17.7

HPSEB's Proposed Projects and Capacity in MW

No.	Name of Project	Installed Capacity	Proposed Developer	Expected Year of Completion
1.	Kashang	160 MW	HPSEB	Phase - I 2005-06 Phase - II 2006-07
2.	Siul	13 MW	HPSEB/MNES	2004-05
3.	Sorang	100 MW	HPSEB	2009-10
4.	Tidong	100 MW	HPSEB	2010-11
5.	Kerang	16/15 MW	HP+SEB/MNES	2004-5
6.	Ganvi - II	8 MW	HPSEB/MNES	2004-05
7.	Barahl	9 MW	HPSEB/MNES	2004-05
8.	Thirthan	25 MW	HPSEB	2005-06
9.	Shalvi	7 MW	HPSEB/MNES	2004-05
	Total	**438 MW**		

Source: Himachal State Electricity Board.

By 2011-2012, HPSEB proposes to add another 438 MW to the 326 MW already installed, and 284 MW under implementation, and have a total installed capacity of 1048 MW. Though current efficiency levels are stagnating at around 40 per cent, if we assume the targeted levels of 50 per cent load factor, this will give about 4300 million units of HPSEB generated power by 2012.

Central Sector

Name of Project	Capacity (MW)	Status	Proposed Developer	Expected Year of Completion
Kuther	260	DPR Ready	Central Sector	2007-08
Hibra	231	DPR Ready	Central Sector	2006-07
Rampur	400-600	DPR Ready	NJPC	2006-07
Thopan Powari	400	DPR Ready	Central Sector	2011-12
Bajouli – Holi	200	DPR Ready	Central Sector	2011-12
Chamba	125	Inv. in progress	Central Sector	2008-09
Karcham Shongtong	225	Inv. in progress	Central Sector	2011-12
Gypsa Dam	240	Inv. in progress	Central Sector	2010-11
Total	**2081**			

IPP Sector

Name of Project	Installed Capacity (MW)	Expected Year of Completion
Sawara-Kuddu	144	2008-09
Saini	100	2006-07
Malana – II	100	2006-07
Dhaula-Sidh	80	2006-07
Chirgaon-Majhgaon	46	2005-06
Paudital-Lassa	36	2005-06
Tangnu-Romai	44	2005-06
Saikothi	17	2005-06
Lambadug	15	2004-05
Baragaon	10.5	2004-05
Total	**592.5**	

Considering the totality of projects under execution, and those for which DPR is ready or investigations are in an advanced stage, the total planned capacity addition in MW is as under:

	Short Term (2001-07)	Medium Term (2007-12)	Total By End of 2001-12
Under State Sector	522	200	722
Under Central/Joint Sector	3260	3472	6732
Under Private Sector	1245	1336	2581
Total	**5027**	**5008**	**10035**

There have been some good developments in 2003, auguring well for the overall scenario:

- Malana H.E.P 86 MW was commissioned by IPP in a record time.
- Out of the lists drawn, recently Himachal Pradesh Government has allocated Rampur HEP (400-600 MW) to NJPC and Hibra HEP (231 MW) to NHPC.
- Policy of incentives/disincentives shall now be applicable on Central Agencies also, to ensure efficiency irrespective of ownership pattern.
- It is very welcome that HP is also proposing to take some projects as Joint Venture with neighbouring States.
- Gujarat Government has also shown keen interest in Hydro-Power Development in the Pradesh.
- GoI has been requested to permit increasing the capacity from 100 MW to 300 MW for allotment through MoU route, leading to further speed in decision making.

A major development is the likely scenario of "unbundling" being contemplated by HPSEB, which has proposed projects for execution through HPSEB, but with provision of following goods and services from Private Agencies as consortium/JV partner:

- Overall project management
- Engineering
- Supply of equipment
- Construction Management
- Project financing

Free Power as Royalty

Himachal Pradesh gets free power as royalty from central, joint, and private sector projects set up in the state. This is a part of the original agreement, which lays down that:

The project developer will be required to provide free energy from the project to the Government of Himachal Pradesh in lieu of right of use of potential site. The free power will be levied at 12 per cent of the deliverable energy of the project for the period starting from the date of synchronisations of the first generating unit and extending up to 12 years from the date of commercial operation of the project. For the balance agreement period of 28 years, the royalty in shape of free power will be charged at 18 per cent of the deliverable energy.

Himachal Pradesh Industrial Development Board has estimated the flow of free power to Himachal Pradesh as shown in Table 17.8:

TABLE 17.8

Tentative Year-wise Detail of the Estimated Free Power Available to the Government of Himachal Pradesh from Various Hydro-Electric Projects

No.	*Description*	*2001-02*	*2002-03*	*2003-04*	*2004-05*	*2005-06*	*2006-07*	*2007-08*	*2008-09*	*2009-10*	*2010-11*	*2011-12*
1.	Private Sector projects											
	(i) Projects executed/under development	40	15	120	32	2	30	34	6	334	408	0
	(ii) Projects for which bids are under evaluation	0	0	0	0	0	0	0	3	60	439	346
	Sub Total (MU)	**40**	**15**	**120**	**32**	**2**	**30**	**34**	**9**	**394**	**847**	**346**
2.	Central PSU Projects											
	(i) Projects executed/under development	290	0	0	35	117	0	90	421	545	84	252
	(ii) Projects for which bids are under evaluation	0	0	0	0	0	0	0	110	286	0	135
	Sub Total (MU)	**290**	**0**	**0**	**35**	**117**	**0**	**90**	**531**	**831**	**84**	**387**
3.	Joint Sector Projects											
	(i) Projects executed/under development	70	0	200	604	0	0	0	0	0	0	0
	Total: 1+2+3 (MU)	**400**	**15**	**320**	**671**	**119**	**30**	**124**	**540**	**1225**	**931**	**733**
4.	Year-wise free power (MU)	400	415	735	1406	1525	1555	1679	2219	3444	4375	5108
5.	T&D losses (%)	19.346	17.636	15.355	13.662	13.099	12.539	12.539	12.539	12.539	12.539	12.539
6.	Units of T&D losses (MU)	77.38	73.19	112.86	192.09	199.76	194.98	210.53	278.24	431.84	548.58	640.49
7.	Energy available for sale (MU)	322.62	341.81	622.14	1213.91	1325.24	1360.02	1468.47	1940.76	3012.00	3826.42	4467.51
8.	Average Sale Rate in paise per unit	229.909	249.433	267.79	287.024	307.598	328.742	345.179	362.438	380.56	399.583	419.587
9.	Expected Revenue at current prices (Rs. in crore)	74.12	85.26	116.6	348.42	407.64	447.1	506.89	703.41	1146.32	1528.97	1874.51

No.	*Description*	*2012-13*	*2013-14*	*2014-15*	*2015-16*	*2016-17*	*2017-18*	*2018-19*	*2019-20*	*2020-21*	*2021-22*
1.	Private Sector Projects										
	(i) Projects executed/under development	0	19	0	0	0	0	14	0	26	320
	(ii) Projects for which bids are under evaluation	346	346	346	346	346	346	346	346	346	447
	Sub Total (MU)	**346**	**365**	**346**	**346**	**346**	**346**	**360**	**346**	**372**	**767**
2.	Central PSU Projects										
	(i) Projects executed/under development	0	0	0	0	0	0	0	0	0	0
	(ii) Projects for which bids are under evaluation	0	0	0	0	0	0	0	0	0	0
	Sub Total (MU)	**0**	**0**	**0**	**0**	**0**	**0**	**0**	**0**	**0**	**0**
3.	Joint Sector Projects										
	(i) Projects executed/under development	0	0	0	0	0	0	0	0	0	0
	Total: 1+2+3 (MU)	**346**	**365**	**346**	**346**	**346**	**346**	**360**	**346**	**372**	**767**
4.	Year-wise free power (MU)	5454	5819	6165	6511	6857	7203	7563	7909	8281	9048
5.	T&D losses (%)	12.539	12.539	12.539	12.539	12.539	12.539	12.539	12.539	12.539	12.539
6.	Units of T&D losses (MU)	683.88	729.64	773.03	816.41	859.8	903.18	948.32	991.71	1038.35	1134.53
7.	Energy available for sale (MU)	4770.12	5089.36	5391.97	5694.59	5997.2	6299.82	6614.68	6917.29	7242.65	7913.47
8.	Average Sale Rate in paise per unit	440.545	462.572	485.700	509.985	585.484	562.258	590.371	619.89	650.884	683.43
9.	Expected Revenue at current prices (Rs. in crore)	2101.45	2354.19	2618.88	2904.15	3511.27	3542.12	3905.11	4287.96	4714.12	5408.30

Thus, in 2001-2002, Himachal Pradesh expects to receive 322 million units of free power, going up to 4467 units by 2011-2012, and finally up to 7913 million units by 2021-22. T&D losses have been kept at an ambitious level of about 12 per cent, as against about 20 per cent now.

The total availability of power in HP in 2001-02 is as under:

Own current generation	1146 million units
Free power	322 million units
Total	1468 million units

The total availability of power in Himachal Pradesh (load factor realistically at 50 per cent) in 2011-12 is likely to be as under:

Own generation	4300 million units (1000 MW)
Free power	4467 million units (1050 MW)
Total	8767 million units (2050 MW)

Demand Scenario

Himachal Pradesh achieved 100 per cent electrification of villages by 1988, and is now almost through with connecting all hamlets too. Even so, it has a low per capita consumption of electricity amongst the northern states, excluding J&K.

TABLE 17.9

Annual Per Capita Consumption of Electricity by States 1999-2000

(KWH)

State	*1980-81*	*1989-90*	*1997-97*	*1999-00*
Haryana	209.5	367.4	508.3	530.8
J&K	74.8	176.4	223.7	267.9
Punjab	303.6	620.5	789.9	921.1
Chandigarh	309.0	686.2	794.4	823.8
Delhi	403.8	673.6	589.7	653.2
Himachal Pradesh	**66.4**	**191.9**	**278.5**	**339.1**

Source: Statistical Abstract quoted in *Tenth Plan* papers, Planning Commission, New Delhi

Sector-wise break-up of consumers is as under:

(MUs)

Consumer Category	*Share (in per cent)*
Agriculture	1
Domestic	28
Commercial	8
Government irrigation and water schemes	9
Small industrial power	2
Medium industrial power	3
Large industrial power	44
Street lighting	–
Bulk	6
Total	**100**

If we look at other parameters, we find that against a growth rate of 5.6 per cent and 6.5 per cent during the Eight and Ninth Plan periods, Himachal Pradesh recorded a growth rate of 6.7 per cent during 1993-94 to 1998-99 (Central Statistical Organisation).

If we examine the percentage share change in net SDP from 1987-88 to 1999-2000, we find that while the primary sector has decreased by 24.96, the secondary and tertiary sectors have considerably increased by 48.23 and 11.81 respectively.

The percentage change in employment share too has declined for the primary sector by 20.03, increased for the secondary sector by 4.29 in the secondary, and by 76.71 for the tertiary sector.

Percentage of population below the poverty line has declined from 28.44 in 1993-94, to 7.63 in 1999-2000.

The CAGR of urban population at three per cent is twice that of the rural population at 1.5 per cent, and the urban population already accounts for about 10 per cent at present.

These trends give a clear indication that the per capita consumption of electricity will rise in HP in the future. This will also be assisted by the state's programme for encouraging horticulture, agro-processing, and tourism. The secondary and tertiary sector developments in these thrust areas will be power hungry, whether it is the refrigeration needs of partly-processed fruits, or lighting and heating needs of tourist hubs.

According to HPSEB, the status of connected load is as shown in the diagram below:

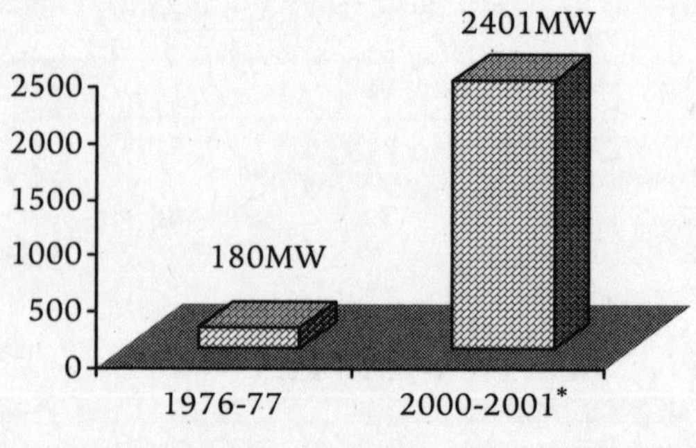

Note: * Up to March 2001

According to HPSEB, the demand is in the region of 3500 million units. In MW, HPSEB estimates the requirement at 600 MW, and growing to about 900 MW by 2015. In the light of a rise in per capita consumption taking place, and the factors brought out above, this appears to be an underestimate. In fact, the connected load has already exceeded 2500 MW now, and it is reasonable to presume that about one-third of the connected load can be seen as demand.

The power requirement, if the development of Himachal Pradesh is not to be fettered, should be realistically seen to be in the region of about 800 MW today, and rising to about 1500 MW by 2012. This is based on an achieved annual SDP growth rate of 6.7 per cent, large shifts from primary to secondary and tertiary sector, and growing urbanisation.

Demand Forecast: 16th Electric Power Survey (EPS) Report

The demand forecast as per 16th EPS report is as under:

Total Consumption (MUs)	*T&D Losses (MUs)*	*Total Requirement (MUs)*	*Peak Load (MW)*
2325	787	3113	610
2542	856	3399	662
2737	918	3656	708
2920	973	3894	750
3118	1034	4153	795

A comparison of this study's forecast appears to be in consonance with the expected forecast of the 16th EPS report, which estimates current demand to be about 800 MW.

Is Himachal Pradesh Power Surplus?

In today's scenario, Himachal Pradesh is buying power from outside for its need of about 3500 million units. It is not power surplus today.

If all its schemes under implementation and under consideration come on steam by 2011-2012, then it will be self-sufficient in power by that time. This will be a world class state, with clean and reliable power ensured for advanced agro processing and tourism industries.

From 2012 onwards, Himachal Pradesh will start to have a sizeable trade in power through the national grid, when the last tranche of projects are undertaken to move towards a full tapping of the hydro resource.

This study would like to recommend a word of caution on the optimism being expressed at using power as a commodity for sale since it is felt that it needs to be used in the service of HP's own development first. The forecast of sale right now, if implemented, would be at the cost of the state's own development. While farmers, processors, and tourists would be clamouring for power (and dependent services – water, cable cars, ropeways, etc), it might be wheeled out of the state. Himachal Pradesh's power will facilitate as an infrastructure in some other regions, while its own citizens' growth will suffer.

Himachal Pradesh power policy should clearly lay down a single cut/shortage scenario as a serious event. A tourist may never come back, and prevent ten others from coming in, if he had to leave his hotel without a hot bath. A 15-minute power outage may cause irreparable loss to the state, because it seeks to enter in the future the difficult area of hospitality, where reputations are lost quickly.

Financial Status of HPSEB

As a commercial organisation, HPSEB is in the doldrums (Table 17.10).

TABLE 17.10

Profit and Loss Account, HPSEB

(Rs. in crore)

Sr. No.	*Year*	*Total Receipt*	*Total Expenditure*	*Total Profit (+) or Loss (-)*	*Rate of Return*
1.	1997-1998	448.54	419.09	+29.45	5.31%
2.	1998-1999	499.48	505.75	-6.27	0.98%
3.	1999-2000	587.58	693.80	-106.22	0.37%
4.	2000-2001	660.84	697.72	-36.88	5.10%
5.	2001-2002	670.48	777.04	-106.56	11.29%

Source: Annual Account of HP State Electricity Board, 1997-2002.

TABLE 17.11

Revenue, Expenditure, Profit and Loss per kWh

(in Rs.)

Sr. No.	*Year (Units sold excluding wheeling in bracket)*	*Revenue per kWh*	*Expenditure per kWh*	*Profit/Loss per kWh*
1.	1997-1998 (2668 MU)	1.68	1.57	0.09
2.	1998-1999 (2797 MU)	1.79	1.81	-0.02
3.	1999-2000 (2864 MU)	2.05	2.42	-0.37
4.	2000-2001 (2821 MU)	2.34	2.47	-0.13
5.	2001-2002 (2881 MU)	2.33	2.70	-0.37

Source: Annual Account of HP State Electricity Board, 1997-2002.

Thus, since 1998-99, HPSEB has entered a financial downturn. It is now even entering the beginnings of a debt trap, where its interest payments have doubled in five years to Rs 80 crore, and it is breaking open reserves to pay back loans.

TABLE 17.12

Statement of Fund Flow

(Rs. in crore)

Year	Source					Application					
	Internal Resource of Loans	Reserves & Others	Govt. Loans	Loans from Financial Institutions	Total	Expenditure on Works	Other Investment	Repayment of Loans	Payment of Interest (Net)	Net change in Working Capital	Total
1997-1998	90.80	55.70	60.70	163.30	370.50	170.90	60.20	38.30	41.90	58.20	370.50
1998-1999	58.30	79.50	88.90	118.10	344.80	212.50	359.10	41.80	43.00	-311.60	344.80
1999-2000	-31.70	75.10	4.20	404.30	451.90	230.00	-329.8	527.50	51.10	-26.90	451.90
2000-2001	50.20	109.50	2.50	244.70	406.90	314.80	52.50	31.30	63.40	-55.10	406.90
2001-2002	3.69	68.30	-	539.16	611.15	297.00	43.80	325.55	78.40	-133.60	611.15

Source: Annual Account of HP State Electricity Board, 1997-2002.

Experience of State Governments in Power Reforms, and Lessons

Faced with a deteoriating condition of the SEBs in India, a Common Minimum National Action Plan was drawn up in 1996, with input from Chief Ministers of the states, that called for:

(i) setting up of Central and State Regulatory Commissions;

(ii) Rationalisation of Retail Tariffs,

(iii) unbundling of the SEBs into more manageable entities with defined functions;

(iv) private sector participation in distribution.

We will examine the case of the pioneer – Andhra Pradesh – and events in two neighbouring states of Haryana and Punjab.

Key stakeholders:

- Government – officials and political parties, both in treasury and opposition benches
- Andhra Pradesh State Electricity Board (APSEB) – over 74,000 employees
- Farmers — the largest user group but dispersed in rural areas
- Households — also important consumers and concentrated in urban areas
- Industry – significantly affected by energy cuts; largest firms may pursue alternative sources

The following steps were taken to address the stakeholders:

Attempt at Information Dissemination

Andhra Pradesh government appointed a high-level committee in 1996 that included two former chairmen of the APSEB. This report was generally considered impartial and professional. Also in 1996, the APSEB began circulating bulletins in English and the local language, Telugu, about the urgent problems in the power sector and the need to address them quickly. The bulletins highlighted the growing gap between supply and demand, the increasing price of generating power and the rising deficits. Later bulletins discussed metering and billing, explaining commercial losses and theft of energy. An inexpensive, pocket-size explanation of the key issues in the power sector and the case for reform was circulated all over the state, reflecting a government commitment to disseminate information on a massive state-wide scale.

Given low literacy rates, particularly in rural areas, additional steps were taken to use audio-visual medium. Several films were produced and aired on the cable network throughout the state. One of the movies used the theme of match-making discussions of an APSEB engineer who, while informing the prospective in-laws about his job, is asked questions about the power sector situation and reforms. In the films, a variety of participants from diverse social and professional backgrounds participated in the discussion and explored the merits of reform.

The government issued two White Papers on the state's finances and the financial condition of the APSEB. These were debated in the state legislative assembly. A discussion of the power sector figured prominently in three successive episodes of the "Dial your C.M.", a weekly televised programme launched by the Chief Minister's office.

Building Support Among Electricity Board Employees

Rank-and-file as well as mid-level engineers and professionals had strong concerns about the impact of reforms on job security and conditions of employment even though, in this case, overstaffing at the aggregate level was not an issue. The government offered assurances to workers and entered into negotiations over revised terms and conditions. A sub-committee for staff matters, which included union representatives, was formed. In late 1997, all but one of the unions representing APSEB employees signed new agreements defining terms and conditions of service, protection of jobs and retrenchment due to restructuring. Compensation levels are negotiated through a separate mechanism with the labour unions. One important union, however, still continued to oppose the reforms and went on strike in April 1998.

Reaching Out to Potential Opponents

The government convened a meeting of all political parties and laid out its proposal to restructure APSEB as the first step in reforming the power sector. The opposition boycotted the meeting and the smaller parties present rejected the government plan. In the months that followed, opposition parties launched their own outreach efforts, contradicting government pro-reform arguments and undermining public support. Failure to secure their support or dent their opposition did create significant problems during implementation.

Soliciting Input on Draft Government Proposals

The commission set up had recommended that the government:

(i) divide APSEB into three separate entities along functional lines (power generation, distribution, and transmission);

(ii) revise the regulatory framework, including rules for tariff-setting and policies for overall sector development;

(iii) take steps to facilitate private sector investment in power generation and distribution. The government endorsed these objectives and stressed the importance of separating the management, regulatory, and policy functions.

APSEB's role, they believed, should be limited to management but given more operational autonomy to meet its obligations. The government should limit its role to policy-making and keep an arm's length from regulatory functions.

After receiving the recommendations of the high-level commission, the AP government issued its Policy Statement in February 1997 that outlined the proposed reforms and initiated a dialogue with diverse groups of stakeholders, including industrialists, agriculturists, non-governmental organisations and journalists. A large open meeting with about 250 representatives of NGOs was held, in which senior government officials, and donor agencies participated.

In April 1998, after fourteen months of public debate on its initial Policy Statement and resolution of key APSEB concerns, the state cabinet moved forward with legislation approving the AP Electricity Reform Act of 1998. It was passed by the Legislative Assembly two weeks later and approved by the President in October 1998.

Implementing Reforms and the Proposed Tariff Hike

Budget preparations for the coming year quickly confronted the government with the need to define the subsidies and estimated tariff increases required for operations of the power sector. The decision whether to approve a tariff hike and the form it would take fell to the newly-created and little-known APERC. Their first step was to prepare a "philosophy paper" on tariff policy. Their second step was to open up the process for debate and discussion. APERC officials organised large public meetings with key stakeholders in three of the largest cities in November 1999.

The nature of the meetings, however, did not lead to a constructive exchange of views on the problems and how to resolve them. Instead, an unwieldy total of over 300 interested participants gathered in each city. Farmers, in particular, dominated the discussions, drowning out other voices and flatly opposing a tariff increase. The gap in understanding here was particularly large since the philosophy paper itself had identified unmetered agricultural consumption as a significant problem to be addressed and, in later discussions, small-scale businesses would effectively argue that they were, in fact, subsidising agricultural users.

Despite the consultation process, there was widespread opposition to the reforms process, and all stakeholders did not feel fully addressed.

These experiences were seen reflected in violence in the neighbouring states of Haryana and Punjab.

In Haryana, police and electricity officials were held in custody by mobs for weeks, and the state highways were closed in the Jind district, protesting against the reforms process. Similarly, in Punjab, an agitation against the reforms process has been an almost continuous activity, and successive governments of different political parties have not been able to satisfactorily resolve the issue.

Lessons

Other than the major issues of participation and communication, some additional important issues that need addressing are:

- One fundamental fact of the reforms process is – higher tariff after implementation.

(Tariff in Rs/unit)

Type	*Pre-Reform*	*Post-Reform*
	Haryana	
Domestic	2.14	3.06
Industry LT	3.19	3.92
Industry HT	3.34	4.07
	Andhra Pradesh	
Domestic <81 units	0.80	1.45
<201 units	1.65	3.90
<401 units	2.90	5.00
>401 units	3.40	5.20

While governments and experts see the opposition as being to the reforms process, paying consumers are only protesting tariff hikes, and the erstwhile free riders are protesting any payment at all. One problem has been an across the board attempt to charge cost plus tariffs, where the consumer is being asked to pay for inefficiencies also.

- Rather, Government must assist SERCs in laying down a long term programme of tariffs, by demonstrating a resolve of bringing in efficiency, lowering cost in the long run, and transferring the advantage to the consumers. For example, unreliable power supply forces farmers to use diesel pumpsets, where the cost per unit is in the region of Rs 10/-. If we calculate the total energy cost to farmers per acre of land, and demonstrate that even with higher tariffs his total energy cost will be less, he will accept the reforms process.
- Governments must give due respect to the statutory institutions of the power sector, and treat the sector as a techno-commercial issue. SERCs must work as independent institutions, and there should be no treading on their domain. In AP, when the government talked of tariff increases before the awards were announced by the APERC, the public perceived it to be a government decision and reacted unfavourably. Government response towards SERC domain should be the same as to sub judice cases and this will build up respect for professional conduct of SERCs and related bodies.
- Government must accept SERC award as a stakeholder only. In case they wish to step in to subsidise certain sectors, provision should be made in the budgets, in accordance with Electricity Act requirements. Unless there is a very good reason to do so, appeals against SERC orders to High Courts will compromise the reforms process at the inception stage itself.
- Public consultations must not be held within a "free expectation" model, but confined to seeking solutions to structured questions. This exercise ensures that stakeholders arrive for consultations with a clearer mental framework, and targeted decisions can be arrived at.

Status of Power Reforms in HP

The following steps have been taken:

- HPERC has been set up and a single member body has commenced work since 6 January, 2001.
- HP has achieved 100 per cent metering, billing, and collection
- HP has entered into a MoU with Ministry of Power, Government of India on 31 March, 2001, laying down specific milestones to be achieved:
  - Creation of independent centres for generation, transmission, and distribution of electricity
  - Reduce surplus staff
  - Reduce CPSU outstanding to two months billing, and securitise earlier outstandings.
  - Implement energy audit at 11 kV distribution feeders and LT sides.
  - Introduce computerised billing for urban customers, and all customers with connected load of 100 kW and above.
  - File Tariff Petition before HPERC by 30 April, 2001
  - Pay subsidy from its own budget, if required.

The basic step of unbundling generation, transmission, and distribution now needs to be taken in HP. These have been declared as separate profit centres from April 1, 2003, and it needs to be taken further as three separate corporate entities.

The Ministry of Power, and Energy Watch has compiled the following comparative status of reforms of the power sector by various states in India:

Milestones	Northen Region								Western Region				
	Delhi	Haryana	H.P	J & K	Punjab	Rajasthan	U.P	Uttranchal	Chattishgarh	Gujarat	Goa	M.P	Mahatashtra
SERC Constituted	☺ 99-00	☺ 8/98	☺ 1/01		☺ 3/99	☺ 99-00	☺ 9/98	☺ 1/02	☺ 01-02	☺ 11/98	☺ 4/02	☺ 8/98	☺ 99-00
Operationalisation of SERC	☺	☺	☺		☺	☺	☺	☺		☺		☺	☺
Last Tarrif Order Issued	☺ 5/01	☺ 12/00	☺ 01/02		☺ 10/02	☺ 3/01	☺ 10/02			☺ 10/00		☺ 9/01	☺ 5/00
Signing of MoU	☺ 3/03	☺ 2/01	☺ 3/01	☺ 4/02	☺ 3/01	☺ 3/01	☺ 2/00	☺ 3/01	☺ 1/01	☺ 1/01	☺ 10/01	☺ 10/02	☺ 3/01
Signing of MoA	☺ 3/03	☺ 12/02	☺ 12/02	☺ 2/03	☺ 8/02	☺ 7/02	☺ 9/02	☺ 12/02	☺ 10/02	☺ 6/02	☺ 11/02	☺ 9/02	☺ 6/02
Signing of TPA		☺ 07/02	☺ 10/02	☺ 7/02	☺ 7/02	☺ 11/02	☺ 7/02	☺ 9/02	☺ 7/02	☺ 6/02	☺ 7/02	☺ 7/02	☺ 3/03
Reform Bill Enactment	☺ 2000	☺ 1998		☺		☺ 2000	☺ 1999	☺ 01/02				☺ 2000	
Unbundling/ Corporatisation	☺ 7/02	☺ 8/99				☺ 7/00	☺ 1/00	☺ 2001				☺ 2002	
Privatisation of Distribution	☺ 7/02												
11 KV for 100% Metering	☺	☺	93%	☺	99%	45%	☺	96%	63%	☺	☺	91%	85%
100% Consumer Metering	☺	☺	☺	40%	85%	90%	59%	87%	65%	93%	95%	63%	86%

	Southern Region				Eastern Region			
	A.P	Karnataka	Kerala	Tamil Nadu	Bihar	Jharkhand	Orissa	West Bengal
SERC Constituted	☺ 7/99	☺ 9/00	☺ 11/02	☺ 3/99	☺ 4/02	☺ 8/02	☺ 5/96	☺ 1/99
Operationalisation of SERC	☺	☺		☺			☺	☺
Last Tarrif Order Issued	☺ 6/00	☺ 2002		☺ 3/03			☺ 4/97	☺ 2001
Signing of MoU	☺ 3/01	☺ 2/00	☺ 8/01	☺ 1/02	☺ 9/01	☺ 4/01	☺ 6/01	☺ 5/01
Signing of MoA	☺ 5/02	☺ 5/02	☺ 10/02	☺ 7/02	☺ 12/02	☺ 11/02	☺ 3/03	☺ 7/02
Signing of TPA	☺ 7/02	☺ 6/02	☺ 8/02	☺ 6/02	☺ 11/02		☺ 9/02	☺ 7/02
Reform Bill Enactment	☺ 1999	☺ 1999					☺ 1996	
Unbundling/Corporatisation	☺ 02/99	☺ 08/99					☺ 4/96	☺
Privatisation of Distribution							☺ 98	
11 KV for 100% Metering	☺	☺	☺	☺	39%		27%	93%
100% Consumer Metering	85%	☺	☺	☺	89%		90%	94%

	North Eastern Region							
	A.P	Assam	Meghalaya	Mizoram	Manipur	Nagaland	Tripura	Sikkim
SERC Constituted	☺ 2/99	☺ 8/01						
Operationalisation of SERC		☺						
Last Tarrif Order Issued								
Signing of MoU	☺ 7/02	☺ 3/01	☺ 11/02	☺ 7/02		☺ 9/02		☺ 12/02
Signing of MoA	☺ 7/02	☺ 7/02	☺ 11/02	☺ 7/02		☺ 9/02		☺ 12/02
Signing of TPA		☺ 7/02	☺ 2/03			☺ 8/02		☺ 11/02
Reform Bill Enactment								
Unbundling/Corporatisation								
Privatisation of Distribution								
11 KV for 100% Metering	19%	34%	30%	79%	21%	34%	☺	24%
100% Consumer Metering	54%	86%	64%	47%	82%	73%	81%	28%

Note: ☺ shows achieved.

It can be seen that power reform process is ahead in western and southern regions, followed by the north. It is lagging most in north east, and with exception of Orissa, in the eastern region also. It is also worth noting that other than Orissa and Delhi, no state has gone in for privatisation of distribution.

Himachal Pradesh has taken some fundamental steps like constitution of SERC, metering of 11 kV lines and customers, and signing of MoU with Government of India. It has however, lagged in putting in place a legal framework for implementing the next phase of reform, which will take it into the area of unbundling generation, transmission and distribution, and finally into hiving off distribution altogether.

What is Wrong with HPSEB?

Consider: As a 100 per cent hydro supplier, Himachal Pradesh must have a cost of electricity comparable to Norway, at one cent (47 paise) per unit, but is actually selling at around five to six cents per unit, almost at thermal price. This inflated cost is also raising the cost of industrial and agro-production in Himachal Pradesh. In reality, if it is to attract industry, then it should be in a position to cover the additional cost of transport of raw material and finished products, through a hugely cheaper power tariff. And this is not happening. And the irony is, HPSEB is still making a loss on every unit sold.

- There are inefficiencies in the generation process. At 70 per cent load factor, 326 MW should produce nearly 1900 million units per year. Against a target of 1480, HPSEB manages only about 1150. This is raising the cost per unit, since in hydro power, fixed costs play an important role, with no fuel cost involved. Thus, improvement of generation efficiency is vital.
- The Planning Commission has specified an indicative norm of 7.8 employees per 1000 customers, whereas HPSEB has 17.
- T&D losses are higher than 20 per cent.

Suggestions

- Himachal Pradesh is ripe for taking power reforms to a logical final step of unbundling and privatisation of distribution.
    - It is a hydro state, with capability to provide power at reasonable rates. If it can move simultaneously on increasing generation efficiency, HP can minimise post-reform tariff hikes.
    - Only 2 per cent of its consumers are in the agriculture sector, thus minimising the stakeholder group that has traditionally caused maximum opposition to power reform.
    - Consumers in the agro-processing and tourism industries will want clean, reliable power in the future, and they are willing to pay, as it increases their own profits.
- Nowadays, it is almost fashionable to talk of privatisation. This is causing a misplaced thrust, because we actually need to talk of efficiency. There are no conclusive studies to establish an ownership pattern as being the determinant of an organisation's business success or failure. HPSEB was making profits till 1998, and was hit hard by the rise in wages by the Pay Commission. Analysis has also revealed inefficiencies both in generation and distribution, and if these are addressed, HPSEB can function well as a generator, and as Himachal Pradesh's State Transmission Utility (STU), both functions performed as separate companies.
- Though now established as separate profit centres, Generation, Transmission and Distribution should be corporatised as separate entities. With respect to the Act, the following must be taken cognizance by Himachal Pradesh immediately:
    - The SERC has now an expanded statutory role to play. The Commission needs to be staffed and provided for to equip it to discharge its obligations under the Act, otherwise either decisions will be delayed, or be sub-optimal.
    - Prepare a Consultation paper for seeking the Central Government notifications on a national Policy for permitting stand-alone systems, especially those based on renewable and non-conventional sources (Section 4 of the Act).
    - Prepare a Consultation paper for seeking the Central Government notifications on a national Policy on rural electrification, and purchase and management of local distribution by PRIs, NGOs, users' associations etc (Section 5).
    - HP should note that as per Section 7, as long as technical standards are adhered to, any company can enter generation. However, as per Section 8, Hydro Electric Projects will need CEA approvals. As per Section 8(1), this is applicable for HEP schemes having capital expenditures beyond a certain sum. HP government should immediately begin consultations so that mini/

micro hydel schemes are kept out of CEA purview, to facilitate quicker decision-making. Presently, projects upto 25 MW are out of CEA purview, and handled by the MNES, but in accordance with Section 8(1), a capital expenditure criterion needs to be established.

- It is felt that rather than focus on a potentially contentious issue of reducing "manpower", we should attempt to reduce "manpower cost", which is the essence of the issue. On the generation side, the inefficiencies highlighted, where stations are working at only 40 per cent load factor, need to be examined, and the load factor brought up to 60-70 per cent, through Renovation & Modernisation. This increased efficiency will reduce the per unit generation cost.
- Distribution operations break even must be reached immediately, and there should be involvement of PRIs/ULBs in this process. It is essential that the power sector reform be made a people's issue, to be achieved through people's participation, and not be seen as a legal/bureaucratic *diktat*. If peoples' participation is not ensured, the reform process will cause alienation.

  Experience shows that post-reform, there is a rise in power price, with withdrawal of subsidies. It takes time for the efficiencies to establish, and there is potential for a public outcry in the interim.
- It should also be kept in mind that HP is a seasonal power producer. In summer, the dams are full, and it sells power, but in winter it needs more power, which it buys back at a higher price. This pattern will continue in the future, and within the framework of the Electricity Act, it is in the interest of the state to enter into long term understanding with its neighbours of J&K, Panjab, Haryana, and the heavy consuming centre of Delhi. It is also a good market situation that its neighbours need more power in the summer, both for domestic and agricultural use, and HP has surpluses at the time. On the other hand, power situation in the plains is easier in winter, and HP will need to augment its own resources then.
- HP should not enter into any PPAs with IPPs. Such agreements will defeat the very purpose of power sector reform of bringing efficiency and lowering costs, and shift the entire risk onto HPSEB. If there is only an attempt to shift risk rather than decrease it, there may be a situation when the IPPs may even work to oppose power sector reform, armed as they are with guarantees, and counter-guarantees (Power Sector Reform and Regulation: The Road Ahead, Sebastian Morris, India Infrastructure Report 2001).

Target dates for adding additional capacity through state, central, joint, and IPP programme appear to be very ambitious. It appears slippages will occur, and the state needs to have a re-look to lay down a revised realistic forecast.

Proposed Model

- Start an initiative to begin people's participation in the reform process. Engage GOs and NGOs in an exercise of dialogue with the people, and SERC can co-ordinate such an exercise. It must be precisely planned, and executed with clear blessings from the highest level. The aim is to build up a consensus for the reforms process by ensuring good quality and assured supply of power at reasonable prices.
- Involve HPSEB employees in the reform-related decision-making process. Employees must be told that they will not be forced to quit their jobs.
- Incorporate a power generation utility consisting of HPSEB's generation wing. Evolve procedures to decentralise decision-making to this generator, while retaining general policy initiative through the Board level, by retaining majority equity capital share. If possible, disinvest through employee stock option plans and public issue to Himachal Pradesh residents, further broad basing the success factor. Build in procedures to ensure efficiency, with minimum PLF achievement at 60-70 per cent. *Do not* offer employee incentives for generation, otherwise plants may refuse to back off when asked, raising grid frequency to dangerous levels. Rather, build in disincentive for not producing according to target. The disincentive will not apply when generator is asked to back off by Regional Transmission Centre.
- Incorporate a power transmission utility, as envisaged under the Electricity Act 2003. Begin talks with CEA, Power Grid, and neighbouring states for establishing and participating in the Regional Transmission Centre/s, and enter into agreements for power sale/purchase with them. Evaluate possibility of multilateral assistance from national and international bodies for strengthening the state's transmission backbone.

The plan should envisage setting up a transmission backbone for handling the anticipated demand for year 2020.

- Handover local distribution to *panchayats, zilla parishads* and urban local bodies. The transmission company will handover power at the local sub-stations, in a metered quantity. The following methodology can be considered:
- Power is metered into the local sub-station, and effectively handed over to the local body. The locally available distribution infrastructure is brought on to the books of the local body, which becomes a franchisee for distribution, and allowed to charge commission for collection of user charges, to cover distribution and administrative costs. The local body will have to be assured that technical hand holding will be done when needed.
- Employees of HPSEB can be offered VRS proposal, linked with a choice of a village/town in which they would like to be associated with the local body in maintenance of distribution infrastructure, distribution of electricity, and collection of user charges. After VRS, they will be working with the local body for a fixed lump-sum on a contractual basis. Considering the "harvesting" absenteeism in linesmen and other staff, if the scheme is worked out thoughtfully, it is likely to succeed.
- Implement rigorous training to local bodies, and the HPSEB staff involved to take on the new role.
- Involve private sector in upgrading distribution systems wherever necessary. Funds for this will come from the user charges for higher loads, etc., and can be collated at a level sufficiently large enough to offer economies of scale.
- The entire package should be worked out in a financially secure manner, with no subsidy input from the government.
- Continue cap on any new recruitment in HPSEB, and strictly implement the same. Special VRS offers should be linked to the distribution scheme as mentioned earlier. Re-deployment of staff will be required in accordance with new corporatised structure.

Current Status of Memorandum of Understanding

Himachal Pradesh has moved on the milestones to be achieved as per the MoU signed with Government of India.

The status of metering is as under:

H V Substation	*Total No. of Feeders*	*No. of Meters Installed*	*Percentage Metering*
33 KV	128	101	78.9
22 KV	114	80	70.17
15 KV	6	1	16.16
11 KV	597	542	90.78
2.2KV	6	6	100.00
DTRs	14600	13222	90.56

- 100 per cent metering of consumers has been achieved.
- Energy Accounting has been started at Circle level, and while 70 per cent of the feeders have being taken up for accounting, 43 per cent are currently under energy audit.

The state position of metering and audit is as under:

	2000-01	*2001-02*	*2002-03*
Input Energy (MU)	2898.793	3104.79	3332.031
Metered Energy (MU)	2206.066	2332.231	2518.909
Billed Energy (MU)	2206.066	2332.231	2518.909
Realised Energy (MU)	2084.723	2120.328	2236.268
Revenue realised (Rs. in crore)	489.3	504.61	541.5

There is still a large gap between input and metering, and metering and realisation.

Supply and sale price per unit is as under:

	2000-01	*2001-02*	*2002-03*
Average cost of Supply (in Paise/Unit)	247	270	266
Average revenue realised (in Paise/Unit)	234	233	250

The differential of 16 paise per unit is proposed to be bridged by the following strategy upto 2005-2006:

	2002-03	*2005-06*
Increase in generation (MU)	1277	2052
Reduction in T&D Loss		
a) Overall	19.35%	13%
b) Within the State	25%	20%
Increase in Revenue (Rs. in crore)	800	2003
Increase in Tariff		16%

With these initiatives, a tentative profit and loss account by 2005-2006 is proposed as under, with economic surplus generation:

(in Rs. crores)

Description	*2001-02*	*2002-03*	*2003-04*	*2004-05*	*2005-06*
Revenue Income	671	800	1030	1759	2004
Expenses	699	757	1083	1634	1756
Net Income before Interest	(-)28	(+)43	(-)53	(+)125	(+)248
Total Interest	138	180	207	247	286
Less IDC Capitalized	60	85	110	120	135
Net Income before income tax	(-)106	(-)52	(-)150	(-2)	(+)97
Asset Base	944	1145	1250	1980	2105
Percentage rate of return	(-)11.29	(-)4.56	(-)12	(-)0.11	(+)4.64

It is assumed that there will be:

- Increase in generation capacity 90%
- Demand Increase 20%
- Reduction in T&D losses 6%
- Increase in Tariff 16%
- Improvement in Billing & Collection efficiency 15%

The proposed business plan makes the right assumptions, and is in consonance with the recommendations made in this study. However, some imperatives must not be lost sight of:

- The interest burden on HPSEB is rising at an alarming rate, and a detailed study of interest liabilities in the long run needs to be assessed.
- Stakeholder participation through the above mentioned recommendations must not be lost sight of.

A long term tariff plan must be finalised, with the consumers clear that short term tariff increases will be balanced out in the long run by greater efficiency.

OTHER INITIATIVES

Fluorescent Lighting

In the domestic lighting sector, people still use incandescent lighting. It would be desirable to impose a higher slab of local taxation such that the incandescent bulb becomes an expensive proposition. At the same time, taxes on fluorescent lighting should be brought down to encourage its use, and it should also be mandated that only electronic ballasts (chokes) are used. This should be coupled with a public awareness programme, and a targeted drive to wipe out incandescent bulbs within a two-year period.

This step is likely to reduce the total lighting load by a margin of 50 per cent.

Energy Saving Equipment

It should be mandated by law that for day to day appliances like fans, pumps, food processors ("mixies"), agricultural motors etc., BIS certification is a must. The market is full of cheap, but power guzzling appliances. They actually cost the buyer much more in its total life-cycle cost, in the form of heavy running charges, and place a great strain on the power system of the state.

An awareness campaign should be conducted for this, and manufacturers asked to seek BIS certification for their products. The energy consumption of the product should be compulsorily mentioned prominently for consumer guidance, and surprise checks of products in the shops conducted to ensure that the product answers its laid down specifications. This should be achieved in a total target time of two years.

Village Broadband Connectivity through HPSEB

In Himachal Pradesh, the cost of digging through rocky terrain to bring telecom connectivity is a costly proposition. While optical fibre cables (OFC) are being laid along national and state highways, the last-mile connectivity to villages and hamlets can be done through HPSEB LT line poles.

While this will lower last-mile telecom costs considerably, it can also help the PRIs run both power, and telecom distribution circuits from the panchayat office.

TRANSPORT

A reading of the Himachal Pradesh Annual Plans, Economic Surveys, and the State Five Year Plans gives an impression of the state's belief that a discussion of the road projects suffices as a Transport Plan.

There is a passing mention of an inter-modal vision, and in fact, it is misspelt as "inter model" at some places. The concept of inter-modal also appears to be restricted to a vision of roads connected to lifts or rope-ways, and there is no treatment of inter-modalism as a logistics issue, either in passenger or goods movement. The official website of Himachal (*www.himachal.nic.in*) does not even mention transport as a subject area, but chooses to discuss it under Public Works, focusing on road construction and maintenance activity.

It is felt that a proper analysis of this sector is not being attempted – *Economic Survey 2003* mentions that

"Road Transport is the mainstay of economic activity in the Pradesh as other means of transport namely ....Taxis.....are negligible." Taxis *do* form an important component of road transport in the state for tourist movements, and its consideration as negligible shows a blind spot, and a rather cursory treatment of a vital subject.

"Road Transport" has also been made synonymous with "HRTC" (Himachal Road Transport Corporation), and other than road construction, this remains the only organised transport activity that finds serious mention. It has not been possible to find a cogent Transport Policy of Himachal Pradesh, and whenever it has been attempted, it has again shown a road-HRTC bias. As late as March 2001, when the then Transport Minister spoke of a "Transport Policy", he exhibited the same bias in declaring that "The Himachal Pradesh Government has decided to strongly implement *transport policy* in order to provide better transport facilities to passengers travelling in the Himachal Road Transport Corporation buses in and outside the state" (*The Tribune*, 23 March, 2001, italics added).

The importance of transport for Himachal Pradesh cannot be overstated enough, since it addresses the core issue of accessibility for the people. There is a specific agenda for the infrastructure sector and the transport sub-sector to address, in the context of Himachal Pradesh's development plans. Important issues to consider are:

i. Hydro-power envisages large, medium and mini/micro schemes to be set up in the near future. This will need millions of tonnes of cement, steel, and machinery to be moved to project sites.

ii. Himachal Pradesh has a policy to give a thrust to horticulture and agro-processing. The raw and processed stock will need quick movements from farms to godowns, from cold storages to processing stations, and finally towards national and international markets.

iii. The other major thrust area of tourism needs assured and safe transport network. It needs structuring for a tourist-friendly system, with enquiries, itinerary planning and reservations, and uniform fare systems.

iv. The network should facilitate day-to-day life of Himachal Pradesh residents, and have an effective linkage with a disaster management plan. This is especially important for a state situated in a seismically active area.

Roads

Considering the geography of Himachal Pradesh, roads are an important component. There are National Highways, Border Roads, State Highways, and other arterial and rural roads.

At Independence, Himachal Pradesh started with nearly no roads, but has done well to build an estimated 27,737 km of motorable roads by 31 December 2002. During 2002-2003, data upto September 2002 also shows good progress.

TABLE 17.13

Road Building Progress During 2002-2003

Item	*Unit*	*Target for 2002-2003*	*Achievement Up to September, 2002*
Motorable	Kms.	550	342
Cross-drainage	Kms.	650	376
Metalling & Tarring	Kms.	650	608
Jeepable	Kms.	20	25
Bridges	No.	30	19
Villages connected	No.	50	12

Source: Himachal Pradesh Economic Survey 2003.

However, the achievements are less than the requirements. The Eighth Five Year Plan for Himachal Pradesh laid down the target in this regard as 26,373 km, to achieve a road density of 473.5 km/thousand sq. km, as against the existence of 16883 km and 303.3 km/thousand sq. km, in March 1990.

The Ninth Five Year Plan for Himachal Pradesh raised the requirement to 30,495 km, and a road density of 547.8 km/thousand sq. km, as against achievement of 19,310 km, and a road density of 346.8 km/thousand sq. km, by March 1996.

Thus, the State Plans could not achieve their targets. In fact, the targets specified in the Eighth State Plan, could be achieved only by the beginning of the Tenth Plan.

Comparison of the road density of Himachal on a national scale shows that the state is below the all-India average, and placed at the 20th rank. However, this comparison would not be fruitful, since the data would take into account geographically dissimilar states. If we compare Himachal Pradesh with the hill states of J&K, Uttaranchal, Arunachal Pradesh,

Mizoram, and Sikkim, then Himachal Pradesh is the best.

In this context, as the leader in road development in hill states, Himachal Pradesh has done well, but in comparison to its own targets and needs, the state needs to get its act together.

Major Road Schemes

Pradhan Mantri Gram Sadak Yojana (PMGSY)

PMGSY was launched by the Government of India in 2000-01 with the primary objective of providing connectivity by all weather roads to all habitations with a population of 500 persons (250 persons for the Himachal Pradesh) and above by the end of Tenth Plan Period (2007). It replaced the erstwhile Basic Minimum Services (BMS) programme. In Himachal Pradesh, the Public Works Department is implementing this *Yojana* through its Programme Implementation Units (PIUs), which are mostly headed by Superintending Engineers, except for tribal areas where these are headed by Executive Engineers.

The funds under this *Yojana* are being released every year by the Ministry of Rural Development, Government of India, for execution of eligible road works, recommended by the respective states.

For implementation of project proposals under PMGSY 2002-03, the Government of India specifically directed all the states to ensure inclusion of only such villages under this *Yojana*, which have not been so far connected with any road, including fair weather roads. Further, Himachal Pradesh was told to prepare a shelf of road projects, costing about Rs.250 crore under PMGSY 2002-03. Accordingly, all the MPs/ MLAs/*Zilla Pradhans* made available their lists of priority road works, which they proposed to include under PMGSY 2002-03. The details received were examined by the State Level Standing Committee on PMGSY during its meeting held on 7 January 2003 and a shelf of 452 roads were finalised covering all 75 Blocks of the state, costing Rs. 251 crores, for providing connectivity to 583 villages, each having a population of 250 and above, and 286 smaller villages falling *en route*. It is pertinent to mention that under PMGSY 2000-01 and 2001-02, except for one road belonging to *Chopal* Block, the surfaces of all the approved roads were to be metalled/ tarred. However, in February 2002, a policy decision was taken that the surface of PMGSY roads would not be metalled/tarred in all such areas of the state, where connectivity is quite poor, which get lot of snowfall or where traffic intensity is quite low. It was decided that in all such areas, the roads would be provided with cross-drainage works and essential soling, so that these could function as all weather roads. Accordingly, while finalising proposals under PMGSY 2002-03, the State Level Standing Committee decided that the roads pertaining to Kangra, Hamirpur, Una and Bilaspur districts and to a part of Nalagarh Block of Solan district, be metalled/tarred and in other areas, this need not be done.

Status of Projects under PMGSY

The following final sanction was conveyed for these projects below:

District	*Total No. of Packages*	*Total No. of Roads*	*Pavement*		*CD Works*		*Other Works (Cost Rs. in Lakh)*	*Total Cost (Rs. in Lakh)*
			Length [in Kms]	*Sanctioned Cost (Rs. in Lakh)*	*No. of CD Works*	*Sanctioned Cost (Rs. in Lakh)*		
Bilaspur	7	16	62.88	657.67	101	117.09	41.98	816.74
Chamba	11	28	136.18	1315.49	255	199.57	69.47	1584.53
Hamirpur	13	34	110.43	1343.07	204	432.44	36.01	1811.52
Kangra	19	105	356.15	3329.42	558	441.23	200.22	3970.87
Kinnaur	6	10	41.55	586.55	80	99.87	4.30	690.72
Kullu	7	15	76.52	869.85	149	126.87	44.52	1041.24
Lahaul and Spiti	2	5	23.30	257.51	45	59.17	44.05	360.73
Mandi	16	49	221.97	1974.08	530	456.86	235.98	2666.92
Shimla	16	36	158.58	1826.65	372	328.67	56.35	2211.67
Sirmaur	8	22	70.53	925.06	149	184.65	47.86	1157.57
Solan	10	25	97.58	1087.60	227	168.23	103.25	1359.08
Una	9	28	113.39	896.14	144	157.53	168.15	1221.82
Total	**124**	**373**	**1469.06**	**15069.09**	**2814**	**2772.18**	**1052.14**	**18893.41**

District	Value of Proposals (Rs. in Lakh)	No. of Roadworks	No. of Roadworks Completed (upto Oct. 2003)	Per cent Roadworks Completed	Expenditure upto Oct. 2003 (Rs. in Lakh)
Bilaspur	816.74	16	10	62.50	660.89
Chamba	1584.53	28	15	53.57	1128.44
Hamirpur	1811.52	34	14	41.18	1377.01
Kangra	3970.87	105	69	65.71	3283.14
Kinnaur	690.72	10	3	30.00	414.78
Kullu	1041.24	15	5	33.33	557.68
Lahaul and Spiti	360.73	5	3	60.00	205.35
Mandi	2666.92	49	24	48.98	1933.98
Shimla	2211.67	36	21	58.33	1508.37
Sirmaur	1157.57	22	9	40.91	833.00
Solan	1359.08	25	10	40.00	952.47
Una	1221.82	28	22	78.57	1011.80
Total	**18893.41**	**373**	**205**	**54.9598**	**13866.91**

In the 12 districts, a total of 373 roads comprising 1469.06 kilometers for Rs 150.69 crore, 2814 cross drainage (CD) projects at a cost of Rs 27.72 crore, and other works costing Rs 10.52 crore, were sanctioned for HP under PMSGY.

The current status upto October 2003 is as tabulated in the table above.

Thus, 205 out of the 373 have been completed to record a progress of 56 per cent physical completion, and out of the total sanction of Rs. 188.93 crore, Rs. 138.66 crore have been spent.

The progress of works is thus good, considering that the monsoon months with conventionally slow progress have passed, and there is likely to be faster progress in the remaining part of the year.

The quality of work done as assessed by the National Quality Monitor shows the following data:

District	Block	Inspection Date	Road Name	Grade
Bilaspur	Bilaspur Sadar	22-04-2002	NH.21 at R.D 125/0 Kothipura to Noa.	Good
-do-	Gehrwin	22-04-2002	Baroha to Dahad road.	Very Good
-do-	Gehrwin	05-08-2002	Baroha to Dahad road.	Good
-do-	Gehrwin	22-04-2002	Chhad Sandyar road.	Very Good
Hamirpur	Bijhri	22-04-2002	Panjot Bagwara road.	Good
-do-	Bijhri	22-04-2002	Samirpur to Khansan	Good
-do-	Hamirpur	22-04-2002	Marial to Miharpura.	Good
-do-	Tihra Sujanpur	22-04-2002	Thalotu to Kuthrin road.	Good

Out of the eight projects inspected, two were judged as Very Good, and the remaining as Good. It is a presumption that the inspections were meaningful, since seven inspections over the districts of Bilaspur and Hamirpur are shown as having been conducted on the same day.

Areas of Concern

- A total of 747 habitations are proposed to be covered under these sanctioned projects, still leaving 10585 habitations unconnected.
- There is a wide variation in cost per kilometer of the road projects executed, ranging from Rs. 7.68 lakh per km (Una) to Rs. 13.95 lakh per km (Solan). The State government is advised to get this investigated through an independent agency.
- The quality of the roads for a tourism destination cannot be anything but perfect. The government should examine the specifications, and ensure that the specified quality is maintained, with constant monitoring right through the construction phase.

NABARD

In 1995-96, the Government of India created the Rural Infrastructure Development Fund (RIDF) with NABARD, which is a subsidiary of the Reserve Bank of India, for providing loan funds to state governments for creating durable assets in rural areas of the country. During the first year the emphasis was on agriculture, horticulture and minor and medium irrigation sectors.

From 1996-97 onwards, the road-and-bridge sector was also included in this scheme, when two road projects of Lal Dhank-Paonta-Rajban-Rohru-Sungri and Sidhpur-Sungri-Dharanghati-Sarahan-Jeori roads, were proposed for loan assistance.

Starting with RIDF-I, Himachal Pradesh is now in RIDF for 2002-2003. Up to February 2003, 298 schemes costing to Rs. 523 crore with Rs. 500 crore as NABARD loan and Rs. 23 crore as the state share have been sanctioned. Total expenditure for all tranches up to February 2003 is Rs. 286 crore only.

The progress of works in NABARD roads needs speeding up.

Central Road Fund

The Central Road Fund (CRF) is a non-lapsable fund. The Central Government determines accruals and allocation of funds to various states under CRF. Central Government allocates the funds, out of the entitled allocation to various states and gives administrative approvals to the proposals of the state governments. After the accord of administrative approvals to proposals by this Ministry, the project estimates for the proposals are approved technically and financially by the state government and works are executed by them. The quality control and proper utilisation of funds is the responsibility of the state government. One-third of the accrual was released initially in November 2000. Thereafter, funds are released based on utilisation of funds by the states. Most of the states have not fully utilised the funds released to them. State governments are being pursued at various levels, including at that of Chief Minister, for expediting completion of works and utilisation of funds.

The status of use of these funds is as below:

Thus, as per the report of the Ministry of Road Transport and Highways, the CRF utilisation by HP is only one-third of the total availability, reflecting a need to watch progress in this area.

(in Rs. Crore)

Sr. No	*Name of the State/UT*	*CRF Accruals for the year 2001-2002*	*Total Accruals Out of CRF from 2000-2001 to 2002-2003*	*Total Funds Released out of CRF*	*Balance (col. 4-5)*	*%age of Utilisation/ Release to the Accruals*
(1)	(2)	(3)	(4)	(5)	(6)	(7)
1.	Andhra Pradesh	162.49	243.94	125.969	117.9718	52
2.	Arunachal Pradesh	21.93	32.79	7.4200	25.3708	23
3.	Assam	29.81	45.21	24.8300	20.3808	55
4.	Bihar	51.81	85.71	16.1100	69.6008	19
5.	Chhattisgarh	45.59	62.87	37.4500	25.4208	60
6.	Goa	7.73	11.82	1.3100	10.5108	11
7.	Gujarat	137.92	206.05	79.7900	126.2608	39
8.	Haryana	63.45	99.20	31.4100	67.7908	32
9.	Himachal Pradesh	20.70	31.45	10.7044	20.7464	34
10.	Jammu & Kashmir	60.57	91.62	21.2502	70.3706	23
11.	Jharkhand	36.07	47.32	6.0700	41.2508	13
12.	Karnataka	113.00	171.13	50.0100	121.1208	29
13.	Kerala	53.83	81.54	9.2300	72.3108	11
14.	Madhya Pradesh	124.42	191.01	50.8205	140.1903	27
15.	Maharashtra	211.98	313.39	68.3500	245.0408	22
16.	Manipur	6.50	9.74	2.2200	7.5208	23
17.	Meghalaya	8.81	13.10	5.7385	7.3623	44
18.	Mizoram	5.92	8.88	7.9200	0.9608	89
19.	Nagaland	4.97	7.44	3.3700	4.0700	45
20.	Orissa	57.71	87.53	9.7000	77.8308	11
21.	Punjab	84.15	124.58	35.7300	88.8508	29
22.	Rajasthan	151.66	228.37	84.4400	143.9308	37
23.	Sikkim	2.19	3.29	0.7400	2.5500	22
24.	Tamil Nadu	133.46	200.68	82.3400	118.3408	41
25.	Tripura	3.80	5.73	2.0770	3.6530	36
26.	Uttaranchal	21.78	29.37	8.2000	21.1708	28
27.	Uttar Pradesh	176.46	272.89	30.5568	242.3340	11
28.	West Bengal	72.00	108.88	32.5605	76.3203	30

National Highways in Himachal Pradesh
(The 1235 km of National Highways in Himachal Pradesh, as shown below)

Name of National Highway	*NH No.*	*Name of Circle*	*Name of Division*	*Length in Division (in Kms)*
Jallandhar-Pathankot-Jammu-Srinagar Road	1-A	NH Circle HPPWD Shahpur	NH Division Jogindernagar	10.000
Pathnkot-Chakki-Mandi Road	20	NH Circle HPPWD Shahpur	NH Division Jogindernagar	197.000
Chandigarh-Mandi-Manali Road	21	NH Circle HPPWD Shahpur	NH Division Pandoh	151.250
Ambala-Kalka-Shimla-Wangtoo-Kaurik Road	22	NH Circle HPPWD Narkanda	NH Division Solan	130.450
			NH Division Rampur	160.000
Jallandhar-Hoshiarpur-Mubarikpur-Amb-Nadaun-Hamirpur T/Devi Dharampur-Kotla Mandi Road	70	1st Circle HPPWD Mandi	Dharampur Division	38.000
		1st Circle HPPWD Mandi	Mandi Division No. II	40.530
		1st Circle HPPWD Mandi	Sarkaghat Division	21.865
		8th Circle HPPWD Hamirpur	Touni Devi Division	22.000
		8th Circle HPPWD Hamirpur	Hamirpur Division	33.265
		9th Circle HPPWD Nurpur	Dehra Gopipur Division	17.050
		15th Circle HPPWD Una	Bharwain Division	32.420
Pinjore-Nalagarh Swarghat Road	21-A	3rd Circle HPPWD Solan	Nalagarh Division	48.875
Shimla-Barahampukhar-Ghagus Hamirpur-Nadaun-Ranital Kangra(Mataur) Road	88	3rd Circle HPPWD Solan	Arki Division	35.600
		4th Circle HPPWD Shimla	Shimla Division No. II	25.000
		5th Circle HPPWD Palampur	Kangra Division	21.300
		8th Circle HPPWD Hamirpur	Hamirpur Division	31.000
		8th Circle HPPWD Hamirpur	Barsar Division	10.000
		8th Circle HPPWD Hamirpur	Touni Devi Division	10.000
		9th Circle HPPWD Nurpur	Dehra Gopipur Division	29.700
		10th Circle HPPWD Bilaspur	Bilaspur Division No. I	16.000
		10th Circle HPPWD Bilaspur	Bilaspur Division No. II	18.400
		10th Circle HPPWD Bilaspur	Ghumarwin Division	27.000
Ambala-Naraingarh-Kala Amb-Paunta-Dehradun Haridwar Road	72	12th Circle HPPWD Nahan	Nahan Division	14.000
		12th Circle HPPWD Nahan	Paonta Division	43.000
Chandigarh-Mandi- Manali Road	21	10th Circle HPPWD Bilaspur	Bilaspur Division No. I	29.750
		10th Circle HPPWD Bilaspur	Bilaspur Division No. II	45.000

MAJOR ROADS OF HIMACHAL PRADESH

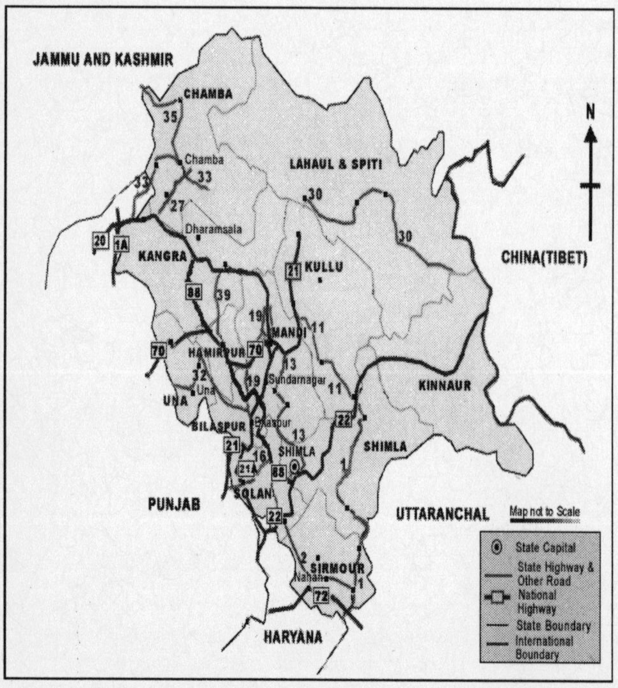

Inadequacies in Road Network

Less All-weather Roads

The total road length was 27,737 km in the state as on 31 December 2002. However, following major issues emerge:

The total road length mentioned is only a count of the total road *formation* in the state. Only 45 per cent of this road formation is metalled and tarred, the remaining being bare road surface.

Thus, less than 50 per cent of the roads are all-weather roads. This is a startling data for a state which seeks to move quickly on the tourism front. This is not restricted only to remote areas, but is seen all over the state.

Poor Village Connection

There are 16807 inhabited villages in Himachal Pradesh. At the end of 2002, less than 50 per cent of them were connected by roads, as shown in Table 17.15:

TABLE 17.14

District-wise Fair Weather and All Weather Roads

District	*Fair Weather Road*	*All Weather Road*
Bilaspur	504.464	717.942
Chamba	520.681	708.471
Hamirpur	573.865	1120.119
Kangra	1828.711	2404.187
Kinnaur	330.619	197.544
Kullu	895.686	420.266
Lahaul and Spiti	584.509	162.705
Mandi	2095.331	1546.721
Shimla	2446.757	1015.701
Sirmaur	802.584	1039.624
Solan	1324.123	856.116
Una	445.798	957.285

Source: Himachal Pradesh PWD Department Records.

TABLE 17.15

Villages Connected with Roads

Villages connected	*As on 31 March*			
	1999	*2000*	*2001*	*2002*
Villages with population more than 1500	184	184	185	186
1000-1500	223	224	224	224
500-1000	839	843	847	849
200-500	2517	2551	2575	2588
Below 200	3973	4001	4036	4063
Total	**7736**	**7803**	**7867**	**7910**

Source: Himachal Pradesh Economic Survey 2003.

Poor Road Quality

The road quality is not up to the mark, causing unsafe conditions, slowing down transport throughout, and raising maintenance costs. The Ministry of Surface Transport, Central Road Research Institute, and the Indian Road Congress have laid down and circulated a number of technical specifications to be observed in road construction, including bridges and drainage practices.

It is usual to see the road surface assuming a wave form at curves. This is the result of over-tarring, used to hide a thin formation of the road.

Poor compacting and drainage design also cause the roads to disintegrate quickly under water flows, as a result of rain.

Environmental Consideration Disregarded

Road design and construction in hills must be undertaken with environment preservation in mind. The parameters of concern are:

- Geological disturbance
- Land degradation and soil erosion
- Interruption in natural drainage system
- Siltation of river basin
- Aesthetic degradation

These issues are not being strictly implemented at road construction sites, thus causing immense air pollution.

As Kachroo and Sinha have brought out, construction of road will involve cutting of the natural inclination of terrain slopes, which may induce landslides during the rainy season. By the removal of vegetation, etc., the exposure of the sloping surface will become prone to erosion by water and may lead to the formation the deep gullies. The disposal of excavated rock mass from road construction, if allowed to slide down the slopes into stream beds will cause huge damage to the down-slope vegetation including forests, pastures and agricultural lands. The sliding of debris may cause widespread destruction of valuable agricultural lands, which are at lower altitudes. This will have an adverse impact on the growth of the vegetation causing imbalance of the ecosystem.

Road Design Keeping in Mind Multi-modalism

Road design should ensure that the national and state highways can handle container trucks with at least 20 foot containers. The gradients and turning radii need to be planned to conform to these requirements. Lay-by areas should be planned for container stuffing and de-stuffing operations.

Recommendations

The following facts emerge:

- While the progress in HP is not tardy, its own need to move on the tourism area needs a quicker build-up of the road sector.
- The need to broad-base its tourism appeal to all-season all-district fronts brings forth the requirement to open up the interiors. For this, rural roads are a must.
- The proportion of all-weather and metalled roads needs to go up.
- National and State highways need to be capable of handling multi-modal container vehicles.

It is necessary to put in place an institutional arrangement to manage the road sector on a professional footing.

Experience of NHAI in NHDP was commenced on the Build-Operate-Transfer model, using toll collection as a basis. However, experience has made it clear that the "tolls" model can succeed in very limited area, and the experience of earlier projects like the Coimbatore bye-pass have given clear indications (G. Raghuram & Geeta Kheskhani). A significant new factor in the BOT programme is the induction of annuities. Instead of, or in conjunction with concessions, the developer is paid an annuity over a fixed period, subject to a certification of the availability of the facilities to the users, as per specifications. This certification is done through an independent engineer, who examines the project in accordance with required specifications, and certifies their availability to the users. This has rightly shifted the emphasis from a mere "build" to "build and maintain" paradigm. The real bane of Indian road sector is the abysmal post-construction maintenance; in addition project developers use materials that pass short term technical testing, but prone to long term maintenance flaws. (The India Infrastructure Sector in India, 2001-02, India Infrastructure Report, 2003, Anupam B. Rastogi)

The annuity principle is ensuring that since payments are made on the basis of continued maintenance of standards, the developer must ensure relevant specifications right from the start.

HP has commenced its private participation in roads exercise by identifying six interstate barriers on which widening, four-laning, computerisation and commercial development will be undertaken on a public-private partnership basis. ILFS has prepared a concept note for structuring the bidding process and attracting private investment which is being finalised. These barriers include Parwanoo, Kala Amb, Mehatpur, Swarghat.

This should be carried further in involving private sector in a clear endeavour to maintain state highways and rural roads to specifications. These roads should be contracted out for maintenance to private agencies, for at least ten year periods, to allow the entrepreneur to effectively recover his investments. The payments should be on the basis of the annuity principle, with linkage to the continued availability of a well-maintained road. At present, construction and one time maintenance contracts allow payments on the basis of work executed, but is not linked to the quality of construction, and long term maintenance. As a result HP PWD is continuously on an exercise of departmental and private road repairs, with highways becoming one long joining of such repaired patches.

Roads – both for new construction and for maintenance of existing ones - in HP, should be thus contracted out over a longer length of chainage, and for a longer period of time, which allows entrepreneurs to develop their business models, linked to annuities, subject to satisfactory maintenance. Road development and maintenance can also be taken up by investors in the tourism business, who may need a right of way to open up their proposed properties to better communication.

Enact Road Fund Act

Recognising the need for mobilising greater non-budgetary resources for development and maintenance of the PWD road network, regulatory and institutional initiatives were undertaken for generating more user charges and mobilising greater private sector involvement in road projects, The Kerala Road Fund was constituted under the Kerala Road Fund Act 2001 which became law on November 23, 2001. The purpose of the Road Fund is to finance.

- routine recurrent and periodic maintenance of PWD roads.
- development of existing road network system including upgrading of any road maintained by the PWD.
- construction of new roads wherever necessary.
- such road safety projects as are found essential for safe and smooth traffic.
- research related to maintenance and development of roads.
- any cost-sharing, donor-funded project intended for all or any of the purposes mentioned above.

The Road Fund shall consist of:

a) all moneys received from the Central Road Fund established under the Central Road Fund Act, 2000.

b) the contribution made by the Government.

c) all fees, fines and other amount collected by the Government as per the provisions of the Kerala Highway Protection Act, 1999.

d) all payments made by the concessionaire as per the concession agreement.

e) all amount standing to the credit of the Bridges Fund established under Section 12 of the Kerala Tolls Act, 1976.

f) the user fees collected by the Government agency or the statutory body under the Kerala Road Fund Act.

g) grants or loans or advances made by the Government of India or any institution.

h) grants or loans or advances made by the Government.

i) all returns on investments made by the Road Fund Board directly or through a Government agency or statutory body.

j) any amount borrowed by the Road Fund Board.

k) any other amount authorised for credit to the Fund under the provisions of Road Fund Act or rules made thereunder or any other law for the time being in force.

The Fund is headed by the CM, with cabinet ministers of finance, PWD, and transport, along with officials and experts from transport and finance areas.

The Government shall contribute to the Fund every year an amount equal to ten per cent of the tax collected by them in the previous year under the provisions of the Kerala Motor Vehicles Taxation Act, 1976, and the said amount shall be charged on the Consolidated Fund of the State.

It is recommended that HP should also enact and create an institutional mechanism for the Road Fund, and place the road sector on a professional basis.

It is also recommended to make the PWD into a separate profit centre, with grants linked to specific maintenance and construction projects. The works of PWD will also be subject to an audit by an independent engineer, to bring transparency and professionalism into its working. After sufficient experience of working as an independent profit centre, PWD department could be corporatised as HP Construction Limited.

Note on Himachal Road Transport Corporation (HRTC)

On the advent of independence, Himachal was formed as a "C" class state. Consequent to nationalisation of passenger and goods service, Himachal Government Transport came into existence in July 1949 and continued to function as such till 1 October 1974. During 1958, a Corporation was floated jointly by the Governments of Punjab and Himachal and the Railways under the Road Transport Corporation Act., 1950 with a name and style as "Mandi-Kullu Road Transport Corporation", basically to operate on the joint routes in Punjab and Himachal. With the re-organisation of Punjab in 1966, certain hilly areas of the state were merged in Himachal and the operational areas of Mandi-Kullu Road Transport Corporation came entirely within expanded Himachal. This Corporation also continued to function as such till October 1, 1974. On October 2, 1974, Himachal Government Transport was merged with Mandi-Kullu Road Transport Corporation and was renamed Himachal Road Transport Corporation, under the Road Transport Corporation Act, 1950.

An operational snapshot of HRTC operations can be seen as in Table 17.16.

TABLE 17.16

Operational Snapshot of Himachal Road Transport Corporation

Indices	*1974*	*2001*	*2003*
Routes	379	1733	1784
Buses	733	1728	1711
Coverage (in lakh km)	303.29	1409.41	1423.06
Fuel consumption (km/litre)	2.90	3.54	3.56
Fleet Utilisation	79%	98%	98%
Accident/lakh km	0.17	0.12	0.13
Accidents/year	52	169	
Km/bus/day	113	223	221

Besides its operation in the entire Himachal Pradesh, including the tribal districts of the State, HRTC operates its buses in the neighboring states of Punjab, Haryana, Rajasthan, Uttar Pradesh, Jammu & Kashmir, Union Territories of Chandigarh and Delhi. Its buses cross through the three highest mountain passes of Bara-Lacha, Kunjam and Rohtang.

Operations indices reveal a good picture on the transport production front. While the number of buses increased 2.5 times, routes went up five times, and total kilometerage increased 4.5 times.

This is reflected in km per bus per day, which has doubled from 113 km per day in 1974, to 221 in 2003.

Fuel consumption data have also improved, and the average consumption is reasonable for hill haulage.

The safety factor, however, remains an area of concern. HRTC has not given any data of fatalities, but its accident rate in terms of accidents per lakh kms shows that the absolute number of accidents has tripled from 52 accidents per year in 1974 to 169 in 2001. Bus-holding has gone up less than three times, indicating a higher per bus accident rate. These issues need close examination.

Staff Efficiency

Since the inception of Himachal Road Transport Corporation, the staff from Mandi-Kullu Transport was absorbed in HRTC. During 2000-2001 the staff strength in HRTC was 9084. The Corporation has fixed the norm for staff of each category. The details are as under:

TABLE 17.17

Category-wise Norms for Staff

Sr. No.	*Description*	*Staff per Bus*
1.	Drivers	1.40
2.	Conductors	1.45
3.	Inspectors	0.18
4.	Administration	0.75
5.	Workshop	1.60
6.	Store	0.18
7.	Others	0.24
	Total	**5.80**

This means that that are three operations and frontline staff (driver + conductor + inspector) per bus, and an equal number of support staff in the workshops and offices. This teeth (frontline) to tail (support) ratio of 1:1 is unacceptable in any production situation.

It is the equivalent of 1 office staff (administration + store) and 2 others (workshop + others), a total of three staff permanently on each bus!

The trend of increase in number of buses and staff for the last ten years is shown in Table 17.18. This clearly shows that bus-to-staff ratio has remained constant for more than a decade.

Transport technology has improved over time. The vehicles have higher fuel averages, longer service intervals, are safer, and afford better ride quality, while increasing available engine power. All these translate into lower operation and maintenance costs. These should have a direct impact on the number of staff required to run and maintain a bus. These efficiencies have not been translated within the organisation, and the improvements in technology have not been exploited.

TABLE 17.18

Year-wise Number of Buses and Staff Strength

Financial Year	*Number of Buses*	*Staff Strength*	*Ratio*
1988-1989	1379	7530	5.46
1989-1990	1503	7986	5.31
1990-1991	1525	8256	5.41
1991-1992	1606	8643	5.38
1992-1993	1614	8659	5.36
1993-1994	1598	8561	5.35
1994-1995	1670	8647	5.17
1995-1996	1666	8810	5.28
1996-1997	1711	8917	5.21
1997-1998	1742	9270	5.32
1998-1999	1777	9229	5.19
1999-2000	1734	9282	5.35
2000-2001	1728	9084	5.26
2001-2002	1747	8964	5.13
2002-2003	1711	8494	4.96

Financial Results

The operational income of HRTC during 2002-2003 was Rs. 201.53 crore. By allowing free/concessional facilities, the corporation is suffering financial loss to the extent of Rs.40.57 crore yearly (as per HRTC reports). In addition to this, the corporation is also operating uneconomical routes in public interest. HRTC provides free and concessional travel facilities as under:

Free Travelling Facility

The Corporation provides free travelling facility to the following categories:

- Handicapped (35,844 persons)
- Press correspondents/MLAs/MPs/Ex-MLAs/Ex-MPs and social workers
- War widows and gallantry award winners - keeping in view the services rendered by the defence personnel for the nation, free travel facility to these two categories is only a mark of honour.
- Padam Shree awardees.
- Freedom fighters.

Concessional Facilities

The Corporation provides concessional travelling facility to the following categories:

TABLE 17.19

Losses Sustained on Account of Providing Cencessional/Free Travelling Facilities by HRTC

(Rs in lakh)

Sr. No.	*Category*	*1995-96*		*1996-97*		*1997-98*		*1998-99*		*1999-00*	
		Nos.	*Amount*	*Nos.*	*Amount*	*Nos.*	*Amount*	*Nos.*	*Amount*	*Nos.*	*Amount*
1	Students	137088	1275.0	150000	1400.0	157500	1700.00	184000	2040.00	228800	2448.0
2	Employees	28179	152.00	31300	170.00	32850	205.00	39420	305.00	47304	366.00
3	Freedom Fighters	2520	18.00	2800	20.00	2940	24.00	3528	29.00	4233	34.00
4	War Widows	680	03.00	750	04.00	790	05.00	948	06.00	1137	07.00
5	Physical Handicapped	8620	24.00	9500	26.00	10000	31.00	12000	37.00	14400	44.00
6	Press Correspondents	135	02.00	150	03.00	160	04.00	192	05.00	230	06.00
7	Police, MP, MLAs & Others	14147	502.00	15700	550.00	17470	615.00	20964	706.00	14788	807.00
	TOTAL	191369	1976.0	210200	2173.0	221710	2584.00	261052	3128.00	310892	3712.0

Source: Himachal Road Transport Corporation, *Annual Accounts*

- Students of Government Schools/Colleges pay 10 single fares a month, and those of Public Schools, who are provided earmarked buses, pay 30 single fares a month.
- Employees: state government employees from place of residence to offices against payment of 30 single fare a month.
- Police officials/jail wardens: Presently, police personnel upto the rank of Inspector and jail wardens travel free within and outside the state, on payment of Rs. 50 a month, deducted from the salary and deposited in the government treasury.

An independent study of the level of subsidies prevalent in HRTC under the subject of Social Accounting found that the level of subsidy enjoyed by target groups under orders of the government amounted to Rs. 37.12 crore in 1999-2000. The claim by HRTC of the current level at Rs. 40 crore therefore seems reasonable.

The losses for 2002-2003 are Rs. 23.36 crore, and projected to be Rs 28.03 crore in 2003-2004 by HRTC.

The data from Table 17.19 read with the profit and loss statement (Table 17.20) make it clear that if HRTC was not forced to provide subsidised travel, there was a possibility of it breaking even.

It was surprising to note that while Himachal Pradesh deducts Rs. 50 from the salary of each police and jail staff for free travel by HRTC, this is not given to HRTC, but deposited in the government treasury!

TABLE 17.20

Profit and loss position of HRTC (1979-80 to 1999-2000)

(Rs. in Million)

Year	*Total Receipts*	*Total Expenditure*	*Profit/Loss*
1979-80	143.14	138.61	+4.53
1983-84	254.24	296.13	-41.89
1987-88	493.72	498.69	-4.97
1991-92	708.66	924.42	-215.76
1995-96	1239.36	1367.82	-128.46
1999-00	1741.12	2226.51	-485.39
2000-01	2038.29	2385.90	-347.61
2001-02	2217.29	2505.83	-288.54
2002-03	2370.67	2669.31	-298.63

Recommendations for HRTC

It is always easy to tell the government that "it has no business in business", but HRTC is not poorly run. It is in a financial fix because of government policies, and if Himachal Pradesh reorients HRTC on business lines, it can do well. The pattern of ownership is a decision that the government can take as it deems fit, but HRTC can be turned around with the following measures:

- Start an aggressive technical training programme, particularly for drivers and workshop staff. This will improve safety and bring down maintenance and operations costs.
- Conduct radical BPR to reassess the staff requirement in the maintenance and

administrative staff. In view of improvements in technology and induction of information technology, current levels of one support staff for every operations staff in unacceptable. Clerical staff can be re-deployed against vacancies in other government departments.

- Safety, better amenities, and punctuality are needed to lift occupancy ratios. CAG has noted in 2001 that "the actual occupancy ratio was 67 per cent, 57 per cent and 59 per cent against the breakeven occupancy ratio of 73 per cent, 76 per cent and 69 per cent during the period 1998-99, 1999-2000 and 2000-01 respectively." Occupancy decreased because of large-scale privatisation, which affected the traffic potential of the corporation on profit earning routes, while the corporation could not withdraw buses from uneconomical routes. There is a need to rationalise the route permits in accordance with traffic needs.
- HRTC has started a number of initiatives for better service and cost reduction. These include computerised and networked advance ticketing, group discount, return ticket incentives, smart cards, etc. These should be vigorously pursued to enhance efficiency.
- Either remove subsidies, or compensate HRTC for the same, in accordance with the Transport Corporation Act.
- The tariff policy of HRTC is not clear, and the fare has not undergone any revision since 1999. The State government should take steps to lay down a clear tariff policy, which would apply to both HRTC and private operators.

Response from HP to these Recommendations

Road Safety Factor

Data has been quoted in support to emphasise that "accident rate" has dropped. However, the data is as under:

Accident Rate Per Lakh Kms

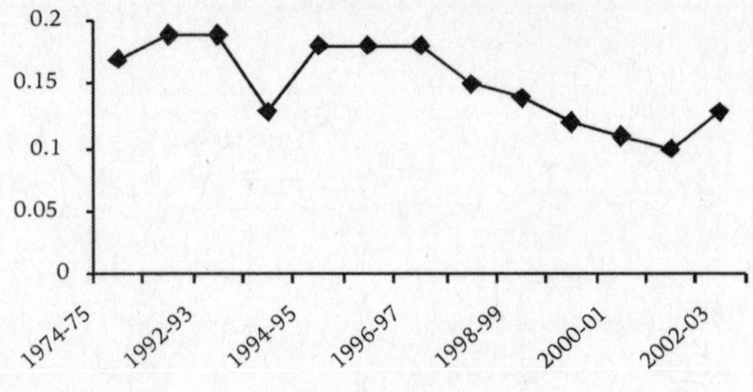

Source: HRTC

The data shows that the rate has decreased slowly since 1997-98, but risen sharply in 2002-2003, and hovered at an average of about 0.15. This needs as serious analysis.

However, HRTC should adopt the additional norm of "fatality per lakh kilometers" also, to arrive at the real passenger impact of safety improvement. Further, HRTC should introduce a mandatory breathalyzer test at duty sign-on, by both driver and conductor, with surprise checks on run.

Staff Ratio

As against the actual per bus staff of 5.40 in 90s, the norm has been fixed at 5.80. HRTC has said the ratio of support staff per bus is 0.75, but as per the data sent by them, it is still 1 per bus (administrative 0.65 + Store 0.16 + Others 0.19). Meaningful steps need to be taken to bring down the staff cost.

Railways

In all its plan papers, Himachal Pradesh has given up on railway as a transport medium. It mentions the existing railway lines in passing, and then moves on to its familiar fixation with Road-HRTC.

The following traffic surveys were done in Himachal Pradesh in the last five years by the Railways:

Surveys Done During Last Five Years in Himachal Pradesh

Sr. No	*Name of Survey*	*Month/year of Report Submission*	*Length in Km*	*Project Cost (in Rs crore)*	*Rate of Return*
1	Kalka-Kamli new line	11/1997	5.35	25	-26.00
2	Hoshiarpur-Una	3/2000	40.5044.50	143156	-24.55-23.14
3	Pathankot-Jogindernagar – Gauge Conversion & BG line from Jogindernagar to Bhanupalli	3/2001	352.13	3566	-27.48
4	Una-Jaijon-Doaba	3/2002	40.14	269	-46.84

EXISTING RAIL NETWORK OF
HIMACHAL PRADESH

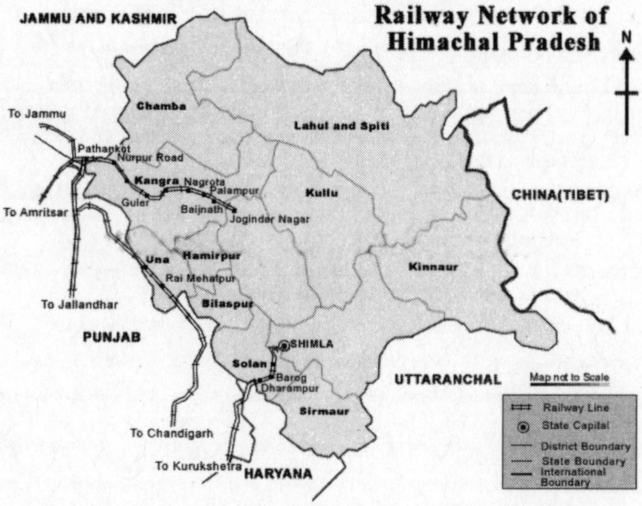

Status of New Line Works

- After commissioning of Nangaldam–Una section, work on the Nangal Dam-Talwara new line was frozen by the Railway Board. Work was defrozen in 1997-98 and is in progress in one block section, i.e., for Una-Himachal to Churaru Takarala (17 km), with a targeted date of completion of December 2003. The original estimate of cost was Rs 210 crore, but the expenditure upto Churaru Takarala is likely to be Rs 68 crore, and the estimates will need revision.
- Kalka-Parwanoo new line (4 km). Work was sanctioned in 1999 at a cost of Rs 37 crore. There has been no progress in this project, because of the prohibitive cost of land. Himachal Pradesh government has now suggested that the line be taken to Tipra village, where the land cost is likely to be less. Fresh survey work has been taken up.

Passenger Railway

Himachal Pradesh is home to two of India's five heritage hill railway networks, the Kalka-Shimla line (96 km) and the Pathankot-Jogindernagar line (113 km).

Kalka-Shimla completed its century in November 2003. The Railways claim that while they spend Rs. 14 crore in maintaining the section, earnings are only Rs.7 crore, and that they run the line primarily as a tourist attraction, and as a heritage value.

Pathankot–Jogindernagar also passes through some of the most breathtaking rail journey views in the world, and its vast tourist potential remains under-utilised.

Himachal Pradesh government should approach Northern Railways to enter into joint tourist promotion packages, especially for attracting foreign tourists for steam tourism. The heritage tourist is willing to pay, provided the package is right. Steam engines are available both for the narrow and the metre guage sections, and time-tabled services should be announced for the same.

Goods Movement

This is a critical area in which Railways can help. Essentially there are two streams of traffic to cater to:

- High value or special-purpose container traffic: In the container segment will fall high value industrial produce, and agro-processing industry produce.
- Medium or low-value bulk traffic: This constitutes raw materials for Himachal Pradesh's cement plants, and movement of finished produce. It will also cater to increased fertilizer requirements for horticulture. It can be a major facilitator in the movement of bulk cement and steel, to as far away as economically possible, for Himachal Pradesh's medium and large hydro projects under construction, and under planning.
- Special Purpose Vehicles (SPVs) should be thought of, with investments from Railways, HP Govt, and the private sector, to develop a railway network that is capable of moving millions of tonnes of bulk raw materials required for hydro projects. When this work is over, the lines will be put to alternate passenger usage, but the business model should break-even with the targetted goods movement only, with extended passenger use as earning additional revenues for the SPV.

Containerisation

HP needs to encourage containerisation of the state. In consultation with Container Corporation of India, nodal points for establishing Container Freight Stations should be set up. To encourage direct shipping of agro-products to international markets, possibility of setting up an ICD should be explored.

Air Transport, Ropeways, Cable Cars

With Himachal Pradesh's vision of a high growth curve, it must be accepted that alternative means of transport must be developed, so that they can take the pressure off the roads. Otherwise, tourists will simply not be able to reach, and goods delivery schedules will go haywire.

The possibility of using ropeways, with abundant power supplies predicted in the future, must be evaluated as a serious option for point-to-point movement of horticulture produce like apples.

Onward air linkages to the existing airports at Jubbar Hatti, Bhuntar, and Kangra by helicopters must also be evaluated. They cannot be a serious option for the average tourist, but the helicopters at Vaishno Devi and Kedarnath are booked in advance, and giving good returns. Circuits where paying tourists are available can be planned for this. Cable cars are also a great attraction, and HP needs to weave all these modes into a plan to encourage private participation in these sectors.

References

Central Electricity Authority, *15th, 16th Electric Power Survey of India*, Ministry of Power, New Delhi

———. *"Perspective of National Power Plan Development up to 2006-07"* New Delhi, 1991.

Chandrasekharam, D, *"Geothermal Power Asia 2000"* Paper presented at IBC, Conference Manila, Philippines, 2000.

Government of Himachal Pradesh, *Annual Plans 1998-2002*, Shimla.

Government of Himachal Pradesh, *Economic Survey, 1998-2003*, Shimla.

Government of Himachal Pradesh, *Eighth and Ninth Five Year Plans*, Shimla.

Harshe Rajen, *Stakeholder Participation in Andhra Pradesh Reform Process*, 2001

ICRA Limited, *Report on Himachal Pradesh to the Power Finance Corporation*, January 2003.

Kachroo, P.N. and Ashish Sinha. *Environmental Concerns in Highway Development with Special Reference to Road Projects in Hill Areas*. 62nd Session, Indian Roads Congress, Kochi.

Kohler, Thomas, Hans Hurni, Urs Wiesmann, and Andreas Kläy, *Mountain Infrastructure: Access, Communication, and Energy*, Bishkek Global Mountain Summit (Background Paper).

Mahajan S.K., *Social Accounting and Performance of Road Passenger Transport: A Case Study, Annual Conference of IASIA*, Athens (Greece) July 2001.

Ministry of Railways, *Union Railway Budget Papers, 1997-2003*, New Delhi.

Morris Sebastian (ed) : *India Infrastructure Report* 2003, 3i Network,

Northern Railway, Annual Progress Reports, Construction Office, 2001, 2002, 2003. New Delhi.

Planning Commission, *Five Year Plan 2002-2007*, Vols. 1, 2, & 3, New Delhi

Srivastava, R.N. *et al. "Planning Power Development in India - Emphasis on Hydro Projects"*. Paper presented at World Energy Council, 17th Congress, Houston, USA - 13-18 September 1998.

World Bank, *Andhra Pradesh Sector Restructuring Project*, Project Appraisal Document.

www.himachal.nic.in (official website of HP government).

www.hpseb.com (website of HP State Electricity Board).

www.hrtc.nic.in (website of Himachal Road Transport Corporation).

www.morth.nic.in (website of Ministry of Road Transport & Highways)

Chapter 18

Information Technology

Introduction

Information technology (IT), a knowledge-based industry, with the potential to become an engine of accelerated economic growth, productivity improvement, provide efficient means of governance, holds large employment potential, provides new opportunities to tackle problems related to rural poverty, health, illiteracy and environmental degradation. The Government of India has been emphasising from time to time the role of information technology in the development process.

During the Eighth Plan period, i.e., 1992-97, there was hardly any activity in the IT sector in Himachal Pradesh. Recognising the role of IT in socio-economic development, Himachal Pradesh, engaged NASSCOM (National Association of Software and Service Companies), a premier national body, to suggest a plan for developing the IT industry in the state.

NASSCOM submitted its report, *Himachal Pradesh: Millennium IT Vision 2010,* exhorting the state to create a state-of-the-art world class IT infrastructure, develop high quality human resource and redefined role for the government in the new digital setup. Beside the IT Vision 2010 for Himachal Pradesh, the NASSCOM report has recommended an IT action plan for human resource development, developing IT infrastructure and implementing e-governance.

According to the NASSCOM, the IT industry in Himachal Pradesh can grow at a highly accelerated pace to achieve an annual turnover of Rs. 20,000 crore (US$ 4.7 billion) by the year 2009-10, which is four to five per cent of the projected turnover of US$ 100 billion for the same year by the Indian IT software and service industry, subject to the implementation of the recommendations of the NASSCOM by the state.

Information Technology Policy – 2001

The state announced *Information Technology Policy – 2001,* spelling out Himachal Pradesh as an attractive IT destination after different industry associations, academia and government departments were consulted and deliberated upon for their views on the IT policy. Most of the recommendations made by NASSCOM were accepted. The state has embarked upon a plan for using IT in the overall development process by involving masses at all levels.

Himachal Pradesh has a number of positive indicators for the growth and development of IT industry. It has good climatic conditions with dust free and cool environment, good telecom infrastructure, adequate power supply, road network, hospitality industry and relatively low cost of living. However, the state has some specific constraints, which needs immediate attention for the growth of IT industry. These are:

- Development of high-grade human resource suitable for IT industry
- Availability of high-tech infrastructure suitable for IT industry
- Insufficient allocation of funds to IT
- Inadequate transport facilities including international airports

In the last three years, the state government has taken some positive steps and declared IT savvy policies but it has not resulted in any perceptible growth in IT software and service industry in the state. As compared to some of the other leading states in India, such as Karnataka, Andhra Pradesh, Maharashtra, Tamil Nadu, Delhi and Haryana, the growth of IT software and service industry in the state has been negligible.

IT Human Resource Development

Human resource development is the single most important factor in the IT industry and has played a key role in developing India as a software hub. Himachal Pradesh has to undertake effective measures to produce quality IT human resource.

The IT industry can be divided into three categories: 'A' - Software Product and Technology Services; 'B' - IT Services; and 'C' - IT Enabled Services (ITES). For categories 'A' and 'B', the qualifications required are MS/M.Tech/B.Tech in Computer Science, MCA or B.Tech from the non-computer stream with training of one to two years in specialised IT technologies. For category 'C', the qualifications required are BA/B.Sc/ B.Com/MA/M.Sc/Diploma/ITIs with a specialised six months training in ITES.

Categories 'A' and 'B': NASSCOM has projected a turnover of Rs. 12,500 crore by 2009-10 for these two categories. Based on the Ministry of Information Technology (MIT) Report, for achieving this turnover, it could be estimated that 38,000 IT engineers would be required to achieve this target.

Out of 660 degree holders, (see the table below) at the most, only one-third would be available for the IT industry. These could be direct IT graduates and those from other engineering fields opting for the IT industry after getting necessary IT specialised training.

Level of the Programme	*Institution*		*Intake*		*No. of Courses*
	Govt.	*Self Financing*	*Govt.*	*Self Financing*	
Degree	1	2	240	420	7
Diploma	7	—	820	—	11
Certificate Course	54	5	2839	276	36

Source: Technical Education Quality Improvement Programme of GoI, Himachal Pradesh State Report for Appraisal Mission, June 2002, Department of Technical Education, H.P.

Presently, the state has one Regional Engineering College at Hamirpur and two private engineering colleges at Kala Amb and Baddi. The Jaypee Institute of Information Technology has come up in the private sector in Solan District. Taking into consideration the existing capacity, assuming a growth of 20 per cent new seats in the existing engineering colleges every year, new graduates from the Jaypee Institute of Information Technology, and the possibility of setting up at least one new engineering institute in the state every year, the total number of IT engineers graduating in Himachal Pradesh would be about 10,000 by 2009-10 against the requirement of 38,000 as per the NASSCOM projections. The growth in this segment of the IT industry is slow as it has a longer gestation period.

For achieving a target of 10,000 IT engineers in categories 'A' and B' by 2009-10, the state has to play a very proactive role in promoting and brand building the IT industry in the state. Such companies as Infosys, Wipro, HCL, TCS and multinationals must be encouraged to set up their development centres in the state. The training of faculty should be ensured to meet the required standards, through their interaction and exchange with institutes of higher learning in India and abroad.

As also recommended by NASSCOM in their Vision 2010 report, the state must set up an IIIT for creating a high quality education hub. This will have far reaching multifarious effects on the state's higher education system. A beginning has been made in the private sector by setting up the Jaypee Institute of Information Technology.

Category 'C': ITES

IT Enabled services, such as Medical Transcription, Call Centres, Data Processing, Back-Office operations, GIS, Revenue Accounting are a niche area. It has emerged as a key engine of growth for the Indian IT industry and the technology-led services industry. Exports of ITES have increased to Rs. 11,300 crore in 2002-03 from Rs. 7,300 crore in the previous year, registering a growth of 59 per cent and is expected to grow 54 per cent during 2003-04. ITES exports from India have been projected to reach Rs, 72,900 crore by 2008.

The employment potential in ITES is large and the gestation period is less as compared to the other categories of the IT industry. The success of ITES will mainly depend on the quality of manpower and infrastructure. Knowledge-based skill-oriented training is the key to the quality of manpower. ITES, to succeed, requires top-class infrastructure with adequate bandwidth, fault-free and continuous power with two layers of redundancy to avoid any breakdown. Segment-wise skill sets required for different services under the ITES industry is as follows:

ITES: Skill Sets Required for Different Services

Segment	*Skill Set Required*
Customer services	Language, accent
Data processing	Computer literate
Human resource	HR skills, legal
Remote education	Domain knowledge
Engineering design	Domain knowledge
Translation & localisation	Language
Medical transcription	Computer literate, medical knowledge
Animation	Creative, computer literate
Finance	International/country-specific accounting
Web hosting	Computer literate
Market research	Knowledge of MR, statistics
Network consulting	Computers, LAN

Source: Mahindras Reality and Infrastructure Developers Ltd. Feasibility Report by Cushman & Wakefield, March 2000.

The NASSCOM report has projected a turnover of Rs. 7500 crore by 2009-10 for this category in Himachal Pradesh. This would require 92,000 ITES trained manpower. Presently, Himachal Pradesh enrols about 30,000 graduate students annually. Even if one-third of them are given special ITES-related training in their final year, the maximum number of students available would be 5000 taking into consideration the average pass ratio of 50 per cent. Further assuming an annual increase of 20 per cent, the total number available would be 36,000 by 2009-10.

For achieving this target, the development strategy would be to train the trainers; 500 teachers from the existing Arts/Science graduate colleges have to be trained by 25 ITES-expert trainers for a period of six months. These 500 teachers, after successful training would be the resource persons for training the graduates starting from 2004-05 onwards. Private institutions should also be encouraged to prepare the students for the ITES industry.

The state government has taken an initiative in this direction by introducing IT and computer education form classes IX to XII in 536 senior secondary schools in the state through a tie-up with ECIL, Hyderabad; MIAECT, Mumbai; and DOEACC, Shimla.

However, the state must ensure the quality of manpower in close association with the needs of the industry. It is strongly recommended that a **State Council of IT Education,** an autonomous body of experts, must be set up for looking after the quality and standardisation in both government and private sector institutes. This body should have all the necessary legal powers to check the unwanted mushrooming of private education institutions.

The state needs to take very effective measures to meet the target of 46000 IT manpower for the IT industry (for all categories) by 2009-10. The projected targets for the IT industry in the state need to be reduced from the NASSCOM projection of Rs. 20,000 crore to Rs. 7000 crore, which may be achievable if the state is decisively proactive.

E-Governance

E-governance is a must for efficient and effective government, facilitates more accessible government services, allow greater public access to information and make government more accountable to citizens. It is customer-driven and service oriented tool. It involves activities at three levels i) Office automation and Computerised Transactions Processing/Information Systems in various departments and Training, ii) Web Sites/Applications of the State Government/Departments/ Corporations/Boards on Internet and iii) Citizen-Government Interface. For implementing e-governance the major components of core infrastructure are statewide intranets, state data centres and service delivery infrastructure at state, district, block and village level.

E-governance is a process that requires sustained political will, resources and interaction among the government, private and public sectors. The suggested road-map and work plan for the implementation of e-governance in the state is as follows:

Road-Map

i) Clear vision

ii) State specific needs and priorities

iii) Political and administrative will

iv) Identification of nodal agency

v) Promoting governmental and non-governmental stakeholders

vi) Optimal selection of priority projects

vii) Planning, implementation and monitoring

viii) Ensuring long term self-sustainability

Work-Plan

i) Content development

- Development of applications

- Open standards
- Local language interface
- User guides
- e-learning materials

ii) Competency building

- Human resource and training programmes at all levels

iii) Connectivity

- Local networks and Internet connections

iv) Cyber laws

- Legal framework

v) Citizen interfaces

- Appropriate delivery channels

vi) Capital

- Identification of revenue streams like user charges, subscription or
- budgets

In Himachal Pradesh, the National Informatics Centre (NIC) has played a key role in implementing computerisation and e-governance projects. The satellite-based computer communication network (NICNET) of NIC connects all districts and the state headquarters with each other and with all such locations in the country. It facilitates services such as Internet, interactive communication, data transfers, e-mail and other value-added network services available on the NICNET to the state. The whole network has been provided with KU-band VSAT for higher speed connectivity to NICNET and Internet and facilitates high-speed data communication.

The use of IT or PC penetration and availability of I-net nodes is low in Himachal Pradesh. Effective implementation of e-governance will take IT to the common man, particularly the poor and those located in remote areas, spread IT culture and improve PC penetration.

The state government is also actively implementing HP State Wide Area Network (HPSWAN) connecting districts with the state headquarter. It should be extended to the block level and subsequently at the village level so that the benefit of IT percolates to the masses at large.

The state has also launched the official website of the Himachal Pradesh Government providing detailed information relating to various aspects of the state and the various Departments/Corporation/Boards of the state. However, it must be ensured that the websites are regularly maintained and updated with the latest data and information.

The state government has shown keen interest in implementing web-enabled interface of the government in providing clean, efficient, responsive and transparent administration. The **Lokmitra Project** has been a success. The project has been implemented on a pilot basis in Hamirpur district with district-wide Intranet having 25 Citizen Information booths located in the rural areas of the district with the active involvement of NIC, HP State unit with a loan of Rs. 40 lakh from NABARD. The population of 175 *panchayats* out of 225 has benefited from these 25 centres, which have also given employment to 25 educated unemployed youth in running these centres. The project has resulted in various direct/indirect social as well as economic benefits/deliveries to the rural masses like rural services such as land records, acquisition of land and registration of deeds, social services such as family pension, old age pension, registration of licences, ration cards, birth and death certificates etc.

It is essential that the Lokmitra project is expanded to all the other districts, thereby increasing employment generation and also facilitating the growth of ISPs throughout the state. To implement this project in other districts, the state is finding it difficult to fund the project from its own sources. Therefore, a financial support/grant-in-aid from Government of India is essential. A one-time grant-in-aid of a minimum of Rs. 50 lakh per district will go a long way in implementing this project in other districts. The state has to ensure project's long-term viability and sustainability. Selective private sector financial participation can go a long way for much needed funding.

According to the recommendations of the Working Group on IT for Masses, set up by the Government of India, five per cent of the state's total budget should be allocated for IT induction. Himachal Pradesh has already set up Department of Information Technology (DoIT). It is proposed that it should be further strengthened in terms of expertise and funds. It is recommended that at least one per cent of the budget in the first year, progressively increasing it to three per cent in the terminal year of the plan period, should be utilised for promoting and implementing e-governance.

It is strongly recommended that e-governance of the state should be implemented in a holistic and integrated manner through a monitoring cell, with defined rules and procedures based on principles of equity, responsibility, transparency and accountability. It should be able to monitor the performance and the status of all the projects, departments and ministries against the set targets. In case of non-performance, the monitoring cell will receive an alert signal and an explanation of the cause of the failure.

IT For Masses

IT for Rural Development

The special IT Task Force, constituted by the Government of India, has recommended the use of state-of-the-art information technology for the development of agriculture and rural development, on the lines of the successful Warana project in the Kolhapur and Sangli districts of Maharashtra. The project aims to utilise IT to increase the efficiency/productivity of the existing co-operative enterprise, by setting up a computer communication network and create a data-base of villages on different socio-economic aspects such as health, education, water supply, sanitation and population. It also provides information on agricultural-related schemes, employment generation schemes, and government procedures for getting ration cards, birth and death certificates etc., to the villagers.

For accelerated socio-economic development in Himachal Pradesh, where the rural population constitutes 90.20 per cent of the state's population, it is recommended that the concept of Community Information Dissemination Centres (CIDCs) be implemented at block/*panchayat* level. This will necessitate the setting up a computer centre at every panchyat, which is to be linked with the server located at the block level. This whole network will be connected to the state headquarters. This will facilitate both government-public interface and effective dissemination of information related to the 29 subjects transferred to the *Panchayats* under the 73rd Amendment to the Constitution. CIDCs will also function as IT kiosks and will provide direct linkages between the masses and the government. CIDCs will further organise training of *panches* and *sarpanches* in the use of IT and its benefits for their day-to-day requirements. This project is essentially on the lines of "Samadhan Kendras' project implemented by the Rural Electronics Division of Department of Information Technology, Government of India in North-Eastern states. For this whole project, a detailed financial and technical report needs to be prepared with the basic aim of its long-term self-sustainability.

CIDCs will also help in improving productivity and performance of agriculture. Support and services of various stakeholders and extension agencies, such as Himachal Agriculture University, Palampur, State Agriculture Department, Mandi Board and other agriculture-related agencies/industries should also be taken up for updating the latest information on products and services, new technologies and practices.

IT can be used in all aspects of agriculture. It can play a major role in crop management, enhancing productivity and crop yields through information on farm practices, seeds, other inputs of production, weather information, better pre- and post-harvest management, water utilisation and management, pest and disease control, etc. IT applications can be effectively used, particularly in Himachal, for management and monitoring of environment resources, pollution warning systems, environmental emergency management systems for floods, forest fires and other natural disasters. IT can also be suitably employed in small and tiny industries for online and real-time information to help small and marginal artisans in their sales and marketing efforts. This will not only help them earn better and boost their morale, but preserve these rare skills, which otherwise are on the verge of extinction.

IT Education for Masses in Rural Areas

The Government of India has proposed the setting up of a network called *Vidya Vahini* to carry the benefit of IT to students. Under this programme, schools and higher learning institutes are proposed to be connected with an integrated voice, data and video network. The Government of India has proposed to introduce this programme in two phases. In the first phase, i.e., in the first two years of the plan, 60,000 schools are proposed to be connected to the network. Himachal should get 5,000 schools networked in the first phase and 5,000 more in the second phase. It is also recommended that all these schools should be only in rural areas. Timely and speedy implementation of the project by the state will go a long way in furthering the use of IT for the masses.

IT Infrastructure

Sound IT infrastructure is the key to the growth of the IT software and services sector. Himachal Pradesh already has one of the finest telecom infrastructures in the country with all digital interconnected optical fiber cable laid (OFC) telephone exchanges. All the districts have 2 Mbps connectivity and blocks headquarters at least 33 kbps. The strong telecommunication facilities are a shot in the arm for developing the IT software and service industry, including distance learning and the implementation of the IT policies for the masses.

The state government has established a Software Technology Park and an Earth Station at Shimla, which are proposed to be co-located later with hi-Tech City. An international gateway has also been commissioned at Shimla for providing reliable speed data communication. All such facilities are likely to facilitate IT related activities in and around Shimla, making it the IT hub for the state. The State is also developing an IT hub in the Solan district on Shimla-Kalka highway, about 25 km from Shimla. It has earmarked 174 acre of land with all the necessary infrastructural facilities for attracting IT related investment. The much-needed upgradation of three existing airports in the state at Shimla, Kullu and Kangra should be taken up at a fast pace.

However, to attract reputed Indian software companies and MNCs to the state, it is essential to market and promote the state in terms of its existing and proposed infrastructure.

Development Strategy and Recommendations

Existing IT Models in Different States

Bangalore Model

Karnataka, in spite of low incentives, continues to be one of the most favoured places for software companies. Bangalore has grown on the strength of private sector rather than market-friendly state government policies. The government in its role of an infrastructure provider failed, though, government-promoted knowledge institutions have acted as catalysts in the explosive growth of IT in Karnataka. For sustaining a knowledge cluster, a superior social and business infrastructure is a pre-requisite in the long run. Bangalore has grown steadily with an initial thrust from Indian companies like Wipro, HCL, Infosys, followed by MNCs setting up their development centres

Andhra Pradesh (AP) Model

It offers an interesting model, which is quite different from Karnataka. Here the government initiative has been the engine of growth, to which the private sector responded very positively. Historically, Hyderabad has never been a knowledge hub, but because of the proactive approach adopted by the state it has been able to attract world IT players like Microsoft, Oracle, IBM and GE. The government has moved towards creating knowledge-based human resource required for the IT industry, by setting up apex institutes like IIIT and Mckinsey Institute of Management in Hyderabad, to produce necessary human capital. Further, to build an IT culture, the state has taken many dynamic measures such as making computer education compulsory at primary and secondary levels of education. The growth of the IT industry in Andhra Pradesh proves that state-government initiative can go a long way in building an IT base in a state.

Maharashtra Model

Maharashtra in spite of being an early starter, has lost it importance as an IT destination, because of the high cost of living and high operational cost for running any unit, although SEEPZ is one of the largest and oldest software parks in Mumbai and has been a trend-setter in the country. It still employs more than 8000 software professionals and has software exports of more than Rs. 10,000 crore every year.

Delhi/Noida/Gurgaon Model

Uttar Pradesh (Noida), Haryana (Gurgaon) and Delhi have developed in last couple of years into a pocket of IT excellence. The Golden Triangle of Noida, Gurgaon and Delhi have been very successful in attracting many IT companies especially ITES companies. This is due to its proximity to Delhi and its well-developed infrastructure. The area offers comparatively lower infrastructure cost and has been able to attract and retain skilled manpower.

Model for Himachal Pradesh

Taking into consideration the various factors involved, it is suggested that HP may follow the extremely dynamic model of Andhra Pradesh to spur the IT sector in the state with necessary local-base variations. The state has to lay more emphasis on developing IT for the masses and high quality human resource needed for IT.

The State Government accepted the recommendations of NASSCOM and announced the Information Technology Policy 2001, wherein most of the recommendations suggested by NASSCOM were accepted. The State has also taken some initiatives in IT infrastructure, IT Human Resource Development and e-governance. The National Informatics Centre (NIC), HP Unit has played a pivotal role in implementing some of the e-governance projects in the State. However, if we compare the projections made by NASSCOM and the achievements made by the state so far, there is a huge gap, which could be attributed to the widening resource gap in terms of financial allocations made by the state government and the availability of human resource.

The projections for the IT industry In Himachal Pradesh by 2009-10 needs to be reduced to one-third of what has been recommended by NASSCOM. Even to achieve the revised projections, the state must focus on high-grade human resource development and high quality infrastructure. The state must make concerted efforts towards the following:

- The government machinery of the state government has to become proactive and aggressively market the state in terms of the infrastructure offered and the conducive atmosphere for setting up IT industry in the state. The state needs to have a conscious policy to welcome private initiatives.
- The State's development strategy should be to develop quality human resource for the IT industry. Draw a charter for implementing the training programme, regular interaction and exchange with institutes of higher learning in India and abroad to upgrade the professional level of existing faculty to meet the international standards. Set up a statutory body like the State Council of IT Education to monitor the quality and standardisation aspects in both government and private institutions.
- Set up an Indian Institute of Information Technology (IIIT) in the state to meet its demand for high-grade human resource. A proactive policy with attractive incentives should be formulated so that private sector particularly, reputed IT companies come forward to setup institutes of excellence in the state.
- The State has to lay more emphasis on socio-economic development in rural areas and for this the concept of Community Information Dissemination Centres (CIDCs) should be implemented by Rural Development department after preparing a detailed financial and technical project report, keeping in view their long-term self-sustainability. HPSWAN infrastructure project, conceived with the primary objective of ensuring linkages with the rural areas, once completed, will pave the way for implementing CIDCs.
- The State must pursue Vidya Vahini Programme recommended by the Government of India for setting up an education network. The state must plan for 5000 schools in the first phase and the same number in the next phase. These schools should only be from rural areas.
- The successful implementation of Lokmitra project in Hamirpur district should be replicated in other districts of the state. E-governance is to be implemented in a holistic and integrated manner through a monitoring cell, with defined rules and procedures, based on principles of equity, responsibility, transparency and accountability.

References

Information Technology Policy-2001, Department of Information Technology, HP.

IT Task Force, Ministry of Information Technology, Government of India.

Mahindras Reality and Infrastructure Developers Ltd. *Feasibility Report* by Cushman & Wakefield, March 2000.

Ministry of Information Technology (MIT), *Report for Tenth Plan (2002-07)*.

NASSCOM Report on *Himachal Pradesh: Millennium IT Vision 2010.*

Punjab Development Report, Planning Commission, Government of India

Technical Education Quality Improvement Programme of GoI, Himachal Pradesh State Report for Appraisal Mission, June 2002, Department of Technical Education, HP.

Chapter 19

Tourism

British Tourist Authority defines tourism as "a stay of one or more nights away from home for holidays, visits to friends or relatives, business conferences or any other purpose, except such things as boarding, education, or semi-permanent employment."

People travel for many reasons nowadays. These include

- Recreational travel
- Adventure and sports tourism
- Cultural tourism
- Health tourism
- Conference and conventions travel

Tourism has been one of the world's fastest growing industries, and there are large societies entirely dependent upon the visitor for their sustenance. Spain with a population of about 10 million, has 40 million tourists per year, and Singapore with a population of 1.2 million has about 6 million tourists.

However, successful countries exhibit a great capacity to continuously change their product, and not get stuck in a mould. It is an eye opener that the highly acclaimed Singapore Tourism Board is re-packaging the destination for the 21st century tourist, and "re-formulating the tourism product". In a policy statement, it emphasises:

> "Evoke one's memories of great cities and invariably, places like Paris, New York, and London come to mind. Cities like these leave deep impressions because they have one thing in common - they are world-class in many ways. From food to fashion to culture, they appeal to visitors in their own unique ways. More than a tourist attraction, these cities possess that magical sense of place, an evocative mixture of factors that spell the difference between a must-stay and stopover.
>
> Singapore is a successful tourist destination in its own right. But it can and should be more - it should be able to reach out to visitors on an emotional level in the same way as these world-class cities, and be a place where memorable experiences are created and cherished."

HP tourism has to address this urgent need of re-formulating its own product and attendant strategy, to emerge as a serious player in the industry.

According to the Ninth Five Year Plan of Himachal Pradesh, the total number of tourists in the state in 2002 were 60 lakh. The actual achievement is in the region of 50 lakh, and HP will need a sustained initiative to improve.

National Tourism Policy 2002 and Tenth Plan

India's share in the tourism industry is below par.

Tourist Arrivals Worldwide and India's Share (1992-2001)

Year	*World Arrivals*	*South Asia*	*India's Arrivals*	*% Share of India in World Arrivals*
1992	500.9	3.6	1.8	0.37
1993	515.7	3.5	1.7	0.34
1994	550.3	3.9	1.8	0.34
1995	550.3	4.2	2.1	0.39
1996	597.4	4.4	2.2	0.38
1997	618.2	4.8	2.3	0.38
1998	626.5	5.2	2.3	0.38
1999	650.4	5.8	2.4	0.38
2000	696.7	6.1	2.6	0.38
2001	692.7	5.7	2.5	0.37

The Tenth Plan documents reveal a distinct shift in the government's approach to tourism. While tourism is indeed a promoter of national integration (domestic tourism), it is also a facilitator of international understanding (international tourism). At the same time, it is seen as having a large share of tertiary sector growth, with a great potential for development, especially for hill states, which are endowed with natural beauty.

The *National Tourism Policy 2002* document exhibits this changed approach. It recognises that tourism emerged as the largest global industry of the 20th century and is projected to grow even faster in the 21st century, and that India has immense possibilities of growth in the tourism sector with vast cultural and religious heritage, varied natural attractions, but a comparatively small role in the world tourism scene. It lays down its mission to promote sustainable tourism as a means of economic growth and social integration and to promote the image of India abroad as a country with a glorious past, a vibrant present and a bright future. This is based around six concepts of:

1. Welcome (swagat),
2. Information (suchana),
3. Facilitation (suvidha),
4. Safety (suraksha),
5. Cooperation (sahyog) and
6. Infrastructure Development (samrachana)

Public and Private Sector Partnership

A constructive and mutually beneficial partnership between the public and the private sectors through all feasible means is an absolute necessity for the sustained growth of tourism. It is, therefore, the policy of the government to encourage emergence of such a partnership. This will be achieved by creating a Tourism Development Authority consisting of senior officials of the government and tourism experts and professionals from the private sector.

Involvement of PRIs/ULBs

It will be the policy of government to encourage peoples' participation in tourism development, including the involvement of Panchayati Raj Institutions, local bodies, co-operatives, non-governmental organisations and enterprising local youth to create public awareness and to achieve a wider spread of tourist facilities. However, attention will be focused on or given for the integrated development of identified centres with well-directed public participation.

Linkage and Synergy in Policies

The government will aim to achieve necessary linkages and synergies in the policies and programmes of all concerned departments/agencies by establishing effective co-ordination mechanisms at Central, State and District levels. The focus of national policy, therefore, will also be to develop tourism as a common endeavour of all the agencies vitally concerned with it at the Central and State levels, public sector undertakings and the private sector.

Role of the Government in the New Policy

Tourism is a multi-sectoral activity and the industry is affected by many other sectors of the national economy. The state has, therefore, to ensure inter-governmental linkages and co-ordination. It also has to play a pivotal role in tourism management and promotion. The specific role of the government will be to:

1. Provide basic infrastructural facilities including local planning and zoning arrangements.
2. Plan tourism development as a part of the over-all area development strategy.
3. Create nucleus infrastructure in the initial stages of development to demonstrate the potential of the area.
4. Provide the required support facilities and incentives to both domestic and foreign investors to encourage private investment in the tourism sector.
5. Rationalise taxation and land policies in the tourism sector in all the States and Union Territories and in respect of land owned by government agencies like the Railways.
6. Introduce regulatory measures to ensure social, cultural and environmental sustainability, as well as safety and security of tourists.
7. Ensure that the type and scale of tourism development is compatible with the environment and socio-cultural milieu of the area.
8. Ensure that the local community is fully involved and the benefits of tourism accrue to them.
9. Facilitate availability of trained manpower, particularly from amongst the local population jointly with the industry.
10. Undertake research, prepare master plans, and facilitate formulation of marketing strategies.
11. Organise overseas promotion and marketing jointly with the industry.
12. Initiate specific measures to ensure safety and security of tourists and efficient facilitation services.

13. Facilitate the growth of a dynamic tourism sector.

Thus, the government is moving from an active investor to:

- Infrastructure provider and manager
- Planner for tourism
- Regulator for conservation and preservation
- General facilitator

As a consequence to this new role of the government, it is expected that the private sector will expand, providing new direction to the industry.

The private sector has to consider investment in tourism from a long-term perspective and create the required facilities including accommodation, time-share, restaurants, entertainment facilities, shopping complexes, etc., in areas identified for tourism development. Non-core activities at all airports, major stations and inter-state bus terminuses such as cleanliness and maintenance, luggage transportation, vehicle parking facilities, etc., should be opened up to private operators to increase efficiency and profitability. The specific role of the private sector will be to:

- Build and manage the required tourist facilities at all places of tourist interest.
- Assume collective responsibility for laying down industry standards, ethics and fair practices.
- Ensure preservation and protection of tourist attractions and give the lead in green practices.
- Sponsor maintenance of monuments, museums and parks and provision of public conveniences and facilities.
- Involve the local community in tourism projects and ensure that the benefits of tourism accrue to them in right measure.
- Undertake industry training and man-power development to achieve excellence in quality of services.
- Participate in the preparation of investment guidelines and marketing strategies and assist in database creation and research.
- Facilitate safety and security of tourists.
- Endeavour to promote tourism on a sustained and long-term perspective.
- Collaborate with Government in the promotion and marketing of destinations.

These are moves in the right direction, based upon international experience in this regard.

Data on Tourist Arrivals in HP

(in lakh)

Year	*Domestic Tourist*	*International Tourist*	*Total*
1997	38.30	0.63	38.93
1998	41.20	0.75	41.95
1999	43.52	0.91	44.43
2000	45.70	1.11	46.81

Source: HP Tourist Economic Survey 2002.

Published data for HP beyond this is not available, but *http://www.himsuchana.org* mentions that in 2002, tourist arrivals have been pegged at 1.44 lakhs for international tourists, and about 49 lakh domestic tourists, for a total of 50.44 lakh tourists.

Tourism Policy of Himachal Pradesh

The policy was laid down in 2000, and takes note of the fact that Rs 10 lakhs invested in tourism industry generates 47 jobs, whereas even a labour-intensive sector like agriculture provides 44 jobs only. There is the stark realisation that tourism contributes only two per cent to the state domestic product, in a state like HP, where the possibilities are endless.

The Mission Statement of HP's tourist policy is:

- To create prosperity for the people of Himachal Pradesh through travel and tourism;
- Tourism that is in harmony with the social and cultural values of the local communities and is environmentally sustainable;
- And to create direct, indirect and ancillary new employment opportunities for the people of this state.

Objectives

- To promote economically, culturally and ecologically sustainable tourism in Himachal Pradesh.
- To promote responsible tourism, that will be welcomed as both preferred employer and a community industry.
- To use tourism as a means of providing new employment opportunities in rural, tribal and remote areas.
- To increase private sector participation in tourism, both as a means of generating employment and providing new infrastructure.

- To develop activity-based tourism to increase the duration of tourists' visits.
- To develop adventure tourism by providing facilities and safety standards at internationally-required levels.
- To devote special attention to the promotion of religious tourism.
- To promote new concepts in tourism, such as time-share.
- To transform the role of the government into that of facilitator.

To be fair, the new HP Tourist policy mentions relevant and important areas for action. The strategy is based on:

- Breaking the seasonality factor: Himachal has always been a popular tourist destination in the summer. Tourism products must be diversified to attract visitors in other seasons as well.
- Dispersal of tourism to lesser known areas of the state: This includes promoting tourism in rural and tribal areas, and developing National Parks and wildlife sanctuaries.
- Developing pilgrimage sites: These can become important tourism destinations by improving access, internal roads, sanitation and drainage, and pilgrim facilities. In addition, other tourism activities can be developed in nearby areas.

For achieving this, the plan of action is based on:

- Basic infrastructure
- Tourism - specific infrastructure
- Entertainment infrastructure
- Accommodation, transport and catering
- Policy/Legislation

The HP government, in general is aware of the efforts needed to bring tourism on a professional level, as evident from directives laid out in its policy statement.

Tourism Clusters

The Department of Tourism will identify sites at new destinations in order to set up tourism clusters. These clusters will be designed and developed as tourism cities/tourist villages. The government will organise the civic infrastructure at these clusters such as water, road, electricity, communication etc. and will also meet the full cost of preparing such projects and shall accord priority for allocation of funds for such ventures from the financial institutions. Activities like amusement parks, resorts, cafes, handicrafts, etc., will also be integrated into the projects. The plots in these clusters will be offered on the pattern of Industrial Plots.

Land Policy

The laws for the purchase of land are being simplified. A single officer will be made responsible so as to co-ordinate clearances from all the departments, thereby saving time and effort of the entrepreneurs. Government land, which is available in the state at important places, will be transferred to the tourism Department. The department will further lease-out these sites to private sector for the development of tourism-related activities in the state. The sites will be advertised in press to attract prospective entrepreneurs. The government will also create a land bank of private land, by inviting consent of owners to sell land for tourism projects. After initial scrutiny of possible use, the land will be shown in pool and put on the website. Parties themselves will enter into the transactions, but the department will impose a nominal fee as service charges from the buyer and the seller. Permission under Section 118 of the Tenancy and Land Reform Act will be readily given for such sales, approval provided for the concept of the project is summed in advance.

Tourism Development Councils

The State Government shall constitute Tourism Development Councils for specific areas or destinations of tourist importance. These Councils will have membership from the tourism and travel trade in addition to a few government officials and shall be entrusted with management of tourism destination within their jurisdiction. These Councils shall maintain and operate a Tourism Destination Fund and shall be allowed to raise resources for the development of the infrastructure and related facilities by way of fees, cess etc.

Tourism Development Board

A Tourism Development Board, under the chairmanship of the Chief Minister and with representations from amongst officials/non-officials, shall also be set up to formulate policy guidelines for the development and promotion of the tourism industry in the state and to advise the state government on matters regarding regulation and licensing in the tourism industry.

A Good Policy *Sans* Action

A policy is only as good as its follow-up, and this is lacking in this case. Some issues to consider are:

- There is little development of tourist clusters, or large-scale initiative for amusement parks.
- Land policy has to undergo a major overhaul. In fact, this is one single factor that can bring in tourism entrepreneurship and capital investment into the state, which it severely lacks today. The state was also to advertise sites for lease, and upload them on the HPTDC website. However, under a link called "investments", the website places some photographs and maps, without any instruction on what to do, and whom to contact.
- To the contrary, the government sent a confidence-destroying signal to the investors, when the state Revenue Minister announced that Himachal Pradesh Government would screen all permissions given by the previous government for the purchase of land in the state in relaxation of Section 118 of the HP Tenancy and Land Reforms Act (The Tribune 27 April 2003). This sends a clear signal to the investor to stay away, as subsequent governments may strike down previous agreements.
- Tourism Development Boards and Councils were to be the future of tourism policy and strategy, with large-scale involvement of non-official members. This vital re-orientation has not been brought about.
- Himachal Pradesh still over-sells Shimla-Kullu-Manali circuit, and under-sells the rest of the state. As a result, while there is wasted capacity in other parts of the state, the entire infrastructure and facilities are under severe stress in this alignment. This causes water shortages, traffic snarls, and power outages, and lowers the overall impression about Himachal Pradesh, not inviting as many "return" or "recommended visits" as it should.
- Concrete action to sell Himachal Pradesh as a winter destination is still lacking, and the seasonal nature of tourism continues. It is also a fact that during winter, infrastructure facilities like power and transport get affected adversely.

Confusion with Regard to Role of HPTDC

- The state talks of private sector initiative and participation as a corner-stone of future policy, but wants to hold on to HPTDC. It states that HPTDC has been a catalyst, trend-setter and a prime mover for the promotion of domestic and foreign tourism, and has established, developed, promoted and executed various projects and schemes to facilitate and accelerate the development of tourism in the state. The government iterates that HPTDC will continue to play a pioneering role in the state to develop and open virgin destinations for tourists and provide healthy competition to the private sector.
- The state government will, however, "explore possibilities of privatisation and disinvestment of existing properties of HPTDC, to raise resources for development of new projects in hitherto virgin areas". HPTDC will also prepare, organise and operate new packages and promote adventure activities. Further it will produce literature for disseminating information to tourists about Himachal Pradesh as a tourist destination.
- While confusion with regard to the role HPTDC continues, there are little signs of improvement of services in its establishments. The staff are not courteous and not muti-lingual. They are not even in a position to communicate with most of the guests. The status of provision and maintenance of services is poor, and there is little evidence of any standardisation of practices across the establishments.
- On Himachal Pradesh tourism websites, the following two nuggets, among others, of non-professionalism were found:
  - Police Orientation Programme in May was listed as a tourist calendar event! No description was available as to the justification for its inclusion here.
  - The information listed in boldest letters says "Luxury Tax Detail of Hotels". It is actually a hyper-link to a facility where hotels can calculate their luxury tax due, but it has been placed in a public site where tourists are expected to visit!
- Food and Beverage practices in Himachal Pradesh need immediate upgradation. Even on the Mall at Shimla, the taste of Chinese cuisine is different in different establishments. There is no standarised, ratified authenticity in any cuisine offering, and this can be a serious deterrent for foreign tourists.

- Hotel accommodation is diverse, even within the same premises. The tourist has no idea of what accommodation to expect at what price.
- The Himachal Police, particularly the Traffic Police, perceive the tourist as a good "milking" opportunity. Tourist vehicles are stopped at random, repeatedly at different check-posts, and corruption is rampant. Himachal Pradesh has started an idea of forming a "tourist police", but wants to induct regular policemen into this facilitating outfit. With police experience being what it is, there is going to be little help, and more harassment.

RECOMMENDATIONS

Change Policy Focus to Tourists

Reading tourism policy statements and related policy documents, it becomes clear that the *focus of Himachal Pradesh tourism is on Himachal Pradesh itself*. Tourism is viewed as a socio-developmental necessity, in order to bring about the development of the state and its citizens. It is treated minimally in its five year plans, annual plans, and the *Economic Survey* – clubbed as "Tourism and Civil Aviation", or a small part of "General Economic Services".

This focus is not correct, and is leading to the formation of incomplete and mis-targetted policies on the tourism front.

The tourism sector has to be seen as an industry (not merely in government documents or taxation and accounting procedures), by re-orienting the entire philosophy to a marketing concept, focusing singularly on the customer, i.e., the tourist. There has to be a clear realisation that the development of Himachal Pradesh will take place as a by-product of looking after the tourist customer.

Disinvest in HPTDC

In its current state of focusing on itself, the state is talking in terms of continuation of the role of HPTDC in the tourism business, because it has employees, who are citizens of the state, who must continue to get their employment. But the moment customer focus is regained, there is realisation that only that is good for the HPTDC employee, which is in the interest of the tourist. In the long run, the Himachal Pradesh government cannot sustain non-professional business operations, and the company can sustain itself only upon customer support.

The existing properties of HPTDC should be put up for disinvestment, both on the national and international markets. If existing employees want to form cooperatives, and take over the properties, this should also be encouraged, and assistance from financial institutions should be facilitated.

Do not Wait for Tourist, Get Him

Himachal Pradesh should not be under a mistaken impression that merely by participating in five annual tourism promotion events, and placing an occasional advertisement, it is going to attract the tourist. It is absolutely clear nowadays that the customer-tourist is looking for a complete-chain solution, from home, back to home. If Himachal Pradesh Tourism will begin from the borders of Himachal Pradesh, or Himachal Bhavan in Delhi, the paying tourist may never turn up. If the intervening roads are not good, or if the airlines are not offering reasonable fares, or the airport handling is inefficient, the tourist will not come.

Himachal Pradesh cannot afford to wait for the tourist to arrive – it has to pluck him from his home. This means marketing research to identify and target him, and reach him. It means tying up credit card companies, airlines, road transport, hotels and guides in one smooth logistics chain, such that the tourist has a re-visit plan, and also recommends the destination to others.

Destination Marketing

Himachal Pradesh has to be marketed as a macro destination, with micro points within it. Even the tourism brand name, brand ambassadors, sites and sounds – all have to be chosen after meticulous research, so that positive associations are permanently built up, and place HP as amongst first-choice destinations.

Even a random line sketch of Eiffel Tower or Statue of Liberty conjures up an image of a city and a nation, and attracts tourists. Malaysia started its "Truly Asia" campaign for the country and focused on Kuala Lumpur, using the Twin Petronas Towers as the icon.

Himachal Pradesh needs to generate these internationally recognisable brand icons. There are competing mountains slopes and pine forests around the world, and the Himachal Tourism logo does not promise anything different.

Devise a Marketing Campaign

The average budget allotment for tourism development has been in the region of Rs. 5 crore annually, and this is too meager to sustain a cohesive destination marketing campaign. A mega input over a period of 10 years is needed to sell Himachal Pradesh in a professional manner, with inputs from trade professionals. The expectation sold must be fulfilled by actual experience on the ground, with a marketing campaign must be based on ground realities.

Himachal Pradesh Tourism Authority

The government should lay down tourism standards, and oversee their strict observance.

The Himachal Pradesh Tourist Board needs to grow into these roles of the Authority to oversee policy, accreditation, standardisation, and certification procedures. From the non-official side, the association of all concerned will be formalised, to broad-base decision-making (hotel and restaurant owners, transporters, guides, porters etc.) The Authority will sustain itself from the membership charges paid by various constituents. It will be charged with the following responsibilities:

1. Coordination of tourism research, for information dissemination to members. Assist in development of market strategy.
2. Interaction with other government agencies to ensure availability of adequate infrastructure in power, transport, telecom and municipal services.
3. Representation in major tourist market points, and the running of information offices.
4. Organisation of and participation in trade shows.
5. Familiarisation trips for key partners from distribution channels and travel writers.
6. Arrange support for new and small business.
7. Consumer assistance and certification practices will form a major part of the Authority's work. The Authority will:
   a. Ensure that tourist developmental activities are conducted in an environment-friendly manner.
   b. Classify services – hotels, restaurants, taxis, guides, porters etc., into clear categories, based upon tourist requirement.
   c. Standardise services, by devising a clear service criteria. For example, it may say that every restaurant must have at least one waiter on duty, who can converse in English and at least one foreign language (depending upon visitor profile), at all times when it is open for business. Standardisation will extend to both, infrastructure facilities fixed and moveable, and to services.
   d. After standardisation, certify the services provided.
   e. For certification, the Authority will authorise training and certification centres across the state. A syllabus for the various services will be prepared, and the training centres will conduct training and certification on the Authority's behalf.
   f. The Authority will ensure through checks that the training centres and their programmes are as per specifications. The training centres shall not become certification shops, where they start certification without training, to the detriment of industry.
   g. Keep track of all individuals and organisations, and their certifications. Arrange certification renewal at a reasonable periodicity to refresh skills.
   h. Withdraw certification upon failure to observe norms, and effectively enforce the withdrawal.
   i. Bring out clear and concise certification information for the guidance of the tourist. The tourist would see certain simple certification graphics on hotels, taxis, porters etc., and know the exact service he can expect. For example, a taxi with the relevant symbol would mean that the driver can speak English, carries a rate chart, help line numbers, an identity card, and a mobile phone for emergency services.
   j. For these services, the Authority will charge member organisations and individuals a reasonable sum to sustain its activities.
   k. The hospitality industry will be encouraged to take membership by announcing suitable incentives and concessions. This will raise standards across the state.
   l. Recommend the rationalisation of taxation and land policies affecting the tourism industry.
   m. Ensure participation of local communities, and PRIs/ULBs.

The government may grant the Himachal Pradesh Tourism Authority a one time corpus of a reasonable amount, and then it grows on its own as a professional organisation.

Change in Land Laws

It is necessary that the best professionals and entrepreneurs be brought in from around the world, to invest in Himachal Pradesh, and upgrade the level of tourism technology to international levels.

Change in land laws remains central to the possibility of inducting large private capital into HP. As a first step, long term lease exceeding fifty years can be offered, so that the investor can work on a secure business model.

Current Indicators

(i) India gets 25 lakh foreign tourists, and thus HP taps into this at 1.44 lakh, which is a share of 5.76 per cent. This needs drastic enhancement by reaching out to the tourist.

Country-wise distribution of tourists in HP is as under:

Country	*Percentage*
USA	9.8
UK	16.1
France	5.1
Canada	3.9
Australia	4.3
Germany	6.6
Holland	3.5
New Zealand	1.6
Sweden	2.0
Nepal	2.0
Iran	0.8
Japan	3.1
Pakistan	1.2
All Others	40.0

Source: HP Tourist Survey 2002

The major countries contributing to tourist arrivals in HP are US, UK, Germany and France.

In the domestic tourist sector, the break-up of arrivals is as under:

Zone	*Percentage*
Eastern Zone	7.96
Western Zone	12.99
Northern Zone	73.31
Central Zone	3.39
Southern Zone	2.35

The major arrivals are from North zone, with potential to market in East, South and Central zones. This also displays the known fact of domestic arrivals from Punjab, Haryana, Jammu areas for religious tourism in the Kangra belt.

(ii) The tourist in Himachal Pradesh has the following reason of the visit:

Reason	*Indian (%)*	*Foreign (%)*	*Total (%)*
Climate	23.42	17.91	22.85
Peaceful Atmosphere	15.19	19.40	15.63
Natural Beauty	40.33	48.26	41.15
Less Expensive	0.58	2.49	0.77
Publicity	1.67	1.49	1.65
Other	18.81	10.45	17.95

It is worth noting that only 1.65 per cent of the tourist felt that he has been drawn by marketing and publicity, highlighting the need for this aspect.

(iii) District-wise patronisation pattern shows the Kullu-Manali-Shimla-centric tourist strategy.

District	*Percentage of Tourists*
Bilaspur	3.6
Chamba	7.3
Hamirpur	4.6
Kangra	14.5
Kinnaur	2.1
Kullu	24.5
Lahaul & Spiti	3.1
Mandi	3.8
Shimla	24.8
Sirmaur	5.9
Solan	4.0
Una	1.8

Thus, the two districts of Kullu and Shimla account for 50 per cent of the total tourist traffic. Even in these districts, the arrivals are not uniform spaced, but concentrated over 3-4 months in a year. There is a need to highlight all-HP all-season tourist product availability to the customer.

(iv) For accommodation, the pattern of stay is as under:

Type of Accommodation	*Indian %*	*Foreign %*	*Total %*
Private Hotel	51.2	47.2	50.9
HPTDC	6.4	7.5	6.5
Dharamshala	13.3	3.0	12.2
Govt Rest House	8.6	3.0	8.0
Other places	20.5	39.3	22.4

Two facts have emerged from this data:

The high percentage of private stay is because of the greater availability, but HPTDC accommodation is preferred by the tourist. This highlights the need for security and standardisation in the provision of tourist services. The tourist first attempts to stay in HPTDC hotels, because he has a perception that he will get standard service at a reasonable price. The tourist is wary of private hotels. This is also seen from the fact that ratio of private-HPTDC accommodation is 17:1, but the tourist ratio is only 8:1. Thus occupancy ratio for private hotels is half of HPTDC.

"Other places" includes camping sites, which are an important element in hill tourism. Safe and clean camp sites need to be proliferated.

(v) Tourists largely visit HP for leisure tourism, or "pleasure trip", as classified by HP.

Purpose of Visit	*Indian*	*Foreign*	*Total*
Business/Official	15.13	4.98	14.08
Pleasure Trip	55.81	68.16	57.09
Sports	3.91	7.46	4.28
Social/Religious Functions	5.41	4.98	5.36
Pilgrimage	11.22	8.45	10.93
Health	1.90	1.49	1.86
Other	6.62	4.48	6.40

There is a potential for health and sports related tourism in HP, which is waiting to be exploited.

(vi) Quality of services needs quantum upgradation.

For public buses and private taxi, 10 per cent of the tourist rated them as "below expectations", while 50 per cent rated them as just "good".

The following ratings were received for hospitality industry:

Attribute	*Excellent*	*Very Good*	*Good*	*Below Expectation*
Behaviour	383	625	854	24
Food	127	687	967	93
Beverages	130	631	1002	61
Cleanliness	150	616	932	160
Total	790	2559	3755	338

Thus, 10 per cent excellent, 35 per cent very good, 50 per cent good, and 5 per cent poor ratings were received. As any hotel industry manager can see, these ratings are not good enough, and do not reflect well for repeat visits.

(vii) Availability of Accommodation

The following accommodation is available:

Private Hotels	714
HPTDC Complex	42
Dharamshala	85
Rest Houses	135
Others	295

A Focused Tourism Strategy for Himachal Pradesh

While missions are the statements of an organisation's intent and vision, objectives lay down achievement targets, and how to get there is strategy. If the objectives are confused, the defined strategy will be difficult to lay down. It is always desirable that after a general vision statement, the objectives – as the word itself indicates – must be *objective*. This is a missing element in the Tourist Policy of Himachal Pradesh. A reading shows general issues of:

- To promote economically, culturally and ecologically sustainable tourism in Himachal Pradesh.
- To promote responsible tourism, that will be welcomed as both preferred employer and community industry.
- To use tourism as a means of providing new employment opportunities in rural, tribal and remote areas.
- To increase private sector participation in tourism, both as a means of generating employment and providing new infrastructure.
- To develop activity based tourism to increase the duration of tourists visits etc.

Instead, HP should lay down clear and unambiguous objectives. A draft objective statement is indicated below:

(i) Himachal Pradesh has currently 50 lakh tourists, 1.44 lakh in the foreign segment. By 2010, this will be enhanced to 1.5 crore tourists, with a component of 15 lakh foreign tourists.

(in lakh)

Year	*Domestic*	*Foreign*	*Total*
2004	58.5	1.5	60
2005	77.5	2.5	80
2006	95.5	4.5	100
2007	113.0	7.0	120
2008	121.5	9.5	130
2009	128.0	12.0	140
2010	135.0	15.0	150

(ii) For domestic zones, we will focus on central and eastern sectors, enhancing their percentage in domestic tourist segment to 10 per cent each from 2007 onwards.

(iii) In the foreign segment, Himachal Pradesh will concentrate on its high contributing countries (US, UK, France, Germany) and raise the numbers of tourists from them by 15 times each by 2010.

(iv) By 2010, no district shall have less than 5.5 per cent of overall tourist traffic.

(v) Place specific focus on health and sports tourism, and increase their share. For health tourism, 1 lakh domestic and 3000 foreign visitors were recorded for 2002, and this will be enhanced to 3 lakhs and 1 lakh respectively.

(vi) The Himachal Tourism Authority will be established by March 31, 2004, with clearly defined role, and powers. It will start performing its functions by June 1, 2004.

(vii) Put in place a land laws regime for encouraging tourism industry, by involving all stakeholders, by March 31, 2004.

(viii) Disinvest in HPTDC by March 31, 2005, by involving all stakeholders.

(ix) Enhance the share of tourism in SDP of Himachal Pradesh to 6 per cent by 2010.

For achieving these draft objectives, the desired strategy could be:

(i) Set up distribution partners in US, UK, France, and Germany. Hire market research teams to identify tourist segments and their needs, and match it to facilities available in the short run. In the long run, plan for ensuring availability of desirable facilities. Offer door to door packages through distribution partners, tying up airlines, airport transfers, road/rail transport, hotels, guides, equipment suppliers etc.

(ii) Organise an investor meet in New Delhi, and other metros, inviting industry representatives. This will be preceded by groundwork to announce changes in land laws and concessions, and gathering complete details of the proposed projects and properties. This programme should commence in June 2004, and be followed by site visits. Every serious lead should have an identified Himachal Pradesh officer to chase with the party and provide information, till the agreement is finalised.

(iii) Market HP as a health destination. Bring in foreign and domestic investors to set up health resorts and spas, preferably as part of an international chain. The investors will be given required assistance through land law and tax concessions. A policy statement in this regard will be issued by March 31, 2004, after consultations with investors.

(iv) Ensure total establishment of certification practices by December 31, 2004, and bring the tourism sector under effective supervision of HP Tourism Authority. The tourists will be offered guaranteed service standards, with the guarantees clearly specified.

(v) Set up an easy system of tourist grievance registration, with quick-response handling and redressal, under the overall superintendence of the Authority.

(vi) Set up distribution partners in Central and Eastern states, and offer door to door packages.

(vii) Start English, French, and German language courses, in keeping with targeting of US, UK, France and Germany for tourism promotion. Lay down norm of knowledge of two out of three languages spoken as a criteria for certification by HP Tourist Authority. Set up Tourist Facility Certification regime, implemented through private partner training institutes.

(viii) Commence state-wide consultation process for change in land laws, and disinvestment if HPTDC.

(ix) Select a mascot (building etc), to publicise as the symbol for future icon marketing.

(x) Continuous marketing research exercise is conducted to define requirements, and then feedback to measure satisfaction levels.

(xi) Facilitate the private sector to set up two entertainment parks of international standards, to be in place by 2008.

(xii) Encourage tourist service providers to offer net-bookings, and acceptance of payments on the net through credit cards, and secure payment gateways. Encourage acceptance of plastic money through the State, to facilitate the tourist.

(xiii) Allocate required funds for tourist promotion. The quantum will depend on the final strategy, but Rs. 5 crore per annum needs quantum enhancement.

(xiv) For manning and managing the Himachal Pradesh Tourism Authority, select the best talent from across the nation. They will be employees of the Authority, not the Himachal Pradesh government, and the jobs will be time-bound and performance-bound contracts.

The Basis of the Strategy

The strategy is based on the following assumptions:

Differentiation

Through market research and analysis, Himachal Pradesh will define its distinctive appeal for the foreign and domestic tourist sectors. This is based upon a realisation that Himachal Pradesh is not the only place in the world with mountains, snow, and pines. Our promotion will have to be based on more than this, and attempt to carve out a different niche, which can be used as a marketing pitch.

Focus

Himachal Pradesh will focus on those foreign countries, where it is most popular already, because the top four tourist-contributing nations of US, UK, France, and Germany are also having high per capita income. The tourist will have a higher spending propensity.

In the domestic sector, the focus will be on generating more tourists from hitherto low contributing central and eastern zones of India. The North already contributes 73 per cent of tourists to Himachal Pradesh, and they will continue to patronise, for reasons of proximity, and familiarity.

Security

The tourist dreads insecurity. Himachal Pradesh will remove this insecurity absolutely by launching door to door tourist packages that take care of complete logistics.

Standards

Tourists dread non-standard practices. The Himachal Pradesh Tourism Authority through a standardisation and certification regime will remove this fear from the tourist experience, encouraging repeat visits, and recommendations as a preferred destination.

Conclusion

The more one thinks of the idea of how the entire tourism policy is NOT focused on the customer-tourist, the greater is the clear realisation of why we are failing to attract him. *In a way, we have become obsessed with "tourism", but forgotten the "tourist"*. It appears we want him so that our need for economic development is satisfied, while he can manage with just some good views of nature. There is an immediate need to focus on the tourist, find out what he needs, and make arrangements to provide it.

- Amend Himachal Pradesh land laws to bring in entrepreneurship, technology, and capital.
- Himachal Pradesh Government to move out of tourism as a business activity, and shift to become a facilitator.
- Set up Himachal Pradesh Tourist Authority to oversee policy, accreditation, standardisation, and certification procedures.
- There should be clear, unambiguous, and objective targets laid down for achievement, backed up with a milestone-based strategy for implementation. This study has proposed a draft objective and strategy statement, and the same can be suitably modified.
- Currently, Tourism has a narrow focus on the development of the state. This must be re-oriented along marketing lines, and clearly target the tourist as a customer. The satisfied tourist will automatically look after the State's economy.

References

Bhat S.S. and P.N. Seth: *An Introduction to Travel and Tourism*, Sterling Publishers, 1993.

Government of Himachal Pradesh: *Annual Plans 1998-2002*, , Shimla.

Government of Himachal Pradesh: *Economic Survey, 1998-2003*, Shimla.

Government of Himachal Pradesh: *Eighth and Ninth Five Year Plans of Himachal Pradesh*, Shimla.

Government of Himachal Pradesh: *Tourist Economic Survey, 2002*, , Shimla.

Kotler, Philip *et al.*: *Marketing for Hospitality and Tourism*, Pearson Education Pte. Ltd., 2003.

Planning Commission: *Tenth Five Year Plan 2002-2007*, Vols. 1, 2, & 3., New Delhi.

www.himachal.nic.in (official website of Himachal Pradesh Government).

www.stb.com (website of Singapore Tourism Board).

www.hptdc.nic.in (website of HP Tourism Development Corporation).

Chapter 20

Urban Development

Urbanisation Pattern in Himachal Pradesh

The formation of Himachal Pradesh as a part 'C' state on April 15, 1948, with the merger of 30 erstwhile princely states marked the onset of urbanisation in the state. Himachal Pradesh experienced a sudden growth of its urban population from 0.86 lakh in 1941 to 1.54 lakh in 1951. The rate of urbanisation grew from 3.80 per cent to 6.45 per cent in the respective census decades. The compound annual growth rate (CAGR) of urban population rose from 1.5 per cent during 1931-41 to 5.99 per cent during 1941-51. Since then, the growth of urban population has been steady. The gradual urbanisation of a predominantly rural society has been set into motion and the urban population of Himachal Pradesh has more than doubled between 1971 and 2001. The absolute increase of urban population during 1991-2001 is 1.46 lakh against 1.23 lakh during 1981-1991 and 0.84 lakh during 1971-81. Though the growth of urbanisation has slowed down in the 1990s, yet the net increase of the state's urban population during the period 1991-2001 has been only slightly less than the total urban population of the state in 1951. The projected higher growth of the economy, industry, trade, commerce and tourism in Himachal Pradesh may lead to faster urbanisation. Table 20.1 indicates the trends in urbanisation in Himachal Pradesh.

From 1971 onwards, urbanisation has been constant, with the CAGR of urban population varying between 2.86 per cent to 3.25 per cent. During the period 1971 to 2001, the average CAGR of the urban population i.e. 9.41 per cent has been considerably higher than the CAGR of the rural population i.e. 5.47 per cent. This difference is likely to increase in the future due to the higher growth of population in the urban areas, which offer better employment opportunities. The consequent economic, environmental and physical changes are likely to exert pressure on the

TABLE 20.1

Trends in Urbanisation in Himachal Pradesh

Census Year	*Total Population (in lakh)*	*Urban Population (in lakh)*	*Rural Population (in lakh)*	*Percentage of Urban Population*	*Compound Annual Growth Rate** (%)*		*Number of Towns/ Urban Agglomerations*
					Rural	*Urban*	
1971	34.60	2.42	32.18	6.99	-1.98	3.12	36
1981	42.81	3.26	39.55	7.61	4.15	3.02	47
1991	51.71	4.49	47.22	8.69	1.79	3.25	58
2001	60.77	5.95	54.82	9.79	1.50	2.86	57
2011*	71.42	7.89	63.64	11.05	1.50	2.86	-
2021*	83.93	10.45	73.88	12.45	1.50	2.86	-

Source: (i) *Census of India 1981, Town Directory, Himachal Pradesh, Series-7, Part XA.*
(ii) *Census of India 1991, Town Directory, Himachal Pradesh, Series-9, Part IX.*
(iii) *Census of India 2001, Rural Urban Distribution, Himachal Pradesh, Series –3, Paper-2 of 2001.*

Note: * Projections: Based on CAGR of 1991-2001 decade.
** The CAGR for 1971, 1981, 1991, 2001, 2011 and 2021: Calculated from the actual decadal values of 1961-71, 1971-81, 1981-91,1991-01 and projected values of 2001-11 and 2011-2021 respectively.

Urban Local Bodies (ULBs) to meet the growing demand for infrastructure such as land, water supply, sewerage, solid waste management, housing, roads etc.

District-wise trend of urbanisation indicates that Shimla, Solan and Sirmaur districts have 23.12 per cent, 18.26 per cent and 10.38 per cent urban population respectively and are the top three urbanised districts with higher level of urbanisation as compared to the state average. The urban population of Himachal Pradesh is not growing in an equitable manner. The inequalities have increased considerably in the last five decades. The two most urbanised districts of the state have 18 towns of different sizes i.e. 10 in Shimla and 8 in Solan, and these indicate a linear/corridor pattern of urbanisation. There is a ribbon type of growth of towns in other districts also i.e. Bilaspur, Mandi, Kullu, Una, Hamirpur, Kangra and Chamba except Kinnaur and Lahaul & Spiti, which have no urban population.

Shimla, the only Class I town is highly urbanised. There are 6 Class III towns, 7 Class IV towns, 17 Class V towns and 26 Class VI towns. Two new towns i.e. Baddi (Solan district) and only the census town of Mant Khas (Kangra district) came up in 2001. Pandoh, a census town in Mandi district in 1991, lost its status in 2001. Table 20.2 shows class wise trend of urban population in Himachal Pradesh from 1971 to 2001.

The number of towns has increased from 36 in 1971 to 57 in 2001 and the urban population of Himachal Pradesh is converging in the larger towns. It is also interesting to note that the smaller towns with a small urban population have started exhibiting a decadal rate of growth, which is as high as that of the larger towns or even higher. Manali Nagar Panchayat, a Class V town in Kullu district, experienced the highest decadal growth rate of +157.50 per cent during 1991-2001, which is largely due to the growth of tourism in Manali, which is emerging as an alternative to Jammu and Kashmir. With the growth of urban population, the number of municipal councils is likely to increase. The spatial pattern of urbanisation emerging from the growth of tourism, trade and industrial activities needs to be observed and monitored for sustainable development of the urban areas.

The population base and growth trend of municipal towns/cantonment boards (CBs) confirm the unequal trend in towns of various size and class. Shimla is the largest and the only municipal corporation town of the state. Among the 20 municipal councils, Solan (0.34 lakh) is the largest and Naina Devi (0.01 lakh) in Bilaspur district the smallest. Among the 28 Nagar Panchayats, the recently constituted Nagar Panchayat of Baddi (0.23 lakh) is the largest and Narkanda (0.007 lakh) is the smallest. Among the seven cantonment boards, Yol (0.11 lakh) in Kangra district is the largest and Bakloh (0.02 lakh) the smallest. Some municipalities in the upper areas (inner Himalyas) of Kangra, Chamba and Kullu districts are very small in size, weak in fiscal base and are unable to initiate projects for infrastructure development. There is a wide variation of size, population base and the growth of population between towns of the same class and

TABLE 20.2

Class-wise Trend of Urban Population in Himachal Pradesh

Years	*Different Size Class Towns*						
	Class I	*Class II*	*Class III*	*Class IV*	*Class V*	*Class VI*	*Total*
1971	- (-) [-]	01 (22.89) [55,368]	01 (8.81) [21,304]	05 (27.18) [65,739]	06 (17.51) [42,362]	23 (23.61) [57,117]	36 (100.00) [241,890]
1981	- (-) [-]	01 (21.66) [70,604]	02 (12.54) [40,869]	05 (22.08) [71,985]	09 (19.83) [64,637]	30 (23.89) [77,876]	47 (100.00) [325,971]
1991	01 (22.75) [102,186]*	- (-) [-]	04 (19.42) [87,228]	07 (21.73) [97,617]	10 (15.81) [71,018]	36 (20.29) [91,147]	58 (100.00) [449,196]
2001	01 (24.31) [144,578]	- (-) [-]	06 (25.87) [153,912]	07 (19.06) [113,376]	17 (19.10) [113,633]	26 (11.66) [69,382]	57 (100.00) [594,881]

Source: (i) Same as in Table 20.1 (i, ii & iii).

Note: (i) Number of towns in each class (without bracket).
(ii) Percentage of urban population in each class ( ).
(iii) Total population in each class [ ].
(iv) Size of population : Class I = 100,000 and above; Class II = 50,000–99,999; Class III = 20,000–49,999; Class IV = 10,000–19,999; Class V = 5,000 –9,999; Class VI = Below 5,000.
(v) * includes out growth population.

between towns of different classes. A few issues relating to changes in the growth pattern of urban areas have not been discussed in this section due to non-availability of data.

The level and growth of urbanisation in Himachal Pradesh has been poor in comparison to neighbouring states as shown in Table 20.3.

TABLE 20.3

Comparative Picture of Urbanisation in Himachal Pradesh, Punjab, Haryana and J&K (1971 to 2001)

State	*Urban Population (%)*				*Decadal Variation of Urban Population (%)*		
	1971	*1981*	*1991*	*2001*	*1971-81*	*1981-91*	*1991-2001*
Himachal	**6.99**	**7.61**	**8.69**	**9.79**	**+34.76**	**+37.80**	**+32.43**
J&K	18.59	21.05	23.83	24.88	+45.86	+45.94	N.A.*
Haryana	17.67	21.88	24.63	29.00	+59.47	+43.41	+50.79
Punjab	23.73	27.68	29.55	33.95	+44.51	+28.95	+37.58
India	**19.91**	**23.31**	**25.71#**	**27.78#**	**+46.39**	**+36.24**	**+31.13**

Source: (i) Same as in Table 20.1 (i, ii & iii).

Note: i. * decadal variation of J&K for 1991-2001: is not available as census of 1991 was not conducted in J&K due to disturbed law and order situation.

ii. # includes projected population of J&K.

Though the urban centres of Himachal Pradesh are not growing at par with those of Punjab, Haryana, and Jammu and Kashmir, yet the consequences of the urbanisation pattern in the state seem to be more complicated and can have long-term implications on the ecology of Himachal Pradesh as well as that of its neighboring states. Comparatively, the absence or poor growth of industry, trade and commerce and the difficult mountainous terrain have controlled the expansion of urban areas and their economies. Disparities in the growth of urbanisation, the economy of the cities and the level and quality of urban infrastructure are growing within the state as well as between the states of north-west region. Poor investment in the various sectors in a large number of towns due to their limited economic base is affecting the development of urban infrastructure/services in Himachal Pradesh.

The spatial pattern of urbanisation in Himachal Pradesh is creating imbalances of resources and deficiencies in the coverage of urban infrastructure and municipal services. Despite the growing contribution of the urban sector, particularly the urban service sector, to the state domestic product (SDP), the quality and quantity of urban infrastructure continue to be poor in Himachal Pradesh. With the decreasing share of the primary sector and the increasing share of the secondary and tertiary sectors in the SDP, in terms of generation of employment and total output, the share of the urban areas in SDP has increased disproportionately.

One of the major concerns in Himachal Pradesh is the growing environmental pollution due to the disposal of untreated sewage in most of the rivers by a large number of towns. Even solid waste such as garbage, polythene bags and other domestic waste, is thrown in the rivers or dumped on the slopes. 'One of the major concerns in Manali is growing environmental pollution due to disposal of untreated sewage in the river Beas and unscientific disposal of non-biodegradable waste' (Gupta, J.P. & Manoj K. Teotia, 2003). Open defecation is common in the urban areas. This can lead to a serious ecological crisis not only in Himachal Pradesh but also in the neighboring states of Punjab and Haryana. Himachal Pradesh does not have any 'urbanisation strategy' or 'urban development policy' to meet the demand and shortfalls in the supply of urban infrastructure/services.

The growth of new and the existing urban centres should be planned. 'Health for All' goal of the state government can be achieved only by providing safe drinking water, improving the urban environmental infrastructure by scientific management of liquid and solid waste to control air, water and soil pollution. Upgradation of the urban environmental infrastructure will improve ecology not only of the state but also of the neighboring states.

There is need for addressing issues relating to the negative impact of urbanisation and evolving an *"urbanisation strategy"* and *"urban development policy"* comprising area/region specific economic frameworks, rural–urban continuum/connectiveness/interdependence, backward and forward linkages and inter-sectoral as well as spatial and environmental dimensions of infrastructure development. Emphasis should be put on localisation so that the urban areas are able to meet the needs of the residents without affecting the interests of the future generations. The strategy/policy should comprise long-term city/environment friendly goals such as empowerment of the ULBs by transferring funds, functions and functionaries and adequate urban infrastructure/services like water supply, sewerage, solid waste management, roads, street lights, housing and transport facilities.

Environmental conservation should be a major thrust area for the urban policymakers and stakeholders in infrastructure development. Creation of an enabling legal, financial and regulatory framework for infrastructure development should be the immediate policy initiative of the state government. Urban development policy must emphasise on capacity building of the elected and appointed functionaries of local self-governments and other officers responsible for infrastructure development in urban areas. Training of urban managers is necessary for institutional development and functional strengthening of local self-government and housing and urban development/ irrigation and public health (IPH) departments responsible for the development of urban infrastructure. Considering that the resources of the ULBs are poor and budgetary support from the state government and transfers/grants from the central government are unlikely to increase, the strategy should suggest ways and means of resource mobilisation from capital markets/non budgetary sources for financing the urban infrastructure.

Urban Infrastructure Scenario in Himachal Pradesh

The urban infrastructure scenario in Himachal Pradesh is grim. Deficiencies in water supply, sewerage, solid waste management, municipal roads, streets and streetlights are becoming acute with growing urbanisation. According to the *State of Environment Report (SER)-HP* (2000), 'most towns lack sewerage systems, and solid waste management is also inadequate. These twin factors expose water to severe pollution hazards' (p.107). The situation becomes acute in peak tourist months in summer as well as in winter. The urban infrastructure and municipal services have been deteriorating in the larger towns and have been grossly unsatisfactory in the small towns. A considerably high proportion of the urban population remains uncovered by municipal services. The cost of providing urban infrastructure services is higher in the urban centres of Himachal Pradesh because of the difficult mountainous terrain, inadequate supply of low-cost raw material and labour. At the same time, pricing and cost recovery of the urban infrastructure is negligible. The technology used for providing and maintaining the urban infrastructure services is old and inappropriate to meet the growing needs.

Urban decay is visible in Himachal Pradesh in the form of water and air pollution, ecological degradation and traffic congestion. It is largely due to unplanned and uncontrolled urbanisation and faulty urban management/development systems. The pronounced inadequacy of urban infrastructure services is affecting the quality of life in the urban areas. It could be attributed to the poor fiscal health of the ULBs. The ULBs of small and medium towns have more serious problems due to planning bias in favour of the larger towns. Disparities in the level and quality of infrastructure between the small and large towns are expected to increase in the future. The *'Report of the Committee on India Vision 2020'* (Planning Commission, Government of India, 2002, p.59) has mentioned that 'greater inequality may be expected in the level of basic services across urban centres of different sizes by the year 2020, unless concerted initiative is taken to reverse the trend'. The major issues relating to the status of urban infrastructure and municipal services in Himachal Pradesh have been discussed in this section.

Water Supply

Himachal Pradesh is no exception to the critical urban water supply position in the major states of India i.e. Andhra Pradesh, Rajasthan, Maharashtra, Gujarat, Karnataka, Tamil Nadu and Delhi. Water supply in the urban areas is inadequate, in terms of quantity as well as quality. According to the *SER-HP* (2000, pp 94-95), 'the water supply systems in most of the towns are quite old and have outlived their utility, their sources need augmentation and the distribution systems in almost all the supply schemes need replacement and rehabilitation'. Table 20.4 shows per capita availability of water in the urban areas maintained by IPH Department.

TABLE 20.4

Per Capita Availability of Water in Urban Areas of Himachal Pradesh

Per-capita Availability of Water (LPCD)	*Number of Towns*	*Name of Towns*
80-120	27	Arki, Chopal, Chowari, Chamba, Dehra, Daulatpur Ghumarwin, Gagret, Jogindernagar, Jubbal, Jawalamukhi, Kangra, Kullu, Kotkhai, Mehatpur, Manali, Nadaun, Nahan, Palampur, Rampur, Rohroo, Rewalsar, Santokhgarh, Sujanpur, Sri Naina Devi, Suni and Una
50 –80	10	Bilaspur, Dharamsala, Dalhousie, Hamirpur, Mandi, Nagrota, Shimla, Solan, Sarkaghat and Sundernagar
25-50	12	Banjar, Bhuntar, Bhota, Baddi, Mant Khas, Narkanda, Nurpur, Nalagarh, Paonta Sahib, Rajgarh, Theog and Talai

Source: Irrigation and Public Health Department, Government of Himachal Pradesh.

Though all the towns of Himachal Pradesh have water supply facility, yet the per capita availability of water in a large number of towns is well below the desired norms. The major populated towns, i.e., Shimla, Solan, Mandi, Hamirpur, Bilaspur, and Dharmsala have a per capita water supply of less than 80 lpcd and the industrial towns of Baddi, Paonta Sahib and Nalagarh have a per capita water supply of less than 50 lpcd. Not all households have individual water connections in most of the towns and not all localities and areas are covered by the water distribution network. The supply is unreliable due to irregular supply, inadequacy, short duration as well as the poor quality of water. A large number of people use drinking water from traditional sources without ascertaining the quality of the water. Due to the unreliability of the water supply, consumers have made additional investments on installing individual tubewells, handpumps, storage facilities (ground as well as overhead), pumping sets, booster pumps and filtration systems.

In a survey of drinking water in the six towns of Chamba, Dharamshala, Manali, Mandi, Shimla and Solan done by the Health Department in 1994, it was found that water-borne diseases were a major health problem in the urban areas of the state. Nearly one-third of the water samples tested were found contaminated with enteric bacterial pathogens (*SER-HP*, 2000, p.109). The situation is no better in other towns as a large number of cases of water-borne diseases are reported in hospitals every year.

Water Supply in Shimla: Some Critical Issues

The per capita availability of water in Shimla is less than 80 lpcd. The situation becomes acute in summer as the demand for water rises to almost double, when hotel occupancy is 100 per cent due to a heavy influx of tourists. It affects the tourists as well as the local citizens. A CRRID study (1999) shows that per capita revenue expenditure (PCRE) on water supply and sewerage in Shimla increased from Rs. 55.67 in 1992-93 to Rs. 61.89 in 1997-98. The PCRE has further increased and is affecting development works as fewer funds are available for improving water crisis management capabilities. Unaccounted water is high due to network losses/wastage and the duration of supply is 30-60 minutes twice a day.

The current system of pricing and cost recovery of water supply in SMC is unsustainable and has serious fiscal implications on the corporation. There is a huge gap between the cost of the water supply and the recovery of water rates. There is no system of periodical review of the tariffs with general inflation rates and costs, due to political interference in fixing water tariffs in Shimla. SMC has been unable to pay arrears to IPH which have accumulated over the time.

The deficiencies of water supply multiply in summer due to the increase in demand and the drying up of several sources. Shimla's water crisis in summer is well known. The supply of water is not volumetric in all towns and it is a major factor in its wastage. Rich and poor sections pay the same rates and hence the consumption of more water by the higher income groups becomes a 'social good' for them as they get it at a nominal cost. There is no system of cross subsidisation. The cost is not linked with consumption and the rates are not revised periodically with the hike in electricity charges, labour charges, and the cost of material. The principle of cost recovery has not been applied to the water supply and plan allocations have been inadequate to cope with the demand. The arrears of Rs. 17.13 crore are due at ULBs on account of water bills to be paid to IPH.

One of the crucial aspects of water supply in Himachal Pradesh is that in most of the towns it is maintained either by the Irrigation and Public Health (IPH) Department (49 towns) or the Cantonment Boards (6 towns) or the Himachal Pradesh Housing Board (1 town) and not by the ULBs. Only Shimla, Solan (distribution of water) and Palampur (O&M and distribution of water) ULBs have this function under their jurisdiction but in a limited manner. Though the 74th Constitutional Amendment envisages the transfer of water supply to the ULBs, yet even after 11 years after the passage of this amendment water supply in Himachal Pradesh continues to be looked after by the IPH Department of the state government. It is time to transfer this function along with funds and functionaries to the ULBs. Their active involvement in prioritising the works according to the needs of the people can help to provide potable water to the citizens in an efficient manner. The involvement of the local people in the operation and maintenance of the water supply systems can be secured through water users associations.

According to the *India Infrastructure Report* (1996), technological upgradation and improved design can increase efficiency and rationalise consumption. Regularity in supply could mean lower project cost and greater willingness of the consumers to pay. The report recommends differential treatment of water for different uses. Micro level system needs to be designed to recycle water at the household level. The supply should be metered to plug leakages. Water conservation, recycling and volumetric supply are necessary to tide over the crisis and sustain the water supply system in the urban centres of Himachal Pradesh in the long run.

Sewerage

The sewerage system in the urban areas of Himachal Pradesh is grossly inadequate. Sewage treatment facilities exist only in seven towns i.e, Shimla, Palampur, Sri Naina Devi, Chamba, Mandi, Bilaspur and Rohroo. Untreated sewage in other towns is disposed of in rivers. It is polluting the drinking water and damaging the ecology of the state. The cost of water treatment is also going up as river water, which is used for drinking purposes in several towns, is becoming polluted day by day due to the disposal of untreated sewage. The pollution level in the major rivers of Himachal Pradesh *viz.* Beas, Satluj, Ravi and Parbati is on the rise and it has serious implications on the health of the people of Himachal Pradesh and of the neighboring states. The Pollution Control Board of Himachal Pradesh, under a national programme called 'Monitoring of National Aquatic Resources' regularly assesses the quality of the water in the major rivers and their tributaries, covering 22 important parameters (*SER-HP*, 2000). It has observed and recommended that:

- frequent sampling should be done if river water is used for drinking and the water for drinking should be properly treated and disinfected.
- all towns on the banks of the rivers should be provided with sewage treatment facilities and should not be allowed to discharge urban waste without treatment into or on the banks of the river.
- a number of hotels and tourist resorts are coming up on the banks of the rivers. These must have proper sewage treatment plants.
- industrial units should not be allowed to discharge untreated effluents into rivers/khads/ nallahs.

These recommendations should be implemented by the state government without any delay as it is important to protect the ecology and the natural beauty of the state. The sewerage facility should be extended to all major towns. The treatment of sewage is necessary and urgent steps are required to be taken for the disposal of treated sewage in the rivers. In several towns, sewage water after proper treatment can be recycled for domestic use. Since sanitation is a municipal function, it should be transferred to the ULBs along with staff working in the urban areas for maintaining and augmenting the sewerage system. The cost of O&M of sewerage should be recovered progressively.

Sewerage and Drainage in Shimla: Emerging Concern for Ecology

The sewerage system in Shimla is almost 100 years old. With the growing population, use of water and increased volume of sewage, the deficiencies in sewerage and drainage have become serious. The construction of sewage treatment plant with financial assistance from OPEC is likely to improve the situation but partially and still several sewage disposal streams have to be covered by treatment facilities.

A study (CRRID, 1999) found that the area covered by sewer lines as a percentage of the area of the SMC declined from 60 per cent in 1992-93 to 54 per cent in 1997-98. We hope situation has not improved much in the last five years. The length of drains per sq. km of area of the SMC also declined from 5.76 km to 4.27 km during the same period. It was largely due to the extension of the municipal area from 19.55 sq.km in 1991 to 28.53 sq.km in 1998. The increase in per capita revenue expenditure on sewerage and drainage from Rs. 13.66 to Rs. 25.34 also affected augmentation of sewerage and drainage as funds for capital expenditure were siphoned off by the increase in salaries and wages.

The augmentation and maintenance of sewerage is with IPH Department and the lack of coordination between the IPH Department and the SMC is affecting proper management and upgradation of the sewerage system. The role of the SMC in prioritising development works has been undermined by the IPH Department. It is against the spirit of the 74th Constitutional Amendment as sewerage is a municipal function listed in its 12th schedule. The involvement of the SMC is necessary to expand the sewerage services according to the needs of the people. 100 per cent collection and treatment of sewage is essential for protecting ecology of Shimla and its neighboring areas.

The *India Infrastructure Report* (1996) recommends that the use of low-cost technologies, the unbundling of services to involve the private sector and proper packaging i.e. clubbing together water supply and drainage projects can reduce the project cost and improve its viability. Similarly, road development and storm water drain management can be clubbed with commercial development of the adjoining areas.

Solid Waste Management

There are serious deficiencies in solid waste management (SWM) in the urban areas and environmental decline is visible in almost all towns. The sudden influx of tourists puts tremendous pressure on the sanitary services. The SWM services are inadequate and the accumulation of garbage can be seen in most of the towns. Diseases like diarrhoea and malaria break out frequently in many towns due to the poor sanitary conditions. The situation has been worsening despite the favourable climatic and environmental conditions in

Solid Waste Management in Shimla: Some Growing Concerns

The capital of the state and the most important tourist town of Himachal has serious deficiencies in SWM. According to a study (CRRID, 1999), the per capita collection of solid waste declined from 294 gm. to 286 gm. during the period 1992-93 to 1997-98. Though solid waste collected as a per cent of the waste generated increased from 64 per cent in 1992-93 to 67 per cent in 1997-98, it has now decreased to 60 per cent (in 2002-03). The uncollected waste is degenerating the environmental conditions of Shimla.

The study also reveals that the per capita revenue expenditure on sanitation and conservancy grew from Rs.105.82 in 1992-93 to Rs. 173.94 in 1997-98, which affected the capital works for augmentation of sanitation services. The SWM services are still poor, as the revenue receipts of the SMC are not growing in proportion and the corporation has been depending on the state government for financing its growing revenue expenditure and committed liabilities on SWM.

The recommendations of the committee, constituted by the Supreme Court of India, to improve SWM in Class I towns, have not been considered and implemented seriously by the Class-I corporation town of Shimla. A waste treatment plant has been set up for bioconversion of waste, but it is not getting enough segregated wastes. The time consumed in conversion is long and people's participation is poor in providing segregated waste. The non-biodegradable/hazardous waste is not disposed of scientifically, which is affecting ecology of the city as well as neighboring areas.

Himachal Pradesh. The municipalities complain of the shortage of sanitation staff but discussions with the local people in several towns reveal that the existing sanitation staff do not work or irregularly sweep the streets and collect the garbage. The cost of collection, transportation and disposal is high due to certain outdated practices and old technologies. Unscientific disposal of waste is common and biodegradable waste is not taken care of at the household level.

One of the factors for poor SWM in the urban areas is the gap in the physical targets and achievements in several SWM activities i.e. construction of dustbins, toilets, purchase of vehicles and construction of waste treatment plants during the Ninth Five Year Plan. This gap is likely to increase with the existing fiscal, institutional and functional deficiencies in the development of the urban infrastructure.

Though the ULBs of Shimla, Kullu, Manali, Nahan and Solan have solid waste treatment plants, the problem of poor SWM continues due to the lack of support of the local people in providing segregated waste to the sanitary staff. These ULBs have to segregate waste at the sites of treatment plants, which is a costly and time-consuming affair. In a few towns i.e. Una, Hamirpur, Dharamshala and Kangra works for construction of treatment plants are in progress. A large number of towns do not have treatment facilities and are creating environmental pollution. Heaps of polythene bags are seen in all major towns. The tourists leave a lot of garbage including polythene bags in the urban areas, which is affecting the ecology of the state. The Himachal government is the first to enact legislation to manage non-biodegradable garbage but the law has not been implemented effectively. Throwing of garbage in drainage channels/nallahs and in the streets is a common practice and the ULBs have to start special campaigns to desilt the nallahs/channels time and again. Sanitation charges are collected by a few municipalities, which are grossly inadequate to maintain even O&M of SWM.

The need of funds for providing adequate treatment facilities and covering the uncovered areas is colossal. *Solid Waste (Management and Regulation) Rules 2000*, formulated by the Ministry of Environment and Forests, Government of India call upon the ULBs to take urgent steps to address problems relating to solid waste management. No doubt the ULBs are making efforts to improve the sanitary conditions in their areas but still a lot remains to be done to create a people-friendly sustainable environment in the urban areas of Himachal Pradesh.

According to *India Infrastructure Report* (1996, p.28), the cost of collection, treatment and disposal of solid waste is to be reduced through various mechanisms. Technological innovations to improve the reusability of the recycled waste will increase the returns and make the projects viable. Privatisation of as many operations as feasible will improve efficiency and reduce the cost. The report suggests:

- greater attention to segregation of different kinds of waste at the collection point to reduce the cost of disposal.
- biodegradable waste should be tackled locally to avoid storage and transportation over long distances.
- wherever environmentally acceptable, disposal can be decentralised to reduce the transportation cost.
- separate collection and disposal of toxic waste.
- use of right technologies to improve the quality of processed waste.
- landfills can be scientifically organised to minimise pollution.

According to the Tenth Five Year Plan of Himachal Pradesh, there are about 152 units which produce hazardous wastes. Sites have been identified for their disposal but there are yet to be notified. This needs to be expedited and disposal facilities created on the ground. Hospital waste management is also important. The United Nations Population Fund (UNFPA) has supplied three incinerators to the zonal hospitals at Mandi, Dharmshala and Nahan. Another incinerator will be installed at the district hospital at Recong Peo in the tribal areas. As a part of the integrated solid waste management project, a common incinerator has been installed near IGMC, Shimla. The Government should install more incinerators, at least one in each major district town, to create a people-friendly environment in the cities of Himachal Pradesh.

The State government should prepare a *'solid waste management strategy'* for urban areas to manage solid waste efficiently, in view of the ecological sensitivity and importance of this hilly state. The small and medium sized ULBs can have a common waste treatment facility, as the construction of a treatment plant in a *nagar panchayat* or even in a medium size municipal council will not be feasible or viable. Since solid waste management in hills requires specific skills and technology due to difficult topography, climatic and environmental factors, the training/capacity building of staff is essential.

Municipal Roads and Streets

Municipal roads in Himachal Pradesh are inadequate, dilapidated and congested. Encroachment of municipal roads is a common practice. Maintenance of roads is poor due to the poor fiscal position of the ULBs and therefore, the flow of traffic is slow in the major cities of the state. Excessive pressure on the roads in cities like Shimla, Solan, Kullu, Manali, Dharmshala, Dalhousie, Mandi, Bilaspur and Kangra is harming their quality. The heavy influx of tourists in the peak seasons aggravates the situation.

The length of roads in municipal areas is 750.84 kms, which comprises 162.48 kms of Shilma MC, 353.82 kms of municipal councils and 234.54 kms of *nagar panchayats* (SSFC, 2002). The length of streets in the ULBs was 396.76 km in 1996 which has increased to 570.87 kms due to the expansion of city limits and addition of new towns. A large number of streets in several towns are not even *pucca* and these should be upgraded to ensure better flow of traffic and convenience to the people. Specific funds should be provided for maintenance of the municipal roads and streets.

Municipal Roads and Streets in Shimla: Some Grey Areas

The total length of roads and streets (roads=162.48 kms + streets 40.58 kms) in SMC is approximately 203 kms. Out of these about 60 per cent are metalled and tarred and the remaining 40 per cent are unmetalled. The municipal roads and streets in Shimla, the capital town and the centre of all major political, economic and administrative activities, are over burdened due to movement of thousands of vehicles every day along with the commuters. The condition of several roads is far from satisfactory and their maintenance is very poor. In many areas, roads have been encroached by shopkeepers, hoteliers and residents. The neglected streets, dilapidated and encroached roads affect the movement of vehicles, and harm the environmental conditions.

Due to its poor fiscal condition, the SMC has been unable to maintain and upgrade several of its important roads properly. According to a CRRID study (1999), surface roads per sq. km of the area of the SMC decreased from 5.76 kms in 1992-93 to 4.27 kms in 1997-98. The augmentation of roads could not be taken up with expansion of the city limits, which resulted in a decline of per sq. km surface road. The situation has not improved much in the last five years.

Metalling, tarring, resurfacing, widening, repair and maintenance of roads, paths, streets and steps by Roads and Building Department of the SMC has been poor due to inadequate and irregular flow of funds under municipal fund, EIUS and SJSRY schemes and grants in aid from the state government.

The First State Finance Commission (FSFC) estimated an annual requirement of Rs. 62.15 lakh for the maintenance of municipal roads in SMC, the municipal councils and *Nagar Panchayats*. This requirement has gone up now and the ULBs need about Rs. 2 crore per annum for the maintenance and augmentation of municipal roads and streets.

The *India Infrastructure Report* (1996), recommends that 'technological upgradation should be used to reduce maintenance cost'. Better coordination with other departments i.e. Telecommunication and IPH can reduce the frequency and cost of leveling of dug up roads.

Street Lights

The maintenance of street lights in the urban areas is not satisfactory. The total number of street lights in the ULBs is 24,555 comprising 3,173 in Shimla Municipal Corporation, 16,568 in Municipal Councils and 4,814 in *Nagar Panchayats* (FSFC, 1996). With the expansion of city limits, the requirement of street lights has gone up especially in larger ULBs but they have been unable to provide adequate number of street lights.

The ULBs are unable to pay street light bills to the Himachal Pradesh State Electricity Board (HPSEB). On

31.3.2002, arrears worth Rs. 6.32 crore were due at SMC against electricity bills for street lights. Many ULBs are in a similar situation. Against the physical target of installating 6000 street light points during the Ninth Five Year Plan, only 1000 points could be installed.

There is no doubt that installation and maintenance of street lights need considerable expenses which the ULBs are unable to bear due to their poor fiscal base. In this situation, the possibility of associating the private sector should be explored on the pattern of Pune, Ahmadabad, Tirunelveli Municipal Corporations and several other towns. Participation of the local community should also be obtained in the maintenance of street lights in some localities.

Parkings

Parkings are grossly inadequate in the urban areas. The situation is grim in towns like Shimla, Manali, Dalhousie, Bilaspur, Solan, Dharamsala, Kangra, Kullu and many others which receive a large number of vehicles due to the growing influx of tourists. The situation in industrial towns like Parwanoo, Nalagarh and Baddi is even grimmer. The tourists as well as the local citizens have to face inconvenience in parking their vehicles. A large numbers of vehicles are challaned for parking at wrong places such as prohibited roads, market places and congested tourist spots. With the growth of tourism in Himachal Pradesh, an adequate number of parkings should be constructed, especially in towns relevant from the tourist and pilgrimage point of views. It is a capital-intensive activity and is not possible to be financed through the budgetary sources of the ULBs.

It is suggested that the ULBs should access the capital market to raise non-budgetary sources for financing this urban infrastructure service. The private sector can play an important role in augmenting parking facilities in the urban areas on Build-Operate-&-Transfer (BOT) or Build-Own-Operate-&-Transfer (BOOT) basis. ULBs like Kullu, Mandi and a few other towns have constructed parkings under various schemes i.e. Integrated Development of Small and Medium Towns (IDSMT). O&M and recovery of the cost of construction of a parking near the High Court in Shimla has been handed over to the private sector on BOT basis. Now it is not possible to construct the large number of parkings under Integrated Development of Small and Medium Towns (IDSMT) and other municipal schemes. It is therefore suggested that the national and international capital market should be accessed for financing parking facilities in urban areas. For a town like Manali, which has come into the limelight due to growing tourism and visits of foreign and national dignitaries like the Prime Minister of India, it is suggested that specific funds should be provided from the Central Finance Commission and the Tourism department for augmentation of parking facilities.

Other Urban Infrastructure Services

Urban forestry, construction of rain shelters, toilets, railings, steps, small bridges on *nallas* and drainage channels, maintenance of round-abouts, shops, palika bhawans and beautification of streets are important urban infrastructure services but there are deficiencies in their provision and maintenance. Though these services do not require large funds individually, yet together these services require a considerable amount of funds. It is therefore suggested that some of the municipal services should be handed over to the private sector and ULBs should prioritise development of these services.

Land development in urban areas of Himachal Pradesh has serious deficiencies. According to a note provided by the Town and Country Planning Department of Himachal Pradesh, 'haphazard development on fringes of towns, ribbon development along roads, sporadic development on raw land and scattered constructions over eco-fragile slopes are major areas of concern'. At present, with casual approach to land subdivision and building permissions, the violation of existing land use and provisions of development plans have increased. Due to limited availability of serviced land, haphazard development in and around urban centres, has been taking place. 'The landscape in Manali is under strain due to haphazard and uncontrolled construction of hotels and guest houses/restaurants' (Gupta, J.P. and Manoj K. Teotia, 2003).

Traffic and transportation problems have multiplied in larger towns due to poor land use and development pattern. Land development therefore, represents one of the major challenges, for urban policymakers and it is likely to become critical in future. There is a need to formulate effective 'land use/land development policy' to promote eco-friendly sustainable development of urban areas. The State should facilitate all round development of towns and villages so that they can grow in a harmonious manner. Housing and urban development plans/policies should be formulated in such a manner that they do not pose threat to the ecosystem in the state. Perspective plans for land use, traffic and transportation planning should be adhered strictly and proper planning and regulation of subdivisions of land are important aspects of land development in Himachal Pradesh. The development of commercial areas, industrial focal points and other establishments should be allowed to grow in harmony with surrounding environments and ecologically sensitive areas should not be affected by their activities. The state policy on development of new townships should take care of environmental implications, and to the extent possible new emerging towns should be planned and developed rather than developing new towns which will be highly capital intensive and ecologically dangerous.

The active participation of local people and institutions including urban local bodies should be secured for planned development and management of land resources in urban areas. Their involvement can help in recovery of encroached lands and commercial exploitation of such land by streamlining/resettlement of unauthorised colonies.

Housing is not a big problem in urban areas as number of houseless people is negligible in Himachal Pradesh. Himachal Pradesh Housing Board has not projected physical and financial targets for construction of houses for economically weaker sections (EWSs). The Board is of the view that urban areas of Himachal Pradesh do not have housing shortage for EWSs and there are no takers for a large number of houses in several towns constructed by the Board. The growing towns with small volumes of houseless persons and people living below poverty line can take benefit of centrally sponsored scheme of Valmiki Ambedkar Awas Yojana (VAMBAY), launched in 2001 on 50:50 basis between the Central and the State Governments. Despite construction of new dwelling units, the existing dwelling units in poor conditions can be upgraded under this scheme.

'Himachal Pradesh is endowed with exotic natural beauty' (Gupta, J.P. and Manoj K. Teotia, 2003). The large number of tourists visit Himachal for adventure, educational, religious and other purposes. Tourism infrastructure is inadequate in the state to meet the demand and expectations of growing tourists and local urban population. This is affecting tourism infrastructure as well as prospects of higher growth of tourism in Shimla, Manali, Dalhousie and many other small and medium towns. The deficiencies in tourism infrastructure in urban areas must be mitigated to promote tourism and satisfy local people.

The institutional set-up in Himachal Pradesh is not conducive to efficient management and improvement of urban infrastructure. Water supply and sewerage, the most important urban infrastructure service, is provided by the IPH Department of the state government, which is already overburdened with a variety of functions in urban as well rural areas. According to 'Conjunctive Utilisation of Ground Water and Surface Water Resources – A Case Study', over-dominance of civil engineers in the IPH department has led to non-development of ground and surface water resources in the hill state. The case study also mentions under the title 'wastage of public money' that the design of the scheme for water supply has been on seasonal sources and in a majority of cases the lean period discharge was not available and therefore, the systems become non-functional immediately after their completion in summer because of drying up of the water sources (*SER-HP, 2000*, p.102). The functions of urban planning including town planning and regulation of land use are listed in the XIIth Schedule of the 74th Constitutional Amendment and are supposed to be performed by the ULBs. But the Town and Country Planning Organisation (TCPO) of the state government performs these functions. The fragmented functioning, illustrated by the performance of several municipal functions by parastatal departments is affecting the functioning of the ULBs. The Himachal Pradesh Infrastructure Development Board (HPIDB) was created as a Special Purpose Vehicle (SPV) to improve the infrastructure in the state but it has not made any investment to upgrade the urban infrastructure. The funds raised by the SPV, were diverted by the state government to the budget account/consolidated fund of the state. This is a bad practice as far as institutional restructuring for infrastructure development is concerned. It is suggested that specific-purpose funds raised by the HPIDB should not be diverted to the budget account and the HPIDB should be allowed to work independently and invest funds in identified critical sectors of infrastructure including the urban infrastructure.

According to *SER-HP* (2000), environmental issues need to be focused. Unfortunately, low cost sanitation (LCS) is not suitable for hill areas. Further, treatment by septic tanks is not adequate and the effluent is not treated up to the required level of IS:4283. In a cold climate and a rock base, the absorption and digestion of sewage is slow and partial. Sewerage schemes with proper sewage treatment plants seem to be the only alternative. Collection and transportation of solid waste need to be made more effective as every crude dump is an environmental hazard and a health risk because of flies, rats and air pollution from deliberate or accidental burning. Disposal through landfills, composting and incineration needs to be done more effectively (p. 107).

Deficiencies in terms of access to municipal services and O&M requirements need to be addressed to improve the quality of life in urban areas. The institutional mechanism should be strengthened to manage urban infrastructure services efficiently. The services being capital intensive should be considered 'economic goods'. Therefore, progressive recovery of user charges is necessary to sustain the delivery of quality services. With growing revenue and fiscal deficits and loan repayments, the state government is not in a position to continue to finance the growing deficits in pricing and cost recovery of the urban infrastructure and municipal services largely due to excessive subsidisation. In this situation, there is possibility of low budgetary transfers or grants. It is likely to affect the quality and quantity of the urban infrastructure services. The requirement of funds for the urban infrastructure is increasing faster than the revenues of the ULBs. This calls for reforms in the resources of the ULBs and explore avenues of resource mobilisation from non-budgetary sources i.e. capital market.

The technological upgradation is a must. Cost minimisation needs appropriate technology, proper attention to maintenance, curbing the misuse of services and efficient service provision. Also to promote cost effectiveness, different infrastructure projects may be packaged together such as water supply and drainage projects. Coordination between departments providing different services will also reduce the overall cost and should be encouraged through appropriate institutional engineering (*IIR, 1996*, p.28).

There is need for a state level *'urban infrastructure policy'* which could project demand and supply of infrastructure/services, monitor quality and quantity, suggest pricing and cost recovery, develop alternative sources and arrange financial resources for augmentation of the infrastructure and the services. Political will is necessary for pricing and cost recovery. The state should draw up a formula for cross subsidisation of municipal services. Since capital cost of the urban infrastructure is comparatively high in Himachal Pradesh, pricing and cost recovery should be improved to sustain the delivery of important basic urban environmental infrastructure to the growing urban population.

Financing Urban Infrastructure in Himachal Pradesh: Need for Investment and Limitations of Traditional Sources

As at the national level, the investment needs of Himachal Pradesh for financing the urban infrastructure are huge as shown in Table 20.5.

The existing sources of ULBs and IPH are inadequate to meet this demand and the state government has been providing a nominal budgetary support for these urban infrastructure services which are treated as 'social goods' to be provided with or without nominal

TABLE 20.5

Estimated Investment Needs for Financing Urban Infrastructure in Himachal Pradesh

(Rs. in crore)

Particulars	*Coverage up to 2006-07 (%)*	*Estimated Investment Needs for Urban Infrastructure (time frame)*					*Total (2002-03 to 2006-07)*
		2002-03	*2003-04*	*2004-05*	*2005-06*	*2006-07*	
Water supply	100	26.08	26.08	26.08	26.09	26.09	130.42
Sewerage including sewage treatment	100	76.46	76.46	76.46	76.46	76.47	382.31
Solid waste management							
a) Extension/augmentation of collection & transportation	100	4.00	4.00	4.00	4.00	4.00	20.00
b) Treatment and disposal	100	4.00	4.00	4.00	4.00	4.00	20.00
Municipal roads and streets	100	2.00	2.00	2.00	2.00	2.00	10.00
Parkings	100	2.00	2.00	2.00	2.00	2.00	10.00
Street lighting	100	1.00	1.00	1.00	1.00	1.00	5.00
Parks, gardens, railings, urban forestry, rain shelters, bus stands, guest houses, palika bhawans & shops etc.	100	6.00	6.00	6.00	6.00	6.00	30.00
Total		121.54	121.54	121.54	121.55	121.56	607.73

Source: Department of Irrigation and Public Health, Government of Himachal Pradesh.
Department of Urban Development, Government of Himachal Pradesh.

charges. The political will has been against the rationalisation of user charges. Unwillingness of the consumers to pay, along with the unwillingness of the decision makers to charge has caused deterioration of the urban infrastructure and municipal services in Himachal Pradesh. The traditional financial sources are inadequate and have outlived their utility. This has been resulting in a low-level equilibrium trap.

Limitations of Traditional Sources of Financing at Local Level

Budgetary allocations, grants from the state and central governments and own sources of revenue are the traditional sources of income of the ULBs, which have been financing the urban infrastructure. Table 20.6 shows details of income of the ULBs from 1999-2000 to 2001-2002.

The traditional sources of income have been grossly inadequate due to a variety of reasons. According to the FSFC, there is a high degree of heterogeneity not only in the imposition of taxes or levies but also in the efforts to levy or collect these and there is no uniformity of taxes or rates of taxes in different ULBs. House tax/property tax and sanitation/*safai* taxes are not levied by all ULBs. Flow of funds under centrally sponsored schemes (CSSs) and externally aided projects vary from year to year. It leads to a wide variation in the quantum of their resources along with their fiscal dependence on the state government.

Before implementation of recommendations of the FSFC, about half the ULBs were getting octroi compensation grants and the rest were largely dependent on other grants from the state government to meet their staff liability. The ULBs were so dependent on octroi, that a majority of the municipal councils and *nagar panchayats* opined to the FSFC that the state government should re-impose octroi to provide them with a dynamic source of revenue, which can help them in the discharge of routine municipal functions. One of the crucial limitations of the existing sources of income is apparent from the fact that when 'octroi grants' and 'other grants' decreased from Rs.18.49 crore and Rs. 12.09 crore in 2000-01 to Rs. 16.67 crore and Rs. 11.21 crore in 2001-02 respectively, the total income from taxes/fees and shops/stalls also decreased from Rs. 14.61 crore to Rs. 13.44 crore. Own revenues, which are non-buoyant due to the poor tax base, have been unable to finance the growing needs of the urban infrastructure and the cost of their maintenance expenditure.

Resource mobilisation efforts at the local level are totally missing. There is absolutely no change in the fiscal and functional domain of the ULBs after the 74th Constitutional Amendment and conformity legislation by the state government i.e. Himachal Pradesh Municipal Act, 1994 and Himachal Pradesh Municipal Corporation Act, 1994. The FSFC noted that the areas of revenue generation were regulated by the state government. Poor urban governance manifested in poor service delivery, growing wasteful expenditure on committed liabilities, weak fiscal and functional domain of the ULBs and their inability to recover even O&M cost of the municipal services is one of the key factors impinging on the development of urban infrastructure in the state. This section describes the limitations of the traditional sources of financing, particularly property tax and user charges, budgetary transfers, loans, grants and shared taxes. An effort has also been made to analyse issues relating to municipal expenditure and budgetary surplus/deficits, which are important in the context of financing the urban infrastructure.

Own Sources of Revenue

The past trend of own revenues shows that their growth and base have been poor to finance the growing needs of the urban infrastructure and services. There is no fiscal discipline among the ULBs and no state policy has been formulated to mobilise their own sources of

TABLE 20.6

Total Income of Urban Local Bodies of Himachal Pradesh from 1999-00 to 2001-02

(Rs. in crores)

Years	*Taxes & Fees*	*Shops/Stalls*	*Interest*	*Misc.*	*Sub Total*	*Octroi Grants*	*Sub Total*	*Other Grants*	*Grand Total*
(1)	*(2)*	*(3)*	*(4)*	*(5)*	*(6) (2+3+4+5)*	*(7)*	*(8) (6+7)*	*(9)*	*(10) (8+9)*
1999-00	8.03	3.81	0.98	5.21	18.03	16.25	34.28	12.93	47.21
2000-01	10.83	3.78	0.78	4.47	19.86	18.49	38.35	12.09	50.44
2001-02	9.02	4.42	0.97	5.38	19.79	16.67	36.46	11.21	47.67

Source: Department of Urban Development, Government of Himachal Pradesh.

revenue. The recommendations of the FSFC of Himachal Pradesh to mobilise own resources have not been considered seriously and there is a huge shortfall in the projections of own revenues and the actual income of the ULBs as is the case of the Shimla Municipal Corporation (Table 20.7).

TABLE 20.7

Shortfall in the Own Revenues of Shimla Municipal Corporation

(Rs. in crores)

Particulars	*1996-97*	*1997-98*	*1998-99*	*1999-00*	*2000-01*	*Total*
Recommended by the FSFC	5.52	6.18	6.92	7.75	8.68	35.05
Actual income	4.89	4.77	5.10	6.58	7.39	28.73
Shortfall	0.63	1.41	1.82	1.17	1.29	6.32

Source: The First State Finance Commission of Himachal Pradesh. Municipal Corporation of Shimla.

With the poor base of own revenues coupled with decreasing grants, little or no funds are left with the ULBs for capital expenditure and asset creation. The memorandum submitted to the SSFC by the Department of Urban Development (2000) shows huge deficits in own income and expenditure of the ULBs of Himachal Pradesh though there is scope for exploiting the full potential of their own sources and to utilise the surplus for financing the urban infrastructure. Own sources can be classified as tax and non-tax revenue.

Tax Revenue

The sources of tax revenue are property tax, entertainment tax, electricity duty, water tax and advertisement tax. According to the FSFC, house or property tax is the major source of tax revenue. Despite its large share, property tax has not grown to its full potential. Other sources of tax revenue yield a negligible income due to the low tax rates. The tax revenue is less than the non-tax revenue. Table 20.8 shows the rates of various sources of tax revenue collected in the urban areas.

The rates of taxes are lower than in Punjab, Haryana and many other states. It is adversely affecting the fiscal position of the ULBs in the state. Since detailed information on the sources of tax revenue is not available at the state level, an effort has been made to analyse the trend of tax revenue of the Shimla Municipal Corporation as shown in Table 20.9.

TABLE 20.8

Rates of Various Sources of Tax Revenue in Urban Areas of Himachal Pradesh

Particulars	*Rates*
General tax*/property tax	7.5% to 15% of ARV
Show tax	Rs. 50/- per show
Tax on consumption of electricity duty	Rs. 0.01 to 0.02** per unit
Sale of liquor	Rs. 1.00 per bottle
Cess on transfer of immovable properties	2% of stamp duty
Tax on advertisements	Rs. 300 per sq. meter per annum

Source: Department of Urban Development, Government of Himachal Pradesh.

Note: * In Shimla general tax is levied @ 15 per cent of ARV on land and buildings. In other ULBs the maximum limit of general tax is 12.5 per cent of ARV.

** the rate limit of two paisa per unit tax on consumption of energy is for municipal corporation only. In other towns the rate of tax on consumption of electricity to be transferred to ULBs has been fixed @paisa one per unit.

TABLE 20.9

Major Sources of Tax Revenue of Shimla Municipal Corporation (1997-98 to 2001-02)

(Rs. in Lakh)

Sources of Tax Revenue	*1997-98*	*1998-99*	*1999-00*	*2000-01*	*2001-02*
General tax/property tax	206.98	226.07	251.52	281.95	294.80
Show tax, stamp duty, electricity duty & excise duty	0.35	1.07	1.02	45.48	58.89
Sewerage tax*	-	-	-	16.97	20.83
Sanitation** and water tax***	3.72	0.45	0.63	0.47	0.64
Vehicle tax on cycles, animal tax and entry Tax****	0.02	0.02	0.01	14.11	0.09
Total	**211.07**	**227.61**	**253.18**	**358.98**	**375.25**

Source: Municipal Corporation of Shimla

Note: * Sewerage tax is charged on commercial buildings only @ 15 per cent of general tax on buildings.

** Sanitation tax discontinued after 1997-98.

*** Water tax is levied @ 2.5 per cent of ARV on properties/lands without meter based water supply.

**** Entry tax was withdrawn from the SMC by the State Government of Himachal Pradesh.

There is considerable scope for improvement in show tax, water tax, share of stamp duty, electricity duty and excise duty etc. Though the share of property tax in the tax revenue of the SMC is good yet it is beset with a variety of problems, which are not different from the deficiencies in property tax in other ULBs of the state.

Property tax

Property tax is a major source of tax revenue in the urban areas but it has a variety of problems as given below: -

- the annual rental value (ARV) system is outdated and has outlived its utility due to deficiencies in assessment, collection and administration of the tax
- many municipalities are not levying property tax
- no survey has been done to identify un-assessed properties and proper assessment of existing properties that could widen the tax net
- collection of property tax in most of the ULBs is far below the demand, achievable targets/ standards resulting in accumulation of arrears
- a large proportion of properties are exempted from property tax
- the existing system does not have an in-built mechanism for periodic determination of ARV to cope with inflation
- billing and collection procedures are manual, time consuming and can be manipulated
- the fixation of ARV of any building or land leaves scope for manipulations and
- rates which are low and vary from municipality to municipality are further lowered with the intervention/discretion of the elected members of the municipalities

Due to these deficiencies, property tax collection remains meager in most of the ULBs and arrears are accumulating. Other sources of tax revenue also suffer from multiple deficiencies and income from these taxes is not enough even to finance their administration.

After visits to the ULBs of Shimla, Mandi, Kullu, Solan, Sundernagar, Manali and Rewalsar, and discussions with their elected and appointed members on various issues including their fiscal and functional domain, we found that tax compliance was poor as the ULBs did not have adequate powers to attach the immovable properties of defaulters. The process of recovery of arrears was lengthy and unfruitful with excessive interference of politicians, which affected collection efficiency of ULBs. During 2001-02, SMC was able to realise only 43.25 per cent of the total tax collection, 67.33 per cent of the current demand collection and only 17.01 per cent of arrears demand collection from tax revenues. On March 31,2001, outstanding tax arrears of the SMC from taxes were Rs. 4.07 crore, that was almost equal to their demand of Rs. 4.43 crore during 2001-02.

Non-tax Revenue

Non-tax revenue consists mainly of grants in lieu of octroi, fees, fines, rents and user charges on water supply and sewerage. Fees and fines include the charges for licences, copying, permits and other municipal services while rents are collected on municipal properties and lands. Octroi grants have been contributing the major share and have been about half the total non-tax revenue of Shimla Municipal Corporation and even more in several ULBs. The non-tax revenue in Himachal Pradesh is not adequate to meet even the growing demand of O&M of the municipal services and the growing committed expenditure, leave aside the augmentation of urban

TABLE 20.10

Non-tax Revenue of Shimla Municipal Corporation (1997-98 to 2001-02)

(Rs. in lakh)

Sources of Non-tax Revenue	*1997-98*	*1998-99*	*1999-00*	*2000-01*	*2001-02*
Grants in lieu of octroi	349.60	385.33	423.37	459.02	459.01
Sale of water, meter rent, recoveries, plugging charges etc.	147.11	156.63	173.88	170.57	172.32
Rent of municipal land/ buildings/ markets	55.48	45.22	121.37	92.97	93.28
Sale of municipal assets	—	—	—	29.56	21.08
License fees for trade and vehicles, copying and tehbazari fees etc.	7.15	4.75	7.53	10.78	9.62
Forest income	3.29	4.63	4.30	1.77	8.51
Library, laboratory, birth/death registration, removal of carcasses/ slaughter house fee, dak bungalow/rest house charges	2.69	2.83	3.07	4.01	5.65
Contribution towards pay of health staff	6.00	21.00	36.92	18.17	35.75
Interest	13.47	22.21	19.31	9.69	40.33
Miscellaneous unclassified receipts	30.66	24.87	38.50	42.21	75.04
Total	**615.45**	**667.47**	**828.25**	**838.75**	**920.59**

Source: Municipal Corporation of Shimla.

infrastructure. Table 20.10 indicates the trend in non-tax revenue of the Shimla Municipal Corporation.

There is almost stagnation in most of the sources of non-tax revenue. Income from the sale of water, meter rent and recoveries and income of rent from municipal lands/buildings and markets decreased during 1999-00 & 2001-02. On March 31, 2001, the arrears of rent of municipal properties in Shimla were Rs. 1.67 crore against the current demand of Rs. 1.15 crore for 2001-02 which could not be realised in full. Income from fees and fines is not growing. This is affecting the fiscal domain of the Shimla Municipal Corporation and its development works. The position of non-tax revenue in other ULBs is even worse and leaves tremendous scope for improvement. The user charges are negligible and are not growing enough to recover even a small portion of the O&M costs, not to speak of capital costs.

USER CHARGES

Cost recovery in urban environmental infrastructure is effected through user charges and taxes or a combination of both. Therefore, user charges should ideally be linked to recover the full cost of O&M and provision of infrastructure/services. At present, user charges are grossly inadequate in almost all the towns. None of the ULBs collects user charges for water supply and sewerage except those of Shimla, Solan and Palampur municipalities as this function is with the IPH Department of the state government. The income and expenditure on water supply and sewerage (WSS) in towns managed by the IPH Department are shown in Table 20.11.

TABLE 20.11

Income and Expenditure on Water Supply and Sewerage in Urban Areas

(Rs. in crores)

Years	*Income*	*Expenditure*	*Surplus(+)/ Deficit(-)*	*Ratio of expenditure to income*
1	*2*	*3*	*4(2-3)*	*5(3/2)*
1997-98	1.86	25.03	-23.17	13.4
1998-99	1.99	40.40	-38.41	20.3
1999-00	1.01	35.00	-33.99	34.6
2000-01	1.05	31.90	-30.85	30.4
2001-02	3.75	29.66	-25.91	7.9
Total	9.66	161.99	-152.33	16.8

Source: Department of Irrigation and Public Health, Government of Himachal Pradesh.

As is obvious from the Table 20.11, there is a huge gap between the income and expenditure on water supply and sewerage. Sewerage is provided almost free and income from water tax/charges is not growing. It is largely due to lack of periodic revision of water rates, which are already low and non payment of water bills by ULBs. SMC alone has not paid water bills of Rs. 15.47 crore to IPH (as on March 31, 2002). At the same time the expenditure is huge and is growing fast. The rates of water supply are given in Table 20.12.

The rates of water supply were revised by the IPH Department in 2001, after nine years and that too nominally. In the latest revision (w.e.f. March 1, 2001), one of the good initiatives was to suggest volumetric (meter based) supply of water and fix penalties for not installing meters within a stipulated time. As a result

TABLE 20.12

Rates of Water Supply in Urban Areas*

Particular	*Rates Charged in Towns where Service is Maintained by the Irrigation and Public Health Department*				*Rates Charged by Shimla Municipal Corporation*			
	Domestic		*Commercial*		*Domestic*		*Commercial*	
	1992	*2001*	*1992*	*2001*	*1992*	*2003***	*1992*	*2003***
Metered water supply (in Rs./ kl/month)	0.20/kl=up to 4.5 kl 0.35/kl=4.5 to 9.0 kl 0.55/kl =9.0 kl and above	2.00/kl	1.35/kl	4.00/kl	1.80/kl= up to 100 KL 2.40/kl= More than 100 kl	No charges= upto 1kl 30/ month=1 to 6 kl; 3.5/kl=above 6 kl	6.00/kl	100/month= upto 6 kl 12.5/kl= above 6 kl
Un-metered flat rates (in Rs./month per connection)	40.00	NA	NA	NA	NA	NA	NA	NA

Source: Department of Irrigation and Public Health, Government of Himachal Pradesh.

Note: * Bulk water rates charged by the IPH from i) ULBs & Housing Board (except SMC) = Rs. 1.50/KL ii) SMC = Rs.4.00/KL; NA= Not specified in *Notifications i) IPH (3)-18/86-Vol.III dated August 6,1992 ii) LSG-C (I)-29/83-II dated August 11,1992 iii) IPH (3)/86-Vol.III dated February 28,2001 iv) IPH (3) 18/86-Vol.III dated July 13,2001.*

** SMC passed resolution on 16/07/03 but rates have yet to be notified by the State Government.

TABLE 20.13

Pricing and Cost Recovery of Water Supply in Shimla: Some Crucial Aspects

Particulars	*Cost (Rs./kl)*	*Recovery (Rs./kl)*
Cost of water produced by State Government for Shimla Municipal Corporation	Rs. 22/- kl	Negligible, as huge arrears are due at Shimla Municipal Corporation (Rs. 15.48 crore as on 31.3.2002)
Cost of water supplied by Shimla Municipal Corporation	i) O&M cost =Rs. 4.65/kl ii) Paid to IPH = Rs.4.00/kl Total cost = Rs. 8.65/kl	Rs. 1.80/kl-Domestic supply* Rs. 6.00/kl- Commercial supply* Deficit Rs. 6.85/kl–Domestic supply Rs. 2.65/kl-Commecial supply (Huge arrears are due at consumers)

Source: *Annual Report of SMC, 2001-02.*

Note: * -These rates have been revised by SMC on 16.07.2003 @ Rs. 3.5/kl (above 6 kl) for domestic and Rs. 12.5/kl (above 6 kl) for commercial consumption, but have not been notified by the state government.

of increase in income from water supply, the revenue from WSS more than doubled between 2000-01 and 2001-02 (Table 20.11), the highest growth of income in the last five years. But this clause was withdrawn by another notification on July 13, 2001, and flat rates of water for domestic consumers were reintroduced and frozen at Rs. 40 per month. With this change, the income of the IPH from water supply and sewerage will decrease considerably.

The income of Shimla Municipal Corporation from water supply & sewerage has also been poor. It revised its water rates in January 2003 and then July 2003, after 11 years. This is a good initiative but even with the revised rates, the corporation is likely to bear the burden of deficits from domestic as well as commercial water supply. The pricing and cost recovery of water supply in Shimla has been poor as shown in Table 20.13.

Cost recovery is negligible and the arrears are growing. It is unfortunate that despite the growing per capita income of the people, user charges continue to be poor and there are no efforts to recover even O&M costs. Water rates are not in proportion to the consumption and paying capacity of the people. The rich and the poor pay the same rates and the higher income groups are drawing the maximum benefit form subsidisation. In the present system, the gap between income and expenditure on WSS is likely to increase if immediate steps are not taken to recover O&M costs. Table 20.14 shows income and expenditure of SMC on water supply (since O&M of water supply in Shimla is looked after by the corporation) from 1997-98 to 2001-02.

Table 20.14 shows that the growth of income from the sale of water has been poor while expenditure has increased considerably. The expenditure on establishment and contingency, which was about Rs. 4 lakh less than the income of the SMC from the sale of water in 1997-98, overtook the income in 1998-99 and in 2001-02 it was Rs. 19 lakh above the income from water. One of the reasons for the slow increase in the income from water has been the lack of revision of water rates for a decade. With increasing deficits on revenue as well as capital accounts, the corporation has been depending on budgetary transfers and grants for works and O&M of the urban infrastructure and the municipal services. There are no monthly charges for sewerage by IPH except one-time connection charges, security and application fee which are nominal as shown in Table 20.15.

TABLE 20.14

Income and Expenditure of Shimla Municipal Corporation on Water Supply

(Rs. in lakh)

Particulars	*1997-98*	*1998-99*	*1999-00*	*2000-01*	*2001-02*
Income	129.30	141.90	159.98	156.18	159.52
Expenditure	153.78	189.67	206.04	228.98	209.04
i) On establishment	93.97	122.56	134.81	152.02	150.53
ii) Contingency/office expenses	31.19	29.60	28.70	39.67	27.87
iii) Works/maintenance	28.62	37.51	42.53	37.29	30.64

Source: Municipal Corporation of Shimla.

Note: Expenditure excludes bulk water charges paid to the IPH @ Rs. 4.00/kl.

Sewerage is a highly capital-intensive activity, and is more costly in Himachal Pradesh due to the difficult hilly terrain. Despite this, it is highly subsidised in comparison with other states. SMC has recently revised the rates of sewerage connection charges. These rates

TABLE 20.15

Connection Charges, Security and Application Fee for Sewerage in Urban Areas

(In Rs. per connection)

Particulars	Connection Charges		Security		Application Fee	
	Domestic	Commercial	Domestic	Commercial	Domestic	Commercial
Towns under IPH	150	300	150	300	10	50
Shimla Municipal Corporation*	1000	1000	500	2000	10	10

Source: Department of Irrigation and Public Health, Government of Himachal Pradesh, Municipal Corporation of Shimla.
Note: * Connection charges have been fixed by SMC @ Rs. 1000 per seat w.e.f. January 1, 2003.

are very poor in the towns under IPH. The rates of connection charges for sewerage should be revised by IPH and sewerage tax should be introduced in all the towns at the pattern of SMC for progressive recovery of O&M cost of this service.

Pricing and cost recovery of water supply and sewerage is totally unsustainable. The cost recovery of sewerage is almost negligible. Institutional arrangements are not favourable to cost recovery of water supply and sewerage as there is no interaction between the IPH department and the ULBs. IPH has been unable to formulate or implement a demand-based and cost-indexed pricing mechanism for water supply and sewerage. Similar is the fate of efforts of the ULBs, which have failed to recover even a part of O&M of user charges.

Recovery of other sources of non-tax revenue is also negligible due to the low rates and poor administrative and management practices. The ULBs have been depending on budgetary transfers and grants to maintain even O&M, leave aside capital works.

Fiscal Transfers/Budgetary Allocations

Historically, the revenue and capital account requirements of the ULBs have been met by the state government through budgetary allocations and fiscal transfers, which have been grossly inadequate to meet the growing investment needs of the ULBs. The mismatch in functional and fiscal position of ULBs is likely to grow with growth of urban population and expansion of the cities. At the same time, the state government may not be able to continue budgetary support to the ULBs in the same manner due to growing revenue and fiscal deficits of the state. The ULBs with poor institutional capacities do not bargain for fiscal autonomy with the state government, which has been using 'fiscal transfers' as a means of state control over the ULBs.

Though investment needs of the ULBs in the wake of growing urbanisation are likely to increase, yet public sector institutions (PSIs) with their limited financial resources may not be able to provide the desirable level and quality of services. Moreover there is a regime at central and state levels to reduce budgetary allocations and grants to the PSIs, i.e. local bodies and various urban development departments of the state. According to the *Report of the Committee on India Vision-2020* (Planning Commission, 2002), 'decentralisation of municipal governance has led to a substantial reduction in budgetary allocations for infrastructural development.'

The 74th amendment seeks to provide more fiscal powers to the ULBs through the State Finance Commission, which suggests fiscal devolution to them by assigning a share in state taxes, imposition of new taxes by the ULBs and devolution of grants-in-aid. Despite this, the ULBs are unable to function as powerful institutions of local self-government. It is largely due to inadequate transfers and irregular grants-in-aid (unpredictable and grossly inadequate) to meet the growing expenditure of the ULBs on wage bills, higher costs of O&M and new capital works.

Loans and Grants

The ULBs have been raising institutional loans from HUDCO, which have been inadequate to finance the growing needs of the urban infrastructure. Moreover, the pattern of infrastructure financing through institutional loans is undergoing a change due to huge inflow of funds from the national and international capital markets at comparatively low interest rates and even without government guarantees. Private sector loans can now be raised directly from the financial institutions. *ESCROW* mechanism, a simple and transparent procedure, is increasingly used for assured loan repayments. In future, the government of Himachal Pradesh with its growing fiscal and financial burden may be reluctant to give guarantees on behalf of the

TABLE 20.16

State and Central Government Grants to Shimla Municipal Corporation

(Rs. in lakh)

Source of Grants	*1997-98*	*1998-99*	*1999-00*	*2000-01*	*2001-02*
NORAD	5.74	141.00	40.00	226.50	292.50
TFC/EFC grants	17.94	13.31	12.21	14.71	26.20
GIA for committed liabilities (amount received for payment of arears of revised pay scale)	418.12	128.00	—	—	—
EIUS/ NSDP	20.95	75.82	69.36	39.63	—
SJSRY	12.03	14.39	62.14	8.57	—
GIA for payments of cost of water to IPH department	100.00	100.00	34.56	—	—
GIA for maintenance of roads, salary of safai karamcharis Land repair of revoli tunnel	145.58	—	—	25.21	—
Urban development, roads and buildings, rain damages, toilets and street lights	128.88	—	—	—	—
GIA for rain damages and different schemes (DC Shimla)	65.90	93.60	61.70	74.03	36.05
GIA for different schemes (Tourism Deptt)	43.75	24.79	3.60	—	—
GIA received from the Governor of Himachal Pradesh	—	—	—	—	1.00
Modern slaughterhouse	0.00	75.00	—	0.00	0.00
Total	**958.89**	**665.91**	**283.57**	**388.65**	**355.75**

Source: Municipal Corporation of Shimla.

ULBs to raise loans for urban infrastructure projects. This is the right time for ULBs to go for loans for commercially viable infrastructure projects, which are now available without government guarantees.

As far as grants are concerned, the ULBs cannot rely on these unpredictable and inadequate sources. This has been one of the major limitations of the ULBs as they cannot plan their future strategy in the absence of a clear, regular and growth-oriented source of finance. Table 20.16 shows the trend of grants (central as well as state) to SMC. The grants declined nearly three times between 1997-98 and 2002-02 and were the lowest in 1999-2000, in the five years under consideration. The Tenth/Eleventh Finance Commission (TFC/EFC) grants have been irregular as these come through the state government. The same is the fate of other grants for centrally sponsored schemes such as the National Slum Development Programme (NSDP), Swarna Jayanti Shahri Rojgar Yojana (SJSRY), and grants-in-aid from the state government for the maintenance and creation of assets and meeting other liabilities.

Grants to other ULBs, have also been irregular and inadequate. The grants in lieu of abolition of octroi, has been poor. The octroi grants recommended by the FSFC have not been transferred in full as shown in Table 20.17.

A large number of ULBs (25 out of 53) have been the victim of non-devolution of octroi grants, as 11 ULBs were not levying octroi at the time of its abolition and 14 ULBs came into existence after the abolition of octroi (1.4.1982). These ULBs are fiscally weak and unable to maintain even the minimum level of services. The FSFC recommended allocation of octroi grants to all ULBs to meet their expenditure on establishment, development and maintenance in proportion to their population. But this has not solved the problems of the small ULBs with huge liabilities due to poor growth of own resources and the heavy influx of tourists. Capital costs in some of the ULBs are also high due to climatic and topographic factors. The effects of poor urban infrastructure and municipal services on ecology are serious not only for these municipalities but for other rural and urban settlements. In the light of these facts, it is suggested that higher share of octroi grants should be transferred to the ULBs not on the basis of population alone. The

TABLE 20.17

Grants-in-Lieu of Abolition of Octroi Recommended by the First State Finance Commission

(Rs. in crore)

Year	*Amount Recommended*	*Amount Released*	*Shortfall*
1996-97 to 2000-01	74.55	64.61	9.94

Source: Department of Urban Development, Government of Himachal Pradesh.

factors like area, committed expenditure on wages and salaries, the funds required for important and commercially viable projects sensitive from the point of view of environmental infrastructure development and growth of tourism should also be taken into account.

Recently the Second State Finance Commission (SSFC) of Himachal Pradesh has renamed "grants-in-lieu of octroi" as "developmental grants", as department of urban development (DUD) could not apprehend the basic issue which was taken care of while fixing the base year figure and mistook this grant only as the 'grant-in-lieu of octroi', whereas it covered grants required to perform delegated functions by ULBs as recommended by the FSFC. Still, the scheme of distribution of grants and base amount has not been changed much and therefore the fate of ULBs seems to be uncertain.

Receipts from Taxes Shared with the State Government

It has been observed that the ULBs are not receiving adequate funds in the form of shared taxes such as electricity duty, excise duty, entertainment duty and stamp duty. After visiting a large number of ULBs we found that the share of electricity duty which goes to the ULBs at the rate of Rs. 0.01 to Rs. 0.02 per unit on consumption of electricity in the urban areas does not go to them in full and hence huge arrears have accumulated with the HPSEB. The share of the ULBs in electricity duty in HP is negligible in comparison with Punjab and many other states. There is scope for enhancing the income of the municipalities from electricity duty by revising the rates and collecting arrears.

Excise duty on sale of the liquor in the urban areas, which is transferred to the ULBs @ Rs. 1 per bottle is negligible in comparison with the share of excise duty transferred to the ULBs in other states such as Punjab. In Punjab, an additional excise duty of 7 per cent of the auction money of country made liquor and 16 per cent of the Indian made foreign liquor is collected by the state government in lieu of octroi on the import of liquor to municipal areas and reimbursed to the municipalities. The government of Himachal Pradesh must enhance the share of ULBs in excise duty and transfer the due amount to these bodies.

Show tax which is charged @ Rs. 50 per show is also negligible against the burden on the ULBs of maintaining cleanliness around the cinema halls. The rates of show tax are as low as Rs. 5 in some of the ULBs. It is suggested that show tax should be revised immediately and at least Rs. 2 to 3 per ticket should be imposed on the cinema halls instead of a flat rate per show.

The share of the ULBs in stamp duty collected by the state government on the sale or transfer of property is only 2 per cent. In Punjab, the FSFC recommended 20 per cent of net proceeds of stamp duty to be shared by the ULBs and panchayats on derivative principles. To improve the fiscal health of the ULBs, Himachal Pradesh can also transfer a higher share of stamp duty to the ULBs and PRIs, on the basis of derivative principles.

The trend of revenue receipts from shared taxes indicates near stagnation. It is largely due to the low rates and non-payment of arrears by the departments concerned. The state government has not been taking it seriously and the ULBs continue to suffer on this account. The DUD in its memorandums to the First and Second State Finance Commissions of Himachal Pradesh sought share for the ULBs in some major state taxes such as general sales tax, passenger and goods tax, excise duty on liquor, entertainment duty/tax (cinematography) etc. The DUD has requested the commissions that luxury tax on hotels, tax on professions/trades/callings and employment, stamp duty on transfer of properties and tax on vehicles should be exclusively collected and utilised by the ULBs or can be collected by the state and transferred to ULBs. Since about 80 per cent of the major state taxes are collected in municipal areas, the ULBs have the rights to a higher share in these taxes.

Limitations of Traditional Sources of Financing at Central Level

Grants through the Central Finance Commission and development grants for centrally sponsored schemes such as Accelerated Urban Water Supply Programme (AUWSP), National Slum Development Programme (NSDP), Swarna Jayanti Shahari Rozgar Yojana (SJSRY) and Integrated Development of Small and Medium Towns (IDSMT), Low Cost Sanitation etc. have been irregular and inadequate to meet the growing need for the urban infrastructure.

There is a need for enhancing the grants for centrally sponsored schemes for the development of the urban infrastructure and improvement of the municipal services. Efforts should be made to transfer these grants directly to the ULBs so that they can prioritise the development activities according to the needs of the people. The following section describes the shortfalls in the amounts recommended and released for centrally sponsored schemes and problems relating to grants recommended by the Central Finance Commissions.

Shortfalls in Amounts Recommended and Released for Centrally Sponsored Schemes

Amounts recommended for implementing centrally sponsored schemes (CSSs) are not released in full. Table 20.18 shows the shortfall in the amount recommended and released for centrally sponsored schemes.

TABLE 20.18

Shortfall in the Amount Recommended by the State Finance Commission and Amount Released for Centrally Sponsored Schemes

(Rs. in crore)

Year	*Amount Recommended*	*Amount Released*	*Shortfall*
1996-97 to 2000-01	13.75	7.25	6.50

Source: Department of Urban Development, Government of Himachal Pradesh.

There is a huge gap between the central government grants recommended by the FSFC and the amount released. The impact of CSSs on infrastructure development in the urban areas has not been good. It is largely due to the poor control of the ULBs as well as the state government on implementation of the schemes. The non-receipt of the recommended grants aggravates the situation. One of the factors for the shortfall in grants for CSSs is that the state government does not contribute its matching share and the unutilised central government grants go back. Another problem is that the central government does not release adequate grants regularly. This aspect needs to be tackled seriously and 100 per cent grants should be utilised by the state by contributing its due share. Strict monitoring and regular evaluation/assessment of the CSSs are necessary for their effective implementation, better utilisation of grants and greater quantitative and qualitative impact on the quality of life in the urban areas.

Grants to ULBs based on Recommendations of the Central Finance Commissions

Article 280(3)(c) of the Constitution empowers the Central Finance Commission (CFC) to make recommendations on the measures needed to augment the consolidated fund of the state to supplement the resources of the municipalities. After the implementation of the 74th Amendment, the ULBs of Himachal Pradesh have received grants recommended by the TFC, which were very nominal. The share of the ULBs of Himachal Pradesh in the grants recommended by the EFC is shown in Table 20.19.

TABLE 20.19

Grants to Urban Local Bodies Recommended by the Eleventh Finance Commission

(Rs. in crore)

2000-01	*2001-02*	*2002-03*	*2003-04*	*2004-05*	*Total*
0.78	0.78	0.78	0.78	0.78	3.90

Source: Report of the Eleventh Finance Commission (2000), Government of India.

The EFC grants allocated to ULBs of the Himachal Pradesh are grossly inadequate. It is largely due to the methodology adopted by the commission for determining the allocation to the ULBs of Himachal Pradesh. The state has not yet benefited from the EFC allocations for ULBs due to the poor composite weightage (w), decided on the basis of percentage of urban population (w=40 per cent), urban areas (w=10 per cent), distance from highest per capita income (w=20 per cent), own revenue efforts of ULBs (w=10 per cent) and index of decentralisation (w=20 per cent). On the basis of this methodology, the composite index for the state's share comes to only 0.195 per cent against 15.813 per cent for Maharashtra, 12.582 per cent for UP, 9.874 per cent for West Bengal and 9.668 per cent for Tamil Nadu. The EFC allocation to the ULBs of Himachal Pradesh for five years comes to only Rs. 3.9 crore against Rs. 316.2 crore for Maharashtra. Himachal Pradesh, no doubt has a small urban population but the size of their problems is very big. The towns of Himachal Pradesh have proportionately larger areas to cover, which results in higher costs. Their obligations to protect the ecology and natural resources are important in comparison with those of the ULBs in plains. Hence many aspects of the EFC formula become irrelevant for allocations to the ULBs in Himachal Pradesh. Being a special category state, Himachal Pradesh has been receiving huge amounts of central assistance from the Government of India but its ULBs are suffering for want of funds in the form of grants, which come through the CFCs or the Government of India. The ULBs should be allocated higher share by the Twelfth Finance Commission for protecting natural resources i.e. river water, forests and air, conserve environment and preserve the heritage of tourist spots. Any discussion on the limitations of traditional sources of financing is incomplete without

TABLE 20.20

Total Expenditure of Urban Local Bodies in Himachal Pradesh

(Rs. in crore)

Year	*Establishment*	*Development Grants*	*Development/Maintenance from Own Income*	*Centrally/State Sponsored Schemes*	*Total*
1	2	3	4	5	6 (2+3+4+5)
1999-00	26.13	8.80	6.04	6.80	47.77
2000-01	26.76	10.45	4.96	7.57	50.44
2001-02	28.14	16.91	11.83	—	56.88

Source: Department of Urban Development, Government of Himachal Pradesh.

discussing the limitations of the municipal expenditure pattern and its effects on urban infrastructure.

Municipal Expenditure

Municipal expenditure comprises revenue and capital expenditure, apart from various financial and banking-related expenditure such as deposits, advances and employees compensation etc. Table 20.20 shows the expenditure of the ULBs on establishment, development through grants from the state and central governments and own revenues and expenditure on the creation of assets under the centrally sponsored schemes.

Revenue expenditure on establishment accounts for a major share of municipal expenditure in Himachal Pradesh. The main source of capital expenditure for the creation of assets, is state and central government development grants. Development and maintenance from own income is nominal due to lack of buoyancy in tax and non-tax revenues. The ULBs have been financing their capital investments through institutional loans which have been nominal and have been routed through lengthy procedures backed by state government guarantees. This is resulting in deficiencies in the urban infrastructure and services. No efforts have been made to mobilise additional sources to finance the growing needs of developmental works and reduce wasteful expenditure. Establishment expenditure is growing unabatedly. The committed expenditure of SMC on salary and contingency has increased considerably between 1997-98 and 2001-02 as shown in Table 20.21.

The salary and contingencies in Shimla and other ULBs are eating up a major share of the total income and are much higher than their own income. This is despite the fact that some of the ULBs like Rewalsar and Banjar do not have adequate regular staff. The situation is grim, as developmental activities have been suffering due to less availability of funds for urban infrastructure.

TABLE 20.21

Share of Salary and Contingencies in Total Expenditure and Revenue Income of Shimla Municipal Corporation

(Rs in crore)

Particulars	*1997-98*	*1998-99*	*1999-00*	*2000-01*	*2001-02*
Salary and contingencies	7.29	9.68	9.92	10.83	10.71
Expenditure(excluding SA*)	11.16	12.79	12.39	12.33	12.41
Income (Excluding SA)	8.27	8.95	10.81	11.98	12.96
Own income (excluding grants)	4.77	5.10	4.23	4.59	4.60
%age of salary/contingencies to expenditure	65.3	75.6	80.0	87.8	86.3
%age of salary/contingencies to income	88.2	108.1	91.7	90.4	82.6
%age of salary/contingencies to own income	152.83	189.8	243.5	236.0	232.8

Source: Municipal Corporation of Shimla.

Note: * SA=Suspense Account.

According to the SSFC, present system of centralised cadre of employees merits (except Secretary/Executive Officers) to be reviewed and status-quo-ante restored as it will lead to reduction in expenditure and better local control. The smaller local bodies should not have any permanent staff except Secretary, as system of engaging staff on part time or contractual basis would lead to reduction in expenditure.

The Trend of Budgetary Surplus/ Deficit of Urban Local Bodies

An analysis of the budgetary surplus or deficit of the ULBs is necessary. The growth of income and expenditure depends on the tax base and its effective exploitation, effective use of resources, transfer from higher levels of the government and the expenditure on revenue and capital obligations. The income and expenditure of the ULBs in last three years is in shown Table 20.22.

TABLE 20.22

Trend of Budgetary Position of Urban Local Bodies in Himachal Pradesh

(Rs. in crore)

Year	*Income*	*Expenditure*	*Surplus (+)/ Deficit(-)*
1	2	3	4 (2-3)
1999-00	47.21	47.77	(-0.56)
2000-01	50.44	49.75	(+0.69)
2001-02	47.66	56.87	(-9.21)

Source: Department of Urban Development, Government of Himachal Pradesh.

The trend of budgetary surplus or deficit is unpredictable and unimpressive. Budgetary deficit has grown considerably due to a shortfall in the octroi grants, taxes, fees and higher expenditure on establishment and maintenance. It is also due to variation in the flow of funds under CSSs and externally aided projects. One of the major aspects of this budgetary trend is that GIA decided at the end of financial year are released to ULBs during next financial year and are accommodated in the year of receipt. The ULBs of Himachal depend heavily on grants in lieu of octroi and other grants, which have been declining and are not likely to increase. The deficit in 2001-02 is not realistic as data regarding the carry forward amount was not available with the department. Moreover, arrears of water charges and electricity dues payable to IPH and HPSEB were cleared recently.

A review of the performance of plan outlays, programmes and policies during the five year plans of Himachal Pradesh indicate that the urban infrastructure has been one of the most neglected areas for investment. Urban infrastructure activities were determined by the availability of funds, which has been a major problem in this resource scarce state. Himachal Pradesh government has largely been depending on central government assistance, which is higher than the own resources of the state. The fiscal over dependence of Himachal Pradesh on central government has affected urban infrastructure development in the state, as plan outlays for urban development have been inadequate. This has resulted in backlog of urban infrastructure and services and promoted top-down approach with or without nominal role of local institutions i.e. ULBs in prioritising infrastructure development works. Multiple programmes, targeting the development of urban infrastructure, municipal services and poverty alleviation have been initiated by the central and state governments during various five year plans, but not much progress is visible because of inadequate outlays, lack of convergence to avoid duplication and poor participation of the local people.

With the 74th Amendment, there is a good opportunity for the state government to adopt people oriented planning and change the policy framework with an active role of grass root level institutions in the development of urban infrastructure. Strict and regular monitoring of centrally sponsored infrastructure development programmes is necessary. Plan outlays for financing urban water supply, sewerage, urban development and housing for the poor should be enhanced for sustainable development of urban areas.

Limitations of Municipal Financial Reporting, Budgeting and Accounting System

The cash based single entry system of accounting prevalent in the ULBs of Himachal Pradesh does not guarantee any management information/financial disclosures and has several deficiencies. It has failed to achieve accountability in the municipal financial reporting and accounting system. The cash basis of accounting has been unable to meet most of the financial reporting objectives. Measures of performance, which depend on this system, are altered by postponing the payment of certain bills to conceal budgetary deficit and separate information about receipts or payments on capital and revenue account cannot be prepared. One of the major deficiencies of this system is that most of the time, measurement of performance and financial position yield incorrect results. The 'single entry accounting system lacks self-balancing mechanism. This system is susceptible to error propagation, which affects the credibility of the financial statement' (Joshi, 2003).

The financial reporting system in the ULBs is not proper even for internal users at the local level and also at the level of the Directorate, leave aside external users such as lending agencies or private sector service organisations. Only a few municipalities prepare their annual administrative reports. The annual budgets prepared by the ULBs have several structural deficiencies. There is no system to prepare exclusive annual financial reports comprising a meaningful annual budget, an administrative report and an audit report.

The budgeting system in the ULBs has a defective structure and improper classification. Preference is given to incremental approach based on the income and expenditure of the previous year. The system of making expenditure conditional on actual receipt or resource mobilisation in a particular year does not exit in the ULBs. They use their allocations irrespective of their revenue receipts or availability of funds.

The relevance of revised budget estimates in reviewing the income and controlling the expenditure to correct deficits of the original budget passed on the experience of the last few months is ignored to enhance the budget allocations. There is no tradition in the ULBs to discuss revised budgets. The ULBs in Himachal Pradesh do not prepare long-term city development plans, which can be the basis of annual budgets. Therefore, there is no continuity of development activities and several times there is no co-relation between the present and past budgets. In most of the ULBs, in-house services are not charged and therefore, there is wasteful expenditure on several municipal activities.

The present financial reporting and budgeting system in the ULBs is ad hoc in nature and does not contain monitorable targets to measure performance indicators. Therefore, most of the practices in financial reporting, accounting and budgeting become roadblocks to cost analysis which leaves hardly any scope for cost reduction, improvement of efficiency and productivity. The larger municipalities, such as the Shimla Municipal Corporation, excessively depend on 'suspense account' by incurring expenditure and drawing advances against budget allocations. This is not considered a good practice in financial management.

Alternative Funding Mechanism for Financing Urban Infrastructure

As discussed in Section III, the fiscal health of the urban local bodies has deteriorated due to the mismatch between the sources of revenue devolved to them and functional responsibilities, increasing concentration of population in the urban areas, control of the state on pricing and cost recovery of urban infrastructure services and parastatal involvement in municipal affairs. This has been affecting the development of urban infrastructure and civic services.

The new economic policy has given a boost to commercial, industrial and trade-related activities in towns of all major states, but the urban centres of Himachal Pradesh have not experienced any significant change. There is a competitive environment between the states and the ULBs to attract investment from the domestic and international capital markets but Himachal Pradesh has not benefited from these new trends and the major chunk of investment has gone to Tamil Nadu, Gujarat, Maharashtra, Andhra Pradesh and West Bengal. Economic competitiveness of the state depends on the level and quality of its infrastructure, specially the urban infrastructure as it plays an important role in economic development. In a recent study on *Infrastructure and Economic Development in Himachal Pradesh,* Tiwari (2000) has summarised that "there is a positive association between infrastructure and economic development in almost all the districts of the state".

The changing urban scenario in post 74th Amendment era and the also post- economic reforms scenario demand a change in the existing financing mechanism. There is need for diversification of revenue sources of the ULBs and for mobilising non-budgetary resources for urban infrastructure. The new orientation, emphasising demand-based provision of services and market-based financing mechanism is important to mobilise non-budgetary financial resources and bring in private sector participation. Commercial orientation, institutional restructuring and fiscal reforms are required to attract funds from the capital market. Improved fiscal and financial management, project development and implementation capabilities of the ULBs should be promoted. Decentralisation of the decision-making process will improve the willingness of the ULBs to introduce institutional changes and manage urban reforms.

Considering the inability of the ULBs to mobilise adequate revenue from their own sources and their increasing dependence on plan and non-plan grants/ allocations from the state, there is a need to devise alternative mechanism for financing urban infrastructure comprising additional resource mobilisation from their own sources, market borrowings, partnership with the private sector, and access to the capital market as discussed in this section.

Additional Resource Mobilisation for Financing Urban Infrastructure

To meet the growing need for funds for urban infrastructure and O&M needs of municipal services, the ULBs need to maximise their internal resource mobilisation from tax and non-tax sources. It is possible if the ULBs are entrusted with adequate powers to fix the rate of taxes subject to the maximum laid down in the municipal acts/laws of the state. The power to grant exemption from the taxes should be given to the ULBs. The financial targets of urban infrastructure and municipal services could be met by reforming property tax, rationalising user charges and introducing innovations in municipal management.

Tax Reforms

Tax reforms through the revision of tax rates, corrective measures in the tax administration and reduction of exemptions should be central to additional resource mobilisation. Imposition of all taxes provided in the *Himachal Pradesh Municipal Act, 1994* and *Himachal Pradesh Municipal Corporation Act, 1994* will strengthen the fiscal base of the ULBs.

Property Tax Reforms

Property tax reform is the need of the hour in Himachal Pradesh as "this tax is a premier local tax and a very buoyaut and elastic source of municipal finance. It is not affected by economic boom or slowdowns" (Teotia, 2001). The ULBs in HP have been following the annual rental value (ARV) system of property tax, which has outlived its utility. According to Jha (2001) "tax on annual rental value of land and buildings (property tax) has lost its buoyancy and elasticity due to a host of administrative, legal and behavioral reasons (discretionary considerations and corrupt practices)". The position of property tax in Himachal Pradesh is worse. A sizeable proportion of property tax is not collected and arrears are accumulating. Exemptions have worsened the position. The following initiatives are suggested to improve collections from property tax in Himachal:

a) Area based property tax system should be adopted as it has been found transparent and simple and has stood the scrutiny of the courts. Property tax reforms initiated by Bihar (Patna Municipal Corporation), Andhra Pradesh, Tamil Nadu, Gujarat and Kerala are worth looking at for reforms in this tax in Himachal Pradesh. Several other states and municipal corporations have followed this system. In a recent judgement on the Andhra Pradesh property tax system, the Supreme Court upheld the area detail system of property tax, provided the methodology and procedure of valuation and assessment of rental value are stipulated in the municipal laws.

b) The Himachal Pradesh Government should follow *'Guidelines for Property Tax Reforms'* prepared by the Ministry of Urban Development, Government of India, which suggests that a good property tax structure should be based on the following principles:
   - low rate of property tax so as to make it acceptable by the public at large
   - minimise the discretion on the part of the assessors in tax levy
   - make the process of assessment, levy and collection transparent and simple
   - ensure equity between classes of tax payers/ property owners
   - facilitate self-assessment of property by property owners/occupiers

c) West Bengal and some other states have initiated reforms in the system of property taxation with provisions for self-assessment, mandatory periodic revision, dispensing with the demand notice for the tax and putting the onus on property owners for timely tax payment etc. Such measures have yielded good results and need to be pursued by all states. The property tax/house tax legislation should be suitably modified to overcome the impediments in the growth of property tax due to rent control laws (Eleventh Finance Commission, 2000).

d) Innovative practices in valuation, assessment and collection of property tax as given below have been found suitable in Ludhiana and several other municipalities (Gupta & Teotia, 2002). The ULBs of Himachal Pradesh can also initiate these practices:
   - mapping of properties and developing geographical information system (GIS) to enhance the property tax net and to improve its administration
   - computerisation of property tax records for effective billing and collection
   - reducing wasteful expenditure through privatisation of billing and collection procedures
   - a scheme of penalties and incentives for tax payers
   - transparency in administration and up-to-date records on computer for public view

e) To improve house tax collections, the grant-in-aid recommended by the SSFC have been linked with collection of house tax by ULBs as below:

- 75 per cent of the grants be released provided the local body imposes and collects house tax on a minimum of 7.5 per cent of ARV.
- 25 per cent of the grant, will be released provided the local body commits to raise the rate of house tax by a percentage point each year so that it reaches 12.5 per cent of ARV by the end of 2006-07.

f) For rationalisation of existing house tax structure, the SSFC has recommended following zonation scheme for urban areas based on the principle of equity and justice:

a) Commercial

b) Residential

c) Peripheral slum area

If the rate of house tax is at a flat rate of Rs. 2 per unit of area in zone "a", then in zone "b" it could be 0.5 of the zone "a" and in zone "c" it could be 0.1 of the zone "b" or say Rs. 2, Re.1 and paisa 10 respectively.

With these reform initiatives, the ULBs of Himachal Pradesh should be able to generate in the next five years additional revenue of about Rs. 2 crore per annum.

There is good scope for mobilising additional revenue from other sources of tax revenue i.e. shared taxes such as stamp duty, excise duty, electricity duty and show tax, water/sewerage tax, conservancy/sanitation tax, profession tax and advertisement tax to strengthen the fiscal base of the ULBs. As discussed in the previous section, the government of Himachal Pradesh should consider steps for enhancing the share of the ULBs in state taxes. The sources of tax revenue, other than property tax should be able to generate about Rs. 1 crore per annum.

Non-Tax Reforms

The major initiatives/reforms in non-tax sources are necessary to generate additional resources for the urban local bodies.

Rationalisation of User Charges

User charges are used to finance the growing needs of the urban infrastructure. One time deposits (Rs. 500 to 1000) and monthly sewerage maintenance charges (Rs. 150 to 750) by Alandur, annual sewerage charges of Rs. 2,019 per household by Amrawati, Government of Karnataka's order for ULBs to set water charges in line with actual costs (minimum O&M costs and debt services), parking fee and eco fee for using municipal garden by Bangalore, fees for 'tatkal' (quick) delivery of services by some ULBs of Tamilnadu and West Bengal, cable charges by ULBs of Tamil Nadu and street tax by Pune municipality helped them to mobilise their income from user charges for financing urban infrastructure (Vaidya and Vaidya, 2003).

In Himachal Pradesh, there is tremendous scope for mobilising resources from user charges. The state government should prepare a strategy for pricing and cost recovery of user charges. According to the EFC (2000), the rate structure of user charges should be revised regularly to keep pace with inflation and to recover as far as possible, the full O&M cost of providing these services. The ULBs should have the power to fix the rate of user charges. The people would be willing to pay, if they get better service. The EFC has also given its perception on the maintenance of civic services including water and sanitation and has recommended that the transfer of these responsibilities to the local bodies should be speeded up, accompanied by transfer of funds and staff. The cost of O&M of services should be met by raising user charges and by the devolution of funds from the state. The SSFC (2002) has suggested that "cost of services being provided to the people should invariably cover at least running and maintenance cost of the services".

To generate additional funds, through rationalisation of pricing and cost recovery of water supply and sewerage the following steps can be initiated: -

- rationalisation of water tariffs linked with electricity tariffs, labour and maintenance costs
- volumetric supply for all types of consumption
- sewerage charges based on water consumption and sewerage tax, as charged by Shimla Municipal Corporation (at the rate of 15 per cent of the general tax/property tax) should be introduced by all ULBs
- extension of user charges to all civic services that qualify for user charges
- collection of arrears through incentives and penalties. The SSFC has decided to reward ULBs who will hike water rates. For every additional rupee raised, the ULBs will be entitled to an incentive grant of Rs. 2 and this will apply to the ULBs having no arrears.
- computerisation of billing and collection procedures and records for improving efficiency in

identifying arrears, preparation of bills and collection of charges

- creation of a strong database to plan for the future demands of services and resources
- adoption of suitable technology to save wasteful expenditure on electricity, material and staff
- off-loading some of the activities to the private sector to check the growth of expenditure of the ULBs on establishment/contingencies
- ensuring involvement of the citizens in fixing tariffs, checking misuse of the services and detecting wastage or theft

A strong political will backed by local support is needed to rationalise the user charges. The transfer of O&M of water supply and sewerage to the ULBs is necessary as their active participation in prioritising augmentation schemes; mobilising resources and ensuring pricing and cost recovery will help in implementing these reforms.

Cross Subsidisation of User Charges through Slab System

Water rates in some selected towns of India as given in Table 20.23 may be looked into while finalising the pricing mechanism and administering a subsidy scheme for economically weaker sections.

Introduction of the slab system is recommended as it is found equitable and takes care of the poor who consume less and have a low paying capacity.

Service Charges/Taxation on Central Government Properties

The debate on taxation of central government properties, being subject to the provisions in the constitution, has now ended with the decision of the Government of India to allow the ULBs to levy service charges on central government properties. The EFC (2000) has recommended that 'all government properties whether they belong to the central or the state governments, should be subject to the levy of user charges and should be regulated by a suitable legislation'. The Government of Himachal Pradesh should consider this recommendation and direct all ULBs to levy service charges on central/state government properties.

With the reforms in user charges and introduction of service charges, it should be possible to generate additional resources worth Rs. 3 crore per annum. The sources of non-tax revenue such as rent from municipal

TABLE 20.23

Water Tariffs in Selected Cities of India* (1998-99)

Cities	Metered Rates (non-slab) (in Rs/kl/month)			Unmetered Flat Rates			Metered Slab Rates (in Rs./kl/ month)		
	Domestic	Non-domestic	Industrial	Domestic	Non-domestic	Industrial	Domestic	Non-domestic	Industrial
Bangalore	—	—	60.00	—	—	—	65.00 (minimum) 3.50 upto 25 kl 7.00-25-50 kl 19.00-50-75 kl 26.00-75-100 kl	33.00 upto 10 kl 39.00-10-20 kl 44.00-20-40 kl 51.00-40-60 kl 57.00-60-100 kl 60.00 above 100 kl	—
Chennai	—	—	—	600.00 per annum	—	4800.00 per annum	2.50 upto 10kl 10.00-10-15 kl 15.00-15-25 kl 25.00-above 25 kl	—	25.00 upto 500 kl 40.00-above 500 kl
Jaipur	—	—	—	—	—	—	1.56 upto 15 kl 3.00-15-40 kl 4.00 above 40 kl	4.68- upto 15 kl 8.25-15-40 kl 11.00- above 40 kl	11.00- upto 15 kl 13.75-15-40 kl 16.50 above 40 kl
Chandigarh**	2.5 (drinking water consumed for lawn irrigation)	9.00 (Institutional 12.00) (Govt. offices)	11.00#	3.25 per sq. feet##	1% of total cost of construction###	—	1.75 upto 15 kl 3.50- 15 –30 kl 5.00-30-60 kl 6.00 above 60 kl	—	—

Source: 1) * National Institute of Urban Affairs (2001), *Urban Water Supply and Sanitation: Status and Investment Implications*, NIUA, New Delhi.
2) **Municipal Corporation of Chandigarh (December 2002).

Note: # Also for semi industrial and commercial consumptions.
For new private residential/non-residential constructions.
For government construction work.

properties, fair fees, map approval fees, *adda* fees, entry fees and other sources of fees, fines and miscellaneous revenues should also grow and contribute an additional income of Rs. 1 crore per annum.

Internal Revenue Efforts and Management Innovations for Resource Mobilisation

There is need for devolving buoyant fiscal sources of revenue to the ULBs to reduce the existing mismatch between functions and finances. Despite the 74th Amendment, the functional and fiscal domain of the ULBs indicate a status quo and nothing concrete has been done to improve the fiscal base of the ULBs through internal resource mobilisation. The rates of most of the taxes and charges were fixed long time ago and remain the same, and all powers to fix the rates and charges vest in the state government. This subject was not dealt comprehensively even by the FSFC which recommended devolution of grants only and did not suggest share in major state taxes. Water supply and sewerage, the major urban infrastructure/municipal services having multiple deficiencies, were not dealt by the FSFC as well as by the SSFC. The SSFC observed that ULBs were not levying the statutory taxes in a uniform manner. It was also seen that the exemptions and concessions were a matter of rule than rare exceptions. The next SFC should look into the matter and devolve adequate share of the major state taxes to the ULBs, recommend introduction of buoyant taxes, cover all major services for assessing revenue and capital account requirements and suggest measures to reduce state control in municipal affairs.

The ULBs are opting for management innovations to improve efficiency and strengthen municipal resource base. For example self assessment system (SAS) in property tax by Hyderabad, periodic revision of ARV and introduction of optional SAS by Bangalore, introduction of SAS by Chennai, Indore and Vishakhapatnam, computerised information system by Chennai, Indore and Ludhiana, outsourcing of bill distribution and municipal asset management by Ludhiana, Surat and Vijayawada, identification and collection of arrears through computerisation of records by Ludhiana, Indore and Mirzapur, online service by Vishakhapatnam and Guntur Municipalities helped these ULBs to mobilise their resources considerably (Vaidya and Vaidya, 2003; Gupta & Teotia, 2002; Planning Commission, 2003).

Management innovations can be introduced by the ULBs of Himachal Pradesh to strengthen their fiscal base and to become a stable and vibrant unit of local self-government.

Using Land as a Resource and Property and Asset Management

The importance of land as a resource has not been considered seriously by the ULBs in Himachal Pradesh. The ULBs should identify all scattered municipal lands including encroached lands and prepare an inventory of their locations and value. It will be a great asset with municipalities, which can be used for raising resources from the capital market. The potential of properly identified and inventorised land in urban areas to generate revenue can be worth several crores. This technique was used by the Ludhiana Municipal Corporation (LMC) and according to Gupta & Teotia (2001), the LMC identified 865 additional properties with a total value of Rs. 350 crore. According to the authors 'the mapping, survey of properties and inventory of old and newly identified assets was a distinctive achievement of the corporation towards tightening control on taxable properties and its own assets'. The municipalities of Himachal Pradesh can adopt the same practice for strengthening their fiscal domain.

Property and asset management by the ULBs in Himachal Pradesh is poor and valuable buildings, rest houses, community halls and shops are deteriorating due to carelessness and lack of proper maintenance. Illegal encroachments and unauthorised occupation of municipal land and buildings are depriving the ULBs of considerable income. Computerised management and information about municipal properties and assets can help ULBs to preserve, maintain and compute the orderly growth of municipal assets and use them for resource generation.

Raising of External Aid from International Agencies

External aid is becoming an important source of financing urban infrastructure in India. The World Bank, Asian Development Bank, Organisation of Petroleum Exporting Countries (OPEC), Norwegian Agency for International Development (NORAD), Australian Agency for Development (AUSAD), European Commission, Department for International Development (DFID), United States Agency for International Development (USAID), European Union (EU) and several other international agencies have been providing grants for financing urban infrastructure, preserving urban environment and reducing urban poverty. Large number of projects in Maharashtra, Gujrat, Tamil Nadu, Rajasthan, Uttar Pradesh, Punjab, Kerala, Hyderabad, Kerala and Karnataka have been financed by international agencies.

Except the Integrated Waste Management Project, Shimla (initiated in 1997-98, with a financial assistance of Rs. 5 crore from NORAD) and Kullu-Manali (initiated in 1997-98, with a financial assistance of Rs. 2.73 crore from NORAD) both under the Indo-Norwegian Environment Cooperation Programme, and Sewerage Augmentation Project in Shimla (initiated in 1997-98 with a financial assistance of Rs. 36 crore from OPEC), and some small projects on environment conservation with a financial assistance of Rs. 3.5 crore, no external assistance has been raised for financing a major urban infrastructure project in Himachal Pradesh.

There is no doubt that Himachal Pradesh has serious deficiencies in urban infrastructure and services and needs huge funds to remove these deficiencies. Funds are unlikely to come from budgetary sources. Therefore, it is necessary that the Himachal Pradesh government should explore the possibility of external aid for financing its urban infrastructure projects. Matching contribution from the central government in several important areas such as solid waste management, sewerage and water supply etc. can give a boost to infrastructure development in the state.

Urban Reform Incentive Fund

In the budget of 2002-03, the Government of India announced an 'urban reform incentive fund' (URIF) with an allocation of Rs. 500 crore to provide reform-linked assistance to the states. The purpose of this fund is to promote urban infrastructure development through public-private partnerships and provide incentives to the states to initiate reforms in urban development i.e. pricing and cost recovery through rationalisation of user charges, introduction of new taxes, better tax administration and improvement in service delivery etc. During the current financial year Rs. 1.05 crore has been allocated to Himachal Pradesh for this purpose. The state government should raise more resources under URIF by implementing financial and institutional reforms in the urban areas. The ULBs showing good reforms should be encouraged by providing adequate special financial incentives out of URIF. The base of this fund can be strengthened through special grant by the state government and equal matching grant by the Government of India.

City Challenge Fund

A 'city challenge fund' (CCF) was also announced by the Government of India in the budget of 2002-03. It was established to support cities by funding transitional cost of moving towards sustainable and creditworthy institutional system of municipal management and service delivery. The fund will assist in partially financing development and economic reform programme and financially viable projects to be undertaken by the ULBs with the help of the private sector. The state government should take advantage of this programme for upgrading its urban infrastructure and municipal services and provide matching share from state exchequer.

With the mobilisation of external aid from international agencies, using land as a resource, and funds raised under URIF and CCF, the state government should be able to generate at least Rs. 3 crore to Rs. 4 crore per annum for the development of its urban infrastructure.

Estimated Additional Resource Mobilisation and Proposed Financing of Urban Infrastructure

The projected financial targets of urban infrastructure and municipal services could be achieved by implementing the above recommendations. O&M cost of user charges should be recovered in the next five years to create confidence among the investors. Revision of user charges, especially for water supply and sewerage, will generate an additional annual revenue of Rs. 3 crore. Himachal Pradesh could take the cue from the water and sewerage tariffs in Chandigarh, Bangalore, Madurai, Vishakhapatnam, Hyderabad and Chennai etc. The break up of additional resource mobilisation from major sources is given in Table 20.24.

TABLE 20.24

Estimated Income through Additional Resource Mobilisation

Particulars	*Amount*
Additional income from property tax	Rs. 2.00 crore per annum
Pricing and cost recovery of user charges including service charges on central government properties	Rs. 3.00 crore per annum
Recovery from other sources of tax and non-tax revenue	Rs. 2.00 crore per annum
Internal revenue efforts and management innovations for resource mobilisation	Rs. 1.00 crore per annum
Using land as a resource and property and asset management	Rs. 1.00 crore per annum
Funds raised under urban reform incentive fund and city challenge fund and external aid from international agencies	Rs. 3.00 crore per annum
TOTAL	Rs. 12.00 crore per annum

The additional resource mobilisation will strengthen the fiscal capability of the ULBs to raise finances from non-budgetary sources. The proposed financing of urban infrastructure and municipal services is given in Table 20.25.

TABLE 20.25

Proposed Financing of Urban Infrastructure and Municipal Services

Particulars	*Amount*
Contribution by ULBs and IPH	Rs. 10.00 crore per annum
Transfers from Himachal Pradesh Infrastructure Development Board or proposed Himachal Pradesh Urban Development Fund (HPUDF)	Rs. 8.00 crore per annum
Earmarked contribution by the state government for water supply, sewerage and urban development	Rs. 32.00 crore per annum
TOTAL	Rs. 50.00 crore per annum

Himachal Pradesh will need Rs. 607.73 crore i.e. Rs. 121.54 crore per annum for financing its urban infrastructure in the next five years. With the proposed annual availability of Rs. 50 crore, it should be possible to raise Rs.71.5 crore per annum from the capital market or the banking institutions. On generation of additional resources, the ULBs will receive a good rating to raise funds. Financial institutions will also support commercially viable infrastructure projects and a part of the assured income of the ULBs can be dedicated to the ESCROW account to assure timely repayment of loans.

On the basis of these parameters, an expert group should prepare a 'project report' to meet the requirements of rating agencies and investors. The report should be acceptable to investors for subscribing loans/bonds in suitable tranches. The aims and objectives of raising funds should be attractive, being developmental, covering all sections of society.

Capital Market

There is consensus on mobilisation of resources from the capital market and financial institutions. The access of funds from the capital markets requires the ULBs and PSIs responsible for urban development to prepare commercially viable and bankable infrastructure projects and also to mobilise additional resources through tax reforms, rationalisation of user charges and improved fiscal discipline. According to the *India Infrastructure Report* (1996) 'it is high time that a commercial approach is adopted'. It is desirable in view of 'the fact that infrastructure services do not pay for themselves and the government does not have the financial capacity to continue to subsidise the beneficiaries'. The report further adds that 'commercialisation of infrastructure projects basically means sufficient provision of services to the consumers' satisfaction on cost recovery basis'. Accessing the capital market to raise non-budgetary resources for financing urban infrastructure and services would necessitate rationalisation of user charges and progressive recovery of costs.

The equity market and the debt market are two streams of the capital market and these new concepts are becoming popular for raising resources through non-budgetary sources i.e. municipal bonds.

Financing Urban Infrastructure through Municipal Bonds

To improve the urban infrastructure in Himachal Pradesh, the ULBs need huge funds, which are unlikely to come through budgetary sources. After the abolition of octroi, the tax base of the ULBs has been poor and they have depended largely on central and state government grants. In this situation, raising funds from the capital market in the form of municipal bonds is a viable alternative for financing urban infrastructure and municipal services.

Municipal Bonds are a primary source of finance for the ULBs in the United States and many other developed and developing countries. The municipal bond market is now emerging as an important source of financing urban infrastructure in several Indian cities. So far, eight municipal corporations, Ahmedabad, Ludhiana, Bangalore, Nasik, Nagpur, Madurai, Hyderabad and Indore, have raised about Rs. 615.3 crore for selected urban infrastructure projects as shown in Table 20.26.

The Municipal bonds were largely raised through private placements and were mainly subscribed by commercial/cooperative banks, financial institutions and public enterprises. The most important aspect of these issues except Banglore and Indore Municipal Corporations has been that these bonds were raised without guarantees of the government. Investment grade credit rating of municipal corporations enabled them to raise bonds as it attracted large number of investors.

The cost of raising funds through municipal bonds depends upon the internal financial strength of the ULBs, which is necessary for the repayment of loans through the ESCROW mechanism. The funds raised by these municipalities were 'structured obligation' and a specified source of municipal revenue was dedicated to the ESCROW account for repayments, as shown in Table 20.27.

TABLE 20.26

Accessing Municipal Bonds for Financing Urban Infrastructure

Cities	*Amount (Rs. in crore)*	*Year of Issue*	*Placement*	*Government Guarantee*	*Assigned Rating*	*Urban Infrastructure Projects*
Bangalore	125	1997	Private	Yes	A-(SO)	City roads/street drains
Ahmedabad-I	100	1998	Private/public	No	AA-(SO)	WSS** projects
Ludhiana	17.8	1998	Private	No	LAA-(SO)	WSS projects
Nashik	100	1999	Private	No	AA-(SO)	WSS projects
Nagpur	50	2000	Private	No	LAA-(SO)	Water supply project
Madurai	30	2001	Private	No	LA+(SO)	Madurai inner ring road project
Indore	10	2001	Private	Yes	A (SO)	Improvement of city roads
Hyderabad*	82.5	2002	Private	No	LAA+(SO)	Road construction and widening
Ahmedabad-II	100	2002	Private	No	AA (SO)	WSS projects

Source: Bagchi, Saumen and Anirban Kundu, 2003, 'Development of Municipal Bond Market in India', *Economic & Political Weekly*, (Feb. 22-28, 2003). Jha, Gangadhar (2002), 'Development of Municipal Bond Market in India', NIUA, New Delhi.

Note: *Hyderabad Municipal Corporation has gone for a double rating AA+(SO) from CRISIL.

**WSS = Water Supply and Sewerage.

The municipal corporation of Shimla, municipal councils of Solan, Kullu, Hamirpur, Nahan, Bilaspur, Mandi and some other municipalities of Himachal Pradesh should go for credit rating, prepare commercially viable or bankable projects and finance them through municipal bonds. A cluster of smaller municipalities can also raise municipal bonds by pooling their resources and ensuring repayments through the ESCROW mechanism.

The credit rating for raising funds through municipal bonds calls for reforms comprising financial reporting and accounting reforms (accrual based double entry accounting system from cash based single entry accounting system), tax reforms (property tax and non property taxes), rationalisation of user charges (water supply and sewerage), introduction of new municipal taxes like sanitation cess and environment tax, effective tax administration and improvement in billing and collection procedures.

Tax-Free Municipal Bonds

The Central Government has announced tax exemption on bonds issued by municipal/local governments and guidelines were issued in February 2001 to regulate the issue of tax-free municipal bonds. The guidelines suggest that the bonds will be issued

TABLE 20.27

Revenue Sources Escrowed by Municipal Bodies

Cities	*Revenue Source Escrowed*	*ER to TR# (%)*
Bangalore	Property tax and grants from the state government	65.3
Ahmedabad-I	Octroi from 10 major octroi *nakas*	45.7
Ludhiana	Revenue from water supply and sewerage	6.3
Nashik	Octroi from four major octroi *nakas*	59.1
Nagpur	Property tax and water charges	27.6
Madurai	Toll tax collection from the newly constructed toll road	25.1
Indore	Na*	Na*
Hyderabad	Non-residential property tax, advertisement tax, profession tax, surcharge on transfer of immovable properties and town planning charges	50.2
Ahmedabad-II	Property taxes of north and central zones	6.2

Source: Bagchi and Kundu (as in Table 20.26).

Notes: # - Share of ER (Escrowed Revenues) of TR (Total Revenue) is the average of last three years, that is 1998-99, 1999-2000 and 2000-01.

Na*- Revenue of the Indore Municipal Corporation is not known.

for raising resources for capital investment in creation of new infrastructure as well as augmentation of existing systems. Ahmedabad and Hyderabad Municipal Corporations have been permitted to issue tax-free municipal bonds worth Rs. 100 crore and Rs. 82.5 crore respectively for improving urban infrastructure. The Municipal Corporation of Shimla and other municipalities can raise tax-free municipal bonds for augmenting their infrastructure and services.

Loan Financing

Loan financing through banks or specialised financial intermediaries is becoming popular for raising resources for urban infrastructure services in many states. The ULBs of Himachal Pradesh should go for loan financing either from general purpose/ commercial/infrastructure banks like IDBI, ICICI and IDFC or Urban Development Funds (special purpose funds) like TNUDF. On the pattern of TNUDF, Himachal Pradesh can create an Himachal Pradesh Urban Development Fund to raise loans for financing urban infrastructure services in the state.

Private Sector Participation

With growing fiscal and financial problems at the central, state and local levels, involving the private sector in urban infrastructure development and delivery in the municipalities is becoming a major necessity. Private sector participation may be in the form of complete privatisation or public-private partnership. Now a growing pool of resources is available to finance commercially viable infrastructure projects.

It is expected that the private sector will help the ULBs in offloading the financial, functional, administrative and managerial burdens. It will help the local communities by introducing management efficiency, quick decision-making and trained skilled manpower for efficient delivery of the services, leading to higher consumer satisfaction.

Private sector participation (PSP) experiences of several ULBs in India particularly Ludhiana, Hyderabad, Tirupur, Alandur, Rajkot, CIDCO (New Mumbai) and Surat have been good and ULBs were able to upgrade quantity and quality of their services and save fiscal resources. ULBs of many other states have also introduced PSP in O&M and augmentation of urban infrastructure.

Himachal Pradesh may introduce private sector participation in urban infrastructure and major activities and projects of the municipalities. The Finance Minister of India in the *Budget 2002-03* announced that 'public-private partnership will be encouraged for the provision of infrastructure facilities, the modalities of which are being worked out by a Task Force'. The central government will develop guidelines for involvement of the private sector in infrastructure, which will ensure competitive bidding process in transparent manner. These guidelines will not only protect the consumers but also ensure integrity of the process.

The World Bank (WB) and the Asian Development Bank have initiated guarantee schemes (IHS-India, 2002) to promote international capital for financing urban infrastructure projects in India. Since the access by lengthening the maturity of related borrowings is facilitated by the WB, it provides good opportunity for the ULBs of Himachal Pradesh to go for infrastructure/ service related projects by accessing funds from international financial institutions, that too without state government guarantee.

People's Participation

The increasing demand for urban infrastructure due to growing urbanisation and the inability of the ULBs to provide these facilities call for promoting people's participation in the augmentation of the urban infrastructure and municipal services. The government of Himachal Pradesh introduced an innovative programme i.e. '*Vikas Mein Jan Sahyog*' (VMJS) in 1994 as part of its strategy for decentralised planning. The share of the government and the local community is 75: 25 in the construction of drinking water and sewerage schemes including installation of handpumps. But due to poor response from the urban people, a major share of the funds have gone to rural areas. To maintain the assets created under various programmes, a scheme '*Rakh Rakhav Mein Jan Sahyog*', was introduced by the state government in 1995-96 on 50:50 basis between the local community and the government. Departmental charges of 17 per cent charged by the Irrigation & Public Health and the Public Works Departments under decentralised planning were waived. There is need for sensitising the local people to contribute their share in small urban infrastructure development projects in their localities and take advantage of these programmes of the state government.

Several towns i.e. Ludhiana (mohalla sanitation committees), Baroda (citizens council), Chennai (EXNORA), Lucknow (muskan jyoti samiti) and Ahmedabad (SEWA) have involved local people in the management of municipal services and mobilisation of resources for infrastructure development (Gupta & Teotia, 2001; Planning Commission and United Nations Development Programme, India, 2003; NIUA, 2001). Sanitary conditions in Chandigarh have improved considerably with the introduction of 'Garbage Bin Free Sector/Sehaj Safai Kendra Scheme' by involving local community through resident welfare associations (Gupta, J.P. and Manoj K. Teotia, 2003). These successful experiments with people's participation in selected areas of infrastructure development, poverty alleviation and municipal service delivery can be replicated in the urban areas of Himachal Pradesh to offload some of the functional and fiscal responsibilities of the ULBs and the IPH department, and mobilise resources for infrastructure development.

Prerequisites for Initiating Alternative Funding Mechanism

To raise funds from alternative sources for achieving financial viability, it is desirable to go for pricing and cost recovery of urban infrastructure and municipal services. In principle, the full O&M cost should be recovered from service users and at the most, the vulnerable sections can be cross-subsidised. In this section, an effort has been made to discuss the major pre-requisites for promoting alternative funding mechanism for financing urban infrastructure in Himachal Pradesh.

Institutional Restructuring and Reform Perspective

Institutional inefficiencies at the policy level have been a constraint on the augmentation of the urban infrastructure and municipal services and the pace of private sector participation in this sector. The suitable institutional and management environment should be created to promote rationalisation of user charges, accessing the capital market and maintaining the services with a greater role for the private sector. ULBs in Tamil Nadu, Gujarat, Karnataka, Maharashtra and West Bengal have demonstrated greater institutional re-structuring, reforms in functional and fiscal domain and regulatory mechanism to raise external funding, improve financial management and urban governance. The ULBs of Himachal can go for similar experiments.

Pooled Financing Mechanism for Development of Urban Infrastructure

In the changing financing scenario, access to the capital market has become a necessity and several municipalities are accessing funds from financial institutions directly. Only large municipal corporations and councils have taken advantage of this and the small and medium municipalities have been deprived of it due to their poor financial position and the lack of capacity to prepare viable projects. For the small and medium municipalities, the Government of India has initiated a Pooled Finance Development Scheme and a state level pooled financing mechanism is proposed to be set up. The scheme will provide credit enhancement to access market borrowings on a creditworthy basis. The main objectives of the state level mechanism will be to facilitate:

- small and medium ULBs to access the capital market for investment in essential municipal infrastructure
- the development of bankable urban infrastructure projects
- the introduction of necessary reforms (e.g. tariff and financial) in the ULBs
- development of the municipal bond market

A tentative allocation of Rs. 400 crore under the Tenth Five Year Plan has been made for this scheme and a provision of Rs. 80 crore has been proposed in the 2003-04 annual plan. This is an important scheme for the small and medium municipalities of Himachal Pradesh to raise funds for financing their urban infrastructure.

The Himachal Pradesh Urban Development Fund (HPUDF)

A special purpose vehicle i.e. the HPUDF can be created to help the ULBs to raise funds for infrastructure development. It will be useful for smaller ULBs, which do not have a sound financial base but need funds. Groups of municipalities can access the debt market on the strength of their collective financial wherewithal. Large and medium municipalities like Shimla, Solan, Kullu, Bilaspur, Mandi, Chamba, Una and Hamirpur can also raise municipal bonds under this scheme.

The ESCROW account is an essential component of the scheme which will be created from general funds (current account) to cover at least one to two years of debt service. A financial intermediary, preferably at the national level, will provide 100 per cent guarantee of the debt service reserve fund, which will be established by separate funds of state government and managed by a special purpose vehicle or an asset management company i.e. Himachal Pradesh Urban Development Fund. This will advise ULBs about various important projects, help them raising resources, preparing project reports and work as a nodal agency right from the stage of formulation of the project, its management, operation and monitoring during different phases.

For this purpose, revenue income of ULBs will have to be enhanced for assured repayments of principal and interest. It is possible to attract national level financial intermediaries such as IDFC, IL&FS and ICICI to contribute to the fund on agreed sharing basis. This type of fund is already functional in Tamil Nadu, Maharashtra and Gujarat.

Functional Decentralisation

The 74th Amendment has provided an illustrative, legal and constitutional framework for devolution of functions to the ULBs. The SSFC (2002) noticed that ULBs were not performing requisite functions as notified in August 1994 in conformity with 12th Schedule of 74th Amendment. But it was largely due to apathy of the state government which did not transfer the delegated functions to ULBs. The government of Himachal Pradesh should take this amendment seriously and go in for functional decentralisation to empower the ULBs. There is need for legislative changes both at the state and the local government levels to achieve functional decentralisation. The empowered institutions of local government will be able to generate funds from internal and external sources, involve private sector and local communities for efficient delivery and management of services.

The functioning of local self-government institutions at various levels should be strengthened. The district planning committees, which are required to consolidate the plans prepared by the ULBs and Panchayati Raj Institutions should be made functional and effective in all respects. They will help to bring about development at the grassroot level. The major functions listed in the Twelfth Schedule should be transferred to the ULBs along with funds and functionaries. Parastatal involvement in the development of urban infrastructure should be reduced as urban local bodies after two elections in post 74th Amendment period have become mature to perform these functions. If the functions of parastatals cannot be transferred immediately they can work as subordinate to the ULBs or as consultants till their abolition. The present Mayoral system in Shimla municipal corporation and President system in municipal councils should be replaced by 'Mayor-in-council and 'President-in-council system' as in West Bengal. "The present Mayoral system is weak and ineffective as the Mayor has limited autonomy for discharging functional and financial obligations. The powers of Mayor and other councilors are not adequate" (Teotia, 2001; 2002).

Devolution of Funds as Recommended by the State Finance Commission

The state finance commission is mandated to recommend devolution of funds to match functional decentralisation. But the SSFC observed that "actual average per capita receipts remained below the forecast made by the FSFC". The transfers recommended for delegated functions were not in toto and this resulted in accumulation of arrears of electricity and water bills to be paid by ULBs to HPSEB and IPH respectively. The SSFC has now recommended to give grants of Rs. 27.52 crore to ULBs to liquidate arrears of electricity charges of street lights (Rs. 10.39 crore) and arrear of bulk water supply (Rs. 17.13 crore). The transfer of these grants and other devolution recommended by the SSFC will pave way for strengthening fiscal domain of ULBs and hence financing urban infrastructure in the State.

Legislative Reforms for Market Borrowings

The market borrowing powers of the ULBs are governed by Local Authorities Act of 1914, amended in 1917 and 1935. This Act has become meaningless with the onset of second generation fiscal reforms as it inhibits the borrowing powers of the ULBs. The state government is empowered to enact legislation under Section 4(i) and 7. The government of Himachal Pradesh should pass legislation to enhance the limits set by the state government on municipal borrowings and a clear strategy, preferably with a single window system should be chalked out to enhance the market borrowing capacity of the ULBs.

Reforms in Financial Management, Creation of Database and Quality of Urban Governance

The ULBs should restructure their tariffs and increase own revenues by initiating reforms in their fiscal and financial management. To become capable of raising funds to finance the growing requirements of infrastructure, the ULBs will have to introduce transparency in their financial management, improve their creditworthiness and generate clear time-series data on various aspects of municipal finances, infrastructure and services. The EFC has initiated reforms to create a database by providing grants to the ULBs for this purpose. The Central Ministry of Urban Development is also interested in improving the information base of the municipalities. The Department of Urban Development (Himachal Pradesh) can take advantage of these reforms and create a sound database not only at the municipal level but also at the directorate level, which at present has serious deficiencies.

Improvement in the quality of urban governance is necessary not only to have citizen-friendly services but also to develop an environment-friendly infrastructure for sustainable development of the urban areas. The political will should support fiscal reforms, as it will help the ULBs to provide adequate and quality service to the people. Smooth coordination between the deliberative and executive wings is necessary to implement reform initiatives and to manage urban affairs efficiently.

Municipal Financial Reporting, Budgeting and Accounting Reforms

It is recommended to introduce the double entry system of accounting to address the deficiencies in financial reporting and budgeting practices in Himachal Pradesh. The ULBs in Himachal Pradesh may adopt the double entry system of accounting, successfully adopted in Tamil Nadu, Gujarat and Karnataka, to install accounting transparency and efficiency in financial reporting, accounting and budgeting procedures. The Directorate of Urban Development can involve a specialised institution to prepare and implement a double entry accrual based accounting manuals in the ULBs. This system will enable the ULBs to prepare information that would reflect their financial position and their capacity to service debts. This system will also help them to attract investment for financing urban infrastructure and municipal services.

Institute of Charted Accountants of India (ICAI) has prepared a technical guide on accounting and financial reporting by the ULBs. The municipalities of Himachal Pradesh should comply with the accounting standards set by the ICAI to provide the users with a broader and complete understanding of the local government and the trends in their financial affairs. For development, standardisation and regularisation of the new accounting system in the ULBs, the standard model of accounting (accrual type) should be prepared by the Government of India. Recommendations of the Task Force constituted by the Ministry of Urban Development on Municipal Accounting Reforms should be circulated to all state governments and implemented on priority basis. The state government should revise the municipal accounting and budgeting code, using the national model of municipal accounting and budgeting code and manual for upgrading the accounting and budgeting systems of the ULBs.

Regulatory Framework

The state government should set up a regulatory authority for urban infrastructure 'to monitor quality of services provided and price charged' (*India Infrastructure Report, 1996*). It would help to promote the private sector participation in project development, financing, rationalisation of user charges and quality control. Such a body should be free from populist political interference and take care of the interests of investors as well as the consumers, particularly the underprivileged sections through cross subsidisation.

Commercial Viability of Projects

Private sector investment largely depends on the commercial viability of the project which means that the project should able to generate project-specific costs including debt service obligations.

The Planning Commission, in response to the problems of less developed states, which are unable to prepare projects of the requisite standard to attract institutional and external funding, has set up a Project Preparation Facility to finance the preparation of development projects by the states for external funding. Himachal Pradesh can utilise this facility for preparing urban infrastructure development projects with the help of professional consultants selected by the Planning Commission through open competitive bidding. Andhra and Maharashtra state governments have been able to access financing for their projects.

Institutional Development through Capacity Building/ Training of Elected and Appointed Representatives of Urban Local Bodies

The training of about 2960 functionaries i.e., 430 elected and 2530 appointed persons of the ULBs is important for efficient delivery of services and municipal management. Urban infrastructure is a technical and complex subject and therefore, the municipal staff should be adequately trained to understand efficient municipal management and to act accordingly. Though elected and appointed representatives of ULBs are trained by Himachal Pradesh Institute of Public Administration (HIPA), Shimla and Centre for Research in Rural and Industrial Development (CRRID), Chandigarh, the state government is of the view that a new Institute specialising in capacity building for urban development may be opened and funded by the Government of India and state government on sharing basis.

The state government should prepare a strategy for capacity building of urban managers, which should be based on realistic assessment of human, financial and technical resources required by the urban local bodies. The elected or appointed members should be aware of various provisions of the Act, the organisational and institutional set-up, the budgeting and accounting practices and also the practices of municipal management. A trained staff will be able to prepare projects, raise funds, attract private sector, involve local community in service delivery and infrastructure development and improve urban governance for sustainable development of urban areas in Himachal Pradesh.

Action Plan

There is need for addressing issues relating to the negative impact of urbanisation and evolving an *"urbanisation strategy"* and *"urban development policy"* comprising area/region specific economic frameworks, rural urban continuum/connectiveness/interdependence, backward and forward linkages and inter-sectoral as well as spatial and environmental dimensions of infrastructure development. Emphasis should be put on localisation so that the urban areas are able to meet the needs of the residents without affecting the interests of the future generations. The strategy/policy should comprise long-term city/environment friendly goals such as empowerment of the ULBs by transferring funds, functions and functionaries and adequate urban infrastructure/services like water supply, sewerage, solid waste management, roads, street lights, land use/development, housing and transport facilities.

There is need for a state level *'urban infrastructure policy'* which could project demand and supply, monitor quality and quantity, suggest pricing and cost recovery, develop alternative sources and arrange financial resources for augmentation of the infrastructure and the services. Political will is necessary for pricing and cost recovery. The state should draw up a formula for cross subsidisation of municipal services. Since capital cost of the urban infrastructure is comparatively high in Himachal Pradesh, pricing and cost recovery should be improved to sustain the delivery of important basic urban environmental infrastructure to the growing urban population.

There is a need to formulate effective 'land use/land development policy' to promote eco-friendly sustainable development of urban areas. Housing and urban development plans/policies should be formulated in such a manner that they do not pose threat to the eco-system in the state. The development of commercial areas, industrial focal points and other establishments should be allowed to grow in harmony with surrounding environments and ecologically sensitive areas should not be affected by their activities. The state policy on development of new townships should take care of environmental implications and to the extent possible new emerging towns should be planned and developed rather than developing new towns which will be highly capital intensive and ecologically dangerous. The active participation of local people and institutions including urban local bodies should be secured for planned development and management of land and other resources in urban areas.

The functioning of local self-government institutions at various levels should be strengthened. The major functions listed in the Twelfth Schedule should be transferred to the ULBs along with funds and functionaries. Parastatal involvement in the development of urban infrastructure should be reduced as urban local bodies after two elections in post 74th Amendment period have become mature to perform these functions. Considering that the resources of the ULBs are poor and budgetary support from the state government and transfers/grants from the central government are unlikely to increase, the strategy should suggest ways and means of resource mobilisation from capital markets/non budgetary sources for financing the urban infrastructure.

The suitable institutional and management environment should be created to promote rationalisation of user charges, accessing the capital market and maintaining the services with a greater role for the private sector. Himachal Pradesh Urban Development Fund (HPUDF) may be created to help the ULBs to raise funds for infrastructure development. It will be useful for smaller ULBs, which do not have a sound financial base but need funds. This will advise ULBs about various important projects, help them in raising resources, preparing project reports and work as a nodal agency right from the stage of formulation of the project, its management, operation and monitoring during different phases.

It is suggested that specific purpose funds raised by the HPIDB should not be diverted to the budget account and the HPIDB should be allowed to work independently and invest funds in identified critical sectors of infrastructure including the urban infrastructure. The state government should set up a regulatory authority for urban infrastructure 'to monitor quality of services provided and price charged'.

Reform in financial management, information and data management is a must for improving quality of urban governance. Municipal financial reporting, budgeting and accounting practices should be upgraded to promote better urban management in the state. It is recommended to introduce the double entry system of accounting to address the deficiencies in financial reporting and budgeting practices in Himachal Pradesh.

Environment conservation should be a major thrust area for the urban policymakers and stakeholders in infrastructure development. Creation of an enabling legal, financial and regulatory framework for infrastructure development should be the immediate policy initiative of the state government. Urban development policy must emphasise on capacity building of the elected and appointed functionaries of local self-governments and other officers responsible for urban governance/infrastructure development.

Vision for the Future

'As Indian cities continue to swell, the challenge of improving the urban infrastructure will be magnified' (Planning Commission, 2002). With the growing level of urbanisation, the challenge of upgradation of urban infrastructure and improvement of urban environment will be major challenges for Himachal Pradesh. The disparities between infrastructure and services of the urban and rural areas should not be allowed to widen in future in this ecologically sensitive state. This demands acceleration of development process for overall improvement of infrastructure services and quality of life in rural as well as urban areas. The trend of urbanisation in Himachal Pradesh is indicative of concentration of population and resources in a few larger towns only. The future population and economic growth is likely to concentrate in and around six to seven towns in Himachal Pradesh. 'The demographic trends towards urbanisation are accompanied by a change in the management and financing of urban development, as a result of liberalisation' (Planning Commission, 2002). The large towns, with strong economy due to growth of tourism, industry and strong fiscal base of ULBs can upgrade their infrastructure and services but small and medium towns with poor economic base and weak fiscal health of ULBs are likely to grow with serious deficiencies in infrastructure development, municipal management and environmental conservation. Towns in difficult hilly terrain and backward regions are unlikely to grow as towns in better terrain and developed regions. Therefore, innovative efforts for infrastructure development, resource mobilisation and urban management as discussed in the previous sections should be initiated so that towns can grow in a sustainable manner.

The 'urbanisation strategy/urban development policy' should be formulated to improve institutional, fiscal, functional and administrative capacities of urban development institutions in the state. Decentralisation of powers by transfer of funds, functions and functionaries, to ULBs is a must for strengthening these institutions of local self-government. Existing policies regarding land development, urban and rural planning and environmental conservation should be suitably modified for sustainable development of urban areas. The new towns should not be allowed to grow in a haphazard manner. Some growth corridors can be identified and developed to meet requirements of rural population in remote and backward areas, with emphasis on employment, education, health and municipal services.

Creation of enabling legal, financial and regulatory frameworks for infrastructure development should be important thrust areas for urban policy makers. Pricing and cost recovery of municipal services and commercialisation of urban infrastructure are important requirements to sustain delivery of municipal services. Additional resource mobilisation from exiting sources i.e. property tax and user charges will help to strengthen fiscal base of ULBs and reduce dependency on higher level of governments. With constraints of budgetary transfers and grants, ULBs should access funds from non-budgetary sources for financing urban infrastructure and meet growing demand of municipal services. Tourism infrastructure must be upgraded in tune with growing number of tourists. Private sector participation and people's involvement in development, delivery and operation and maintenance of infrastructure and services should be promoted through institutional restructuring and legislative reforms. Reform in accounting, budgeting, financial management, data base/ management information system and wasteful revenue expenditure is important pre-requisite for improving quality of urban governance in Himachal Pradesh.

Last but not least, capacity building of urban policymakers (elected and appointed representatives of ULBs) and implementers of infrastructure development programmes is necessary for institutional development and sustainable management and use of resources in urban areas.

References

Bagchi, Saumen and Anirban Kundu, 2003, "Development of Municipal Bond Market in India", *Economic & Political Weekly* (Feb. 22-28, 2003),Vol. XXXVIII, No. 8

Centre for Research in Rural and Industrial Development (1999), *A Survey for Estimating the Revenue Account Requirements of Municipalities for the Years 2002-2005 AD for the State of Himachal Pradesh,* prepared for NIPFP, New Delhi (Chief Coordinator: J P Gupta; Assistant Coordinator: Manoj K Teotia).

Guidelines for Property Tax Reforms (2002), Ministry of Urban Development, Government of India, New Delhi.

Gupta, J.P. and Manoj K. Teotia (2003), *Urban Management in a Hill Town: A Case Study of Manali in Himachal Pradesh,* CRRID, Chandigarh (Draft Report submitted to NIUA, New Delhi under FIRE(D) Programme of USAID).

————. (2003), *Innovative Municipal Management for Mobilisation of Financial Resources and Upgradation of Environmental Infrastructure (A Case Study of Chandigarh Municipal Corporation),* Draft Report submitted to NIUA, New Delhi under FIRE(D) programme of USAID.

————. (2002), "Urban Development" in *Punjab Development Report 2002,* prepared by CRRID and published by the Planning Commission of India.

————. (2001), *Innovative Urban Management: Resource Mobilisation and Privatization in Ludhiana Municipal Corporation,* CRRID, Chandigarh (unpublished Report, submitted to NIUA, New Delhi under FIRE(D) programme of USAID).

IHS-India (2002), *Financing Urban Infrastructure,* Training Manual, prepared by Institute of Housing and Urban Development Studies: India for FIRE(D) Project of USAID and NIUA, New Delhi.

————. (2002), *Project Development for Urban Local Bodies,* Training Manual, prepared by Institute of Housing and Urban Development Studies: India for FIRE(D) Project of USAID and NIUA, New Delhi.

Jha, Gangadhar (2001), 'Municipal Resource Mobilization; Issues and Experiences', Working paper for the Workshop on Municipal Revenue Mobilization, organized by the Municipal Association of Nepal and Urban Management Programme, South Asia (UNDP, UNCHS) at Dhulikhel, Nepal (May 14-16, 2001).

————. (2002), "Development of Municipal Bond Market in India", paper presented at the Workshop on *Development of Municipal Bond Market in India,* organised by NIUA, New Delhi, 31 May, 2002.

Joshi, Ravikant (2003), "Succeeding in Municipal Accounting Reforms: The Gujarat, Tamil Nadu and Karnataka Experiments", in *India Infrastructure Report 2003,* published by Oxford University Press, New Delhi.

Mathur, Mukesh P. (2001), "Alandur Sewerage Project : A Success Story of Public-Private Partnership Arrangements", paper prepared for the *India Infrastructure Report, 2002.*

Municipal Solid Wastes (Management and Handling) Rules, 2000, Ministry of Environment and Forests, Notification dated 25 September 2000.

NCAER (1996), *The India Infrastructure Report* (known as Rakesh Mohan Committee Report), National Council of Applied Economic Research, New Delhi.

NIUA (2001),'Mobilising Communities: Communities in Action', Series 2, National Institute of Urban Affairs, New Delhi.

————. (2001), *Urban Water Supply and Sanitation: Status and Investment Implications,* National Institute of Urban Affairs, New Delhi.

Planning Commission (2002), *Report of the Committee on India Vision 2020,* Planning Commission, Government of India, New Delhi.

Planning Commission, Government of India (2003), *Successful Governance Initiatives and Best Practices: Experiences from Indian States,* published by Academic Foundation, New Delhi.

Planning Commission (2003), *Tenth Five Year Plan 2002-07,* Government of India, New Delhi.

Report of the Himachal Pradesh State Finance Commission (1996), Government of Himachal Pradesh (referred as FSFC).

Report of the Himachal Pradesh Second State Finance Commission (2002), Government of Himachal Pradesh (referred as SSFC).

Report of the Eleventh Finance Commission (2000), Department of Economic Affairs, Ministry of Finance, Government of India, New Delhi.

Solid Waste Management in Class I Cities in India (1999), Report of the Committee Constituted by the Hon'ble Supreme Court of India.

State of Environment Report- Himachal Pradesh (March 2000), State Council of Science, Technology and Environment, Shimla.

Tenth Five Year Plan 2002-07, Department of Planning, Government of Himachal Pradesh, Shimla.

Teotia, Manoj Kumar (2002), "Need to Define and Expand Functional and Financial Domain of Municipal Corporation," Guest Column, *Hindustan Times,* January 3, 2002,Chandigarh.

————. (2001), "Go the Calcutta Way: Introduce Mayor-in-Council System", Guest Column, *Hindustan Times,* December 10, 2001, Chandigarh.

————. (2001), "Property Tax: Need of the Hour", Guest Column, *Hindustan Times,* January 15, 2001, Chandigarh.

The Constitution (74th Amendment) Act, 1992, Ministry of Urban Development, Government of India, New Delhi.

The Himachal Pradesh Infrastructure Development Act 2001 (Act No. 1 of 2002), Government of Himachal Pradesh.

The Himachal Pradesh Municipal Act, 1994.

The Himachal Pradesh Municipal Corporation Act, 1994.

Tiwari, A K (2000), *Infrastructure and Economic Development in Himachal Pradesh,* Indus Publishing Company, New Delhi.

TNUDF (2001), *Report on the Activities and Annual Accounts of Tamil Nadu Urban Development Fund for the Financial Year 2000-01,* Department of Housing and Urban Development, Government of Tamil Nadu, Chennai.

Union Budget 2002-03, Ministry of Finance, Government of India, New Delhi.

Urban Finance (2002), 'MCD Decides to Privatize Toll Tax Collection', Volume 5 Number 1, Quarterly Journal of NIUA, New Delhi.

Vaidya, Chetan and Hitesh Vaidya (2003), "Management Innovations for Municipal Resource Mobilisation in India", in *Governance,* March 2003, Urban Management and Development Centre, RCVP Noronha Academy of Administration, Bhopal.

Descriptions of West Bengal, Karnataka, Mumbai, Rajasthan Urban Infrastructure/ Municipal Development / Environmental Improvement Programmes, Technical Assistance for Calcutta Municipal Environmental Improvement Programme and programmes / reform initiatives relating to housing, urban development and poverty alleviation etc. were obtained from the Ministry of Urban Affairs and Employment, Government of India's Website *http:urbanindia.nic.in/prg.htm7*

Discussions with Elected and Appointed Representatives of Shimla, Solan, Kullu, Manali, Sunder Nagar and Rewalsar and suggestions received from the Department of Urban Development, Government of Himachal Pradesh, Shimla and Planning Commission, Government of India, New Delhi

Various Annual Reports (ARs) of the of Municipal Corporation of Shimla (1997-98 to 2001-02), Budget Documents of ULBs, Notifications of Department of Irrigation and Public Health, Department of Urban Development, Planning Documents (Five Year Plans), Note provided by the Town and Country Planning Department, Action Taken Report on First State Finance Commission and some other papers / documents and website *http:// www.himachal.nic.in*

- I am grateful to Shri J P Gupta, IAS (Retd), Former Chairman, Punjab State Finance Commission and Senior Advisor CRRID and Dr Gangadhar Jha, Former Professor, NIUA, New Delhi and currently Team Leader, Agra Municipal Reforms Project, IPE, New Delhi for their valuable suggestions and comments on this chapter.

Chapter 21

Employment and Unemployment

Introduction

One of the serious problems of Himachal Pradesh is its rising level of unemployment. Disguised unemployment in agriculture and the large volume of low-quality employment are causes of concern. Unemployment among the educated youth is serious, considering that the state is one of the highly literate ones. The growth of employment has not kept pace with the state's domestic product, and the result is underutilisation of the labour force. An important objective of development planning has been to increase employment opportunities so as to meet the backlog of the unemployed and also take care of the new entrants to the labour force. One of the important monitorable targets of the Tenth Five Year Plan at the national level that has rightly been given prominence is to provide gainful high quality employment to the labour force. Similarly, a thrust area in the Tenth Five Year Plan of Himachal Pradesh is the generation of additional employment opportunities in the private sector by promoting investment, improving marketable vocational skills with the help of information technology. The growth rate of eight per cent or above as envisaged in the Tenth Plan period will generate higher employment opportunities, raise the standard of living of the people and reduce the poverty level. However, the process of globalisation and privatisation has serious implications for further generation of employment opportunities in the organised sector, especially the public sector, where the disinvestment process is on and there is emphasis on resource efficiency. The higher use of capital-intensive technology has serious implications for the generation of employment opportunities. This indicates possibility of further deterioration of the employment situation in the short run, if not in the long run, and hence, calls for appropriate policy interventions at different levels.

This chapter seeks to examine the dimensions of the employment and unemployment situation in the state, its status and quality of employment, sector-level changes, especially non-farm employment, employment in the organised sector and the role of special employment generating schemes for alleviating poverty. Trends and the structure of employment and unemployment have been analysed at the area, gender, age, and education level over specific periods for which relevant information is available. After an analysis of various aspects of the employment and unemployment situation in the state and other related aspects, recommendations have been made from a policy point of view. The main sources of data used in this chapter are NSSO surveys, population censuses, Labour and Employment Department of Himachal Pradesh and various state publications.

Employment and Unemployment Scenario

The analysis of the measure, trends and structure of employment and unemployment in the state is based mainly on quinquennial surveys carried out by the National Sample Survey Organisation (NSSO). Estimates of employment and unemployment by NSSO are derived from three concepts, usual status (US), current weekly status (CWS) and current daily status (CDS). These concepts take only time utilisation into account and do not reflect the quality of work or income.

Changes in Work-Participation Rates (WPRs)

Work participation rate is an important indicator of development showing the proportion of the working population in an economy. Table 21.1 indicates that WPR in Himachal Pradesh, based on the UPS criterion for rural and urban males, was 50.4 per cent and 49.9 per cent respectively in 1999-00. On the other hand,

WPR based on UPSS was 53.6 per cent for rural males and 49.7 per cent for urban males over the same period. The female WPR in the state during 1999-00 was 28.1 per cent on the UPS and 47.1 per cent on the UPSS criterion in the rural areas.

This indicates that a large number of women in the rural areas work in a subsidiary capacity. The female WPRs based on CWS and CDS, which are comparatively higher, support this fact. The female WPR in the urban areas is very low on all criteria. A glance at Table 21.1 shows that the WPR based on US, CWS and CDS has declined for rural males and females and urban females during 1993-94 to 1999-2000. However, the WPR for urban males has increased on all approaches during the same period. The decline in the WPR in the rural areas suggests that more people are going to school and that there is a reduction in the growth of population.

The age-specific worker-population ratio (ASWPR) for the younger age groups, especially 10-14 years and 15-19 years, based on the UPSS criterion sharply declined for rural males and females and urban females in 1999-2000 as compared to 1993-94. However, the ASWPR for younger urban males has risen during this period. It is interesting to note that the ASWPR for rural females in the age groups of 40-44 to 55-59 years increased over this period (NSSO 1997, 2001).

TABLE 21.1

Worker-Population Ratio in Himachal Pradesh

	1977-78	*1983*	*1987-88*	*1993-94*	*1999-00*
Usual Principal Status					
Rural Male	62.3	58.1	49.2	51.0	50.4
Rural Female	51.9	45.8	34.8	36.3	28.1
Urban Male	61.2	57.9	45.5	47.4	49.8
Urban Female	15.3	16.8	12.8	14.3	9.6
Usual Principal and Subsidiary Status					
Rural Male	69.5	61.4	53.9	59.0	53.6
Rural Female	65.9	54.4	48.0	52.0	47.1
Urban Male	63.2	58.8	46.6	48.8	49.9
Urban Female	17.9	19.2	15.6	20.1	13.0
Current Weekly Status					
Rural Male	60.6	57.9	48.8	54.0	51.0
Rural Female	45.5	39.8	33.5	46.2	42.4
Urban Male	60.9	58.7	45.5	47.9	49.7
Urban Female	14.6	16.7	12.9	17.6	11.7
Current Daily Status					
Rural Male	58.3	57.5	48.8	51.5	49.8
Rural Female	36.6	34.4	31.9	36.2	31.3
Urban Male	60.2	57.7	45.4	47.3	49.4
Urban Female	13.0	15.1	12.4	14.3	10.1

Source: NSSO, 1981, 1988, 1990, 1997, 2001.

Work Participation Rates at the District Level

An analysis of the WPR at the district level based on the census data indicates that the district of Lahaul and Spiti has the highest WPR both for males (68.39%) and females (57.43%) in 2001.On the other hand, Kangra district has the lowest male and female WPR. Table 21.2 shows that the total work participation rate has increased during 1991-2000 in all districts of the state except Lahaul and Spiti. The total WPR in the state as a whole has increased from 42.80 per cent in 1991 to 49.28 per cent in 2001. However, a look at the gender level WPR indicates that the female WPR has substantially increased during this period. Both male and female WPRs have increased in all districts of the state except Lahaul and Spiti. The increase in female WPR is encouraging. However, there has been a significant increase in the proportion of female marginal workers during the decade. Among Indian states and union territories, Himachal Pradesh ranked third, 12th, and second respectively during 2001 in terms of the total, male and female work participation rates.

TABLE 21.2

Work Participation Rate at the District Level, 1991 and 2001

Districts	*Total*		*Male*		*Female*	
	1991	*2001*	*1991*	*2001*	*1991*	*2001*
Lahaul & Spiti	64.93	63.50	68.90	68.39	60.07	57.43
Kinnaur	52.42	60.54	60.08	65.62	43.48	54.78
Kullu	47.93	57.05	54.05	60.63	41.28	53.20
Solan	45.05	52.70	54.14	61.32	35.06	42.60
Shimla	48.62	51.19	55.18	57.46	41.29	44.20
Mandi	45.72	50.44	49.11	52.69	42.38	48.23
Chamba	48.58	50.04	53.99	53.98	42.89	45.94
Hamirpur	41.87	49.90	44.15	51.06	39.81	48.85
Sirmaur	46.59	49.30	55.63	56.49	36.50	41.32
Bilaspur	44.60	48.95	48.39	52.31	40.82	45.56
Una	33.45	45.03	48.66	53.02	18.50	37.41
Kangra	34.37	44.04	46.08	50.84	22.94	37.01
Himachal Pradesh	**42.80**	**49.28**	**50.60**	**54.70**	**34.80**	**43.69**

Source: Director of Census Operations Himachal Pradesh (2002), *Census of India 2001, Provisional Population Totals, Distribution of Workers and Non-Workers, Paper 3 of 2001*, Registrar General and Census Commissioner, Govt. of India.

Changes in the Status of Employment

Employed persons have been categorised into three broad groups according to the status of their employment such as (i) self-employed, (ii) regular employees and (iii) casual labour. Table 21.3 shows usually employed persons per 1000 principal and subsidiary workers. Table 21.3 also reveals that during 1999-2000, a large majority of males and females in the rural areas of the state were self-employed. The proportion of regular employees among women as compared to men was much lower in the rural areas. In the urban areas, the proportion of regular employees, both male and female, was significantly high. The proportion of casual labour was relatively higher for males than females both in rural and urban areas. However, male casual labour in the rural areas at 20.4 per cent was higher than in the urban areas where it was 12.0 per cent.

TABLE 21.3

Per 1000 Distribution of Usually Employed by Status of Employment

Status	*1987-88*	*1993-94*	*1999-2000*
Self-Employed			
Rural Male	738	751	629
Rural Female	977	774	959
Urban Male	384	337	337
Urban Female	564	537	533
Regular Employees			
Rural Male	89	122	167
Rural Female	10	11	29
Urban Male	502	575	543
Urban Female	404	363	406
Casual Labour			
Rural Male	173	127	204
Rural Female	13	215	12
Urban Male	114	88	120
Urban Female	32	100	61

Source: NSSO: 1990, 1997, 2001.

An examination of the changes in the status of employment over the period indicates that the proportion of self-employed rural males has decreased between 1993-94 and 1999-00, whereas the proportion of self-employed rural females has significantly increased. It is interesting to note that regular male employees in the rural areas have increased by five per cent during 1993-94 through 1999-00 and casual male labour by seven per cent. Similarly, whereas self-employment of rural women has increased by 19 per cent over this period, women casual labour has correspondingly decreased by 20 per cent. Changes in the status of urban employment indicate that the ratio of male self-employment remained the same during 1993-94 as well as 1999-00, whereas regular employment decreased by three per cent and correspondingly casual labour increased by three per cent. Over the period, regular female employment in the urban areas increased by five per cent and casual employment by four per cent. Recent changes in the status of employment point to the impact of post-liberalisation policies.

Growth of Workforce According to Census Data

Table 21.4 indicates the growth of the workforce based on census data. The work participation rate of main workers, especially males, declined during 1991-2001. On the other hand, the work participation rate of marginal workers increased. Male marginal workers increased from 1.56 per cent to 11.40 per cent, and female workers from 15.45 per cent to 22.61 per cent during this period (Director of Census, HP 2002). This indicates a deteriorating quality of employment in the state. The growth of main workers declined during the decadal census period. On the other hand, the growth rate of marginal workers increased.

TABLE 21.4

Growth of Workforce in Himachal Pradesh over the Census Periods

Workforce	*1981*	*1991*	*2001*	*Annual Growth Rates*	
				1981-91	*1991-2001*
Population (in lakhs)	42.81	51.70	60.70	1.90	1.62
Work Participation Rate (Main Workers)	34.36	34.41	32.36	0.01	-0.61
Main workers (in lakhs)	14.71	17.79	19.64	1.92	0.99
Work Participation Rate (Marginal Workers)	8.01	8.42	16.92	0.50	7.23
Marginal Workers (in lakhs)	3.43	4.35	10.27	2.40	8.97

Source: Census of India 1981, 1991, 2001.

Trends in Unemployment Rates

Table 21.5 shows unemployment rates in the state according to three approaches. It may be observed that estimates of unemployed persons based on the usual status criterion or even the more restrictive US (adjusted) measure were very low during 1999-00. The unemployed person-days rates were higher than those for persons, based on usual status rates, which indicate a high degree of intermittent unemployment. This means lack of regular employment for many workers. Urban unemployment rates are relatively higher than rural ones. Unemployment rates for rural males on the usual principal status as well as usual status (adjusted) have increased by about one per cent during 1993-94 through 1999-00. On the other hand, urban unemployment among males on these measures remained almost the same. Unemployment rates for urban females on UPS and US (adjusted) measures decreased by five per cent and three per cent respectively, and increased for rural females by one per cent on UPS and remained almost the same on US (adjusted) measure. However, from 1983 to 1999-00, there has been a decline in unemployment rates for rural males until 1993-94, and a rise during 1999-00. The process of economic reforms seems to have had a bearing on this situation. There is a declining trend throughout in female unemployment rates in rural areas on all the three measures. A large majority of women are self-employed in the agriculture sector and their proportion has substantially increased. There has been no definite pattern in the unemployment rates for urban males and females during this period.

TABLE 21.5

Unemployment Rates in Himachal Pradesh

	Usual Status	*Usual Status (adj.)*	*Current Weekly Status*	*Current Daily Status*
Rural Male				
1983	2.1	–	2.1	2.2
1987-1988	4.3	1.3	4.1	4.1
1993-1994	2.3	0.9	1.2	2.6
1999-2000	3.0	1.8	2.7	3.4
Rural Female				
1983	0.7	–	0.7	0.8
1987-1988	0.9	0.4	0.9	0.9
1993-1994	0.6	0.1	0.3	0.5
1999-2000	1.8	0.5	0.7	0.9
Urban Male				
1983	8.2	–	7.7	8.1
1987-1988	6.9	6.6	7.1	7.1
1993-1994	4.1	3.3	3.5	4.0
1999-2000	6.3	6.2	6.7	7.0
Urban Female				
1983	8.6	–	8.6	9.7
1987-1988	10.5	8.8	9.8	10.2
1993-1994	0.4	0.3	0.9	1.2
1999-2000	11.8	7.9	9.9	11.9

Source: NSSO: 1988, 1990, 1997, 2001.

Unemployment Rates of the Educated

The NSSO survey defines educated persons as those who have attained the educational level of secondary and above. Table 21.6 presents unemployment rates on various approaches for educated persons for the latest and the last quinquennial survey. During 1999-2000, unemployment rate among the educated in the state was much higher for females in both rural and urban areas, despite a substantial decline during 1993-94 to 1999-2000. The unemployment rate of educated rural males has increased by one per cent on different approaches over this period. Among urban males, the unemployment rate has declined by one per cent on the different measures. A comparison with total unemployment rates indicates relatively higher rates for the educated in the state. A high literacy rate in the state and the lack of generation of appropriate employment opportunities for the educated might explain such a situation.

TABLE 21.6

Unemployment Rates of the Educated of Age 15 Years and Above

	Usual Status	*Usual Status(adj.)*	*Current Weekly Status*
Rural Male			
1993-1994	8.6	3.4	4.3
1999-2000	8.7	4.9	5.7
Rural Female			
1993-1994	7.8	1.6	3.2
1999-2000	8.4	0.9	1.8
Rural Persons			
1993-1994	8.5	2.8	4.0
1999-2000	8.6	3.7	4.6
Urban Male			
1993-1994	5.5	4.7	4.5
1999-2000	8.7	8.7	8.8
Urban Female			
1993-1994	0	–	1.6
1999-2000	19.1	14.2	17.1
Urban Persons			
1993-1994	4.6	3.8	4.0
1999-2000	4.0	9.6	10.3

Source: NSSO: 1997, 2001.

State Level Comparison of Workforce Growth and Unemployment

Table 21.7 indicates that the growth rate of employment in Himachal Pradesh at 0.37 per cent during 1993-94/1999-00 is one of the lowest in the country except Kerala and Andhra Pradesh. However, the unemployment rate, even after an increase in this period, is still the lowest in Himachal Pradesh compared to these states. It is interesting to note that employment elasticity was very low at 0.052 during 1993-94/1999-00, though the growth rate of the GDP at 7.1 per cent was sufficiently high. This indicates that the employment generation capacity of growth has

TABLE 21.7

Employment and Unemployment in Selected States (CDS Basis)

Selected States	*Employment ('000) 1999-00*	*Employment Growth 1993-94 to 1999-00*	*Unemployment Rate (Per cent)*		*Employment Elasticity 1993-94 to 1999-00*	*Annual GDP Growth 1993-94 to 1999-00*
			1993-94	1999-00		
Andhra Pradesh	30614	0.35	6.69	8.03	0.067	5.2
Assam	7647	1.99	8.03	8.03	0.737	2.7
Bihar	30355	1.59	6.34	7.32	0.353	4.5
Gujarat	18545	2.31	5.70	4.55	0.316	7.3
Haryana	5982	2.43	6.51	4.77	0.420	5.8
Himachal Pradesh	**2371**	**0.37**	**1.80**	**2.96**	**0.052**	**7.1**
Karnataka	20333	1.43	4.94	4.57	0.188	7.6
Kerala	8902	0.07	15.51	20.97	0.013	5.5
Madhya Pradesh	28725	1.28	3.56	4.45	0.272	4.7
Maharashtra	34979	1.25	5.09	7.16	0.216	5.8
Orissa	11928	1.05	7.30	7.34	0.262	4.0
Punjab	8013	1.96	3.10	4.03	0.426	4.6
Rajasthan	19930	0.73	1.31	3.13	0.104	7.0
Tamil Nadu	23143	0.37	11.41	11.78	0.052	7.1
Uttar Pradesh	49387	1.02	3.45	4.08	0.185	5.5
West Bengal	22656	0.41	10.06	14.99	0.056	7.3
All India	**336736**	**1.07**	**5.99**	**7.32**	**0.160**	**6.7**

Source: Ministry of Finance and Company Affairs, 2003.

reduced. Unemployment rate in Kerala was the highest in the country during 1999-00, followed by West Bengal and Tamil Nadu. Only in Gujarat and Haryana, there was a decline in unemployment rates during the period under consideration.

Rural Urban Status of Labour force and Workforce

Table 21.8 shows the growth of population, labour force and workforce in Himachal Pradesh in the rural and urban areas. The growth rate of the labour force in the state during the period 1993-94 to 1999-00 has been 0.54 per cent while that of the workforce has been 0.37 per cent during this period. The growth of unemployed persons during the same period has been 8.50 per cent. The growth rates of population, labour force and workforce are relatively much higher in the urban areas than in the rural areas. Similarly, the rate of unemployment in the urban areas was much higher at 7.77 per cent during 1999-00 than in the rural areas at 2.41 per cent. The growth rate of unemployed persons in the urban areas at 18.77 per cent is higher than in the rural areas. Lack of employment avenues in the rural areas and excessive migration to the urban areas in search of employment aggravate the unemployment situation in the latter. However, according to NSS data, the extent of unemployment in the state is not large.

TABLE 21.8

Labourforce, Workforce and Unemployed in Himachal Pradesh (CDS)

	1993-1994	*1999-2000*	*Annual Growth Rates 1993-1994 to 1999-2000*
Rural			
Population	49,01,482	53,61,076	1.51
Labour force	21,88,017	22,30,092	0.32
Workforce	21,51,103	21,76,301	019
No. of Unemployed	36,914	53791	6.48
Rate of Unemployment	1.69	2.41	
Urban			
Population	4,81,903	5,70,079	2.84
Labour force	1,61,619	1,97,281	3.38
Workforce	1,56,161	1,81,958	2.58
No. of Unemployed	5,456	15,323	18.77
Rate of Unemployment	3.78	7.77	
Total			
Population	53,83,385	59,31,155	1.63
Labour force	23,49,636	24,27,373	0.54
Workforce	23,07,264	23,58,269	0.37
No. of Unemployed	42,372	69,114	8.50
Rate of Unemployment	1.80	2.85	

Source: NSSO: 1997, 2001.

Magnitude of Unemployment According to Employment Exchange Data

In addition to the NSS data, estimates of unemployment are available from the state employment exchanges. According to their live registers, the total number of registered job-seekers, both educated and uneducated, was 9.01 lakh during 2002-03 (Table 21.9). The number of applicants on the live registers has considerably increased over the period. Of the total job seekers during 2002-03, 66.2 per cent were matriculates and undergraduates, 20.7 per cent undermatriculates, 8.9 per cent graduates and 3.3 per cent postgraduates. Thus, matriculates and undergraduates constitute the large majority of those seeking work. Male applicants on the live register were 68.2 per cent and female applicants were 31.8 per cent. Of the total registrants in 2002-03, 19.7 per cent were scheduled castes and 2.9 per cent scheduled tribes (Dept. of Labour and Employment, H.P.)

The number of technically qualified job-seekers, such as degree engineers, diploma engineers and ITI craftsmen was 40,626 during 2001-02. The highest number, i e., 34,064 was that of ITI certificate holders. The number of engineers has declined recently but the number of diploma and ITI certificate holders has increased.

TABLE 21.9

Percentage of Job-Seekers on the Live Register at the Education Level

Education	*1980*	*1990*	*1999-2000*	*2000-2001*	*2001-2002*	*2002-2003*
Post-graduate	1.28	2.5	2.84	2.89	3.11	3.31
Graduate	6.37	6.4	7.83	8.01	8.49	8.87
Matric & above	51.39	55.9	65.21	65.50	66.00	66.18
Below matric	31.09	29.1	22.59	22.37	21.36	20.75
Illiterate	9.86	6.1	1.52	1.23	1.04	0.88
Total (No. in lakhs)	1.42	4.40	8.75	9.00	8.95	9.01
Technically Qualified (No)						
Degree holder			1798	1753	1692	-
Diploma holder			4512	4630	4870	-
Certificate holder (ITI Trade)			30915	31617	34064	-
Total			37225	38000	40626	-

Source: *Statistical Abstracts of H.P. (different years)*, Department of Labour and Employment, Himachal Pradesh

A district-level analysis of the unemployment situation in the state indicates that the three districts of Kangra, Mandi and Shimla, being more urban, account for about 55.38 per cent of the registrants (Table 21.10). On the other hand, Kinnaur and Lahaul and Spiti, being sparsely populated account for less than one per cent each. In the remaining districts, the percentage of job-seekers varies between 4.73 in Chamba and 7.30 in Bilaspur. The ratio of placement to registration is very low and has declined over the period.

TABLE 21.10

District-wise Job-seekers on the Live Register of Employment Exchanges (2002-2003)

District	*Registration*	*Vacancies Notified*	*Submission Made*	*Placement*	*Live Register*
Bilaspur	7,635	129	3,425	136	65,786
Chamba	8,399	240	3,748	188	42,617
Hamirpur	12,469	117	4,896	188	63,976
Kangra	32,585	300	11,001	352	1,67,872
Kinnaur	1,805	9	360	85	7,737
Kullu	6,929	267	2,212	154	45,205
Lahaul & Spiti	1,394	24	450	29	5,584
Mandi	20,337	122	6,266	381	1,66,195
Shimla	15,352	435	5,029	243	1,64,836
Sirmaur	9,686	113	3,453	141	47,479
Solan	9,455	162	4,944	255	64,954
Una	10,172	91	4,468	241	58,711
Himachal Pradesh	**1,36,218**	**2009**	**50,252**	**2393**	**9,00,934**

Source: Department of Labour and Employment, Govt. of H.P., Shimla.

The employment exchange data suffer from limitations and constraints and do not give a reliable picture of unemployment in the state. For instance, a large number of applicants registered with the employment exchanges might be employed but continue to be on the live registers. Further, an applicant may be registered with more than one exchange. The Planning Department of Himachal Pradesh conducted a sample survey of the registrants of employment exchanges in six districts to find out the exact status of registrants on 31 December 1991. A two per cent sample was taken. It was found that 36.18 per cent of the registrants were employed, three per cent in the public sector, 18.31 per cent in the private sector and 14.87 per cent were self-employed. If we exclude 36.18 per cent who were employed from the total of unemployed during 2002-03 i.e., 3.26 lakh out of a total of 9.01 lakh, it leaves the number of unemployed to be 5.75 lakh (*Ninth Five Year Plan of HP*, Chand 1993). Thus, there is need to monitor those registered with the exchanges for multiple registration and for being employed.

Quality of Employment

Besides the problem of open unemployment, the quality of a large part of the existing employment is low and is deteriorating. Table 21.11 shows whether the usually employed were underutilising their available labour-time due to lack of enough work or persons having enough work but not getting sufficient return were seeking or were available for additional and alternative work. About six per cent of the usually employed rural males and four per cent of the usually employed urban males reported seeking or being available for additional work during 1999-2000. The corresponding percentages were 1.6 for rural females and 4.3 per cent for urban females. On the other hand, among those who sought alternative work during 1999-00, 5.2 per cent were rural males, 5.6 per cent urban males, 1.3 per cent rural females and 3.2 per cent urban females. It can be observed that the number of those who seek additional/alternative work has declined during 1999-00 except for urban males seeking alternative work. However, underemployment is still high in the state.

TABLE 21.11

Per Thousand Usually Working Persons of Age 15 Years and above Available for Additional/Alternative Work

Year	*Available for Additional Work*			*Available for Alternative Work*		
	1987-88	*1993-94*	*1999-00*	*1987-88*	*1993-94*	*1999-00*
Rural Male	47	68	63	12	58	52
Rural Female	16	22	16	10	19	13
All	—	49	45	—	41	37
Urban Male	24	54	44	16	54	56
Urban Female	23	50	43	11	32	32
All	—	53	44	—	50	52

Source: NSSO: 1990, 1997, 2001.

Non-Agricultural Employment

Increasing the share of employment and income in non-agricultural activities is identified with the achievement of higher levels of development. The agricultural sector, after a period, cannot absorb any additional labour force and sustain productivity and growth rates. Hence, there is need to diversify into non-agricultural activities for achieving higher growth of the economy.

Table 21.12 indicates the changing structure of the workforce at the broad sector-levels in Himachal Pradesh. The economy of the state is dominated by agriculture, which accounted for 68.90 per cent of the employment during 1999-2000, whereas the non-agricultural sector accounted for 31.10 per cent. The share of the workforce engaged in the primary sector, especially agriculture, declined over the period. On the other hand, the share of the secondary and tertiary sectors increased. The growth rate of non-agricultural employment in the state was 4.38 per cent as compared to the growth rate of agriculture and allied sectors, which was –1.63 per cent during 1993-94 to 1999-00. Thus, Himachal Pradesh has experienced a shift of the labour force from agriculture to the non-agricultural sector. It is interesting to observe that the contribution of the farm sector to the state domestic product during 2001 was about 23 per cent and that of the non-agricultural sector 77 per cent. This indicates low productivity and high disguised unemployment in agriculture.

TABLE 21.12

Percentage Distribution of Non-Agricultural Employment and its Growth Rate (UPSS)

Sectors	*1983*	*1993-94*	*1999-00*	*Growth Rates*	
				1983/ 93-94	*1993-94/ 99-00*
Primary	82.05	75.98	68.90	0.85	-1.63
Secondary	7.66	11.05	15.08	4.99	5.30
Tertiary	10.28	12.97	16.02	3.73	3.56
Non-Agricultural Employment	**17.94**	**24.01**	**31.10**	**4.29**	**4.38**
All (in Lakh)	24.40	28.93	28.90	1.28	-0.02

Source: NSSO 1987, 1997, 2001.

Comparison with Neighbouring States

As compared to the neighbouring states and the all-India average, the share of non-agricultural employment is the lowest in Himachal Pradesh. It is the highest in Punjab, followed by Jammu and Kashmir and Haryana. In Himachal Pradesh, it is also lower than the national average (Table 21.13). Non-agricultural employment is the highest in Kerala at 76.7 per cent and the lowest in Bihar at 22.6 per cent (Director of Census HP 2002).

TABLE 21.13

Rural Non-farm Employment in Selected States, 2001 (per cent)

States	*Farm Employment*	*Non-farm Employment*
Himachal Pradesh	**68.6**	**31.4**
Haryana	51.6	48.4
Jammu & Kashmir	50.1	49.9
Punjab	39.4	60.6
All India	**58.4**	**41.6**

Source: Census of India, 2001.

TABLE 21.14

Percentage of Usually Working Persons (UPSS) at Broad Industry Category by Area and Sex

Industrial Category	*Rural Male*			*Rural Female*			*Urban Male*			*Urban Female*		
	1983	*1993-94*	*1999-00*	*1983*	*1993-94*	*1999-00*	*1983*	*1993-94*	*1999-00*	*1983*	*1993-94*	*1999-00*
Agriculture, forestry, fishing	77.00	65.8	53.8	97.5	95.5	95.1	6.5	8.8	4.2	34.1	44.4	39.1
Mining & quarrying	0.5	0.2	0	-	-	-	-	0.8	-	-	-	-
Manufacturing	5.0	4.8	6.7	1.1	1.6	1.1	12.2	4.11	9.5	5.8	1.6	1.8
Electricity, gas, water etc.	0.5	1.3	2.0	-	0.2	0.1	2.0	4.0	4.1	2.4	1.5	2.1
Construction	5.8	11.9	17.2	-	0.4	0.4	6.2	8.7	11.7	-	3.9	1.7
Trade, hotel & restaurants	1.8	5.2	6.1	0.2	0.6	0.6	16.3	20.8	24.6	1.6	4.1	10.9
Transport, storage communication etc.	1.1	1.6	4.3	0.1	-	0.1	2.7	3.0	5.9	4.1	-	1.4
Finance, insurance, business activities etc.	0.3	0.4	0.7	-	-	-	5.5	4.0	5.7	1.9	1.2	1.0
Public administration, education, community services etc.	7.1	8.8	9.2	1.1	1.5	2.5	48.0	45.8	34.3	48.3	43.2	41.9
All (In Lakh)	12.65	14.53	14.44	11.09	12.68	12.56	1.13	1.29	1.58	0.30	0.44	0.33

Source: NSSO 1990, 1997, 2001.

Note: The total workers in each industry for each year have been worked out by applying the percentage distribution given by National Sample Surveys across industries to absolute numbers of four categories of workers. These categories of workers in each industry have been added to work out estimates of total workers in each industry.

Rural-urban and Gender-wise Non-agricultural Employment

Table 21.14 presents the distribution of usually employed workers by broad industry for principal and subsidiary status workers. During 1999-2000, among the usually employed workers in the rural areas of Himachal Pradesh, about 54 per cent males and 95 per cent females were engaged in agricultural activity. The proportion of males in the agricultural sector has gradually declined. Over the years, there has been a significant increase in the proportion of males engaged in construction, trade, hotels and restaurants, transport, storage and communication services in the rural areas of the state.

In the urban areas of the state, trade, hotels and restaurants employed about 25 per cent of the male workers, while the manufacturing and construction sectors accounted for 10 per cent and 12 per cent respectively of the usually employed males during 1999-2000. Public administration, community services, transport, storage and communications provided employment to about 34 per cent and six per cent respectively of urban male workers. On the other hand, the services accounted for the highest proportion of urban females, that is, 42 per cent, followed by agriculture (40%), trade, hotels and restaurants (11%), and manufacturing (2%). The proportion of urban male workers in manufacturing declined by two per cent and in the services by 14 per cent during 1983 to 1999-2000. Their proportion increased in construction, electricity, gas, water, trade, hotels and restaurants, transport, storage and communications during this period. On the other hand, the proportion of urban female workers increased in trade, hotels and restaurants by nine per cent and decreased in agriculture and manufacturing by five and four per cent respectively, between 1983 and 1999-2000.

Sectoral Growth Rates of Non-agricultural Employment

Table 21.15 indicates growth rates of different sectors from 1983/1993-94 to 1993-94/1999-00. Sectors with comparatively higher growth rates in the post-liberalisation period are transport, storage and communications (17.98%), finance, insurance, etc. (9.18%), construction (6.08%) and manufacturing (4.65%). The growth in these sectors has substantially increased over this period. On the other hand, the growth rate of agriculture has declined from 0.85 per cent during 1983/1993-94 to –1.63 per cent during 1993-94/1999-00. Other sectors which have experienced a decline in their growth rate of employment during this period are trade, hotels and restaurants, electricity, gas, water, public administration, community services etc. However, the percentage of employment in these sectors has increased during this period. The overall growth rate of employment has declined from 1.28 per cent to –0.02 per cent over this period.

TABLE 21.15

Growth Rates of Employment at the Industry Level (UPSS)

Industrial Category	*Employment (per cent)*			*Annual Compound Growth Rates*	
	1983	*1993-94*	*1999-00*	*1983/ 1993-94*	*1993-94/ 1999-00*
Agriculture, forestry, fishing etc.	82.05	75.98	68.90	0.85	-1.63
Mining & quarrying	0.26	0.14	-	-4.21	-
Manufacturing	3.73	3.32	4.37	0.49	4.65
Electricity, gas, water etc.	0.38	0.98	1.29	10.37	4.58
Construction	3.29	6.61	9.42	8.19	6.08
Trade, hotel & restaurants	1.80	3.86	4.77	8.86	3.57
Transport, storage communication etc.	1.05	0.94	2.53	0.52	17.98
Finance, insurance, business activities etc.	0.43	0.40	0.67	0.75	9.18
Public administration, education, community Services etc.	7.00	7.77	8.04	1.03	0.54
All	100.00	100.00	100.00	1.28	-0.02

Source: NSSO 1987, 1997, 2001.

Non-agricultural Employment at the District Level

An analysis of non-farm employment at the district level indicates that Lahaul and Spiti has the highest proportion of workers (45.32%) employed in the non-farm sector followed by Solan (42.94%), Una (37.18%) and Kangra (36.36%) (Table 21.16). On the other hand, Kullu district had the lowest non-farm employment (21.22%) during 2001. Districts, which have non farm employment below the state average, are Sirmaur, Chamba, Hamirpur and Bilaspur. The districts of Kangra, Solan and Una, where non-farm employment is very high, are industrially important. Lahaul and Spiti, being less populated and having desert and snow conditions, a significant proportion of workers depends on non-agricultural activities for employment.

Thus, it may be observed that the share of the non-agricultural sector has increased over the period. However, the pace of the shift from agriculture to non-agricultural activities, especially in the rural areas, needs to be hastened through diversification and other means necessary. The nature and determinants of non-farm employment need to be examined (Chand, 2002). It is interesting to note that in most of the developed countries, only a very small proportion of workers are dependent on the agricultural sector. For instance, in such countries as Canada, Britain, the United States, Australia, Italy, the Republic of Korea, the workforce engaged in the agricultural sector ranged between one per cent and 5.7 per cent in 1997 (ILO 1999). Hence, a speedy diversification into non-agricultural activities is the immediate requirement for generating higher employment opportunities in the state.

TABLE 21.16

Percentage Distribution of Non-Agricultural Workers at the District Level, 2001

Districts	*Farm Employment*	*Non-Farm Employment*
Chamba	73.79	26.21
Kangra	63.64	36.36
Lahaul and Spiti	54.68	45.32
Kullu	78.78	21.22
Mandi	74.09	25.91
Hamirpur	71.58	28.42
Una	62.82	37.18
Bilaspur	70.49	29.51
Solan	57.06	42.94
Sirmaur	74.18	25.82
Shimla	67.16	32.84
Kinnaur	68.87	31.13
Himachal Pradesh	**68.65**	**31.35**

Source: Director of Census Operations HP, 2002.

Employment in the Organised Sector

Table 21.17 indicates that out of 3.13 lakh employees in the organised sector in 2001, about 84.6 per cent were employed in the public sector and 15.4 per cent in the private sector. The total public sector employment declined during 1986-90 but increased thereafter. On the other hand, private sector employment has increased throughout the period. An analysis of employment in the organised sector at the broad industry level indicates that the proportion of employment in the public sector is the highest in community, social and personnel services (48.5%), followed by construction (22.5%), electricity, gas and water (12.2%) accounting for 83 per cent of the public sector employment in 2001. Since 1986, the proportion of employment has constantly increased in these sectors, except construction, which has experienced a decline throughout. Employment in the organised private sector at the industry level has been the highest in manufacturing (69.3%) followed by community, social and personnel services (14.5%) and construction (10.2%), accounting for 94 per cent of the employment in the private sector.

TABLE 21.17

Industrial Distribution of Employment in the Organised Sector (per cent)

Category	*Public Sector*				*Private Sector*			
	1986	*1990*	*1995*	*2001*	*1986*	*1990*	*1995*	*2001*
Agriculture, forestry, fishing	9.6	5.2	4.5	4.8	3.0	2.0	1.8	1.3
Mining and quarrying	0.1	0.1	0.1	0.1	0.1	0.5	—	—
Manufacturing	1.5	1.7	1.4	1.1	52.4	67.4	67.2	69.3
Electricity, gas and water	8.9	10.4	11.6	12.2	0.1	—	—	—
Construction	35.7	26.5	25.0	22.3	18.7	8.3	7.6	10.2
Trade, hotels & restaurants	0.4	0.4	0.5	0.5	5.5	4.0	5.3	4.0
Finance, insurance, real estate & business services	5.3	5.8	6.0	6.2	1.0	0.9	0.7	0.4
Transport, storage & communications	2.7	4.0	4.6	4.4	1.8	0.1	0.1	0.1
Community, social and personnel services	35.8	45.3	46.2	48.5	17.4	17.0	17.3	14.5
All (No.)	265566	240794	247246	264378	22059	30082	39082	48266

Source: Ninth Five Year Plan 1997-2002, Department of Labour and Employment 2002.

The growth rate of organised sector employment as a whole has constantly declined from 2.63 per cent in 1981-85 to 1.36 per cent in 1995-96 and further to 0.10 per cent in 1999-2000.The annual growth rate of employment in the organised public sector has been 1.12 per cent as against 3.58 per cent in the private sector. The growth rate of private sector employment declined from 8.06 per cent during 1986-90 to 5.37 per cent during 1990-95 and further to 3.58 per cent during 1995-2001. On the other hand, the growth rate of public sector employment during the same period has risen from –2.22 per cent to 0.5 per cent and further to 1.12 per cent.

Of the total employment in the organised public sector, 68.9 per cent of the employment during 2001 was in state government establishments, 23.4 per cent in quasi-government, 6.3 per cent in central government and 1.4 per cent in local bodies (Table 21.18).

The share of organised sector employment in the total employment in the state was about ten per cent only in 2001. Obviously, a very large proportion of the workforce (90%) in the state is employed in the informal sector. As compared to Himachal Pradesh, the proportion of workforce engaged in the organised sector in the country is only about seven per cent (Planning Commission 2001a).

Table 21.19 shows that the total number of government employees on 31 March 2001 was 2,35,594, of which 1,39,882 were regular employees and the remaining, about 40 per cent, non-regular employees. About 69 per cent of the regular employees are employed in the departments of Education (41.78%), Police (8.60%), Health and Family Welfare (8.57%), Forests (5.10%) and Public Works (4.79%). Three districts, namely, Shimla, Kangra and Mandi account for about 54 per cent of the employees (Census of Government Employees 1999, 2001). Of the regular employees, about 19 per cent are women. The state has the highest ratio of government employees per 1000 of population in the country. In the absence of large employment opportunities, especially in the non-agricultural sector, people aspire for government jobs, which provide adequate social security. Political considerations also play a significant role in adding to the number of government employees. There has been a continuous addition to the number of government employees since 1990. Regularisation of non-regular employees in 1999 has further enhanced the number of these employees. Large resources are spent on their salaries and pensions.

TABLE 21.18

Percentage Distribution of Public Sector Employees by Establishments

Sector	*Years*					
	1970	*1980*	*1985*	*1990*	*1995*	*2001*
I. Public sector						
State government	75.10	71.9	71.7	67.4	68.6	68.9
Central government	20.00	10.2	6.9	6.7	6.7	6.3
Quasi-government (central+ state)	2.2	15.9	20.3	24.6	23.4	23.4
Local bodies	2.7	2.0	1.2	1.3	1.3	1.4
Total (no.) (public sector)	162243 (92.4)	225104 (95.3)	244443 (92.9)	240794 (88.9)	2477246 (86.4)	264378 (84.6)
II Private sector	13395 (7.6)	11176 (4.7)	18791 (7.1)	30082 (11.1)	39082 (13.6)	48266 (15.4)
Total I & II	**175638 (100.0)**	**236280 (100.0)**	**263234 (100.0)**	**270876 (100.0)**	**286328 (100.0)**	**312644 (100.0)**

Source: Economic Review, Himachal Pradesh, 1971, 1981, 1986, *Ninth Five Year Plan 1997-02, Himachal Pradesh*, Department of Labour and Employment, Himachal Pradesh.

TABLE 21.19

Regular and Other Government Employees

Date of Census	*Regular*	*Ad-hoc*	*Tenure*	*Part-time*	*Work-charged*	*Voluntary*	*Daily Paid*	*Total*
31.3.1990	111700	—	—	4217	6098	—	58617	180632
31.3.1991	113851	—	—	4613	5434	2718	58024	184640
31.3.1992	114831	812	305	4867	6126	5857	65042	197840
31.3.1993	112717	2780	1553	5404	6624	8405	59570	197053
31.3.1994	113039	2677	1834	5426	6455	8860	60124	198415
31.3.1995	115493	2200	1781	5704	12023	8753	56725	202679
31.3.1996	117944	1490	1157	5667	17716	8401	58607	210982
31.3.1997	120703	1216	1721	6308	19294	8295	56318	213855
01.1.1998	123626	1011	2487	7242	21039	7090	54983	217478
31.3.1999	131919	669	3622	8718	23778	4199	54190	227095
31.3.2000	136085	615	4034	9000	27827	3753	52430	233744
31.3.2001	139882	481	3960	9794	31001	4021	46455	235594

Source: Department of Economic and Statistics, Govt. of Himachal Pradesh

There is a strong preference for white-collar jobs in the organised sector, especially government jobs, rather than unorganised jobs because of assured regular income and other social security benefits. If the expectations of the labour force, pertaining to the creation of employment in the organised sector, has to be met, a high rate of growth of the economy has to be achieved. In the absence of the expansion of government employment in the organised sector, the possibility of creating more jobs in the private organised sector has to be explored.

A large proportion of people of the state are serving soldiers and ex-servicemen. Further, due to the dearth of sufficient employment opportunities in the state, people migrate to the adjoining and other states in search of work. The number of ex-servicemen in 2000 was 77,852, that of serving soldiers 1,11,845 and war widows 18,481 (Table 20.20). About 88 per cent of the ex-servicemen are from the districts of Kangra, Hamirpur, Mandi, Una and Bilaspur. Thus, a significant proportion of persons in the state are ex-servicemen who retire at a young age and a number of them get re-employed in the organised sector or take up self-employment occupations in the service sector. The ex-servicemen who have high sense of discipline and other moral values need to be involved in various productive activities intensively so that the youth of the state can be better guided and involved in activities in the rural areas

Employment in the Unorganised Sector

The contribution of the unorganised/informal sector in the state is significant in terms of employment and income generation. About 90 per cent of the workforce is engaged in activities in the informal sector. Similarly, about 93 per cent of the workforce earns its livelihood from the unorganised sector in the country and its share in the net domestic product is 60.5 per cent of the total national net domestic product (CSO 2001). Though this sector provides employment to a large workforce, it has to function under severe constraints and the quality of most of the employment generated is low. The constraints faced by this sector limit its capacity to absorb more workers. Especially, the general lack of credit availability through the formal financial institutions inhibits the expansion of the informal sector activities and hence, the growth of employment (Chand 1997).

TABLE 21.20

Serving Soldiers, Ex-servicemen and War Widows

	1995	*1996*	*1998*	*1999*	*2000*
Serving Soldiers	103654	105294	107004	112390	111845
Ex-servicemen	67562	71312	75466	76357	77852
War widows	15657	16828	18155	18155	18481

Source: Statistical Outline of Himachal Pradesh (different issues)

The economic census provides information on enterprises in the unorganised sector. Table 21.21 shows that the total number of non-agricultural enterprises in the state was 2.14 lakh during 1998 and 5.59 lakh workers were working in them. Of these, 3.71 lakh were in rural enterprises and 1.89 lakh in urban enterprises. The largest proportion of workers in the rural areas were in OAEs followed by NDEs and DEs. On the other hand, the largest proportion of workers in the urban areas were in DEs, followed by NDEs and OAEs. Per enterprise employment generated in the

TABLE 21.21

Non-Agricultural Enterprises and Workers in Them (In lakh)

	Rural		*Urban*		*Combined*	
	Enterprises	*Workers*	*Enterprises*	*Workers*	*Enterprises*	*Workers*
Own Account Enterprises (OAE)	1.18 69.01	1.36 36.66	0.26 60.47	0.33 17.46	1.44 67.29	1.69 30.23
Directory Enterprises (DE)	0.08 4.68	1.33 35.85	0.04 9.30	1.22 64.55	0.12 5.61	2.55 45.62
Non-Directory Enterprises (NDE)	0.45 26.32	1.02 27.49	0.13 30.23	0.34 17.99	0.58 27.10	1.35 24.15
All	1.71 100.00	3.71 100.00	0.43 100.00	1.89 100.00	2.14 100.00	5.59 100.00

Source: *Economic Census 1998.*

Note: Figures in the second row in each column are percentages to totals

OAE: An enterprise run by members of the household

DE: An enterprise, which employs six or more workers on a fairly regular basis

NDE: An enterprise, which employs five or less workers on a fairly regular basis

urban areas were 4.1 persons as compared to 2.1 persons in the rural areas in 1998.

The growth rate of enterprises has declined over the economic census period (Table 21.22). The decline in the growth rate of workers during this period is sharp, especially in the urban areas. A similar trend is witnessed in the country as a whole. The mortality rate of unorganised enterprises is higher due to the constraints they face. It has been observed that under the present economic order, the growth of employment in the organised sector has considerably declined in recent times and there is not much scope of employment expansion, especially in the public sector. It is essential, in the circumstances that special efforts are made to meet the financial requirements of the economically viable enterprises in the unorganised sector.

TABLE 21.22

Growth Rate of Enterprises and Workers Over Economic Censuses

	1980-90		*1990-98*	
	HP	*India*	*HP*	*India*
Rural				
Enterprises	2.49	2.69	2.63	2.27
Workers	2.85	2.88	2.73	2.15
Urban				
Enterprises	4.00	3.55	2.70	2.50
Workers	3.73	2.81	2.43	1.34
Combined				
Enterprises	2.76	3.04	2.64	2.36
Workers	3.13	2.84	2.63	1.71

Source: Economic Census 1998.

Poverty and Employment

In India, the strategy to reduce poverty is pursued through

a) economic growth and economic development

b) directly targeted programmes for poverty eradication through employment generation, training and building up asset endowment of the poor

c) human development with emphasis on health, education and minimum needs

d) a targeted PDS to protect the poor from inflationary pressures and provide them with access to essential foods at affordable prices.

In what follows, we have discussed the impact of direct intervention programmes especially centrally sponsored programmes of employment generation for poverty alleviation.

A number of centrally sponsored and state level programmes are being implemented in Himachal to provide employment and earnings to the vulnerable sections of society in rural as well as urban areas. Programmes with a state share have been especially designed for poverty alleviation in the rural and urban areas. The major centrally sponsored schemes in the rural areas are: Integrated Rural Development Programme (IRDP) with sub-schemes, Training of Rural Youth for Self-Employment (TRYSEM), Million Wells Scheme (MWS), Supply of Improved Toolkits to Rural Artisans (SITRA) and Development of Women and

Children in Rural Areas (DWCRA). These schemes have been brought under Swaran Jayanti Gram Swarozgar Yojana (SGSY) launched in April 1999-2000. The restructuring of IRDP is considered a step in the right direction for improvement in the programmes. The objective of SGSY is to provide sustainable income to the rural poor. The programme aims at establishing a large number of micro-enterprises in the rural areas. This programme emphasises the cluster approach instead of individual benefits, which would enable the beneficiaries to start viable projects in a joint manner to generate income. This approach will also improve the skills of the poor through the inbuilt training component, upgradation of technology, provide backward and forward linkages and a better market arrangement.

Low productivity and unemployment are the factors responsible for rural poverty. It, therefore, becomes imperative to increase productivity and enhance employment in the rural areas. An employment-oriented growth strategy can achieve this goal in the medium and long run. In the short run, supplementary employment has to be provided to the needy, especially in agriculturally lean seasons. To meet this specific requirement, two wage-employment programmes have been put into operation — the National Rural Employment Programme (NREP) and the Rural Landless Employment Guarantee Programme (RLEGP). On April, 1 1989, NREP and RLEGP were merged into Jawahar Rozgar Yojana (JRY). The main objective of JRY has been the generation of additional gainful employment through creation of rural infrastructure and community and social assets. JRY has been replaced by Jawahar Gram Samridhi Yojana (JGSY), which is now conceived as a rural infrastructure development scheme and also provides wage employment to the rural poor.

Another wage employment scheme, Employment Assurance Scheme (EAS) is being implemented for creating additional employment opportunities during periods of acute shortage of wage employment through manual wage for the rural poor and to create durable community, social and economic assets for sustained employment. JRY and EAS will now be part of Sampooran Grameen Rozgar Yojana (SGRY) and would be executed by the PRIs at all levels. The objective of SGRY is to provide additional wage employment besides food security and also to create durable assets. During the Tenth Five Year Plan 2002-2007, Panchayati Raj Institutions and NGOs will be closely associated with the planning and execution of these programmes.

Similar programmes for the urban areas are also being implemented in the state. Migration from the rural areas is seen as the main cause of urban growth as well as urban poverty, making its alleviation an important issue. The Nehru Rozgar Yojana (NRY) and the Prime Minister's Integrated Urban Poverty Eradication Programme (PMIUPEP) are two urban poverty alleviation programmes. NRY, which consisted of three schemes: (i) Scheme for Development of Urban Micro Enterprises, (ii) Scheme for Urban Wage Employment and (iii) Scheme for Housing and Shelter Upgradation, has now been replaced by a new scheme, Swaran Jayanti Shahari Rozgar Yojana (SJSRY). It has three components (i) Urban Self-employment Programme, (ii) Urban Wage Employment Programme and (iii) Development of Women and Children in Urban Areas.

In addition, Drought Prone Area Programme (DPAP), Desert Development Programme (DDP) and Integrated Watershed Development Programme are being implemented under a watershed development approach. In all these programmes, a micro watershed of approximately 500 hectares is taken up for development for a period of five years. The objective of these projects is to promote the economic development of the village community to reduce the adverse effect of drought, to restore ecological balance and generate employment for the people of the watershed areas. Apart from this, a number of state sponsored schemes are in operation.

These programmes have, by and large, performed satisfactorily as far as the percentage of expenditure to available or allocated funds and achievement of the physical targets in terms of employment generation are concerned. On the other hand, a study of all the rural development programmes in Punjab found several lacunae in the implementation of these programmes (Chand, 1999)

It is difficult to measure the impact of growth and employment on poverty reduction. Only some causal linkages can be established. The proportion of people below the poverty line in Himachal Pradesh increased significantly from 16.40 per cent in 1983 to 28.44 per cent in 1993-94 but declined to 7.63 per cent in 1999-00. A vast majority of the people live in the rural areas where poverty is more acute. The number of persons below the poverty line in the rural areas was 4.84 lakh as compared to 0.29 lakh in the urban areas during 1999-00.

Per capita consumption has increased both in rural and urban areas from Rs. 350.63 and Rs 746.92

TABLE 21.23

Change in Poverty Status in Selected States

States	*Percentage of Persons BPL*			*Improvement (+)/Deterioration(-) in Persons BPL*		*Annual Rate of Reduction in Persons BPL*	
	1983	*1993-94*	*1999-00*	*1983/93-94*	*1993-94/99-00*	*1983/93-94*	*1993-94/99-00*
Himachal Pradesh	**16.40**	**28.44**	**7.63**	**-12.04**	**20.81**	**5.66**	**-19.69**
Haryana	21.37	25.05	8.74	-3.68	16.31	1.6	-16.09
Jammu & Kashmir	24.24	25.17	3.48	-0.93	21.69	0.38	-28.09
Punjab	16.18	11.77	6.16	4.41	5.61	-3.13	-10.23
India	**44.48**	**35.97**	**26.10**	**8.51**	**9.87**	**-2.1**	**-5.2**

Source: Planning Commission, 2002a.

respectively in 1993-94 to Rs. 684.50 and Rs. 1242.93 per month in 1999-00. Gini ratio for per capita consumption expenditure has declined for the rural and urban areas from 0.275 and 0.435 to 0.236 and 0.298 during this period, indicating a reduction of inequalities. The annual compound growth rate of per capita consumption expenditure has been 11.79 per cent for the rural areas and 8.86 per cent for the urban areas during 1993-94/1999-00 (Planning Commission 2001a).

It is interesting to note that the growth of employment during 1993-94/1999-00 has declined from 2.9 per cent to 1.4 per cent and the incidence of unemployment has increased from 0.7 per cent to 1.6 per cent on UPSS for workers in the age groups of 15 years and above (Planning Commission 2002) though the growth rate of the economy has been at 7.1 per cent per annum. However, poverty has substantially declined during this period, i. e., by 21 per cent and the rate of poverty reduction during the period has been–19.69 per cent. This suggests that the state has been able to reduce poverty through various poverty alleviation programmes and that higher achievements in the social sector have also contributed to improving the human resource quality in the state (Table 21.23).

An overwhelming majority of the poor are not apparently unemployed, but engaged, for a major part of their time, in some activity, however, at very low level of productivity and income. Thus, the strategy has to focus not only on the generation of new employment opportunities but also on the augmentation of the existing employment in terms of productivity and income through suitable technological, market and institutional interventions.

No macro policy of market-led growth by itself will be successful in dealing with the problem of poverty or employment. Very often development under market-led growth benefits those who are adequately qualified and socially well placed to take advantage of the capital-intensive and labour-displacing technologies. Policies to upgrade the skills of the poorer sections of the population to a reasonable level are needed to enable them to enter the mainstream market activities.

Thus, there is need for direct employment generation measures for the rural poor in the short run. Added emphasis is essential on improving education and training and on creating employment opportunities for the rural poor, spread over medium and long periods so that they can also enter the high productivity areas including non-farm activities or post-harvest activities in rural areas.

According to the Planning Commission (2002a), Himachal ranked first in the urban poverty index and eighth in the rural poverty index among various states and union territories of the country. As for the Human Development Index, the state ranked 1st in the urban index and 12th in the rural index in the country. These indicators are much better than those of the neighbouring states of Haryana, Jammu and Kashmir and Punjab and many other states of the country.

Reorientation of the employment and anti-poverty schemes has to be undertaken during the Tenth Plan. The problem of disguised unemployment and underemployment is serious in the state and the growth process may not fully deal with it during the plan period. The appropriate instrument for addressing this specific problem is the Employment Assurance Scheme (EAS), which has been designed specially for this purpose and should be implemented on the pattern of the Maharashtra Employment Guarantee Scheme, which has been a success (ILO, 2000).

A number of agencies are involved in watershed development programmes with different approaches and guidelines. It is felt that these programmes should be unified with simple common guidelines so that states are free to give priority to activities according to local needs. Periodic evaluation of these programmes needs to be undertaken to assess their efficacy.

The detailed analysis of poverty alleviation programmes will be undertaken elsewhere in the report.

Skills, Training and Employment

Skill-level is what determines labour productivity. Mismatch of the skill requirements of employment and the skill base of the unemployed is one cause of unemployment. This is likely to become more acute with rapid structural changes in the economy.

It is widely recognised that the unplanned rapid expansion of education, particularly of higher education, has contributed to the mismatch in the labour market. High private rates of return from higher education, to a large extent resulting from low private cost, are an important reason for the rush for higher education despite high incidence of educated unemployment. At the same time, after completion of schooling, very few join vocational courses. Efforts to strengthen vocational education are needed. It is, therefore, necessary to orient the educational and training system improving its capability to impart the requisite skills in the medium and long run, so as to enable it to respond quickly to the needs of the labour market in the short run. Besides, the system should also be in a position to impart suitable training to the large proportion of workers engaged as self-employed and wage earners in the informal sector, for upgrading their skills so as to raise their productivity and income levels.

Skill-level and training have a decisive impact on the growth of income and employment. However, quantification of skill-levels is not easy due to data constraints. The level of vocational skills in the labour force in India is very low as compared to other countries. For instance, in the age group of 20-24, only five per cent of the labour force in India has vocational skills, whereas in the developed countries the percentage varies between 60 and 80. The percentage for Korea at 96 is very high. Many developing countries too have a much higher percentage of skilled manpower than India, For example, in Mexico, it is 28 per cent, Mauritius, 36 per cent and Botswana 22 per cent (Planning Commission, 2001a).

The existing training institutions, like industrial training institutes, have undoubtedly been meeting a significant part of the requirements of skilled manpower for organised industry. It, however, seems that expeditious restructuring and reorientation of their courses should be undertaken to enable them to respond quickly to the changing demands of labour market. Greater involvement of industry in planning and running the training system would also be necessary for this purpose.

According to employment exchange data, a large section of the technically trained manpower from ITIs and other institutions has remained unemployed. An evaluation of special training programmes in Punjab (Chand, 1999) has indicated that a number of those who had got training were either unemployed or not employed in the trade in which they had received training, pointing to the mismatch between market demand in terms of technology and supply. Thus, there is immediate need for expansion of specialised training through the ITIs. The role of the private sector in higher general education and technical education must be expanded. The existing ITIs must be strengthened and modernised. The industrial sector should be more involved in the development of training programmes and imparting instruction.

Various aspects of employment, unemployment and related issues have been comprehensively dealt with in reports prepared by the Government of India (Planning Commission 2001a, 2001b, 2002b; Ministry of Labour 2002).

Employment Generation: Potential Sectors

The agriculture sector in Himachal Pradesh is very important in terms of its contribution to employment and income generation and hence cannot be ignored at the policy level, despite its declining share. However, it should be kept in mind that this sector has a limited capacity to engage a large workforce as it suffers from disguised unemployment. From the long-term point of view, expansion of employment opportunities has to be explored in the non-farm sector. A significant shift in the labour force must take place from agriculture to non-agricultural activities.

The potential labour-intensive areas for higher employment and income generation can be listed as:

- Horticulture, animal husbandry, fisheries, agro-forestry, aromatic and medicinal plants, and other allied activities
- Small-scale industries
- Construction

- Tourism
- Information technology
- Education and health infrastructure
- Transport
- Retail trade
- Hydel power
- Biotechnology

Detailed analyses of various aspects of these potential areas will be discussed in the relevant sections of this report.

The Task Force on Employment Opportunities, set up by the Planning Commission, has identified the following five broad areas, which together would constitute an appropriate strategy for employment generation (Planning Commission 2001a):

- Accelerating the rate of growth of the economy especially in sectors, which would ensure the spread of income to the low-income segment of the labour force.
- Pursuing appropriate policies in individual sectors, which are important for employment generation. These sector-level policies must be consistent with the overall objective of accelerating the growth of the state domestic product.
- Implementing focused special employment programmes for creating additional employment and enhancing income generation for existing activity, aimed at helping the weaker sections of society that may not be sufficiently benefited by the more general growth promoting policies.
- Pursuing suitable policies for education and skill development, which would upgrade the quality of the labour force and make it capable of supporting a growth which generates high quality jobs.
- Ensuring that the policy and the legal environment governing the labour market encourage labour absorption in the organised sector.

Future Growth of Employment

The slow growth of employment may primarily be due to the fact that the SDP growth rate actually achieved has fallen short of what was expected during the plan periods and the growth of employment has not taken place according to the elasticity of employment projected in the plans. Thus, in order to generate additional opportunities for productive employment and improve the quality of existing employment during the Tenth Five Year Plan and beyond, the growth of the economy has to be accelerated to higher levels. Hence, the emphasis is on growth-led employment generation. To attain a higher growth rate of the economy in the future, the investment level has to be raised substantially and its efficient use has to be ensured to the extent possible. That would result in higher employment elasticity. The rate of investment (gross state capital formation) as a percentage of GSDP, and the efficiency of investment measured by the incremental capital-output ratio (ICOR), are two critical determinants of growth, which are important from a policy point of view for accelerating growth in the future.

The rate of investment in Himachal Pradesh has been about 23 to 24 per cent in the last two years. The Tenth Plan of the state envisages an increase of more than 32 per cent in the rate of investment for attaining a higher level of growth and employment, whereas the average growth rate during this period has been about 6.0 per cent (Table 21.24). An investment rate of about 23 to 24 per cent resulting in 6.0 per cent growth rate of the economy, roughly gives an ICOR of about 4.0 per cent. By applying this ICOR, an acceleration from 6.0 per cent growth to 8.0 per cent would need an investment rate of 32 per cent. Similarly, acceleration to nine per cent and ten per cent would require investment rates of 36.0 per cent and 40.0 per cent respectively. The growth target of GSDP for the state in the national Tenth Plan has been estimated to be 8.92 per cent per annum, agriculture contributing 4.55 per cent, industry 12.49 per cent and services 8.26 per cent (*Tenth Five Year Plan 2002-07, Vol. III*). To achieve this growth rate, a very high rate of investment is required, which is a difficult task. However, policies to reduce the ICOR resulting in efficient use of capital, can also help attain a higher growth level with a relatively lower investment level. Since the major source of financing investment is domestic savings, it has to be maintained at an adequate level, in addition to raising foreign direct investment (FDI) to meet the shortfall in domestic savings. However, falling interest rates and the slow pace of FDI due to a number of reasons have to be taken care of. Improvement in efficiency in every sector is imperative if the targeted rate of growth has to be achieved. To attain efficiency, domestic and international competition is essential, though initially, it could have some adverse effect on employment. China could achieve a higher growth rate of the economy because of a very high rate of domestic investment and FDI, though mainly by overseas Chinese.

TABLE 21.24

Average Investment Rate and Growth Rate

Rate of investment	24.0
Growth rate	6.0
Incremental capital-output ratio	4.0
To achieve growth rate of:	**Estimated investment required:**
7 per cent	28.0 per cent
8 per cent	32.0 per cent
9 per cent	36.0 per cent
10 per cent	40.0 per cent

Source: Economic Survey H.P., 2001-2002 and Tenth Five-Year Plan, H P 2002-07.

Thus, if accelerated growth of the gross state domestic product (GSDP) has to be the core of a viable strategy for employment generation, then the policy framework for its realisation and necessary action in this regard are essential preconditions for successful employment generation. The following areas can be regarded critical at the level of macro-economic policy (Planning Commission 2001a).

- Achieving high rate of investment.
- Improvement in efficiency.
- Improvement in infrastructure.
- Improvement in financial system.
- Credit availability for informal sector

Keeping in view the seriousness of the unemployment problem, the state authorities concerned have intensified efforts to make available higher employment opportunities, especially for the educated persons including technically qualified, through several measures, such as identifying workers in short supply and high demand in the private sector, identifying skill gaps, improving the quality of training to narrow down the mismatch of demand and supply, promoting on-the-job training by involving employers in the private sector, strengthening overseas employment avenues for those desirous of working abroad, etc.

Employment Strategy of Himachal Pradesh

Planning Department of the state has prepared employment generation plan and strategy to generate higher employment opportunities in the state for the Tenth Five Year Plan (2002-07) (Planning Department, 2003). State Employment Plan as by-product of budget document has the following components:

Government Sector Employment Plan: Employment generated by opening new institutions especially pertaining to education and health.

Organised Sector and Self-Employment Sector Plan: Self-employment generated by various corporations such as HP State SC/ST Corporation, BC Finance and Development Corporation, Department of Social and Women Welfare and Others.

Wage Employment Sector Plan: Employment generated by implementing capital works especially by the Public Works Department and Irrigation & Public Health Department.

Total employment generated by these sector plans was 108070 in 2001-02 and 94750 in 2002-03.

The development strategy of the state envisages implementing of such programmes and schemes, which aim at increasing productive employment in different sectors of the economy. Broad strategy of the government will focus on the following areas for containing the rising unemployment situation in the state:

- Supplementing and complementing land based agricultural activities and animal husbandry and other diversified horticultural activities to make livelihoods of marginal cultivators and agricultural labourers sustainable.
- Diversification of cropping pattern, promoting production of off-season vegetables by increasing new areas under vegetables and fruits crops by raising productivity for all cash crops including maize crop.
- Promoting the production of floriculture in the state.
- Strengthening marketing system for farm products.
- Increasing marginal returns on investment in the Primary Sector.
- Promoting emerging biotechnology for generating employment in the field of agriculture and horticulture.
- Policies for the provision of income generating assets aimed at encouraging small-scale and cottage industries and providing gainful employment opportunities through backward and forward linkages.
- Direct expenditure on employment generation.

- Enhancing labour productivity by investing on health and education.
- Strengthening of industrial units in all districts and backward pockets as per revised Backward Area Industrial Policy announced by the Central Government.
- Improving and locating new tourist destinations for the domestic and foreign tourists by providing ideal infrastructure facilities to the visiting tourists in the state.
- Improving of airstrips at Bhuntar, Kangra and Shimla. This would generate additional employment to the local people, besides significant increase in the foreign tourists flow to the State.
- Accelerating actualisation of power potential.
- Increasing private sector investment in transport and tourism.

Sectoral policy initiatives for generating higher employment opportunities have been spelled out in detail in the Strategy for sectors such as: Agriculture and Horticulture, Power, Forest. Tourism, Animal Husbandry, Fisheries, Cooperation and Information Technology.

In addition, to explore above areas, a number of centrally sponsored and state schemes are in operation to generate additional higher employment by promoting non-farm activities. Important state schemes in this regard are *Vikas Main Jan Sahyog, Dalit Varg Vyavsayak Prashiksan Yojana*, Loan for Self-employment to Ex-servicemen and Granting of Permits to Unemployed Youth for plying of vehicles and ancillary employment.

Besides, a committee was constituted for employment generation and resource mobilisation and Project Proposals to provide employment to 50,000 persons through mushroom cultivation were submitted. Perspective Plan for angora development, proposals on employment generation through olive cultivation and resin tapping through forestry have been submitted and are under consideration of the state government which will help in raising the potential of employment generation.

Micro finance is being made available to the informal enterprises through Self Help Groups (SHGs) already established. In this respect, NABARD is instrumental in strengthening these SHGs. Total number of SHGs operating in the state are 7304. Of these, 3024 stand linked for obtaining group linked micro finance.

Following Committees have been set up to monitor the employment generation in the state:

I) State level Employment Monitoring and Review Committee with Chief Secretary as its Chairperson

II) District Employment Generation and Manpower Planning Committees with Deputy Commissioners with their Chairpersons

These committees monitor the employment targets fixed under different sectors at the district level and take remedial measures for the achievement of the employment targets.

Conclusions and Implications of Employment Policy

- The overall unemployment rate in the state is low as compared to other states. However, it has increased during 1993-94 and 1999-00, which is a matter of concern.
- Unemployment rates in the urban areas are higher than the rural areas, especially unemployment rates for urban females are very high. Excessive migration from rural to urban areas might be responsible for this situation. Efforts need to be made to generate higher productive employment in rural areas through schemes and programmes and conscious policy intervention.
- The growth of employment in the state has been one of the lowest in the country, with the lowest employment elasticity during 1993-94/1999-00, though the growth rate of the economy during this period has been significantly high, indicating lack of strong linkage between growth and employment. There is need for deeper exploration of this situation so that corrective steps can be taken.
- Districts which are industrially important such as Solan, Una and Kangra, have a very high proportion of employment seekers. There is immediate need for appropriate intervention in these areas for enhancing employment opportunities. The backward districts located in the interior of the state should be promoted by using the local resource base for generation of employment opportunities in these districts, which can also result in a balanced development of the state.

- Underemployment in the state has been high, which indicates a low quality of employment. In fact, the major challenge is the replacement of the existing low-quality jobs with high-quality jobs. The proportion of main workers declined, whereas that of marginal workers increased significantly during 1981-91. Casual employment of rural males at 20 per cent and urban males at 12 per cent is high and registered an increase during 1999-00 over 1993-94. There is need to improve the quality of such employment in terms of higher working days and better real wages, which can be ensured through faster growth of the economy.
- Educated unemployment in the state is far more serious, especially of matriculates and under-graduates. Appropriate employment opportunities have to be created for this section, which could ensure a higher income level. A fresh look at the present education policy is required for proper manpower planning.
- Though the rate of female work-participation has been high in the state, a large proportion of women workers are engaged in a subsidiary capacity in low productivity activities. A large majority of them are self-employed in the agriculture sector, which suffers from severe underemployment. Efforts need to be made to provide employment to women in non-farm activities. There is need for a detailed study of various aspects of activities in which women are engaged.
- The private sector has to be encouraged for the generation of higher employment in the state. Regular jobs in the organised sector can be increased if serious and sincere efforts are made to remove the bottlenecks, which discourage rapid expansion of regular employment in the private sector. Inflexible labour laws present a major hurdle in this regard. Changes in labour laws, the process for which has already begun, can provide flexibility for the expansion of employment in potential areas. Creation of regular employment in the near future will not be substantial. A large volume of better-quality employment has to be generated through self-employment. Therefore, adequate policy steps have to be taken to promote self-employment by facilitating credit, raw material and marketing requirements of those involved.
- Activities in the non-agricultural sector have to be promoted and excessive dependence on the agricultural sector has to be reduced for better quality of employment and incomes. Sectors, which have the potential for higher employment generation in the future are, agro-and food-processing industries including horticulture and agro-forestry, small-scale industries, construction, trade, tourism, transport, communication, information technology and other services. Most of these sectors have achieved significant growth during the post-liberalisation period. It is expected that most of the employment to be generated in the next few years will be in the service sector. Thus, improvements in this sector can create quality employment. Extensive economic and social infrastructure development is the need of the time. Private investment needs to be encouraged in this sector. Faster development of non-farm activities, especially in the rural areas, will be helpful in checking rural-to-urban migration. However, there is need for in-depth studies to understand the type of activities pursued and their productivity level, potential areas and constraints to their promotion.
- The Khadi and Village Industries (KVI) sector has the potential for creating new jobs at low cost. This sector not only provides employment in rural areas at low investment per job, but also utilises local skills and resources and provides part-time and full-time work to rural artisans, women and the weaker sections of society. Expansion of village industries will ensure an increase in income levels and the quality of life of rural workers and craftsmen. There is need to restructure KVIC programme to enhance the design and quality of its products. PMRY and other special schemes can be effectively used to promote non-farm activities.
- The unorganised sector assumes greater significance for future expansion of employment, as the growth of employment in the organised sector has substantially declined. However, to promote wage and self-employment in this sector, its different needs, especially finance and marketing have to be met.
- Apart from growth, the impact of resources expended on rural development and direct poverty alleviation programmes has contributed to reducing poverty. Though these programmes seem

to have succeeded in raising the standard of living of the poor, they need to be effectively monitored for optimum results. State-specific features such as topography, geography, work conditions, economic status, cost of execution of development works, etc., should be kept in view while issuing guidelines for centrally sponsored schemes. In view of the high cost of implementation of these schemes in the hilly areas, separate guidelines should be issued for these areas. Availability of funds should be regular and adequate for proper implementation of these schemes. Funds should be provided on the basis of area, population and performance.

- There is a large unmet need for imparting vocational training to new entrants to the labour force, as only about five per cent enter the labour force with some kind of formal vocational training. The ITIs and other technical institutions are in need of upgradation and modernisation of infrastructure, staff and courses. The system of specialised higher technical education needs to be strengthened if the technical manpower is to take advantage of the opportunities in the international labour market. Industry should be involved in the management of these institutions. The private sector has to be encouraged to play an important role in imparting vocational training. Such institutions as IITs and IIMs, which are known for their quality of talent, need to be promoted. Several developed countries have achieved high levels of growth because of a very high level of vocational and technical education. Training systems of these countries need to be studied.

- Social security of workers deserves special attention. Only workers in the organised sector, who constitute hardly 10 per cent of the total workforce, are covered by some form of social security. The rest of the workers, especially in the unorganised sector, are deprived of social security benefits. These workers need to be adequately covered under social security. Vulnerable groups of the labour force such as child labour, migrant labour, building and construction workers need special attention.

- Since the state has the highest number of employees in the public sector per thousand of population in the country, there is need for identifying superfluous jobs, abolishing vacant posts, banning new appointments and preparing VRS package for loss making PSUs. Appropriate manpower planning and judicious use of the human resource is the urgent need.

- At the prevailing growth rate, it will not be possible to achieve any significant improvement in the employment situation. A very high investment rate is required to achieve a higher rate of growth of the state economy during the Tenth Five Year Plan along with increase in efficiency of capital use, i.e., reduction in ICOR. Hence, there is a need for a higher investment rate to ensure growth-led employment generation. A comprehensive review of policies in different areas is needed to identify constraints to efficiency and optimal utilisation of resources.

- In view of the fact that there is limited scope for employment opportunities in the organised sector, the Department of Labour, H.P. wants that the network of 67 employment offices evenly spread throughout the state should be utilised for dissemination of information on all employment and especially self-employment schemes available in Himachal Pradesh. In this regard, it is proposed that the Department of Labour and Employment be actively involved in all the committees formed at government level and all meetings held as such relating to employment and self-employment promotion and monitoring thereof. This shall ensure that this department is kept up-to-date on all the information and schemes relating to employment in the state. Thereby the Employment Exchanges can be utilised to further disseminate this information to the youth visiting these offices.

References

Central Statistical Organisation, Economic Census 1998, Ministry of Statistics and Programme Implementation, Govt. of India, New Delhi.

Central Statistical Organisation (2001), *National Accounts Statistics 2000*, Ministry of Statistics and Programme Implementation, Govt. of India, New Delhi.

Chand, Himal (1993), "Educated Unemployment in Punjab", *Man and Development* 15(1) 82-132.

————. (1997), *Urban Informal Manufacturing Sector: A Study of the Border Districts of Punjab, Jammu & Kashmir and Rajasthan*, CRRID, Chandigarh.

————. (1999), *Impact Assessment Study on Rural Development Programmes in Jalandhar District (Punjab)*, (Project sponsored by the Ministry of Rural Development, Government of India), CRRID, Chandigarh.

————. (2002), "Growth and Determinants of Rural Non-farm Employment in Punjab", *Man and Development*, 24(2), pp. 98-112, June.

Department of Economics and Statistics (2002), *Economic Survey 2001-02*, Govt. of Himachal Pradesh, Shimla.

Department of Economics and Statistics, *Statistical Abstracts of Himachal Pradesh* (Various Issues) Govt. of Himachal Pradesh, Shimla.

Department of Economics and Statistics, *Statistical Outline of Himachal Pradesh and Economic Review* (different issues) Govt. of Himachal Pradesh, Shimla.

Department of Economics and Statistics (2002), *Census of Government Employees 2001*, Govt. of Himachal Pradesh, Shimla.

Department of Labour and Employment (2002), *Annual Administrative Reports, 2001-02*, Govt. of Himachal Pradesh, Shimla.

Department of Planning, *Economic Reviews of Himachal Pradesh 1971, 1981, 1986*, Shimla.

Department of Planning, *Ninth Five Year Plan 1997-2002 of Himachal Pradesh*, Govt. of Himachal Pradesh, Shimla.

Department of Planning, *Tenth Five Year Plan (2002-07)* and *Annual Plan 2002-03*, Government of Himachal Pradesh, Shimla.

Department of Planning (2003) *Employment Strategy of Himachal Pradesh in Tenth Plan (2002-07)* Govt. of Himachal Pradesh, Shimla.

Director of Census Operations, Himachal Pradesh (2002), *Census of India 2001, Provisional Population Totals, Distribution of Workers and Non-Workers, Paper 3 of 2001,Shimla.*

ILO (1999) *World Employment Report, 1998*, International Labour Office, Geneva.

ILO (2000), *World Labour Report, 2000, Income Security and Social Protection in a Changing World*, International Labour Office, Geneva.

Ministry of Finance and Company Affairs (2003), *Economic Survey 2002-03*, Government of India, New Delhi.

Ministry of Labour (2002), *The Report of the Second National Commission on Labour*, Government of India, New Delhi.

NSSO (1981) *Sarvekshana*, Vol.V, Nos. 1&2 July-Oct. Department of Statistics, Ministry of Planning, Government of India, New Delhi.

NSSO (1987), *Report on Third Quinquennial Survey on Employment and Unemployment. Survey Results NSS 38 Round 1983*, Government of India, New Delhi.

NSSO (1988), *Sarvekshana*, Vol.XI, No. 4, Issue NO. 35, April. Department of Statistics, Ministry of Planning, Government of India, New Delhi.

NSSO (1990), *Results of the Fourth Quinquennial Survey on Employment and Unemployment, NSS 43rd Round (July 1987-June 1988), Sarvekshana*, Special Number, Government of India, New Delhi.

NSSO (1997), "Employment and Unemployment in India,1993-94", *Fifth Quinquennial Survey, NSS 50th Round (July 1993-June 1994)*, Report No.409, Department of Statistics, Government of India, New Delhi.

NSSO (2001), "Employment and Unemployment Situation in India 1999-2000 (Part I)", *Sixth Quinquennial Survey, NSS 55th Round (July 1999-June 2000)*, Government of India, New Delhi.

Planning Commission (2001a), *Report of Task Force on Employment Opportunities*, Government of India, New Delhi.

Planning Commission (2001b), *Report of the Steering Committee on Labour and Employment for the Tenth Five-Year Plan 2002-07*, Government of India, New Delhi.

Planning Commission (2002a), *National Human Development Report 2001*, Government of India, New Delhi.

Planning Commission (2002b), *Report of the Special Group on Targeting Ten Million Employment Opportunities Per Year Over the Tenth Plan Period*, Government of India, New Delhi.

Planning Commission (2003), *Tenth Five Year Plan 2002-07 Vol. I-III*, Government of India, New Delhi.

Registrar General and Census Commissioner, Govt. of India, *District Profile Himachal Pradesh, 1991.*

Chapter 22

Wages and Prices

More than 90 per cent of the population in Himachal Pradesh lives in villages and is engaged mainly in agriculture, which is highly unorganised. The question of wages, particularly minimum wages of unskilled labour, thus assumes great importance. Unorganised, mostly illiterate, without any bargaining power and lacking awareness, this huge population is highly vulnerable to exploitation.

With fundamental changes in the labour market in the name of globalisation, wages cannot be left entirely to the interplay of market forces. Government intervention is necessary to provide social security at least to the least privileged sections of society.

Several measures have already been taken to ensure and improve the payment of wages, but these need to be further strengthened. The history of such attempts goes back to the nineteenth century, when the Government of India passed the Employees and Workers (Dispute) Act in 1860. The first direct step in this direction was the Payment of Wages Act in 1936, followed by the Minimum Wages Act in 1948. The Act requires the appropriate government (central or state) to fix minimum wages in scheduled employments and to carry out periodic review/revision of the rates at intervals not exceeding five years.

Of the 275 scheduled employments, for which wages are fixed in different work spheres, 24 are common to Himachal Pradesh.

The minimum wage varies from region to region and employment to employment. In agriculture, it varies from the lowest of Rs. 30 per day in Kerala to Rs. 102.60 per day in Delhi (2001).

The National Minimum Wage Policy introduced a floor-level minimum wage of Rs. 35 per day in 1996. This means that no state government can fix even the minimum wage (in any scheduled employment) below the national floor-level, which was increased to Rs. 40 per day in August 1998 and Rs. 45 per day in November 1999.

Since minimum wage is the subsistence wage (Study Group on Wages, 1991), increased cost of living has to be fully neutralised to maintain real wages, through the mechanism of the variable daily allowances (VDA). How far the revised minimum wage in Himachal Pradesh succeeds in keeping the real wages intact is examined in the context of agriculture in the following exercise. The minimum wage in agriculture is subject to revision on the basis of consumer price indices for agricultural labour. A similar exercise has been carried out for the period 1995-96 to 2000-2001 and the results are shown in Table 22.1.

Consumer price index numbers for agricultural labourers before 1995-96 included Delhi, Haryana, Punjab and Himachal Pradesh. CPIAL from 1995-96 has been used to deflate increase in the cost of living and provide for monetary compensation for increased prices while per capita income (PCY) has been used to account general increase in living standards generated by rising income levels.

Assuming that the actual minimum wage in 1995-96 was as desired, monetary compensation for the increase in prices should have increased the minimum wage by Rs. 8.75 and further to Rs. 4.49 in 1999-00, in order to account for growth rate of economy at large. Going by the exercise carried out for desired increase in minimum wage in Table 22.1, the actual minimum wage raised to Rs. 51 per day in 2000-01 against the notional desired wage of Rs. 40.24 per day was a commendable social welfare measure on the part of the government.

TABLE 22.1

Gap in the Actual and the Desired Level of Minimum Wages for Agriculture Labourers

	1995-96	*1996-97*	*1997-98*	*1998-99*	*1999-00*	*2000-01*
CPIAL (Base 1986-87=100)	**220**	**240**	**256**	**283**	**294**	**292**
Actual minimum wage (Rs./day)	26	26	26	26	26	51
Increase in CPIAL (%)	-	9.09	6.67	10.55	3.89	-0.68
Minimum wage should increase by Rs.	-	2.36	1.89	3.19	1.30	-0.24
Minimum wage should reach at Rs./day	-	28.36	30.25	33.45	34.75	34.51
Per capita income (PCY) in Rs.	**8,966**	**9,140**	**9,625**	**10,131**	**10,514**	**10,942**
Increase in PCY (%)	-	1.94	5.31	5.26	3.78	4.07
Minimum wage should increase by Rs.	-	0.50	1.41	1.47	1.11	1.24
Minimum wage should reach at Rs./day	-	26.50	27.91	29.38	30.49	31.73
Desired increment in minimum wage (Rs.)	-	2.87	3.30	4.66	2.41	1.00
Desired minimum wage (Rs./day)	**26**	**28.87**	**32.17**	**36.82**	**39.23**	**40.24**

Source: Labour Bureau, Ministry of Labour, GoI, *Minimum Wages in India, 2002.*
Labour Bureau, Ministry of Labour, GoI, *Annual Report, Consumer Price Index for Agricultural and Rural Labourers*, different issues.
Government of India, *Various Issues of Statistical Abstracts of Punjab and Haryana.*

The minimum wage for unskilled workers in different states of the northern region (as on October 1, 2001) varies from the highest of Rs. 99.70 per day in Delhi, to the lowest of Rs. 45 per day in Jammu and Kashmir. All northern states or UTs, except Jammu and Kashmir, have a rate of minimum wage higher than that of in Himachal Pradesh.

How far the rates of minimum wage fixed by the government is actually implemented, remains an unanswered question. Government figures, however, are alarming. Data on inspections made, irregularities detected, and prosecutions in Himachal Pradesh are reproduced from the Ministry of Labour's document in Table 22.2.

TABLE 22.2

Irregularities in the Enforcement of Minimum Wages in Himachal Pradesh

Details	*1996-97*	*1997-98*	*1998-99*	*1999-00*	*2000-01*
I. Inspections made (No.)	1,273	871	2,236	1,293	1,562
II. Irregularities detected (No.)	480	574	959	692	1,254
III. Irregularities rectified	380	312	435	526	870
IV. Persons prosecuted (No.)	43	26	165	165	231
(III / II)*100	79.17	54.36	45.36	76.01	69.38
(IV / II)*100	8.96	4.53	17.21	23.84	18.42

Source: Ministry of Labour, *Minimum Wages in India, 2002*

It reveals that while the number of irregularities detected has increased (2.6 times over five years), the percentage of irregularities rectified has actually declined. Only 8.96 per cent persons were prosecuted against 480 irregularities in 1996-97, and only 18.42 per cent were prosecuted against 1,254 irregularities in 2000-01. Although the government makes efforts to check irregularities in the enforcement of minimum wages, gaps still remain and are increasing. These efforts exclude a large number of workers who are beyond the purview of the Act, because of the condition that for inclusion in the scheduled list of employments, there should be at least 1,000 workers engaged in that activity in the state.

Actual Wage Rate in Himachal Pradesh

Since 90.21 per cent of the population in Himachal Pradesh lives in rural areas, and works mainly in the unorganised sector, our main focus is on the actual wage rates of rural workers in agricultural and non-agricultural sectors.

The average daily wage in a particular year is the simple mean of the month-wise average of daily wages in the particular occupations. Month-wise average daily wage figures in respect of 18 occupations were obtained from Labour Bureau Publication *Wage Rates in Rural India*, different issues. One of its limitations is that data for 1996-97 and 1997-98 have not been published. Thus, the analysis is restricted to four agricultural years (1995-96, 1998-99, 1999-00, and 2000-01).

Data about some occupational categories was not available either, because the activity connected with the occupation was not undertaken in the state, or the activity was out of season, or that a particular category of workers (men/women/children) were not engaged in that operation. Out of 18 occupations, the average daily wage of men in rural Himachal Pradesh (in Rs. per day) at all four points of time were available for eight (four agricultural and four non-agricultural) occupations. These are divided into three broad categories as listed in Table 22.3. Children were not reported in any of the occupations while women were reported in limited agricultural operations, namely sowing, weeding, and harvesting, and as unskilled labourers. Table 22.3 shows a comparative analysis of the wages of men in different occupations.

TABLE 22.3

Average Daily Wage Rates (for Men) in Different Occupations (Rupees), Himachal Pradesh

	1995-96	*1998-99*	*1999-00*	*2000-01*	*% Increase (1996-01)*
	(i)	*(ii)*	*(iii)*	*(iv)*	*(v)*
I. Agricultural Operations					
(1) Ploughing	60.95	88.99	90.17	98.67	61.88
(2) Sowing	48.68	78.21	88.77	103.41	112.42
(3) Weeding	45.14	76.15	78.74	98.33	117.84
(4) Harvesting	54.35	77.24	80.57	90.80	67.05
Average (1-4)	52.28	80.15	84.55	97.80	87.07
II. Artisans					
(1) Carpenter	97.98	133.93	143.95	159.19	62.47
(2) Blacksmith	92.17	115.41	128.27	141.79	53.85
(3) Mason	98.87	135.40	144.07	158.13	59.93
Average (1-3)	96.34	128.25	138.76	153.04	58.85
III. Unskilled Labourer	60.15	72.83	79.44	89.83	49.34
II/I	1.84	1.60	1.64	1.56	-
II/III	1.60	1.76	1.75	1.70	-
III/I	1.15	0.91	0.94	0.92	-

Source: Labour Bureau, Chandigarh/Shimla, Ministry of Labour, GoI, *Wage Rates in Rural India, different issues.*

An analysis of average daily wages over five years (1996-01) reveals a huge gap between the actual wages of artisans, agricultural workers and unskilled labourers. The artisans' work has been far more remunerative throughout this period. Occupations such as mason and carpenter commanded all-time high wages. During 1995-96, unskilled labourers were paid relatively better than agricultural workers, but over the years it could not keep pace with the increase in wages in other sectors. However, the reported average daily wage paid to unskilled labourers is far above the minimum fixed for them.

The wage-rate ratio of artisans to that of agricultural workers, and the ratio of the wage rate of unskilled labourers to agricultural workers declined over the period while that of artisans to unskilled labourers increased. The gap between the wages of artisans and agricultural labour has narrowed down while the gap between the wages of artisans and unskilled labourers has increased.

Variations in the average daily wage (for men), as shown in Table 22.3, reveal some interesting feature about fluctuations in wage rates. Although the artisan has been better paid throughout 1996-01, wages in agricultural operations, particularly weeding and sowing, increased at a pace faster than that of the wages of artisans or unskilled labourers.

In this situation, the gap between the wages for artisans and agricultural workers seems to have narrowed down. The percentage increase in wages was the lowest in the case of unskilled labourers and the highest for weeding. However, the increase in the wage of unskilled labourers was more than that of the artisans during 1999-00 and 2000-01.

The average wage rate in agricultural operations in 2000-01 was 1.9 times more than in 1995-96. The corresponding average wage rate for artisans and unskilled labourers in 2000-01 was 1.6 and 1.5 times that of 1995-96.

TABLE 22.4

Average Daily Wage Rate in Different Occupations Across Few Northern States (Rs.)

	Punjab	*Jammu and Kashmir*	*Himachal Pradesh*	*All-India*
Average of agricultural operations				
1995-96	58.94	57.00	52.28	41.68
1998-99	68.19	76.96	80.15	57.43
1999-00	69.93	80.95	84.56	61.06
2000-01	71.07	75.60	97.80	57.09
% Increase (1996-01)	20.72	64.41	95.40	36.59
Average of artisans				
1995-96	119.65	100.74	96.34	68.37
1998-99	141.15	134.72	128.25	90.92
1999-00	147.78	137.10	138.76	98.02
2000-01	154.87	142.93	153.04	93.74
% Increase (1996-01)	29.45	40.70	58.75	36.76
Unskilled labourer				
1995-96	60.60	50.37	60.15	37.95
1998-99	73.06	83.23	72.83	53.12
1999-00	76.18	83.64	79.44	56.85
2000-01	79.63	89.72	89.83	53.16
% Increase (1996-01)	31.40	78.14	49.34	40.07

Source: Labour Bureau, Chandigarh/Shimla, Ministry of Labour, GoI *Wage Rates in Rural India*, different issues.

A comparison of the nominal wage rate in selected northern states and the all-India level, in Table 22.4, reveals that wages in all the three states are far above the all-India rate. Himachal Pradesh has witnessed the maximum increase in the daily wages of agricultural labourers and artisans. The difference in the artisan's wage in Himachal Pradesh and in Punjab that has the maximum wage rate in 1995-96, has narrowed down by 2001 and is almost on a par. Although the wages of unskilled labourers in Jammu and Kashmir have increased sharply and have come close to, but lower than those in Himachal Pradesh. Thus, agricultural labourers, along with other labourers, are in a comfortable position in Himachal Pradesh as compared to those in Punjab and Jammu and Kashmir.

The increase in wages of all occupations in Himachal Pradesh was more pronounced during 2000-01, when there was a fall at the all-India level.

Table 22.5 reveals a different picture of the average daily real wage in some of the northern states. The wage rate in real terms has been obtained by using CPIAL (1986-87=100) as deflator for agricultural operations and CPIRL (1986-87=100) as deflator for the other two occupations.

TABLE 22.5

Average Daily Real Wage Rate (Rs./day)

	Punjab	*Jammu and Kashmir*	*Himachal Pradesh*	*All-India*
Agricultural Operations				
1995-96	24.16	25.22	23.76	17.37
1998-99	22.28	25.40	28.32	19.21
1999-00	22.27	25.06	28.76	19.76
2000-01	22.49	23.19	33.49	18.78
Change % (1995-96 to 2000-01)	-6.89	-8.07	40.94	8.14
Artisans				
1995-96	48.44	44.77	43.59	28.49
1998-99	42.90	45.36	45.16	30.41
1999-00	46.62	43.38	47.04	46.68
2000-01	48.40	44.81	52.05	30.64
Change % (1995-96 to 2000-01)	-0.09	0.07	19.41	7.54
Unskilled Labourer				
1995-96	24.53	22.38	27.22	15.81
1998-99	22.21	28.02	25.64	17.77
1999-00	24.03	26.47	26.93	27.07
2000-01	24.88	28.13	30.56	17.37
Change % (1995-96 to 2000-01)	1.42	25.65	12.26	9.86
CPIRL (% Change)	29.55	41.78	33.03	27.50
CPIAL (% Change)	29.51	44.25	32.73	26.67

Sources: Computed from the data by Labour Bureau, Chandigarh/Shimla, Ministry of Labour, GoI *Wage Rates in Rural India*, different issues.

Labour Bureau, Ministry of Labour, GoI, *Annual Report, Consumer Price Index Numbers for Agricultural and Rural Labourers, different issues.*

Himachal Pradesh is best-placed in terms of real increase in wages. Although the increase in the real wages of artisans and unskilled labourers in H.P. is not at the same rate as that of CPIRL, it is far above the national level and the highest among the three northern states for artisans. However, unskilled labourers are the most vulnerable of all rural workers to increased prices.

Table 22.6 shows the wages of women as compared with those of men in occupations in which women workers were reported. It reveals that men are relatively better paid in all occupations. However, the gap had marginally narrowed in 1999-00 compared to 1995-96, for all occupations, except a marginal increase in sowing. Wage difference was relatively more among unskilled labourers.

TABLE 22.6

Average Daily Wage Rate for Men and Women in Different Occupations in H.P. (Rupees), 1995-96 and 1999-00

	1995-96			*1999-00*		
	Men (M)	*Women (W)*	*M/W*	*Men (M)*	*Women (W)*	*M/W*
	1	2	3	4	5	6
Sowing	48.68	44.51	1.09	88.77	79.41	1.12
Weeding	45.14	42.50	1.06	78.74	78.56	1.00
Harvesting	54.35	49.95	1.09	80.57	79.04	1.02
Unskilled Labourers	60.15	48.00	1.25	79.44	65.83	1.21

Source: Labour Bureau, Chandigarh/Shimla, Ministry of Labour, GoI, *Wage Rates in Rural India, different issues*

Prices

Wages and prices are complementary. An increase in prices must be compensated with an increase in wages. This section is an attempt to examine the movement of wages in relation to the changes in the prices of essential commodities. Before discussing the wage-price relation, it is desirable to examine changes in retail prices. Month-wise retail prices (per unit) of 15 essential commodities from 1991 to 2000 were obtained from Economic and Statistics Office (ESO) Shimla, and the annual averages were calculated from the monthly averages. Figure 22.1 represents the percentage increase in prices over nine years. The annual movement of prices and the changes in the annual average retail prices over the previous year's prices are shown in Table 22.6.

Figure 22.1 shows the maximum increase in retail prices of *urad dal* (150.3%), followed by rice *parmal*

TABLE 22.7

Percentage Change in the Average Annual Retail Prices over the Previous Year

	1991-92	1992-93	1993-94	1994-95	1995-96	1996-97	1997-98	1998-99	1999-00	CARG (1991-00)
Rice Parmal	24.56	12.74	14.89	2.95	10.07	6.33	9.66	10.01	3.51	9.3
Wheat	20.73	1.62	9.11	4.98	6.92	24.31	10.95	9.27	2.26	8.8
Wheat Flour	17.10	1.18	11.61	2.65	16.97	15.14	6.59	8.79	2.09	8.0
Urad Dal	-5.85	-3.82	38.20	57.30	0.78	-11.98	-0.10	16.21	23.47	9.6
Channa Dal	-0.39	34.69	30.62	-23.55	-1.23	33.02	11.39	-8.57	10.76	7.1
Gur	-1.02	47.56	16.45	-2.09	-4.93	9.64	24.05	-3.11	0.22	7.7
Groundnut Oil	6.54	-16.03	7.42	13.14	3.11	0.52	5.82	1.23	-9.32	0.9
Sugar	3.99	15.61	26.89	-4.84	5.82	2.89	6.27	2.32	4.12	6.0
Mustard Oil	-1.67	-8.14	9.30	10.43	0.52	-3.66	37.02	1.67	-16.32	2.1
Vanaspati	0.82	-11.43	7.47	6.50	-3.52	-3.91	22.12	-11.81	-19.54	-2.0
Tea	1.81	18.41	6.73	0.90	12.34	14.17	33.09	7.03	2.33	9.3
Onion	-25.37	58.51	2.21	1.19	-2.40	14.47	162.69	-48.30	-17.40	4.4
Potato	-8.14	10.44	2.49	35.52	12.15	-9.44	57.68	-36.87	-5.67	3.0
Cement	15.88	-1.73	-7.24	22.93	8.66	0.98	-0.57	0.64	3.33	4.0
Kerosene Oil	-5.26	-0.32	1.89	0.22	1.69	0.91	4.04	0.63	102.26	7.7

Source: Computed from the data provided by the Directorate of Economic and Statistics, Government of Himachal Pradesh.

(142.7%) and tea (142.7%). The increase in the price of groundnut oil was the least, while the only commodity that recorded a decline in price was vanaspati. The rate of increase in prices, CARG (Table 22.7) follows the same order. However, annual fluctuations in prices are more significant for examining the impact of the total increase in prices on wages.

FIGURE 22.1

Percentage Change in Prices, 1991-2000

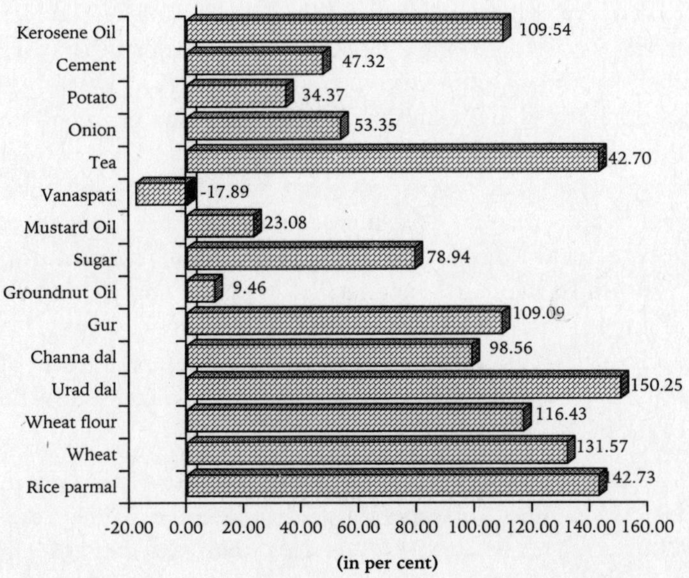

Source: Directorate of Economic and Statistics, Government of Himachal Pradesh.

Table 22.7 reveals that the prices of tea, wheat, wheat flour and rice have increased steadily over the years. Wheat prices recorded a major jump in 1992 and again in 1997. Although no single year recorded simultaneous increase in the prices of all commodities, but many, namely, onion, potato, mustard oil, tea, vanaspati recorded an all-time high, along with a negligible fall in the prices of cement (-0.57%) and urad dal (-0.10%) during 1997-98. Onion and potato prices suddenly increased 162.69 per cent and 57.68 per cent (maximum) during 1997-98, followed by a huge decrease in subsequent years. The price of kerosene showed minor fluctuations until 1999, but increased more than 100 per cent during 1999-2000. CARG shows that a majority of the commodities have recorded an increase of more than five per cent.

A breakdown of the increase in prices in two periods of time, 1991-96 and 1996-2000, shows that the prices of most of the commodities increased more during the first half than in the second. The commodities, prices of which increased more during the second half of the nineties, include tea, onion (mainly during 1997-98), mustard oil (mainly during 1997-98), wheat, and kerosene (mainly during 1999-2000).

The basket of commodities mentioned above has been classified in four broad categories. These are cereals (including rice and wheat), pulses (including *urad dal* and *channa dal*), cooking oils (including mustard oil and *vanaspati*), and vegetables (including onion and potato).

A comparison of the increase in nominal prices (Table 22.8) with the increase in nominal wages (Table 22.3) during 1996-2000 reveals that the percentage increase in the wages of all three categories of workers has been more than the percentage increase in retail prices. Considering that a major part of the wage earnings of the labourers is spent on food, mainly cereals and pulses, a large part of the increased wages of unskilled labourers goes to the food basket, leaving little for other basic minimum needs. Hence they are the worst hit section. Increase in wages especially of unskilled labourers (49.34%) seems to be offset by the increase in the prices of cereals (39.82%) and pulses (34.69%) alone. However, the actual consumption basket includes many more commodities of daily use.

TABLE 22.8

Change in Retail Prices under Broad Categories

Categories	*1991-1995*	*1996-2000*	*1991-2000*
1. Cereals	(+) 56.51	(+) 39.82	(+) 138.55
2. Pulses	(+) 68.26	(+) 34.69	(+) 126.75
3. Cooking Oils	(+) 5.16	(-) 2.11	(+) 1.66
4. Vegetables	(+) 30.10	(+) 7.27	(+) 45.41

Source: Computed from the data provided by Directorate of Economic and Statistics, Government of Himachal Pradesh.

Real Wages

Real wage represents the capacity of the worker to buy, at a given wage and at a given price. Income of an individual, organisation, or country, after taking into consideration the effects of inflation on purchasing power is the real wage or real income.

TABLE 22.9

Consumer Price Index Numbers Himachal Pradesh (Base 1986-87=100)

Year	*CPIAL*	*CPIRL*
1995-96	220	221
1996-97	240	240
1997-98	256	258
1998-99	283	284
1999-00	294	295
2000-01	292	294
2001-02	298	304

Source: Labour Bureau, Ministry of Labour, GoI, *Annual Report, Consumer Price Index Numbers for Agricultural and Rural Labourers, different issues.*

Consumer price index numbers for rural labourers include agricultural and non-agricultural labourers (Table 22.9). The index numbers are provided separately for agricultural labourers but not for the non-agricultural category of rural workers. The consumer price index for agricultural labourers (CPIAL) has been used to deflate the nominal wage rate in agricultural occupations, while the nominal wage rates of artisans and unskilled labourers have been deflated by the consumer price index number for rural labourers (CPIRL).

TABLE 22.10

Average Annual Real Wage Rates (for Men) in Himachal Pradesh (Rs./Day)

	1995-96	*1998-99*	*1999-00*	*2000-01*	*% change 1995-96 to 2000-01*
I. Agricultural operations					
(1) Ploughing	28.00	31.00	31.00	34.00	21.97
(2) Sowing	22.00	28.00	30.00	35.00	60.05
(3) Weeding	21.00	27.00	27.00	34.00	64.12
(4) Harvesting	25.00	27.00	27.00	31.00	25.87
Average (1-4)	24.00	28.00	29.00	33.00	40.94
II. Artisans					
(1) Carpenter	44.00	47.00	49.00	54.00	22.13
(2) Blacksmith	42.00	41.00	43.00	48.00	15.64
(3) Mason	45.00	48.00	49.00	54.00	20.22
Average (1-3)	44.00	45.00	47.00	52.00	19.41
III. Unskilled labourer	27.00	26.00	27.00	31.00	12.26

Source: Computed from the data by Labour Bureau, Chandigarh/Shimla, Ministry of Labour, GoI, *Wage Rates in Rural India, different issues,* and Labour Bureau, Ministry of Labour, GoI, *Annual Report, Consumer Price Index Numbers for Agricultural and Rural Labourers, different issues.*

Note: CPIAL and CPIRL have been used to deflate nominal wage rates to get real wage rates.

The nominal wage rate for all rural labour has recorded a steady increase (Table 22.3). The real wages of all, except unskilled labourers and blacksmiths, have also increased continuously (Table 22.10). Unskilled labourers and blacksmiths actually experienced a fall in their real wages in 1998-99. Although the nominal wages of artisans remained at an all-time high and their real wages stable, the increase in the real wages in agricultural activities has been the maximum. Agricultural workers experienced a major boost, a 40.94 per cent increase. In contrast, money wages in agricultural operations were not as high as those of artisans, but the increase in their real wages was the highest.

Table 22.11 shows a comparison of the increase in real wage rates corresponding to increase in CPIAL and CPIRL. Increase in CPIAL is less than the increase in the real wage rate in agricultural operations (column iv). This implies that the agricultural sector, mainly weeding and sowing, has been more progressive in terms of increase in real wages. The same is not true of other two categories of workers. The percentage increase in their real wages is far less than the increase in CPIRL. Agricultural labour in Himachal Pradesh is in the most comfortable position. The position of all workers improved in 2000-01, corresponding to a fall in CPI value. The situation was the worst in 1998-99.

TABLE 22.11

Percentage Change in Average Annual Real Wage Rates (for men) in Himachal Pradesh in Rs./Day

	1995-96 to 1998-99	*1998-99 to 1999-00*	*1999-00 to 2000-01*	*1995-96 to 2000-01*
	(i)	*(ii)*	*(iii)*	*(iv)*
I. Agricultural operations				
(1) Ploughing	13.50	-2.47	10.18	21.97
(2) Sowing	24.90	9.26	17.29	60.05
(3) Weeding	31.14	-0.47	25.73	64.12
(4) Harvesting	10.48	0.41	13.47	25.87
Average (1-4)	19.18	1.54	16.46	40.94
II. Artisans				
(1) Carpenter	6.37	3.47	10.96	22.13
(2) Blacksmith	-2.56	7.00	10.92	15.64
(3) Mason	6.57	2.44	10.13	20.22
Average (1-3)	3.59	4.16	10.67	19.41
III. Unskilled labourer	-5.78	5.01	13.46	12.26
IV. CPIAL	28.64	3.89	-0.68	32.73
V. CPIRL	28.51	3.87	-0.34	33.03

Source: Computed from the Data by Labour Bureau, Chandigarh/Shimla, Ministry of Labour, GoI, *Wage Rates in Rural India, different issues*, and Labour Bureau, Ministry of Labour, GoI, *Annual Report, Consumer Price Index Numbers for Agricultural and Rural Labourers, different issues.*

Note: CPIAL and CPIRL have been used to deflate nominal wage rates to get real wage rates.

Although labourers in Himachal Pradesh enjoy a comfortable position in terms of real wages, as compared to Punjab, J & K, and India as a whole, unskilled labourers are the most vulnerable among the rural workers in the state. A second look at the level of minimum wages fixed for unskilled labourers and strict action against irregularities in the enforcement of these wages are required, to maintain the real increase in wages.

No sustained improvement in real wages can be brought about unless it is accompanied by a corresponding improvement in productivity (*Report of the National Commission on Labour, 2002*). Productivity does not depend only on labour and has many other dimensions to it. Thus, the issue of linking productivity with wages is a complex one and requires a separate study.

Such marked difference in real wages calls for action by the government at all levels, not only for unskilled labourers but also for artisans and agricultural labourers. In a fast changing world, the concept of wage can never be absolute, and has to be determined in relation to the changing priorities as well. Further attempts to address the problems of the workforce in the unorganised sector, in the context of fast changing priorities in the name of globalisation, will provide fresh light on the working as well as living conditions of these workers in Himachal Pradesh.

Conclusion

- The actual minimum wage raised to Rs. 51 per day in 2000-01 against the notional desired wage of Rs. 40.24 per day was a commendable social welfare measure on the part of the government.
- It is also revealed that the revision of the minimum wage has not been regular.
- The increase in real wages to workers other than agricultural labourers was also far less then the warranted.
- Among the three categories of the workers, the artisans are the better paid both in terms of nominal and real wages. But, agricultural operations, particularly weeding and sowing, have seen the highest increase in wages during 1996-01 and hence have been more progressive.
- Although labourers in Himachal Pradesh are better placed than at the all-India level and the selected neighbouring states, unskilled labourers are most vulnerable to increased prices. This could be said more in respect of unskilled women labourers.

References

Chattopadhyay, M. *Conditions of Labour in Indian Agriculture: Apparent and Real*, K.P. Bagchi & Company, Calcutta, 1985.

Labour Bureau, *Report on the Working of Minimum Wages Act 1948*, different issues, Chandigarh/Shimla.

Labour Bureau, Ministry of Labour, *Annual Reports, Consumer Price Indices for Agricultural and Rural Labourers*, different issues, Ministry of Labour, Government of India.

Labour Bureau, *Wage Rates in Rural India*, different issues, Ministry of India, Government of India.

Labour Bureau, *Minimum Wages in India, 2002*, Ministry of Labour, Government of India.

Mishra, L., *Unorganised Labour: Deprivation & Emancipation*, Manak Publications Pvt. Ltd., 1999

Report of the National Commission of Rural Labour, Reports of Study Group, 1991.

Report of the National Commission of Labour, 2002.

Unni, J., "Wages and Employment in Unorganised Sector: Issues in Wage Policy", in *Informal Sector in India (ed.)* by Amitabh Kundu and Alakh N. Sharma, 2001, Institute of Human Development, New Delhi.

Chapter 23

Science and Technology

The methodology followed in the chapter on Science and Technology is based on identifying Drivers, Enablers, and Processes in the context of Himachal Pradesh to provide with recommendations. This conceptual framework can be better understood with the help of the following figure

Drivers

(Important factors instrumental for its socio-economic development)

- Natural Resources
- Forest Resources
- Agriculture
- Infrastructure
- Rural Development
- Industry

→

Enablers

(Science and Technology vehicles to undertake specific tasks)

- Remote Sensing Technology
- Geographical Information System
- Solar Passive Building Technology
- Zoning Atlas
- Bio Technology
- Plasma Pyrolysis

→

Processes

(Specific projects to deliver results)

- Information Technology
- E-Governance
- Technical Education
- Industrial Consortiums

Drivers

Important factors instrumental for its socio-economic development

- Natural Resources
- Forest Resources
- Agriculture
- Infrastructure
- Rural Development
- Industry

Natural Resources

Natural Resources of Himachal Pradesh which should draw the attention of Science & Technology have been grouped, for the purpose of this note, as follows:

- Physiographic Zones
- Drainage Network
- Soil Types
- Land Resources
- Water resources
- Mineral Resources
- Natural Disasters

Natural Resources of Himachal Pradesh have direct relationship to its physiographic conditions including relief, drainage, climate and geology. These in turn influence the type of soils and kind of vegetation cover. Integrating Remote Sensing based thematic information, meteorological and collateral data for scientific management of various natural resources should be an important priority for S&T. Using GIS to provide information regarding

- District/Block Boundaries (With Areas)
- Settlement/Roads (With Names),
- Contour/Elevation Points (In Meters),
- Watershed/Drainage (With Area),
- Soils (Types),
- Lithology/Geology,
- Hydro-Geomorphology (Water Potential Zone, Land Use/Cover (Latest Satellite Information),
- Hazard Zonation (Risk Prone Area),
- Action Plan For Water Management (Number of Locations),
- Action Plans For Land Resource Development (Spatial)

Physiographic Zones

Himachal Pradesh has been divided physiographically into four distinctly identified zones based on the variations in altitude, climate, geology, soil, flora, fauna and topography namely:

- Outer Himalayas/Shivalik Hills
- Lesser or Lower Himalayan Zone
- Main or Great Himalayan Zone and
- Trans-Himalayan Zone

Drainage Network

The state is drained by nine major river systems and thereby has nine catchments areas. Some of these are: the Satluj, the Beas, the Chenab, the Yamuna, the Ravi and the Indus.

The system of sustainable water management has to be preceded by understanding the dynamics of the hydrological regime. This would involve studying the movement of glaciers and their role in water regulation, the role of precipitation, percolations and fluctuations of ground water

Soil Types

The soils of Himachal Pradesh vary from thin and bare soils of High Mountain to rich deep alluvial soils of valleys and to snow covered soils. These can be classified into

- Udalfs-Ochrepts Soils
- Othents-Ochrepts Soils
- Udolls Soils
- Glaciers and Snow-capped Soils

Soils are under gully and sheet erosion. About two-fifths of the state's area is under the impact of very high soil erosion. The unsurveyed parts of the state need to be studied and mapped by remote sensing cell using satellite data.

Land Resources

The total state area is 55673 kms. Hardly 10 per cent of the total area is cultivated and actual forest cover make 22.5 per cent of the total area. Permanent pastures and other grasslands account for 24 per cent of the total area. Barren and Unculturable land covers about 14 per cent of the area of the state. About 23 per cent of the total area remains unsurveyed.

On the basis of land use Himachal Pradesh can be divided into three broad regions.

- Intensively Ploughed, moderately forested, southern region with marginal presence of pastures and other grazing lands;
- Moderately Cultivated, highly forested central region, with a considerable proportion of pastures and other grazing lands; and
- Poorly cultivated, sparsely forested, northern region with a high proportion of pastures and other grazing lands

Considerable improvements are required for an optimum utilisation of land resources.

- The forest cover needs to be extended to more areas, as it is much below the target of the National Forest Policy according to which a hill state should have 60 per cent of its area under forest.
- There is a need for proper management of extensive wastelands.
- The policy of shifting of management of common lands from the community to the state has not proved beneficial as it reduced the scope of people's participation in resource management.
- Using satellite data (IRS-1D) for preparing risk maps and landslide management maps to

formulate the strategies for minimising the social impact of land slides

Water Resources

The state is richly endowed with the hilly terrain with significant volume of water of its perennial rivers flowing down in steep gradient in the mountain catchments. This permits the required natural head for the generation of hydroelectric power, refer Annexure A–23.3.

The State also has many water resources in the form of (a) surface water resources (glaciers, rivers, lakes, reservoirs Table 2.1 & 2.2, Chapter 2 of the present Report), (b) ground water resources, and traditional sources of water (Table 2.3, Chapter 2) (refer Annexure A–23.4)

S&T issues related to water are

- Ensuring infrastructure facilities for ground water management,
- Tapping hydro-power potential,
- Keeping in view the ecological impact on upstream and downstream parameters,
- Realising the importance of glaciers as "Frozen Water Banks",
- Emphasis should be given to the collection of hydrological and hydro-geological data for exploration of surface and groundwater resources,
- Using GIS to access Hydro-geomorphology (water potential zones)
- Using Remote Sensing Satellite data for delineation of potential groundwater zones (IRS-1A, 1B, IC & 1D satellite data)
- Using Remote Sensing Techniques for the selection of sites for setting of hand pumps/bore wells.
- Construction of low cost Ferro-cement rainwater harvesting structures.
- Setting up Hydrams (an apparatus which utilises the kinetic energy of moving column of water to pump up a part of this water to a greater height than that of supply head).

Mineral Resources

The state has rich mineral resources such as limestone, gypsum, rock salt, manganese, silica sand and quartzite etc. In addition, building materials like slate, granite, clay and sandstone are available. Other minerals reported are iron, beryl, copper, lead, silver, uranium, kyanite etc. (Table 2.7, Mineral Resources of Himachal Pradesh, Chapter 2 and refer to Annexure A–23.5)

Data in Zoning Atlas should be used for granting future permissions for establishing new industries, particularly plants that use mineral resources e.g. cement plants.

Natural Disasters

Himachal Pradesh is exposed to natural disasters of various intensity, which prominently hamper the development process of the state.

Disasters in the form of earthquakes (Table 3.1 & 3.2 Chapter 3), landslides, flash flood and cloudbursts (Table 3.3, Chapter 3), avalanches (Table 3.4, Chapter 3), soil erosion, forest fires (Annexure A–23.6) have caused substantial loss to the state.

Using information generated from IRS-1D satellite data should be used for:

- Base map
- Lithological Map
- Rock Weathering
- Soil Map
- Geomorphological Map
- Slope Map
- Slope Aspect
- Slope Morphology
- Drainage Density,
- Intersection of Lineament
- Density of Lineament
- Proximity to Fault
- Land Use/Land Cove
- Anthropogenic Factors
- Land Slide

Forest Resources

Forests are a key natural asset of the state. The striking feature is the diversity of woody plant species, representing soft wood conifers and hard wood deciduous flowering plant species occupying temperate climate zones. Of the 45,000 species of plants found in the country as many as 3,295 are reported in the state. Himachal Pradesh comprises four forest zones:

- Sub-tropical Forests

- Sub-temperate Forests
- Wet-temperate Forests
- Dry-temperate Forests

(Table 4.1, Chapter 4)

The forest cover in Himachal Pradesh is 14,360 sq km, which is 25.79 per cent of the geographical area. This includes area under orchards and natural regenerated area. Forest classification shows a decline in the total forest area during 1995-96 over 1990-91 due to decrease in unclassed forest area and protected forest area. In 2000-2001, the total forest area exceeded that of 1995-96 but remained below what it was in 1990-91 (Table 4.5 & 4.6 Chapter 4).

The data on annual prescribed yield and growing stock of commercially important species (Table 4.9, Chapter 4) reveal that Fur/Spruce followed by Deodhar are the important species which the state government exploits for different purposes. District-wise percentage of the forest cover to the total geographical area of Himachal Pradesh in 1999 varies from 1.1 per cent in Lahaul-Spiti to 46.6 per cent in Shimla (Table 4.10, Chapter 4).

S&T actions in the area should include

- Use of plant biotechnology for reforestation (involving micro propagation)
- Systematic organic cultivation of appropriate species of medicinal plants in proper ecosystem for sustained availability with suitable regulation on extraction of Wild Flora
- Development of processing technology for all the year round, harnessing of the crops in appropriate harvesting season and preservation thereof without loss of quality for the year round consumption

Agriculture

Major aspects under agriculture that should draw S&T actions in the State are:

- Horticulture
- Medicinal and Aromatic plants
- Irrigation
- Watershed Development

The state is dominated by agriculture including horticulture and animal husbandry. Important crops grown in the state are Cereals-Maize, Wheat, Rice and Barley, Pulses, Oil seed, Buckwheat, Minor Millets, Cash crops—Potato, Ginger, Tea, Peas, Kuth, Hops, and a variety of vegetables including out of season and exotic vegetables and fruits particularly Pome, Stone and dry fruits like *Chilgoza*, Walnut, Pecan nut, Pistachio etc. and vegetables like Seed potato, Ginger, Chickery seed, Olives, Figs, Apples and Mushrooms besides certain medicinal and aromatic plants.

The texture of the soil, climate and rainfall vary in the four zones and so does the cropping pattern (Table 11.1 & 11.2, Chapter 11).

IRS-1C, 1D remote sensing data should be extensively used for crop acreage and production estimation for providing pre-harvest district/state level crop acreage estimate and integrating these estimates with yield relationship for district/state level production forecasting

Horticulture

Himachal Pradesh has the advantage of the climate and topography in the cultivation of a variety of fruits. Temperate fruits cover about 64 per cent of the total cultivated area of the state of which more than 40 per cent is under apple cultivation. The area under fruits more than doubled in the last two decades.

Similarly the productivity of apples almost doubled to 4500 kg per hectare during 2000-01 but the productivity of Nuts, Dry fruits, Citrus and other subtropical fruits decreased even though the area under these crops increased (Table 11.9, Chapter 11).

Fruit production which was 1200 metric tonnes in 1950-51 increased to 4.3 lakh metric tonnes but the yields are about 10 to 12 times below what is produced in European countries (Table 11.11, Chapter 11)

The S&T activities in the area of horticulture should include

- Use of low cost and easy to use fertilisers –Bio Fertilisers
- Popularising fertilisers which rejuvenate the soil strata and add organic fertilisers to the soil
- Popularising use of fertilisers, which provide nitrogen and phosphorus and liberate growth regulators

Medicinal and Aromatic Plants

The state is a rich repository of medicinal and aromatic plants because of its situational advantage. It is estimated that about 500 medicinal, 150 aromatic and a large no of potent alternative and substitute drug plant species are available in the area (Table 11.15, Chapter 11). Some of the herbs and plants available in the state are *Guchhi, Tejpatta, Patish, Banka Kari, Dhooproots, Bharami, Katha, Kala Jira, Karu, Banaksha, Kesar,* Hyphopia etc.

Besides, there are many species which remain unidentified due to lack of knowledge and research. Unsustainable ways of harvesting and unrestricted marketing have led to the reduction in population of some of the high demand medicinal plants leading to sudden escalation of prices.

This calls for urgent measures for *in-situ* and *ex-situ* conservation of such species coupled with cultivation for sustained development of growing herbal drug industry. To identify new species and to avoid unscientific ways of extraction training programs should be organised in the state.

Setting up of herbal-based clusters has been suggested. These clusters will provide high quality infrastructure in terms of marketing, financial and technical support. Other important horticulture activities include Mushroom Cultivation and Bee Keeping.

Suggested actions for S&T are:

- To develop agro technology of endangered and commercial species of medicinal and aromatic herbs/plants
- Use of GIS and Remote Sensing for the study of bio-diversity supported by ground truth realities
- Use of biotechnology for multiplication of species, shy seed bearer or have low germination rate

Irrigation

While there is plenty of water in the hills, yet water used for irrigation is limited to over 1.05 lakh hectares out of nearly 6 lakh hectares of cultivated land. More than 50000 hectares of cultivated land can be brought under irrigation through major and medium irrigation projects, which are underway, and the remaining area can be provided with irrigation through minor and other irrigation schemes.

Using satellite data interpretation for mapping of glaciers and snow fields/disaster warning/estimation of irrigation potential/planning and operation of mini and micro hydel electric power stations is required.

Watershed Development

The objective of the Watershed Development Projects is to promote economic development of the village community and to check the adverse affects of drought by restoring the ecological balance and generating the employment for the people of the watershed area. Nearly 70–75 per cent of the rain occurs during the monsoon season, which flows as run-off without much use or conservation.

As a consequence all areas which are without assured irrigation suffer from water stress and low productivity. For the Tenth Five Year Plan, 70 water-sheds have been identified in 8 districts of Himachal Pradesh. These watersheds when commissioned will irrigate about 44000 hectares of cultivated land in the dry season (Table 11.18, Chapter 11).

Infrastructure

Two areas, namely, Energy and Transport-Roads are suggested as focus for S&T.

Energy

The state has a Hydro Power Potential of 20000 MWs of which only 20 per cent has been harnessed so far. Power can be tapped from both renewable and non-renewable resources. Himachal Pradesh has the highest heat flow and highest thermal gradient geothermal basin in India (Table 17.1, Chapter 17).

The non-conventional sources of Geothermal and Solar Power have potential for rural and hamlet electrification schemes. As of now, 20 per cent of the total available potential has been harnessed with another 7060 MWs under various stages of execution (Table 17.4, Chapter 17).

S&T actions proposed in this area are:

- Use of solar passive housing technology for public and industry
- Simulation of solar passive buildings using computer software

Transport-Roads

Considering the geography of the state, roads in the form of National Highways, border roads, state highways and other arterial and rural roads are an important component. Various schemes like The Pradhan Mantri Gram Sadak Yojna, The Rural Infrastructural Development Fund (RIDF), Central Road Fund are being undertaken to fill the inadequacies of the road network like less all-weather roads (Table 17.14, Chapter 17), poor village connection (Table 17.15, Chapter 17), poor road quality, lack of environmental consideration in road design and construction etc.

Remote Sensing Technology, Satellite data and 3-D Modelling software (surface modellers, surface modellers, polygon modellers) for economical position and structure assessment of roads and bridges should be used.

Rural Development

The proposed areas of focus for S&T are rural industrialisation and rural informatics.

The State with 90.2 per cent of its population in the rural areas (Table 13.1, Chapter 13) has a sizeable deprived population consisting of marginal farmers, landless labourers, besides schedule castes, the schedule tribes and other backward castes. This component of population has to be brought into focus for upliftment with emphasis on the skill up-gradation, removal of unemployment and vertical growth.

A better network of physical infrastructure facilities is essential for development of rural economy. Table 13.3, 13.4, 13.5 and 13.6, of Chapter 13 highlight inter-district disparities with regard to some of the basic development indicators. For this purpose S&T thrust in this area should include:

- Using information technology for governance by focussing the tension on improvement of production, consumption and social services
- Using IT for marketing rural goods
- Maintaining and upgrading existing rural infrastructure and promoting facilities such as cold chains, marketing intelligence network to facilitate the agro processing industries

Rural Industrialisation

Rural development requires a positive change in the rural areas, both qualitatively and quantitatively, which is possible by providing gainful employment, proper utilisation of land resources, introduction of modern technology industries and micro planning under the Panchayati Raj setup with decentralisation of finances and delegation of powers

Rural Informatics

Components of rural development, *viz.*, agricultural growth, infrastructure development, human resource development, rural industrialisation and grassroot level rural governance, can benefit from information technology by focusing attention on improvement of production, consumption and social services.

Computerised information can be used in decision making at the village, block and district levels for maintaining land records, afforestation, beneficiary details, development schemes, rural banking, rural environment and other socio-economic indicators.

Industry

The focus areas for S&T concern in Himachal Pradesh are suggested to be:

- Concentration of Industry
- Industrial Infrastructure
- Agro/Food Processing
- Textile and Hosiery
- Cement
- Handloom Industry
- Sericulture
- Waste Management

Concentration of Industry

By March 2002 the total production for SSI and L&M sectors was worth Rs. 5000 crore providing direct employment to 1.556 lakh persons with an investment of Rs. 3048 crore (Table 16.2, Chapter 16)

Industrial development in the state has been uneven. The state has been classified into two categories *viz.*, industrially developed and backward areas/districts. The periphery districts of Solan and Sirmaur are the most developed and have been categorised as developed districts, while Kangra and Una are less developed and come under the category of backward districts.

In the industrially developed areas of Solan and Sirmaur districts, L&M units account for 88 per cent, investment 70 per cent and employment 34 per cent, while in the remaining 10 districts categorised as backward areas/districts SSI and tiny sector units account for 82 per cent, investment 30 per cent and employment 66 per cent (Table 16.3, 16.4, and 16.5, Chapter 16)

S&T should take help of Zoning Atlas to:

- Zone and classify the environment in a district;
- identify locations for siting of industries; and
- identify industries suitable to the identified sites

Industrial Infrastructure

Himachal Pradesh has developed 30 industrial areas and 10 industrial estates with all basic amenities like roads, power, sewerage, water and communication etc. (Table 16.7, Chapter 16). The existing industrial areas and estates provide the basic infrastructure but modern and technological infrastructure is highly inadequate.

The State with diverse agro climatic conditions and geographical features, horticulture, floriculture, sericulture, forestry, hydro-power generation, handicrafts, handlooms, herb based and aromatic, minerals, wool based industries are comparatively better developed. These industries have been identified as thrust industries.

This makes it imperative to develop modern and appropriate infrastructure setting up clusters at conducive destinations (for example, Table 16.8 of Chapter 16 gives an overview of recommended clusters location wise).

Agro/Food Processing

The number of units in this area is 8000 in the SSI and tiny sectors and 27 in L&M sector and employ approximately 30000 people. This industry at present is mainly limited to traditional processing of agricultural and horticultural raw materials using low-grade technology. The production of all kinds of fruits has decreased sharply during the year 1999-2000 evident from the fact that as against the production potential of 4.92 lakh tonnes, the production of fruits during the year 1999-2000 was 0.89 lakh tonnes.

S&T initiatives should take effective steps to raise the productivity and quality of apples and other fruits and to evolve an integrated strategy for fruit farming and food processing.

Textile and Hosiery

This industry accounts for 60 per cent of the total employment offered in the large and medium sector. The major hosiery industries are in SSI and tiny sectors located in the backward areas. The main products of this industry are shawls, patti, caps, jackets, sweaters and mufflers. Kullu, Shillai, Udaipur and Hamirpur have been identified for setting up the textile and hosiery clusters.

Cement

Mining in recent years has intensified in the state due to abundance of Limestone, Gypsum, Slates etc. In the aftermath of this activity many adverse environmental factors have arisen. The exploitation of limestone and the quarrying of slate have affected the ecosystem of the state, leading to encroachment and destruction of forests.

At present there are four cement plants in the L&M sectors in addition to three mini plants (Table 16.9, Chapter 16). Quality limestone which is one of the important ingredients in the manufacture of grey port land cement is available in plenty in Himachal Pradesh.

Three more large-scale cement plants based on limestone have been approved to be set up in Sundernagar, Alsindi (Mandi District) and Chamba. These private sector plants are being set up by M/s Larsen and Toubro Ltd, M/s Grasim Industries Ltd and M/s Harishchanra Ltd. M/s Gujrat Ambuja Cement Ltd. has proposed to set up new plans near their plant already in production in Solan district. In addition, one at Koti and in Gumma in Shimla district are also under consideration.

The installation of these plants poses a threat to the ecology and environment of Himachal Pradesh.

Handloom Industry

With 42000 handlooms in the state, primarily based on wool, the handloom industry is an important cottage industry providing gainful employment to about 45000 weavers. The main products woven in handlooms are Woollen Ladies' Shawls, Woollen Gents' Shawls, Woollen Tweeds, Shirting, Dress Material and Woollen Carpets etc. This industry is mainly concentrated in Kullu, Mandi, Kinnaur, Kangra, Lahaul and Spiti and Chamba districts of the state.

Sericulture

Climatic conditions of Himachal Pradesh are most favourable for the growth of this industry. It is a village oriented labour intensive industry in all its phases from cultivation of silk worms and food plants to silk worm rearing, silk reeling and other processes such as twisting, dying, weaving, printing and finishing. At present this industry provides subsidiary occupation to more than 10000 families mainly belonging to the poorer section.

Waste Management

As Solan and Sirmaur have the maximum number of L&M units, they also have the largest concentration of hazardous waste generating industries. The waste generated by different towns and industries is polluting rivers, their tributaries and streams. A major pollutant in the river is the synthetic waste. The condition of major rivers like Gumbher, the Kuni, the Kaushalya, the Asni, and the Sarsa are receiving industrial waste which carry filth and non-biodegradable waste [refer to Annexure 8 (a) and (b)]

Productivity and quality improvement initiatives in each of the above sectors should be taken up by S&T.

The Enablers

Science and Technology vehicles to undertake specific tasks

- Remote Sensing Technology
- Geographical Information System
- Solar Passive Building Technology
- Zoning Atlas
- Bio-Technology
- Plasma Pyrolysis

Remote Sensing Technology

Geographical Information System

- Tax (Parcel) Map Maintenance
- Producing Mailing Labels for Abutter Notifications
- Standard Theme Maps
- Custom Maps
- Providing Basic Information for Building Permit
- Public Access Terminal
- Network Infrastructure Maintenance Tracking
- Export Data to Computer Assisted Drawing (CAD) Software
- Fire Equipment Response Distance Analysis
- Preparation of Existing Land Use Map
- Analysis of Urban Sprawl
- Land Suitability Analysis
- Transportation and Network Analysis
- GIS in Municipal Governance
- Land Use/Cover Analysis
- Land Use Change Detection

The broad spectrum of application areas in GIS suggests that GIS can be a promising tool to the urban planners in finding the solutions to the problems confronting them today.

Remote Sensing is of immense use in field of scientific mapping of natural resources, especially in the remote and inaccessible areas of the state. The capability of high resolution, synoptic prospective and repetitive coverage over the same area from Remote Sensing Satellite orbiting the earth have been an added advantage for monitoring the seasonal changes on vegetation and timely forecasting of the future events on the earth's surface.

Facilities for the analysis, interpretation and use of satellite data have been created in the state. Using these facilities, the following studies have been completed.

- Hydro-geomorphologic mapping on 1:250000 scale
- Land use/land cover mapping on 1:250000 scale
- Lineament mapping on 1:250000 scale delineation of prospective areas for mineral exploration
- Delineation and generation of digital database of the wasteland in nine districts of the state namely Shimla, Mandi, Kullu, Lahaul & Spiti, Sirmaur, Una, Solan, Kinnaur and Bilaspur districts on 1:50000 scale
- Wetland inventory prepared and digital database made available to the fisheries department
- Integrated evaluation of natural resources of Chamba district on 1:50000 scale and generation of digital database for planning.
- Assessment of tea plantation in Kangra district
- Glacier and snow cover mapping for the Satluj and Beas basins

Remote Sensing Techniques can further help in providing consultancy services in the field of ground-water management, micro Hydel project pre-feasibility study, environmental impact assessment studies etc.

Geographical Information System

GIS is a computer aided decision support and planning tool, which integrates data from maps and other auxiliary information from geographical area of interest. It does a complex analysis of spatial data and non-spatial information. Its objective is to bring data from a multitude of sources together and to uncover complex relationships otherwise difficult to comprehend.

The enormous data on natural resources, socio-economic and demographic set-up required for district level planning could be efficiently handled and analysed using GIS. Different management scenario can also be processed allowing the planners/managers to analyse various alternatives before selecting the most appropriate plan.

GIS can be used as an effective tool for civic administration. However, till date most of the organisations are manually creating and utilising a variety of maps in their daily activities. With the ever-exploding population, the basic infrastructures in urban and rural areas could crack down in the absence of an adequate planning due to these analogue maps. GIS tools can effectively be used as front ends, if designed appropriately for use of novice officers in the administration".

Suggested Applications of GIS

Tax (Parcel) Map Maintenance

As property boundaries change, the Assessor's tax maps need to be updated. Once property boundaries are part of the GIS database, they can be edited using the GIS software. The system of property tax management can also be upgraded while using GIS and preparing property tax information system.

Producing Mailing Labels for Abutter Notifications

Zoning board of appeals hearings or proposed actions by a town/city require notifying abutting property owners. A GIS application for producing abutter mailing labels enables you to identify abutting property owners in different ways ("within 300 feet", "abutters and abutters-to- abutters", "abutters on a Main Street between house numbers 23 and 77"). Once the properties are identified this kind of GIS application can produce mailing labels and be integrated with a word processing "mail merge" capability.

Standard Theme Maps

Many communities produce or need maps for specialised purposes (e.g., property maps for revaluation by the assessor, maps of the water system, police zone maps, urban zoning maps, etc.). A GIS typically includes a programming capability that makes it possible to create a standard map set. When the program is run it produces one of each sheet in the set and sends them to a colour printer.

Custom Maps

GIS allows you to make maps of virtually any size and scale for any area of your jurisdiction. In addition, these maps can combine any set of features you want from the database. This is simply not practical without a GIS.

Providing Basic Information for Building Permit

At its simplest level this involves using the GIS to find a property location using an address. Once the property to which the permit applies is identified, the GIS can be used to provide some of the essential information (e.g., address, property ID, zoning classification, lot area, street frontage) needed for filling out the permit.

Public Access Terminal

GIS can be used at public counters, either by the public or by town staff assisting the public, to view information such as properties and related information about assessed value. Similarly information about streets, open space, natural features, school districts, election wards or zoning districts can also be displayed. If provided, such a terminal might also enable users to make maps of the requested information.

Network Infrastructure Maintenance Tracking

Public Works Department may systematically and annually perform certain kinds of maintenance on road, sewer, water or storm drain networks. These actions might consist of street re-paving, water main flushing or similar activities. A GIS could be used to track work that has been performed in prior years, the work planned for the current year and the work proposed for future years. This information can then be summarised on a map and/or in tabular form.

Export Data to Computer Assisted Drawing (CAD) Software

GIS software will be able to export your data to other file formats, such as DXF or drawing exchange format. This format is read by many software packages including the CAD software AutoCAD. This kind of application might allow you to select features (e.g. property boundaries, building outlines, sewer pipes) for an area you select and then save them to .DXF file format for use in creating engineering design drawings.

Fire Equipment Response Distance Analysis

A GIS can be used to evaluate how far (as measured via the street network) each portion of the street network is from a firehouse. This can be useful in evaluating the best location for a new firehouse or in determining how well the fire services cover particular areas for insurance ratings.

Preparation of Existing Land Use Map

A remote sensing and GIS can be used to prepare an existing land use map and update the old town planning scheme maps.

Analysis of Urban Sprawl

To study the extent and direction of the city expansion, also to understand the underlying driving forces for the expansion. Assessment of Land use conversion in different parts of the city to help understanding of the impact of the policy pursued.

Land Suitability Analysis

Expansion of any activity requires land. And the purpose of the land use requires the suitability of the land. It depends upon several parameters such as soil, topography, slope, drainage, etc., A GIS can be used to integrate all these parameters and identify the land suitability for the required purpose.

Transportation and Network Analysis

Besides these, there are many planning tasks that can be carried out using GIS for meaningful applications. It is essential to look into the technical, financial and institutional processes and lacuna in order to make the use of GIS in municipal organisation for its effectiveness.

GIS in Municipal Governance

In the municipal administration GIS can contribute to improved productivity and streamlining of internal government administration by helping to remove paper work from the process or by facilitating coordination and consolidation of information.

Land Use/Cover Analysis

Remote Sensing and GIS finds a major role in detecting changes in land use. Through remote sensing, one can get various season data, clearly indicating the changes in the land. Through visual interpretation, the changes can be identified. However GIS is essential for detailed land use/land cover analysis. The interpreted data when taken into GIS through R to V conversion and the relevant database attached to land use/land cover map, different types of overlay analysis can be done in no time.

Land Use Change Detection

GIS can be effectively used in detecting the changes in land use. Base map of the area for which the change in land use needs to be analysed needs to be prepared over two time periods. One would be the present land use map and the other would be the land use map for preceding time. The two base maps of different time periods when overlaid and if required rubber sheeted (is done to equalise the analysis areas), the changes can be interpreted for different parcels or layout subdivisions. Land use change detection is very critical for tax planners for tax assessment of the parcels, urban planners for planning for land use changes/land use analysis, detecting land use violations etc.

The endless list of application areas in GIS suggests that GIS can be a promising tool to the urban planners in finding the solutions to the problems confronting them today.

Solar Passive Building Technology

Major areas of focus for S&T are suggested as follows:

- Solar Buildings with no additional costs
- Solar Buildings with incremental costs of 5-10 per cent
- Buildings requiring retrofitting

Himachal Pradesh is the first state in the country to introduce Solar Passive Building Technology for the design and construction of Government and Semi-Government buildings on a large scale. Solar Passive Building Technology utilises the orientation of the building for the availability of solar energy at the site for natural heating or cooling of the building resulting in saving of large amounts of fossil fuels and electricity and will also result in considerable savings of the Government Exchequer.

The dependence on conventional fuels like firewood, charcoal, coal, and electricity for space heating is also lessened, thus saving forest and conserving energy. This technology is an environmentally sound and economically viable technology in which the site planning, climatic conditions, and movements of the sun during summers and winters are considered to create comfortable living conditions.

Solar Buildings with No Additional Costs

Buildings for which there is a freedom of proper site planning, appropriate building materials and efficient functional planning at initial stages, the solar passive design features will cost very little extra expenditure

Solar Buildings with Incremental Costs of 5-10 per cent

Buildings for which there is less independence in selecting the site and orientation, there may be a small incremental cost of 5-10 per cent.

Buildings Requiring Retrofitting

Buildings above 2000 meters requiring roof collector solar space/air/water heating systems with electric backups or in which solar passive systems are to be retrofitted, the costs can go up to 15 per cent. However, due to lesser fuel consumption these incremental costs can be recovered with in 2-3 years

Solar Passive Designs Should be Used for

- Innovative Designs For Rural Buildings- incorporating earthquake resistant and solar passive designs
- Consultancy For Innovative Housing Technologies To Public- incorporating Solar passive technology, earthquake resistant features etc. thereby helping in proper utilisation and planning of the land area
- Passive Solar Cooling Technology for Hot Climates – incorporating features of passive cooling for low altitude regions of Himachal Pradesh.
- Retrofitting of Rural Houses with Solar Passive Heating System-retrofitting existing houses with low cost Thermo Symphoning Air Heating Panels, Sunspaces and Trombe Wall Systems
- Thermal Comfort Evaluation of Buildings
- Solar Passive Designs of Primary Schools and
- Training & Field Demonstration of Technologies

Zoning Atlas

The overall deterioration of the environment has given a fresh impetus to physical planners to include environmental parameters in planning. At present, the industries and the related activities in our country are expanding at a fast rate, but the siting of these industries is not carried out in a planned manner. This has serious repercussions on the environment. The carrying capacity of the environment is not unlimited. Some areas like forests, human settlements, the flora and fauna and water bodies or air shed might be affected and the ecosystem might be harmed.

Environmental planning is a proven tool for reducing the impact from such risks.

The Zoning Atlas is not only the solution for the problems caused by haphazard industrial siting, but tackles the cause of the problem itself. The Zoning Atlas identifies suitable sites for siting of industries based on environmental considerations. The environmental parameters and conditions are evaluated and quantified and the suitability of sites is determined based on their sensitivity to air, water and land pollution. The present report deals with the Zoning Atlas for siting of industries, based on environmental considerations, for Kullu District of Himachal Pradesh.

The Zoning Atlas for siting of industries, zones and classifies the environment in a district and presents the pollution receiving potential of various sites/zones in the district and the possible alternate sites for industries through easy-to-read maps.

The objectives of preparing a Zoning Atlas for siting of industries are:

- To zone and classify the environment in a District;
- To identify locations for siting of industries; and
- To identify industries suitable to the identified sites.

The type of decisions that can be taken at various levels are given below:

The Government	Plan better pollution control and monitoring programmes and speed up the sanctioning of industries.
The Industrialists	Develop policies and plan sustainable industrial development.
Regulatory Authorities	Both environmental and economic considerations. Identify the most suitable industrial site, matching.
The Public	Participate in the decision making process on the type of industrial development in their neighbourhood.

Bio Technology

Suggested focus areas are:

- Bioengineering of Medicinal Plants
- In Vitro Propagation Techniques
- Biotechnology based industries
- Herbal And Floriculture Plant Production
- Floriculture

Himachal Pradesh is endowed with immense diversity of food, fruit crops, fodder, vegetables, minor forest products, diversity of micro organisms and richest wealth of forest and medicinal herbs. The state offers unlimited opportunities and has most suitable and ideal conditions for setting up biotechnology-based industries.

Himachal Pradesh has immense microbial diversity, which needs further inputs for its meaningful exploration, documentation and usage in many industrial applications. Biotechnology as a tool has helped in the recovery of degraded eco-system.

Some of the methods based on plant biotechnology include reforestation involving Micro propagation and use of Mycorrhizae. Micro propagation has resulted in increasing plant cover preventing erosion and giving a climatic stability. It can also help in rejuvenation of degraded land, which is in plenty in Himachal Pradesh and to stop genetic erosion by Lantana and other weeds.

Bioengineering of Medicinal Plants

The biosynthetic pathways for the biologically active chemical compounds in medicinal plants are usually complex. Genetic manipulations can help increase/ decrease the contents of specific compounds in the medicinal plants. Detailed understanding of these pathways will be a prerequisite for the identification, cloning and genetic engineering of the concerned structural and regulatory genes. These genetic techniques will also help develop designer medicinal plants.

In Vitro Propagation Techniques

Biotechnological tools are important to select, multiply and conserve the critical genotypes of medicinal plants by adopting techniques such as micro propagation, creation of somacional variations and genetic transformations. Biotechnological tools can also be harnessed for production of secondary metabolites using plants as bioreactors.

Plant cell culture is of importance for improvement of medicinal plants. Complete plants have been regenerated from callus cultures, excised anthers and isolated protoplasts of many medicinal and aromatic plants. Many of the regenerated plants showed somaclonal variation and selections were made for high active principle yielding cell lines. Protoplast fusion plant is regenerated and micropropagation techniques can be used to multiply and clone the desired species. Gene transfer is possible from wild and related species to desired cultivators through wide hybridisation including embryo rescue systems.

Various components of the application of Tissue Culture Technology are:

- Microporpagation
- Conservation through cryopreservation
- Bio production of value added secondary metabolites
- Biotransformation of bioactive molecules
- Genetic upgradation for improvement
  - Somatic Hybridisation
  - Somaclonal Variations
  - Transgenic Plants

Himachal Pradesh, a fruit bowl of India, needs immediate replacement of old orchards with high yielding disease-free fresh planting stock. Biotechnology can play an important role by use of Micro propagated plants. There is also need to improve present fruit processing units and technologies, which can help industries for Cider, Vinegar, Wine and Juice to match the international standards. In agricultural sector there is need for diversification of farming for economic rehabilitation and self-sufficiency.

High yielding improved crop varieties, transgenics specially stress tolerant (cold, rain-fed conditions), bio-fertilisers, bio-pesticides etc. (Table 11.19 to 11.23, Chapter 11) are other areas where biotechnology can play a major role.

Biotechnology Based Industries

- Commercial Micro Propagation
- Fermentation
- Pharmaceuticals
- Bio-pesticides and Bio-fertilisers
- Phyto chemicals
- Transgenic seeds
- Bio-fuels
- Post Harvest Technology
- Bio Processing
- Enzyme Production
- Environment Protection and Animal Husbandry
- Gene Therapy and
- Bio Informatics

Himachal Pradesh has a diverse and fragile eco-system, which harbours rich flora of about 4000 plant species including a large number of rare medicinal and aromatic plants and wild relatives of cultivated crops. Documentation of diversity of such resources including agro-bio diversity is urgently required. The recent development in biotechnology infrastructure and sound industrial base of a vast market development ensure opportunities for biotech products and business in bio-pharmaceuticals, agriculture, food and nutrition sector.

Himachal Pradesh is an ideal destination to invest in bio-technology based industry because of its Bio-diversity, Eco-diversity, pollution-free environment, mild climate, availability of adequate land water and electricity, excellent law and order situation and research and development backing.

Herbal and Floriculture Plant Production

Herbal Products are gaining popularity as medicines, nutraceuticals, and skin care products across the world and the market potential is enormous. The present weaknesses of a herbal scenario include the paucity of adequate raw material, lack of large-scale cultivation activities, non-availability of standards of production and processing, age-old non-mechanised operation and non-availability of validity and claims.

Himachal Pradesh has a clear edge because of its potential of physio diversity in varying ecological zones. Emphasis need to be given at the R&D level to deeper knowledge based products via phyto genomics and studies for discovering novel bio molecules. For this it is important to create access to the testing facilities and centres within the state for this purpose.

Floriculture

In Himachal Pradesh, total production in floriculture was worth Rs. 4 crore in the year 1999-2000. Gladiolus, Lilium, and Carnations are the major floriculture crops in Himachal Pradesh.

Scientific Techniques and measures can assist the floriculture industry with:

- High quality flower bulb production
- Identifying the right crop and right variety with respect to climate.
- Developing infrastructure for forcing flower bulbs.
- Developing the Chrysanthemum industry.
- Interaction with industry, financial institutes/ banks via proper networking.

Plasma Pyrolysis System for Disposal of Plastic Carry Bags

Himachal Pradesh is the first state in the country to have enacted an act for dealing with solid waste management and the menace of plastic carry bags. The "Himachal Pradesh Non-Biodegradable Garbage [Control] Act" was formulated by the Department of Science, Technology and Environment, Government of Himachal Pradesh and enacted in 1995 to prevent throwing or depositing non-biodegradable garbage in public drains, roads and places open to public view in the state.

The natural process of degradation is inefficient in respect of plastic bags. Recycling generates toxic gases dangerous to human health. Incinerators have also proved to be inefficient as some gases such as Phosgene, Carbon Monoxide, Chlorine, Sulphur Dioxide, Nitrogen Dioxide and deadly Dioxin are released during combustion. Dumping leads to the leaching of heavy metal like lead and cadminium into the soil affecting not only soil quality but also ground water. The special problems of problems of plastic bags in the hilly state of Himachal Pradesh are

- Availability of open slopes where municipal wastes are indiscriminately thrown. The generally prevalent low temperature averages only serves to aggravate the problem further.
- The retention of wastes on the slopes causes further problems as these wastes enter into the drainage system and pollute the water sources, specifically of the lower lying rural areas.
- The polythene bags have created problems by choking the sewerage and drainage systems and also by virtue of the fact that polythene is non-biodegradable there by remaining on the slopes as such for years.
- The municipal wastes are not easily collected because of the problem of access (transport and roads). Also the rag pickers cannot collect these wastes from steep slopes.
- Disposal of solid wastes is presently being done on the slopes, as large landfill sites are not available.
- Many chemicals are added during production of polythene bags to impart strength; these chemicals leach into the food products resulting in contamination of stored food, drinks, soil and water sources.

It has been estimated that 5200 plastic bags reach a middle class colony of thousand households everyday and plastic forms 20 per cent of the total waste (*Vatavaran*).

Hence the need for an appropriate technology- "Plasma Pyrolysis" which can safely dispose the plastic material is strongly felt.

Pyrolysis is the process of disintegration and decomposition of carbonaceous material by heat. At lower temperature ash and liquid by-products are formed. At optimised temperature carbonaceous matter yields methane, carbon monoxide, hydrogen, carbon dioxide, and water.

The gas emission will be within the environment emission standards set by Central Pollution Control Board (CPCB). The Facilitation Centre for Industrial Plasma Technologies has been set up by the Institute for Plasma Research, the centre has processed development and material characterisation laboratories, technology demonstration facilities and pilot plants. FCIPT has designed and engineered plasma pyrolysis system for disposal of medical waste (Medical waste consists of all kinds of polymers including polyethylene).

The Processes

Specific projects to deliver results

- Information Technology
- E-governance
- Technical Education
- Industrial Consortiums

Information Technology

The state government should encourage private sector participation in laying High Bandwidth backbone in the state. The government should endeavour to computerise the process of governance, so that the citizens can file the documents required by the government electronically.

Priority area should include:

- Rural services such as Land Records, Acquisitions of Land and Registration of Deeds.
- Police services such as FIR Registration
- Social services such as Family Pension, Old Age Pension etc.
- Registration of Licences, Ration Cards, Birth Certificate, Death Certificate, Caste/Tribe Certificate, Driving Licence, etc.
- Public Information/Utility such as Employment Exchange Registration, Employment Opportunities, Examination Results, Hospitals/Beds Availability, Road Transport Time Tables, Government Notifications, Government Schemes, etc.
- Agriculture/Horticulture Sector-providing the information about Mandi Rates in respect of identified Commodities in important Mandis.
- Electronic filing of Tax Returns, State Excise Duty, House Tax, Property Tax, Road Tax, etc.

Departments should be encouraged to establish web-sites. Departments where databases already exist should be asked to upgrade the same to provide dynamic information and use their sites as platforms for citizen-government interface.

Internet Kiosks should be encouraged to serve the information needs of the citizens and to provide a large number of employment to educated youth (Table 7.20, Chapter 7), work contracts with leading and reputed Information Technology service vendors can be established to avail a wide range of IT consultancy, specialist services and IT products at lower cost with shortened procurement cycle.

Boosting e-commerce in all activities of the state is a must for Himachal Pradesh. This will facilitate local industries to compete in the global market. The following initiatives can be followed up:

- Net Banking - Net Based Banking would catalyse increase in use of Internet for e-commerce and also reduce high overhead costs for banks.
- Encourage e-Commerce, EDI Implementation in Government Departments.
- Encourage e-commerce in items/goods in which the state has comparative/distinct advantage example Horticulture produce, Handicrafts etc.
- Himachal has an excellent Telecommunication infrastructure wherein all the telephone exchanges are digital and are interconnected to each other. The state has probably the highest density of OFC (Optical Fibre Cable) penetration per unit area as compared to any other state in the country. This strong background can help Himachal to emerge as a regional gateway for the "North Indian" Internet, e-Commerce and Digital Services Traffic.

In order to promote the growth of IT in the state it is imperative that Hi-Tech Habitats are built in and around all major towns. Such space would be extremely useful to promote the growth of IT enabled services

Technical Education

The state government should make concerted efforts to market the state as an ideal location for setting up institutes of excellence on the national and international scale. Himachal Pradesh has technical institutions like N.I.T. Hamirpur, I.I.T.T. College of Engineering, Kala Amb, Institute of Engineering and Emerging Technology, Baddi, Green Hill Engineering College, Kumar Hatti, Solan, The Jai Prakash University of Information Technology, Wakanaghat, Solan, with high quality education and training facilities in subjects and vocations in demand by the industry (Table 7.22, Chapter 7).

Efforts should be made to set up more institutes, which can offer courses in fields of education, which are relevant in the modern context especially in the field of Information Technology and related areas. Strong directions and measures should be undertaken to introduce the subject of IT education at the primary and secondary school level (as of now these courses are being imparted in more than 150 senior secondary schools).

The use of IT or PC penetration and availability of I-NET nodes is low in Himachal Pradesh. Presently the state government is actively implementing Himachal Pradesh State Wide Area Network (HPSWAN), connecting districts with the state headquarters. This facility should be extended to the block level and subsequently to the village level so that the benefits of IT percolate to the masses at large.

E- Governance

The Enabling Technology

Groupware technology can offer dramatic improvements in the intra-government synchronisation, optimisation of government resources, and decision support systems to boost the efficiency and efficacy of the public policy. The major contributions of groupware in improving organisational performance include on-line collaborative work, electronic community development, knowledge management and workflow applications.

In such a scenario, information will be more directly accessible to decision-makers and flow smoothly across departments through a common database and compatible systems inter-linked under a secure high-speed networked environment. In addition to a tangible improvement in the functioning of the administration, the government-public interface shall undergo a radical change for the better.

Industrial Consortium

With the infrastructural development, and implied industrial emphasis in the state plans, the number of registered industrial units has shown a sizable increase (Table 16.2, 16.3, 16.4, 16.5 and Table 16.7, Chapter 16). Besides the identified clusters, some of the District Industries Centres (DICs) of the industry department have recommended activities, which could be viable under the industrial cluster programme (Table 16.8, Chapter 16).

In addition to these, some herbal-based clusters could be set up in the state as the higher reaches are endowed with the precious herbs (Table 4.16, Chapter 4, and Table 11.15, Chapter 11). Similarly sericulture could be taken up through clusters in the districts of Kangra, Mandi and Sirmaur. The rich mineral resource of Himachal Pradesh also endows it with a conducive environment for the cement industry, slate tiles, calcium and ammonium nitrates etc (Table 2.7, Chapter 2).

Following steps can be taken to ensure this:

- Creation of dense vegetation buffers around cement plants and other industries so that pollutant particles are restricted to go beyond a certain limit. Remote Sensing Techniques can be used to assess the appropriate landscape for setting up cement plants and other industries.
- Assessment of impact of industrial emissions and pollutants on human and cattle health and also on agriculture. Need to take appropriate steps to maintain pollution control standards to conserve climatological and pollution-free industrial environment of the state.
- Provision of incentives for eco-friendly industries. Inclusion of Small Scale Industries for environmental clearance.

The state government has already developed 30 industrial areas and 10 industrial estates with all basic amenities like roads, parks, sewerage, water and communication etc. Apart from new technologies, in most industries, there is an increased demand to keep pace with national and international development. The concern is vital for development of long-term markets for the industry. The pressure mainly comes from cost effectiveness, quality and technology upgradation.

The state government should make efforts to formulate an Industrial Consortium, which will develop as a powerful vehicle to propel the technological advancement of the industry by providing a forum for interaction, exchange of ideas and a platform to carry out technological development and services for example, The National Research and Technology Consortium (NRTC) at Parwanoo which functions as an autonomous, non-profit R&D organisation by the State Council for Science, Technology and Environment, Government of Himachal Pradesh.

NRTC programs are in the form of industrial projects, technology development, R&D facility provision to the industry, consultancy and training workshops and seminars to strengthen the skill base of people from the industries and institutions. Wherever specific expertise and knowledge base are required, links are established with national laboratories and universities to acquire the appropriate knowledge base. Various projects initiated by NRTC, which has helped the industry can be summarised as

H.P. Science & Technology Initatives

The Himachal Pradesh State Council for Science, Technology and Environment came into being in 1985.

The council plays an advisory role in bringing up contemporary developments in the notice of the state government apart from providing active support in drafting guidelines/policies for mitigating environmental problems. The main objectives of the council are:

- To advice state government on science and technology policy issues and interventions.
- To transfer, develop and demonstrate appropriate technologies for hilly regions.
- To exchange scientific knowledge with national and international scientific institutions/ organisations.
- To promote, popularise and disseminate science and technology.
- To create and strengthen science and technology facilities in the state.
- To promote research and development studies relevant to state needs.
- To establish linkages with state universities, R&D institutions.
- To provide consultancy services in successfully demonstrated/developed technologies.

Achievements During the Year 2002-03

The programs of the State Council for Science, Technology and Environment were focussed in the following areas:

- Popularisation and assessment of the potential of Remote Sensing Technology.
- Demonstrating the Potential of natural sources of energy.
- Educating and creating awareness on different facets of environment.
- Popularising and demonstrating appropriate technologies in science.

Remote Sensing Cell

Remote Sensing Technology has emerged as a modern technology for acquiring the information about the earth surface with remote access. It has been found to be of immense use in the field of scientific mapping of natural resources especially in the remote and inaccessible areas of the state.

ISRO IGBP Programme: Effect of Climatic Variation in Himalayan Glacier

International geo-sphere biosphere program is a project funded by Department of Space, GoI which will help the state in finalisation of glacier inventory for the Ravi basin in Himachal Pradesh. The main objective of this investigation is to have the systematic inventory of glaciers and snowfields for overall assessment of water availability in the Himalayan region (Annexure A–23.2 (a) and A–23.2 (b).

Snow Cover Monitoring in Himachal Pradesh

The main objective of snow cover monitoring will be to know about the change in snow pattern in Himachal Pradesh during the last five years.

NRIS Project

NRIS is a computer-based information system that provides various sets of capabilities to handle geo-referenced data such as data input, data storage/ management, data manipulation/analysis and data output.

Land Hazard Zonation Project

This project was used to prepare landslide hazards zonation maps along NH-22 and NH-88 at 1:25000 scale using IRS-1D satellite data to generate digital database for landslide related parameters such as lithology, lineament, slope, land use/land cover etc.

To prepare risk maps along Manali-Bilaspur-Shimla-Sumdo section and to prepare landslide management maps to formulate the strategies for minimising the societal impact of landslides. Remote sensing technology should be used to prepare risk maps along the selective perpetual problematic zones along the highway corridor in the state and to prepare landslide management maps to formulate the strategies for minimising the societal impact of iandslides.

Bio-Geo Database Project

The Bio-Geo Database Project funded by the Department of Science & Technology, GoI, New Delhi for evolving programmes on Bio-Geo Data Ecological Modelling of Himalayan region would be helpful to the state in terms of generation and overall development of the watershed in a scientific manner.

Disaster Management in Himachal Pradesh

As a follow-up of the government notification *vide* which the state council for science, technology and environment has been considered as the nodal agency for the management of Geological hazards in Himachal Pradesh for which a committee was constituted under the Chairmanship of Principal Secretary (S & T) to the government of Himachal Pradesh. The main recommendation was to establish a disaster management cell in the state which will look after the strategies to be adopted at the state level for the management of Geological hazards mainly the earthquakes, landslides, avalanches and floods.

Appropriate Technology Dissemination

Passive Solar House Action Plan

A passive solar house action plan for Himachal Pradesh is being implemented in the state and is being coordinated by the council in collaboration with the HPPWD, and HP Housing Board. Himachal Pradesh is the first state in the country to make the solar passive design of all Government/Semi-Government buildings mandatory. More than 50 Government buildings, offices, hospitals, primary school buildings, teacher's hostels and residential buildings have been designed and constructed until now.

- Innovative Designs for Rural Buildings.
- Consultancy for Innovative Housing Technologies to Public.
- Passive Solar Cooling Technology for Hot Climates.
- Retrofitting of Rural Houses with Solar Passive Heating System.
- Thermal Comfort Evaluation of Buildings
- Solar Passive Designs of Primary Schools under DPEP Project.
- Training & Field Demonstration of Technologies

Creation & Strengthening of Science & Technology Facilities in Himachal Pradesh.

- Support to National Research & Technology Consortium (NRTC) for Industries - Science & Technology Inputs to Industry.
- Establishment of Solar Energy Research Centre for hilly areas.
- Establishment of Science & Technology Information Network.
- To Set up Himachal Pradesh Science Academy.
- To Set up a Planetarium & Sub-Regional Science Centre in Himachal Pradesh.
- Support Patent Information Centre for Himachal Pradesh.
- Science Popularisation & Promotion Programmes in Himachal Pradesh.
- Ecology and Environment.
- Conservation of Wetlands and Biodiversity.
- Integrated Garbage Management Programme.
- Execution of Bio-Diversity Strategy and Action Plan.
- Eradication of Weeds Lantana, Parthenium, and Ageratum.
- Biomass Waste Management in the State.
- Strengthening of Meteorological Network in the State.

ANNEXURE A–23.1 (a)

Wheat Acreage and Production Estimates for the Year 2000-2001

(Using Satellite Data in Respect of 6 Districts of Himachal Pradesh)

Sr. No.	District	Acreage ('000 ha)	Yield (q/ha)	Production ('000 t)
1.	Kangra	69.029	16.53	114.105
2.	Una	22.593	20.07	45.344
3.	Bilaspur	14.167	17.09	24.353
4.	Hamirpur	13.796	14.38	19.839
5.	Mandi	61.769	15.16	93.642
6.	Solan	19.031	14.64	27.861
	Total	**200.385**	**16.226**	**325.144**

Source: State Council for Science, Technology and Environment, Himachal Pradesh.

ANNEXURE A–23.1 (b)

Wheat Acreage and Production Estimates for the Year 2001-2002

(Using Satellite Data in Respect of 6 Districts of Himachal Pradesh)

Sr. No.	District	Acreage ('000 ha)	Yield (q/ha)	Production ('000 t)
1.	Kangra	93.942	17.85	167.686
2.	Una	33.574	21.75	73.023
3.	Bilaspur	27.234	18.25	49.702
4.	Hamirpur	27.772	16.75	46.518
5.	Mandi	77.61	17.65	136.98
6.	Solan	23.528	16.85	39.645
	Total	**283.66**	**18.1**	**513.55**

Source: State Council for Science, Technology and Environment, Himachal Pradesh.

ANNEXURE A–23.2 (a)

Distribution of Glaciers & Snow Fields in Himachal Pradesh

Basins	No. of Glaciers	Aerial Extent (Sq. Km.)	No. of Snow Field	Aerial Extent (Sq. Km.)
Satluj	55	154.762	194	110.843
Spiti	71	258.273	597	368.366
Baspa	25	203.3	66	64.964
Beas	6	15.843	47	72.442
Parbati	39	450.627	131	188.188
Saini	9	37.255	59	51.934

ANNEXURE A–23.2 (b)

Glacial Retreat in Baspa Basin, Himachal Pradesh from 1962-2001

Glacier Number	Glacier Number in Data Sheet	Glacier Area (sq. km.)		Loss in Area (%)	Snout Altitude (m)	
		1962	2001		1962	2002
1.	53107001	10.5	8.7	17	4480	4560
2.	53107002	4.6	4.3	6.5	4520	4720
3.	53107003	2.2	2	9	4600	4640
4.	53107004	4.6	4.1	11	4720	4720
5.	53107005	1.7	1.2	29	3920	4360
6.	53111013	3.2	3.2	0	4920	4920
7.	53111014	1.5	0.8	47	5000	5080
8.	53112001	5.9	5.6	5	4760	5000
9.	53112002	38.4	33.5	13	4320	4360
10.	53112003	2.7	2.2	19	4480	4480
11.	53111009	7.1	5	30	4600	4600
12.	53111010	6.9	5.8	16	4640	4640
13.	53111011	8.7	4.5	48	4760	4760
14.	53107006	35.2	30.4	14	4200	4200
15.	53107007	11.6	9.9	15	4240	4240
16.	53107008	5.5	4.1	26	4360	4360
17.	53107009	3.9	1.9	51	4200	4440
18.	53107010	8	7	13	4360	4400
19.	53107011	10.8	6.1	44	4080	4320
Total Area/ Average Altitude		173	140.3	18.9	4482	4570

Source: State Council for Science, Technology and Environment, Himachal Pradesh.

ANNEXURE A–23.3

Hydro Electric Potential in Himachal Pradesh

Basin	*Projects Under Operation*	*MW Generated*	*Projects Under Construction*	*MW Generated*	*Projects Under Investigation*	*MW Generated*
Yamuna	Andhra	16.95	Gumma SHP	3.00	Rupin	39.00
	Yamuna Projects	537.37			Chirgaon-Majhgaon	46.00
	Giri	60.00			Renuka Dam	40.00
	Gumma	3.00			Paudital Lassa	40.00
					Tangnu Romai	44.00
					Shalvi	8.25
					Sawara Kuddu	144.00
					Nerwar	4.70
Satluj	Rongtong	2.00	Bhaba Aug. Scheme	3.00	Thopan Powari	400.00
	S V P Bhaba	120.00	Ghanvi	22.50	Baspa Stage-I	210.00
	Chaba	1.75	Nathpa Jakri	1500.00	Keshang	120.00
	Bhakra Dam	1200.00	Rampur	680.00	Shongtong Karcham	225.00
	Rukti	1.50	Baspa		Rampur	680.00
	Nogli-Stage I	2.50			Nogli Stage-I	3.50
Beas	Beas Satluj Project	990.00	Larji	126.00	Sarvari	12.00
	Uhl Stage-II	60.00	Parbati Stage -II	800.00	Kalath	60.00
	Baner	12.00	Uhl Stage-II	60.00	Parbati Stage I,II & III	2051.00
	Pong Dam	360.00			Patikari	20.00
	Uhl Stage-I	110.00				
	Binwara	6.00				
	Gaj	10.50				
Ravi	Gharola	0.05	Holi	3.00	Bajoli Holi	200.00
	Bhuri Singh P/House	0.45	Chamera Stage -II	300.00	Kutehar	240.00
	Chamera Stage -I	540.00	Sal-II	2.00	Bharmour	40.00
	Bharmaur Micro	0.02			Sal -I	8.25
	Baira Sieul	180.00			Holi	3.00
					Harsar	60.00
					Chamera Stage-II	300.00
					Siul	7.50
Chenab	Sissu	0.10				
	Shansa	0.20				
	Killar	0.30				
	Billing	0.20				
	Thirot	4.50				
Total		4219.39		3499.50		5006.20

Source: State Council for Science, Technology and Environment, Himachal Pradesh.

ANNEXURE A–23.4

District Wise Water Resources of Himachal Pradesh

Name of the District	Ground Water	Surface Water	Rain Water	Traditional Resources	Other Conventional Sources
Bilaspur	827	786	0	461	0
Chamba	1717	2433	30	2598	836
Hamirpur	1057	485	0	231	1
Kangra	1602	1317	11	1369	466
Kinnaur	76	217	0	24	2
Kullu	0	3392	0	0	0
Lahaul Spiti	1	290	0	57	0
Mandi	833	3924	0	1483	840
Shimla	233	3917	5	2518	9
Sirmaur	644	2249	0	535	9
Solan	344	1090	0	1215	316
Una	832	123	1	21	116
Himachal Pradesh	**8186**	**20223**	**20**	**10512**	**2595**

Source: *Water Resource of Himachal Pradesh by R.G. Arya (Council of Science, Technology and Environment).*

ANNEXURE A–23.5

Important Minerals Reported in Himachal Pradesh

District	Minerals
Bilaspur	Limestone, Coal, Quartzite, Glass, Sand, Gold, Pyrites
Chamba	Copper, Coal, Gypsum, Limestone, Magnesium, Phosphate, Pyrites, Sulfur, Slates, Tale
Kangra	Asbestos, Bismuth, Coal, Glass sand, Gold, Copper, Ore, Limestone, Rocksalt, Slate and Nautral Gas.
Kinnaur	Beryl, Copper, Flourspar, Kyanite, Lead, Gypsum, Silver, Stealite
Kullu	Copper, Iron, Lead, Silver-Re, Limestone, Mica, Nickel, Cobalt, Pyrite, Beryl, Kyanite, Uranium
Lahaul-Spiti	Asbestos, Antimony, Gypsum, Copper, Iron-Ore, Lead, Sulfur, Zinc
Solan	Barytes, Coal, Lead, Phosphate, Gypsum, Limestone, Copper
Una	Glass sand, Calctufa
Mandi	Coal, Copper, Gold, Iron Ore, Limestone, Rock Salt, Slates
Hamirpur	Uranium, Calctufa, Glass, and Oil and Natural Gas
Shimla	Asbestos, Coal, Lead, Barytes, Limestone, Glass, Glass sand, Slates and Iron
Sirmaur	Barytes, Bauxite, Lead, Copper, Gold, Silver Ore, Phosphate, Limestone, Gypsum, Zinc, Pyrite

Source: *Introduction to Himachal Pradesh-Rajendra Attri.*

ANNEXURE A–23.6

Forets Fires, their Causes and Area Burnt (1991 to 1996)

Causes	1991-92		1992-93		1993-94		1994-95		1995-96	
	Number of Cases	Area Burnt (ha)	Number of Cases	Area Burnt (ha)	Number of Cases	Area Burnt (ha)	Number of Cases	Area Burnt (ha)	Number of Cases	Area Burnt (ha)
Fire caused by accident or through carelessness in burning fire lines	93	2157	96	1732	46	569	16	127	58	4165
Fire entering the forets by cross exterior fire traces	12	744	16	205	5	144	5	160	15	599
Fire originating owing to carelessness or accident	331	2257	127	2597	348	7188	1603	9509	1315	41848
1) By workman employed in forests by purchasers or forest produce										
2) By villagers/travellers etc. passing through the forests										
3) By sparking from Railway engines										
4) By lighting or fire ballons										
Intentional firing										
1) in order to obtain new grass										
2) In order to turn out grass										
3) Maliciously fired										
Causes Unknown	96	1167	86	3245	187	2269	82	1054	281	6562
Total	**532**	**6325**	**325**	**7779**	**586**	**10170**	**1706**	**10850**	**1669**	**53174**

Source: State Council for Science, Technology and Environment, Himachal Pradesh.

ANNEXURE A–23.7

Productivity of Different Crops in Himachal Pradesh, India and Best in the World (2000-01)

Crop	H.P.	India	World's Best
	Food Grains		
Rice	1423	2914	12090 Australia
Wheat	1266	2756	8656 Ireland
Maize	2272	1769	10226 New Zealand
	Vegetables		
Tomato	34645	15068	377667 Ukraine
Beans (green)	9921	9600	12471 Israel
Pea (Green)	9574	10000	16010 France
Cabbage	28663	18085	57641 Germany
Cauliflower	18164	15000	45134 New Zealand
Capsicum	9355	9074	49639 Kuwait
Potato	23890	18657	46662 Bosnia

Source: FAO Abstract 2002.

ANNEXURE A–23.8

Geophysical Zones of Himachal Pradesh

Geophysical Zones	Biomes	District
A	Sub-Artic	Kinnaur
	Alpine	Lahaul & Spiti
	Cold Temperature	
B	Alpine	Kullu
	Cold Temperature	Chamba
	Warm Temperature	
C	Cold Temperature	Shimla
	Warm Temperature	Kangra
D	Warm Temperature	Sirmaur
	Sub Tropical	Solan
		Bilaspur
		Una
		Hamirpur
		Mandi

Source: Human Development Report Himachal Pradesh: Section on Environment.

ANNEXURE A–23.9

Rankings of Districts as per Stress Analysis

S. No.	Ranking of Primary Parameters	Ranking of Secondary Parameters	Cumulative Ranking (Primary and Secondary Parameters)
1	**Shimla** (groundwater dependancy for irrigation, water deficiency,Tourism Hotspots)	**Solan** (% increase in cultural waste)	Solan
2	**Bilaspur** (reserve forest as % to total forest, decrease in dense forest area,Increase in Barren land)	**Kinnaur** (% forest area as compared to geographic area, % agricultural area as compared to geographic area, % increase in cultural waste, % increase in non agriculture)	Shimla
3	**Una** (fuel wood dependancy hotspots, groundwater dependancy for irrigation)	**Shimla** (% increase in current fallow, urbanisation)	Blaspur
4	**Kangra** (forest cover decrease, water deficiency, % distribution of small scale industrial activities)	**Bilaspur** (gross density, % increase in other fallow, % decrease in pastures)	Kinnaur
5	**Kullu** (decrease in open forest area, groundwater dependancy for irrigation, tourism hotspots, grazing hotspot, workers engaged in biological resource based activities)	**Hamirpur** (Gross Density,% decrease in agricultural land, urbanisation)	Kangra
6	**Mandi** (fuel wood dependancy hotspots, groundwater dependancy for irrigation,% distribution of small scale industrial activities)	**Sirmaur** (% increase in non-agriculture)	Una
7	**Sirmaur** (% distribution of large-scale industrial activities, distribution of hazardous waste generating industries, grazing hotspots, workers engaged in biological resource based activities)	**Kangra** (% decrease in agricultural land, % increase in current fallow, % decrease in pastures)	Sirmaur
8	**Solan** (% distribution of large-scale industrial activities, distribution of hazardous waste generating industries, increase in cultural waste)	**Chamba** (growth rate)	Mandi
9	**Hamirpur** (fuel wood dependancy hotspots, increase in barren land)	**Una** (% increase in other fallow)	Hamirpur
10	**Chamba** (forest cover decrease, groundwater dependancy for irrigation)	**Mandi**	Chamba
11	**Kinnaur** (decrease in open forest area, groundwater dependancy for irrigation, increase in cultural waste)	**Lahaul & Spiti** (% forest area as compared to geographic area, % agricultural area as compared) to geographic area, % increase in non-agriculture)	Kullu
12	**Lahaul & Spiti** (reserve forest as % to total forest, decrease in dense forest area, groundwater dependancy for irrigation)	**Kullu** (growth rate)	Lahaul & Spiti

ANNEXURE A–23.10

Biotechnological Research Institutes of Himachal Pradesh

University/Institution	*Biotechnological Area of Research*
C.S.K. Krishi Vishvavidyalya, Palampur	Micropropagation
	DNA fingerprinting of plants and microbes
	Molecular markers and gene tagging, pyramiding and marker assisted selection
	Double Haploidy breeding
	Transgenics
Dr. Y.S. Parmar University of Horticulture & Forestry, Solan	Micropropagation of horticulture and plants forest
	In Vitro conservation of endangered plants
	Biofertilisers and bio-pesticides
H.P. University, Shimla	Micro-propagation of ornamental crops
	Fermentation Technology
	Biochemicals
	Bioinformatics
Institue of Himalayan Bioresource Technology, Palampur	Micropropagation of tea and medicinal plants
	Gene expression and cloning
	Bioresource conservaton
	Secondary metabolites
	Transgenic
Central Potato Research Institute, Shimla	Micropropagation
	Molecule markers
	Transgenic

Chapter 24

Sectoral Perspectives and Development Strategy

Context

- Imagine a state, half of which was segmented into 30 princely states (26 Shimla Hills and 4 Punjab Hills) during the colonial days, functioning separately with some degree of internal autonomy, and other half was directly under the hegemony of the British rule;
- Imagine a state which was previously much smaller and non-contiguous in the early years of its development history after independence; and
- Imagine a state which could not look after its interests effectively before it gained statehood in 1971

This is, of course, Himachal Pradesh, which made a transition from a patchwork of feudatory states, to the status of a Chief Commissioner's Province in 1948, Part C State in 1951, union territory in 1956, a consolidated geographical entity in 1966, and a full-fledged state in 1971. On the way, the Part C State of Bilaspur was merged into it in 1954. Such a territorial evolution of the state had a profound influence on the structure and style of its politics and administration. Thereby, the development process too got defined in diverse ways in terms of priorities and pace over time.

Himachal Pradesh covers an area of about 56 thousand sq. kms, and has a population of 6.1 million, according to the 2001 Census. It is one-third larger in area and one-sixth smaller in population than Switzerland. Its population is projected to increase to 6.9 million in 2011 and 7.9 million in 2025 (Sharma and Parthi, 2001). Administratively, the state is organised into 12 districts, 75 *tehsils*, and as many development blocks.

Vision

Which is the most appropriate vision for Himachal Pradesh?

- A 'model' hill state, analogous to Kerala in human development, Punjab in economic development, and Andhra Pradesh in e-governance;
- A 'modern' hill state, in terms of a physical and social infrastructure of the best quality; an economy which is based on horticulture belts, industrial clusters, tourism circuits and hydel-power complexes; an investment climate which is conducive to entry of multinationals, in particular; and a society which is responsive to the emerging global scene;
- A 'beautiful' state, manifest in landscapes exquisitively designed by nature, professional management of water, soil and vegetation on watershed basis, and a harmony between economy and ecology; and
- A 'local governance' state, wherein development is based on local resources, requirements and adaptive technology; management of affairs is by the people rather than for the people; and tradition and modernity have been meaningfully blended to invigorate the native culture.

The vision leads us to some specific questions. How can a progressive upgradation of the standard of living and quality of life of the people be ensured? How can the prevailing subsistence foodgrain agriculture of the state be transformed into widespread commercial horticulture, appropriate to different altitudinal zones and seasons? How can the state attract massive investment in power, tourism, industry, and information technology? How can the dynamism of the state be stirred by raising the core competency of the people, promoting entrepreneurship and breaking their insular psyche? And, above all, how can all this be accomplished without causing damage to ecology?

Guiding Principles

As a response to the questions raised above, it is imperative to enunciate some guiding principles. These are listed below:

- We have to work for a recipe which can be worked into a delectable dish; a strategy that is implementable. The actual task boils down to identification of micro-level projects, which will spur the development process, or solve some chronic problem, or create something special.
- A policy has to be formulated which is free from any political bias or prejudice and which can survive any electoral change. The critical issues facing the state are fairly well defined and choices are limited.
- A policy has to be designed which does not permit erosion of the development gains already made, especially in the sphere of human development.
- The resource gap in every individual sector has to be assessed, and effective measures to fill it worked out.
- Note has to be taken of the interconnectivity of every individual sector of the state with its counterpart in the neighboring states, in terms of both complementarity and competition.
- Since the Government of Himachal Pradesh has already announced policies for a number of sectors, including Environment (undated), Transport (1999), Industry (1999), Tourism (2000), Information Technology (2001), Youth (2002), Forestry (2002), and Biotechnology (2003), it will be desirable to review these within the framework of their specifications, and suggest improvements, if necessary.
- Reforming the existing structure is better than replacing it by a new one. Revolutionary measures can be made to wait. This is said with special reference to the respective roles of the public and private sectors in running the system.

Distinctive Features

For defining such a development strategy, we may first take note of what makes Himachal Pradesh a distinct entity. This is summarised below:

- The state is a macro-watershed for the entire north-west region. Three major rivers, namely the Beas, Ravi and Chenab, originate from here. The Satluj traverses through it for a long distance and the Yamuna defines its eastern boundary. The ecological criticality of the watersheds formed by these rivers transcends the territorial limits of the state into Punjab, Haryana and Jammu & Kashmir. This calls for an inter-related planning to protect the ecological health of the entire region, and realise mutual economic benefit.
- The state experienced frequent and extensive territorial changes in its physical contours. The reorganisation of Punjab in 1966 led to the doubling of its area over what then existed. This gave it a physical contiguity and compactness too. On acquiring statehood in 1971, it inherited an administrative set-up and infrastructure base, which could be maintained only with liberal financial assistance from the Central Government. Such a situation persists even today.
- Four successive phases - 1947-66, 1966-71, 1971-91 and 1991 to date - can be identified in the history of development of the state since independence. The temporal divides, as indicated, coincide either with a change in its political status, or territorial arrangement or management paradigm. The post-1991 phase is linked to the adoption of the new economic policy, at the all-India level.
- Himachal Pradesh is noted for its relative political stability. National parties held a sway; regional parties could not make a dent. For 20 years, Y.S. Parmar was the Chief Minister; Virbhadra Singh was earlier Chief Minister for as many as 12 years and has again returned with a five year mandate; and P.K. Dhumal recently had a five-year uninterrupted stint. Such a political regime gave a continuity to the development process, and transformed the state from a problem one to a progressive one. By that token, Himachal Pradesh is a peaceful state; caste and class conflicts are minimal; and there is hardly any law and order problem.
- The state is credited for its relative efficiency and efficacy. It has ranked consistently high at the all-India level in the implementation of the 20 Point Programme. It has been quick in its response to every natural disaster. In all earnestness, it has prepared policy documents for

TABLE 24.1

Special Category States: Some Select Development Indicators

	Per Capita Net State Domestic Product (1999-2000) (Rs.)	*Per Capita Public and Private Investment (1999-2000) (Rs.)*	*Credit/Deposit Ratio (1999-2000)*	*Per Capita Tax Revenue (1999-2000) (Rs.)*	*Road Length Per 1000 sq. km. (1999-2000)*
Himachal Pradesh	**15012**	**52102**	**26**	**2512**	**542**
Jammu & Kashmir	12228	16916	34	1863	97
Uttaranchal	NA	19943	24	NA	NA
Sikkim	13356	122629	15	2913	258
Arunachal Pradesh	14338	37888	22	3089	168
Nagaland	NA	1372	14	3051	1107
Manipur	11370	5053	41	1846	490
Mizoram	NA	13422	29	3599	229
Tripura	10213	17577	22	1754	1405
Meghalaya	11678	3022	17	1939	378
Assam	9720	42158	38	1070	872

Source: Tenth Five Year Plan: 2002-2007, Volume III, State Plans, Concerns and Strategies, p. 71 for items 1, 2 and 3, and Statistical Abstract of Punjab, 2002, pp. 806-807 for item 4.

the promotion of several sectors of the economy and society. The ground experience is that people have an easy access to those in political power or administration. Grievances are generally taken care of expeditiously. The state delivery system is fairly regulated.

- There is a long tradition of service in the army. Himachal Pradesh accounts for almost 10 per cent of the serving soldiers in the Indian Army. Ex-servicemen constitute a big constituency. There is considerable inflow of financial resources to the state through remittances and pensions, thereby.
- Out-migration under conditions of intense population pressure on agricultural land has been sizeable over the years. The outflow was mainly of males, with families staying back to look after the land. This is true particularly of those areas of the state which were earlier part of Punjab
- Practically every family nurtures the dream of having at least one of its members in government service on considerations of security of job, social status and administrative/political networking.
- Himachal Pradesh scores high on indices of human development. Its per capita outlay for the social sector is the highest among all the states in the country. The relatively high status of women has been promotive of household economy, education and self-help groups. Using data for 46 indicators, classified into 8 categories of prosperity and budget, law and order, health, education, consumer market, agriculture, infrastructure, and investment, and employing the technique of principal component analysis, *India Today*, in its May 19, 2003 issue, described Himachal Pradesh as a trail-blazing success story in human development and social infrastructure scripted by a remarkable synergy between government initiative and community participation.
- Above all, it is a 'special category' state. Among 11 states of the kind, it ranks the highest on per capita income, and also on percentage of households having the facility of tap water supply, electricity connection, television and telephone (Tables 24.1 and 24.2). Likewise, Himachal Pradesh is best placed in respect of tap water supply and electricity connections among the neighbouring states (Table 24.3). During 1970-2000, the 'special category' states received financial transfers from the Centre which, on per capita basis, were nearly three times of what other states got, Within its own group, what Himachal Pradesh received was 15 per cent higher than the others (Table 24.4).

In a relative sense, Himachal Pradesh is a success story in hill-area development. It is covered also under the partially Tribal Area and Border Area Development programmes. The World Bank and other such international agencies have provided considerable financial support to its development projects as a part of the state efforts. No less crucial has been the NABARD's contribution to the extension of rural infrastructure, particularly irrigation and road transport, during the recent years.

TABLE 24.2

Special Category States of India: Some Select Indicators of Quality of Living, 2001

State/India	*Percentage of Households with the Facility of*					
	Pucca House	*Tap Water Supply*	*Electricity*	*LPG*	*Television*	*Telephone*
Himachal Pradesh	**64.5**	**84.1**	**94.8**	**28.1**	**53.3**	**16.6**
Jammu & Kashmir	66.0	52.5	80.6	22.1	40.7	6.8
Uttaranchal	86.3	65.9	60.3	33.5	42.9	9.9
Sikkim	37.7	70.3	77.8	18.8	30.9	13.2
Arunachal Pradesh	20.4	67.8	54.7	20.2	26.7	9.2
Nagaland	16.3	42.0	63.6	9.5	18.1	5.2
Manipur	8.4	29.3	60.0	21.8	24.2	5.3
Mizoram	53.0	31.9	69.6	37.7	20.4	14.1
Tripura	9.9	24.6	41.8	12.9	23.7	5.2
Meghalaya	22.2	34.5	42.7	7.7	20.9	7.0
Assam	19.7	9.2	21.9	13.2	18.3	4.3
INDIA	**51.8**	**36.7**	**55.9**	**17.5**	**31.7**	**9.1**

Source: Census of India, 2001, Housing Tables.

Carriers of Development

Let us now review the factors, which have been favourable to the overall development of the State.

- By virtue of its status as a 'special category' state as also its earlier status as a 'union territory' till 1971, Himachal Pradesh has been beneficiary of relatively liberal devolution of funds from the Central Government. During 1990-2000, the average annual transfer of resources from the Centre to the state was Rs. 4717, on per capita basis. The figure for all the states put together was only Rs. 1520. Such a pattern has been consistent over the decades (Table 24.4).
- Credit is due also to 'quality of political leadership', to a considerable degree for the socio-economic transformation of the state. The contributions of Y.S. Parmar have been vital, in this respect. A scam-free functioning of administration, by and large, has also played a positive role. The social milieu, defined by interaction of the masses with the politico-administrative set-up, and the minimal strife based on caste, class or region have been no less favorable for the overall progress of the state. All this has added up to a comparatively high level of 'human development'. This is expected to serve as a solid foundation for the future economic development of the state.

TABLE 24.3

Himachal Pradesh and the Neighbouring States: Some Select Indicators of Quality of Living, 2001

State/India		*Percentage of Households with the Facility of*					
		Pucca House	*Tap Water Supply*	*Electricity*	*LPG*	*Television*	*Telephone*
Himachal Pradesh	**Rural**	**61.8**	**82.9**	**94.5**	**21.8**	**50.4**	**13.9**
	Total	**64.5**	**84.1**	**94.8**	**28.1**	**53.3**	**16.5**
Jammu & Kashmir	Rural	45.6	40.7	74.8	9.4	28.8	2.3
	Total	55.0	52.5	80.6	22.1	40.7	6.8
Uttaranchal	Rural	85.1	60.6	50.4	21.3	32.3	4.4
	Total	86.3	65.9	60.3	33.5	42.9	9.9
Punjab	Rural	83.3	15.8	89.5	18.1	61.3	11.9
	Total	86.1	33.6	91.9	23.7	67.7	18.9
Haryana	Rural	58.2	37.8	37.8	15.3	44.0	6.2
	Total	65.8	48.1	82.9	30.2	53.0	12.7
INDIA	**Rural**	**41.1**	**24.3**	**43.5**	**5.7**	**18.9**	**3.8**
	Total	**51.8**	**36.7**	**55.9**	**17.5**	**31.6**	**9.1**

Source: Census of India, 2001, India: Housing Tables

TABLE 24.4

Special Category States: Gross Transfer of Resources From the Centre: 1975:2000

State	Average Annual (Rs. in million)					
	1970-75	1975-80	1980-85	1985-90	1990-95	1995-2000
Himachal Pradesh	**533 (154)**	**1108 (320)**	**2290 (535)**	**5463 (1276)**	**9983 (1931)**	**17895 (2786)**
Jammu & Kashmir	1036 (224)	1926 (417)	3684 (615)	9303 (1554)	19326 (2504)	30182 (3165)
Uttaranchal*	—	—	—	—	—	—
Sikkim	—	190 (905)	451 (1427)	1070 (3386)	1801 (4436)	2626 (4964)
Arunachal Pradesh	—	—	—	2156 (3426)	4528 (5235)	8329 (7384)
Nagaland	343 (665)	650 (1260)	1350 (1742)	3253 (4197)	5848 (4833)	8392 (5275)
Manipur	248 (231)	586 (546)	1306 (919)	2825 (1988)	4959 (2700)	6805 (2853)
Mizoram	—	—	—	2309 (4674)	4280 (6203)	5665 (6287)
Tripura	260 (167)	513 (330)	1222 (595)	3324 (1619)	5617 (2037)	9031 (2521)
Meghalaya	218 (215)	437 (432)	977 (731)	2341 (1752)	4299 (2422)	5950 (2581)
Assam	1475 (97)	2248 (136)	5126 (272)	12619 (614)	21655 (923)	36302 (1416)
Special Category States	4113 (150)	7658 (266)	16406 (469)	44663 (1180)	73260 (1596)	131177 (2428)
All States	**32459 (60)**	**60225 (111)**	**126748 (187)**	**270927 (401)**	**520843 (596)**	**897181 (924)**

Source: Reserve Bank of India: *Monthly Bulletins, Various Issues, RBI, Mumbai*

- The relatively high ratio of the government public sector employees, that is four for every 100 persons or one in every four households, is generally seen as a heavy liability for the state exchequer. This fact cannot be denied. There is another side of this picture as well. The comparatively high proportion of government/public sector employees has been crucial to the formation of the middle class in the state. This segment of the population, ever eager to raise its standard of living, has adopted the small family norm, and attaches great importance to the education of children. A similar contribution has been made by the defence personnel from the state. Through their greater exposure to the external world, they were able to raise their families on progressive lines. On their retirement, they themselves constitute a disciplined and trained human resource. In the process, human development receives a great fillip.
- Himachal Pradesh has an impressive record on plan implementation. The state's outlay for the Ninth Plan was Rs. 5700 crore. The actual expenditure was of the order of Rs. 7900 crore. Expenditure exceeded outlay by 40 per cent. This is the evidence of the state having succeeded in securing additional resources from the Central Government under various development schemes.
- Above all, the development of the state is rooted in the variety of its natural resource base. It has enormous hydel-power potential; horticulture finds all variety of climatic range for its flowering; tourism sites exist in exquisite physical, religious and historical settings; and forest wealth is extensive and rich. If intelligently managed, Himachal Pradesh has all the ingredients of a bright future. A thrust on the high yielding sectors—power, industry, tourism and horticulture—is essential. It is also imperative to sustain and enhance the gains already made, especially in 'human development'.

Barriers to Development

Equally essential is to take a note of the constraints to which the development process in the state is subject. The most significant among these are discussed below:

- The per unit cost of development is high in Himachal Pradesh due to peculiarities of its physiography, population distribution and distance factor. This has particular reference to laying of infrastructure, such as transport, telecommunications, electrification and water supply. A straight line distance of one km here is actually two km, on an average, thereby giving the detour index of 2 for the state as a whole. This adversely affects access to health, educational, administrative and other services for the public.
- Climate, though highly conducive to the promotion of tourism, horticulture, and forestry, is not without some negative features affecting the daily life of the people. The tribal belt of Kinnaur and Lahaul & Spiti districts and Bharmour and Pangi subdivisions of Chamba district, remains cut off from rest of the state for about six months in a year. Natural disasters in the form of landslides, cloud bursts, and avalanches are frequent. Rainy and snowy spells of weather shorten the duration of working hours.
- Forests, a natural wealth of Himachal Pradesh, are no longer a source of non-tax revenue. This is the cost which the state has to bear for preserving the ecological health not only of its own but also of the neighbouring states. Likewise, the mineral wealth of the state, particularly limestone, can be harnessed only to a limited extent for reasons of ecology and transport.
- Himachal Pradesh is envied for its water resource as a source of power. This is not easy to exploit. Hydel-power generation makes a huge demand on investment, carries immense rehabilitation and ecological costs, and requires a long gestation period. The cost of generating one MW is estimated at Rs. 6 crore. If power generation is to be augmented by 1000 MW, it will entail an investment of about Rs. 6000 crore.
- The scattered pattern of population distribution invokes its own cost for provision of public utilities and basic services, such as electricity, drinking water supply, telephones, LPG, school and dispensary. The state's population is distributed amongst as many as 20,118 villages and 57 towns. The problem is compounded by the fact that villages are mostly fragmented into a number of habitations. Even the towns are not compact physical entities, with localities separated by open spaces. For that reason, it is often not possible to ensure a threshold population for a given service to make it break even. A 'welfare state' has limited options and is obliged to bear such liabilities.
- Finally, Himachal Pradesh has a peripheral location on the map of India, placed at a considerable distance from the large and lucrative markets of the country. Shimla, the state capital, is situated at a rail distance of 1728 km., from Mumbai, 1781 km., from Kolkata, and 2534 km. from Chennai. This not only works as a disincentive to investment by any potential external source but also raises the cost of importing raw materials or exporting finished products. Added to this is the factor of state's own small internal market, and that too highly dispersed.

Core Concerns

Fully aware of its strengths and constraints, the state is earnest in giving a spurt to socio-economic development. At the initial stage, Himachal Pradesh defined its concerns more in the political domain in terms of ensuring its separate identity as a political entity; seeking integration of left-out areas which should have been its part on a linguistic-cultural basis; and attaining statehood. After acquiring the status of a state in 1971, Himachal Pradesh gave priority to transport and agriculture. With the passage of time, social sector, education and health by and large, also gained prominence. Alongside, power generation too started receiving an increasing attention The scene became complex gradually. The state's fiscal position acquired several infirmities, and issues became diverse. The following could be listed as the core concerns of Himachal Pradesh, at present:

- Progressive rise in standard of living and quality of life of the people;
- Correction of fiscal imbalance;
- Acceleration in implementation of hydel-power generation projects;

- Diversification of subsistence agriculture towards horticulture, with enhanced productivity;
- Dispersal of horticulture to new areas;
- Promotion of tourism;
- Addressing the unemployment problem, especially of educated youth;
- Strengthening of grassroot institutions, public distribution system and quality of service provision; and
- Sustaining ecology.

Sectoral Perspectives

Economy

The most serious problem facing the state government could be succinctly put: How to correct the fiscal imbalance and accelerate the economic growth rate?

Available data are indeed staggering. These reveal that 71 per cent of the state's revenue receipts are in the form of financial transfers and grants from the Central Government; 110 per cent of the total revenue receipts go towards meeting the committed expenditure on salaries, pensions and interest payments, and revenue expenditure exceeds total revenue by 32 per cent. Loan liability is about Rs. 15000 crore. Most worrisome is the fact that the share of development expenditure to total expenditure declined from 82 per cent 1970-71 to 53 per cent in 2000-01.

The irony of the whole situation is that the potential sectors which could give a boost to the economy are low yielding at present. Agriculture demands maximum care as it absorbs around two-thirds of the working force but remains a low productivity case. Horticulture-based industry is crucial to the state's economy but it has not made the desired impact. Tourism is a lucrative proposition but its potential is yet to be fully harnessed. Power generation holds a big promise but its gestation period is long. Above all, there is no easy way to downsize or rightsize the bureaucracy.

The situation is not without some positive features. The ratio of plan expenditure to the gross state domestic product has risen from 14 per cent in the Eighth Plan to 16 per cent in the Ninth Plan. Further, the growth rate of the gross state domestic product by 6.7 per cent during 1993-94 to 1998-99 was higher than that of all the neighbouring states. The per capita income of the state is now higher than the national average. District-wise disparities in per capita income have declined. Tribal areas absorb development funds three times of their share in the population.

The Planning Commission, New Delhi, has targeted an annual growth rate of 8.9 per cent for Himachal Pradesh during the Tenth Plan. The primary sector is expected to grow by 4.6 per cent, secondary sector by 12.5 per cent, and tertiary sector by 8.3 per cent. The State's Planning Department considers this growth rate as achievable. The recommended strategy is to double the area under high yielding variety of maize, and increase the area under vegetables by 1.5 times for realising the growth rate earmarked for the primary sector. The secondary sector is expected to grow rapidly through a big investment in industry in response to the new incentive package, completion of ongoing power projects, and a stimulus to construction activity. The tertiary sector would benefit from expansion of tourism, information technology, transport and financial services. All this is contingent upon a well thought-out strategy and earnest action by the government. In particular, the new industrial incentive package is to be marketed most effectively.

Agriculture

Engaging two-thirds of the workforce and contributing about one-fourth of the net state domestic product, agriculture is the staple economy of Himachal Pradesh. Almost two-thirds of the cultivators eke out their living from holdings of less than one hectare each. The stark reality is that an agricultural worker earns just one-third of what the workers in other sectors do. A clear message is that the economic well being of a vast majority of the population in the state depends on the intensification and diversification of agriculture. A shift of the agricultural workforce to non-farm employment is essential for reducing the pressure on agricultural land, as nearly two-thirds of the landholdings in the state are smaller than one hectare each.

Trends in outlay/expenditure for agriculture under successive plans do not present an encouraging picture. Agriculture accounted for about one-fourth of the total expenditure under the Fourth Plan (1969-74); its share came down to only one-tenth in the Ninth Plan (1992-2002). The same could be said about irrigation for which expenditure dwindled to hardly 4 per cent in the Ninth Plan. Irrigation in the state can be ignored only at the peril of its agriculture economy, which is subject to the vagaries of the monsoons, subject to variability, both in time and space. It is estimated that only one-third of the state's irrigation potential has been realised so far.

The crux of the matter lies primarily in raising agricultural productivity and adding value to agricultural produce through necessary processing. This is possible through extension of irrigation (which covers hardly one-fifth of the cultivated area), especially by following the strategy of watershed management; increase in area under high yielding varieties of major crops, especially maize; an accelerated shift from grain crops to horticulture; and forward linkage of horticulture with industry. The process will generate additional employment too. The per hectare human power requirement for vegetables is estimated as four times of that for rice.

A great challenge, which the state faces, is dispersal of horticulture to new areas so as to address the issue of spatial equity. The Ministry of Agriculture, Government of India, defines horticulture as raising of all types of fruits, vegetables, flowers, honey, nuts, spices and herbs (Government of Himachal Pradesh, 2002-03, p.68). The state can hope to realise rich revenue, estimated at around Rs. 5000 crore by the experts at the Planning Commission, through cultivation of medicinal and aromatic plants, particularly lavander, Indian barberry, *jatamansi*, *kutki*, and *sugandha-walla*.

Of the nearly one million hectors of land under agriculture in 2001-02, about 22 per cent was devoted to raising of fruits, and of this 42 per cent was under apple alone. As of today, three-fourths of the area under fruits is shared by only three districts of Shimla, Kullu and Kangra, and two-thirds of that under vegetables by three districts of Shimla, Mandi and Sirmaur. Four-fifths of the area under 'apple' is confined to Shimla, Kullu and Mandi districts. Spatial dispersal of pomiculture and vegetable cultivation has to be made a vital component of the agricultural development strategy of the state. The scope for organic farming is immense, as the use of fertilisers and pesticides is already low in the state. Since agricultural produce is highly perishable and its prices fluctuate widely from time to time, a chain of controlled/modified atmosphere cold storages, which can preserve the freshness of fruits like apples up to nine months, is a must for Himachal Pradesh. Equally essential here is to promote contract farming and marketing cooperatives. All this requires a package approach consisting of drip and sprinkle irrigation, appropriate technology, road transport and extension services.

Above all, promotion of livestock subsector is both a need and relief for Himachal Pradesh where agriculture is mainstay of livlihood for a large proportion of population, landholdings are inordinately small, and pasture lands are extensive. The primary task is to upgrade the quality and raise the productivity of the livestock. It is ironical that while the veterinary infrastructure has been laid on an impressive scale, there is acute shortage of personnel to manage it. Veterinary institutions must turn out trained persons in much larger number. Veterinary sector is the one which offers great employment opportunities, both direct and indirect.

Forestry

Himachal Pradesh forests are a wealth whose value lies primarily in preserving rather than utilising it for ensuring the ecological well-being of the entire north-west region. Among around 45 thousand plant species in the country, the state has over one-fifth. This represents the degree of biodiversity which Himachal Pradesh enjoys.

In 2001, 26 per cent of the geographical area of the state was under tree cover, a rise from 21 per cent in 1991. The World Bank's Integrated Watershed Development, Indo-German Changer, and U.K. assisted forestry projects contributed significantly to this increase. The state proposes to bring ultimately 50 per cent of the state's feasible area under tree cover by 2020. Going by an increase of 5 per cent points during 1991-2001 decade, it may take some longer time to achieve the target. Per hectare cost of afforestation is estimated at Rs. 1.2 lakh.

Under the Tenth Plan, the 'Forestry' sector received 4.5 per cent of the total outlay. Despite all the restrictions imposed, this sector contributed 4.7 per cent to the net state domestic product. A great scope exists for increasing this share through reform of the contracting out system for collection of minor forest produce, and by placing more emphasis on products for which a lucrative international market exists.

Some forest cover is inevitably lost, agricultural land gets submerged, and settlements are displaced wherever a power project is implemented. The existing practice is to compensate only the upstream inhabitants. This requires a policy change. The downstream displaced families also deserve to be compensated. Loss in their case is as huge, if not larger.

Quite worrisome is the estimated survival rate of saplings, estimated at 55 per cent. The reason adduced is the lack of fencing. 'Sanjhi Van Yojna' has to be made more effective for meeting the situation. This will help in checking of forest fires also, which are quite a frequent menace.

Further, road construction inevitably depletes some forest cover. To minimise such damage, it is desirable to construct roads passing through a protected forest under the supervision of the Forest Department.

Finally, 'the watershed development' strategy has demonstrated itself as the most effective for the promotion of forestry. This needs to be adopted in all cases.

Rural Development

It goes to the credit of Himachal Pradesh that despite severe constraints imposed by terrain, land cover, and climate, its record of providing infrastructure in rural areas has been highly commendable: 95 per cent of rural households have domestic electricity connection as compared with 44 per cent in India; 83 per cent of rural households avail of tap water supply as compared with 16 per cent in Punjab; and one-half of the households have television as compared with one-third in Uttaranchal (Table 24.2). The relative proportion of rural households using LPG and having telephone connection is the highest in Himachal Pradesh as compared with all its neighbouring states (Table 24.3).

It is commendable that, over the years, Himachal Pradesh has consistently followed a sensible policy of locating service institutions, such as school, dispensary, veterinary centre, regulated agricultural market and fair price shop, at panchayat headquarters. This has led to a fairly equitable distribution of such basic services for the rural masses. The outcome is evident. Himachal Pradesh has acquired a pride of place in 'human development' among different states in the country.

This is not to say that all is well on the rural front. While the basic services and facilitates have been made available to a great extent, the issue of ensuring the 'quality of services' still remains to be addressed. In 2001, among 45,367 rural habitations, 29 per cent were either not covered or partially covered by water supply (Government of Himachal Pradesh, 2001). The weak monsoons during 2001 and 2002 caused serious water scarcity in about 10 per cent of the rural habitations and a number of towns, including Shimla, Dharmshala and Solan. In Shimla and Kangra districts this proportion was about one-half. Several village roads are not all weather and are subject to frequent landslides. Moreover, quite some villages, including panchayat headquarters, still remain without a connection to a metalled road. There are glaring gaps on the development map of Himachal Pradesh.

The scene may change with the devolution of functions, finances and functionaries to the *panchayats*. Already 15 out of 29 subjects have been transferred and more will follow. *Gram panchayats* have been empowered to monitor and report on the grassroots functionaries, such as *patwari*, constable, peon and forest guard. Now they can undertake development works up to Rs. 5 lakh. For this, it is most essential that the elected representatives are made aware of their obligations and are trained for the functions to be performed by them. This would be in the nature of 'capacity building' of those who are to manage development at the grassroot level.

There are, at present, 3037 *gram panchayats*, 75 *panchayat samitis* and 12 *zila parishads* in the state. These together have around 27 thousand representatives. To train them, about 600 workshops need to be organised, each covering 40 to 50 elected representatives. The estimated cost of such an exercise is about Rs. 4 crore. Indeed, training of this nature has to be a continuing affair since several new members will be elected every five years. This calls for establishment of training centres for the purpose, spread all over the state. The two existing training institutes at Mashobra and Baijnath are most inadequate to meet the need. One practical way of spreading awareness about the powers and obligations of panchayati raj institutions would be to incorporate a comprehensive chapter on this theme in the school syllabus at 10+2 level, for compulsory learning

A most missed item on the agenda of any State Development Report is the issue of 'sustaining the regional and local culture'. These reports, going by their terms of reference, have an inordinate emphasis on economic parameters of development. Needs of the soul are neglected at the expense of requirements of the body. Such a paradigm should be unacceptable to a state like Himachal Pradesh, whose each valley and ridge has its distinctiveness of folk culture. Though over 90 per cent of its population speaks 'western pahari', more than 30 dialects are specific to different parts of the state; such as Sirmauri in Sirmaur district, Keonthali in areas surrounding Shimla, Kochi in Rampur Bushahr, Kului in Kullu district, and Mandiali in Mandi district. There are as many as 124 communities based on caste, tribe and locality (Singh, 1996, p. xiii). It will be in the fitness of things to spare some resources of the state for building a chain of mini-museums focusing on the display of artifacts of local culture. A pragmatic way of doing this would be to adopt a 'place of worship' as the repository of local art and culture too. Measures should also be taken to help the practioners of the folk graphic and performing arts, economically viable in the modern socio-cultural context.

Industry

The share of the secondary sector (which includes the sub-sectors of manufacturing, construction, and electricity, gas and water supply) in the net state domestic product experienced a rise from 19 per cent in 1971-72 to 32 per cent in 2000-01. This increase was of the order of 5 per cent to 14 per cent in the case of the manufacturing sector. Manufacturing seems to have picked up. The data further reveal that most of this increase took place only during the nineties. This was a positive outcome of the three industrial policies announced by the state government in 1991, 1996 and 1999.

In 2003, the 194 large and medium scale industrial units in the state had a total investment of Rs. 2400 crore and employed nearly 30 thousand workers. By comparison, about 30 thousand small-scale units, with an investment of Rs. 710 crore, employed 130 thousand workers. As such, investment per worker was of the order of Rs. 8 lakh in the large and medium scale industry and Rs. 55 thousand in small-scale industry.

A notable feature of industrialisation in the state is the virtual concentration of the large and medium scale units, to the extent of 95 per cent, in the districts adjoining Punjab and Haryana, and predominance of the small scale units, to the extent of 60 per cent, in the inner districts. Only the two districts of Solan and Sirmaur account for almost 90 per cent of the large and medium scale units in the state. Industry in these periphery districts has grown in response to the special incentives announced by the government from time to time. Their proximity to Chandigarh did help. The difficult political situation in Punjab during the eighties also seems to have favoured Himachal Pradesh in deflecting some industry towards it.

On the whole, incentives have played a very critical role. Virtually all the entrepreneurs are from outside. Some of them have shown a tendency to exit on the expiry of the tenure of incentives. A question mark on sustainability of incentive–driven industry is justified. Ways and means have to be identified to prevent the flight of the beneficiary units when no longer entitled to special benefits.

There are four imperatives which have to be pondered over for ensuring the desired success of any industrial policy for the state. The first is to identify the industries which are cost effective and employment generative. Fruit processing in Sirmaur district, agricultural implements in Kangra district, shawl weaving in Kullu district, and wooden products in Mandi district are indicated as possible candidates. Cement industry, by reason of its capacity to generate both direct and indirect employment, cannot be ignored in the scheme of things for the state. At the same time, the cement plants must be made to adopt all pollution control measures, most strictly.

The second imperative is an identification of optimal locations for industrial parks/clusters for the promotion of small-scale industry, particularly in the inner districts. These clusters must offer training and marketing facilities, in addition to state-of-the-art infrastructure. Such an observation is based on a realisation that small-scale industry, including handicrafts, must be a priority for Himachal Pradesh and this goal can be best achieved if the quality of goods is constantly upgraded through a regular input of the latest technology, and new products are manufactured to meet the demands of both domestic and international markets.

The third imperative hinges on the issue of encouraging the local entrepreneur to invest in industry. The credit/deposit ratio of the state was hardly 30 per cent in 2002, signifying an outgo of a large proportion of its scarce resources to outside places for investment. Industry and technical education have to work together to generate native entrepreneurship. The effort on the part of the Himachal Pradesh Centre for Entrepreneurial Development to generate industrial awareness and cultivate human resource through training programmes is commendable. There is a need to assess their impact through evaluation studies.

The final imperative pertains to ensuring sustainability of the 'incentive-led' industry', attracted to the periphery districts. It must be seen that the beneficiary large and medium scale industrial units install the requisite physical infrastructure. They should set up or facilitate the establishment of ancillary units. Also, they must have in-house research, design and training cells, not only for themselves but also for the associated ancillary units.

It is beyond dispute that incentives to industry have to stay in the case of Himachal Pradesh. The impact of the new industrial package announced by the Central

Government for the State in January 2003 had an encouraging impact. During only nine months of January-October 2003, 138 large and medium scale industrial units with an investment exceeding Rs. 2000 crore, and 500 small scale industrial units with an investment of around Rs. 300 crore got themselves provisionally registered with the state's Department of Industries. This promises a bright future for industry in the state.

Urban Development

According to the 2001 Census, Himachal Pradesh is hardly 10 per cent urban, the lowest for any state in India. In March 2003, there were 53 urban local bodies, including Shimla Corporation, beside 7 cantonment boards in the state. Shimla, with a population of nearly 1.5 lakh is the only city here. It accounts for one-fourth of the state's total urban population.

This exceptionally low level of urbanisation is attributed mainly to a largely subsistence agricultural economy, the incipient stage of modern industrialisation, and the modest scale of transport development. Functional links of towns with their surrounding areas are weak. This is due partly to the limited scope for economic exchange and partly to mobility constraints associated with hilly/mountainous topography. Stimulus for growth of towns is weak. Inter-town interaction is feeble. The irony of the whole situation is that most of the functionally dynamic towns, such as Shimla, and fruit producing belts, such as Kullu Valley, and Kotgarh–Kotkhai tract, have more active links with places outside the state than within. A large part of the economic surplus generated in the process is not invested internally. This is detrimental to the urbanisation process.

There is another aspect of spatial organisation, which also needs to be understood. The frequency of rural service centres is quite high in Himachal Pradesh. For example, Sirmaur district has only three towns but is dotted with as many 30 rural service centres. These provide the essential services of retailing, high school education and medical facilities, among others. Such places perform some of the urban functions but fail to qualify as towns for not being in a position to acquire a statutory urban status from the state government or satisfy the demographic criteria as laid down by the Indian Census.

Above all, over one-third of Himachal Pradesh is virtually devoid of any habitation, not to speak of towns. This is due to physical constraints imposed by high altitude, extremely cold climate, and snow cover. A sizeable part of the state just does not have any scope of urbanisation.

Hill towns are popularly perceived as ideal from the environmental angle. This is as it appears at a macro-level. The picture that emerges is different when examined at the micro-level or from within. The inner conditions of the hill towns present a contrast to their splendid outer environmental quality. Only six towns in the state have a sewerage system. Hardly four towns, namely Shimla, Kullu, Mandi and Solan have solid waste treatment plants. Most critical is the situation pertaining to water supply. Per capita daily supply of water in large towns, such as Shimla, Solan and Dharamsala, is hardly 50-80 litres. Summers are more acute scarcity time. Notably, most of the towns in the state depend on Irrigation and Pubic Health Department and the Housing Board for water supply. It is only in the case of Shimla, Solan and Palampur and, of course, the six cantonment towns that the urban local bodies come into picture. It is expected that the things will improve if the due function of water supply is devolved to the urban local bodies, along with necessary financial and technical support.

The infrastructure base of the hill towns in terms of water supply, sanitation, local transport, fire protection and other such services, is being made to bear far heavier load than that for which they were originally raised. Municipal bodies are starved of funds and staff. Estimates of investment required for augmenting the urban infrastructure are 2.5 times the total revenue (including grants) of the municipal bodies.

Of special concern is the haphazard physical expansion of the two major tourist centres – Shimla and Manali. The former is suffering severe water shortage and the latter from intolerable congestion of structures, including hotels and restaurants. A distant view of Shimla gives a picture of two concrete carpeted segments, with much of greenery lost. Manali has acquired a physical disposition which does not permit a convenient intra-city mobility. One wonders as to how it will be possible to sustain the tourism eminence of these two places in the long run.

No less worrisome is the extensive and unplanned ribbon development along the main highways, such as Kalka-Shimla, Shimla-Dharmsala and Kullu-Manali. A number of traffic bottlenecks have already started appearing on these routes. The scenic beauty around, itself a tourist attraction, is fast disappearing. It is high time that these developments were monitored and appropriate action initiated. There is a need for a rigorous appraisal of any new construction activity before it is approved. If necessary, the relevant laws may be reformed.

Tourism

Informed opinion is in favour of adopting tourism as one of the lead sectors for both generating employment and strengthening economy. The cost of generating a job in tourism sector is just around Rs. 20,000, which is fairly comparable to that one in agriculture (Government of Himachal Pradesh, 2000, p.1). It is undisputedly a fast growing sector. The number of tourists to the state had doubled from 25 lakh in 1991 to 50 lakh in 2001. Foreign tourists multiplied six times from 15 thousand to one lakh during the same period. Tourism has, however, been receiving highly inadequate allocations under the plans. It is estimated as currently contributing about 2 per cent of the net state domestic product but the Tenth Plan outlay for this sector is merely Rs. 27 crore. This works out just a quarter of one per cent of the total plan outlay. Perceptions could not have been less unimaginative.

Recently, the state has formulated a 'new tourism policy', which seeks to promote a variety of tourisms: leisure, pilgrimage, business, heritage, health, and eco-adventure. There are plans to involve the private sector in a big way. The essential features of the strategy are to develop pilgrimage sites on priority, disperse tourism to new areas, and break the seasonality factor.

The state must take effective measures, to achieve the desired results. For instance, the pilgrimage places of Chintapurni, Jawalamukhi and Nainadevi should be developed on the pattern of the highly applauded Vaishnodevi model. Secondly, the tourists with Shimla as their destination are to be intelligently managed. A strategy of peoples' participation should be adopted in this case. Villages and towns along the Kalka-Shimla national highway and beyond should be surveyed to identify households who are willing to provide paying guest facility of requisite standard for the tourists. Credit facility should be made available to them, if required. Further, a private, professional agency can be invited to operationalise the scheme. It should function as a link between the client (tourist) and the service provider (household offering paying guest facility). The entire system must be efficient and dependable. Such an arrangement will achieve at least the following objectives: keep the tourists in close proximity to Shimla, without crowding the city and putting pressure on its infrastructure; distribute economic gains of tourism over a wider populace; and generate avenues of self-employment. Thirdly, the areas/regions of origin of tourists at home and abroad should be identified and entrepreneurs from these very places be encouraged to invest in tourism. This will be an effective way of developing tourism on a sustainable basis. Professional marketing agencies can be hired for the purpose. Fourthly, Himachal Pradesh can be marketed as a health, ayurveda and meditation destination. Finally, what a delight it would be if the tops of the front ridges facing Kalka-Shimla highway were illuminated imaginatively and tastefully as a night display. This in itself could be a tourist attraction of a unique kind.

The management of tourism, as envisaged, will call for professional training of personnel interested in joining this sector. Further, tourism has to be promoted on a selective basis, in terms of both type and destination. It will be most effective to begin with the religious tourism to only three places of Chintpurni, Jwalamukhi and Naina devi. Meleodganj also requires improvement and strengthening of its infrastructure. Moreover, if the private sector is to be attracted for investment in this sector, the state's land policy has to be appropriately modified. Above all, if tourism is to make a dent as a key sector of economy, the selected projects have to be macro-enterprises for real effect. Scattered tourism sites will be low yielding.

Finally, the proposal to convert the Himachal Pradesh Tourism Development Corporation/Board into a Tourism Commission is worthy of consideration. The Commission will have representatives from all the stakeholders – the government, corporate sector, hoteliers, taxi-operators, and labour unions. They should work together on all issues pertaining to tourism sector. In particular, certification and rating procedures should be laid out and monitored regularly. This will build confidence amongst tourists and give them a sense of security.

Education

This sector has been a high priority for the state through all the plans. It has been outlayed 22 per cent per cent of the total provisions under the Tenth Plan. This level of allocation is the highest for any state in India. The state claims to be the first one in the country to provide free education to girls at all levels, from the time of enrolment in a primary school to the university education, including technical and professional courses. No wonder, Himachal Pradesh scores high on several parameters of education; its literacy rate at 77 per cent is higher by 12 per cent points than over the national average; primary education is almost universal with a drop-out rate of barely 1 per cent; and accessibility to all types of educational institutions is fairly high for a hilly and mountainous state. What is in question is the quality of education: one-fourth of the primary school teachers are untrained ones and failure rate of students is 54 per cent at the high school level.

The situation in respect of infrastructure in schools leaves much to be desired. The Sixth All India Educational Survey 1999 revealed that one-third of the higher secondary schools functioned from a semi-*pucca* or *kutcha* building, over one-third of high schools did not have toilets, and around one-third of the primary schools were without drinking water facility. One in every seven primary schools has less than 10 students each. A happy feature is that the state is aware of these gaps and is taking remedial measures.

The time has come when education as a sector has to be reinvented for addressing job opportunities that may emerge as a consequence of the growth of other sectors, such as industry, information technology, tourism and horticulture. There is a need to shift its thrust from formal learning to technical and professional training. The state does have one national institute of technology, two engineering colleges, 7 polytechnics and 57 I.T.I.s, fairly equitably distributed over space. The desired quality of education and training and their linkage with the relevant economic sectors must be ensured. Technical education is yet to be anchored to industry; education in tourism management is yet to find a niche in the promotion of this sector through private investment, and medical education has to be brought to a level which will spare patients from seeking treatment outside the state. All this is possible only when the best of faculty is appointed, latest equipment is installed, and new courses in environment, chemical, automobile and food processing are introduced. Likewise, professional courses in hotel and tourism management should receive a priority.

One has to figure out systemic constraints in every case. It is a pity that technical education gets only Rs. 50 crore or half of 1 per cent of the total outlay under the Tenth Plan. Where do we stand in respect of its desired upgradation?

In point of fact, 'quality education' can be an economic enterprise in itself. Himachal Pradesh is reputed for several of its residential schools, such as at Sanawar and Chail. As a seat of higher learning, St. Bede's College at Shimla has its own eminence. Can the state extend this model and replicate the same for all kinds of educational institutions, particularly technical and professional? This calls for heavy investment in the best of faculty, state-of-the-art infrastructure, and innovative management. The state must facilitate the private sector entry into this sector. This may require some appropriate modification in land policy. Future development of Himachal Pradesh is to be worked largely through private investment. State funding is going to be more scarce, with passage of time. Setting up an Institute of Information Technology at Rachchiana in Solan district through Jai Prakash Seva Sansthan is a commendable step in this direction.

Health

The health sector offers substantially a better scope for setting up quality institutions. Himachal Pradesh provides an ideal natural setting for health resorts, sanatoria and spas. This asset can be capitalised through requisite investment in health infrastructure, research and education of excellence that would attract even foreign clients.

In other words, the state may think of raising world class institutions of health care. Even a single institution of international repute can go a long way in strengthening the economy of the state. Such ventures may be highly capital intensive in the initial stage but dividends are going to be compensatory and rich in the long run.

It is anomalous that despite clean environmental conditions, fairly laid out health care network of 50 civil hospitals, 66 community health centers, 152 dispensaries and 2067 sub-centres and relatively higher literacy rate, Himachal Pradesh is noted for a morbidity incidence which is 1.5 times that of India. Chronic ailments are far more prevalent. This is not the end of the story. The incidence of fatal bronchial and cough cases in Himachal Pradesh is reported to be almost double of that in India; and of diseases of the circulatory system and digestive disorder 1.5 times. The elderly, in Himachal Pradesh, are far more prone to problems of joints, cough, blood pressure and heart than in India. The frequency of deaths through accidents and injuries, at 8.2 per cent of the total, is frightening. Of special concern is the spread of HIV/AIDS. Of the 35,773 serum samples tested in 2003, as many as 531 were found HIV positive, among whom 143 were full blown cases of AIDS.

The encouraging news is that the incidence of tuberculosis at around 2.5 per 1000 persons is half of that in India. The same holds good for leprosy at 0.5 per 1000 persons. Incidence of complete blindness at 4.6 per 1000 persons exceeds the national average of 4.2.

Available data suggest that 60 per cent of the patients availed of the public sector health facilities for non-hospitalised ailments. The figure is as high as 90 per cent in respect of hospitalised episodes. Child immunisation and emergency services remain the domain of public sector. Allopathy is the preferred mode of treatment, with 94 per cent of the patients opting for it. None the less, the number of ayurvedic dispensaries in the state is around half of the allopathic ones. Ayurvedic system, as a supplementary source, seems to be retaining its traditional popularity.

The state government has been responding to such a situation in a fairly satisfactory manner. Under the Tenth Plan, it has outlayed 8 per cent of the total for the health sector. This figure is one of the highest for any state in the country. About three-fifths of this outlay are assigned to allopathy (medical and public health), about one-fifth to ayurveda and other systems of medicine, and the remaining one-fifth to medical education and miscellaneous items. The public health delivery system has followed a sensible policy of locating the health services at the *panchayat* headquarters, by and large. Nearly one-fifth of such places, however, still remain without this facility, a gap which needs to be filled on priority basis.

All in all, government will have to continue playing a big role in the provision of health services. The private sector often tends to be selective of location and clientele, and is not enthused to take up emergency cases, particularly of accidents which are not infrequent in the state. None the less, the private sector is gradually making a headway especially in the form of clinics. The need here is to monitor their functioning through regular registration. The private sector can also be encouraged to come into diagnostic services, including within the premises of government hospitals and dispensaries.

Power

It is the 'power sector', which holds the most lucrative promise for the state economy. Himachal Pradesh generates today about 4000 MW of hydel-power while its potential exceeds, 20,300 MW. Under execution are several projects which will add over 6000 MW to the existing base by 2010.

To be more precise, of the 3967 MW generated in the state, only 332 MW or 8 per cent is generated by the HPSEB. The rest comes from other public sector undertakings, namely BBMB, PSEB, NPHC and UPSEB, which are linked to the Central Government or other states. What comes as a surprise is that in terms of availability of power, Himachal Pradesh is a deficit state. In 2001-02, it sold power worth Rs. 188 crore in summer months and purchased power worth Rs. 361 crore during the winter.

The total availability of power to the state was 3984 MU in 2001-02. Around one-third of it was generated by the HPSEB, one-third received as free power and share, and the remaining one-third was purchased from outer sources. Situation is expected to improve by the end of the current year when an additional 500 MU will became available as its share from the new hydel projects.

Himachal Pradesh State Electricity Board, which looks after generation, transmission and distribution of power, employs around 31 thousand persons, that is one in every nine government/public sector employees in the state. It serves around 1.5 million consumers, of which 86.8 per cent are domestic, 10.6 per cent commercial, 2 per cent industrial and the remaining 0.4 per cent agricultural and others. Household coverage is the highest for any state in India. In terms of consumption, half of the power goes to industry, nearly one-third for domestic use, 1 per cent for agriculture and the rest for other uses.

Transmission and distribution losses are about 20 per cent level. The corresponding figure for Punjab is 26 per cent but under a situation in which one-third is being given free to the agriculturists, thereby hiding a sizeable component of the losses. Transmission and distribution losses of Haryana and Delhi are as high as 37 per cent and 47 per cent respectively. The acceptable norm is 16 per cent (12 per cent transmission and 4 per cent distribution).

Electricity tariffs in Himachal Pradesh are the lowest in the country. The state has achieved 100 per cent metering and is on the fast track to electronic metering. Such a situation is favourable for rationalisation of the tariffs to raise additional revenue for the state. It may also be advisable to follow a zonal pattern of levying tariffs in place of going in for a uniform rate.

Despite the low cost of power generation, its actual cost is high due primarily to excessive cost of distribution. Against a per unit revenue of Rs. 2.33, the expenditure is Rs. 2.70, representing a loss of Rs. 0.37 on every unit distributed. This is attributed to overstaffing of the Himachal Pradesh State Electricity

Board. The solution lies in immediate implementation of the Central Electricity Act, 2003. A desired way out is to reduce manpower cost rather than manpower. In other words, manpower efficiency is to be raised through additional power generation with the same number of employees and rationalisation of the distribution system. Voluntary Retirement Scheme can be promoted, and those opting for VRS can be invited to work with the panchayati raj institutions and urban local bodies for the distribution of power and maintenance of services.

Transport

This sector was accorded the top priority right in the First Plan of Himachal Pradesh. It can be compared with the "power sector' which is receiving the highest attention at present. In the Tenth Plan, one-sixth of the total outlay has been earmarked for the transport sector. Almost 95 per cent of it will go towards the sub-sectors of roads and bridges. The remaining paltry 5 per cent is left for other means of transport, such as civil aviation, inland water ways, and ropeways.

About 27,737 km. of motorable roads snail their way on the ridges, across the spurs and along the valleys of the state. Over 90 per cent of these are the state highways and the remaining central roads, including national highways and border roads. The road density works out as about 50 kms. per 100 km^2 of area as compared with 75 in India.

To render connectivity to every village, the state requires around 40 thousand kms of metalled roads. On a rough estimate, the average cost of constructing one km. of road, along with bridges and drains, works out to about Rs. 40 lakh. To meet the additional target of 13,000 km. of metalled roads, an investment of no less than Rs. 5200 crore is required.

Apart from construction of new roads, straightening the curves of the existing ones is also necessary. This is said with special reference to the busy corridors, such as Shimla-Dharmsala, Bilaspur-Kullu, and Kalka-Shimla. This will reduce transport cost in a big way, in both time and fuel.

Though the railways play a small role in the state yet the existing rail-routes of Kalka-Shimla (96 km.) and Pathankot–Jogindernagar (113 km.) can be imaginatively developed for heritage tourism in collaboration with the Central government. The same could be said about Nangaldam-Una (16 km.) rail route. A feasible plan will give desired results in revenue earning.

Ropeways can be laid over more for carriage of goods than passengers. These have a special significance for areas specialising in horticulture. The effort should be geared towards bringing the produce from remote areas to convenient transit points on the main routes. A well designed multi-modal scheme, combining ropeways, road and rail transports can effectively serve both the economy and people of the state.

Telecommunications

With every sixth household enjoying the facility of a telephone, Himachal Pradesh scores high on this parameter. The corresponding figure for India as a whole is one telephone for every eleventh household. Teledensity of Himachal Pradesh is 8.4 telephones per 100 persons whereas the all-India figure is 5 only. This facility is certainly very critical to Himachal Pradesh where physical mobility is constrained by hilly and mountainous topography, population distribution is scattered, and extensive areas are not only remote but also remain cut off during winter. The facility is, however, highly unevenly distributed, with Mandi district having a great edge. Inter-district disparities need to be resolved.

Employment

One of the ways of looking at the planning process is to define its primary task as (hu) manpower budgeting. The basic question is: How to apportion the labourforce to various sectors and activities so that productivity is maximised, equity is ensured, poverty is ameliorated and every willing hand gets adequate and remunerative work. The task is extremely complex for it has to deal with both the stock and flow of those who are already in work and others who are looking for it. Equally imponderable is the growth behaviour of different sectors of the economy and their capacity to generate and provide employment. It is immensely difficult to preview the job preferences of the people.

The 2001 Census of India data show that nearly one-third (32.4 per cent) of the population in Himachal Pradesh are main workers and another one-sixth (16.9 per cent) marginal workers. The latter figure points to a high incidence of underemployment.

By comparison, National Sample Survey Organisation data for 1999-2000 shows that the work participation rate of males at around 50 per cent is virtually the same in both rural and urban areas of the state. Female participation rate in rural areas at 28 per cent is almost three times of that (10 per cent) in urban places. In the rural segment of the state, nearly two-thirds are self-employed, one-sixth regular employees, and about one-fifth casual workers.

One is always on slippery ground when dealing with data on 'unemployment'. National Sample Survey Organisation data put the unemployment rate in the state at 3 per cent as compared with 7.3 per cent in India. It is also learnt that 8.5 per cent of the labour force is available for additional or alternative work. This means that the incidence of underemployment is almost three times that of unemployment.

'Employment Exchange' data are staggering. The number of persons registered with it was 9 lakh in December 2002, that is, one in every four in 18+ age-group. Among the registered, 78 per cent were at least matriculate and 5 per cent technically trained. Unemployment in Himachal Pradesh is essentially of educated youth, hence sensitive for they are looking for specific kinds of jobs in the organised sector which are not easy to create. For most of them, a government job is the only one worth chasing.

Data from the same source further reveal that during 2002 alone, there were 1.4 lakh registrations but notified vacancies were less than 2 thousand, and submissions exceeded 37 thousand. The scene is dismal. The state's government/public sector of the state is already over-saturated. It has 248 thousand employees, or about 4 for every 100 persons. The comparable all-India figure is 2. The organised private sector employs 48 thousand persons or 15 per cent of the labourforce in organised sector as a whole; all-India figure is 30 per cent. Opportunities in this sphere are also highly limited. Above all, the state's employment elasticity, that is the ratio between growth rate of economy and that of employment, is hardly 0.05 per cent as compared with 0.16 per cent in India. This means that direct jobs are to be generated in place of depending merely on an accelerated growth rate of economy for creating employment avenues.

For decades, out-migration to other parts of India for a job and recruitment in the army have been two regular responses to the chronic unemployment situation. The state has 1.2 lakh serving men, that is nearly 10 per cent of the Indian Army, while its share in total population of the country is hardly 0.6 per cent. But then the state is also left with 85 thousand ex-servicemen; most of whom retire at an early age of around 40. Many of them enter the job market and offer a kind of competition to the youth.

A perusal of the National Sample Survey Organisation data further reveals that tertiary sector activities of transport, hotel/restaurant and financial services, and secondary sector activities of construction, manufacturing and electricity have been growing fast during the nineties. The message is clear: the industry, transport, tourism and above all 'repair and maintenance' services hold the key to generation of additional employment in the state. Since employment elasticity of the economic growth rate is not much obliging, it is critical to promote entrepreneurship and create climate for self-employment among the youth who otherwise look only to a government job as ultimate-in-life.

Governance

It is indeed the quality of governance which determines the functional quality and development dynamics of any system. On a popular plane, Himachal Pradesh is credited for its relatively committed and efficient administration. Indicators include a relatively happy law and order situation, highly creditable performance of the state on the basic needs programme, and announcement of appropriate policy on practically every important sector. This is attributed to the close proximity which has evolved over the years between the people and their representatives and also the bureaucracy. This itself has roots in the political stability, for which Himachal Pradesh is reputed.

In the context of what has already been achieved, the pressure for hastening the pace of development is ever mounting, but the capacity of the administration to deliver the aspired level of goods and services is proving inadequate. It is necessary to reinvent the government. The critical question is: How? Which are the salient parameters of this desired change? How to ensure public-private sector partnership in management of affairs? In which proportion should this mix differ in various sectors? How can the unions of government employees, school teachers, truck operators and others be involved in governance as active stakeholders? How can the functioning of the panchayati raj institutions and urban local bodies be strengthened? How can their operational capacity be raised?

Answers to all these questions are imbedded in the dictum that governance has always to be efficient, just and effective. It must be oriented to technology, knowledge and development. The politico-administrative culture has to be responsive also to the issues of regional disparity and structural inequality. The poor are to be rendered positive discrimination. A right kind of political will and a change in bureaucratic mindset can only bring the desired change.

The need to reinvent the governance has become all the more critical in the context of adoption of new economic policy, coupled with structural reforms, since 1991. Now the emphasis is upon liberalisation of the system from any unnecessary and restrictive government regulations; involvement of all stakeholders, including the private sector, community based organisations, grassroots institutions, households, and of course, the government itself; and opening of the economy to a competitive culture as a part of the globalisation process. As a strategy toward that end, the central government has earmarked 'Fiscal Incentive Fund' of over Rs. ten thousand crore for the Tenth Plan period, to facilitate monitorable fiscal reforms on the part of state governments. The intended reforms pertain to efficiency, transparency and accountability in governance; reduction in subsides; invitation to private sector for investment; and participation of people in management and development activities at the local level. Himachal Pradesh is already in a pursuit of such reforms. The effort at present is, however, piecemeal. There is a need to have a holistic perspective and devise integrated measures. This process will be facilitated if an 'Economic, Fiscal and Administrative Reforms Division' is constituted by the state government for coordinating and monitoring the reforms.

Some specific tasks for governance in Himachal Pradesh include: elimination of any pilferage of development funds, especially in remote, inaccessible areas, capturing the surplus capital generated in the apple belt for investment within the State; managing the induction of the private sector in various sectors of economy, such as industry, tourism, information technology and health; and creating conditions wherein the activities of all kinds of unions promote rather than impede the functioning of the system. Above all, the mind-set of the youth has to be engineered towards self-employment by providing necessary facilities.

A reform of the administrative map of the state is also called for. Should Lahaul & Spiti district be bifurcated into two or retained as one? Is it possible to rationalise the highly unwieldy disposition of Shimla district? Can the territorial size of the exceptionally small district of Hamirpur be enlarged? Is there a case for retaining only districts and development blocks and doing away with sub-divisions/tehsils? If so, what is the optimal number of districts for the state?

Above all, what is the feasibility of relocating highly scattered populations in remote areas to some planned central habitations so as to economise on the provision of services and reduce the cost of development? Mizoram did so in the nature of progressive villages during the sixties. A 'Reorganisation Commission' may be set up to look into all these issues pertaining to the reform of spatial dimensions of development administration.

Interconnectivity with Neighbouring States

There is now a growing realisation that regional cooperation is basic to optimal utilisation of resources, cost-effective solution of problems, and unfettered functioning of the interdependent systems. In other words, the neighbouring states, in particular, have to work in a spirit of interconnectivity while charting out their own road maps of development. This is no less relevant for Himachal Pradesh.

At a macro-level, Himachal Pradesh is a 'watershed' for its neighbouring states of Punjab, Haryana, Jammu & Kashmir, and to a limited extent for Uttaranchal. The prominent rivers, namely Satluj, Beas, Chenab and Yamuna, either originating in or traversing through Himachal Pradesh, are a source of water and power to the states forming its 'command' areas. This fact deserves to be placed at the centre of any effort at harnessing and enhancing interconnectivity between the states involved. Himachal Pradesh deserves due recognition as a critical watershed for preserving and promoting the ecological health of its neighbours.

Himachal Pradesh bears a cost on this count. It loses scarce agricultural land to power and irrigation projects, has to make additional investment in natural resource management, and forgo possible benefits accruing from utilisation of forest wealth. The beneficiary neighbouring states must realise this and share the cost.

At the same time, Himachal Pradesh must take a note of certain situations while placing itself in the regional context. It has to be conscious of the fact that the state has to compete with Jammu & Kashmir in tourism, with Uttaranchal in horticulture, and with Punjab in attracting industrial investment. Meanwhile it has also to collaborate with Jammu & Kashmir in matters of internal security, with Uttaranchal in building of transport linkages, and with Punjab in generation and utilisation of hydel-power. The state must weigh its relative strengths and weaknesses in each case and devise appropriate strategies.

Parwanoo in Himachal Pradesh, Panchkula in Haryana, Mohali in Punjab and Chandigarh are emerging as dynamic centres of industry and services. Though located in different political territories, they have already developed considerable interconnectivity. This process can be carried forward by promoting their industrial, information technology and tourism base on a collaborative basis. The concerned states should make a collective effort at getting Chandigarh airport upgraded into an international airport. This will spur the economic activity of all.

Himachal Pradesh is not without some grievances against Punjab. It alleges to have suffered internal colonialism in relation to this state in exploitation of natural resources. It points out to the fertile agricultural land it lost under the Bhakra and Pong dam reservoirs, whose waters essentially irrigate the states constituting the command area. It also bemoans the treatment it met as a weaker brother at the time of Punjab's reorganisation in 1966. Himachal Pradesh got only 2.5 per cent of the power generated at Bhakra as its share against the due share of 7.19 per cent. In respect of the Beas-Satluj link, it got only 1.6 per cent of the power generated. It got no power from the Pong dam. Such grievances need to be looked into and perceptions corrected.

In any case, interconnectivity between Himachal Pradesh and its neighbouring states has to be strengthened to every one's benefit. The constitution of a North-West Council, on the pattern of the North-East Council, is most desired. Member states would include Himachal Pradesh, Jammu & Kashmir, Uttaranchal, Punjab and Haryana, and the union territory of Chandigarh. The Council could serve as a statutory forum for deliberating and designing development projects for member states in a co-ordinated manner. It has to adopt a wider perspective and prepare an integrated plan for the constituent states.

Salient Messages

The messages distilled from the foregoing discussion can be succinctly put as follows:

- Politico-administrative peculiarities of Himachal Pradesh demand a continuing big role for the State. At the same time, future investment in development is contingent largely upon the entry and vigour of the private sector. The state has to acquire a professional proficiency in managing private sector and privatisation.
- Factors of topography, scattered pattern of population and distance make the involvement of panchayati raj institutions indispensable for the development process to be effective and sustained. Simultaneously, the elected members need to be trained on regular basis for their capacity building.
- Bio-business, based on medicinal and aromatic plants, holds a highly lucrative market for Himachal Pradesh at the international level. Lavander, Indian barberry, *kutki*, *jatamansi*, and *sugandhwalla* are among the plants, which can be rendered a priority.
- People have to grow into an enterprising society beyond the prevailing mindset of acquiring a government job as the goal of life.
- For attracting external investment, relaxation of the land policy is desired. Some appropriate steps have already been taken through amendments in 1999 of the Himachal Pradesh Ceiling and Land Reforms Act 1972, and of Himachal Pradesh Tenancy and Land Reforms Act 1975, in favour of industries, tourism and hydel projects.
- The watershed principle is most appropriate for organisation of space for administration and development. The boundaries of the districts and blocks should preferably coincide with those of watersheds.
- A sub-regional perspective internally and extra-regional perspective vis-à-vis neighbouring states are imperative for the state's integrated development.
- The role of science and technology is emerging as paramount. Preparation of watershed plans, identification of appropriate tourism sites and assessment of glacial retreat by employing remote sensing and geographic information systems, techniques; use of bio-fertilisers in horticulture, in particular; and promotion of interconnectivity between various localities, and government departments through telecommunication, are some of the illustrations.

In an overall assessment, Himachal Pradesh does display certain contrasting features. The State is high on social development but lags in economic development. While the economic health of the State is feeble its people are relatively well-off. Where it is sound on macro-level indicators, its micro-level realities leave much to be desired.

TABLE 24.5

Percentage Share of Different Sectors and Sub-sectors in Net State Domestic Product 1970-71 to 2000-01 (at 1993-94 prices)

Sector/sub-sector	*1970-71*	*1971-72*	*1972-73*	*1973-74*	*1974-75*	*1975-76*	*1976-77*	*1977-78*	*1978-79*	*1979-80*
Agriculture and animal husbandry	39.02	39.35	35.60	38.00	37.30	41.68	34.70	35.25	35.79	33.37
Forestry and logging	17.13	15.37	16.99	15.36	15.58	13.28	15.67	16.45	16.71	12.76
Fishing	0.06	0.06	0.06	0.07	0.07	0.07	0.08	0.13	0.15	0.17
Mining and quarrying	0.09	0.10	0.19	0.27	0.14	0.15	0.23	0.20	0.18	0.35
Primary Sector	56.29	54.88	52.84	53.69	53.09	55.19	50.68	52.04	52.83	46.65
Manufacturing	5.30	5.01	4.82	4.38	4.57	4.17	4.64	5.92	5.12	4.88
Registered	2.36	1.96	1.87	1.67	1.72	1.48	1.91	2.90	2.19	1.97
Unregistered	2.95	3.05	2.95	2.71	2.85	2.69	2.74	3.02	2.93	2.90
Construction	13.58	14.48	16.41	15.74	15.10	14.16	16.56	15.72	13.98	15.30
Electricity, gas and water supply	0.06	0.07	0.13	0.13	0.16	0.16	0.18	0.19	0.33	0.32
Secondary Sector	18.95	19.55	21.37	20.25	19.83	18.49	21.38	21.82	19.43	20.50
Transport, storage and communication	2.01	2.05	2.08	2.01	2.12	2.04	2.16	1.97	2.04	2.42
Railways	0.09	0.10	0.09	0.08	0.08	0.10	0.10	0.10	0.09	0.06
Transport by other means and storage	1.43	1.44	1.45	1.40	1.47	1.36	1.41	1.29	1.31	1.55
Communication	0.49	0.51	0.54	0.53	0.57	0.58	0.64	0.58	0.64	0.80
Trade, hotel and restaurants	3.11	3.10	3.08	3.13	1.99	3.90	4.42	4.59	5.48	6.55
Subtotal: Transport and Trade	**5.12**	**5.15**	**5.16**	**5.15**	**5.45**	**5.94**	**6.57**	**6.56**	**7.52**	**8.98**
Banking and insurance	0.62	0.80	0.85	0.90	0.93	0.91	1.09	1.19	1.51	1.74
Real estate and ownership of dwellings and business services	6.41	6.49	6.55	6.37	6.62	6.25	6.53	6.02	6.09	7.15
Subtotal: Finance and Real Estate	**7.03**	**7.29**	**7.39**	**7.27**	**7.55**	**7.16**	**7.63**	**7.21**	**7.59**	**8.89**
Public administration	4.89	5.20	5.43	5.72	5.81	5.62	5.98	5.19	5.46	6.61
Other services	7.72	7.92	7.81	7.91	8.28	7.60	7.76	7.17	7.17	8.37
Subtotal: Community and Personal Services	**12.61**	**13.13**	**13.24**	**13.64**	**14.09**	**13.22**	**13.74**	**12.37**	**12.62**	**14.99**
Tertiary Sector	24.76	25.56	25.79	26.05	27.09	26.32	27.94	26.14	27.74	32.85
Total	**100.00**	**100.00**	**100.00**	**100.00**	**100.00**	**100.00**	**100.00**	**100.00**	**100.00**	**100.00**

Sector/sub-sector	*1980-81*	*1981-82*	*1982-83*	*1983-84*	*1984-85*	*1985-86*	*1986-87*	*1987-88*	*1988-89*	*1989-90*
Agriculture and animal husbandry	34.95	35.52	31.92	35.76	34.96	34.97	35.81	30.16	28.99	33.98
Forestry and logging	12.11	12.72	11.30	10.64	7.47	6.90	6.37	5.46	6.53	5.66
Fishing	0.27	0.29	0.32	0.29	0.31	0.30	0.23	0.39	0.35	0.33
Mining and quarrying	0.76	0.72	0.83	0.91	1.07	1.38	1.47	1.98	2.02	2.02
Primary Sector	48.09	49.24	44.37	47.59	43.81	43.54	43.88	37.98	37.88	41.99
Manufacturing	2.26	2.97	3.22	3.37	4.16	3.99	0.41	4.54	6.39	5.82
Registered	1.05	1.71	1.90	2.00	2.72	2.54	2.57	3.13	5.06	4.38
Unregistered	1.21	1.27	1.32	1.37	1.44	1.45	1.43	1.41	1.32	1.44
Construction	18.23	16.15	14.00	12.02	11.99	15.29	13.42	16.20	15.46	10.60
Electricity, gas and water supply	-0.40	0.34	4.23	3.28	2.89	2.48	2.59	2.11	2.51	2.43
Secondary Sector	20.09	19.46	21.44	18.68	19.04	21.76	20.00	22.86	24.36	18.85
Transport, storage and communication	1.79	1.65	1.89	2.04	2.25	2.03	2.15	2.31	1.46	1.32
Railways	0.10	0.11	0.09	0.09	0.09	0.10	0.11	0.12	0.09	0.08
Transport by other means and storage	0.67	0.54	0.61	0.69	0.71	0.71	0.72	0.85	0.84	0.76
Communication	1.02	1.00	1.18	1.26	1.45	1.23	1.32	1.34	0.52	0.48
Trade, hotel and restaurants	7.66	8.17	8.32	8.78	8.62	8.29	8.85	8.41	8.97	8.54
Subtotal: Transport and Trade	**9.45**	**9.82**	**10.20**	**10.82**	**10.86**	**10.32**	**11.01**	**10.72**	**10.43**	**9.86**
Banking and insurance	1.43	1.68	2.05	2.14	2.44	2.41	3.27	3.61	2.84	4.02
Real estate and ownership of dwellings and business services	6.60	6.38	6.72	6.61	7.20	6.44	6.22	6.34	5.78	6.32
Subtotal: Finance and Real Estate	**8.03**	**8.06**	**8.77**	**8.75**	**9.64**	**8.85**	**9.50**	**9.95**	**8.62**	**10.34**
Public administration	5.90	5.46	6.79	6.02	7.10	6.87	6.96	8.40	8.41	8.64
Other services	8.43	7.96	8.42	8.15	9.54	8.65	8.66	10.09	10.31	10.33
Subtotal: Community and Personal Services	**14.33**	**13.42**	**15.21**	**14.17**	**16.64**	**15.52**	**15.62**	**18.49**	**18.72**	**18.97**
Tertiary Sector	31.82	31.30	34.19	33.74	37.14	34.69	36.12	39.16	37.76	39.17
Total	**100.00**	**100.00**	**100.00**	**100.00**	**100.00**	**100.00**	**100.00**	**100.00**	**100.00**	**100.00**

Contd. ...

Contd. ...

Percentage Share of Different Sectors and Sub-sectors in Net State Domestic Product 1970-71 to 2000-01 (at 1993-94 prices)

Sector/sub-sector	*1990-91*	*1991-92*	*1992-93*	*1993-94*	*1994-95*	*1995-96*	*1996-97*	*1997-98*	*1998-99*	*1999-00*	*2000-01*
Agriculture and animal husbandry	31.77	30.47	28.79	27.17	24.64	24.37	23.31	21.78	20.99	18.27	19.52
Forestry and logging	6.62	6.71	7.10	7.77	7.55	6.54	6.38	6.09	5.24	4.95	4.67
Fishing	0.36	0.42	0.40	0.39	0.27	0.30	0.29	0.28	0.24	0.22	0.21
Mining and quarrying	1.49	0.93	0.70	0.66	0.81	0.94	0.86	1.09	1.09	1.17	1.10
Primary Sector	40.24	38.53	36.99	35.99	33.27	32.14	30.84	29.23	27.57	24.61	25.50
Manufacturing	6.05	7.35	6.71	7.05	9.02	10.04	11.87	11.79	11.33	11.88	11.23
Registered	4.54	5.73	5.00	5.30	7.02	7.73	9.23	8.91	8.81	9.23	8.84
Unregistered	1.51	1.62	1.71	1.75	2.00	2.31	2.64	2.88	2.52	2.65	2.40
Construction	12.90	12.76	14.75	15.03	14.62	15.54	15.45	14.63	14.93	15.42	15.54
Electricity, gas and water supply	3.44	2.59	2.68	3.21	6.77	5.97	5.17	5.79	5.78	5.19	5.22
Secondary Sector	22.38	22.70	24.14	25.29	30.41	31.55	32.49	32.21	32.03	32.49	32.00
Transport, storage and communication	1.24	1.32	1.56	1.80	1.53	1.55	1.40	1.85	2.18	2.17	2.40
Railways	0.07	0.08	0.04	0.07	0.02	0.05	0.05	0.05	0.07	0.08	0.07
Transport by other means and storage	0.66	0.67	0.98	1.11	0.93	1.05	0.91	1.38	1.39	1.34	1.61
Communication	0.51	0.57	0.54	0.62	0.58	0.46	0.45	0.42	0.72	0.75	0.71
Trade, hotel and restaurants	8.83	9.47	9.44	9.00	9.15	8.99	9.15	9.18	9.40	8.92	8.76
Subtotal Transport and Trade	**10.07**	**10.79**	**10.99**	**10.80**	**10.68**	**10.54**	**10.55**	**11.03**	**11.58**	**11.09**	**11.16**
Banking and insurance	3.93	4.53	4.81	4.35	4.40	4.01	4.36	4.24	4.36	5.15	4.86
Real estate and ownership of dwellings and business services	5.51	5.69	5.57	5.52	5.18	5.08	5.02	4.85	4.46	4.35	4.22
Subtotal: Finance and Real Estate	**9.44**	**10.22**	**10.38**	**9.87**	**9.59**	**9.09**	**9.38**	**9.09**	**8.82**	**9.50**	**9.09**
Public administration	7.86	7.37	7.21	7.63	6.52	6.50	6.84	7.25	7.57	8.56	9.27
Other services	10.01	10.38	10.28	10.41	9.54	10.17	9.90	11.18	12.43	13.75	12.99
Subtotal: Community and Personal Services	**17.87**	**17.75**	**17.49**	**18.05**	**16.05**	**16.67**	**16.74**	**18.43**	**20.00**	**22.32**	**22.26**
Tertiary Sector	37.38	38.76	38.87	38.72	36.32	36.30	36.67	38.56	40.40	42.90	42.50
Total	**100.00**	**100.00**	**100.00**	**100.00**	**100.00**	**100.00**	**100.00**	**100.00**	**100.00**	**100.00**	**100.00**

Source: Calculated from data provided by the Directorate of Economic and Statistics, Government of Himachal Pradesh, Shimla.

TABLE 24.6

Percentage Distribution of Net State Domestic Product by Major Sectors, 1970-71- 2000-01

Year	*Percentage*		
	Primary	*Secondary*	*Tertiary*
1970-71	56.29	18.95	24.76
1971-72	54.88	19.55	25.56
1972-73	52.84	21.37	25.79
1973-74	53.69	20.25	26.05
1974-75	53.09	19.83	27.09
1975-76	55.19	18.49	26.32
1976-77	50.68	21.38	27.94
1977-78	52.04	21.82	26.14
1978-79	52.83	19.43	27.74
1979-80	46.65	20.50	32.85
1980-81	48.09	20.09	31.82
1981-82	49.24	19.46	31.30
1982-83	44.37	21.44	34.19
1983-84	47.59	18.68	33.74
1984-85	43.81	19.04	37.14

Contd. ...

Contd. ...

Year	*Percentage*		
	Primary	*Secondary*	*Tertiary*
1985-86	43.54	21.76	34.69
1986-87	43.88	20.00	36.12
1987-88	37.98	22.86	39.16
1988-89	37.88	24.36	37.76
1989-90	41.99	18.85	39.17
1990-91	40.24	22.38	37.38
1991-92	38.53	22.70	38.76
1992-93	36.99	24.14	38.87
1993-94	35.99	25.29	38.72
1994-95	33.27	30.41	36.32
1995-96	32.14	31.55	36.30
1996-97	30.84	32.49	36.67
1997-98	29.23	32.21	38.56
1998-99	27.57	32.03	40.40
1999-00	24.61	32.49	42.90
2000-01	25.50	32.00	42.50

Source: Calculated from Data provided by the Directorate of Economic and Statistics, Government of Himachal Pradesh, Shimla.

TABLE 24.7

Percentage Share of Different Sectors in Expenditure Under Five Year Plans

Five Year Plans	*Expenditure (per cent)*
Fourth Five Year Plan: 1969-74	
Agricultural programme	24.12
Cooperative and community development	3.18
Water, irrigation and power	21.67
Industrial and mining	3.65
Transport and communication	29.08
Social services	18.01
Miscellaneous	0.29
Fifth Five Year Plan: 1974-78	
Agriculture and allied services	26.34
Cooperation	1.10
Water and power development	26.93
Industry and minerals	3.37
Transport and communication	23.02
Social and community services	16.92
Economic services	0.08
General services	2.24
Sixth Five Year Plan: 1980-85	**15.81**
Agriculture and allied services	4.66
Rural development	0.08
Special area programme	5.84
Irrigation and flood control	26.97
Energy	3.08
Industries and minerals	17.82
Transport	0.03
Scientific services and research	22.45
Social and community services	0.12
Economic services	3.15
General services	106.838
Seventh Five Year Plan: 1985-90	
Agriculture and allied services	19.63
Rural development	3.71
Special area programme	0.00
Irrigation and flood control	5.39
Energy	26.55
Industries and minerals	3.22
Transport and communication	14.78
Science and technology and environment	0.07
General economic services	1.80
Education sports art and culture	7.41
Health	3.28
Water supply, housing, urban development and sanitation	10.61
Information and publicity	0.25
Welfare of SCs/STs/OBCs	0.42
Labour and Labour welfare	0.08
Social welfare	0.66
General services	2.13
Eighth Five Year Plan: 1992-97	
Agriculture and allied services	13.91
Rural development	3.34
Irrigation and flood control	4.24
Energy	18.89
Industry and minerals	2.47
Transport and communication	12.56
Science, technology and environment	0.14
General economic services	7.39
Education	13.00
Health	4.65
Water supply, sewerage, housing and urban development	14.91
Other social services	2.10
General services	2.40
Ninth Five Year Plan: 1997-2002	
Agriculture and allied services	11.34
Rural development	4.38
Irrigation and flood control	4.44
Energy	18.41
Industry and minerals	1.29
Transport and communication	14.36
Science, technology, environment	0.10
General economic services	2.90
Social services	41.28
General services	1.45
Tenth Five Year Plan	
Agriculture and allied services	9.60
Rural development	3.32
Irrigation and flood control	3.62
Energy	24.19
Industry and minerals	0.84
Transport and communication	16.14
Science, technology, environment	0.05
General economic services	2.41
Social services	39.00
General services	0.84

Contd. ...

Contd. ...

Source: Government of Himachal Pradesh, *Various Five Year Plans*, Shimla

TABLE 24.8

Per Capita Income (at 1993-94 prices) of Himachal Pradesh, Neighbouring states and India 1970-71 to 2000-2001

Year	*Himachal Pradesh*	*Haryana*	*Punjab*	*Jammu and Kashmir*	*India*
1970-71	5659	6141	6591	5165	4967
1971-72	5676	6267	6677	5155	4920
1972-73	5584	5923	6764	5071	4739
1973-74	5784	5734	6819	5269	4873
1974-75	5659	5608	6899	5335	4849
1975-76	6160	6575	7343	5401	5186
1976-77	5726	6834	7644	5212	5100
1977-78	6085	6939	8131	5759	5438
1978-79	6193	7450	8550	6107	5618
1979-80	5392	6757	8408	5966	5202
1980-81	5792	7429	8501	6343	5469
1981-82	6035	7510	9032	6329	5650
1982-83	5707	7758	9183	6364	5643
1983-84	5864	7702	9145	6407	5972
1984-85	5516	7720	9749	6561	6083
1985-86	6042	8708	10172	6543	6214
1986-87	6362	8507	10283	6461	6311
1987-88	6202	8144	10571	5611	6408
1988-89	6553	9915	10880	6200	6972
1989-90	7420	10200	11787	6179	7237
1990-91	7280	10999	11794	6379	7455
1991-92	6986	10968	12087	6339	7297
1992-93	7734	10723	12422	6443	7512
1993-94	7870	11090	12710	6543	7690
1994-95	8489	11617	12784	6619	8070
1995-96	8966	11570	12989	6732	8498
1996-97	9140	12664	13705	6978	9007
1997-98	9625	12544	13812	7128	9242
1998-99	10131	13003	14279	7296	9647
1999-00	10514	13709	14698	7384	10067
2000-01	10942	14331	14916	7383	10306

Source: Calculated from different volumes of *Statistical Abstracts of Himachal Pradesh, Punjab and Haryana.*

Note: Provisional

References

Ahluwalia, M.S. (1988), *History of Himachal Pradesh*, Intellectual Publishing House, New Delhi.

Balokhra, Jag Mohan (2002), *The Wonderland Himachal Pradesh*, H.G. Publications, New Delhi.

Cranney, Brenda (2001) *Local Environment and Lived Experience: Mountain Women of Himachal Pradesh*, Sage Publications, New Delhi.

Government of Himachal Pradesh (Undated) *Himachal Pradesh – India: A Himalayan Experience*, Government of Himachal Pradesh, Shimla.

Government of Himachal Pradesh (2000), *Tourism Policy*, Department of Tourism and Civil Aviation, Shimla.

Government of Himachal Pradesh (2001) *Rural Habitations Coverage by Water Supply Schemes*, Department of Irrigation and Public Health, Shimla.

Government of Himachal Pradesh (2002), *Himachal Pradesh Human Development Report*, Government Printing Press, Shimla.

Government of Himachal Pradesh (2002-03), *Work Plan for Accelerated Growth of Agriculture and Horticulture in Himachal Pradesh*, Shimla

Government of Himachal Pradesh (Years as listed), *State Policy Documents on Environment (undated), Transport (1999), Industry (1999), Tourism (2000),Information Technology (2001), Forestry (2002) and Biotechnology (2003)*, Shimla.

Government of Himachal Pradesh (2003), *Budget Speech of Shri Virbhadra Singh to the State Assembly*, Shimla.

Himalayan Jal Sanskriti (2003), *Survival Lessons*, Sterling Preferred Printing, New Delhi.

International Institute of Population Sciences (2002), *Himachal Pradesh: National Family Health Survey*, India 1998-99, Mumbai.

Kanwar, Pamela (1999), *Essays on Urban Patterns in Nineteenth Century Himachal Pradesh*, Indian Institute of Advanced Study, Shimla.

Laws, Sohie (2003), *Research for Development*, Vistaar Publications, New Delhi.

Negi, S.S. (1993), *Himachal Pradesh, Land and People*, Indus Publishing Company, New Delhi.

Planning Department (undated), *Tenth Five Year Plan: 2002-2007*, Government of Himachal Pradesh, Shimla.

Planning Commission (undated), *State Plans – Trends, Concerns and Strategies, Tenth Five Year Plan (2002-2007)*, New Delhi.

Reserve Bank of India (2002), *State Finances: A Study of Budget of 2001-02*, New Delhi.

Sharma, D.K. (2003), *Growth Scenario for the Tenth Plan of Himachal Pradesh*, Department of Planning, Shimla (A paper communicated in personal capacity).

Sharma, Pawan Kumar and Komila Parthi (2001), "Population Projections for a Hill State: Himachal Pradesh", *Population Geography*, Volume 23, pp. 61-68.

Singh, K.S. (1996), *People of India: Himachal Pradesh (Volume XXIV)*, Manohar, New Delhi.

State Council for Science Technology and Environment (2000), *State of Environment Report – Himachal Pradesh*, Government of Himachal Pradesh, Shimla.